Communications
in Computer and Information Science 2577

Series Editors

Gang Li⬤, *School of Information Technology, Deakin University, Burwood, VIC, Australia*

Joaquim Filipe⬤, *Polytechnic Institute of Setúbal, Setúbal, Portugal*

Zhiwei Xu, *Chinese Academy of Sciences, Beijing, China*

Rationale
The CCIS series is devoted to the publication of proceedings of computer science conferences. Its aim is to efficiently disseminate original research results in informatics in printed and electronic form. While the focus is on publication of peer-reviewed full papers presenting mature work, inclusion of reviewed short papers reporting on work in progress is welcome, too. Besides globally relevant meetings with internationally representative program committees guaranteeing a strict peer-reviewing and paper selection process, conferences run by societies or of high regional or national relevance are also considered for publication.

Topics
The topical scope of CCIS spans the entire spectrum of informatics ranging from foundational topics in the theory of computing to information and communications science and technology and a broad variety of interdisciplinary application fields.

Information for Volume Editors and Authors
Publication in CCIS is free of charge. No royalties are paid, however, we offer registered conference participants temporary free access to the online version of the conference proceedings on SpringerLink (http://link.springer.com) by means of an http referrer from the conference website and/or a number of complimentary printed copies, as specified in the official acceptance email of the event.

CCIS proceedings can be published in time for distribution at conferences or as post-proceedings, and delivered in the form of printed books and/or electronically as USBs and/or e-content licenses for accessing proceedings at SpringerLink. Furthermore, CCIS proceedings are included in the CCIS electronic book series hosted in the SpringerLink digital library at http://link.springer.com/bookseries/7899. Conferences publishing in CCIS are allowed to use Online Conference Service (OCS) for managing the whole proceedings lifecycle (from submission and reviewing to preparing for publication) free of charge.

Publication process
The language of publication is exclusively English. Authors publishing in CCIS have to sign the Springer CCIS copyright transfer form, however, they are free to use their material published in CCIS for substantially changed, more elaborate subsequent publications elsewhere. For the preparation of the camera-ready papers/files, authors have to strictly adhere to the Springer CCIS Authors' Instructions and are strongly encouraged to use the CCIS LaTeX style files or templates.

Abstracting/Indexing
CCIS is abstracted/indexed in DBLP, Google Scholar, EI-Compendex, Mathematical Reviews, SCImago, Scopus. CCIS volumes are also submitted for the inclusion in ISI Proceedings.

How to start
To start the evaluation of your proposal for inclusion in the CCIS series, please send an e-mail to ccis@springer.com.

Riccardo Guidotti · Ute Schmid · Luca Longo
Editors

Explainable Artificial Intelligence

Third World Conference, xAI 2025
Istanbul, Turkey, July 9–11, 2025
Proceedings, Part II

Editors
Riccardo Guidotti
University of Pisa
Pisa, Italy

Ute Schmid
University of Bamberg
Bamberg, Germany

Luca Longo
Technological University Dublin
Dublin, Ireland

ISSN 1865-0929　　　　　　ISSN 1865-0937　(electronic)
Communications in Computer and Information Science
ISBN 978-3-032-08323-4　　ISBN 978-3-032-08324-1　(eBook)
https://doi.org/10.1007/978-3-032-08324-1

© The Editor(s) (if applicable) and The Author(s), under exclusive license to Springer Nature Switzerland AG 2026. This book is an open access publication.

Open Access This book is licensed under the terms of the Creative Commons Attribution 4.0 International License (http://creativecommons.org/licenses/by/4.0/), which permits use, sharing, adaptation, distribution and reproduction in any medium or format, as long as you give appropriate credit to the original author(s) and the source, provide a link to the Creative Commons license and indicate if changes were made.
The images or other third party material in this book are included in the book's Creative Commons license, unless indicated otherwise in a credit line to the material. If material is not included in the book's Creative Commons license and your intended use is not permitted by statutory regulation or exceeds the permitted use, you will need to obtain permission directly from the copyright holder.
The use of general descriptive names, registered names, trademarks, service marks, etc. in this publication does not imply, even in the absence of a specific statement, that such names are exempt from the relevant protective laws and regulations and therefore free for general use.
The publisher, the authors and the editors are safe to assume that the advice and information in this book are believed to be true and accurate at the date of publication. Neither the publisher nor the authors or the editors give a warranty, expressed or implied, with respect to the material contained herein or for any errors or omissions that may have been made. The publisher remains neutral with regard to jurisdictional claims in published maps and institutional affiliations.

This Springer imprint is published by the registered company Springer Nature Switzerland AG
The registered company address is: Gewerbestrasse 11, 6330 Cham, Switzerland

If disposing of this product, please recycle the paper.

Preface

Over the last decade, Explainable Artificial Intelligence (XAI) has developed into an ever-growing research field dedicated to approaches that make AI systems—especially those based on machine-learned black box models—more transparent, interpretable, and comprehensible to humans. The demand for XAI methods rises with the growing number of application areas for AI methods, from image-based medical diagnostics to personalised recommenders to scientific discovery. In the context of the European AI Act, requirements for trustworthy AI systems have been defined, including human agency and oversight, robustness, fairness, and transparency. Trustworthiness is crucial for critical application domains, such as healthcare, industrial production, and finance. XAI methods can help meet these requirements.

A growing variety of XAI methods has emerged over the last decade. Initially, a strong focus has been placed on feature relevance methods for classification models applied to images and tabular data. These methods are beneficial for model developers to assess the quality of learned models, particularly in addressing issues such as overfitting to training data or unwanted biases. Soon, the importance of non-expert users of AI systems was recognised, especially professionals in the respective application domain of an AI system and end-users who interact with AI systems in a private context. Consequently, the need for XAI methods that consider the specific information needs of these user groups has been recognised. This has resulted in a rich set of XAI methods, including counterfactual or contrastive explanations, prototype-based explanations, and concept-based explanations. Furthermore, it has been recognised that XAI must be an interdisciplinary endeavour to consider the cognitive demands of the explainees and design helpful human-AI interfaces.

While most XAI research has focused on local, post-hoc explanations for classifiers, XAI methods have expanded to unsupervised learning and generative AI approaches. Additionally, methods for explaining inherently interpretable AI models and providing global explanations are investigated. Methods of explanatory interactive learning broaden the scope of XAI research, shifting from explanation to understanding and revision. Over recent years, the need to systematically evaluate XAI methods has been recognised. To support understanding the output of a model, an explanation needs to be faithful concerning its inferential mechanisms.

To bring together the growing number of researchers dedicated to developing and evaluating XAI methods, the World Conference of Explainable Artificial Intelligence (xAI) was established in 2023. This conference aims to connect researchers from AI, computer science, cognitive science, human-computer interaction, social sciences, law, philosophy, and practitioners from all continents to share and discuss knowledge, new perspectives, experiences, and innovations in XAI. The Third World Conference on Explainable Artificial Intelligence (xAI 2025) took place in Istanbul, Turkey, from July 9 to 11, 2025. It attracted 224 submissions worldwide for the main track, as well as over

60 submissions for the late-breaking work and demo tracks. The conference also had a doctoral consortium, and 14 doctoral proposals were accepted.

Split over five volumes, the proceedings aggregate the best contributions received and presented at xAI 2025, describing recent approaches, methods, and techniques for explainability. The acceptance rate has been roughly 40 per cent, with 96 accepted papers for the main track. The accepted contributions were selected through a rigorous, single-blind peer-review process. Each article received at least three reviews, with an average of four reviews per paper, from more than 300 scholars in academia and industry. All accepted research contributions are included in these proceedings and their authors were invited to give oral presentations.

Several thematic sessions were organised, each proposed and chaired by various researchers. A parallel track was organised for work in progress, specifically preliminary novel research studies relevant to xAI, which were presented as posters during the event. A demo track was held, where researchers from academia and industry presented their software prototypes, focusing on explainability or real-world applications of explainable AI-based systems. A doctoral consortium was organised, with lecturers for PhD scholars who submitted their doctoral proposals on future research in XAI. Finally, two panel discussions were organised with renowned scholars in XAI, offering multidisciplinary views while inspiring the attendees with tangible recommendations to tackle challenges toward designing responsible, trustworthy AI-based technologies through explainable AI.

We would like to thank the volunteers who helped in the xAI 2025 organising committee, our local chair, Berrin Yanikoglu, and Pınar Karadayı Ataş. Thank you to the doctoral consortium chairs, Przemysław Biecek and Slawomir Nowarczyk, and the late-breaking work and demo chair Gitta Kutyniok. Also, a special thank you goes to Wojciech Samek, the keynote speaker for xAI 2025. A word of appreciation goes to the proposers of the special tracks and those who chaired them during the conference, and to all the senior chairs, including Charlie Abela, Christopher Anders, Omran Ayoub, Pietro Barbiero, Przemysław Biecek, Enrico Ferrari, Pascal Friederich, Francesco Giannini, Paolo Giudici, Julia Herbinger, Verena Klös, Tuwe Löfström, Gianmarco Mengaldo, Maurizio Mongelli, Anna Monreale, Grégoire Montavon, Francesca Naretto, Ann Nowe, Ruairi O'Reilly, Roberto Pellungrini, Alan Perotti, Salvatore Rinzivillo, Christin Seifert, Francesco Sovrano, Lenka Tětková, Giulia Vilone, Philipp Wintersberger, and Bartosz Zieliński. A word of appreciation goes to all the moderators and panellists of the two engaging sessions "Integrating XAI in industry processes challenges for responsible AI" and "From Explanations to Impact". Special thanks go to the researchers and practitioners who submitted their work, the various program committee members who provided valuable feedback during the peer-review process, and all who attended the event, making it a fantastic networking opportunity to share findings and learn from one another as a community.

July 2025

Riccardo Guidotti
Ute Schmid
Luca Longo

Organization

Programme Committee Chairs

Riccardo Guidotti — University of Pisa, Italy
Ute Schmid — University of Bamberg, Germany

Doctoral Consortium Chairs

Przemysław Biecek — Warsaw University of Technology, Poland
Slawomir Nowarczyk — Halmstad University, Sweden

Late-Breaking Work and Demo Chair

Gitta Kutyniok — LMU Munich, Germany

Local Chairs

Berrin Yanikoglu — Sabancı University, Turkey
Pınar Karadayı Ataş — Istanbul Arel University, Turkey

General Chair

Luca Longo — Technological University Dublin, Ireland

Steering Committee

Sebastian Lapuschkin — Fraunhofer Heinrich Hertz Institute, Germany
Paolo Giudici — University of Pavia, Italy
Luca Longo — Technological University Dublin, Ireland
Christin Seifert — University of Marburg, Germany
Grégoire Montavon — Freie Universität Berlin, Germany

Programme Committee

Ad Feelders	Utrecht University, Netherlands
Adrian Byrne	CeADAR UCD/Idiro Analytics, Ireland
Alan Perotti	CENTAI Institute, Italy
Alberto Fernández	University of Granada, Spain
Alberto Freitas	University of Porto, Portugal
Alberto Tonda	INRAE, France
Alessandro Antonucci	IDSIA, Switzerland
Alessandro Renda	Università degli Studi di Firenze, Italy
Alex Freitas	University of Kent, UK
Alexander Schulz	Bielefeld University, Germany
Alexandros Doumanoglou	Information Technologies Institute, Greece
Amparo Alonso-Betanzos	University of A Coruña, Spain
André Artelt	Bielefeld University, Germany
André Panisson	CENTAI Institute, Italy
Andrea Apicella	University of Naples Federico II, Italy
Andrea Campagner	Università degli Studi di Milano-Bicocca, Italy
Andrea Passerini	University of Trento, Italy
Andrea Pazienza	NTT DATA Italia SpA & A3K Srl, Italy
Andrea Pugnana	University of Pisa, Italy
Andreas Holzinger	University of Natural Resources and Life Sciences, Vienna, Austria
Andreas Theissler	Aalen University of Applied Sciences, Germany
Andres Paez	Universidad de los Andes, Colombia
Andrew Lensen	Victoria University of Wellington, New Zealand
Angela Lombardi	Politecnico di Bari, Italy
Angelica Liguori	ICAR-CNR, Italy
Ann Nowe	Vrije Universiteit Brussel, Belgium
Anna Monreale	University of Pisa, Italy
Annalisa Appice	Università degli Studi di Bari Aldo Moro, Italy
Antonio Mastropietro	Università di Pisa, Italy
Antonio Moreno	Universitat Rovira i Virgili, Spain
Antonio Jesús Banegas-Luna	Universidad Católica de Murcia, Spain
Anurag Koul	Microsoft Research, USA
Arianna Agosto	University of Pavia, Italy
Aris Anagnostopoulos	Sapienza University of Rome, Italy
Astrid Rakow	German Aerospace Center (DLR) e.V., Germany
Athanasios Voulodimos	University of West Attica, Greece
Autilia Vitiello	University of Naples Federico II, Italy
Axel-Cyrille Ngonga Ngomo	Paderborn University, Germany
Barbara Hammer	Bielefeld University, Germany

Bartosz Zieliński	Jagiellonian University, Poland
Benoît Frénay	Université de Namur, Belgium
Bernard Zenko	Jožef Stefan Institute, Slovenia
Bettina Finzel	Otto-Friedrich-Universität Bamberg, Germany
Björn-Hergen Laabs	Universität zu Lübeck, Germany
Bruno Martins	INESC-ID - Instituto Superior Técnico, University of Lisbon, Portugal
Bruno Veloso	University of Porto & LIAAD - INESC TEC, Portugal
Carlo Metta	University of Florence, Italy
Carlos Soares	University of Porto, Portugal
Caroline Petitjean	Université de Rouen - LITIS EA 4108, France
Carsten Schulte	University of Paderborn, Germany
Caterina Senette	IIT-CNR, Italy
Cèsar Ferri	Universitat Politècnica de València, Spain
Charlie Abela	University of Malta, Malta
Chiara Renso	ISTI-CNR Pisa, Italy
Chirag Agarwal	University of Illinois Chicago, USA
Christian Lovis	University Hospitals of Geneva, Switzerland
Christin Seifert	University of Marburg, Germany
Christoph Schommer	University of Luxembourg, Luxembourg
Christophe Labreuche	Thales R&T, France
Christopher Anders	Technische Universität Berlin, Germany
Christos Dimitrakakis	University of Neuchâtel, Switzerland
Ciara Heavin	University College Cork, Ireland
Clemens Dubslaff	Eindhoven University of Technology, Netherlands
Corrado Mencar	Università degli Studi di Bari Aldo Moro, Italy
Damiano Verda	Rulex Innovation Labs Srl, Italy
Dariusz Brzezinski	Poznań University of Technology, Poland
Dave Braines	IBM United Kingdom Ltd., UK
David Leake	Indiana University, USA
David H. Glass	University of Ulster, UK
Diego Borro	CEIT and University of Navarra, Spain
Dino Ienco	IRSTEA, France
Domenico Talia	University of Calabria, Italy
Donato Malerba	Università degli Studi di Bari Aldo Moro, Italy
Duarte Folgado	Associação Fraunhofer Portugal Research, Portugal
Edel Garcia	CCG, Portugal
Eliana Pastor	Politecnico di Torino, Italy
Elio Masciari	University of Naples Federico II, Italy
Elvio Gilberto Amparore	Università di Torino, Italy

Emmanuel Müller	TU Dortmund University, Germany
Enea Parimbelli	University of Pavia, Italy
Enrico Ferrari	Rulex Innovation Labs Srl, Italy
Erasmo Purificato	Joint Research Centre, European Commission, Italy
Fabian Fumagalli	Bielefeld University, Germany
Fabio Fassetti	University of Calabria, Italy
Fabrizio Angiulli	University of Calabria, Italy
Fabrizio Marozzo	University of Calabria, Italy
Federico Cabitza	Università degli Studi di Milano-Bicocca, Italy
Florije Ismaili	South East European University, North Macedonia
Floris Bex	Utrecht University, Netherlands
Francesca Naretto	Scuola Normale Superiore, Italy
Francesco Flammini	University of Florence, Italy
Francesco Giannini	Scuola Normale Superiore, Italy
Francesco Guerra	Università di Modena e Reggio Emilia, Italy
Francesco Marcelloni	Università di Pisa, Italy
Francesco Sovrano	University of Zurich, Switzerland
Francesco Spinnato	University of Pisa, Italy
Françoise Fessant	Orange Labs, France
Frederic Jurie	University of Caen Normandie, France
Gabriella Casalino	Università degli Studi di Bari Aldo Moro, Italy
Ganna Grynova	University of Birmingham, UK
Georgiana Ifrim	University College Dublin, Ireland
Gesina Schwalbe	University of Lübeck, Germany
Gianmarco Mengaldo	National University of Singapore, Singapore
Giovanna Dimitri	University of Siena, Italy
Giovanni Ciatto	University of Bologna, Italy
Giulia Vilone	Technological University Dublin, Ireland
Giulio Rossetti	KDD Lab ISTI-CNR, Italy
Giuseppe Casalicchio	Ludwig-Maximilians-Universität München, Germany
Giuseppe Manco	ICAR-CNR, Italy
Giuseppe Marra	KU Leuven, Belgium
Gizem Gezici	Scuola Normale Superiore, Italy
Gjergji Kasneci	Technical University of Munich, Germany
Grégoire Montavon	Freie Universität Berlin, Germany
Grzegorz J. Nalepa	Jagiellonian University, Poland
Guido Bologna	University of Applied Sciences and Arts of Western Switzerland, Switzerland
Hamed Ayoobi	Imperial College London, UK

Heike Buhl	Paderborn University, Germany
Hendrik Baier	Eindhoven University of Technology, Netherlands
Henning Müller	HES-SO and University of Geneva, Switzerland
Henrik Boström	KTH Royal Institute of Technology, Sweden
Henrique Lopes Cardoso	University of Porto, Portugal
Heta Gandhi	Nurix Therapeutics, USA
Howard Hamilton	University of Regina, Canada
Ilir Jusufi	Blekinge Institute of Technology, Sweden
Iordanis Koutsopoulos	Athens University of Economics and Business, Greece
Isacco Beretta	Università di Pisa, Italy
Isel Grau	Eindhoven University of Technology, Netherlands
Jaesik Choi	Korea Advanced Institute of Science and Technology, South Korea
Jan Arne Telle	University of Bergen, Norway
Jane Courtney	Technological University Dublin, Ireland
Jaromir Savelka	Carnegie Mellon University, USA
Jasper S. van der Waa	TNO, Netherlands
Jaumin Ajdari	South East European University, North Macedonia
Jenny Benois-Pineau	LaBRI Université de Bordeaux, CNRS, France
Jérôme Guzzi	IDSIA, Switzerland
Jerzy Stefanowski	Poznań University of Technology, Poland
Jesús Alcalá-Fdez	University of Granada, Spain
João Gama	Porto University, Portugal
Jörg Hoffmann	Saarland University, Germany
Johannes Fürnkranz	Johannes Kepler University Linz, Austria
Johannes Langer	University of Bamberg, Germany
John Gilligan	Technological University Dublin, Ireland
John Lawrence	University of Dundee, UK
Jonathan Ben-Naim	Institut de Recherche en Informatique de Toulouse (IRIT-CNRS), France
Jonathan Dunne	IBM, Ireland
Jose Juarez	Universidad de Murcia, Spain
Jose M. Molina	Universidad Carlos III de Madrid, Spain
Jose Paulo Marques dos Santos	University of Maia, Portugal
Josep Domingo-Ferrer	Universitat Rovira i Virgili, Spain
Juan Corchado	University of Salamanca, Spain
Juan A. Recio-Garcia	Universidad Complutense de Madrid, Spain
Julia Herbinger	Ludwig-Maximilians-Universität München, Germany
Julien Delaunay	Université Rennes, France

Juri Belikov	Tallinn University of Technology, Estonia
Kary Främling	Umeå University, Sweden
Katharina Rohlfing	University of Paderborn, Germany
Katharina Weitz	Fraunhofer Heinrich Hertz Institute, Germany
Kirsten Thommes	Padeborn University, Germany
Konstantinos Makantasis	University of Malta, Malta
Kristoffer Wickstrøm	UiT The Arctic University of Norway, Norway
Larisa Soldatova	Goldsmiths, University of London, UK
Lars Kai Hansen	Technical University of Denmark, Denmark
Lenka Tětková	Technical University of Denmark, Denmark
Luca Ferragina	University of Calabria, Italy
Luca Oneto	University of Genoa, Italy
Lucas Rizzo	Technological University Dublin, Ireland
Lucie Charlotte Magister	University of Cambridge, UK
Luis Galárraga	Inria, France
Luis Macedo	University of Coimbra, Portugal
Luís Rosado	Fraunhofer Portugal AICOS, Portugal
Maguelonne Teisseire	Irstea - UMR Tetis, France
Malika Bendechache	University of Galway, Ireland
Manuel Mazzara	Innopolis University, Russia
Marcelo G. Manzato	University of São Paulo, Brazil
Marcilio De Souto	LIFO/University of Orléans, France
Marcin Luckner	Warsaw University of Technology, Poland
Marco Baioletti	Università degli Studi di Perugia, Italy
Marco Podda	University of Pisa, Italy
Marco Polignano	Università degli Studi di Bari Aldo Moro, Italy
Maria Kaselimi	National Technical University of Athens, Greece
Maria Riveiro	Jönköping University, Sweden
Marija Bezbradica	Dublin City University, Ireland
Mario Brcic	University of Zagreb, Croatia
Mario Giovanni C. A. Cimino	University of Pisa, Italy
Mark Hall	Airbus, UK
Markus Löcher	Berlin School of Economics and Law, Germany
Marta Marchiori Manerba	Università di Pisa, Italy
Martin Atzmueller	Osnabrück University, Germany
Martin Gjoreski	Università della Svizzera italiana, Switzerland
Martin Holeňa	Czech Academy of Sciences, Czechia
Martin Jullum	Norwegian Computing Center, Norway
Marvin Wright	Leibniz Institute for Prevention Research and Epidemiology - BIPS & University of Bremen, Germany
Massimo Guarascio	ICAR-CNR, Italy

Mathieu Roche	Cirad, TETIS, France
Mattia Cerrato	Johannes Gutenberg University Mainz, Germany
Mattia Setzu	University of Pisa, Italy
Maurizio Mongelli	CNR-IEIIT, Italy
Mauro Dragoni	Fondazione Bruno Kessler, Italy
Md Shajalal	University of Siegen, Germany
Megha Khosla	Delft University of Technology, Netherlands
Meiyi Ma	Vanderbilt University, USA
Melinda Gervasio	SRI International, USA
Mexhid Ferati	Linnaeus University, Sweden
Michail Mamalakis	University of Cambridge, UK
Michelangelo Ceci	Università degli Studi di Bari Aldo Moro, Italy
Miguel Couceiro	Inria, France
Miguel A. Gutiérrez-Naranjo	University of Seville, Spain
Miguel Angel Patricio	Universidad Carlos III de Madrid, Spain
Mirna Saad	Scuola Universitaria Professionale della Svizzera Italiana, Switzerland
Myra Spiliopoulou	Otto von Guericke University Magdeburg, Germany
Nick Bassiliades	Aristotle University of Thessaloniki, Greece
Nicolas Boutry	EPITA Research Laboratory (LRE), Le Kremlin-Bicêtre, France
Niki van Stein	Leiden University, Netherlands
Nikolay Tcholtchev	Fraunhofer FOKUS, Germany
Nikos Deligiannis	Vrije Universiteit Brussel, Netherlands
Nikos Karacapilidis	University of Patras, Greece
Nirmalie Wiratunga	Robert Gordon University, UK
Nuno Silva	INESC TEC & ISEP - IPP, Portugal
Oliver Eberle	Technische Universität Berlin, Germany
Oliver Ray	University of Bristol, UK
Omran Ayoub	Scuola Universitaria Professionale della Svizzera Italiana, Switzerland
Özgür Lütfü Özcep	University of Hamburg, Germany
Pance Panov	Jožef Stefan Institute, Slovenia
Paola Cerchiello	University of Pavia, Italy
Paolo Giudici	University of Pavia, Italy
Paolo Pagnottoni	University of Insubria, Italy
Paolo Soda	Umeå University, Sweden
Pascal Friederich	Karlsruhe Institute of Technology, Germany
Pascal Germain	Inria, France
Paulo Cortez	University of Minho, Portugal
Paulo Lisboa	Liverpool John Moores University, UK

Paulo Novais	University of Minho, Portugal
Pedro Sequeira	SRI International, USA
Peter Kieseberg	St. Pölten University of Applied Sciences, Austria
Peter Vamplew	Federation University Australia, Australia
Philipp Cimiano	Bielefeld University, Germany
Prasanna Balaprakash	Oak Ridge National Laboratory, USA
Przemysław Biecek	Polish Academy of Sciences, University of Wrocław, Poland
Renato De Leone	Università di Camerino, Italy
Ricardo Prudêncio	Universidade Federal de Pernambuco, Brazil
Riccardo Cantini	University of Calabria, Italy
Richard Jiang	Lancaster University, UK
Rita P. Ribeiro	University of Porto, Portugal
Rob Brennan	University College Dublin, Ireland
Roberta Calegari	Alma Mater Studiorum–Università di Bologna, Italy
Roberto Capobianco	Sapienza University of Rome, Italy
Roberto Interdonato	CIRAD - UMR TETIS, France
Roberto Pellungrini	University of Pisa, Italy
Roberto Prevete	University of Naples Federico II, Italy
Rocio Gonzalez-Diaz	University of Seville, Spain
Romain Bourqui	Université Bordeaux 1, Inria Bordeaux-Sud Ouest, France
Romain Giot	LaBRI Université de Bordeaux, CNRS, France
Rosa Lillo	Universidad Carlos III de Madrid, Spain
Rosa Meo	University of Turin, Italy
Rosina Weber	Drexel University, USA
Ruairi O'Reilly	Munster Technological University, Ireland
Ruben Laplaza	École Polytechnique Fédérale de Lausanne, Switzerland
Ruggero G. Pensa	University of Turin, Italy
Rui Mao	Nanyang Technological University, Singapore
Sabatina Criscuolo	University of Naples Federico II, Italy
Salvatore Greco	Politecnico di Torino, Italy
Salvatore Rinzivillo	ISTI-CNR Pisa, Italy
Salvatore Ruggieri	Università di Pisa, Italy
Sandra Mitrović	IDSIA, Switzerland
Sang Won Baae	Stevens Institute of Technology, USA
Santiago Quintana Amate	Airbus, UK
Sebastian Lapuschkin	Fraunhofer Heinrich Hertz Institute, Germany
Severin Kacianka	Technical University of Munich, Germany
Shahina Begum	Mälardalen University, Sweden

Shai Ben-David	University of Waterloo, Canada
Shujun Li	University of Kent, UK
Silvia Giordano	Scuola Universitaria Professionale della Svizzera Italiana, Switzerland
Simon See	Nvidia, Singapore
Simona Nisticò	University of Calabria, Italy
Simone Piaggesi	University of Bologna, Italy
Simone Stumpf	University of Glasgow, UK
Slawomir Nowaczyk	Halmstad University, Sweden
Sriraam Natarajan	University of Texas at Dallas, USA
Stefano Bistarelli	Università di Perugia, Italy
Stefano Mariani	Università di Modena e Reggio Emilia, Italy
Stefano Melacci	University of Siena, Italy
Stéphane Galland	Université de Technologie de Belfort-Montbéliard, France
Sylvio Barbon Junior	University of Trieste, Italy
Szymon Bobek	AGH University of Science and Technology, Poland
Takafumi Nakanishi	Musashino University, Japan
Tania Cerquitelli	Politecnico di Torino, Italy
Telmo Silva Filho	University of Bristol, UK
Teodor Chiaburu	Berliner Hochschule für Technik, Germany
Thach Le Nguyen	University College Dublin, Ireland
Thomas Guyet	Inria, France
Thomas Lukasiewicz	University of Oxford, UK
Tiago Pinto	Universidade de Trás-os-Montes e Alto Douro/INESC-TEC, Portugal
Tjitze Rienstra	Maastricht University, Netherlands
Tomáš Kliegr	Prague University of Economics and Business, Czechia
Tommaso Turchi	University of Pisa, Italy
Tran Cao Son	New Mexico State University, USA
Tuan Pham	Queen Mary University of London, UK
Tuwe Löfström	Jönköping University, Sweden
Udo Schlegel	University of Konstanz, Germany
Ulf Johansson	Jönköping University, Sweden
Vân Anh Huynh-Thu	University of Liège, Belgium
Vedran Sabol	Know-Center GmbH, Austria
Verena Klös	Carl von Ossietzky Universität Oldenburg, Germany
Vincent Andrearczyk	HES-SO, Switzerland
Vincenzo Moscato	University of Naples, Italy

Vincenzo Pasquadibisceglie	Università degli Studi di Bari Aldo Moro, Italy
Weiru Liu	University of Bristol, UK
Werner Bailer	JOANNEUM Research, Austria
Wojciech Samek	Technical University of Berlin, Germany
Yazan Mualla	Université de Technologie de Belfort-Montbéliard, France
Zahraa S. Abdallah	University of Bristol, UK

Contents – Part II

Rule-Based XAI Systems and Actionable Explainable AI

CFIRE: A General Method for Combining Local Explanations 3
    *Sebastian Müller, Vanessa Toborek, Tamás Horváth,
and Christian Bauckhage*

Which LIME Should I Trust? Concepts, Challenges, and Solutions 28
    Patrick Knab, Sascha Marton, Udo Schlegel, and Christian Bartelt

Explainable Bayesian Optimization 53
    Tanmay Chakraborty, Christian Wirth, and Christin Seifert

Bridging the Interpretability Gap in Process Mining: A Comprehensive
Approach Combining Explainable Clustering and Generative AI 78
    *Jonas Amling, Emanuel Slany, Christian Dormagen,
Marco Kretschmann, and Stephan Scheele*

Balancing Fairness and Interpretability in Clustering with FairParTree 104
    *Cristiano Landi, Alessio Cascione, Marta Marchiori Manerba,
and Riccardo Guidotti*

Features Importance-Based XAI

Antithetic Sampling for Top-K Shapley Identification 131
    Patrick Kolpaczki, Tim Nielen, and Eyke Hüllermeier

Detecting Concept Drift with SHapley Additive ExPlanations
for Intelligent Model Retraining in Energy Generation Forecasting 156
    Brígida Teixeira, Tiago Pinto, and Zita Vale

Counterfactual Shapley Values for Explaining Reinforcement Learning 169
    Yiwei Shi and Weiru Liu

Improving the Weighting Strategy in KernelSHAP 194
    Lars Henry Berge Olsen and Martin Jullum

POMELO: Black-Box Feature Attribution with Full-Input, In-Distribution
Perturbations 219
    Luan Ademi, Maximilian Noppel, and Christian Wressnegger

Novel Post-hoc and Ante-hoc XAI Approaches

Explain to Gain: Introspective Reinforcement Learning for Enhanced Performance 247
   Santiago Quintana-Amate, Delaney Stevens, Varniethan Ketheeswaran, Patrick Capaldo, Dylan Sheldon, and Mark Hall

Extending Decision Predicate Graphs for Comprehensive Explanation of Isolation Forest 271
   Matteo Ceschin, Leonardo Arrighi, Luca Longo, and Sylvio Barbon Junior

Mathematical Foundation of Interpretable Equivariant Surrogate Models 294
   Jacopo Joy Colombini, Filippo Bonchi, Francesco Giannini, Fosca Giannotti, Roberto Pellungrini, and Patrizio Frosini

Interpretable Link Prediction via Neural-Symbolic Reasoning 319
   Rodrigo Castellano Ontiveros, Ehsan Bonabi Mobaraki, Francesco Giannini, Pietro Barbiero, Marco Gori, and Michelangelo Diligenti

CausalAIME: Leveraging Peter-Clark Algorithms and Inverse Modeling for Unified Global Feature Explanation in Healthcare 332
   Takafumi Nakanishi

XAI for Scientific Discovery

Interpreting the Structure of Multi-object Representations in Vision Encoders 359
   Tarun Khajuria, Braian Olmiro Dias, Marharyta Domnich, and Jaan Aru

Leveraging Influence Functions for Resampling Data in Physics-Informed Neural Networks 383
   Jonas R. Naujoks, Aleksander Krasowski, Moritz Weckbecker, Galip Ümit Yolcu, Thomas Wiegand, Sebastian Lapuschkin, Wojciech Samek, and René P. Klausen

Safe and Efficient Social Navigation Through Explainable Safety Regions Based on Topological Features 396
   Victor Toscano-Duran, Sara Narteni, Alberto Carlevaro, Jérôme Guzzi, Rocio Gonzalez-Diaz, and Maurizio Mongelli

A Biologically Inspired Filter Significance Assessment Method for Model
Explanation 422
   Emirhan Böge, Yasemin Gunindi, Murat Bilgehan Ertan,
   Erchan Aptoula, Nihan Alp, and Huseyin Ozkan

Author Index 437

Rule-Based XAI Systems and Actionable Explainable AI

CFIRE: A General Method for Combining Local Explanations

Sebastian Müller[1,2](✉), Vanessa Toborek[1,2], Tamás Horváth[1,2,3], and Christian Bauckhage[1,2,3]

[1] University of Bonn, Bonn, Germany
`semueller@uni-bonn.de`
[2] Lamarr Institute for Machine Learning and Artificial Intelligence, Bonn, Germany
[3] Fraunhofer IAIS, Sankt Augustin, Germany

Abstract. We propose a novel eXplainable AI algorithm to compute faithful, easy-to-understand, and complete global decision rules from local explanations for tabular data by combining XAI methods with closed frequent itemset mining. Our method can be used with any local explainer that indicates which dimensions are important for a given sample for a given black-box decision. This property allows our algorithm to choose among different local explainers, addressing the disagreement problem, i.e., the observation that no single explanation method consistently outperforms others across models and datasets. Unlike usual experimental methodology, our evaluation also accounts for the Rashomon effect in model explainability. To this end, we demonstrate the robustness of our approach in finding suitable rules for nearly all of the 700 black-box models we considered across 14 benchmark datasets. The results also show that our method exhibits improved runtime, high precision and F1-score while generating compact and complete rules.

1 Introduction

Explainable artificial intelligence (XAI) focuses on bringing transparency to the decision-making process of black-box machine learning models (see, e.g., [24]). Due to their inherent interpretability (see, e.g., [21,22,37]), *decision rules* are among the most popular target languages of various XAI rule extraction methods [6,15,32]. Several algorithms have been developed in XAI to generate *local* explanations for single instances of the input space (see, e.g., [23,31,32,35]). While useful in some scenarios, these instance-specific local explanations fall short in terms of comprehensibility and generalisability. To address these shortcomings, existing efforts focus on aggregating *local* explanations into *global* models [6,32].

In this work we propose CLOSED FREQUENT ITEMSET RULES FROM EXPLANATIONS (CFIRE), a novel local-to-global XAI algorithm for extracting rules from black-boxes trained on tabular data. It produces global rule models in disjunctive normal forms (DNFs) that are: (i) *faithful*, (ii) *compact*, (iii) *complete*, i.e., can explain all classes in both binary and multi-class settings, (iv) *robust* against the Rashomon effect in XAI, and (v) *flexible*, i.e., can work with different local explainers.

While the first three properties are quite standard in the literature (see, e.g., [6,15,32,33]), the last two, to the best of our knowledge, have so far been completely neglected. In particular, (iv) is motivated by the *Rashomon effect* [9] in XAI, where different yet equally well-performing models can make the *same prediction* for *different reasons*, with certain models even being more difficult to explain than others [26]. Property (iv) addresses this effect by requiring the method to produce equally well-performing global explanations for equally well-performing black-box models.

Finally, property (v) is motivated by the *disagreement problem* [20], i.e. the general observation that *different local explainers* produce *different explanations* for the *same black-box prediction*. Our experimental results show that the ability of dynamically choosing the local explainer can strongly impact the quality of the resulting rule model. Hence the demand for flexibility is of crucial importance.

In brief, CFIRE works as follows: Given a black-box model, a local explainer, and a set of input samples, CFIRE first generates a set of important feature sets by using *closed frequent itemset* mining [29] from the local explanations computed for the samples. Each closed frequent itemset is a subset of the feature set and thus defines a subspace of the input space. For each subspace, it generalizes the samples by creating a set of axis-aligned boxes, ensuring that samples with different predicted class labels are placed in separate boxes. Finally, using the greedy heuristic for the set cover problem, it selects a compact set of boxes from this set of box systems and returns it in the form of a set of DNFs.

A key distinction from related approaches [6] lies in the use of *closed* frequent itemsets rather than *all* frequent itemsets. The number of frequent itemsets grows exponentially with the number of important features, requiring some small bound on the number of features to keep computations feasible. However, as we demonstrate experimentally, this constraint leads to overly general rules. In contrast, closed frequent itemsets provide a *lossless* compression of frequent itemsets and can be listed *efficiently* (see, e.g., [8]) regardless of the number of important features. This allows CFIRE to generate more specific important feature combinations.

Unlike traditional surrogate models, our algorithm ensures that the resulting DNFs reflect the black-box model's behavior in at least two key aspects: First, the properties of closed frequent itemsets ensure that the rules are directly restricted to the *specific input dimensions* indicated by the local explanations. Second, the rules provide the most specific generalizations possible: for any set of training examples inducing a box, the smallest box containing the examples is calculated. In other words, CFIRE does *not* extrapolate beyond observed subspaces *nor* does it compute box rules with unbounded edges.

Our experimental results on 14 benchmark datasets clearly show that CFIRE generates *faithful*, *compact* and *complete* global rule models for both binary and multi-class problems (properties (i), (ii) and (iii)). To show that CFIRE fulfills property (iv), we evaluate it on 50 high-performing black-box models per task, confirming its robustness against the Rashomon effect. Our results clearly show that its flexibility in choosing among multiple local explainers (property (v)) has a large positive impact on performance in terms of properties (i)-(iii).

Finally, our experiments focusing on the (dis)agreement between CFIRE and the local explainers show that CFIRE is able to retain key semantic properties of the local explanations, even on unseen data. Furthermore, compared to its strongest competitor in terms of all properties described above, we observe a runtime improvement for CFIRE by a factor of up to two orders of magnitude.

The rest of the paper is organized as follows: Sect. 2 reviews related work, while Sect. 3 covers the necessary background on quality metrics for rules and on closed frequent sets. In Sect. 4, we state and motivate the problem setting. Section 5 details our algorithm, which is evaluated on benchmark datasets in Sect. 6. Finally, Sect. 7 concludes and outlines future research directions. The code to reproduce all experiments is available on github.com/semueller/CFIRE.

2 Related Work

Building global rule-based explanations from a given black-box model generally involve two steps: 1) *rule extraction* and 2) *rule composition*. Rule extraction generates candidate rules based on the behavior of the black-box model, while rule composition selects a subset of these rules to form a global explanation.

A common way to categorize explainability methods is along the axis of *local* versus *global* explanations. Local methods provide explanations for individual predictions, focusing on why a model made a particular decision for a single input. In contrast, global methods aim to explain the overall behavior of a model across multiple inputs or the entire input space.

Our goal in this work is to compute a global explanation in the form of a rule-based model from local explanations. We focus on the most prominent representatives of local explanations, in particular, feature attribution methods.

Attribution methods such as KernelSHAP [23], LIME [31], and Integrated Gradients [35] assign weights to individual input features, quantifying their influence on a model's output for a given input sample. A high positive or negative value indicates that the feature strongly supports or opposes the model's prediction, respectively, while values close to zero suggest that the feature had negligible influence. Users typically focus on the most highly weighted features, but the exact magnitude of these scores is difficult to interpret [20]. To address this lack of interpretability, the authors of LIME later developed ANCHORS [32].

ANCHORS is a local explanation technique that represents explanations in the form of local decision-rules. Given a sample, a precision threshold, and a background distribution, ANCHORS searches for a term with the highest coverage applicable within the local neighborhood of the sample that still satisfies the precision threshold. Starting with an empty term, it generates high coverage candidate predicates to add to the term. By repeatedly drawing samples from a background distribution, it determines the most precise candidate, adds it to the final term, and starts over by generating more candidates. The process terminates once no additional candidates are found. Similarly to LIME, the background distribution can be defined over an interpretable ambient space, instead of the data space directly, and can be purely synthetic. While the focus of ANCHORS clearly lies on the rule extraction, the authors also experimented with a simple technique to select multiple local rules to jointly explain the model behavior more globally. Given a user defined integer k, the method selects k of the highest-precision terms where all terms cover at least one distinct sample. We refer to the construction of a globally applicable rule model from local rules as *bottom-up*. Note that this k has to be fixed in advance. This is a weakness of ANCHORS because there is no guarantee of completeness – meaning it may not generate an explanation for every class – if this parameter is set too low. We have observed this behavior across many model initializations. Hence, in our experiments we will also consider an idealized variant, ANCHORS-∞, which continues to select terms until it reaches maximum coverage. This will serve as a reference for the maximal local-to-global performance of ANCHORS. While ANCHORS, in principle, can naturally handle multi-class settings, it cannot work with different local explainers (property (v)).

A very different approach to computing a rule model is taken by CEGA [6]. Instead of computing rules for individual samples one by one, CEGA starts with a set of attribution scores computed for a set of input samples. Because multiple samples are considered at the same time, regardless of their position in the input space, we refer to this paradigm as *top-down*. In a first step, it uses the Apriori algorithm [5] on the attribution scores to obtain *sets of input features* that are frequently marked as 'important' simultaneously. A drawback of this approach is that the cardinality of frequent itemsets considered must be limited by some small constant in advance for complexity issues. In the next step, it uses the training samples, corresponding labels, and sets of input features to perform association rule mining. This step determines the relationship between the actual values observed in the marked input dimensions and the class labels. This produces a set of rules that describe an association between feature values and one or multiple classes. Rules that contain more than one class label are filtered out. The authors state that in scenarios where classes are highly imbalanced, association rule mining only finds rules for one of the classes. To counter this problem, the authors limit their method to binary problems only. This allows CEGA to use not only the positive attribution scores as evidence for one class but also the negative ones for evidence towards the *other* class. Our algorithm is not restricted to binary problems because rules are learned in a one-vs-rest scheme for each class individually. This addresses the rule extraction from CEGA. For rule composition, CEGA distinguishes between two modes: *discriminatory* and *characteristic*. In the discriminatory mode, the class label is in the consequent; in the characteristic mode, it appears in the antecedent. Rules of the opposite form are omitted based on the selected mode, and the remaining rules are filtered by a confidence threshold. We note that CEGA's itemset mining based approach allows it to not only work with attribution scores as inputs but with any input that provides some form of description of input samples, including rules. In summary, CEGA fulfills property (v) but not property (iii).

3 Preliminaries

In this section we collect the necessary background for our work. In particular, we discuss established performance measures for global rule-based explanations (Sect. 3.1) and provide the most important notions concerning closed frequent itemsets (Sect. 3.2).

3.1 Evaluation Criteria and Methods

Evaluating the quality of explanations is an active research field of XAI [3,28]. A fundamental contention arises between the need of explanations to be *faithful*— reflecting the actual decision process of the black-box model as best as possible— and the need to be *understandable* by the target user [7,18]. In Sect. 1 we have formulated five natural properties that should be fulfilled by every local-to-global XAI rule extraction algorithm. In this section we specify how we assess the performance of CFIRE in terms of these requirements.

Property (i) from Sect. 1 requires the output of CFIRE to be *faithful*. Accuracy, precision, F1-score, and coverage are established measures to assess this property in rule based explanations [6,15,31]. In particular, accuracy and precision address the aspect that a valid explanation needs to agree with the black-box output and coverage quantifies the extent to which a global rule-based model is even applicable in the black-box's input domain. We therefore assess faithfulness by reporting *precision* as the accuracy of a rule at face value and *F1-score* as a joint measure for error rate and coverage.

Property (ii) requires the rules to be *understandable* to the target user. For each class, CFIRE returns a rule in the form of a DNF with literals defined by interval constraints. Accordingly, the comprehensibility of a global model formed by the union of such DNFs depends strongly on its size. In case of rule-based models, this is often measured by the number of independent rules that comprise this model [6,33]. We follow this approach and define the *size* of this kind of global rule models by the total number of terms in it, across all classes.

According to (iii), the output is expected to be *complete* in the sense that all instances of the domain are covered by at least one "powerful" rule. This measure is of particular importance for algorithms, including CFIRE, that can handle multi-class problems. We quantify completeness by the proportion of the cases in which 1) the algorithm provides a rule model with above chance precision and 2) at least one rule for each of the classes.

Property (iv) requires the algorithm to show *robustness* against the Rashomon effect [9] in XAI. This requirement is motivated by the recent experimental study [26], which shows that explanations obtained by the same XAI method for two different but equally well-performing models will likely diverge and that some models are easier to explain than others. The results in [26] highlight that it is not sufficient to demonstrate the effectiveness of an explanation method on a single instance of a black-box hypothesis class, but that explanation methods need to be evaluated across *several* instances. To the best of our knowledge, the robustness of the methods against the Rashomon effect has, up to now, been disregarded. To evaluate CFIRE for this property, we conduct all experiments for not one, but 50 equally well-performing black-box models per task and calculate mean values and standard deviations for all measures (F1-score, precision, size). *Low* standard deviations in F1-scores and precision indicate robustness, while *high* variability in rule size suggests the algorithm adapts to individual models.

The requirement for *flexibility* (property (v)) results from the *disagreement problem* [20]. It is the phenomenon that different local explainers may produce different explanations for the same black-box prediction, yet no single attribution method can consistently outperform others across models and datasets. While the disagreement of feature attribution methods has been further quantified in previous work [26], its downstream effect on methods that take such attributions as input has not been studied so far. As a first step towards this direction, we perform an ablation study on CFIRE. We compare the results for rule models based on different local attribution methods and show that *flexibility* can have a strong *positive* effect on the outcome, in particular for properties (i)–(iii).

Besides the five properties discussed above, we further quantify the agreement between the rules and local explanations by measuring, for each sample, the *precision* with which the applicable rules align with the dimensions identified as important by the local explanation, given that the rules assign the sample the same label as the black-box model.

3.2 Closed Frequent Itemsets

We recall some basic notions and results from *frequent pattern mining* (see, e.g., [4]). For a finite ground set U, let $\mathcal{D}$ be a multiset of subsets of U (i.e., a subset of U may occur in $\mathcal{D}$ with muliplicity greater than one). Given $\mathcal{D}$ over U and a (relative) frequency threshold $\tau \in (0, 1]$, the problem of *frequent itemset mining* [5] is to generate all subsets of U that are subsets of at least t sets in $\mathcal{D}$ for $t = \lceil \tau |\mathcal{D}| \rceil$. The subsets of U satisfying this property are referred to as *frequent (item)sets*. It follows that if $F \subseteq U$ is frequent then all proper subsets of F are also frequent, implying that the number of frequent itemsets is exponential in the cardinality of a frequent itemset of maximum cardinality. Instead of frequent itemsets, one may consider the collection (also called family) of closed frequent itemsets [29]; a subset $F \subseteq U$ is *closed frequent* if it is frequent and for all $F' \supsetneq F$, there exists $T \in \mathcal{D}$ with $F \subseteq T$ and $F' \not\subseteq T$.

As an example, consider the ground set $U = \{a, b, c, d, e\}$ and the family

$$\mathcal{D} = \{bce, abde, abde, abce, abcde, bcd\} \ ,$$

where the strings in $\mathcal{D}$ represent sets of elements (e.g., bce denotes $\{b, c, e\}$). Note that $\mathcal{D}$ is a multiset, as $abde$ appears more than once in $\mathcal{D}$. Let the frequency threshold be $\tau = 0.5$. Then bde is frequent, as it is a subset of $3 = \lceil 0.5 \cdot 6 \rceil$ sets in $\mathcal{D}$. However, bde is not closed. Indeed, if we extend bde by a, then $abde$ is a subset of all three sets in $\mathcal{D}$ containing bde. In contrast, bce is not only frequent, but also closed. For all proper supersets of bce, none is a subset of *all* three sets in $\mathcal{D}$ that contain bce (i.e., $bce, abce, abcde$). One can check for $\mathcal{D}$ and τ above that while the number of frequent itemsets is 19, that of closed frequent itemsets is only 7. In Sect. 5 we will discuss some attractive algebraic and algorithmic properties of closed frequent sets that are also utilized by our algorithm.

4 Problem Setting

In this section we define the problem setting considered in this work. Given a black-box classifier model Φ mapping the domain $\mathbb{R}^d$ to a finite set of target classes for some positive integer d, our goal is to construct a *global explanation* formed by a set of rule-based explanations, each computed for one of the target classes. In the following, the set $\{1, \ldots, d\}$ is denoted by $[d]$.

Explanation Language. We consider class explanation rules of the form $E \to c$, where the antecedent E, the *explanation*, is a DNF and the consequent c is one of the target classes. More precisely, the *language* $\mathcal{L}$ for the explanations is formed by the class of DNFs over variables defining *interval constraints*. That is, all variables V in all *terms* (i.e., conjunctions) of a DNF in $\mathcal{L}$ are of the form $A_i \in [a, b]$ for some $a, b \in \mathbb{R}$ and $i \in [d]$, where A_i denotes the i-th feature. Without loss of generality, we require that each term of a DNF contains at most one interval constraint for A_i, for all $i \in [d]$. The terms in E represent *boxes*, i.e., axis-aligned hyperrectangles, in subspaces of $\mathbb{R}^d$. Thus, a rule $E \to c$ with $E \in \mathcal{L}$ approximates the set of instances with predicted class c by the union of a finite set of such boxes. Although this limitation of $\mathcal{L}$ may seem too restrictive at first glance, our experimental results and those in [32] using the same language clearly show that $\mathcal{L}$ has a sufficiently large expressive power. Needless to say, DNFs in $\mathcal{L}$, containing only a few terms, are undoubtedly *easy* for domain experts to interpret, provided the terms do not contain too many literals (i.e., interval constraints). We emphasize that for all classes c, we are interested in rules that explain the predicted and *not* the (unknown) true class label.

The Problem. To compute $E \in \mathcal{L}$ for a rule $E \to c$ for some class c, the algorithm receives as input a finite subset X of the domain generated by the *unknown* target distribution. The input set X is required to contain at least one instance with predicted class c. We assume that the algorithm has access to the *black-box model* to be explained and to a *local explainer* algorithm. The black-box model, denoted Φ, is a function mapping the domain $\mathbb{R}^d$ to $\mathcal{Y}$, where d is the dimension of the domain and $\mathcal{Y}$ is the set of target classes. We deal with *classification* models, i.e., $\mathcal{Y}$ is some finite set. For an input sample $\mathbf{x} \in \mathbb{R}^d$, it returns the *predicted* class $\Phi(\mathbf{x}) \in \mathcal{Y}$ of $\mathbf{x}$. The *local explainer*, denoted L_Φ, returns for the black-box model Φ and $\mathbf{x}$ an *attribution vector* $\mathbf{w} \in \mathbb{R}^d$. It is a d-dimensional vector with real valued entries, where entry i indicates how much feature i contributes to the black-box model's prediction of the class of $\mathbf{x}$. Finally, the set of instances of X predicted as c is denoted by X_c, i.e.,

$$X_c = \{\mathbf{x} \in X : \Phi(\mathbf{x}) = c\} \;.$$

Note that X_c depends on Φ. We omit Φ from the notation because it is always clear from the context. Our goal is to compute a *compact* explanation for each class c that is *consistent* with the predicted labels of all instances in X, i.e., it covers all instances in X_c and none of the elements of $X \setminus X_c$. More precisely, we consider the following problem:

Problem 1. Given a black-box model $\Phi : \mathbb{R}^d \to \mathcal{Y}$ for some positive integer d and finite set $\mathcal{Y}$ of class labels, a local explainer L_Φ for Φ, and a finite set $X \subset \mathbb{R}^d$ with $X_c \neq \emptyset$ for all $c \in \mathcal{Y}$, *compute* a set

$$\mathcal{E} = \{E_c \to c \text{ with } E_c \in \mathcal{L}\}_{c \in \mathcal{Y}}$$

of class explanations that is

(i) consistent with Φ on X, i.e., for all $\mathbf{x} \in X$, $c \in \mathcal{Y}$, and $E \to c \in \mathcal{E}$, $\mathbf{x}$ satisfies E iff $\Phi(\mathbf{x}) = c$ and
(ii) all explanations in $\mathcal{E}$ have the smallest size with respect to this property, i.e., for all $c \in \mathcal{Y}$, there is no $E' \to c$ with $E' \in \mathcal{L}$ that satisfies the consistency condition above and E' has strictly less terms than E.

We note that Problem 1 is NP-complete. Indeed, it is in NP and the NP-hardness follows from a straightforward reduction from the following decision problem from computational learning theory: *Given* disjoint sets $P, N \subseteq \{0,1\}^d$ for some d and a positive integer k, *decide* whether there exists a k-term-DNF (i.e., which consists of k terms) that is consistent with P and N (i.e., which is satisfied by all instances in P and by none in N). This consistency problem is NP-complete already for $k = 2$ [30].

The NP-completeness of the problem implies that we need to resort to some *heuristic* approach to approximately solve Problem 1. In the next section we present such a heuristic algorithm. Among other things, it makes use of some nice algebraic and algorithmic properties of *closed sets* that are relevant for our context. Note that Problem 1 allows the rules in $\mathcal{E}$ to be approximated for each class separately, as we only require the explanations in the rules to be consistent with the predicted classes of the instances in X; the family of subsets of $\mathbb{R}^d$ represented by the class explanations in $\mathcal{E}$ are *not* required to be pairwise disjoint. This observation allows the instances in X with the same predicted class to be handled separately for every class.

5 The Algorithm

In this section we present our *heuristic* algorithm CLOSED FREQUENT ITEMSET RULES FROM EXPLANATIONS (CFIRE) for Problem 1. A schematic representation and the pseudocode of the algorithm are given in Fig. 1 and Algorithm 1,

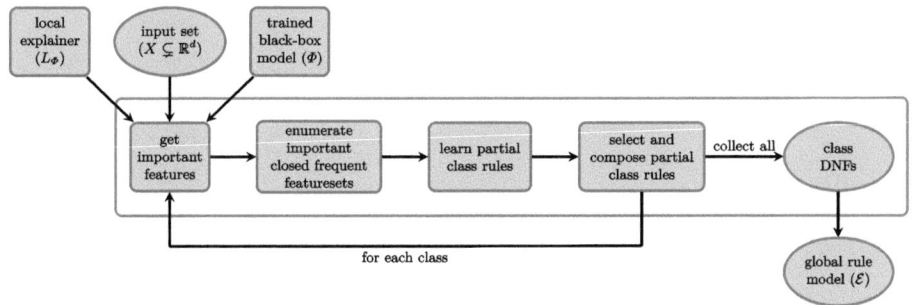

Fig. 1. Schematic overview of our algorithm CFIRE. Given black-box model Φ, local explainer L_Φ, and input data X, our algorithm computes DNFs as explanations for each class independently.

respectively.[1] The input to the algorithm consists of a black-box model Φ, a local explainer L_Φ, and a finite subset X of $\mathbb{R}^d$, as defined in Problem 1. It is important to emphasize that the algorithm can be parameterized by *any* local explainer that computes explanations which specify the dimensions that are important for a given black-box prediction (cf. property (v) on flexibility in Sect. 1). In this work we will consider attribution methods for their popularity and ease of use. The downstream effect of the *disagreement problem*, that is, the impact of using *different* local explainers, is evaluated experimentally and discussed in Sect. 6.2. The algorithm processes every target class $c \in \mathcal{Y}$ separately (cf. lines 2–12) and returns a set of class explanations, one for each class, in $\mathcal{E}$ (cf. line 13). The explanation for the current class c, variable DNF in Line 11, is computed in five main steps, as described below.

(Step 1) Initialization. We initialize $\mathcal{T}$, the set of candidate terms for the explanation of class c, and $\mathcal{D}$, a multiset of subsets of the feature set, by the empty set. Then, we compute X_c, which contains all input samples from X that were predicted as class c by the black-box model Φ (cf. lines 3–4).

(Step 2) Selection of Important Features. In this step we calculate for all instances $\mathbf{x} \in X_c$ the set of features that are important for the class prediction of $\mathbf{x}$. Formally (cf. lines 5–6), for all $\mathbf{x} \in X_c$, the algorithm calls the local explainer L_Φ for $\mathbf{x}$. By condition, it returns an attribution vector $\mathbf{w} \in \mathbb{R}^d$ (i.e., $\mathbf{w} = L_\Phi(\mathbf{x})$). Normalizing the importance scores in $\mathbf{w}$ by the sum of their absolute values, a feature is regarded as *important* if its absolute value is greater than a threshold ι after normalization. As a rule of thumb, we used $\iota = 0.01$ in *all* of the experiments.

(Step 3) Closed Frequent Feature Sets. For each target class, only features that are *important* for the prediction of *sufficiently many* instances in the block of the class are considered as candidates for the interval constraints in the

---
[1] For simplicity we omit the hyperparameters from the description because they were constant in all our experiments (see Sect. 6).

Algorithm 1. CFIRE

Input: black-box model $\Phi : R^d \to \mathcal{Y}$ for some positive integer d and finite set $\mathcal{Y}$, local explainer L_Φ for Φ, finite input set $X \subset \mathbb{R}^d$ with $X_c \neq \emptyset$ for all $c \in \mathcal{Y}$
Output: $\mathcal{E} = \{\text{DNF}_c \to c : c \in \mathcal{Y}\}$
1: $\mathcal{E} \leftarrow \emptyset$
2: **for all** $c \in \mathcal{Y}$ **do**
3:     $\mathcal{T}, \mathcal{D} \leftarrow \emptyset$ ▷ $\mathcal{D}$ is a multiset
4:     $X_c \leftarrow \{\mathbf{x} \in X : \Phi(\mathbf{x}) = c\}$
5:     **for all** $\mathbf{x} \in X_c$ **do**
6:         $T_\mathbf{x} \leftarrow \text{GET\_IMPORTANT\_ATTRIBUTES}(L_\Phi(\mathbf{x}))$
7:         add $T_\mathbf{x}$ to $\mathcal{D}$
8:     $\mathcal{C} \leftarrow \text{ENUMERATE\_CLOSED\_FREQUENT\_SETS}(\mathcal{D})$
9:     **for all** $F \in \mathcal{C}$ **do**
10:        $\mathcal{T} \leftarrow \mathcal{T} \cup \text{LEARN\_RULES}(F, \sigma(F), X \setminus X_c)$
11:    $\text{DNF} \leftarrow \text{SELECTANDCOMPOSERULES}(\mathcal{T}, X_c)$
12:    add DNF $\to c$ to $\mathcal{E}$
13: **return** $\mathcal{E}$

---

class explanations. This *frequency constraint* is necessary for the explanations' *compactness*, as each selected feature will induce at least one interval constraint.

Accordingly, our goal is to generate a family of feature sets in which *all* features in a set contribute significantly to the prediction of *several* instances in the block. In other words, we aim to compute subsets of features, each being a candidate for inducing a term in the DNF, where the features within a particular subset *jointly* contribute significantly to the class prediction for *several* instances. Note that this family can be incomplete in the sense that the binarized attribution vector of an instance in X is not covered by any of these frequent feature sets. However, this does not imply that none of the interval constraints computed from the frequent sets will cover the instance itself. When regarding the binarized attribution vectors as the characteristic vectors of subsets of the entire feature set, the above problem of generating all frequent sets of important features is precisely an instance of the *frequent itemset mining* problem (see, also, Sect. 3.2): Given a transaction database, where each transaction is a subset of the set of all items and a relative frequency threshold, the task is to generate the set of all frequent itemsets, i.e., the subsets that appear in at least a certain number of the transactions specified by the threshold.

As already mentioned, each frequent set of important features induces a term in the class explanation DNF by taking the conjunction of the interval constraints computed for the features in the set. Although this idea may seem straightforward at first glance, it raises a serious complexity problem: If there exists a frequent set of cardinality k, then the number of frequent itemsets is $\Omega(2^k)$, as all subsets of a frequent set are also frequent. To overcome this problem, one may control the number of frequent itemsets by bounding the size of the frequent itemsets by some small constant s. However, this restriction results in terms that contain at most s interval constraints. Hence, the corresponding boxes of $\mathbb{R}^d$ are unbounded in at least $d-s$ coordinates (features). For example, in the open source code for CEGA [6], which we use in our experiments, the number of literals in a term is bounded by 3 (cf. Sect. 2). Our experimental results presented in Sect. 6 clearly show that the corresponding boxes are too general, implying that CEGA is unable to generate global class explanations of high accuracy.

We tackle this complexity issue by considering *closed* frequent itemsets. Recall from Sect. 3.2 that a frequent itemset is closed if it is maximal for the following property: its extension by a new item leads to a drop in the number of supporting transactions. Closed frequent itemsets have several advantages over frequent itemsets that can be utilized in our application context:

(a) For any frequent itemset F with a support set (i.e., the set of instances in X_c with important feature sets containing F), there exists a *unique* closed itemset with the same support set as F. Thus, closed frequent itemsets are a lossless representation of frequent itemsets.
(b) The above mentioned maximality property of closed frequent itemsets implies that the boxes determined by the interval constraints for the features in closed frequent sets are more specific (i.e., have a lower degree of freedom) than those in frequent itemsets, addressing the problem of overly general boxes mentioned above.
(c) The number of closed frequent itemsets can be exponentially smaller than that of frequent itemsets.
(d) The set of closed frequent itemsets can be generated *efficiently* (more precisely, with polynomial delay, meaning that there is an algorithm such that the delay between two consecutive closed frequent itemsets generated by the algorithm is bounded by a polynomial of the size of the input).

Properties (a), (c), and (d) together imply that closed frequent itemsets form a *lossless* representation of frequent itemsets, can achieve an exponentially large compression ratio, and can be listed efficiently, independently of their maximum cardinality (see, e.g., [8, 14, 29]). These nice algebraic and algorithmic properties together with (b) make closed frequent itemsets more suitable for our purpose than ordinary frequent itemsets.

Formally, for $c \in \mathcal{Y}$ and instance $\mathbf{x} \in \mathbb{R}^d$, let $I(\mathbf{x})$ be the set of important features selected in Step 2 for $\mathbf{x}$ and denote

$$\mathcal{D}_c = \{I(\mathbf{x}) : \mathbf{x} \in X_c\}$$

the family of important feature sets for the instances in X_c. The *support* of a set F of features in $\mathcal{D}_c$ is the family of sets in $\mathcal{D}_c$ that contain F, i.e.,

$$\sigma(F) = \{S \in \mathcal{D}_c : F \subseteq S\} \ .$$

We note that $\mathcal{D}_c$ and $\sigma(F)$ are regarded as multisets. For $\mathcal{D}_c$ and relative frequency threshold $\tau \in (0,1]$, let $\mathcal{C}_c$ denote the family of closed frequent sets of $\mathcal{D}_c$ for τ, i.e., for all subsets F, F' of the set of features with $F \subsetneq F'$,

$$F \in \mathcal{C}_c \iff \frac{|\sigma(F)|}{|\mathcal{D}_c|} \geq \tau \text{ and } \sigma(F') \subsetneq \sigma(F) \ .$$

It holds that $\mathcal{C}_c$ can be computed in time polynomial in the combined size of $\mathcal{D}_c$ and the cardinality of the set of all features (see, e.g., [8]). In the realization of line 8 we use the closed frequent set generation algorithm in [14]. It is a highly effective enumeration algorithm based on the divide and conquer paradigm. This paradigm implies some nice algorithmic properties that are utilized by our implementation of Algorithm 1. For *all* experiments, $\tau = 0.01$ was used.

(Step 4) Learning Incomplete Class Explanations. For a closed frequent feature set F generated for class c, we take the projection of all training examples to the subspace in $\mathbb{R}^d$ spanned by the features in F. Let X' denote the set of training examples $\mathbf{x}$ with predicted class c such that the important feature set $I(\mathbf{x})$ of $\mathbf{x}$ supports (i.e., contains) F, that is,

$$X' = \{\mathbf{x} \in X_c | F \subseteq I(\mathbf{x})\} \ .$$

Finally, let B be the smallest box in the subspace induced by F that contains the projections of the elements in X'. We distinguish two cases: If B is consistent with the training examples predicted as classes different from c, we associate F with the term representing this box and continue. Otherwise, we frame the problem as a binary classification task (X' vs $X \setminus X_c$) and apply a decision tree learning algorithm within the subspace. We allow a certain amount of inconsistency for the tree learner in order to avoid too complex decision trees and hence overfitting rule models. We associate F with a refined B, extended by the disjunction of the terms representing the paths to leaf-nodes that correspond to samples in X'.

(Step 5) Learning Complete Class Explanations. The set of terms computed in Step 4 for a given class c represents a set of boxes in $\mathbb{R}^d$, each (almost) consistent with $X \setminus X_c$. Each term is associated with the set of samples in X_c that satisfy it (or equivalently, whose corresponding projections are contained by the corresponding box). By construction, a particular instance in X_c can satisfy several terms. The goal is to select a smallest set of terms such that the union of their associated samples covers all instances in X_c. Note that this selection problem can be regarded as an instance of the *set cover* problem. Since this problem is NP-hard, we resort to the standard greedy heuristic designed for it (see, e.g., [11]). Our results in Sect. 6.2 show that the selected rules reproduce the characteristics of the local explanations surprisingly well. Finally, we return the explanation for class c by taking the disjunction of the set of terms selected with this heuristic.

Using CFIRE with Multiple Local Explainers. Given multiple L_Φ, we compute a set $\mathcal{E}_{L_\Phi}$ of class explanations for each of them and select the one, denoted $\mathcal{E}$, that achieves the highest accuracy on X.

Applying $\mathcal{E}$. For an instance $\mathbf{x}$, we predict its class by the rule $E_c \to c \in \mathcal{E}$ that is satisfied by $\mathbf{x}$. In case that more than one E_c is satisfied by $\mathbf{x}$, we break the tie by choosing the rule where the term satisfied by $\mathbf{x}$ has the highest accuracy.

6 Experimental Evaluation

In this section we present our experimental results. In particular, we compare the performance of CFIRE against that of ANCHORS [32] and CEGA [6], and show that our algorithm fulfills all five properties required in Sect. 1.

Datasets and Black-Box Models. We consider seven binary and seven multi-class learning tasks. Table 1 provides a summary of the datasets and performance of our black-box NNs. The corresponding datasets are publicly available at either OpenML.org, UCI Machine Learning Repository or Harvard Dataverse. In some cases categorical variables trivialised the learning problem; these features were removed from the respective datasets. All datasets obtained in this way became subsets of $\mathbb{R}^d$ for some d. Each dataset was split into three *disjunct* parts: Roughly 80% were used to train the black-box neural networks (NNs), 10% were used as input to the algorithms (i.e., X in Table 1), and the remainder for testing the rule models. For very small datasets (such as iris or wine), the split was 60-20-20. Set X is guaranteed to contain samples from all classes. We train 50 NNs for each task, all of which achieve similarly good performance (see Table 1)[2]. Since CEGA is not applicable to multi-class tasks, we compare our method CFIRE against the ANCHORS variants only in those cases. All algorithms were given the same input set X to compute global rule models.

Setup and Hyperparameters. For *all* experiments with CFIRE, we set the importance threshold $\iota = 0.01$, the frequency threshold $\tau = 0.01$, and the maximum depth of the decision trees learned in Step 4 (cf. Sect. 5) to 7^3. As motivated

Table 1. Overview of datasets used in the experiments. $|\mathcal{Y}|$ describes the number of classes, d the dimensionality of the data, and $|X|$ the cardinality of the input set for the rule algorithms. Φ reports the average black-box accuracies on X.

(a) Binary classification datasets.

Dataset	d	$|X|$	Φ
[39] btsc	4	150	0.81 ±0.00
[10] spf	24	389	0.76 ±0.01
[19] breastw	9	1000	0.99 ±0.00
[17] spambase	57	921	0.94 ±0.00
[3] heloc	23	1975	0.73 ±0.00
[38] breastcancer	30	114	1.00 ±0.00
[34] ionosphere	34	71	0.96 ±0.01

(b) Multiclass classification datasets.

Dataset	$|\mathcal{Y}|$	d	$|X|$	Φ
[13] iris	3	4	38	0.92 ±0.01
[16] autouniv	3	5	140	0.42 ±0.01
[27] abalone	3	7	627	0.64 ±0.00
[2] wine	3	13	36	1.00 ±0.00
[25] vehicle	4	18	170	0.81 ±0.01
[1] beans	7	16	1050	0.91 ±0.00
[12] diggle	9	8	124	0.96 ±0.00

---

[2] All NNs consisted of 512 neurons or less, details can be found in the repository.
[3] The choice of threshold parameters proved robust across all tasks, we leave further optimization to future work.

by the disagreement problem, we run CFIRE with three local explainers: KernelSHAP (KS) [23], LIME (LI) [31], and Integrated Gradients (IG) [35]. For KS, LI we use the implementation provided in Captum. For each black-box we choose the CFIRE output for a single L_Φ as described in the previous section.

The results for ANCHORS were computed using the anchors implementation available on PiPy. The precision threshold was set to 0.9 for all experiments. To obtain a global model from ANCHORS, we use the greedy selection approach outlined in [32]. It requires the user to set an upper bound k on the number of rules to be selected *in advance*. For a fair comparison at the same *compactness-level*, we set k to the same number of terms that CFIRE computed. To compare against the best *theoretical* result for ANCHORS, we also report results with an unconstrained k, denoted by ANCHORS-∞. This *idealized* version can select as many terms computed on X as needed to reach maximum coverage on the input set. Since ANCHORS does not provide a prediction function, we use the same strategy as for CFIRE for both variants of ANCHORS.

To compute the CEGA explanations, we used the code available on Github. CEGA was also run with all three local explainers. Here, the maximum length parameter (i.e., the upper bound on the cardinalities of frequent sets) is kept at its default of 3 and the confidence threshold for association rule mining for the Apriori algorithm [5] is lowered to 0.04 to increase options during rule selection. To perform rule selection, CEGA filters the rules using another confidence threshold. To obtain discriminatory explanations, we used nine thresholds between $[0.05, \ldots, 0.95]$ and likewise, nine thresholds for characteristic explanations between $[0.05, \ldots, 0.8]$ (cf. Sect. 2). Combined with the three different L_Φ, we thus obtain 54 different rule models from CEGA for each black-box model it is tasked to explain. As with CFIRE, we select the rule model with the highest accuracy on X and report results on the test data.

To compute local explanations, KS and LI were given a sampling budget of 300 and IG performed 200 steps to approximate the integral. The empirical mean of the black-box training data was used as baseline for all attribution methods.

6.1 Algorithm Comparison: Properties (i)-(iv)

In this section, we compare CFIRE against CEGA and the two variants of ANCHORS. First we show an example output of all three algorithms. Then, we present the results from four different aspects: faithfulness, comprehensibility, completeness, and robustness against the Rashomon effect (see Properties (i)–(iv) in Sect. 1). Lastly, we compare the runtime of the rule extraction step for every algorithm.

Example Rule Models. Table 2 provides an example output on the btsc dataset for all three algorithms, each for the same black-box model. The DNFs in the table are intended to illustrate compactness and comprehensibility. CFIRE and CEGA contain 2 terms each (i.e., Size = 2) with 2 or fewer literals each; ANCHORS provides 5 terms with up to 3 literals. ANCHORS' rules consist of half open intervals in this example. While half open intervals do not impede performance in terms of accuracy, we argue that it is questionable for an *empirically*

Table 2. Rules generated by CFIRE, ANCHORS and CEGA for the same black-box model Φ on btsc. Labels {0,1} indicate whether an individual donated blood during a certain time period.

Algorithm	Rules
CFIRE	Precision = 0.933, F1 = 0.835 0 : (Amount $\in$ (250, 4 250]) 1 : (Recency $\in$ (1, 4] $\wedge$ Amount $\in$ (1 250, 8 500])
ANCHORS	Precision = 0.893, F1 = 0.893 0 : (Recency $\in$ (4.03, ∞]) $\vee$ (Amount $\in$ ($-\infty$, 997.01]) $\vee$ (Time $\in$ (50.11, ∞]) 1 : (Amount $\in$ (997.01, ∞] $\wedge$ Recency $\in$ ($-\infty$, 4.03] $\wedge$ Time $\in$ ($-\infty$, 50.11]) $\vee$ (Amount $\in$ (1 930.35, ∞] $\wedge$ Recency $\in$ ($-\infty$, 4.03])
CEGA	Precision = 0.176, F1 = 0.036 0 : (Time $\in$ (14.82, 42.43]) 1 : (Frequency $\in$ (5.35, 8.86])

obtained rule to suggest that model behavior will not change before $\pm\infty$. Both CFIRE and CEGA, by design, always provide bounded intervals.

Regarding the five properties listed in Sect. 1, consider Tables 3a and 3b. They contain quantitative results on binary and multi-class tasks, respectively. For each dataset, the first three rows show the average values and the standard deviations of the F1-score, precisions, and rule sizes over the 50 black-box models. Recall that the rule size (Size) counts the number of terms across all classes for the final global rule model. The fourth row (Compl.) denotes the proportion of the cases where the corresponding algorithm was able to produce rules for every class with an overall better than random precision on the test set. Since CEGA is restricted to binary class problems, it is omitted from Table 3b.

Properties (i) and (ii). Regarding faithfulness and comprehensibility, a closer look at the F1-score and the precision results show that CFIRE always outperforms CEGA, in most of the cases ANCHORS, and is comparable even to the idealized version of ANCHORS (i.e., ANCHORS-∞) in terms of faithfulness. In addition, CFIRE, almost always returns (much) more compact rules than ANCHORS-∞ (see row Size).

Comparing the idealized variant ANCHORS-∞ to CFIRE, it outperforms CFIRE in terms of F1-score and precision in 8 out of 14 cases, while requiring up to 3× more terms at the same time. In 5 out of the 6 other datasets, CFIRE outperforms ANCHORS-∞ on average, while requiring the same or only half the amount of terms. On one of the dataset (i.e., abalone), CFIRE needs more than twice the amount of terms (25.24 cmp. to 11.8). Comparing standard deviations, CFIRE and ANCHORS-∞ actually overlap in half of the tasks.

Comparing against the normally budgeted ANCHORS, CFIRE outperforms it on average in 13 out of 14 cases, but with overlapping standard deviations in 5 cases. We note that both algorithms show notable gaps between F1-score

Table 3. Performance on binary tasks (3a) and multi-class tasks (3b). Size counts the number of terms in a global explanation across all classes. Compl. is the proportion of the 50 models for which the algorithm provides a rule model with above chance precision and at least one rule for each of the classes. All but the last row report mean±std over all 50 black-box models per task. ANCHORS-∞ is the idealized version of ANCHORS.

(a) Binary tasks

Task	Metric	CFIRE	CEGA	ANCHORS	ANCHORS-∞
btsc	F1	0.93±0.02	0.09±0.06	0.71±0.26	0.90±0.02
	Precision	0.94±0.02	0.54±0.28	0.81±0.15	0.90±0.02
	Size	4.36±1.54	2.22±0.58	4.10±0.99	5.58±0.81
	Compl.	0.98	0.	0.3	0.7
spf	F1	0.76±0.03	0.55±0.05	0.27±0.03	0.84±0.02
	Precision	0.76±0.03	0.57±0.05	0.76±0.05	0.85±0.02
	Size	17.80±6.01	43.34±35.03	17.80±6.01	70.10±8.24
	Compl.	0.94	0.02	0.	1.
breastw	F1	0.96±0.01	0.36±0.06	0.79±0.20	0.96±0.02
	Precision	0.97±0.01	0.70±0.03	0.90±0.08	0.96±0.02
	Size	15.12±4.43	6.70±2.84	13.76±3.19	18.24±3.51
	Compl.	1.	0.02	0.72	1.
spambase	F1	0.87±0.03	0.29±0.15	0.45±0.10	0.76±0.03
	Precision	0.90±0.02	0.85±0.06	0.70±0.07	0.76±0.03
	Size	9.22±6.95	8.42±13.79	8.66±5.48	21.66±2.13
	Compl.	1.	0.14	0.1	1.
heloc	F1	0.86±0.02	0.20±0.13	0.56±0.01	0.89±0.01
	Precision	0.89±0.01	0.76±0.07	0.80±0.06	0.89±0.01
	Size	13.98±10.55	3.98±2.10	13.98±10.55	68.48±8.83
	Compl.	1.	0.29	0.	1.
breastc.	F1	0.88±0.03	0.57±0.07	0.70±0.05	0.93±0.01
	Precision	0.92±0.01	0.63±0.02	0.98±0.02	0.97±0.01
	Size	3.34±1.98	25.26±10.71	3.34±1.98	12.88±1.77
	Compl.	1.	0.1	0.06	1.
ionos.	F1	0.75±0.05	0.53±0.14	0.33±0.09	0.81±0.02
	Precision	0.78±0.05	0.58±0.10	0.77±0.11	0.85±0.03
	Size	4.60±1.44	67.32±32.18	4.60±1.44	15.86±2.86
	Compl.	0.86	0.04	0.08	1.

(b) Multi-class tasks

Task	Metric	CFIRE	ANCHORS	ANCHORS-∞
iris	F1	0.87±0.02	0.72±0.08	0.92±0.03
	Precision	0.96±0.01	0.94±0.02	0.94±0.02
	Size	4.62±0.73	4.62±0.73	9.14±0.95
	Compl.	1.	0.	1.
autouniv	F1	0.41±0.04	0.40±0.06	0.54±0.04
	Precision	0.44±0.04	0.65±0.08	0.66±0.05
	Size	24.82±5.60	24.80±5.57	43.92±4.63
	Compl.	0.96	0.36	1.
abalone	F1	0.81±0.02	0.77±0.02	0.77±0.02
	Precision	0.86±0.03	0.77+0.02	0.77±0.02
	Size	25.24±8.75	11.80±2.81	11.80±2.81
	Compl.	1.	1.	1.
wine	F1	0.66±0.08	0.50±0.11	0.87±0.04
	Precision	0.85±0.07	0.88±0.07	0.95±0.02
	Size	4.30±1.27	4.30±1.27	10.44±0.97
	Compl.	1.	0.02	1.
vehicle	F1	0.55±0.04	0.57±0.05	0.61±0.03
	Precision	0.61±0.05	0.72±0.04	0.70±0.03
	Size	19.48±4.91	19.48±4.91	36.60±4.65
	Compl.	1.	0.06	1.
beans	F1	0.91±0.02	0.80±0.03	0.87±0.01
	Precision	0.93±0.01	0.86±0.02	0.87±0.01
	Size	34.50±7.10	34.50±7.10	63.98±6.65
	Compl.	1.	0.02	1.
diggle	F1	0.85±0.02	0.61±0.05	0.71±0.04
	Precision	0.99±0.01	0.71±0.06	0.74±0.04
	Size	9.58±0.64	9.58±0.64	16.78±1.76
	Compl.	1.	0.	0.

and precision on the multi-class tasks. For ANCHORS this also holds true on the binary tasks, but not for CFIRE. In the results for CEGA, the F1-scores and precision are notably lower compared to the other algorithms. It does provide the smallest rule models in 4 cases but also produces vastly larger rule models without notable performance gains in the other three cases.

Property (iii). In terms of completeness (row Compl.), CFIRE achieves a consistently high level of completeness, compared to the poor completeness results of CEGA and ANCHORS. In particular, it only loses 11 models across three binary tasks and two in a single multi-class task out of the $2 \times 7 \times 50 = 700$ models. ANCHORS, using the same size budget as CFIRE, loses models on all tasks except abalone, producing insufficient rule models in a total of 564 cases. Similarly, CEGA fails to produce sufficient explanations in the vast majority of cases. When ANCHORS-∞ is allowed to select as many rules as needed to reach maximum coverage, the number of insufficiently explained models drops to 65, though at the expense of increasing size by $2.2\times$ on average.

Property (iv). Recall from Sect. 3.1 that the robustness of a method against the Rashomon effect is measured by the standard deviations of the mean F1-score and precision values. The remarkably low standard deviations obtained for the F1-scores and precisions by CFIRE and ANCHORS-∞ show that they are of comparably high stability with regard to the Rashomon effect. CFIRE matches or exceeds ANCHORS and CEGA in all tasks.

More precisely, the standard deviation of the F1-scores is at most 0.05 in most cases, it is ≤ 0.1 for CEGA in three out of 7, and for ANCHORS in four out of 14 cases. By providing similarly accurate rules for all black-boxes, both CFIRE and ANCHORS-∞ show higher robustness against the Rashomon effect.

The standard deviation on the size indicates that all algorithms adapt to individual black-boxes by increasing complexity. For CFIRE and CEGA, the standard deviation can exceed half the total value of the mean, whereas for ANCHORS-∞, it seldom exceeds 15% of the mean. This suggests a saturation of representation in ANCHORS-∞, where increasing the number of rules provides diminishing returns on novel information. In contrast, our top-down approach CFIRE adapts more effectively, providing new insights with fewer terms and avoiding the redundancy seen in bottom-up methods.

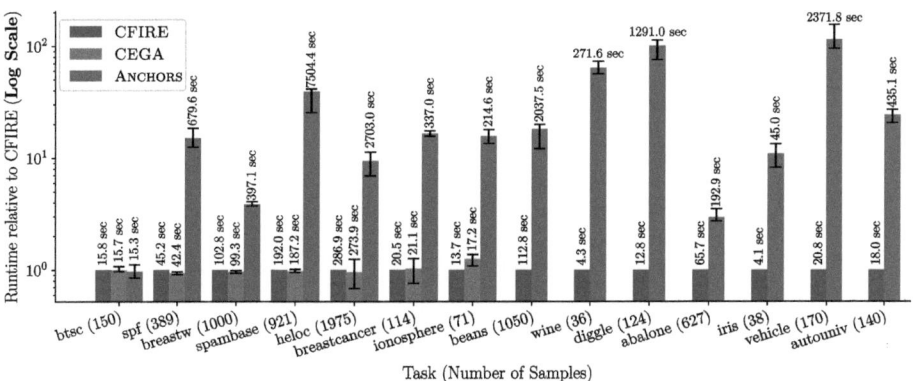

Fig. 2. Runtimes (Y-axis) of ANCHORS-∞ and CEGA *relative* to CFIRE on the 14 datasets (X-axis). Note the *log* scale of the Y-axis. The average runtime in seconds are provided atop the bars. Bar height is average runtime, whiskers indicate min-max values across the 50 black-boxes per task.

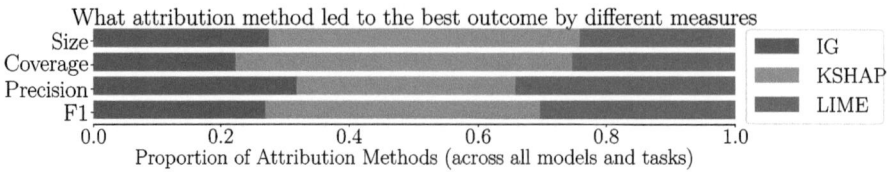

Fig. 3. Summarized over all tasks and black-boxes, the *frequency* of each attribution method leading to the best model for a given measure (Size, Coverage, Precision or F1).

Runtime. Figure 2 presents a runtime comparison for the initial rule extraction step. Each bar shows the average single-core runtime of the respective algorithm *relative* to CFIRE over all 50 models for each task on a *logarithmic* scale[4]. The black whiskers displayed atop each bar indicate minimum and maximum relative values, with absolute runtime in seconds above. CFIRE's and CEGA's runtimes also account for the computation of all three local explainability methods. The runtime for ANCHORS is accumulated over all samples in X. Rule selection is not contained in the runtime. Hence, we only report a single time for ANCHORS and ANCHORS-∞.

The runtimes for CFIRE range from 4 to 290 s across all tasks. Where applicable, CEGA demonstrates comparable performance. ANCHORS is faster only on btsc than CFIRE for certain models, taking on average 0.5 s less. For all other datasets, CFIRE is faster by a factor of 2.95 to 113. For all algorithms, the runtime depends not only on the cardinality of X, but also on the dimensionality of the data. For example, consider the runtimes for breastw ($d = 9$) and spambase ($d = 57$). For these tasks, where $|X| \approx 1\,000$, CFIRE takes twice as long on spambase (192 sec) compared to breastw (102 sec). While this increase is notable, ANCHORS takes 397 s on average on breastw, but 7 504 s (i.e., more than two hours) on spambase. For a 6.3× increase in dimensionality this reflects an 18.9× increase in runtime. Overall, both CFIRE and CEGA offer compelling runtime advantages over ANCHORS.

Summary. The results show a significant runtime advantage of the top-down methods compared to ANCHORS, despite them calculating multiple global explanations based on different local explainability methods. CEGA falls behind in the faithfulness measures and shows mixed results regarding compactness. Our algorithm CFIRE is well equipped to provide explanations in binary as well as multi-class settings, providing high precision rules and insights into all classes in nearly all cases. The results indicate that our approach is *robust* against the Rashomon effect, effectively adapting the number of terms used to describe a black-box model. ANCHORS-∞, the theoretically unbounded version of ANCHORS, shows similar stability, however, at the expense of a disproportionately higher complexity.

---

[4] Experiments run on a machine with an Intel Xeon E5-1680 CPU and 60GB RAM.

6.2 Flexibility: Property (v)

In the analysis above we computed rule models for all three attribution methods and chose the best. We now move on to analyze the impact of flexibility (Property (v)) on the results for CFIRE by asking the following questions: Which $L_\Phi \in \{\text{KS, LI, IG}\}$ would have been the best choice, according to target measures other than accuracy on the test set? How large would the performance difference be if we used a single method? For that, Fig. 3 provides a summarizing overview for F1-score, precision, coverage, and size as target measures. The plot aggregates over all datasets. For this plot we filter out results for all black-box models that were not explained using any L_Φ. This completely removes explanations for 4 of the 700 black-boxes we trained. Recall that CFIRE lost 13 models, meaning that for 13-4 = 9 models it would have provided an explanation but they were not chosen by our selection criterion of highest accuracy. Of the 696 remaining black-boxes, only 120 were best explained by a single attribution method according to all measures simultaneously. In those 120 cases KS led to the best outcome in 52% of cases, IG in 27% and LI in 21%. While KS represents the majority of the cases, in 48% of cases a different method would have been better overall. Looking at the individual measures in Fig. 3 across all models, KS dominates in terms of F1-score, coverage, and size, but the number of cases where LI and IG are the best choice is non-negligible. For precision, all methods are equally represented. This already demonstrates the beneficiality of flexibility.

Example Rule Models. Table 4 shows examples of rule models computed by CFIRE given IG and LI as L_Φ for the same black-box model. One can see that the different local explainers lead to semantically different rule models. More precisely, for the binary task btsc, we see that both methods lead to rule models with Size = 2. For LI, the rules rely on the features 'Amount' and 'Recency', while for IG, the rules also use 'Time'. Most notably, 'Recency' is used strictly in different classes by both rule models. They achieve very similar F1-scores. The examples for the iris dataset are also quite different. Rule models for LI and IG use 4 and 5 terms, each across all three classes. For class Setosa, IG leads to three terms with a single literal each, focusing on different intervals on the Sepal Width feature. In comparison, LI produces a single term that evaluates both Petal Length and Width.

Faithfulness and Compactness. In addition to the qualitative example above, Tables 5a and 5b quantitatively confirm that there is indeed a notable downstream effect caused by the disagreement problem. Column CFIRE is given as reference, again depicting average scores for the best result according to accuracy on X. Columns CFIRE-{KS, LI, IG} show results for the individual feature attribution methods.

The last three columns show that restricting CFIRE to a *single* local explainer may result in entirely different outputs. Notable performance differences with respect to F1-score and precision are observed on 8 datasets. Explanations based on CFIRE-IG underperform notably on breastw, wine, diggle, abalone, and iris, with performance differences of up to 25% compared to

Table 4. CFIRE Rules generated using IG or LI for the same black-boxes on btsc and iris.

btsc		
LI	Precision = 0.911, F1 = 0.899	
	0 : (Amount ∈ (250, 4 250])	
	1 : (Recency ∈ (1, 4] ∧ Amount ∈ (1250, 8 500])	
IG	Precision = 0.904, F1 = 0.895	
	0 : (Recency ∈ (0, 23] ∧ Time ∈ (2, 98])	
	1 : (Amount ∈ (4 625, 8 500])	
iris		
LI	Precision = 0.939, F1 = 0.886	
	Setosa : (Petal Length ∈ (1, 1.7] ∧ Petal Width ∈ (0.1, 0.5])	
	Versicolour : (Sepal Length ∈ (5.85, 6.6]) ∨ (Sepal Width ∈ (2.2, 2.95])	
	Virginica : (Petal Length ∈ (4.8, 6.7] ∧ Petal Width ∈ (1.6, 2.4])	
IG	Precision = 0.933, F1 = 0.835	
	Setosa : (Sepal Width ∈ (3.05, 3.15]) ∨ (Sepal Width ∈ (3.35, 3.7]) ∨ (Sepal Width ∈ (3.85, 4.2])	
	Versicolour : (Sepal Length ∈ (5.20, 6.65])	
	Virginica : (Petal Length ∈ (4.80, 6.7] ∧ Petal Width ∈ (1.6, 2.4])	

CFIRE. CFIRE-LI deviates negatively on spambase and breastcancer, but actually outperforms CFIRE on ionosphere. On ionosphere, both CFIRE-KS and CFIRE-IG perform equally but worse than CFIRE-LI. Overall, CFIRE-KS delivers solid accuracy and is seldom outperformed by a large margin.

For CFIRE-KS and CFIRE-LI, Size is very similar in 9 cases. In the other cases CFIRE-LI provides an explanation with less terms than CFIRE-KS. However, IG leads to the most compact explanation in nearly all cases. Most importantly, it does so in cases where it does not underperform regarding the other measures.

Completeness. Across all 14 tasks, KS leads to a loss (Compl.) of 95 (out of 700) models, LI 50, and IG 26 compared to just 12 for CFIRE. Conspicuously, the majority of insufficiently explained models does not stem from the multiclass tasks but in fact from the binary tasks. For spf, breastw, spambase, and ionosphere, at least one attribution method fails on 10 or more models.

Robustness Against the Rashomon Effect. Regarding the standard deviation across models, we note that it remains small for F1-score and precision. It exceeds 5% in only 5 cases. The standard deviation for Size is equal or lower for individual L_Φ than for CFIRE, but still exceeds variability of ANCHORS-∞, reaching 20% or more of the total mean value even for datasets with a comparably large size such as spf, beans or abalone. This clearly demonstrates that part of CFIRE's higher robustness against the Rashomon effect is due to its flexibility to work with different local explainers.

(Dis)agreement Between Rules and Local Explanations (Prec. L_Φ). Recall that this property is measured by the precision with which the applicable

Table 5. Comparison of individual attribution methods against CFIRE on binary and multi-class tasks. Size and Compl. are the same as in Table 3. Prec. L_Φ quantifies the agreement between rule models and local explanations. All rows but Compl. report mean±std over all 50 black-box models per task.

(a) Binary tasks

Task	Metric	CFIRE	CFIRE-KS	CFIRE-LI	CFIRE-IG
btsc	F1	0.93±0.02	0.92±0.02	0.91±0.02	0.90±0.01
	Precision	0.94±0.02	0.93±0.02	0.93±0.02	0.91±0.01
	Size	4.36±1.54	3.78±1.15	3.56±1.80	2.42±1.31
	Compl.	0.98	0.98	0.98	0.92
	Prec. L_Φ	0.72±0.09	0.77±0.02	0.58±0.05	0.98±0.06
spf	F1	0.76±0.03	0.74±0.03	0.73±0.03	0.76±0.03
	Precision	0.76±0.03	0.74±0.03	0.73±0.03	0.77±0.03
	Size	17.80±6.01	18.02±5.69	14.34±4.76	13.76±5.48
	Compl.	0.94	0.56	0.56	0.94
	Prec. L_Φ	0.78±0.14	0.72±0.09	0.51±0.10	0.83±0.12
breastw	F1	0.96±0.01	0.97±0.01	0.95±0.02	0.91±0.03
	Precision	0.97±0.01	0.97±0.01	0.96±0.02	0.94±0.03
	Size	15.12±4.43	15.68±4.27	10.02±3.41	2.94±1.02
	Compl.	1.	1.	1.	0.76
	Prec. L_Φ	0.74±0.22	0.87±0.02	0.35±0.04	0.49±0.29
spam	F1	0.87±0.03	0.83±0.07	0.83±0.01	0.87±0.01
	Precision	0.90±0.02	0.83±0.07	0.87±0.04	0.88±0.01
	Size	9.22±6.95	16.06±7.48	8.84±3.15	4.90±1.30
	Compl.	1.	0.64	1.	1.
	Prec. L_Φ	0.87±0.21	0.73±0.07	0.47±0.05	0.99±0.00
heloc	F1	0.86±0.02	0.87±0.03	0.87±0.01	0.85±0.02
	Precision	0.89±0.01	0.87±0.03	0.88±0.01	0.88±0.02
	Size	13.98±10.55	23.28±7.40	8.40±5.29	10.52±5.58
	Compl.	1.	1.	1.	1.
	Prec. L_Φ	0.85±0.15	0.71±0.04	0.57±0.08	0.92±0.06
breastc.	F1	0.88±0.03	0.89±0.04	0.82±0.07	0.88±0.03
	Precision	0.92±0.01	0.90±0.04	0.85±0.06	0.92±0.02
	Size	3.34±1.98	6.96±2.05	5.58±2.17	2.66±1.08
	Compl.	1.	1.	1.	1.
	Prec. L_Φ	0.96±0.13	0.88±0.04	0.31±0.07	0.98±0.04
iono.	F1	0.75±0.05	0.74±0.06	0.86±0.03	0.74±0.05
	Precision	0.78±0.05	0.74±0.06	0.87±0.02	0.78±0.05
	Size	4.60±1.44	2.46±1.01	4.36±0.96	4.56±1.45
	Compl.	0.86	0.02	0.58	0.88
	Prec. L_Φ	0.96±0.07	0.93±0.07	0.63±0.18	0.97±0.02

(b) Multi-class tasks

Task	Metric	CFIRE	CFIRE-KS	CFIRE-LI	CFIRE-IG
beans	F1	0.91±0.02	0.92±0.01	0.89±0.03	0.91±0.01
	Precision	0.93±0.01	0.93±0.01	0.92±0.02	0.93±0.01
	Size	34.50±7.10	36.68±6.16	36.64±6.50	27.32±4.23
	Compl.	1.	1.	1.	1.
	Prec. L_Φ	0.88±0.06	0.89±0.02	0.82±0.04	0.93±0.03
wine	F1	0.66±0.08	0.66±0.07	0.70±0.07	0.40±0.04
	Precision	0.85±0.07	0.86±0.06	0.85±0.05	0.53±0.06
	Size	4.30±1.27	3.96±1.03	5.08±1.26	5.12±1.33
	Compl.	1.	1.	1.	1.
	Prec. L_Φ	0.96±0.03	0.96±0.03	0.93±0.04	0.98±0.03
diggle	F1	0.85±0.02	0.85±0.02	0.84±0.02	0.68±0.06
	Precision	0.99±0.01	0.99±0.01	0.98±0.04	0.88±0.07
	Size	9.58±0.64	9.58±0.64	10.42±0.70	12.94±1.46
	Compl.	1.	1.	0.96	1.
	Prec. L_Φ	0.99±0.01	0.99±0.01	0.90±0.05	0.96±0.03
abalone	F1	0.81±0.02	0.81±0.02	0.80±0.03	0.75±0.02
	Precision	0.86±0.03	0.83±0.02	0.85±0.04	0.77±0.03
	Size	25.24±8.75	31.62±6.26	21.84±5.79	19.00±5.57
	Compl.	1.	1.	1.	1.
	Prec. L_Φ	0.76±0.07	0.71±0.07	0.77±0.08	0.90±0.04
iris	F1	0.87±0.02	0.87±0.02	0.87±0.03	0.83±0.01
	Precision	0.96±0.01	0.96±0.01	0.96±0.02	0.93±0.02
	Size	4.62±0.73	4.62±0.73	3.06±0.24	5.92±0.27
	Compl.	1.	1.	1.	1.
	Prec. L_Φ	0.94±0.09	0.94±0.09	0.92±0.09	0.94±0.03
vehicle	F1	0.55±0.04	0.53±0.04	0.52±0.04	0.56±0.04
	Precision	0.61±0.05	0.56±0.05	0.58±0.05	0.61±0.04
	Size	19.48±4.91	22.70±5.27	21.06±3.83	17.42±3.92
	Compl.	1.	0.94	0.98	1.
	Prec. L_Φ	0.91±0.07	0.74±0.08	0.80±0.08	0.93±0.03
autouniv	F1	0.41±0.04	0.43±0.04	0.40±0.04	0.43±0.04
	Precision	0.44±0.04	0.44±0.05	0.43±0.04	0.46±0.04
	Size	24.82±5.60	23.02±5.28	24.50±5.35	19.80±4.27
	Compl.	0.96	0.96	0.94	0.98
	Prec. L_Φ	0.70±0.08	0.73±0.08	0.65±0.07	0.75±0.08

rules match the dimensions that are important according to the local explanation, provided that the rules are consistent with the black-box model on the sample. Overall we observe a large agreement between the local explanations and the final rules but there are differences between the individual local explainers. For CFIRE-KS and CFIRE-IG, the precision is always above 0.7 and often even above 0.8, whereas for CFIRE-LI it only exceeds 0.7 in 6 cases and at the lowest drops down to 0.31. CFIRE reaches Prec. L_Φ of ≥ 0.85 on seven datasets, with values > 0.7 in the other cases. CFIRE, naturally, seldom reaches the top score for each row, however, it surprisingly ranks at least second in all but four cases. The overall good alignment on test data of nearly all methods indicates that the rules successfully capture key semantic properties of the local explanations. This indicates that a high train accuracy (our selection criterion) is related to a good alignment, also validating CFIRE's bias towards high-coverage boxes during the greedy rule selection step.

Summary. Comparing CFIRE variants using a single local explainer we found: CFIRE-IG lost the least amount of models but also showed the least reliable performance regarding accuracy. CFIRE-KS provides strong results regarding accuracy in all cases but struggled with Compl. the most. CFIRE-LI underperformed in accuracy on 3 datasets only, but it did loose double the amount of models compared to CFIRE-IG.

Regarding Compl., each local explainer failed notably on at least one task. While all methods can be summarised by distinctive strengths and weaknesses, Compl. indicates that, regardless what other metric might be regarded most important in a certain context, the Rashomon effect is only accounted for if results from multiple local explainers are considered. This implies that the flexibility to choose different local explainers is a key property for robustness of local-to-global explainers.

7 Concluding Remarks

We presented CFIRE, a novel XAI algorithm computing global rule models from local explanations for black-box models in form of a set of class DNFs. We experimentally demonstrated that, in contrast to the state-of-the-art methods, it fulfills all five desirable properties outlined in Sect. 1. In particular, CFIRE computed faithful, compact, and complete DNFs for nearly all black-box models. The flexibility to choose among different local explainers proved to be a key property to CFIRE's success in several cases. It was as fast as CEGA and up to two magnitudes faster than ANCHORS. In comparison, ANCHORS struggled with faithfulness and completeness, ANCHORS-∞, the idealized version of ANCHORS, required considerably more rules, and CEGA failed in every regard. CFIRE exhibited the greatest adaptability in adjusting its rule complexity to different black-box models, demonstrating its ability to adjust to model-specific characteristics when needed. In assessing CFIRE's flexibility, our experiments, to the best of our knowledge, also provide the first sizable empirical evidence of the downstream effects of the disagreement problem. Additionally, our evaluation scheme builds on recent results on the Rashomon effect in XAI [26] and our results underscore that accounting for this effect is crucial for an adequat experimental evaluation of explanation methods. Future work could improve the empirical methodology further by including more hypothesis classes besides NNs.

While CFIRE provided good precision scores in nearly all cases, its coverage could be improved in multi-class settings. One possible solution could be to allow

CFIRE to generate synthetic samples and query the black-box to enrich the data available, similar to how ANCHORS also explores the data space locally. Although the greedy set cover heuristic proved effective at the rule composition stage, it would be interesting to see how closed itemset mining and more sophisticated composition approaches like GLocalX [33] interplay.

Our ablation study on the downstream effects of the disagreement problem showed that each local explainer that we considered has led to distinct outputs. We picked a particular local explainer based on a rule model's predictive performance on the instance set, but as we also saw, a single local explainer seldom led to the best outcome according to other criteria. Further research is needed to understand the specific qualitative differences in attribution methods that make one particularly effective for generating strong explanations with desired properties for specific tasks or models. Alternatively, future work could explore combining explanations from different methods before itemset mining, rather than running CFIRE separately for each explainer.

The rules produced by CFIRE for different classes can overlap (see Table 2 for an example). In this work, we resolve ambiguity for specific instances by assigning the class of the empirically more accurate rule (cf. Section 5). While our experimental results justify this approach, the trade-off between faithfulness (avoiding ambiguity) and comprehensibility (remaining compact) should be explored further. One way could be to associate the rules with a reliability or certainty score for conflicting areas. While not resolving the fundamental conflict, it provides additional information to the user. We are working on a more sophisticated approach based on van Fraassen's model for explanations [36].

References

1. Dry Bean. UCI Machine Learning Repository (2020). https://doi.org/10.24432/C50S4B
2. Aeberhard, S., Forina, M.: Wine. UCI Machine Learning Repository (1992). https://doi.org/10.24432/C5PC7J
3. Agarwal, C., et al.: Openxai: towards a transparent evaluation of model explanations. Adv. Neural. Inf. Process. Syst. **35**, 15784–15799 (2022)
4. Aggarwal, C.C., Han, J.: Frequent Pattern Mining, 1 edn. Springer Cham (2014)
5. Agrawal, R., Mannila, H., Srikant, R., Toivonen, H., Verkamo, A.I.: Fast discovery of association rules. In: Fayyad, U.M., Piatetsky-Shapiro, G., Smyth, P., Uthurusamy, R. (eds.) Advances in Knowledge Discovery and Data Mining, pp. 307–328. AAAI/MIT Press (1996)
6. Alkhatib, A., Boström, H., Vazirgiannis, M.: Explaining predictions by characteristic rules. In: Joint European Conference on Machine Learning and Knowledge Discovery in Databases, pp. 389–403. Springer (2022)
7. Beckh, K., Müller, S., Rüping, S.: A quantitative human-grounded evaluation process for explainable machine learning. In: LWDA, pp. 13–20 (2022)
8. Boley, M., Horváth, T., Poigné, A., Wrobel, S.: Listing closed sets of strongly accessible set systems with applications to data mining. Theor. Comput. Sci. **411**(3), 691–700 (2010)

9. Breiman, L.: Statistical modeling: the two cultures (with comments and a rejoinder by the author). Stat. Sci. **16**(3), 199–231 (2001)
10. Buscema, M, T.S., Tastle, W.: Steel Plates Faults. UCI Machine Learning Repository (2010). https://doi.org/10.24432/C5J88N
11. Cormen, T.H., Leiserson, C.E., Rivest, R.L., Stein, C.: Introduction to algorithms, 4 edn. MIT press (2022)
12. Diggle, P.J.: Time series: a biostatistical introduction. Oxford University Press (1990)
13. Fisher, R.A.: Iris. UCI Machine Learning Repository (1936). https://doi.org/10.24432/C56C76
14. Gély, A.: A generic algorithm for generating closed sets of a binary relation. In: Formal Concept Analysis: Third International Conference, ICFCA 2005, Lens, France, February 14-18, 2005. Proceedings 3, pp. 223–234. Springer (2005)
15. Guidotti, R., Monreale, A., Giannotti, F., Pedreschi, D., Ruggieri, S., Turini, F.: Factual and counterfactual explanations for black box decision making. IEEE Intell. Syst. **34**(6), 14–23 (2019)
16. Hickey, R.: AutoUniv. Online database (2010). https://www.openml.org/d/1553. Accessed 19 Sept 2024
17. Hopkins, Mark, R.E.F.G., Suermondt, J.: Spambase. UCI Machine Learning Repository (1999). https://doi.org/10.24432/C53G6X
18. Jacovi, A., Goldberg, Y.: Towards faithfully interpretable NLP systems: how should we define and evaluate faithfulness? In: Proceedings of the 58th Annual Meeting of the Association for Computational Linguistics, pp. 4198–4205 (2020)
19. Jan van Rijn: BNG (breast-w) Dataset. Online database (2014). https://www.openml.org/d/251. Accessed 19 Sept 2024
20. Krishna, S., Han, T., Gu, A., Pombra, J., Jabbari, S., Wu, S., Lakkaraju, H.: The disagreement problem in explainable machine learning: a practitioner's perspective. arXiv preprint arXiv:2202.01602 (2022)
21. Lakkaraju, H., Bach, S.H., Leskovec, J.: Interpretable decision sets: A joint framework for description and prediction. In: Proceedings of the 22nd ACM SIGKDD International Conference on Knowledge Discovery and Data Mining, pp. 1675–1684 (2016)
22. Letham, B., Rudin, C., McCormick, T.H., Madigan, D.: Interpretable classifiers using rules and bayesian analysis: Building a better stroke prediction model (2015)
23. Lundberg, S.M., Lee, S.I.: A unified approach to interpreting model predictions. Advances in neural information processing systems **30** (2017)
24. Molnar, C.: Interpretable Machine Learning. 2 edn. (2022). https://christophm.github.io/interpretable-ml-book
25. Mowforth, P., Shepherd, B.: Statlog (Vehicle Silhouettes). UCI Machine Learning Repository. https://doi.org/10.24432/C5HG6N
26. Müller, S., Toborek, V., Beckh, K., Jakobs, M., Bauckhage, C., Welke, P.: An empirical evaluation of the Rashomon effect in explainable machine learning. In: Joint European Conference on Machine Learning and Knowledge Discovery in Databases, pp. 462–478. Springer (2023)
27. Nash, Warwick, S.T.T.S.C.A., Ford, W.: Abalone. UCI Machine Learning Repository (1994), https://www.openml.org/d/183, https://doi.org/10.24432/C55C7W
28. Nauta, M., Trienes, J., Pathak, S., Nguyen, E., Peters, M., Schmitt, Y., Schlötterer, J., Van Keulen, M., Seifert, C.: From anecdotal evidence to quantitative evaluation methods: A systematic review on evaluating explainable ai. ACM Comput. Surv. **55**(13s), 1–42 (2023)

29. Pasquier, N., Bastide, Y., Taouil, R., Lakhal, L.: Efficient mining of association rules using closed itemset lattices. Inf. Syst. **24**(1), 25–46 (1999)
30. Pitt, L., Valiant, L.G.: Computational limitations on learning from examples. J. ACM **35**(4), 965–984 (1988)
31. Ribeiro, M.T., Singh, S., Guestrin, C.: "Why should i trust you?" Explaining the predictions of any classifier. In: Proceedings of the 22nd ACM SIGKDD international Conference on Knowledge Discovery and Data Mining, pp. 1135–1144 (2016)
32. Ribeiro, M.T., Singh, S., Guestrin, C.: Anchors: High-precision model-agnostic explanations. In: Proceedings of the AAAI Conference on Artificial Intelligence, vol. 32 (2018)
33. Setzu, M., Guidotti, R., Monreale, A., Turini, F., Pedreschi, D., Giannotti, F.: Glocalx-from local to global explanations of black box ai models. Artif. Intell. **294**, 103457 (2021)
34. Sigillito, V., W.S.H.L., Baker, K.: Ionosphere. UCI Machine Learning Repository (1989). https://doi.org/10.24432/C5W01B
35. Sundararajan, M., Taly, A., Yan, Q.: Axiomatic attribution for deep networks. In: International Conference on Machine Learning, pp. 3319–3328. PMLR (2017)
36. Van Fraassen, B.C.: The Scientific Image. Oxford University Press, New York (1980)
37. Wang, F., Rudin, C.: Falling rule lists. In: Artificial Intelligence and Statistics, pp. 1013–1022. PMLR (2015)
38. Wolberg, William, M.O.S.N., Street, W.: Breast Cancer Wisconsin (Diagnostic). UCI Machine Learning Repository (1993). https://doi.org/10.24432/C5DW2B
39. Yeh, I.C.: Blood Transfusion Service Center. UCI Machine Learning Repository (2008). https://doi.org/10.24432/C5GS39

Open Access This chapter is licensed under the terms of the Creative Commons Attribution 4.0 International License (http://creativecommons.org/licenses/by/4.0/), which permits use, sharing, adaptation, distribution and reproduction in any medium or format, as long as you give appropriate credit to the original author(s) and the source, provide a link to the Creative Commons license and indicate if changes were made.

The images or other third party material in this chapter are included in the chapter's Creative Commons license, unless indicated otherwise in a credit line to the material. If material is not included in the chapter's Creative Commons license and your intended use is not permitted by statutory regulation or exceeds the permitted use, you will need to obtain permission directly from the copyright holder.

Which LIME Should I Trust? Concepts, Challenges, and Solutions

Patrick Knab[1]($^{\boxtimes}$), Sascha Marton[2], Udo Schlegel[3,4], and Christian Bartelt[1]

[1] Technical University of Clausthal, Clausthal-Zellerfeld, Germany
`patrick.knab@tu-clausthal.de`
[2] University of Mannheim, Mannheim, Germany
[3] Ludwig-Maximilians-Universität München, Munich, Germany
[4] Munich Center for Machine Learning (MCML), Munich, Germany

Abstract. As neural networks become dominant in essential systems, Explainable Artificial Intelligence (XAI) plays a crucial role in fostering trust and detecting potential misbehavior of opaque models. LIME (Local Interpretable Model-agnostic Explanations) is among the most prominent model-agnostic approaches, generating explanations by approximating the behavior of black-box models around specific instances. Despite its popularity, LIME faces challenges related to fidelity, stability, and applicability to domain-specific problems. Numerous adaptations and enhancements have been proposed to address these issues, but the growing number of developments can be overwhelming, complicating efforts to navigate LIME-related research. To the best of our knowledge, this is the first survey to comprehensively explore and collect LIME's foundational concepts and known limitations. We categorize and compare its various enhancements, offering a structured taxonomy based on intermediate steps and key issues. Our analysis provides a holistic overview of advancements in LIME, guiding future research and helping practitioners identify suitable approaches. Additionally, we provide a continuously updated interactive website, Which LIME Should I Trust?, offering a concise and accessible overview of the survey.

Keywords: LIME · XAI · Survey

1 Introduction

Artificial intelligence (AI) has transitioned from a futuristic concept to an integral part of our daily lives in the last decade. As computing power continues to become more affordable, intelligent models can increasingly be leveraged to enhance process efficiency through automation, elevate user experiences, and enable innovative solutions across diverse sectors such as healthcare, finance, and transportation [51,104]. Despite its impressive capabilities, the decision-making processes, primarily driven by neural networks (NNs), remain opaque and challenging to interpret. This lack of transparency challenges trust, accountability, and ethical considerations in AI applications. Therefore, users and stakeholders increasingly demand explanations for AI decisions, particularly in high-stakes areas such as medical diagnoses, loan approvals, and legal judgments. These explanations have the goal of helping the user (explainee [60]) to build trust in these systems and understand the rationale behind specific outputs [10,51].

Explainable AI (XAI) aims to make AI models more interpretable, addressing the challenges posed by opaque decision-making. The concept of interpretability has been widely applied across various domains and to different types of opaque models, such as convolutional neural networks (CNNs) in the imagery domain and transformer-based architectures for textual modalities [15,62,83,95]. However, because each problem presents unique characteristics, there is a need for diverse explainability techniques [91]. For instance, one might seek to approximate the behavior of a model [72], while in other cases the goal might be to explain the intrinsic properties of the model itself [84]. Moreover, developing or extending explanatory approaches to meet new challenges becomes essential as models grow in complexity. This could involve incorporating additional data modalities or enhancing the robustness of existing methods to handle more sophisticated architectures or specific data characteristics.

LIME (Local Interpretable Model-agnostic Explanations) [72] has become one of the most widely adopted techniques in the XAI domain, offering local explanations for complex models by providing insights into how individual decisions are made. Despite its popularity, LIME faces several challenges, including instability [21,33,59,63,85,93,103], computational inefficiency [97], and limitations in the handling of certain types of data [31,54]. In response, numerous studies have proposed enhancements to address these issues [19,40,46,48,88,98]. Notwithstanding the numerous enhancements, there is a significant need for a thorough and systematic evaluation of LIME and its variants from a research perspective. Our new analysis helps guide future developments and expand its application in various domains. In addition, practitioners often face challenges in identifying the most suitable LIME methodology or even recognizing the advancements that have been made. A comprehensive overview of these techniques supports their ability to explain their models more effectively.

1.1 Contribution and Organization

This work presents a comprehensive and focused review of LIME and its diverse adaptations. Rather than comparing LIME to other interpretability methods such as SHAP [53] or Grad-CAM [84], we exclusively examine its modifications and extensions to provide a detailed analysis of its evolution, limitations, and research challenges. By systematically categorizing existing LIME variations, we bridge key gaps in prior research, particularly regarding stability, robustness, and domain-specific adaptations. Additionally, this survey serves both researchers and practitioners, offering a structured framework to identify suitable LIME techniques based on data modality (e.g., text, images, tabular data) and application domain constraints (e.g., healthcare). This study also investigates the challenges and limitations of LIME's application and development. To address these, we perform a detailed literature analysis, introduce a novel categorization framework, and review advancements aimed at improving LIME's interpretability and efficiency.

The main contributions of this study are as follows:

- To the best of our knowledge, this paper presents the first comprehensive survey of LIME-related techniques, synthesizing a wide range of modifications and improvements from the literature.
- We introduce a novel taxonomy that categorizes LIME extensions along two key dimensions: (1) the technical modifications within the LIME framework and (2) the specific issues they address. Based on this taxonomy, we systematically analyze the strengths and limitations of existing methods and provide insights into promising directions for future research.
- Beyond categorization, this survey provides a practical resource by mapping research challenges to LIME techniques, helping researchers identify relevant modifications based on specific properties and practitioners select suitable methods for their applications.

Furthermore, we host a webpage dedicated to this work that will continue to monitor LIME-related techniques, as illustrated in Fig. 1.

1.2 XAI Categorization

In the following, we briefly review the categorization of XAI techniques to provide context for situating LIME within the broader landscape of explainability approaches. XAI techniques can be broadly categorized into ante-hoc (sometimes also intrinsic) and post-hoc methods [10,51,62].

Ante-hoc methods focus on building inherently interpretable models from the ground up, such as decision trees, linear regression, and rule-based systems. These models are designed to be understandable by default but may lack the predictive power of more complex algorithms like neural networks [62].

In contrast, **post-hoc** methods aim to explain already trained, opaque models without altering their structure. These methods are further divided into two types: *model-specific* and *model-agnostic* approaches. Model-specific methods generate explanations tailored to particular types of models, such as activation maps in neural networks, or attention in transformers.

Model-agnostic techniques, like LIME [72] and SHAP (SHapley Additive exPlanations) [53], can be applied to any machine learning model, making them more versatile. Both techniques focus on analyzing the relationship between the model's inputs and outputs rather than examining the internal workings of the model itself. Specifically, LIME explains model predictions by approximating the model locally through an interpretable surrogate model built from perturbations of the input features [72], while SHAP quantifies the contribution of each feature to a prediction using Shapley values derived from cooperative game theory [53]. Explanation methods can further be classified into *local* and *global* explanations. Local methods, like LIME, explain individual predictions for individual samples.

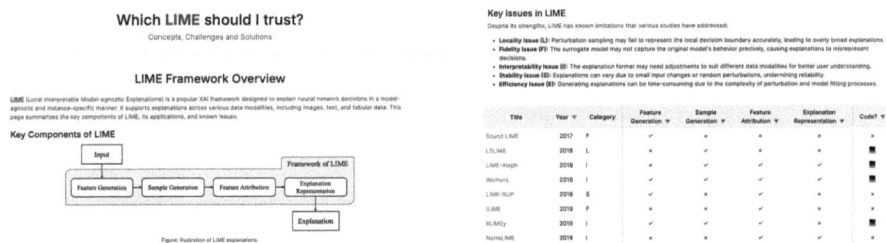

Fig. 1. LIME Webpage. This website is designed to monitor and collect new LIME-related techniques continuously. For an ongoing collection of LIME-related methods, please refer to the webpage: https://patrick-knab.github.io/which-lime-to-trust/.

In contrast, global methods, such as partial dependence plots (PDP) and feature importance measures, offer insights into the overall behavior of the model in general or across an entire dataset [62].

Recent advancements in XAI have been surveyed extensively, with broad overviews offering foundational insights into general trends, methodologies, and challenges [10,51,77]. In parallel, domain-specific reviews have emerged across medical [15,66,95], time-series data [74,94], IoT [42], tabular data [78], finance [58], manufacturing [8], and human-centered contexts [75], each underscoring the growing need for interpretable, transparent AI solutions in specialized settings.

2 Methodology

This section outlines the methodology used to search, identify, and analyze research papers on LIME techniques. To ensure transparency in our literature review process, we detail the steps we followed in accordance with established guidelines. Our methodology follows the structured process recommended by Webster et al. [99], complemented by the documentation approach outlined by Brocke et al. [14].

The literature review began with an extensive exploration of prior research that builds upon and extends the original LIME publication [72][1]. Given the vast number of related studies, we refined our selection by incorporating additional keywords such as 'LIME issues', 'LIME improvements', and 'LIME advancements' to systematically narrow the corpus of relevant articles. Each selected article was rigorously evaluated based on its quality, applied methodologies, and publication venue. Furthermore, we included non-peer-reviewed articles from ArXiv, provided they offered novel and pertinent contributions to our research. Our initial review covered papers published between 2016 and 2025. To further broaden our search, we examined the references cited in these papers to identify additional relevant works. Additionally, we focused exclusively on papers that explicitly mention or address LIME limitations and improvements within

---

[1] As of January 21st 2025, the publication had been cited in 21,343 papers on ArXiv.

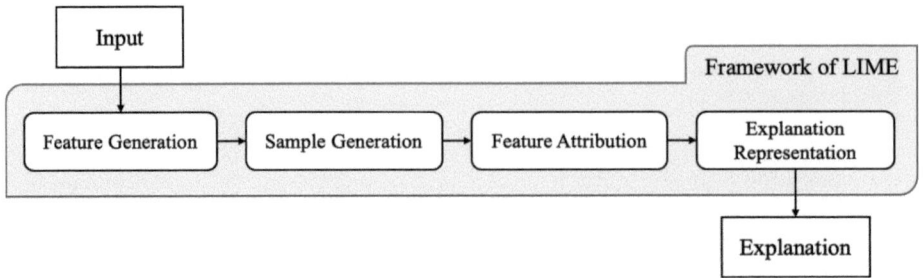

Fig. 2. Steps of LIME: The framework operates in four steps: (1) Feature generation: Extract features (e.g., image segmentation). (2) Sample generation: Create perturbed samples around the instance. (3) Feature attribution: Train an interpretable model (e.g., linear) to approximate the complex model locally. (4) Explanation representation: Use the model's weights to represent feature importance.

the LIME framework, recognizing that other works might create model-agnostic explanations outside of this framework [53]. We acknowledge the possibility of overlooking papers that did not align with our selection criteria, given the challenge of reviewing over 20,000 works. However, as we maintain a continuous record of LIME advancements, any missed works can be integrated into the ongoing online overview (Fig. 1).

To facilitate documentation, we created a concept matrix [99]. It provides comprehensive details on each technique, such as the name, source, the particular problem it addresses, the modality, domain-specific characteristics, a description of any changes made within the LIME framework, the evaluation, and the availability of code for implementation. This concept matrix built the foundation for the creation of the LIME categorization.

3 Fundamentals of LIME

Notation. We consider instances from modalities such as time series, images, text, audio, tabular data, or graphs. Let $\mathbf{x} \in \mathcal{X}$ denote an instance, and $\mathbf{y} \in \mathcal{Y}$ its corresponding label. For classification, $\mathcal{Y}$ is a set of discrete labels, $\{1, 2, \ldots, C\}$; for regression, $\mathcal{Y} \subset \mathbb{R}$. We denote the black-box model as $f : \mathcal{X} \to \mathcal{Y}$, which outputs a prediction $\hat{y}$ for a given $\mathbf{x}$.

LIME explains the decisions of a neural network f in a *model-agnostic* and *instance-specific* (local) manner, applicable to images, text, and tabular data [72]. Its algorithm follows the structure in Fig. 2. Through this survey, we will refer to this structure when addressing LIME enhancements and will discuss them in greater detail in Sect. 4.

Feature Generation. The technique trains a local, interpretable surrogate model $g \in G$ (e.g., linear models or decision trees) to approximate f around an instance $\mathbf{x}$ [72,89]. For text or tabular data, minimal preprocessing is applied before computing feature importance scores. Preprocessing can include tokenization, lowercasing, and possibly stopword removal for text data. Tabular data

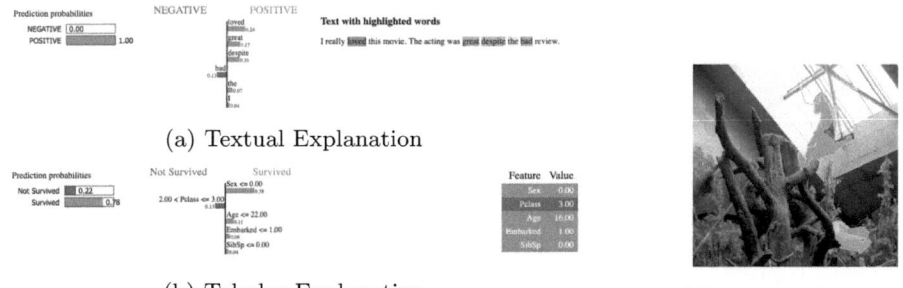

(a) Textual Explanation

(b) Tabular Explanation

(c) Imagery Explanation

Fig. 3. LIME Exemplary Explanations. Fig. 3a shows a sentiment classification from a movie review (IMDB dataset [55]), highlighting words linked to positivity and negativity. Figure 3b depicts a young female passenger from the Titanic dataset, with survival probability mainly influenced by her sex and age. Figure 3c explains an image classified as a gorilla, where green and red superpixels represent positive and negative classification contributions.

might involve normalization, handling missing values, or encoding categorical variables. A common practice for time series is to generate features based on the time series' local context, such as rolling window statistics (e.g., moving averages, trends, or differences) that capture the temporal properties in the data. In contrast, for imagery data, the $n \times m$ pixels are transformed via segmentation into superpixels [3,32,65], which serve as the features.

Sample Generation. LIME generates a set of perturbed samples to locally approximate the behavior of a black-box model around a given instance $\mathbf{x} \in \mathcal{X}$. Let $\mathbf{z} \in \mathcal{X}$ denote a perturbed instance derived from $\mathbf{x}$ by selectively modifying features while maintaining the underlying structure of the original data. The binary vector $\mathbf{z}' \in \{0,1\}^d$ encodes which features are retained (1) or replaced (0) in the perturbed instance. Formally, if the original instance is represented as $\mathbf{x} = [f_1, f_2, \ldots, f_d]$, where d denotes the dimensionality of the feature space (e.g., the number of superpixels in an image, the number of features in tabular data, or the number of tokens in text), then we define $\mathbf{z} = h(\mathbf{x}, \mathbf{z}')$, where $h(\cdot)$ maps the original instance $\mathbf{x}$ and the binary mask $\mathbf{z}'$ to a perturbed instance $\mathbf{z}$ by retaining or replacing individual features according to:

$$z_i' = \begin{cases} 1 & \text{feature } i \text{ is retained} \\ 0 & \text{feature } i \text{ is replaced} \end{cases}.$$

For **image data**, the instance $\mathbf{x}$ is segmented into d superpixels $s_1, s_2, \ldots, s_d$ to produce the feature space. To generate a perturbed sample $\mathbf{z}$, each superpixel s_i is independently toggled on or off as indicated by $\mathbf{z}'$. If $z_i' = 0$, the pixels in the i-th superpixel are replaced by a reference value (e.g., the mean pixel intensity), maintaining the image structure but altering its appearance in selected areas [40]. In the modality type **tabular data**, each feature f_i is either retained or replaced with a perturbed value sampled from a suitable distribution or set to a reference value [26]. This approach preserves the tabular layout but allows variation in feature values. For **text data**, the instance **x** consists of d tokens $w_1, w_2, \ldots, w_d$. A perturbed sample **z** is generated by retaining or masking/replacing each token based on **z**$'$. If a token w_i is replaced (i.e., $z'_i = 0$), it may be set to a common placeholder such as 'UNK' or removed from the text, thus maintaining syntactic structure while altering semantic content [57].

By systematically generating perturbed samples **z** according to the binary vector **z**$'$, LIME explores the local neighborhood of the original instance **x**, providing the basis for fitting an interpretable model that approximates the model's decision in that locality.

Feature Attribution. LIME employs a proximity measure, denoted as $\pi_\mathbf{x}$, to assess the closeness between the predicted outputs $f(\mathbf{z})$ and $f(\mathbf{x})$, which is fundamental in assigning weights to the samples (similarity measurement). In the standard implementation of LIME, the kernel $\pi_\mathbf{x}(\mathbf{z})$ is defined as follows:

$$\pi_\mathbf{x}(\mathbf{z}') = \exp\left(-\frac{D(\mathbf{x}', \mathbf{z}')^2}{\sigma^2}\right),$$

where $\mathbf{x}'$ is a binary vector, all states are set to 1, representing the original instance **x**. D represents the $L2$ distance (can be substituted with a different distance metric depending on the specific context), given by $D(\mathbf{x}', \mathbf{z}') = \sqrt{\sum_{i=1}^{n}(\mathbf{x}'_i - \mathbf{z}'_i)^2}$ and σ being the width of the kernel. Subsequently, LIME trains a linear model (Surrogate Model), minimizing the loss function $\mathcal{L}$, which is defined as:

$$\mathcal{L}(f, g, \pi_\mathbf{x}) = \sum_{\mathbf{z}, \mathbf{z}' \in \mathcal{Z}} \pi_\mathbf{x}(\mathbf{z}) \cdot (f(\mathbf{z}) - g(\mathbf{z}'))^2.$$

In this equation, **z**, and **z**$'$ are sampled instances from the perturbed dataset $\mathcal{Z}$, and g is the interpretable model being learned [72,93].

Explanation Representation. The model's interpretability comes from the coefficients of g, which indicate each feature's influence by their magnitude and sign. Explanation communication varies by modality. For text, keywords or phrases are emphasized (see Fig. 3a); for tabular data, important features or columns are highlighted (see Fig. 3b); and for images, the n most influential superpixels (positive or negative) are visually marked (see Fig. 3c).

4 LIME Categorization

This section constitutes this survey's principal component, wherein we comprehensively elucidate our categorization taxonomy. The first dimension addresses the LIME-specific issues referenced in Sect. 4.1, while Sect. 4.2 delineates the second dimension by succinctly discussing the implementation particulars of the proposed methodologies within the previously established LIME substeps as illustrated in Fig. 2. This section wraps up with an overview of LIME techniques with specific modalities and domains for practitioners in Sect. 4.3.

4.1 Issue Categorization

The model-agnostic property allows LIME to handle various machine-learning models effectively. Consequently, it has been successfully applied to complex models such NNs, CNNs [7], Long-Short-Term-Memory (LSTMs) [4] networks, and transformer architectures [40], as well as decision trees and random forests [19]. Also, its built-in interpretation representation for textual and tabular data makes it easy to use with minimal modifications, as demonstrated in Fig. 3. Therefore, the technique has found numerous useful applications across various domains, including healthcare, finance, and manufacturing [7,28,41,56,67,68, 96].

However, the technique is not flawless. Consequently, various issues have emerged over the years that have been identified and tackled by several studies. In the subsequent part, we will group and define these issues into five distinct categories, constituting the first dimension of our terminology.

- **Locality Issue (L)**: The explanations may not be sufficiently specific to the instance being explained if the perturbed data points used to create the surrogate model do not adequately represent the local decision boundary [13,31,36,80].
- **Fidelity Issue (F)**: The surrogate model used by LIME may not accurately capture the behavior of the original model, leading to explanations that do not fully reflect the original model's decision-making process [12,23,63,89, 98,103]. Fidelity and locality are closely linked. The problem of fidelity may arise not only from locality issues, such as when the sampling process fails to generate meaningful perturbed data points but also from other factors, such as an overly simplistic surrogate model or inadequate feature representations.
- **Interpretability Issue (I)**: The explanation representation may not represent the model's decision in a well-interpretable way by users or need adaptions due to varying modalities [1,6,17,34,46].
- **Stability Issue (S)**: The explanations provided by LIME can vary significantly due to minor changes in the input data, perturbation process, sampling, repeated runs, or the underlying model, resulting in inconsistent and unreliable outcomes. Such behavior undermines confidence in the XAI technique or the model to be explained, as the explainee does not know from which part the instability originates in case of doubt [12,33,35,59,85,93,103].
- **Efficiency Issue (E)**: The time required to generate explanations can be significant due to the steps involved in perturbation generation, obtaining model predictions, and fitting the surrogate model [44,81,97].

The issues presented should not be considered independently of each other. For example, increasing locality can negatively impact efficiency, but decreasing efficiency can positively affect stability. Additionally, many studies discussed here do not focus solely on one issue but address several simultaneously.

4.2 Implementation Categorization

We already described LIME's functionality in Sect. 3 that we split into four main parts. These substeps contain the essence of the technology (Fig. 2), feature (1) and sample generation (2), training an interpretable surrogate model based on the samples (3), and presenting the local explanation with the interpretable model (4), such as its coefficients. The LIME-dependent works we cover in this work adapt at one or multiple points of this pipeline; we categorize the techniques with this scheme to get an overview of how different approaches adjust the framework, and we define them more precisely in this subsection. Table 1 summarizes the techniques, organized by topic, with check marks indicating modifications in the four main components of LIME, which are represented as the table's columns. This provides researchers with a quick reference to specific LIME variants and their technical properties, making it easier to identify relevant approaches for further development or comparison with similar work.

Feature Generation (1): This step encompasses all processes that modify the input instance to generate new or transformed features, enhancing their suitability for the explanation process.

Segmentation-Based: Given the variety of segmentation techniques, the authors of [90] enable individual selection of feature generation methods in their pipeline, similar to the approach in [46]. With the advancement of foundation models like Segment Anything (SAM) [37], Knab et al. integrate these models into their framework to automatically segment images into more interpretable segments for humans [40]. Segmentation variations are not confined to images but extend to preprocessing time series. Several papers investigate segmentation approaches tailored explicitly to time series data [1,2,82]. With more meaningful segments, for example, through semantic correlations [88], the super features can be covered in some coherent regions, allowing the model's decision to be better approximated. For audio input, the authors of [31] employ source separation to decompose the signal into its sources, such as piano, vocals, or drums, and then segment these audio signals. Sound LIME [61] further segments the audio signal into temporal, frequency, and time-frequency parts. When dealing with graph data, GraphLIME [34] uses the nodes within the graph as features.

Clustering-Based: Other methods apply clustering to the training set to incorporate this knowledge into the process. For instance, [102] uses hierarchical clustering to partition the training set into specific clusters, akin to the approach in [30]. The authors of [33] propose a similar method but with a supervised partitioning tree for clustering.

Feature Importance-Based: An et al. [9] calculate feature importance and generate a partial dependence plot (PDP) in advance, feeding the feature importance scores, split feature importance, and the binary PDP plot into LIME. SLICE [11] calculates feature importance for feature selection with the estimation of sign entropy. Conversely, the authors of [49] first run standard LIME on every sample of the training set, aggregating these explanations to create a global

Table 1. LIME Techniques Categorization. This table lists all the covered LIME techniques and their associated issues and indicates with a checkmark the point at which the technique has adaptations within the LIME framework.

LIME-Technique	Issue	Feature Generation	Sample Generation	Feature Attribution	Expl. Representation
Kernel-LIME [21]	L	-	-	✓	-
C-LIME [36]	L	-	✓	-	-
LSLIME [48]	L	-	✓	-	-
QLIME [13]	L	-	-	✓	-
ILIME [23]	F	-	-	✓	-
LIMEtree [89]	F	-	-	✓	-
Sound LIME [61]	F	✓	-	-	-
MPS-LIME [86]	F	-	✓	-	-
US-LIME [76]	F	-	✓	✓	-
TS-MULE [82]	F	✓	-	-	-
SS-LIME [47]	F	-	✓	✓	-
LORE [29]	F	-	✓	-	✓
LIME-Aleph [69,70]	I	-	✓	✓	✓
Anchors [73]	I	✓	✓	✓	✓
bLIMEy [90]	I	✓	✓	✓	-
DIME [54]	I	✓	✓	✓	✓
Explain Explore [17]	I	-	-	✓	✓
GraphLIME [34]	I	✓	✓	✓	-
NormLIME [6]	I	-	-	✓	✓
$\mathcal{G}$-LIME [49]	S	✓	✓	✓	-
DLIME [102]	S	✓	✓	✓	-
LIME-SUP [33]	S	✓	-	✓	-
K-LIME [30]	S	✓	-	✓	✓
S-LIME [104]	S	-	✓	-	-
Attention-LIME [81]	E	-	✓	-	-
survLIME [44]	E	-	-	✓	-
survLIME-inf [97]	E	-	-	✓	-
Specific-Input LIME [9]	L, F	✓	-	-	-
s-LIME [27]	L, F	-	✓	-	-
LIMESegment [88]	L, F	✓	✓	-	-
CBR-LIME [71]	L, F	-	✓	✓	-
GuidedLIME [80]	L, I	-	✓	-	-
audioLIME [31]	L, I	✓	-	-	✓
ExpLIMEable [46]	S, I	✓	✓	-	✓
Sig-LIME [2]	S, I	✓	✓	✓	-
gLIME [20]	S, I	-	-	✓	✓
ALIME [85]	S, F	-	✓	✓	-
BayLIME [103]	S, F	-	-	✓	-
BMB-LIME [35]	S, F	-	✓	✓	-
SLICE [11]	S, F	✓	✓	-	-
OptiLIME [98]	S, F	-	-	✓	-
DSEG-LIME [40]	S, F	✓	✓	✓	✓
UnRAvEL-LIME [79]	S, F	-	✓	-	-
GLIME [93]	S, F	-	✓	-	-
GMM-LIME [63]	S, F	-	✓	-	-
MeLIME [12]	S, F	-	✓	✓	-
SEGAL [59]	S, L	-	✓	✓	-
B-LIME [1]	S, F, I	✓	✓	✓	✓

explanation using NormLIME [6] and Averaged-Importance [52] as priors in a Bayesian framework.

Arbitrary-Based: The authors of the initial LIME pipeline also propose Anchors [73], which create 'anchor' rules by identifying key features and using these rules as explanations; these anchors are linked to features, such as superpixels in images or specific features in tabular data. For multimodal tasks, e.g., Visual Question Answering (VQA), DIME [54] applies the feature generation processes for both modalities (image and text) in parallel.

Sample Generation (2): Generating samples for explanation purposes can be achieved through various methods. Techniques that deviate from the standard LIME process, which typically involves random sampling around an instance, adopt more refined approaches. Many of these methods focus on selective, approximation-based, neighborhood-based, or distribution-based sampling strategies to improve the interpretability and reliability of the explanations.

Selective-Based: Sangroya et al. [80] proposes a method that selects samples, maximizing coverage criteria while minimizing redundancy. BMB-LIME [35] incorporates uncertainty estimation from BayLIME [103] to enrich sample diversity, whereas [36] excludes anomalous samples that deviate significantly from the local neighborhood. LIME-Aleph [70] uniformly selects n instances from a pool of logical representations, while US-LIME [76] pre-generates samples and then focuses on those near the decision boundary. UnRAvEL-LIME [79] employs an uncertainty-driven acquisition function to guide sample selection.

Approximation-Based: In the work of Li et al. [49], they use a modified version of ElasticNet [105] estimator with ℓ_1 and ℓ_2 regularization to generate sparse, informative interpretations in Bayesian linear regression. AttentionLIME [81] narrows the search space by leveraging attention weights from the target label, improving sampling efficiency for text data. S-LIME [104] uses Lasso, a modification of Least Angle Regression (LARs) [22], to estimate the number of samples required for more stable explanations.

Neighborhood-Based: DLIME [102] utilizes the partitions from the feature generation process and applies KNN to find the closest neighbors and samples from those. MeLIME [12] samples from neighbors with different generators (kernel density, principal component analysis, variational autoencoder, and word2vec). In a graph-fashion style, MPS-LIME [86] structures the superpixels in an undirected graph; connected nodes are neighbors and search for cliques for sampling. Similar to GraphLIME [34], it also acts in a graph-like structure but applies neighborhood sampling using the proposed N-hop network. LSLIME [48] generates instances with GrowingSpheres to find close decision boundaries. s-LIME [27] generates n equally-weighted instances independently drawn from the underlying distribution. DSEG-LIME [40] samples from a hierarchical tree, where parent and child segments form the nodes within the tree. Anchors [73] generates samples around the test instance to validate the generated anchors and LORE [29] uses a genetic algorithm. The authors of [71] propose an approach by selecting similar instances with a predetermined set of LIME settings for the instance to be explained to achieve better results.

Distribution-Based: ALIME [85] samples from a Gaussian distribution with a trained autoencoder. [93] employs a local and unbiased sampling distribution to ensure the locality property. SEGAL [59] has a generative model that samples from the underlying data distribution. GMM-LIME [63] utilizes a Gaussian Mixture Model (GMM) to capture the data's underlying distribution and sample from it.

Arbitrary-Based: The authors of [1] use bootstrapping to sample from time series segments. Sig-LIME [2] introduces random noise while sampling time series segments. SLICE [11] employs adaptive blur in its superpixel replacement strategy. In [54], the sample generation process is expanded to incorporate two modalities. The works of [46,90] propose a modular approach, allowing users to switch between various sampling techniques. Sivill and Flach [88] emphasize the significant impact of perturbed backgrounds on LIME's performance and propose an approach to generate realistic perturbations for time series data. SS-LIME [47] generates perturbations by substituting words or tokens with semantically similar alternatives, ensuring that the sampled instances preserve contextual coherence.

Feature Attribution (3): This step includes all interpretable surrogate model training modifications by replacing the interpretable model, altering the proximity measurement or kernel, or other alterations.

Linear Regression Modifications: [103] uses a Bayesian linear regression approach with the optional integration of priors to increase stability. $\mathcal{G}$-LIME [49] utilizes Least Angle Regression (LARs) [22] to rank the importance of every feature in the explanation over the path of ℓ_1-regularization. K-LIME [30] builds a generalized linear model

Replacement of Surrogate Model: LIME-SUP [33] and LORE [29] replace the model with a tree-based technique. Similarly, [1] trains a decision forest as its surrogate model. Another tree-based technique is Sig-LIME [2], which uses random forests to uphold non-linear interactions and use them for the explanation. LIMEtree [89], in contrast, uses multi-output regression trees to improve fidelity. gLIME [93] implements a graphical most minor absolute shrinkage and selection operator (GLASSO) [24] that produces an undirected Gaussian graph for explanation. [44] utilizes the Cox proportional hazards model [50] to approximate a survival model as the surrogate model. [97] improves this approach [44] by using the L_∞-norm for computing the distance between cumulative hazard functions. LIME-Alpeh [70] replaces the model for interpretation with an inductive logic programming system that enables the detection of feature relations. Since decision boundaries are limited by linear regression, BMB-LIME [35] approximates nonlinear boundaries using multivariate adaptive regression splines (MARS) and employs bootstrap aggregation to stabilize the explanation. In contrast, [13] learns non-linear decision boundaries by fitting a quadratic model.

Weighting Modification: [102] calculates the pairwise distance of the instances within the built clusters and uses them as the weights for the training of the surrogate model. [85] uses the embedding of the trained autoencoder for the weighting of the samples used for surrogate model training. ILIME [23] includes the proximity of the generated samples to the original instance as an influencing function. OptiLIME [98] automatically determines the optimal kernel width to balance the explanation stability and fidelity trade-off. Also, [21] improves the locality of the explanation by an automatic kernel adaption during the surrogate model training. US-LIME [76] has a weighting kernel approach that is based on a Gaussian kernel. Other hyperparameters that can be optimized are treated by [59], which utilizes an adaptive weighting method for additional hyperparameter tuning. ExplainExplore [17] leaves this parameter adjustment dynamically adaptive by the explainee during the explanation process.

Training of Surrogate Model: [73] evaluates and assigns importance to its anchors by measuring their coverage and precision in the predictions. [40] iteratively goes through the feature importance calculation in the built tree structure to construct fine or coarse explanations. MeLIME [12] uses a local minibatch strategy, deduced by the neighboring approach, to improve the robustness of the training of the surrogate model. NormLIME [6] shifts from local to global explanations by running multiple LIME instances and aggregating them to estimate the global relative importance of the model's features. [34] trains the model using the Hilbert-Schmidt Independence Criterion Lasso (HSIC Lasso). bLIMEy [90] provides a modular architecture enabling users to select between different feature attribution techniques as in the previous steps. DIME [54] has separate feature attribution methods to calculate the unimodal importance contributions for each modality by disentanglement and the multimodal contribution.

Explanation Representation (4): The explanation derived from the surrogate model is typically static, visualizing the most significant coefficients as a saliency map for images or highlighting the most critical features within text or tabular data. However, this representation might overlook essential properties needed for better interpretation by the explainee.

Expanded Explanation Representation: Anchors [73] generate a set of predicates that serve as explanations for the explainee. For the sentiment analysis, the explanation could include rules like 'not bad' indicating positive sentiment, and 'not good' indicating negative sentiment. Similarly, LORE [29] translates the rule from the decision tree into a logical explanation. In [40], the granularity of the explanation can be controlled by the explainee, allowing visualization of both broad and coarse explanations derived from segmentation hierarchies, shown as feature importance maps for image classification. [93] produces a graph-based explanation, highlighting feature relationships of nodes and information flows between them. Similarly, [70] considers combinations of features and their relationships within an object for explanation. B-LIME [1] extends heatmap visualization to fit time-series data, indicating which points or sequences in the time series are most important based on the segmented data. For sound modali-

Table 2. Modalities and Domains of LIME Adaptions. This table clusters the adaptations covered in this survey into the covered modalities and the additional domain-specific adaptations.

Modality	Domain	LIME-Techniques
Universal	Text, Tabular & Image	LIME [72], BayLIME [103], GLIME [93], MeLIME [12], s-LIME [27], Anchors [73], $\mathcal{G}$-LIME [49], NormLIME [6], OptiLIME [98], S-LIME [104]
Image	Universal	DSEG-LIME [40], SLICE [11], MPS-LIME [86], CBR-LIME [71]
	Archaeology	LIME-Aleph [69, 70]
	Healthcare	ExpLIMEable [46]
Time Series	Universal	SEGAL [59], TS-MULE [82], LIMESegment [88]
	Healthcare	B-LIME [1], Sig-LIME [2], C-LIME [36]
Tabular	Universal	ILIME [23], Kernel-LIME [21], K-LIME [30], LIME-SUP [33], survLIME [44], survLIME-inf [97], bLIMEy [90], GMM-LIME [63], BMB-LIME [35], LORE [29], ExplainExplore [17], GuidedLIME [80], LSLIME [48], QLIME [13], Specific-Input LIME [9], US-LIME [76], LIMEtree [89], ExplainExplore [17], UnRAvEL-LIME [79]
	Healthcare	DLIME [102], gLIME [20], ALIME [85]
Audio	Universal	audioLIME [31], Sound LIME [61]
Text	Universal	AttentionLIME [81]
	Semantic Analysis	SS-LIME [47]
Image-Text	VQA	DIME [54]
Graph	Universal	GraphLIME [34]

ties, AudioLIME [31] provides listenable explanations, improving interpretability and broadening the range of explanation representations. NormLIME [6] transitions the type of explanation from local to global, allowing users to make global assumptions about the behavior of the model. For multimodal expansion, DIME [54] generates unimodal contribution explanations for text and images, along with a multimodal interaction explanation to explore how the different modalities interact.

Interactive Explanation: ExpLIMEable [46] offers an interactive dashboard to the explainee, allowing the modification of the explanation parameters during the explanation phase to improve the output. Similarly, ExplainExplore [17] provides a dashboard with multiple visual explanations, offering different perspectives to aid interpretability.

4.3 Domain Categorization

LIME's fundamental implementation has been utilized for text, tables, and images. Our review of the literature uncovered various specific modes, adaptations for particular domains, and multimodal strategies. Table 2 presents an overview of these approaches, detailing their associated modalities and domains, providing practitioners with a convenient reference for identifying suitable techniques.

As the table illustrates, some implementations are categorized as universal, capable of handling text, tabular, and image data without requiring modifications, and independent of any specific domain. Other approaches are categorized by modality, with some exhibiting domain-specific characteristics, such as those designed for archaeology or healthcare, if the method has been exclusively tested within that domain. Approaches within a particular modality are also considered universal if the authors do not mention any limitations in their work. However, we cannot definitively assess the validity of the claimed universality for each approach, as not all methods have an available code.

5 Discussion, Opportunities and Conclusion

We conclude this paper with a section addressing key research challenges specific to LIME and outlining potential solutions. This is followed by future research directions related to LIME and finalized with the conclusion.

5.1 Discussion

Despite LIME's popularity, a best-practice standard for research and evaluation has not been established. This lack of standardized procedures hinders the scientific rigor and broader application of LIME-based techniques. In this section, we address the most significant issues that have arisen in LIME research and application without explicitly naming specific papers that have not met these standards. By highlighting these problems, we aim to encourage the development of more robust and reproducible LIME-related methodologies, ultimately enhancing the trust and interpretability of model predictions.

Reproduction Issues. We observed a great lack of code availability (50%, see tool in Fig. 1) that creates significant reproducibility issues, making verifying the authors' contributions difficult. This limitation hinders the XAI community's ability to adapt to more advanced LIME frameworks, address known issues, and improve the trust and interpretability of the model's predictions that the explainee seeks to achieve.

Evaluation Practices. A direct consequence of the code availability limitation becomes evident when examining the evaluation sections of the covered articles. This lack prevents authors from comparing their LIME-related approaches to previously published techniques for benchmarking. As a result, many papers begin their motivation by highlighting a known issue of LIME (see Sect. 4.1) and often compare their adapted version solely against the standard LIME version. However, this approach disregards other related works, a practice that undermines the quality of the research. In contrast to the works that include a comparison with previous LIME-related techniques, these often compare against

Table 3. LIME XAI Evaluation Metrics. This table categorizes key properties across different areas, such as content, presentation, and user-centered aspects, to guide researchers and practitioners in selecting suitable metrics for evaluating LIME explanations. We adopt the structure of [64].

Area	Property	Description
Content	Correctness	Reflects how accurately the explanation represents the underlying model'âĂŹs decision-making process.
	Completeness	Measures the extent to which the explanation captures the full behavior of the model, including all relevant aspects that influence its decisions.
	Consistency	Evaluates how stable the explanation is across multiple similar instances, ensuring the same explanation is provided when the inputs are only slightly varied or the same.
	Continuity	Assesses the degree of similarity between explanations for similar instances, ensuring that small changes in input lead to minor adjustments in the explanation.
	Contrastivity	Gauges how well the explanation differentiates the explained instance from others, clarifying why this instance was treated differently than similar cases.
	Covariate complexity	Refers to the complexity of the features and their interactions used in the explanation, with simpler explanations typically being more interpretable.
	Efficiency	Evaluates the computational resources and time required to generate explanations, which are especially important for real-time applications.
	Scalability	Describes how well the explanation method performs as the model or dataset size increases.
Presentation	Compactness	Describes the conciseness of the explanation, focusing on its size and the number of elements included, with smaller explanations generally being more user-friendly.
	Composition	Refers to the structure and organization of the explanation, including how the information is presented and whether it follows a logical format.
	Confidence	Indicates the inclusion and accuracy of probability information within the explanation, helping users understand the certainty associated with the model'âĂŹs predictions.
	Applicability	Evaluates whether the explanation method can be used across various models or if it's tied to specific models.
	Modality Flexibility	Describes whether the explanation method can adapt to different data modalities, such as text, image, or tabular data.
User	Context	Describes how well the explanation aligns with the user'âĂŹs specific needs, goals, and the context in which it is applied.
	Coherence	Refers to how well the explanation fits with the user'âĂŹs prior knowledge, beliefs, and expectations, ensuring that it makes logical sense from their perspective.
	Controllability	Describes the level of interactivity or customization the user has over the explanation, allowing them to explore or adjust different aspects of it.
	Complexity	Refers to how easy or complex it is for a user to generate an explanation, including the required computational resources, technical knowledge, and effort involved.

S-LIME [104] or BayLIME [103], as these provide code for reproducibility and thus enable comparisons.

Another prevalent problem is the selection of evaluation metrics that confirm the stated contributions. This issue is universal within the XAI community and needs to be addressed. The evaluation of the explanations should be divided into qualitative and quantitative evaluations. Many works integrate user surveys for qualitative evaluation, where participants rate XAI-generated explanations. However, there is no standard procedure, with varying sample sizes and differing tasks—some involve interacting with explanations, while others require selecting the best one. We encourage authors to conduct user studies consistently and scientifically, referring to [16].

Concerning quantitative evaluation, numerous metrics have been proposed to assess various aspects of what makes a good explanation. [64] provide a comprehensive overview of these techniques aimed explicitly at explainable AI. However, despite the availability of these metrics, their application remains inconsistent. Many papers address only a subset of evaluation criteria, creating ambiguity about whether the proposed approaches are truly superior or where they may have limitations, which are not always clearly communicated. Regarding this issue, we identified the work of Klein et al. [39] highlighting a similar concern, noting that practitioners often struggle to choose the proper method for their specific problem. Their work demonstrates how evaluation metrics, when paired with different model architectures, can guide the search for appropriate XAI techniques, aligning with the challenges we address in this paper. In Sect. 5.2, we explore how LIME evaluation can be standardized to address these issues. In Table 3, we provide an overview of XAI metrics applicable to LIME, which can guide researchers in selecting proper evaluation metrics for their use cases. Here, we adapt the structure proposed by Nauta et al. [64] and add additional metrics found during the literature review.

5.2 Research Opportunities

Automatic LIME Selection. The challenge of selecting an appropriate XAI technique has been addressed in the literature [38,43,91,101], as the growing number of methods can make it difficult for users to choose the most suitable one. These studies guide users in applying different techniques based on specific requirements. An advancement in this area is presented in [18], which proposes an automated approach for selecting XAI techniques based on factors such as model type and explanation constraints. However, such approaches are limited to the techniques within the original framework, overlooking subsequent improvements and adaptations. This is significant, as standard, out-of-the-box techniques may be insufficient in scenarios requiring tailored solutions, such as applying LIME to audio data for audio sample explanations [31]. To address this, we have created the LIME overview page (Fig. 1), providing a quick overview of available techniques along with corresponding code implementations to facilitate efficient selection and application.

Evaluation of LIME Techniques. The challenge of establishing widely adopted evaluation techniques for LIME-related approaches, as discussed in Sect. 5.1, remains a significant concern. While a broad spectrum of suitable and well-established metrics already exists, their application is inconsistent across the community [64]. To address this inconsistency, developing a tailored evaluation framework specifically for LIME would be beneficial in assessing whether the identified issues are effectively mitigated. Such a framework could draw inspiration from existing XAI evaluation frameworks, which facilitate the comparison of fundamental metrics across various XAI techniques [5,39,87].

Foundation Model Integration. In recent years, foundation models, such as large language models (LLMs), have gained widespread prominence. Trained on diverse datasets, these models encapsulate world knowledge by capturing the underlying structural patterns within the data. For instance, in reinforcement learning (RL) domains, foundation models are increasingly used during the agent exploration phase, leveraging the knowledge embedded in LLMs to enhance the agent's performance [100]. This knowledge can also be utilized in XAI by assessing whether it aligns with the explained model's decisions or by identifying biases in the world model through systematic cross-checking, enabling the deliberate integration of foundation models into explainability. Another promising approach would be integrating a large language model (LLM) into LIME's feature generation and sample generation stages for text explanations. LLMs can enhance the locality of explanations by generating features that are more contextually aligned with the instance being explained. Furthermore, leveraging foundation models for feature generation could soften LIME's strict locality, transitioning it toward a hybrid local-global explanation. This is because LLMs can naturally sample instances from the surrounding neighborhood, broadening the scope of the explanation. For sample generation, foundation models could guide the process by selectively sampling instances where LIME is uncertain, effectively using the LLM's knowledge as an exploration-driven function to improve the overall explanation quality.

However, it is crucial to distinguish between scenarios where, for instance, an LLM is used to simulate a model's decision [45] and those where a foundation model is directly incorporated into an explainability approach. In the latter case, the explanation is not generated by the foundation model itself; instead, its properties are incorporated into the explanation process. Research has already demonstrated this with LIME [40], and similar approaches have been successfully applied to other explainability methods, such as SHAP [92].

Focus on Explainee. For whom are these techniques being developed? The most common motivation is to improve explanations for users seeking to understand the decision-making basis of an AI system within a given input. This assumption often suggests that the work applies to straightforward, user-centric scenarios. However, due to the frequent lack of accessible or complete public implementations, end users have limited or no opportunity to effectively benefit from the insights gained. Additionally, there can be a mismatch between how XAI techniques generate explanations for an instance and what the end user expects or finds useful [25]. The future directions for LIME-based research highlighted here emphasize the importance of involving end users more directly. This could include assisting them in selecting the appropriate LIME techniques, ensuring proper evaluation, or leveraging the contextual knowledge of foundation models. Therefore, this point is not a call for a specific new research direction but a recommendation for how future research should be structured.

5.3 Conclusion

In this survey, we provide a comprehensive overview of XAI techniques built upon the widely used local and model-agnostic framework, LIME. We begin by describing the core principle of LIME: approximating model behavior in a localized region and illustrate how this approach adapts to various data modalities. Building upon this foundation, we organize LIME's underlying processes into a taxonomy, distinguishing the framework's key subprocesses. We map the specific challenges each technique addresses, derived directly from the existing literature, to highlight the unique contributions of each method. Additionally, we examine LIME adaptations across different target modalities and application domains, emphasizing how the framework can be refined to enhance accuracy or adapt to specific domains. Through this systematic analysis, we identify overarching trends within the research community and highlight persistent challenges that warrant further investigation.

Acknowledgments. This research was supported in part by the German Federal Ministry for Economic Affairs and Climate Action of Germany (BMWK), and in part by the German Federal Ministry of Education and Research (BMBF).

References

1. Abdullah, T.A.A., Zahid, M.S.M., Ali, W., Hassan, S.U.: B-lime: an improvement of lime for interpretable deep learning classification of cardiac arrhythmia from ecg signals. Processes **11**(2) (2023)
2. Abdullah, T.A.A., Zahid, M.S.M., Turki, A.F., Ali, W., Jiman, A.A., Abdulaal, M.J., Sobahi, N.M., Attar, E.T.: Sig-lime: a signal-based enhancement of lime explanation technique. IEEE Access **12**, 52641–52658 (2024)
3. Achanta, R., Shaji, A., Smith, K., Lucchi, A., Fua, P., Süsstrunk, S.: Slic superpixels compared to state-of-the-art superpixel methods. IEEE Trans. Pattern Anal. Mach. Intell. **34**(11), 2274–2282 (2012)
4. Adak, A., Pradhan, B., Shukla, N., Alamri, A.: Unboxing deep learning model of food delivery service reviews using explainable artificial intelligence (xai) technique. Foods **11**(14) (2022)
5. Agarwal, C., et al.: Openxai: towards a transparent evaluation of model explanations (2024)
6. Ahern, I., Noack, A., Guzman-Nateras, L., Dou, D., Li, B., Huan, J.: Normlime: a new feature importance metric for explaining deep neural networks (2019)

7. Aldughayfiq, B., Ashfaq, F., Jhanjhi, N.Z., Humayun, M.: Explainable ai for retinoblastoma diagnosis: interpreting deep learning models with lime and shap. Diagnostics **13**(11) (2023)
8. Alexander, Z., Chau, D.H., Saldaña, C.: An interrogative survey of explainable ai in manufacturing. IEEE Trans. Industr. Inf. **20**(5), 7069–7081 (2024)
9. An, J., Zhang, Y., Joe, I.: Specific-input lime explanations for tabular data based on deep learning models. Appl. Sci. **13**(15) (2023)
10. Barredo Arrieta, A., et al.: Explainable artificial intelligence (xai): concepts, taxonomies, opportunities and challenges toward responsible ai. Inf. Fusion **58**, 82–115 (2020)
11. Bora, R.P., Terhörst, P., Veldhuis, R., Ramachandra, R., Raja, K.: Slice: stabilized lime for consistent explanations for image classification. In: Proceedings of the IEEE/CVF Conference on Computer Vision and Pattern Recognition (CVPR), pp. 10988–10996, June 2024
12. Botari, T., Hvilshøj, F., Izbicki, R., de Carvalho, A.C.P.L.F.: Melime: meaningful local explanation for machine learning models. CoRR abs/2009.05818 (2020)
13. Bramhall, S., Horn, H.E., Tieu, M., Lohia, N.: Qlime-a quadratic local interpretable model-agnostic explanation approach (2020)
14. Brocke, J.v., Simons, A., Niehaves, B., Riemer, K., Plattfaut, R., Cleven, A.: Reconstructing the giant: On the importance of rigour in documenting the literature search process, June 2009
15. Chaddad, A., Peng, J., Xu, J., Bouridane, A.: Survey of explainable ai techniques in healthcare. Sensors **23**(2) (2023)
16. Chromik, M., Schuessler, M.: A taxonomy for human subject evaluation of blackbox explanations in xai. Exss-atec@ iui **1** (2020)
17. Collaris, D., van Wijk, J.J.: Explainexplore: visual exploration of machine learning explanations. In: 2020 IEEE Pacific Visualization Symposium (PacificVis), pp. 26–35 (2020)
18. Cugny, R., Aligon, J., Chevalier, M., Roman Jimenez, G., Teste, O.: Autoxai: A framework to automatically select the most adapted xai solution. In: Proceedings of the 31st ACM International Conference on Information & Knowledge Management, CIKM 2022, pp. 315–324. Association for Computing Machinery, New York (2022)
19. Dieber, J., Kirrane, S.: Why model why? assessing the strengths and limitations of LIME. CoRR abs/2012.00093 (2020)
20. Dikopoulou, Z., Moustakidis, S., Karlsson, P.: Glime: A new graphical methodology for interpretable model-agnostic explanations (2021)
21. Duong, H., Hoang, L., Le, B.: Controlling lime kernel width to achieve comprehensible explanations on tabular data. In: Honda, K., Le, B., Huynh, V.N., Inuiguchi, M., Kohda, Y. (eds.) Integrated Uncertainty in Knowledge Modelling and Decision Making, pp. 153–164. Springer, Cham (2023)
22. Efron, B., Hastie, T., Johnstone, I., Tibshirani, R.: Least angle regression. Ann. Stat. **32**(2), 407–499 (2004)
23. ElShawi, R., Sherif, Y., Al-Mallah, M., Sakr, S.: Ilime: local and global interpretable model-agnostic explainer of black-box decision. In: Welzer, T., Eder, J., Podgorelec, V., Kamišalić Latifić, A. (eds.) Advances in Databases and Information Systems, pp. 53–68. Springer, Cham (2019)
24. Epskamp, S., Fried, E.I.: A tutorial on regularized partial correlation networks. Psychol. Methods **23**(4), 617 (2018)
25. Freiesleben, T., König, G.: Dear xai community, we need to talk! fundamental misconceptions in current xai research (2023)

26. Garreau, D., von Luxburg, U.: Looking deeper into tabular lime. arXiv preprint arXiv:2008.11092 (2020)
27. Gaudel, R., Galárraga, L., Delaunay, J., Rozé, L., Bhargava, V.: s-lime: reconciling locality and fidelity in linear explanations. In: Bouadi, T., Fromont, E., Hüllermeier, E. (eds.) Advances in Intelligent Data Analysis XX, pp. 102–114. Springer, Cham (2022)
28. Gawde, S., Patil, S., Kumar, S., Kamat, P., Kotecha, K., Alfarhood, S.: Explainable predictive maintenance of rotating machines using lime, shap, pdp, ice. IEEE Access **12**, 29345–29361 (2024)
29. Guidotti, R., Monreale, A., Ruggieri, S., Pedreschi, D., Turini, F., Giannotti, F.: Local rule-based explanations of black box decision systems. CoRR abs/1805.10820 (2018). http://arxiv.org/abs/1805.10820
30. Hall, P., Gill, N., Kurka, M., Phan, W.: Machine learning interpretability with h2o driverless ai. H2O. ai (2017)
31. Haunschmid, V., Manilow, E., Widmer, G.: audiolime: Listenable explanations using source separation. CoRR abs/2008.00582 (2020)
32. Hoyer, L., Munoz, M., Katiyar, P., Khoreva, A., Fischer, V.: Grid saliency for context explanations of semantic segmentation. In: Wallach, H., Larochelle, H., Beygelzimer, A., d' Alché-Buc, F., Fox, E., Garnett, R. (eds.) Advances in Neural Information Processing Systems, vol. 32. Curran Associates, Inc. (2019)
33. Hu, L., Chen, J., Nair, V.N., Sudjianto, A.: Locally interpretable models and effects based on supervised partitioning (lime-sup) (2018)
34. Huang, Q., Yamada, M., Tian, Y., Singh, D., Chang, Y.: Graphlime: local interpretable model explanations for graph neural networks. IEEE Trans. Knowl. Data Eng. **35**(7), 6968–6972 (2023)
35. Hung, Y.H., Lee, C.Y.: Bmb-lime: Lime with modeling local nonlinearity and uncertainty in explainability. Knowl.-Based Syst. **294**, 111732 (2024)
36. Ito, T., Ochiai, K., Fukazawa, Y.: C-lime: a consistency-oriented lime for time-series health-risk predictions. In: Uehara, H., Yamaguchi, T., Bai, Q. (eds.) Knowledge Management and Acquisition for Intelligent Systems, pp. 58–69. Springer, Cham (2021)
37. Kirillov, A., et al.: Segment anything (2023)
38. Klaise, J., Looveren, A.V., Vacanti, G., Coca, A.: Alibi explain: algorithms for explaining machine learning models. J. Mach. Learn. Res. **22**(181), 1–7 (2021)
39. Klein, L., Lüth, C.T., Schlegel, U., Bungert, T.J., El-Assady, M., Jäger, P.F.: Navigating the maze of explainable ai: A systematic approach to evaluating methods and metrics (2024)
40. Knab, P., Marton, S., Bartelt, C.: Dseg-lime: Improving image explanation by hierarchical data-driven segmentation (2024)
41. Knab, P., Marton, S., Bartelt, C., Fuder, R.: Interpreting outliers in time series data through decoding autoencoder (2024)
42. Kok, I., Okay, F.Y., Muyanli, O., Ozdemir, S.: Explainable artificial intelligence (xai) for internet of things: A survey. IEEE Internet Things J. **10**(16), 14764–14779 (2023)
43. Kokhlikyan, N., et al.: Captum: a unified and generic model interpretability library for pytorch. CoRR abs/2009.07896 (2020)
44. Kovalev, M.S., Utkin, L.V., Kasimov, E.M.: Survlime: a method for explaining machine learning survival models. Knowl.-Based Syst. **203**, 106164 (2020)
45. Kroeger, N., Ley, D., Krishna, S., Agarwal, C., Lakkaraju, H.: In-context explainers: harnessing llms for explaining black box models (2024)

46. Laguna, S., et al.: Explimeable: a visual analytics approach for exploring lime. In: 2023 Workshop on Visual Analytics in Healthcare (VAHC), pp. 27–33 (2023)
47. Lam, S., et al.: Local interpretation of deep learning models for aspect-based sentiment analysis. Eng. Appl. Artif. Intell. **143**, 109947 (2025)
48. Laugel, T., Renard, X., Lesot, M., Marsala, C., Detyniecki, M.: Defining locality for surrogates in post-hoc interpretablity. CoRR abs/1806.07498 (2018)
49. Li, X., et al.: G-lime: statistical learning for local interpretations of deep neural networks using global priors. Artif. Intell. **314**, 103823 (2023)
50. Lin, D.Y., Wei, L.J.: The robust inference for the cox proportional hazards model. J. Am. Stat. Assoc. **84**(408), 1074–1078 (1989)
51. Linardatos, P., Papastefanopoulos, V., Kotsiantis, S.: Explainable ai: a review of machine learning interpretability methods. Entropy **23**(1) (2021)
52. van der Linden, I., Haned, H., Kanoulas, E.: Global aggregations of local explanations for black box models (2019)
53. Lundberg, S.M., Lee, S.: A unified approach to interpreting model predictions. CoRR abs/1705.07874 (2017)
54. Lyu, Y., Liang, P.P., Deng, Z., Salakhutdinov, R., Morency, L.P.: Dime: Fine-grained interpretations of multimodal models via disentangled local explanations (2022)
55. Maas, A.L., Daly, R.E., Pham, P.T., Huang, D., Ng, A.Y., Potts, C.: Learning word vectors for sentiment analysis. In: Proceedings of the 49th Annual Meeting of the Association for Computational Linguistics: Human Language Technologies, pp. 142–150. Association for Computational Linguistics, Portland, Oregon, USA, June 2011
56. Mandeep, Agarwal, A., Bhatia, A., Malhi, A., Kaler, P., Pannu, H.S.: Machine learning based explainable financial forecasting. In: 2022 4th International Conference on Computer Communication and the Internet (ICCCI), pp. 34–38 (2022)
57. Mardaoui, D., Garreau, D.: An analysis of lime for text data. In: International Conference on Artificial Intelligence and Statistics, pp. 3493–3501. PMLR (2021)
58. Martins, T., Almeida, A.M., Cardoso, E., Nunes, L.: Explainable artificial intelligence (xai): a systematic literature review on taxonomies and applications in finance. IEEE Access **12**, 618–629 (2024)
59. Meng, H., Wagner, C., Triguero, I.: Segal time series classification - stable explanations using a generative model and an adaptive weighting method for lime. Neural Netw. **176**, 106345 (2024)
60. Miller, T.: Explanation in artificial intelligence: insights from the social sciences. Artif. Intell. **267**, 1–38 (2019)
61. Mishra, S., Sturm, B.L., Dixon, S.: Local interpretable model-agnostic explanations for music content analysis. In: International Society for Music Information Retrieval Conference (2017)
62. Molnar, C.: Interpretable machine learning. Lulu. com (2020)
63. Mulwa, M.M., Mwangi, R.W., Mindila, A.: Gmm-lime explainable machine learning model for interpreting sensor-based human gait. Eng. Rep. **n/a**(n/a), e12864
64. Nauta, M., et al.: From anecdotal evidence to quantitative evaluation methods: a systematic review on evaluating explainable ai. ACM Comput. Surv. **55**(13s), July 2023
65. Neubert, P., Protzel, P.: Compact watershed and preemptive slic: on improving trade-offs of superpixel segmentation algorithms. In: 2014 22nd International Conference on Pattern Recognition, pp. 996–1001 (2014)

66. Onari, M.A., Grau, I., Nobile, M.S., Zhang, Y.: Trustworthy artificial intelligence in medical applications: A mini survey. In: 2023 IEEE Conference on Computational Intelligence in Bioinformatics and Computational Biology (CIBCB), pp. 1–8 (2023)
67. Park, M.S., Son, H., Hyun, C., Hwang, H.J.: Explainability of machine learning models for bankruptcy prediction. IEEE Access **9**, 124887–124899 (2021)
68. Perez-Castanos, S., Prieto-Roig, A., Monzo, D., Colomer-Barbera, J.: Holistic Production Overview: Using XAI for Production Optimization, pp. 423–436. Springer, Cham (2024)
69. Rabold, J., Deininger, H., Siebers, M., Schmid, U.: Enriching visual with verbal explanations for relational concepts - combining lime with aleph. In: Cellier, P., Driessens, K. (eds.) Machine Learning and Knowledge Discovery in Databases, pp. 180–192. Springer, Cham (2020)
70. Rabold, J., Siebers, M., Schmid, U.: Explaining black-box classifiers with ilp - empowering lime with aleph to approximate non-linear decisions with relational rules. In: Riguzzi, F., Bellodi, E., Zese, R. (eds.) Inductive Logic Programming, pp. 105–117. Springer, Cham (2018)
71. Recio-García, J.A., Díaz-Agudo, B., Pino-Castilla, V.: Cbr-lime: A case-based reasoning approach to provide specific local interpretable model-agnostic explanations. In: Case-Based Reasoning Research and Development: 28th International Conference, ICCBR 2020, Salamanca, Spain, June 8–12, 2020, Proceedings, pp. 179–194. Springer, Heidelberg (2020)
72. Ribeiro, M.T., Singh, S., Guestrin, C.: "Why should i trust you?": explaining the predictions of any classifier. In: Proceedings of the 22nd ACM SIGKDD International Conference on Knowledge Discovery and Data Mining, KDD '16, pp. 1135–1144. Association for Computing Machinery, New York (2016)
73. Ribeiro, M.T., Singh, S., Guestrin, C.: Anchors: high-precision model-agnostic explanations. In: Proceedings of the Thirty-Second AAAI Conference on Artificial Intelligence and Thirtieth Innovative Applications of Artificial Intelligence Conference and Eighth AAAI Symposium on Educational Advances in Artificial Intelligence. AAAI'18/IAAI'18/EAAI'18, AAAI Press (2018)
74. Rojat, T., Puget, R., Filliat, D., Ser, J.D., Gelin, R., Díaz-Rodríguez, N.: Explainable artificial intelligence (xai) on timeseries data: A survey (2021)
75. Rong, Y., Leemann, T., Nguyen, T.T., Fiedler, L., Qian, P., Unhelkar, V., Seidel, T., Kasneci, G., Kasneci, E.: Towards human-centered explainable ai: a survey of user studies for model explanations. IEEE Trans. Pattern Anal. Mach. Intell. **46**(4), 2104–2122 (2024)
76. Saadatfar, H., Kiani-Zadegan, Z., Ghahremani-Nezhad, B.: Us-lime: Increasing fidelity in lime using uncertainty sampling on tabular data. Neurocomputing **597**, 127969 (2024)
77. Saeed, W., Omlin, C.: Explainable ai (xai): a systematic meta-survey of current challenges and future opportunities. Knowl.-Based Syst. **263**, 110273 (2023)
78. Sahakyan, M., Aung, Z., Rahwan, T.: Explainable artificial intelligence for tabular data: a survey. IEEE Access **9**, 135392–135422 (2021)
79. Saini, A., Prasad, R.: Select wisely and explain: Active learning and probabilistic local post-hoc explainability. In: Proceedings of the 2022 AAAI/ACM Conference on AI, Ethics, and Society, AIES 2022, pp. 599–608. Association for Computing Machinery, New York (2022)

80. Sangroya, A., Rastogi, M., Anantaram, C., Vig, L.: Guided-lime: Structured sampling based hybrid approach towards explaining blackbox machine learning models. In: International Conference on Information and Knowledge Management (2020)
81. Santhiappan, S., Reghu, M.K., Saminathan, M., Veerappan, A.: Speeding up lime using attention weights. In: Proceedings of the 7th Joint International Conference on Data Science & Management of Data (11th ACM IKDD CODS and 29th COMAD), p. 444–448. CODS-COMAD '24. Association for Computing Machinery, New York (2024)
82. Schlegel, U., Vo, D.L., Keim, D.A., Seebacher, D.: Ts-mule: Local interpretable model-agnostic explanations for time series forecast models. In: Machine Learning and Principles and Practice of Knowledge Discovery in Databases, pp. 5–14. Springer, Cham (2021)
83. Schwalbe, G., Finzel, B.: A comprehensive taxonomy for explainable artificial intelligence: a systematic survey of surveys on methods and concepts. Data Min. Knowl. Disc. **38**(5), 3043–3101 (2024)
84. Selvaraju, R.R., Das, A., Vedantam, R., Cogswell, M., Parikh, D., Batra, D.: Grad-cam: why did you say that? visual explanations from deep networks via gradient-based localization. CoRR abs/1610.02391 (2016)
85. Shankaranarayana, S.M., Runje, D.: ALIME: autoencoder based approach for local interpretability. CoRR abs/1909.02437 (2019)
86. Shi, S., Zhang, X., Fan, W.: A modified perturbed sampling method for local interpretable model-agnostic explanation (2020)
87. Sithakoul, S., Meftah, S., Feutry, C.: Beexai: Benchmark to evaluate explainable ai. In: Longo, L., Lapuschkin, S., Seifert, C. (eds.) Explainable Artificial Intelligence, pp. 445–468. Springer, Cham (2024)
88. Sivill, T., Flach, P.: Limesegment: meaningful, realistic time series explanations. In: Camps-Valls, G., Ruiz, F.J.R., Valera, I. (eds.) Proceedings of The 25th International Conference on Artificial Intelligence and Statistics. Proceedings of Machine Learning Research, vol. 151, pp. 3418–3433. PMLR, 28–30 Mar 2022
89. Sokol, K., Flach, P.: Limetree: Consistent and faithful multi-class explanations (2024)
90. Sokol, K., Hepburn, A., Santos-Rodriguez, R., Flach, P.: bLIMEy: surrogate prediction explanations beyond LIME. In: 2019 Workshop on Human-Centric Machine Learning (HCML 2019) at the 33rd Conference on Neural Information Processing Systems (NeurIPS 2019), Vancouver, Canada (2019)
91. Spinner, T., Schlegel, U., Schäfer, H., El-Assady, M.: explainer: a visual analytics framework for interactive and explainable machine learning. IEEE Trans. Visual Comput. Graphics **26**(1), 1064–1074 (2020)
92. Sun, A., Ma, P., Yuan, Y., Wang, S.: Explain any concept: Segment anything meets concept-based explanation (2023)
93. Tan, Z., Tian, Y., Li, J.: Glime: General, stable and local lime explanation. In: Oh, A., Naumann, T., Globerson, A., Saenko, K., Hardt, M., Levine, S. (eds.) Advances in Neural Information Processing Systems, vol. 36, pp. 36250–36277. Curran Associates, Inc. (2023)
94. Theissler, A., Spinnato, F., Schlegel, U., Guidotti, R.: Explainable ai for time series classification: a review, taxonomy and research directions. IEEE Access **10**, 100700–100724 (2022). https://doi.org/10.1109/ACCESS.2022.3207765
95. Tjoa, E., Guan, C.: A survey on explainable artificial intelligence (xai): toward medical xai. IEEE Trans. Neural Networks Learn. Syst. **32**(11), 4793–4813 (2021)

96. Ullah, N., Hassan, M., Khan, J.A., Anwar, M.S., Aurangzeb, K.: Enhancing explainability in brain tumor detection: a novel deepebtdnet model with lime on mri images. Int. J. Imaging Syst. Technol. **34**(1), e23012 (2024)
97. Utkin, L.V., Kovalev, M.S., Kasimov, E.M.: Survlime-inf: A simplified modification of survlime for explanation of machine learning survival models. ArXiv abs/2005.02387 (2020)
98. Visani, G., Bagli, E., Chesani, F.: Optilime: optimized lime explanations for diagnostic computer algorithms. ArXiv abs/2006.05714 (2020)
99. Webster, J., Watson, R.T.: Analyzing the past to prepare for the future: writing a literature review. MIS Quarterly **26**(2), xiii–xxiii (2002)
100. Xu, Z., Yu, C., Fang, F., Wang, Y., Wu, Y.: Language agents with reinforcement learning for strategic play in the werewolf game (2024)
101. Yang, W., Le, H., Savarese, S., Hoi, S.: Omnixai: A library for explainable ai (2022)
102. Zafar, M.R., Khan, N.M.: Dlime: A deterministic local interpretable model-agnostic explanations approach for computer-aided diagnosis systems (2019)
103. Zhao, X., Huang, W., Huang, X., Robu, V., Flynn, D.: Baylime: Bayesian local interpretable model-agnostic explanations. pp. 887–896 (2021), 37th Conference on Uncertainty in Artificial Intelligence 2021, UAI 2021 ; Conference date: 27-07-2021 Through 30-07-2021
104. Zhou, Z., Hooker, G., Wang, F.: S-lime: Stabilized-lime for model explanation. In: Proceedings of the 27th ACM SIGKDD Conference on Knowledge Discovery & Data Mining, KDD 2021, pp. 2429–2438. Association for Computing Machinery, New York (2021)
105. Zou, H., Hastie, T.: Regularization and variable selection via the elastic net. J. Roy. Stat. Soc. Ser. B: Stat. Methodol. **67**(2), 301–320 (03 2005)

Open Access This chapter is licensed under the terms of the Creative Commons Attribution 4.0 International License (http://creativecommons.org/licenses/by/4.0/), which permits use, sharing, adaptation, distribution and reproduction in any medium or format, as long as you give appropriate credit to the original author(s) and the source, provide a link to the Creative Commons license and indicate if changes were made.

The images or other third party material in this chapter are included in the chapter's Creative Commons license, unless indicated otherwise in a credit line to the material. If material is not included in the chapter's Creative Commons license and your intended use is not permitted by statutory regulation or exceeds the permitted use, you will need to obtain permission directly from the copyright holder.

Explainable Bayesian Optimization

Tanmay Chakraborty[1,3](✉) , Christian Wirth[2] , and Christin Seifert[3]

[1] Continental Automotive Technologies GmbH, AI Lab Berlin, Berlin, Germany
[2] Continental Automotive Technologies GmbH, Frankfurt, Germany
christian.2.wirth@continental-corporation.com
[3] Marburg University, Marburg, Germany
tanmay.chakraborty@continental-corporation.com,
christin.seifert@uni-marburg.de

Abstract. Manual parameter tuning of cyber-physical systems is a common practice, but it is labor-intensive. Bayesian Optimization (BO) offers an automated alternative, yet its black-box nature reduces trust and limits human-BO collaborative system tuning. Experts struggle to interpret BO recommendations due to the lack of explanations. This paper addresses the post-hoc BO explainability problem for cyber-physical systems. We introduce TNTRules (Tune-No-Tune Rules), a novel algorithm that provides both global and local explanations for BO recommendations. TNTRules generates actionable rules and visual graphs, identifying optimal solution bounds and ranges, as well as potential alternative solutions. Unlike existing explainable AI (XAI) methods, TNTRules is tailored specifically for BO, by encoding uncertainty via a variance pruning technique and hierarchical agglomerative clustering. A multi-objective optimization approach allows maximizing explanation quality. We evaluate TNTRules using established XAI metrics (Correctness, Completeness, and Compactness) and compare it against adapted baseline methods. The results demonstrate that TNTRules generates high-fidelity, compact, and complete explanations, significantly outperforming three baselines on 5 multi-objective testing functions and 2 hyperparameter tuning problems.

Keywords: Explainable artificial intelligence · Bayesian optimization · Hyper-parameter optimization · Hierarchical agglomerative clustering

1 Introduction

Manual parameter tuning of cyber-physical systems by experts has been the industry norm [32, 34]. To reduce the manual effort, Bayesian Optimization (BO) has been introduced for parameter tuning [48]. BO is a model-based optimization technique with a Gaussian Process (GP) backbone that returns black-box recommendations. Since the recommendations provided by BO may not be accurate, due to simplified objectives and approximation errors, the parameter tuning process cannot be fully automated and still requires expert intervention [10, 51].

Typically, experts in domains such as automotive tuning, engine calibration, laser alignment, and other hardware-oriented fields have limited computer science backgrounds. Therefore, they primarily use BO results in a post-hoc manner (experts not involved in the BO development process), usually as a tool for fine-tuning physical systems [34,57]. In addition, complex industrial design processes for aerospace components [22], mechanical bearing designs for fault tolerance [35], as well as instrumentation designs in particle accelerators can also use BO as a tool to explore design spaces, making the design more autonomous and easier [42]. In this case, collaboration refers to receiving recommendations from BO and using them on the hardware system.

However, BO is a black box algorithm. Thus, it only returns suggested parameter settings without explanations, which hinders the expert's trust in the tuning process [1,4,41]. This interpretability challenge in BO mirrors similar challenges in AI that led to the rise of Explainable AI (XAI) [43]. While several techniques have been developed to explain AI decisions, explanations for optimization algorithms are rare. Explainable Bayesian Optimization aims to make BO recommendations transparent by providing explanations to experts. Explanations for BO would instill trust in the BO recommendations and provide a better collaborative experience for the expert [1,4,41]. The main goal is to elaborate the design spaces of the optimization problem, as learned by BO, using simple and easy to understand rules, so that users can use the recommendations in an interpretable way.

In this paper, we address the post-hoc BO explainability problem. More specifically, we present a method for explaining BO recommendations to experts who calibrate and tune cyber-physical systems (Fig. 1). Based on the literature, we identified two main requirements for providing these explanations [4]: i) identifying optimal solution bounds and ranges for tuning, and ii) identifying and providing bounds and ranges for tuning potential alternative solutions (in the case of local minima).

Current XAI methods are designed to explain machine learning models, such as classification and clustering algorithms, and do not meet the requirements [45]. We address this gap by introducing TNTRules (Tune-No-Tune Rules), a post-hoc rule-based explanation algorithm for BO. TNTRules provides local explanations through visual graphs and actionable rules that indicate which parameters should be adjusted or left unchanged to improve results. For global explanations, TNTRules generates a ranked "IF-THEN" rule list. We use Hierarchical Agglomerative Clustering (HAC) to identify rules within the optimization space, including their associated uncertainties [37]. Unlike many XAI methods, TNTRules is controllable, allowing adjustments for high-quality explanations. Controllability means adjusting the number of rules mined. In BO, this means changing the size of the bounding boxes that divide the optimization space, which affects explanation quality. In terms of explanation, it means allowing the user to have different views on the optimization space. We provide high-quality explanations through multi-objective optimization, aiming to maximize explanation quality by automatically tuning a threshold t_s and balancing different quality metrics.

We evaluate the explanation quality (qualitative and quantitative) of TNTRules using metrics derived from the XAI literature (Co-12 framework) [33]. Although there are numerous, competing metrics for evaluating explanation quality, we focus on the three evaluation criteria from the Co-12 framework, that are relevant to our use case: Correctness (quantitative), Completeness (quantitative and qualitative), and Compactness (qualitative). Ideally, explanations should be consistent with the model they

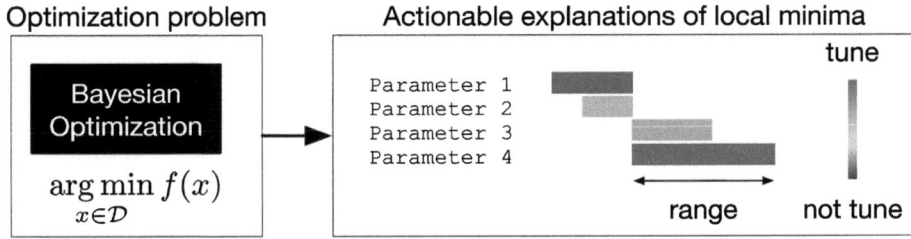

Fig. 1. Explainable Bayesian Optimization with actionable local explanation for one minimum (multiple minima would have multiple graphs): red/yellow bars indicate optimal parameters, green bars indicate tunable parameters. Bar lengths indicate tuning ranges. (Color figure online)

are explaining (correctness), thorough in their coverage (completeness), and concise enough for users to easily understand (compactness). A high-quality explanation would score well on all three metrics.

Current literature lacks directly comparable methods for evaluating TNTRules – apart from RXBO [4] – which is why we adapted existing approaches (decision rules [3] and RuleXAI [24]) from the XAI literature to provide diverse baselines for comparison. Our results show that TNTRules generate high-fidelity, compact, and complete explanations, which shows substantial improvement from the baseline methods. More specifically, we make the following contributions:

1. We introduce TNTRules, a method for explaining Bayesian Optimization as a set of global rules and local actionable explanations.
2. We introduce a variance pruning technique for hierarchical agglomerative clustering to encode uncertainty.
3. We introduce an optimizaton method based on multi-objective criteria to maximize the quality of explanations.
4. Our functionally grounded evaluation of hyperparameter optimization tasks shows that TNTRules outperform other explanation methods. On common optimization test functions, we show TNTRules' capability to identify the optimal region and its potential to detect other local minima.

2 Related Work

This section provides an overview of XAI, explanation presentations, and evaluation of the XAI method. This is followed by rule-based explanations and optimizing the quality of explanations.

2.1 Explainable AI

XAI can be broadly classified into transparent models and post hoc explanation methods, which are either specifically designed for certain model classes or applicable to a wide range of models (model agnostic) [14]. The resulting explanations can be global, explaining the entire model, or local, explaining a single sample. TNTRules generates a global surrogate model [8] as a set of rules and local actionable rules.

Explanations for Bayesian Optimization are either post-hoc, i.e. explaining the minima and their bounds [4], or online, i.e. explaining BO's next point selection strategy [1,41]. There has been additional work on explaining hyperparameter optimization tasks [28,46]. These works are not directly comparable to ours because they i) do not explain the black-box function in BO, ii) do not address or bound minima in the optimization space, iii) do not provide tuning ranges, and iv) are not rule-based systems.

The **post-hoc method** of [47] explains the core of BO, i.e., Gaussian Process (GP), primarily by producing feature rankings, possibly uncertainty-aware [47], but they do not meet the explainable Bayesian optimization's requirements i)-ii). RXBO, the closest work to ours, introduces a rule miner for optimization, but does not deal with uncertainty during clustering and lacks multiple minima identification [4]. We take inspiration from the literature on rule-based surrogate models [2,7,29]. These methods distill a base model into sets of rules by using a (probabilistic) surrogate model. **Online methods** are suitable for domains such as drug discovery, materials exploration, and manufacturing, where experts rely heavily on computer simulations for discovery processes [6,12]. In such domains, understanding BO's next point selection (while the algorithm is running) helps experts make informed decisions. Unlike online methods, post-hoc methods (this work and [4]) focus on the user group that uses BO results in a post-hoc manner (not involved in the algorithm running phase, but using BO as a tool) [57].

Explanation generation is typically tightly coupled to a **presentation format**. Following the model inspection pipeline of [14], we argue that explanation generation and visualizations are distinct aspects, emphasizing the central role of explanation presentation in improving understandability. TNTRules translates rules into visual explanations, following design patterns from popular visual-centric approaches such as SHAP [23] and LIME [39]. Similar to evaluating machine learning models, explanation methods need to be evaluated. **XAI evaluation** libraries such as Quantus [16] are actively involved in establishing evaluation benchmarks. A comprehensive study [33] has identified 12 properties for evaluating XAI. We adopt an appropriate subset of these properties to evaluate our TNTRules. We use functionally based evaluations, which is standard in XAI [53,62].

2.2 Rule Mining and Rule-Based Explanations

Association rule mining has many established algorithms such as Apriori, and Eclat [61]. XAI has adopted them for rule-based explanations because of their transparency, fidelity, and ease of use [54]. We take a similar stance, choosing rules for their high level of comprehensibility. Similar to [55], we present rules in descending order of utility. TNTRules are not fuzzy rules, meaning rules do not have a degree of uncertainty in themselves, but they represent the uncertainty of the GP model. The rules maintain precision within the domains they define, ensuring clarity and accuracy in the explanations provided [25].

2.3 Optimizing Quality of Explanations

Controllability, i.e., mechanisms for end users to control the explanation method, is a desideratum for explanations [33]. Controlling an XAI method means being able to define and set parameters for an explanation method [11]. Many XAI methods, such as SHAP and LIME, lack control and assume that the explanations they produce are consistently optimal, making them black boxes explaining black boxes (the machine learning models). The existing literature on controllable XAI methods is limited. A recent paper [36] introduced the concept of hyperparameter search for XAI. Building on this foundation, our contribution advances the field by proposing a novel approach to XAI hyperparameter search using multi-objective optimization.

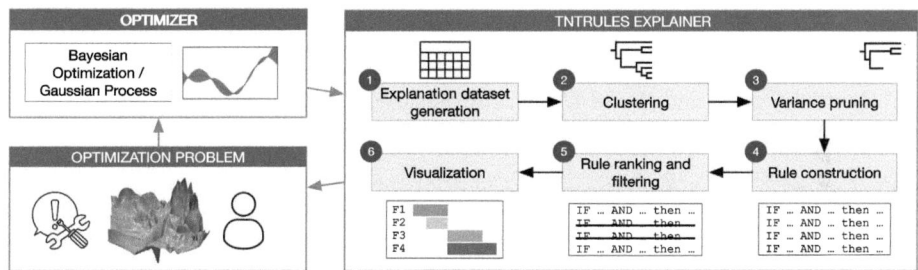

Fig. 2. Given an optimization problem, TNTRules explains the optimizer by identifying parameter bounds for optimal regions in the search space. TNTRules first generates an explanation dataset (1) by sampling the search space. The dataset is clustered (2); these clusters are pruned (3), and rules are constructed for them (4). These rules are then ranked and filtered (5), and the final set is presented as explanations to the end user (6).[4]

3 Background and Problem Setting

This section briefly describes the background of Bayesian Optimization (BO) and Gaussian Processes (GPs) relevant to this paper, followed by the problem setup.

Bayesian Optimization, a sequential model-based optimization technique, uses a probabilistic model, usually a Gaussian Process (GP). BO uses uncertainty-aware exploration/exploitation trade-offs to reduce the required number of iterations [13].

BO identifies minima ($\mathbf{x_{opt}}$) for a black-box objective $f(\mathbf{x})$ defined in a bounded search-space $\mathcal{D} \subseteq \mathcal{R}^d$:

$$\mathbf{x_{opt}} = \arg\min_{\mathbf{x} \in \mathcal{D}} f(\mathbf{x}). \tag{1}$$

f is a black-box function that is *expensive to evaluate, noisy, and not known in closed form*. The GP serves as an approximator of the objective function [48]. We assume that the underlying GP approximates the optimization space sufficiently. Minimizing the GP approximation error is a separate research area [40].

A **Gaussian Process** is a set of random variables with each finite set of those variables following a multivariate normal distribution. The distribution of a GP is the joint distribution of all variables. In a GP, a distribution model is formulated around functions, each having a mean $m(\mathbf{x})$ and covariance function, commonly referred to as the kernel function $k(\mathbf{x}, \mathbf{x}')$. These collectively dictate the behavior of each function $f(\mathbf{x})$ at the specific location $\mathbf{x}$. When the mean is defined as $m(\mathbf{x}) = \mathbb{E}[f(\mathbf{x})]$, and the kernel function is articulated as $k(\mathbf{x}, \mathbf{x}') = \mathbb{E}[(f(\mathbf{x}) - m(\mathbf{x}))(f(\mathbf{x}') - m(\mathbf{x}'))]$, the GP framework is formally denoted as $f(\mathbf{x}) \sim GP(m(\mathbf{x}), k(\mathbf{x}, \mathbf{x}'))$ [38].

Hierarchical Agglomerative Clustering (HAC) [30] groups data points into clusters by iteratively merging the closest pairs, starting as individual clusters and visualized via a dendrogram. The linkage matrix records each merger, noting the merged clusters, their distance, and the new cluster size. Ward's criterion, a variant of HAC, minimizes within-cluster variance by merging clusters that least increase the total variance, producing compact clusters. This is quantified as $\Delta V(A, B) = \frac{|A| \cdot |B|}{|A|+|B|} \cdot \|\bar{A} - \bar{B}\|^2$, where $|A|$ and $|B|$ are the sizes, and $\bar{A}$ and $\bar{B}$ the centroids of clusters A and B [31,56].

Problem Setting: Given the objective function in Eq. (1), the boundaries of the search space $\mathcal{D} = \{\mathbf{x} \in \mathcal{R}^d : lb^j \leq x^j \leq ub^j, \forall j \in 1, .., d\}$, and the GP model, the post-hoc explanation goal is to find rules that bound the minima of this function. An explanation is defined as rules bounding minima of the objective function. These rules must be constrained within the search space, considering the variance of inputs and outputs as modeled by the GP. Let's denote input points that are neighboring minima by a variance v as $\mathbf{X_v}$, the GP mean and standard deviation as μ & σ respectively. An explanation for minima takes the form: $[min(X_v), max(X_v)] => [min(\mu - 2*\sigma), max(\mu + 2*\sigma)]$. This indicates that the bounds of the rule are determined by the minimum and maximum input points, which are grouped based on their variance, with a result representing the confidence interval for the corresponding inputs. Input points that exceed the variance threshold should be separate rules. These rules would need to be checked for relevance, i.e. whether they contain additional local minima. Rules that do not contain a likely minimum must be filtered out. The bounds of the rules provide the expert with tunable ranges for each parameter that can be tuned to maintain a certain level of utility. In case of multiple, local minima similar ranges should be provided for each.

4 TNTRules (Tune-No-Tune Rules)

TNTRules (Fig. 2) is our algorithm (Algorithm 1) for extracting and visualizing BO solution spaces. In TNTRules, we create an explanation dataset (1) for the objective function f, cluster it (2), and prune the cluster tree (3), then generate rules describing the clusters (4), rank and filter them for final explanations (5), and visualize the rules in a user-friendly manner (6) (cf. Fig. 3). Additionally, TNTRules is optimized with multi-objective optimization to produce high-quality explanations (cf. Sect. 6).

4.1 Explanation Dataset Generation

In standard XAI settings, the explanation method has access to a data set. Usually, this is the training data, the ground-truth labels, and the model's predictions. In the BO set-

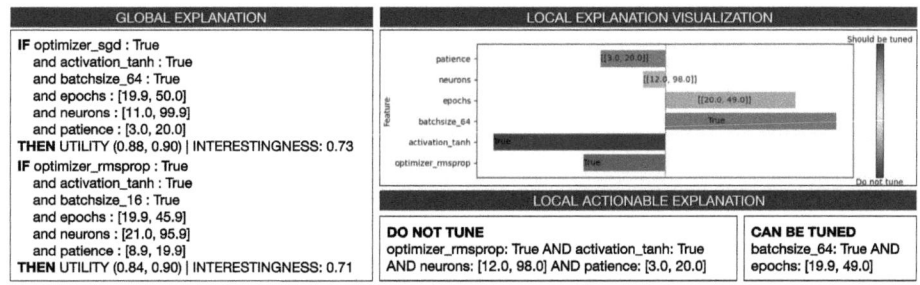

Fig. 3. Example of the three forms of explanations generated using the HPO use case with the MLP model. Global explanations consist of 22 rules; here, we present two as examples. Local explanations include a sensitivity graph and actionable insights detailing which parameters to tune and what ranges.

ting, the data set does not exist a-priori. BO dynamically acquires data during execution from the search space $\mathcal{D}$ [48]. The sampled data is small in quantity and biased toward optimal areas (BO iteratively refines the objective function while avoiding exhaustive sampling of the optimization space). Thus, the sampled data is unsuitable as an explanation dataset.

Therefore, we generate an explanation dataset by uniformly sampling the search space for (N_e) samples $\mathbf{X_e} = \{x_1, \ldots, x_{N_e}\} \sim \mathcal{U}(\mathcal{D})$ (algorithm lines 6–7). Our explanation dataset then has a comprehensive view of the optimization space. Sampling the search space is less computationally expensive than acquiring data during execution. In this setting, we assume that the GP sufficiently approximates the black-box function during the optimization run (cf. Section 8.5). The GP is queried with $\mathbf{X_e}$ to infer the posterior distribution i.e., mean μ and standard deviation σ_y. The resulting explanation dataset is formulated as $\mathbf{E} = [\mathbf{X_e}; \mu; \sigma_y]$ (algorithm line 8).

4.2 Clustering

We use clustering to identify significant regions in the approximated posterior distribution ($\mathbf{E}$), considering the uncertainty within each region. Using the Ward criterion, we apply HAC to the explanation dataset $\mathbf{E}$ (algorithm line 10). The resulting linkage matrix $\mathbf{E}_{\text{link}}$ consists of links and distances between clusters. $\mathbf{E}_{\text{link}}$ is of size $(N_e - 1)$, where each row corresponds to a merge or linkage step in the clustering process. The resulting clustering can be visualized in the form of a dendrogram which represents the hierarchical tree structure of the linkage matrix. Pruning at different distances/levels of $\mathbf{E}_{\text{link}}$ produces clusters with varying coverage [44]. It is a challenge to determine the optimal clustering threshold (t_s) or pruning distance for pruning that produces meaningful explanations, i.e., clusters that are both localized and cover areas around minima (cf. Sect. 7.2).

Algorithm 1. TNTRules Algorithm

Require: BO search space: $\mathcal{D}$,
1: No. of explanation samples: N_e,
2: Clustering threshold: t_s
3: Interestingness threshold: t_α
4: BO backbone GP: GP
5: **procedure** $TNTRules(\mathcal{D}, N_e, t_s)$
6:    # Explanation dataset generation (Sec. 4.1)
7:    $\mathbf{X_e} \leftarrow \{x_1, \ldots, x_{N_e}\} \sim \mathcal{U}(\mathcal{D})$
8:    $\mu, \sigma_y \leftarrow GP_{predict}(\mathbf{X_e})$
9:    $\mathbf{E} \leftarrow [\mathbf{X_e}; \mu; \sigma_y]$
10:   #Clustering (Sec. 4.2), Variance pruning (Sec. 4.3), and Rule construction (Sec. 4.4)
11:   $\mathbf{E_{link}} \leftarrow Clustering(\mathbf{E})$
12:   $\mathbf{K} \leftarrow VariancePruning(\mathbf{E_{link}}, t_s)$
13:   $\rho_\dashv, \rho_\vdash \leftarrow RuleConstruction(\mathbf{E}, \mathbf{K})$
14:   # Rule ranking and filtering (Sec. 4.5)
15:   **for** i in $\rho_\dashv$ **do**
16:      $\rho^i_{temp} \leftarrow find(\mathbf{X_e} \in [\rho^i_\dashv; \rho^i_\vdash])$
17:      $Rel^i \leftarrow max(likelihood(GP_{predict}(\rho^i_{temp})))$
18:      $Covr^i \leftarrow ECDF(\rho^i_\dashv, \mathbf{X_e})$
19:      $Supp^i \leftarrow ECDF([\rho^i_\dashv; \rho^i_\vdash], [\mathbf{X_e}; \mu])$
20:      $Con^i \leftarrow Supp^i/Covr^i$
21:      $\alpha^i \leftarrow weightedSum(Rel^i, Covr^i, Supp^i, Con^i)$
22:   **end for**
23:   $\rho \leftarrow FilterRules([\rho^i_\dashv; \rho^i_\vdash], \alpha, t_\alpha)$
24:   **return** ρ
25: **end procedure**

4.3 Variance Pruning

Instead of using a traditional dendrogram threshold to merge clusters, we employ the HAC method to obtain only the linkage structure $\mathbf{E_{link}}$, followed by a distance-based pruning mechanism. However, conventional distance metrics often fail to separate clusters effectively in cases of high variability or outliers [20].

To overcome this, we propose a variance-based pruning approach that captures data uncertainty through the linkage matrix (cf. Sect. 8.5). Variance reflects uncertainty in BO, making it a meaningful metric for clustering. The intuition here is that highly uncertain areas would require more human attention and thus must be separated from very certain areas.

Let μ represent the target values of the leaf nodes (produced by the GP), n the number of leaf nodes, and t_s a predefined clustering threshold. The merging condition is:

$$\begin{cases} \text{Merge leaf nodes} & \text{if } \text{Var}(\mu) \leq t_s \\ \text{Do not merge leaf nodes} & \text{if } \text{Var}(\mu) > t_s \end{cases}$$

Here, $\text{Var}(\mu)$ denotes the variance of μ, and t_s serves as a hyperparameter controlling cluster formation.

4.4 Rule Construction

Based on the formed clusters $\mathbf{K}$, we extract the data points $\mathbf{X}^i_e$ belonging to the subtree/cluster from $\mathbf{X_e}$ to generate rules for each cluster. The antecedent's rule bounds

($\rho_\dashv$) are determined by taking the minimum and maximum over the extracted data points represented by each subtree. Similarly, for the consequent part ($\rho_\vdash$), we calculate the confidence interval for the corresponding GP posterior, capturing the uncertainty: $\mu^i \pm 2 * \sigma_y^i$ (algorithm line 12). A single rule looks like $[min(X_e^i), max(X_e^i)] => [min(\mu^i - 2 * \sigma_y^i), max(\mu^i + 2 * \sigma_y^i)]$. This step produces the full rule set denoted as ρ_{all}.

4.5 Rule Ranking and Filtering

The initial rule set ρ_{all} must be filtered and ranked based on their quality for producing the final explanations. We employ a quantitative framework to assess rule quality, focusing on localization within the optimization space and the ability to cover meaningful regions around potential solutions. Our evaluation integrates four metrics:

1. Coverage ($Covr$): how much a rule's antecedent covers a region within the search space relative to the total area (algorithm line 17).
2. Support ($Supp$): evaluates the alignment of a rule's domain with regions containing actual data (algorithm line 18).
3. Confidence (Con): is the ratio of Support to Coverage (algorithm line 19).
4. Relevance (Rel): is the maximum log-likelihood derived from the GP applied to the subset of data that conforms to a particular rule. Let $\mathbf{l_s}$ denote the log-likelihood values for such instances, and l represent the log-likelihoods of the entire dataset $Rel = max_{\mathbf{l_s} \in \mathbf{l}}(\mathbf{l_s})$ (algorithm line 16) [38, Chapter 2].

Coverage, and Support are standard in rule mining and computed using an empirical cumulative probability distribution (ECDF) [58]. While effective in measuring the quality of the generated bounding boxes, they have limitations in locating optimal solutions. We introduce the Relevance metric to address this limitation. Relevance effectively identifies regions where the GP is most likely to locate optimal solutions.

Finally, we define the overall interestingness of a rule, bounded between (0,1], as the weighted sum: $\alpha = w_1 * Covr + w_2 * Supp + w_3 * Con + w_4 * Rel$, higher is better (algorithm line 20). The most interesting rules are presented by filtering the rule set ρ_{all} based on the interestingness threshold t_α resulting in explanations ρ (algorithm line 22).

4.6 Visualization

TNTRules presents explanations ρ to the recipient through three visualization modes: global textual rules, local visual graphs, and local actionable explanations. The global explanations are expressed as an ordered list of "IF-THEN" rules, organized in decreasing order of interestingness α (cf. Fig. 3, left). Textual rules provide a simpler and interpretable model but are challenging to comprehend for an explanation recipient, especially in scenarios with long antecedents. Local explanations are given as a rule extracted from our global rule set that explains a particular sample. This allows for easier comprehension than a full rule set.

In Fig. 3, local explanation visualizations appear on the right. To generate these graphs, we perform a sensitivity analysis of the GP model [60], focusing on data samples covered by a rule. The sensitivity analysis identifies optimization model parameters that, when adjusted, can improve results. Tailored to the use case, we generate local, actionable explanations that cover all the input parameters of the problem. This representation abstracts non-essential rule components during tuning, improving user understanding. The graph and actionable explanations guide the user by indicating parameters that require attention and those that can be ignored, simplifying interpretation, especially in cases with long antecedents. Aptly, these rules are called "TUNE-NO-TUNE" rules. The interpretation of the local actionable explanation given in the figure is as follows: do not tune the parameters $optimizer\_rmsprop$, $activation\_tanh$, $neurons$, and $patience$ because they are already in their optimal state according to the backbone GP model. While tuning is required from your side for parameters $batchsize\_64$ and $epoch$, this means that for this MLP model, a good batch size is not 64 but some other value from the search space, and also the epoch value can be adjusted from 19 to 49 for better results.

5 Illustrative Example

We provide an illustrative example for TNTRules in Fig. 4. The first step is to uniformly sample $\mathbf{X_e} = 40$ points from $\mathcal{D}$, visualized as the x-axis in Fig. 4a. We then apply the GP model, trained to approximate our optimization target $f(x) = e^{-(x-2)^2} + e^{-(x-6)^2/10} + \frac{1}{x^2+1}$, to obtain predictions $\mu; \sigma_y$. This is visualized in Fig. 4b. (cf. Algorithm 1 and Sect. 4.1).

Subsequently, the explanation dataset $\mathbf{E} = [\mathbf{X_e}; \mu; \sigma_y]$ is formed and clustered using HAC (Sect. 4.2). Following, distance- and variance-pruning are employed (Sect. 4.3), forming different clusters as given by different bounding boxes in Fig. 4c.

Finally, we construct rules from the bounding boxes (Sect. 4.4), which are then ranked based on how interesting they might be to a user (Sect. 4.5), rule-based explanations or visual explanations are generated for the most interesting rules, and the rest are filtered out (Sect. 4.6) Fig. 4c.

This example demonstrates that variance-based pruning offers a more effective clustering strategy for TNTRules than traditional distance-based pruning. In the given scenario, the global optimum is enclosed within cluster 4. While distance-based pruning groups a large area into this cluster—overlooking the underlying uncertainty of the GP model—variance-based pruning adapts to the model's uncertainty. Regions with higher uncertainty, where human intervention might be necessary, are clustered more densely, whereas areas with higher GP certainty form larger, less granular clusters.

6 Optimizing for Explanation Quality

We formulate the challenge of providing good explanations as an optimization problem. We maximize the quality of explanations by exploiting the controllability property of TNTRules. We argue that explanation quality depends on a trade-off between several

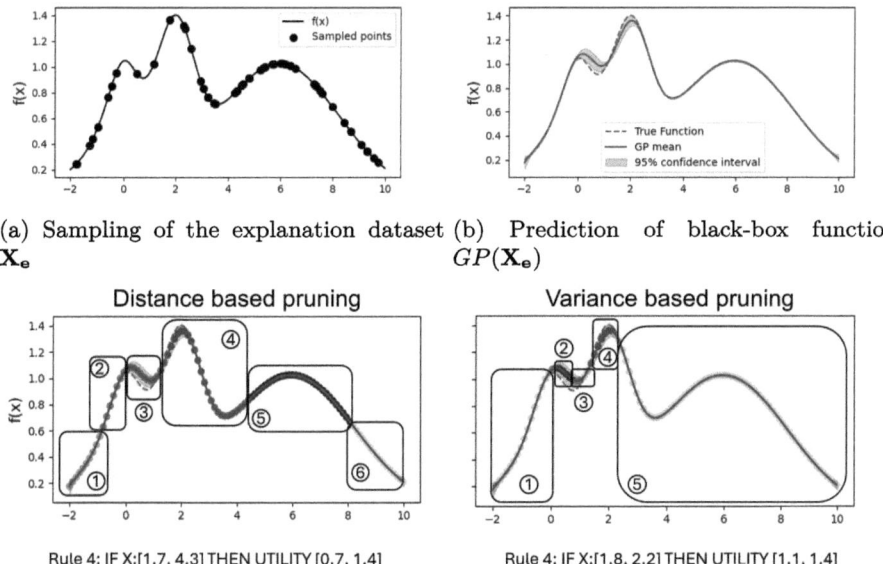

(c) HAC based clustering and distance and variance pruning of explanation dataset **E** along with rule explanation for the optimal area (cluster 4)

Fig. 4. (a) Generate X samples for the explanation dataset $\mathbf{X_e} = 40$ from the search space $\mathcal{D}$. (b) Apply the GP model, trained to approximate our optimization target $f(x) = e^{-(x-2)^2} + e^{-(x-6)^2/10} + \frac{1}{x^2+1}$, to obtain predictions $\boldsymbol{\mu}$ and $\boldsymbol{\sigma_y}$. (c) Form the explanation dataset $\mathbf{E} = [\mathbf{X_e}, \boldsymbol{\mu}, \boldsymbol{\sigma_y}]$ and cluster it with HAC. To have meaningful clusters, prune the hierarchical structure. Finally, generate rules as an explanation for the different clustered areas.

metrics. We formulate this as multi-objective optimization. Multi-objective optimization is a process of finding optimal values when multiple competing objectives need to be met.

We seek an optimal t_s value (cf. Sect. 4.2) that simultaneously maximizes support, relevance, and rule set length (equivalent to minimizing the coverage of each rule): $\mathbf{t_{s_{opt}}} = \arg\max_{t_s \in [0,1]}[Supp, Rel, |\boldsymbol{\rho}|]$. The range between [0,1] is set because we are normalizing the variances in the data to be in [0,1].

We choose these metrics to ensure that the explanations effectively identify solutions (Relevance) and provide accurate localization with valid data support (Support and rule set length). While maximizing the rule set length may seem counterintuitive to having a small explanation set, in our case we filter the rule set in the last step of the algorithm 1 to keep the final explanations (*FilterRules*, Sect. 4.5), so the overall length of the explanation set remains small. We get a Pareto front of solutions in this case.

We can also frame this as a scalar optimization problem $t_{s_{opt}} = \arg\max_{t_s \in [0,1]} \alpha(t_s)$ with interestingness α as the metric. In this case, the choice of weights for α becomes crucial, as it involves balancing the different aspects of all the metrics. Nevertheless, we found the multiobjective optimization method easier to automatically balance the different metrics, at the cost of more time due to multiple runs.

7 Experimental Setup

This section describes our evaluation metrics and criteria, threshold tuning, and experimental setup. For our experiments, we selected benchmark functions with known ground truth and a common Bayesian Optimization (BO) problem: hyperparameter optimization (HPO) of machine learning models, using publicly available data. [50].

7.1 Evaluation Criteria and Metrics

We use the three evaluation metrics suitable for our use case from the Co-12 properties to evaluate TNTRules [33]: correctness, completeness, and compactness.

Correctness: Measures the correctness of explanations with respect to the model (also called fidelity). Traditional decision boundary fidelity measures are inappropriate for continuous distributions, so we use a sampling-based approach. Let **N** be the number

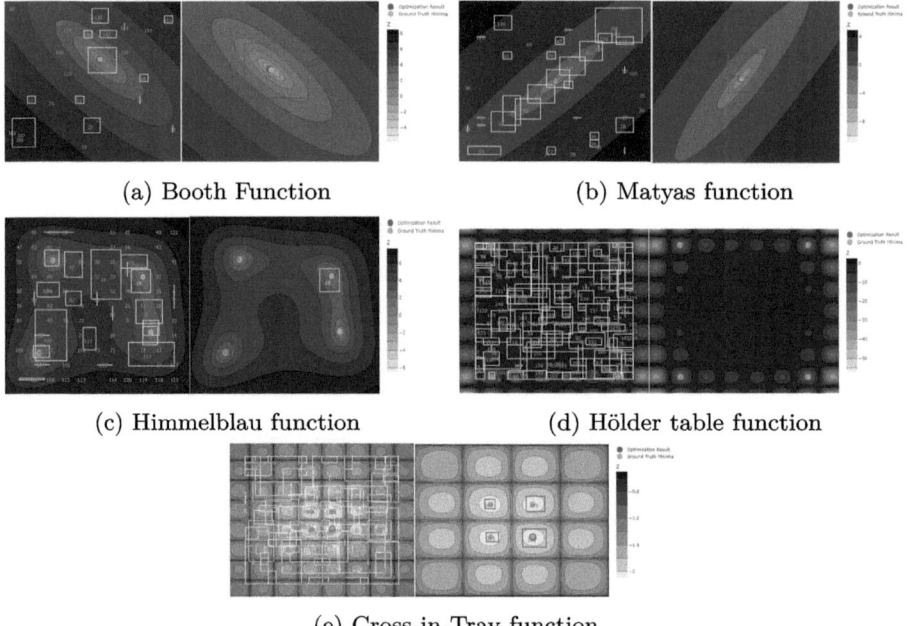

(a) Booth Function

(b) Matyas function

(c) Himmelblau function

(d) Hölder table function

(e) Cross-in-Tray function

Fig. 5. Results of benchmark test functions marked with minima locations, red dot indicates BO found minima. Bounding boxes represent rule-based explanations. White boxes on the left show all rules from the HAC method. The final explanations after filtering are shown on the right. Highly relevant rules are shown in red boxes, moderately relevant rules are shown in yellow boxes, and irrelevant rules are omitted. (Color figure online)

of uniformly sampled points from the rule antecedents. Define $F(x)$ as a function that returns 1 if the GP prediction of N_i is within the bounds of the rule consequent and 0 otherwise. The mean fidelity, $\bar{F}$, is computed as $\bar{F} = \frac{1}{N}\sum_{i=1}^{N} F(x_i)$ where $x_i \in \mathbf{X}$. High correctness ensures that the explanations are reliable and can be trusted by the users. In practical terms, the expert can depend on these suggestions to make adjustments that agree with the learned model and are not based on erroneous or misleading information.

Compactness: Measures the global size of the ruleset ($|\rho|$) (Sect. 4.5) to determine how large the ruleset is, which is directly related to the effort required to understand it. The practical benefit of compactness is that it makes the explanations accessible and actionable. Users are more likely to utilize insights that are easy to understand. Compact explanations would reduce cognitive load, making it easier for experts to quickly grasp and act on recommendations without extensive analysis.

Completeness: Measures how well input parameters are represented in a rule. It is the ratio of the parameters represented in the longest rule in a set to the total number of input parameters. ($\frac{|\rho_{\neg}|_{max}}{|p|}$) (Sect. 4.4). Completeness ensures that the explanation is completely describing all parameters of the problem. For practical purposes, the explanations should offer recommendations that consider all parameters without ignoring any. This is crucial for ensuring that no significant aspect of the tuning process is ignored, potentially leading to clear explanations.

7.2 Optimizing Clustering Threshold (t_s)

To determine t_s, we use the pymoo NSGA II implementation[5] with 25 iterations. We set the population size to 25, the number of generations to 10, and initialized the algorithm with no constraints. We select the solution with the highest rule set length from the Pareto front.

7.3 Optimization Problems

We evaluate TNTRules on two sets of optimization problems: First, we benchmark using test functions for optimization (Booth, Matyas, Himmelblau, Hölder table, and Cross-in-tray functions) [17,27,49], and second, HPO with deep learning models (MLP, ResNET [15], and XceptionNET [5]). We set the weights for interestingness α as $w_1 = 0.2, w_2 = 0.2, w_3 = 0.1, w_4 = 0.5$ (Sect. 4.5) for all experiments in this paper as recommended by the multi-objective optimization. Ablation for different weights was also explored to show how well the optimization step performs (cf. Sect. 8.3). We perform a comparative analysis of TNTRules with the XAI methods Decision trees (DT) [18], RXBO [4], and RuleXAI [24].

Optimization Benchmark Functions. We evaluate TNTRules on five optimization benchmark functions (Booth, Matyas, Himmelblau, Hölder table, and Cross-in-tray

---
[5] https://pymoo.org/algorithms/moo/nsga2.html.

functions). These domains allow the collection of inexpensive baseline samples that allow for direct evaluation. BO samples data from the respective search spaces for the benchmark functions to perform optimization. For the TNTRules explanation set generation, we also use the same search space to sample the explanation set.

Hyperparameter Optimization Problems. We evaluate the performance of TNTRules in a practical deep-learning context involving HPO tasks for both classification and regression problems. We use the MNIST [9], CIFAR-10 [21], and California Housing [59] datasets for the study. All datasets were randomly divided into 80-10-10 training, testing, and validation sets. We used Tensorflow and Keras for the experiments. We normalize the data as a pre-processing step for MNIST and CIFAR-10. For California Housing, we one-hot encode the categorical features as a preprocessing step. We also use the standard Keras tuner to optimize the model parameters using BO[6]. We set validation accuracy as the objective for the optimization problem in the Keras tuner. The BO algorithm behind the Keras tuner framework also samples the hyperparameters from a defined search space. For the declarative set in TNTRules, we use the same search space definition as the Keras tuner to perform the sampling. In these tasks, the number of minima is unknown beforehand; thus, selecting a threshold is difficult. We create the training data set for TNTRules and use it as input for all methods. The fidelity of the methods is determined by using GP samples since ground truth samples are too expensive to obtain.

For TNTRules, we focus on rules with interestingness $\alpha > 0.7$, i.e. rules that have a higher chance of being an alternative solution.

8 Results

In this section, we first present qualitative and quantitative results on the optimization benchmark functions (Sect. 8.1), confirming that TNTRules extracts relevant regions of interest and significantly reduces the search space. We then present the quantitative evaluation for the HPO use case (Sect. 8.2), showing the superiority of TNTRules over the state-of-the-art XAI baselines. We then show through an ablation study that the GP approximation is a valid way to evaluate TNTRules (Sect. 8.4). Finally, we ablate for clustering choices and pruning (Sect. 8.5).

8.1 Results on Benchmark Functions

Figure 5 shows the resulting explanations for the benchmark functions visualized in function space. The left hand side of each pair of plots shows all detected rules ρ_{all} before filtering, with white boxes indicating their boundaries. The right hand side, shows the rules after filtering: red boxes ($\alpha \geq 0.6$) indicate highly interesting rules, yellow boxes ($0.6 > \alpha \geq 0.4$) indicated moderately interesting rules. Rules with lower interest levels are omitted. *The results show that TNTRules effectively localized high-interest minima identified by BO in four out of five cases* except for the Himmelblau's

---
[6] https://www.tensorflow.org/tutorials/keras/keras_tuner.

Table 1. Results comparing XAI methods on ground truth samples vs. GP surrogate. TNTRules accurately identify minima in the GP surrogate case and outperform other methods in the ground truth case.

		Ground Truth (iter = 1000)		Surrogate GP (N_e = 1000)	
		Compactness $\|\rho\| \downarrow$	Correctness $\bar{F} \uparrow$	Compactness $\|\rho\| \downarrow$	Correctness $\bar{F} \uparrow$
BOOTH	DR	700 ± 0	0.88 ± 0.01	1000 ± 0	0.92 ± 0.01
	RXBO	10 ± 1	0.97 ± 0.01	5 ± 0	0.97 ± 0.01
	RuleXAI	16 ± 0	0.30 ± 0.00	12 ± 1	0.42 ± 0.01
	TNTRules	**3 ± 2**	**1 ± 0.00**	**1 ± 0**	**0.98 ± 0.01**
MATYAS	DR	700 ± 0	0.85 ± 0.02	1000 ± 0	0.90 ± 0.02
	RXBO	15 ± 0	0.98 ± 0.01	6 ± 5	0.97 ± 0.02
	RuleXAI	17 ± 1	0.27 ± 0.00	50 ± 2	0.48 ± 0.02
	TNTRules	**6 ± 1**	**1 ± 0.00**	**1 ± 0**	**0.99 ± 0.00**
HIMMEL.	DR	700 ± 0	0.83 ± 0.01	1000 ± 0	0.98 ± 0.01
	RXBO	30 ± 3	0.94 ± 0.03	25 ± 2	0.94 ± 0.01
	RuleXAI	17 ± 0	0.34 ± 0.01	35 ± 0	0.55 ± 0.01
	TNTRules	**6 ± 2**	**0.99 ± 0.01**	**4 ± 1**	**0.99 ± 0.00**
HOLDER.	DR	699 ± 1	0.88 ± 0.03	1000 ± 0	0.77 ± 0.03
	RXBO	14 ± 1	0.97 ± 0.02	12 ± 2	**0.98 ± 0.01**
	RuleXAI	17 ± 0	0.78 ± 0.00	55 ± 1	0.41 ± 0.02
	TNTRules	**3 ± 2**	**0.98 ± 0.01**	**4 ± 0**	**0.98 ± 0.01**
CROSS.	DR	700 ± 0	**0.99 ± 0.00**	1000 ± 0	0.97 ± 0.02
	RXBO	15 ± 5	**0.99 ± 0.00**	9 ± 3	**0.99 ± 0.00**
	RuleXAI	29 ± 1	0.96 ± 0.02	127 ± 1	**0.99 ± 0.00**
	TNTRules	**4 ± 0**	0.98 ± 0.00	**4 ± 0**	**0.99 ± 0.00**

function where the generated rule showed moderate interestingness. The rule selection process reduced the number of initially discovered rules by 98.5%, highlighting key rules as explanations. Rule curation resulted in a significant 98% reduction in search space exploration when BO was rerun.

8.2 Results on Hyperparameter Optimization Problems

The performance comparison in Tab. 2 shows that, ***explanations generated by TNTRules outperform all the baseline methods in all metrics.*** Both, TNTRules and RXBO, consistently demonstrate high correctness in their explanations, reflecting a robust approximation of the underlying GP model, which is facilitated by the clustering-based surrogate.

Analysing results in more detail, we observe that the decision rules tend to overfit the data, resulting in an excessive number of rules (compactness criterion). In contrast, RuleXAI and RXBO struggle to fit the data adequately, as evidenced by the moderate number of rules they generate. The variance-based pruning method introduced in TNTRules consistently achieves better cluster separations, leading to a reduced number of rules and a more compact rule set. This trend aligns with the findings from the ablation study using test functions.

Table 2. Comparison of XAI methods with TNTRules for HPO with BO for deep learning models (MLP, ResNET, and XceptionNET). We utilized MNIST, California housing (Housing), and the CIFAR10 dataset. TNTRules outperform all methods on all three criteria.

			Compactness $\|\rho\| \downarrow$	Completeness $\|\rho_\dashv\|_{max}/\|p\| == 1.00$	Correctness $\bar{F} \uparrow$
MLP (P = 6)	MNIST	DR	141 ± 5	4.33 ± 0.02	0.02 ± 0.01
		RXBO	62 ± 5	1.00 ± 0.00	0.80 ± 0.01
		RuleXAI	42 ± 1	1.33 ± 0.00	0.01 ± 0.00
		TNTRules	**23 ± 1**	**1.00 ± 0.00**	**0.85 ± 0.01**
	HOUSING	DR	154 ± 6	2.50 ± 0.04	0.01 ± 0.00
		RXBO	34 ± 8	1.00 ± 0.00	0.61 ± 0.02
		RuleXAI	34 ± 1	1.50 ± 0.00	0.01 ± 0.00
		TNTRules	**22 ± 1**	**1.00 ± 0.00**	**0.82 ± 0.03**
RESNET (P = 6)	MNIST	DR	1000 ± 15	2.83 ± 0.02	0.93 ± 0.01
		RXBO	55 ± 2	1.00 ± 0.00	0.97 ± 0.01
		RuleXAI	117 ± 0	1.50 ± 0.00	0.86 ± 0.02
		TNTRules	**3 ± 0**	**1.00 ± 0.00**	**1 ± 0.00**
	CIFAR10	DR	1000 ± 13	1.66 ± 0.00	0.98 ± 0.01
		RXBO	57 ± 5	1.00 ± 0.00	0.99 ± 0.00
		RuleXAI	106 ± 0	2.00 ± 0.00	0.72 ± 0.01
		TNTRules	**12 ± 0**	**1.00 ± 0.00**	**1 ± 0.00**
XCEP.NET (P = 11)	MNIST	DR	56 ± 2	0.54 ± 0.00	0.98 ± 0.01
		RXBO	69 ± 2	1.00 ± 0.00	0.99 ± 0.00
		RuleXAI	141 ± 1	0.72 ± 0.02	0.99 ± 0.00
		TNTRules	**4 ± 0**	**1.00 ± 0.00**	**1 ± 0.00**
	CIFAR10	DR	977 ± 3	2.27 ± 0.02	**0.84 ± 0.02**
		RXBO	21 ± 3	1.00 ± 0.00	0.80 ± 0.01
		RuleXAI	130 ± 0	0.72 ± 0.00	0.14 ± 0.01
		TNTRules	**5 ± 1**	**1.00 ± 0.00**	0.81 ± 0.05

Regarding completeness, we see that methods such as DT and RuleXAI produce rules of variable length. These rules may either repeat parameters across different ranges, increasing overall rule length, or omit parameters completely, resulting in shorter rules. In our case, completeness is greater than 1 for longer rules and less than 1 for shorter ones. In contrast, TNTRules by design creates fixed-length rules that correspond to the number of input parameters. By neither omitting nor repeating parameters, we ensure completeness remains at 1. This comprehensive representation of parameters within the rules eliminates confusion for engineers tuning physical systems, as they require clarity on the fixed ranges of each parameter. Overall, the results indicate that TNTRules outperforms other XAI methods both qualitatively and quantitatively.

An overall qualitative summary of the results is shown in Table 3.

8.3 Ablation for Interestingness Weights

Interestingness is an important factor in TNTRules to generate good explanations. To recall, we defined interestingness of a rule as the weighted sum of Coverage (Covr),

Table 3. Summary of results (Table 1 and 2) explainability methods mapped to evaluation criteria, TNTRules outperforms baselines.

Methods	Compactness	Completeness	Correctness
Decision Rules	High number of rules	No	Low
RXBO	Moderate number of rules	Yes	**High**
RuleXAI	Moderate number of rules	No	Low
TNTRules	Low number of rules	Yes	High

Table 4. Ablation showing the impact of optimized interestingness weights on TNTRules. We test five different weight combinations for TNTRules besides the optimal version and compare them with baseline RXBO to show the impact on metrics compactness and correctness. Results show optimized weights TNTRules outperform the rest, thus highlighting the importance of setting the correct weights.

			Configuration w_1, w_2, w_3, w_4	Compactness $|\rho|\downarrow$	Correctness $\bar{F}\uparrow$
MLP (P = 6)	HOUSING	RXBO	-	34 ± 8	0.61 ± 0.02
		TNTRules	$w_1 = 0.1, w_2 = 0.1, w_3 = 0.1, w_4 = 0.7$	56 ± 1	0.76 ± 0.01
		TNTRules	$w_1 = 0.1, w_2 = 0.2, w_3 = 0.2, w_4 = 0.5$	32 ± 2	0.77 ± 0.02
		TNTRules	$w_1 = 0.2, w_2 = 0.1, w_3 = 0.2, w_4 = 0.5$	30 ± 4	0.72 ± 0.03
		TNTRules	$w_1 = 0.2, w_2 = 0.1, w_3 = 0.1, w_4 = 0.6$	45 ± 1	0.78 ± 0.01
		TNTRules	$w_1 = 0.1, w_2 = 0.1, w_3 = 0.3, w_4 = 0.5$	47 ± 4	0.71 ± 0.04
		TNTRules w Optimization	$w_1 = 0.2, w_2 = 0.2, w_3 = 0.1, w_4 = 0.5$	**23 ± 1**	**0.85 ± 0.01**
	MNIST	RXBO	-	62 ± 5	0.80 ± 0.01
		TNTRules	$w_1 = 0.1, w_2 = 0.1, w_3 = 0.1, w_4 = 0.7$	46 ± 3	0.81 ± 0.02
		TNTRules	$w_1 = 0.1, w_2 = 0.2, w_3 = 0.2, w_4 = 0.5$	26 ± 1	0.81 ± 0.01
		TNTRules	$w_1 = 0.2, w_2 = 0.1, w_3 = 0.2, w_4 = 0.5$	26 ± 2	0.77 ± 0.03
		TNTRules	$w_1 = 0.2, w_2 = 0.1, w_3 = 0.1, w_4 = 0.6$	31 ± 2	0.82 ± 0.01
		TNTRules	$w_1 = 0.1, w_2 = 0.1, w_3 = 0.3, w_4 = 0.5$	39 ± 1	0.80 ± 0.01
		TNTRules w Optimization	$w_1 = 0.2, w_2 = 0.2, w_3 = 0.1, w_4 = 0.5$	**22 ± 1**	**0.82 ± 0.03**

Support (Supp), Confidende (Con), and Relevance (Rel): $\alpha = w_1 * Covr + w_2 * Supp + w_3 * Con + w_4 * Rel$ (cf. Sect. 4.5).

In previous sections, the weights for interestingness, α were determined through a multi-objective optimization process, resulting in the values $w_1 = 0.2, w_2 = 0.2, w_3 = 0.1, w_4 = 0.5$. In this ablation study, we investigate the impact of variations in these weights on the compactness and correctness of explanations. We omit completeness, as TNTRules explanations are complete by design (cf. Sect. 8.2).

We investigated how weight changes influence our quality metrics. We evaluate on two datasets: MNIST for image classification and California housing for regression tasks using the MLP model. TNTRules was applied to the HPO task using BO on the MLP model for both the dataset. We tested five different configurations of the weights w_1, w_2, w_3, w_4, each chosen randomly close to the optimized weights.

The results (Table 4) indicate that ***TNTRules configured with optimized weights consistently outperforms both the non-optimized versions of TNTRules and the*** *baseline method, **RXBO***. The non-optimized versions shows a moderate to low number of rules, compromising the compactness of the explanations. This lack of compactness implies that users are required to analyze more extensive information for tuning, potentially increasing cognitive load. Additionally, the correctness of explanations in the non-optimized configurations was lower, often resulting in rules that poorly represent the parameter space. This issue was primarily due to inadequate data support, leading to overly narrow bounding boxes that fail to cover meaningful regions of the parameter space.

The lower quality of rules in the non-optimized configurations could mislead users, providing suboptimal guidance for system tuning. Thus it is important to carefully calibrate the weights.

8.4 Ablation for GP Approximation

So far, we have assumed that the surrogate GP in BO sufficiently approximates the direct BO evaluation of a function (ground truth (GT)) (cf. Sect. 3). Thus, we can evaluate on GP samples instead of GT samples, which is useful when obtaining GT samples is costly, as in HPO. Since evaluating optimization test functions is cheap, we perform an ablation study to demonstrate the consistency and independence of our results, regardless of whether we used GT directly or the surrogate GP with an explanatory dataset.

We compared TNTRules with XAI methods under two settings: one with 1000 GT samples ($N_e = 0$) and the other with the sampled explanation dataset and the GP surrogate ($N_e = 1000$). For the fidelity calculation in the GT case, we withheld 25% of the GT samples. In the GP-based evaluation, fidelity was computed using randomly generated 300 samples, as introduced in Sect. 7.1.

Table 1 presents results comparing the GT samples and the GP surrogate with an explanatory dataset. ***TNTRules outperforms all other methods in the comparison, identifying all minima with high fidelity.*** RXBO performs second best, with better fidelity than decision rules and RuleXAI, suggesting good data approximation. Decision rules overfit, as evidenced by numerous rules, while RuleXAI underfits, as evidenced by low fidelity scores. An exception is the Cross-in-Tray function, where all methods had high fidelity.

In case the GP is not able to sufficiently approximate the black box function (indicating a bad BO run), our explanations are still faithful to the GP model. The GP model would show high uncertainty, which would also be highlighted in our explanations (through wide ranges of consequences). This visualization of uncertainty can be used as an indication of the quality of the BO run.

8.5 Ablation Clustering Choices and Pruning

We conducted an ablation study to support our design choices for HAC. We compared 16 combinations with seven HAC methods, two distance metrics, distance pruning, and variance pruning. We chose Himmelblau function with four known minima for benchmarking [17]. The study evaluated the performance of the methods in identifying and localizing the four minima. The HAC methods included Complete, Ward,

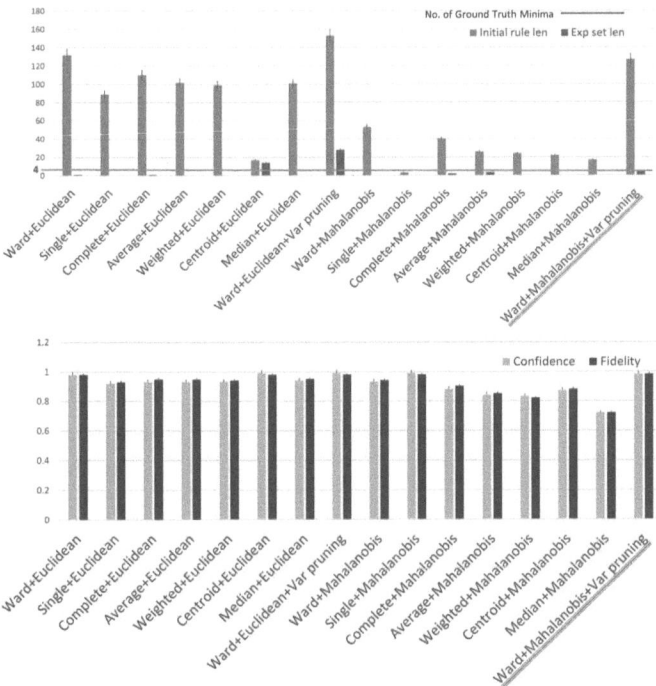

Fig. 6. Ablation study comparing 16 HAC configurations. Left: number of initial rules discovered by each method compared to the resulting explanation set after applying the interestingness filter ($\alpha > 0.6$). Right: rule set confidence and fidelity for each configuration. The optimal method is underlined.

Average, Median, Weighted, Centroid, and Single linkages, with Euclidean and Mahalanobis distances [30]. Each linkage method uses different criteria for clustering the data. Evaluation criteria included the number of initial rules, subset after applying the interestingness filter ($\alpha > 0.6$), correctness, and overall confidence, as shown in Fig. 6.

From our ablation study, *we note the effectiveness of using Ward linkage based on Mahalanobis distance and variance pruning, which accurately identifies all four solutions and provides tight bounding boxes.* Ward and Complete linkages with Euclidean distance, along with distance-based pruning, yield one highly interesting rule ($\alpha > 0.6$) for one minima and three moderately interesting rules ($0.6 > \alpha \geq 0.4$) covering the remaining three minima. However, the dynamic threshold is challenging when the number of minima is unknown. On the other hand, average linkage with Mahalanobis distance successfully identifies high-interest minima, but results in larger bounding boxes, decreasing the explanatory value, as evidenced by fewer rules found.

Further, we conducted another ablation study to evaluate our ability to generate uncertainty-aware clusters within the BO framework. To achieve this, we compared standard distance-based pruning using Mahalanobis distance with Ward linkage to our proposed variance-based pruning method. Our analysis used a synthetic problem where

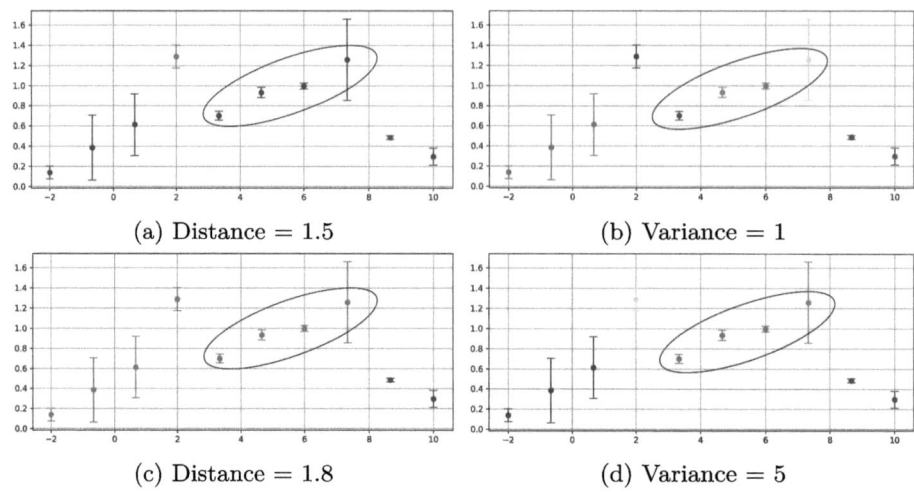

Fig. 7. Ablation study analyzing the difference in clustering based on different thresholds for distance-based pruning and variance-based pruning. Results in circular highlights show that the distance-based pruning method was not able to separate clusters based on uncertainty, while the variance-based method was able to separate clusters based on uncertainty.

we artificially added noise to increase the variance of certain data points. The problem is given as $f(x) = e^{-(x-2)^2} + e^{-(x-6)^2/10} + \frac{1}{x^2+1} + \mathcal{N}(0,1)$ This strategy allowed us to assess whether the methods could accurately identify these high variance points and separate them into distinct clusters.

We used the dendrogram to select threshold points for the distance-based method. For variance pruning, we computed the variance of the subtrees from the linkage matrix and selected different levels of variance as thresholds.

Our results (Fig. 7) show that the *distance-based method failed to account for uncertainty, resulting in inadequate cluster separation*. And this was the expected result since the distance method does not exploit uncertainty [20]. *The variance-based method successfully differentiates clusters based on uncertainty.* The increase in clusters is not a problem for our use case, because TNTRules filters out clusters with insufficient data support and ranks them based on their interestingness to produce the final explanations.

8.6 Results Summary

TNTRules consistently prove effective in localizing the minima identified by BO and generate high-quality explanations compared to baseline methods. When further enhanced with optimized weights, TNTRules outperform its non-optimized variant and the RXBO baseline, reliably identifying all minima. Leveraging Ward linkage with Mahalanobis distance and variance pruning leads to precise cluster separation and meaningful bounding boxes, while distance-based pruning fails to accommodate uncertainty and thus produces non-meaningful cluster separation.

9 Limitations and Future Work

Even though TNTRules is an effective explainability method for BO, certain aspects warrant further investigation. First, the effectiveness of TNTRules is based on the performance of the chosen clustering method. While the fidelity of the explanations is preserved through the data support metric for rule selection, the design choices in clustering can significantly impact the range of rules generated. Investigating alternative approaches for grouping data and establishing dynamic criteria for identifying "good" regions is a promising area of future work.

Second, HAC methods such as clustering with the Ward criterion often struggle with high-dimensional data, leading to challenges in forming meaningful clusters [19]. This limitation can adversely affect the performance of TNTRules when applied to very high-dimensional datasets. Standard mitigation techniques such as dimensionality reduction [52], and approximate clustering [26] can be applied for mitigation. More scenarios need to be explored in the future for generating accurate clusters with high-dimensional data. In addition, if the GP in BO is not sufficiently approximated, TNTRules may produce explanations that are accurate for the model, but not particularly useful to users because they do not accurately reflect the underlying function. Future research could improve the explanations to indicate the degree of GP approximation based on overall uncertainty, thus helping users decide whether to rely on the explanations.

Finally, TNTRules, being a general framework, cover broad industrial application domains; while it is desirable to explore the performance in different domains, we are limited by datasets and access to such industrial applications. Future research could expand upon this by exploring more practical use-cases where TNTRules can be applied.

10 Conclusion

We have introduced and evaluated TNTRules, a post-hoc explainable Bayesian optimization framework designed for collaborative parameter tuning in hardware-centric domains. TNTRules excels at generating high-fidelity, localized rules within the optimization search space, effectively capturing the behavior of the underlying Gaussian Process (GP) model in Bayesian Optimization (BO). This capability allows it to identify alternative solutions that complement traditional BO results, thereby providing actionable tuning recommendations. By delivering comprehensible rules and visualizations, TNTRules enhances the transparency and interpretability of human-AI collaborative tuning in cyber-physical systems. Our experimental results demonstrate that TNTRules surpasses other XAI methods in producing high-quality rules for optimization. In industrial settings, TNTRules could significantly improve the transparency and user-friendliness of automated tuning systems, thus aiding the broader adoption of human-in-the-loop tuning approaches. Future work will involve a user study with a real-world use case to further assess the actionable and human-centric aspects of the explanation formats introduced by TNTRules.

Acknowledgments. This study was supported by BMBF Project hKI-Chemie: humancentric AI for the chemical industry, FKZ 01—S21023D, FKZ 01—S21023G and Continental AG.

References

1. Adachi, M., et al.: Looping in the human collaborative and explainable bayesian optimization (2024)
2. Amoukou, S.I., Brunel, N.J.: Consistent sufficient explanations and minimal local rules for explaining the decision of any classifier or regressor. In: Advances in Neural Information Processing Systems, NeurIPS. Curran Associates, Inc. (2022)
3. Apté, C., Weiss, S.: Data mining with decision trees and decision rules. Futur. Gener. Comput. Syst. **13**(2–3), 197–210 (1997)
4. Chakraborty, T., Wirth, C., Seifert, C.: Post-hoc rule based explanations for black box bayesian optimization. In: Artificial Intelligence. ECAI 2023 International Workshops, pp. 320–337. Springer, Cham (2024)
5. Chollet, F.: Xception: Deep learning with depthwise separable convolutions. In: 2017 IEEE Conference on Computer Vision and Pattern Recognition (CVPR), pp. 1800–1807 (2017). https://doi.org/10.1109/CVPR.2017.195
6. Colliandre, L., Muller, C.: Bayesian optimization in drug discovery. In: High Performance Computing for Drug Discovery and Biomedicine, pp. 101–136. Springer (2023)
7. Coppens, Y., Efthymiadis, K., Lenaerts, T., Nowé, A., Miller, T., Weber, R., Magazzeni, D.: Distilling deep reinforcement learning policies in soft decision trees. In: Proceedings of the workshop on explainable artificial intelligence, IJCAI Workshop, pp. 1–6. IJCAI (2019)
8. Craven, M., Shavlik, J.: Extracting tree-structured representations of trained networks. Advances in neural information processing systems **8** (1995)
9. Deng, L.: The mnist database of handwritten digit images for machine learning research. IEEE Signal Process. Mag. **29**(6), 141–142 (2012)
10. Farrell, P., Peschka, D.: Challenges in drift-diffusion semiconductor simulations. In: Klöfkorn, R., Keilegavlen, E., Radu, F.A., Fuhrmann, J. (eds.) Finite Volumes for Complex Applications IX - Methods, Theoretical Aspects, Examples, pp. 615–623. Springer, Cham (2020)
11. Fernandes, P., Treviso, M., Pruthi, D., Martins, A., Neubig, G.: Learning to scaffold: optimizing model explanations for teaching. Adv. Neural. Inf. Process. Syst. **35**, 36108–36122 (2022)
12. Frazier, P.I., Wang, J.: Bayesian optimization for materials design. Information science for materials discovery and design, pp. 45–75 (2016)
13. Garnett, R.: Bayesian Optimization. Cambridge University Press (2023)
14. Guidotti, R., Monreale, A., Ruggieri, S., Turini, F., Giannotti, F., Pedreschi, D.: A survey of methods for explaining black box models. ACM Comput. Surv. (CSUR) **51**(5), 1–42 (2018)
15. He, K., Zhang, X., Ren, S., Sun, J.: Deep residual learning for image recognition. In: 2016 IEEE Conference on Computer Vision and Pattern Recognition (CVPR), pp. 770–778 (2016). https://doi.org/10.1109/CVPR.2016.90
16. Hedström, A., Weber, L., Krakowczyk, D., Bareeva, D., Motzkus, F., Samek, W., Lapuschkin, S., Höhne, M.M.C.: Quantus: an explainable ai toolkit for responsible evaluation of neural network explanations and beyond. J. Mach. Learn. Res. **24**(34), 1–11 (2023)
17. Himmelblau, D.: Applied Nonlinear Programming. McGraw-Hill (1972)
18. Hutter, F., Hoos, H., Leyton-Brown, K.: An efficient approach for assessing hyperparameter importance. In: Proceedings of the 31st International Conference on International Conference on Machine Learning - Volume 32, pp. I–754–I–762. ICML'14, JMLR.org (2014)

19. Kampman, I., Elomaa, T.: Hierarchical clustering of high-dimensional data without global dimensionality reduction. In: Ceci, M., Japkowicz, N., Liu, J., Papadopoulos, G.A., Raś, Z.W. (eds.) Foundations of Intelligent Systems, pp. 236–246. Springer, Cham (2018)
20. Klutchnikoff, N., Poterie, A., Rouvière, L.: Statistical analysis of a hierarchical clustering algorithm with outliers. J. Multivar. Anal. **192**, 105075 (2022)
21. Krizhevsky, A., Hinton, G., et al.: Learning multiple layers of features from tiny images. Master's thesis, University of Toronto (2009)
22. Liu, R.L., Zhao, Q., He, X.J., Yuan, X.Y., Wu, W.T., Wu, M.Y.: Airfoil optimization based on multi-objective bayesian. J. Mech. Sci. Technol. **36**(11), 5561–5573 (2022)
23. Lundberg, S.M., Erion, G.G., Chen, H., DeGrave, A.J., Prutkin, J.M., Nair, B., Katz, R., Himmelfarb, J., Bansal, N., Lee, S.: From local explanations to global understanding with explainable AI for trees. Nat. Mach. Intell. **2**(1), 56–67 (2020)
24. Macha, D., Kozielski, M., Wróbel, L., Sikora, M.: Rulexai - a package for rule-based explanations of machine learning model. SoftwareX **20**, 101209 (2022)
25. Magdalena, L.: Fuzzy Rule-Based Systems, pp. 203–218. Springer, Heidelberg (2015)
26. Mahmud, M.S., Huang, J.Z., Ruby, R., Ngueilbaye, A., Wu, K.: Approximate clustering ensemble method for big data. IEEE Trans. Big Data **9**(4), 1142–1155 (2023)
27. Mishra, S.K.: Some new test functions for global optimization and performance of repulsive particle swarm method. Available at SSRN 926132 (2006)
28. Moosbauer, J., Herbinger, J., Casalicchio, G., Lindauer, M., Bischl, B.: Explaining hyperparameter optimization via partial dependence plots. In: Proceedings of the 35th International Conference on Neural Information Processing Systems. NIPS '21. Curran Associates Inc., Red Hook (2021)
29. Murdoch, W.J., Szlam, A.: Automatic rule extraction from long short term memory networks. arXiv preprint arXiv:1702.02540 (2017)
30. Murtagh, F., Contreras, P.: Algorithms for hierarchical clustering: an overview. Wiley Interdisciplinary Reviews: Data Mining and Knowledge Discovery **2**(1), 86–97 (2012)
31. Murtagh, F., Legendre, P.: Ward's hierarchical clustering method: Clustering criterion and agglomerative algorithm. CoRR abs/1111.6285 (2011)
32. Nagataki, M., Kondo, K., Yamazaki, O., Yuki, K., Nakazawa, Y.: Online auto-tuning method in field-orientation-controlled induction motor driving inertial load. IEEE Open J. Ind. Appl. **3**, 125–140 (2022)
33. Nauta, M., et al.: From anecdotal evidence to quantitative evaluation methods: A systematic review on evaluating explainable ai. ACM Computing Surveys (2023)
34. Neumann-Brosig, M., Marco, A., Schwarzmann, D., Trimpe, S.: Data-efficient autotuning with bayesian optimization: an industrial control study. IEEE Trans. Control Syst. Technol. **28**(3), 730–740 (2019)
35. Ortiz, R., et al.: An enhanced modeling framework for bearing fault simulation and machine learning-based identification with bayesian-optimized hyperparameter tuning. J. Comput. Inf. Sci. Eng. **24**(9), 091002 (2024)
36. Pahde, F., Yolcu, G.Ü., Binder, A., Samek, W., Lapuschkin, S.: Optimizing explanations by network canonization and hyperparameter search. In: Proceedings of the IEEE/CVF Conference on Computer Vision and Pattern Recognition, pp. 3818–3827 (2023)
37. Ran, X., Xi, Y., Lu, Y., Wang, X., Lu, Z.: Comprehensive survey on hierarchical clustering algorithms and the recent developments. Artif. Intell. Rev. **56**(8), 8219–8264 (2023)
38. Rasmussen, C.E., Williams, C.K.I.: Gaussian processes for machine learning. Adaptive computation and machine learning. MIT Press (2006)
39. Ribeiro, M.T., Singh, S., Guestrin, C.: "why should I trust you?": Explaining the predictions of any classifier. In: Proceedings of the International Conference on Knowledge Discovery and Data Mining, SIGKDD. pp. 1135–1144. ACM (2016)

40. Rodemann, J., Augustin, T.: Accounting for gaussian process imprecision in bayesian optimization. In: International Symposium on Integrated Uncertainty in Knowledge Modelling and Decision Making, pp. 92–104. Springer (2022)
41. Rodemann, J., et al.: Explaining bayesian optimization by shapley values facilitates human-ai collaboration (2024)
42. Roussel, R., et al.: Bayesian optimization algorithms for accelerator physics. Phys. Rev. Accelerators Beams **27**(8), 084801 (2024)
43. Rudin, C.: Why black box machine learning should be avoided for high-stakes decisions, in brief. Nature Rev. Methods Primers **2**(1), 81 (2022)
44. Salvador, S., Chan, P.: Determining the number of clusters/segments in hierarchical clustering/segmentation algorithms. In: 16th IEEE International Conference on Tools with Artificial Intelligence, pp. 576–584. IEEE (2004)
45. Schwalbe, G., Finzel, B.: A comprehensive taxonomy for explainable artificial intelligence: a systematic survey of surveys on methods and concepts. Data Mining and Knowledge Discovery, pp. 1–59 (2023)
46. Segel, S., Graf, H., Tornede, A., Bischl, B., Lindauer, M.: Symbolic explanations for hyperparameter optimization. In: Faust, A., Garnett, R., White, C., Hutter, F., Gardner, J.R. (eds.) Proceedings of the Second International Conference on Automated Machine Learning. Proceedings of Machine Learning Research, vol. 224, pp. 2/1–22. PMLR, 12–15 Nov 2023
47. Seitz, S.: Gradient-based explanations for gaussian process regression and classification models. arXiv preprint arXiv:2205.12797 (2022)
48. Shahriari, B., Swersky, K., Wang, Z., Adams, R.P., Freitas, N.: Taking the human out of the loop: a review of bayesian optimization. Proc. IEEE **104**(1), 148–175 (2015)
49. Silagadze, Z.: Finding two-dimensional peaks. Phys. Particles Nuclei Lett. **4**, 73–80 (2007)
50. Snoek, J., Larochelle, H., Adams, R.P.: Practical bayesian optimization of machine learning algorithms. Advances in neural information processing systems **25** (2012)
51. Sundin, I., et al.: Human-in-the-loop assisted de novo molecular design. J. Cheminform. **14**(1), 1–16 (2022)
52. Velliangiri, S., Alagumuthukrishnan, S., Thankumar joseph, S.I.: A review of dimensionality reduction techniques for efficient computation. Procedia Comput. Sci. **165**, 104–111 (2019)
53. Vilone, G., Longo, L.: A quantitative evaluation of global, rule-based explanations of post-hoc, model agnostic methods. Front. Artif. Intell. **4**, 717899 (2021)
54. Waa, J., Nieuwburg, E., Cremers, A.H.M., Neerincx, M.A.: Evaluating XAI: a comparison of rule-based and example-based explanations. Artif. Intell. **291**, 103404 (2021)
55. Wang, F., Rudin, C.: Falling rule lists. In: Artificial Intelligence and Statistics, pp. 1013–1022. PMLR (2015)
56. Ward, J.H., Jr.: Hierarchical grouping to optimize an objective function. J. Am. Stat. Assoc. **58**(301), 236–244 (1963)
57. Wirth, C., Schmid, U., Voget, S.: Humanzentrierte künstliche intelligenz: Erklärendes interaktives maschinelles lernen für effizienzsteigerung von parametrieraufgaben. In: Hartmann, E.A. (ed.) Digitalisierung souverän gestalten II, pp. 80–92. Springer, Heidelberg (2022)
58. Witten, I.H., Frank, E., Hall, M.A., Pal, C.J.: Chapter 3 - output: Knowledge representation. In: Data Mining (Fourth Edition), pp. 67–89. Morgan Kaufmann, fourth edition edn. (2017)
59. Wu, Z., et al.: Prediction of California house price based on multiple linear regression. Academic J. Eng. Technol. Sci. **3**(7.0) (2020)
60. Xu, C., Gertner, G.Z.: Uncertainty and sensitivity analysis for models with correlated parameters. Reliability Eng. Syst. Saf. **93**(10), 1563–1573 (2008)
61. Yazgana, P., Kusakci, A.O.: A literature survey on association rule mining algorithms. Southeast Europe J. soft Comput. **5**(1) (2016)
62. Zhou, J., Gandomi, A.H., Chen, F., Holzinger, A.: Evaluating the quality of machine learning explanations: a survey on methods and metrics. Electronics **10**(5), 593 (2021)

Open Access This chapter is licensed under the terms of the Creative Commons Attribution 4.0 International License (http://creativecommons.org/licenses/by/4.0/), which permits use, sharing, adaptation, distribution and reproduction in any medium or format, as long as you give appropriate credit to the original author(s) and the source, provide a link to the Creative Commons license and indicate if changes were made.

The images or other third party material in this chapter are included in the chapter's Creative Commons license, unless indicated otherwise in a credit line to the material. If material is not included in the chapter's Creative Commons license and your intended use is not permitted by statutory regulation or exceeds the permitted use, you will need to obtain permission directly from the copyright holder.

Bridging the Interpretability Gap in Process Mining: A Comprehensive Approach Combining Explainable Clustering and Generative AI

Jonas Amling[1]([✉])[iD], Emanuel Slany[1][iD], Christian Dormagen[2][iD], Marco Kretschmann[1][iD], and Stephan Scheele[3][iD]

[1] dab: Daten - Analysen & Beratung GmbH, Deggendorf, Germany
{jonas.amling,emanuel.slany,marco.kretschmann}@dab-gmbh.de
[2] University of Bamberg, Bamberg, Germany
christian.dormagen@uni-bamberg.de
[3] OTH Regensburg, Regensburg, Germany
stephan.scheele@oth-regensburg.de

Abstract. Process mining often yields highly complex "Spaghetti Models", making them difficult to interpret and impeding informed decision-making. Therefore, researchers have explored clustering of event logs to simplify process models and reduce their complexity. However, the unsupervised nature of clustering can introduce an interpretation gap, necessitating manual effort to identify differences and similarities across the resulting process models. To address these issues, we propose an explainable clustering approach that identifies key subprocesses and applies eXplainable Artificial Intelligence (XAI) techniques to clarify the rationale behind model partitioning. Moreover, we integrate a Large Language Model (LLM) into the process discovery procedure to generate natural language descriptions and compare the discovered process models, enhancing user understanding, engagement, and making complex technical details more accessible. A case study demonstrates that our method operates effectively across various LLMs, preserving vital contextual information while simplifying the process discovery workflow. Our findings reveal that larger models generally ensure completeness, whereas smaller ones offer more efficiency at the expense of explanation quality, highlighting the importance of a balanced LLM choice for practical applications.

Keywords: Clustering · Process Mining · XAI-Supported Clustering

1 Introduction

Process mining is an advanced analytical technique that reveals the actual execution of business processes by extracting insights from event data. It provides valuable insights into process flows and facilitates the identification of inefficiencies, deviations, and bottlenecks from intended workflows [8]. However, the complexity of event data in real-world applications often leads to intricate spaghetti models [41], where excessively dense transitions between nodes make process flows difficult to interpret (see Fig. 1). The resulting complexity of such process graphs poses a significant challenge, limiting their practical usability.

1.1 Towards Explainable Process Mining

One way to address this challenge is to apply clustering algorithms, e.g., hierarchical, partitional, or density-based methods. These techniques group data sets into meaningful subsets – called partitions or clusters [27] – and, when applied to process mining graphs, group similar processes to reduce the complexity of graph models [39]. If the resulting clusters capture *meaningful* process variations, clustering can significantly improve the comprehensibility of graph models.

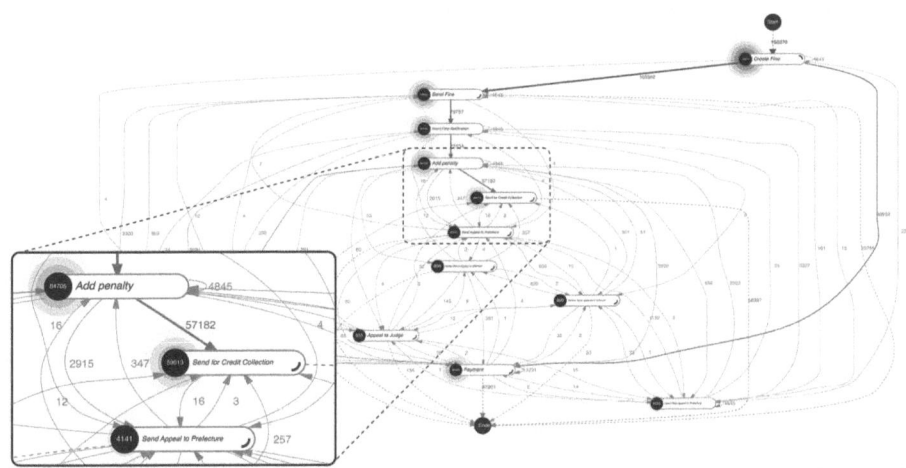

Fig. 1. *Spaghetti Graph* from process mining on the RTFMP dataset.

Due to their unsupervised nature, clustering methods often lack interpretability [11]. In process mining, users must analyze various process groups (clusters) to identify similar and dissimilar characteristics. The rich landscape of distinct clustering algorithms with different optimization paradigms [27] causes deviating process groups even for a single graph model. These challenges underscore the need for methods that enhance the interpretability of clustered process models.

Recent literature proposes various strategies to enhance the *post-hoc interpretability* of clustering techniques. These approaches can generally be distinguished by whether they rely on surrogate models or not: For instance, the *LOcal Rule-Based Explanations* (LORE) [22] method, utilizes decision trees that are trained with cluster identifiers as transparent surrogate model. In contrast, the ClusterExplainR method [11] derives explanatory rules by calculating cluster-inherent feature importance scores. For a comprehensive overview of explainable artificial intelligence (XAI) methods for clustering, see [11]. We identify three core **challenges** with current state-of-the-art XAI techniques for clustering:

1. Even if some methods claim to be model- and data-agnostic [15,22], their task invariance has not been investigated. XAI techniques might be suitable for the clustering algorithm and the instances' data type, but the process mining task still formulates unique challenges, as it requires a semantic understanding of particular process instances [8].
2. Most XAI methods for clustering either assign importance values to features [17], describe the cluster by rules [22], or execute both [11]. Yet, none of the reviewed methods captures the described particularities of process mining or is compatible with process mining graph visualizations.
3. A related third problem addresses the target group shift: Whereas XAI for clustering covers the explanation needs of machine learning (ML) experts, clustered process mining graphs identify relevant, frequently economic, subprocesses [3]. We argue that business analysts have more expressive explanation needs than ML experts.

In our approach, we combine Microsoft's *Power Automate Process Mining* solution[1] with the *Hierarchical Density-Based Spatial Clustering of Applications with Noise* (HDBSCAN) algorithm [30] to segment process graphs into meaningful process groups. To enhance their interpretability, we integrate the method from the ClusterExplainR [11], forming a framework for explainable artificial intelligence (XAI) in process mining. This integration facilitates more transparent process analysis, helping business analysts better understand, interpret, and act on complex process structures.

Our work makes the following contributions: First, we adapt and extend our previous work, ClusterExplaineR – an algorithm-agnostic XAI approach for clustering [11] – to the domain of process mining. Second, we extend our explanation framework by integrating a Large Language Model (LLM) to verbalize rule-based explanations, including rich background knowledge. This allows users to interactively explore and analyze process-related insights, including process explanations, subprocess analysis, cluster differentiation, metric interpretations, and more. Finally, we evaluate the effectiveness of our approach through an empirical study assessing the quality of LLM-generated verbalizations for explaining in the process mining domain.

1.2 Application Use-Case (Running Example)

Consider the following application scenario based on the analysis of a traffic fine management process (RTFM)[2], shown in Fig. 1. Our point is that even seemingly simple processes can contain many complex variations: Some defendants are charged with a traffic violation, but pay the fine immediately. Others refuse to pay the fine even after repeated requests to pay. Finally, a court may find

---

[1] https://learn.microsoft.com/en-us/power-automate/process-mining-overview, Jan. 28, 2025.
[2] https://data.4tu.nl/articles/dataset/Road_Traffic_Fine_Management_Process/12683249, Jan. 28, 2025.

a defendant guilty and the defendant pays the fine, including reminder fees, before the case is closed. The number of variations and their complexity prevent analysts from identifying key processes from the process mining graph.

Our approach is illustrated in Fig. 2. First, after process discovery from an event log, we partition the process mining graph into clusters of similar processes. Second, we induce rules for each process group. Third, an LLM verbalizes the rules, making them more accessible. An analyst might observe that the majority of variants fall into process group {Violation → Create Fine → Payment}, or simply put: most fines are paid immediately after the violation. Furthermore, not all processes might terminate, indicating that some traffic fines remain unpaid. Leveraging the LLM interface and additional domain knowledge, the analyst can ask follow-up questions, such as *"What are the differences between Cluster X and Cluster Y?"* A possible answer: *"Cluster X includes only* Create Fine *and* Payment *with a median duration of 5 days, whereas Cluster Y includes* Create Fine *and* Send Fine *with a median duration of 101 days."* Thus, we argue that our framework advances interpretable process mining by identifying relevant subprocesses, contextualizing them with domain knowledge, and facilitating the interactive explanatory exploration through an LLM-interface.

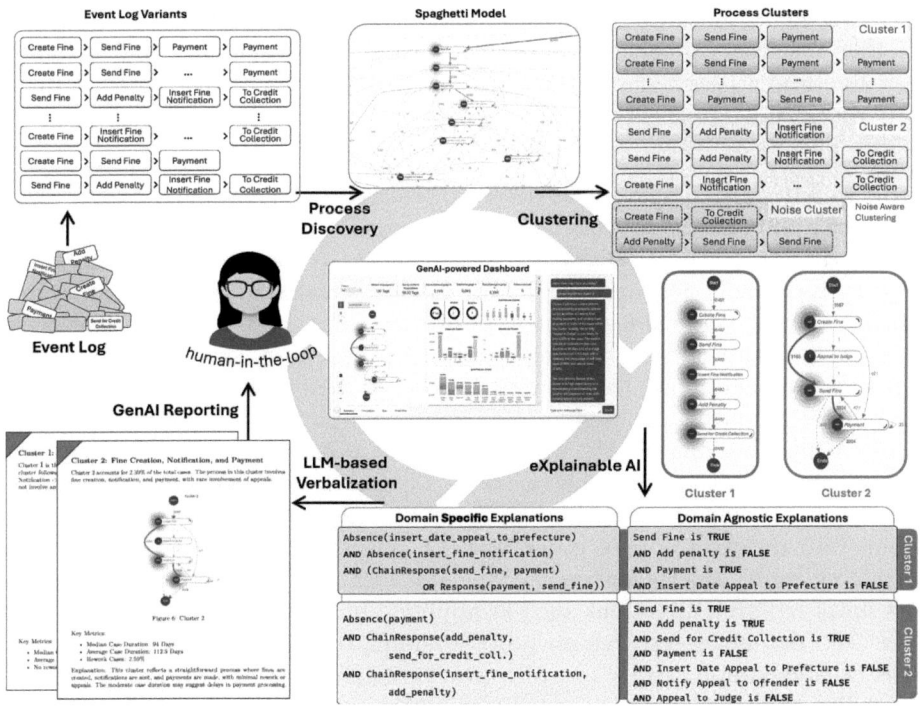

Fig. 2. From process model clustering to interactive verbal explanations: process discovery, clustering, XAI, and LLM verbalization.

The remainder of our article is structured as follows: Sect. 2 discusses related work, ranging from the challenges of XAI for unsupervised ML to the clustering of process mining graphs. Section 3 introduces key mathematical concepts in process mining and formalizes our approach. Section 4 describes the experimental setup and workflow of our approach. Section 5 empirically evaluates LLM-generated verbalizations of cluster explanations within the context of process mining. Finally, Sect. 6 summarizes our key insights, contextualizes our findings within existing research, and highlights open research directions.

2 Related Work

Building on the Introduction, process mining graphs are often tedious to interpret [41]. Clustering algorithms can help by identifying relevant groups of processes [28], but their unsupervised nature frequently hinders the comprehensibility of the results. While some XAI methods for clustering attempt to restore the transparency of the underlying partitioning mechanisms post-hoc [11], their explanations are rarely accessible to non-ML experts.

Our literature review is structured accordingly: First, we examine process mining techniques and the fine granularity of their outputs. Next, we compare clustering algorithms in terms of their suitability for process group identification. We then discuss approaches to improve clustering transparency and highlight their limitations, particularly their lack of consideration of the semantic information embedded in event data. Finally, we review related work and outline the unique advantages of our approach.

Process Mining. For over two decades, researchers have proposed algorithms to discover and analyze processes from event logs [6], optimize the discovery process, or check the process alignment. For instance, [5] have repurposed methods of analysis of social networks to identify interpersonal relations within an organization's event log. Typically, process mining techniques use the entire event log data to obtain process mining graphs. A *divide and conquer* method simplifies this by identifying the relevant portion of the event log and then mining the process graph [25]. A well-known example of process alignment evaluation (conformance checking) is [10], which introduces a cost-function-based approach. Today, commercial solutions like Celonis [13] dominate process mining in practice. Current academic contributions focus on integrating process mining algorithms into the data science ecosystem [13]. Others enhance the formalization by mining event objects instead of single elements of the event log [4] or discuss novel research directions such as applying process mining to unstructured data [24]. Yet, novel research on process mining does not overcome the limitations causing subtle, overly complex process mining graphs, driven by process variability and insufficient standardization [9].

Clustering of Process Graphs. Hence, we argue that simplifying process mining graphs – by clustering them into representative subprocesses – is essential. Broadly, clustering methods in process mining fall into three categories:

vector-based, model-based, and context-aware approaches [28]. Vector-based approaches transform event log traces into trace vector representations, employing various techniques to capture trace characteristics [20,39,43]. For instance, activity profiling [39] represents each trace as a numerical vector based on the count of activities per case, enabling clustering with any algorithm that operates on vector-based data. Model-based approaches take the process graphs as input [16,21,42]. Finally, context-aware approaches cluster the process graph while considering the context of activities, specifically their order and relation to each other [18,32]. Each of these strategies presents a viable approach to simplifying process graphs. However, these solutions add a layer of complexity, as the partitioning process involves intricate tasks that remain opaque to users.

XAI for Clustering. Once humans draw inferences from process models and their subprocesses, revealing the mechanisms behind the generation of subprocesses becomes mandatory. While our preliminary publication [11] has focused on the necessity for XAI for clustering in general, this paragraph interprets existing methods in the context of process mining. Most XAI techniques for clustering fall into one of the following categories: They are either *intrinsically explainable* or rely on *post-hoc methodologies* [11]. Intrinsically explainable methods ensure transparency by providing interpretable cluster models such as decision trees [14,34] or rule-based frameworks [19]. On the other hand, post-hoc approaches use either surrogate models [22] or statistical characteristics of the partitions [11,31]. We argue that rule-based approaches are generally superior for describing process mining partitions. Limiting clustering techniques to rule-based methods may be impractical and restrictive. On the contrary, the reliance on surrogate models has shown to be prone to additional errors depending on the underlying algorithms [36]. Based on our literature review, rule-based XAI methods without surrogate models, such as [11], are superior in the context of process mining.

LLM Verbalization. In XAI, different user groups might prefer different explanation modalities [12]. Domain experts without extensive ML expertise, such as process mining experts [3], benefit from a tailored, verbalized explanation modality [45]. With the rise of LLMs, the usability of XAI methods can be improved post-hoc [29,37]. However, none of the previous works address the process mining domain. Yet, business analysts in this field extensively benefit from verbalized, interactive explanations that support human-in-the-loop exploration of process groups. Through the following chapters, we present and evaluate our solution, contributing to bridging the identified gap in the current literature.

3 Methods

In this section, we semi-formally define our method of the interactive explainer for clustering in the process mining domain. We aim to enable a human-centric exploration experience for business analysts without a strong ML background. As a foundation, let us first introduce the definition of an event log.

Definition 1 (Event Log [1]). Let $c \in \mathcal{C}$ and $a \in \mathcal{A}$ be cases and activities of an *event log* $\mathcal{L} = \{(c_i, a_i, t_i) | i \in \{1, ..., n\}\}$ with arity n and timestamp $t_i \in \mathbb{R}^+$. Then, each case $c \in \mathcal{C}$ can be written as an ordered sequence

$$\sigma_c = \langle (a_1, t_1), ..., (a_{m_c}, t_{m_c}) \rangle$$

of m_c activities of case c sorted by time t such that $\sum_{c \in \mathcal{C}} m_c = n$.

Example 1 (Event Log). Consider the following tabular representation of an event log, based on the RTFM data set.

Case Identifier c_i	Activity a_i	Timestamp t_i
1	violation	2024-02-04 10:00
1	create fine	2024-02-04 10:05
1	payment	2024-02-04 10:15
2	violation	2024-02-05 12:00
2	create fine	2024-02-05 12:05
2	send fine	2024-02-05 17:00
3	violation	2024-02-05 12:00
3	create fine	2024-02-05 12:05
3	payment	2024-02-05 12:15

The ordered sequence $\sigma_{c=1}$ is given as: $\sigma_{c=1} = \langle \text{violation}, \text{create fine}, \text{payment} \rangle$.

Remark 1. For didactic purposes, $t_i \in \mathbb{R}^+$ (Definition 1) is converted into date time notation in Example 1.

An event log (Definition 1) contains multiple cases, of which each case consists of one or more activities ordered by a timestamp [1]. Ordered sequences are activities of a case sorted by the timestamp in ascending order. Traces of a process mining graph (Definition 2) are directed connections between consecutive activities [7]. The weights of traces is typically determined by their occurrences, either in absolute or relative numbers.

Definition 2 (Process Mining Graph [7]). Let $\mathcal{T} = \{\sigma_j | j \in \{1, ..., k\}\}$ be a set of k traces. A *process mining graph* is a triple $G = (\mathcal{V}, \mathcal{E}, w)$, where $\mathcal{V}$ is the set of unique activities from $\mathcal{A}$, $\mathcal{E} \subseteq \mathcal{V} \times \mathcal{V}$ is the set of edges, and weight function $w : \mathcal{E} \to \mathbb{N}$ assigns a frequency value to each edge. A directly-follows edge between two activities a and a' of $\mathcal{A}$ exists if

$$\exists \sigma_j \text{ such that } \langle (a, t), (a', t') \rangle \text{ with } t < t',$$

where t and t' are timestamps of a and a', respectively. The weight function $w(\langle a, a' \rangle)$ represents the number of occurrences of transitions from a to a' in $\mathcal{T}$.

Remark 2. We reinforce the semantic difference between edges that connect activities and activities of an event log by $\mathcal{V}$ and $\mathcal{A}$. Note that the former is the set notation for activities, whereas the latter is indexed by natural numbers ranging from one to the arity of the event log.

Example 2. Example 1 can be transformed into a process graph. Thicker edges indicate more frequent transitions between activities.

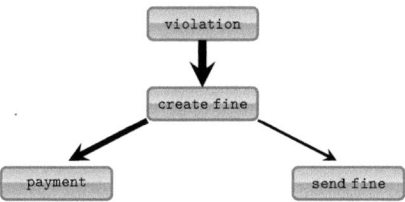

Remark 3. Process mining graphs are characterized by a Pareto optimum [2]: A small number of variants often encapsulates a large number of traces.

By grouping similar instances, clustering transforms a comparatively complex data set into smaller partitions, frequently termed clusters, with lower complexity [27]. We apply this strategy to process mining graphs once the ordered sequences of traces are transformed into a set of boolean vector representations, where each vector indicates the presence or absence of all possible activities (Definition 3). In practice, we apply the HDBSCAN algorithm [30] to group the binary vector representations into meaningful subsets.

Definition 3 (Clustering of Process Mining Graphs [39]). *Clustering for process mining graphs partitions the set of traces $\mathcal{T}$ in three steps:*

(i) Let $f_a : \sigma \to (\{0,1\})^{|\mathcal{V}|}$ transfer an ordered sequence into a boolean representation of the absence or presence of an sequence's activity by:

$$f_a(\sigma) = \begin{cases} 1, & \text{if } \exists s \in \{1,...,|\sigma|\} \text{ such that } \sigma_s = a \\ 0, & \text{otherwise} \end{cases}, \quad \forall v \in \mathcal{V}.$$

(ii) Let the boolean trace set be obtained by:

$$\mathcal{X} = \{f_a(\sigma) | \sigma \in \mathcal{T}\}.$$

(iii) Let $B \in \mathcal{B}$ be a partition (cluster) of $\mathcal{X}$, where $B \subseteq \mathcal{X}$ and $\mathcal{B}$ is the set of partitions. Let $cl : \mathcal{X} \to \mathcal{B}$ with $|\mathcal{B}| = k'$ partition a data set $\mathcal{X}$ into k' subsets.

Example 3. The three ordered sequences of the event log (Example 1) correspond to two traces in the process graph (Example 2). The following table categorizes the sequences into two fictitious clusters based on their activity presence/absence:

Remark 4. In this simple running example, the obtained clusters correspond to the trace variants. In practice, clustering is capable of abstracting from trace variants, such that $|\mathcal{B}| \leq |\text{unique}(\mathcal{T})|$, where $\text{unique}(\mathcal{T})$ returns the unique traces.

sequence σ_c	violation	create fine	send fine	payment	cluster B
σ_1	True	True	False	True	1
σ_2	True	True	True	False	2
σ_3	True	True	False	True	1

We believe that the *meaningfulness* of partitions is crucial for the practical usability of clustering algorithms. Consequently, we envision clustering as a highly interactive and context-dependent process, where human users might revise the algorithm based on an initial suggestion of partitions. In supervised ML settings, XAI is a prerequisite for revealing the model's decision-making mechanism [40]. In our previous work [11], we applied this finding to XAI for clustering. We presented a method that estimates the importance of features for clusters solely by the entropy as a generic statistical characteristic. Definitions 4 and 5 project the mathematical preconditions into the domain of process mining.

Definition 4 (Activity Random Process [11]**).** Let $X \in \mathbf{X}$ with $|\mathbf{X}| = |\mathcal{V}|$ be a Bernoulli *random process* behind each *activity* that models its absence or presence in a sequence. Further, let $z \in Z$ be a realization of the set of possible values of random process X. Finally, let $p_z = Pr(X = z)$ denote the probability of the realization of z given the random process X.

Definition 5 (Shannon Entropy [11,26]**).** Let the *Shannon entropy* be:
$$H(X) = -\sum_{z \in Z} p_z \log_2 p_z.$$

The local activity importance score (Definition 6) assesses the importance of an activity for a specific cluster. It compares the probability of an activity's presence within a cluster to its probability in the global population. Intuitively, an activity is considered important for a partition when it is distributed more homogeneously within a cluster. The greater the difference between its local (cluster) and global distribution, the more crucial the activity becomes in defining the cluster.

Definition 6 (Local Activity Importance Score [11]**).** Let the *local activity importance score* ($lAIS$) be defined as:
$$lAIS(X, B) = 1 - \min(H(X_B) \cdot H(X)^{-1}, 1),$$
where X_B is the random process of X in partition B.

Example 4. The following table showcases the existence probabilities for each distinct activity (Example 3):

data	$Pr(\text{violation})$	$Pr(\text{create fine})$	$Pr(\text{send fine})$	$Pr(\text{payment})$
$B^{(1)}$	1.0	1.0	0.0	1.0
$B^{(2)}$	1.0	1.0	1.0	0.0
$\mathcal{X}$	1.0	1.0	$\frac{1}{3}$	$\frac{2}{3}$

The local importance of the **payment** activity for the first cluster is given as:

$$H(X_{\text{payment},B^{(1)}}) = -(1.0 \cdot \log_2 1.0) = 0.0$$

$$H(X_{\text{payment}}) = -\left(\frac{2}{3} \cdot \log_2 \frac{2}{3}\right) \approx 0.0301$$

$$lAIS(X_{\text{payment}}, B^{(1)}) = 1 - \min\left(0.0 \cdot 0.0301^{-1}, 1\right) = 1$$

The activity **payment** is the determining activity for the first cluster.

Rules are conjunctive statements (Definition 7). Based on the local activity importance score, explanations are generated by a rule selection heuristic [11]: It selects the most important feature and iteratively refines the rule using the F1-score to balance accuracy and coverage. Non-differentiating features are ignored, while rules with false positives are incrementally refined.

Definition 7 (Trace Rules [11]). Let $tr : B \times \mathcal{X} \times \mathbf{X} \to R$ utilize a rule search heuristic [11] for partition B of a boolean *trace* set $\mathcal{X}$ with random processes $\mathbf{X}$ to return a set of conjunctive *rules* R.

Example 5. The execution of $tr(B^{(1)}, \mathcal{X}, \mathbf{X})$ [11] by the aid of Example 6 results in the following rule for cluster $B^{(1)}$:

```
Cluster 1 (accuracy: 1.0, coverage: 1.0):
    payment is True,
    AND send fine is False
```

Remark 5. Compared to [11], $tr(B, \mathcal{X}, \mathbf{X})$ uses Definition 6 instead of the local feature importance score to highlight the specificities inherited by activities of a process mining graph.

Remark 6. Our approach fosters DECLARE [33] constraints as an additional logical representation. Those will also be subject of the empirical evaluation in Sect. 5. Its basic semantics are given as follows:

constraint	explanation	examples			
		$\langle a,b,c \rangle$	$\langle a,c,a \rangle$	$\langle d,b,c \rangle$	$\langle a,c,a,b \rangle$
PRESENCE(a)	a occurs	✓	✓	✗	✓
ABSENCE(a)	a does not occur	✗	✗	✓	✗
INIT(a)	a occurs first	✓	✓	✗	✓
END(a)	a occurs last	✗	✓	✗	✗
RESPONSE(a,b)	b occurs after a if a occurs	✓	✗	✓[a]	✓
CHAINRESPONSE(a,b)	b occurs *immediately* after a if a occurs	✓	✗	✓[a]	✗

[a] In practice, vacuous constraints are treated as False.

Example 6. The DECLARE representative for Example 5 is:

```
Cluster 1 (accuracy: 1.0, coverage: 1.0):
   ChainResponse(create fine, payment)
```

The LLM alters the explanation modality from a logical to a narrative representation. These rule verbalizations correspond to our identified target group shift and account for the presumed information needs of business analysts.

Definition 8 (Verbalization). Let $ve : R \rightarrow \langle str \rangle$ apply a zero-shot `gpt-4o` model[3] for the *verbalization* of a rule set R, where $\langle str \rangle$ is a string.

Example 7. A potential verbalization of the rule from Example 5 with a zero-shot `gpt-4o` model is:

> **Model:** Cluster 1 is characterized by a violation occurring, a fine being created, and the payment being made.

Natural language as explanation modality elevates the interaction ability for human users. Human users interact with the LLM based on its initial output and additionally included background knowledge.

Definition 9 (Interact [38]). Let INTERACT($\langle str \rangle$) be a procedure, which enables a human user to *interact* with the verbalized explanation.

Example 8. Suppose the rule for partition $B^{(2)}$ (Example 7) is given as follows:

```
Cluster 2 (accuracy: 1.0, coverage: 1.0):
    payment is False
    AND send fine is True
```

---

[3] https://platform.openai.com/docs/models#gpt-4o, 28 January 2025.

A user might interact with the model as follows:

> **User:** What distinguishes cluster 1 from cluster 2?

> **Model:** Cluster 1 represents cases where the fine has already been paid, whereas cluster 2 represents cases where the fine has been issued but not been paid yet.

The derived methods are combined in Algorithm 1. Our interactive Process Graph eXplanations (iPGX) procedure first extracts the traces from an event log using process discovery (line 1). Afterwards, iPGX conveys the process traces into the existence feature data set (line 2). Clusters (line 3) based on the existence data are explained by rules (line 4). Verbalizations with LLMs increase their expressiveness and interactivity (lines 5 and 6).

Algorithm 1: iPGX($\mathcal{L}$) (interactive Process Graph eXplanations)

Input: Event log $\mathcal{L}$
Output: Interactive rule set verbalization $\langle str \rangle$
1: $\mathcal{T} \leftarrow \{\sigma_j | j \in \{1, ..., k\}\}$ ▷ *Definition 2*
2: $\mathcal{X} \leftarrow \{f_a(\sigma) | \sigma \in \mathcal{T}\}$ ▷ *Definition 3*
3: $\mathcal{B} \leftarrow cl(\mathcal{X})$ ▷ *Definition 3*
4: $R \leftarrow tr(\mathcal{B}, \mathcal{X}, \mathbf{X})$ ▷ *Partition selected by user, Definition 7*
5: $\langle str \rangle \leftarrow ve(R)$ ▷ *Definition 8*
6: INTERACT($\langle str \rangle$) ▷ *Definition 9*
7: **return** $\langle str \rangle$

In summary, this section has proposed a mathematically sound strategy to cluster and explain traces from event logs with rules. Our approach increases the practicality of rule-based cluster explanations by incorporating LLMs to verbalize and interact with the distinguishing attributes of process traces. The next section will guide readers through the front end of our method. Our demonstrator puts the theoretical derivation of this section into practice.

4 Interactive Exploration of Process Models

To showcase the practical usability of our approach, we develop an interactive demonstrator that integrates Power BI visualizations with an LLM-driven chat (Fig. 3). Our dashboard presents discovered clusters along with key metrics, facilitating intuitive process exploration. It visualizes process mining graphs and generates verbalized rule-based cluster explanations, allowing users to interactively explore and analyze identified process patterns.

The instruction of LLMs plays a vital role for the exploration of subprocesses in process mining. Our interactive cluster exploration framework has continuous access to essential and task-specific background knowledge that is represented as structured JSON-data. Essential background knowledge, illustrated in Table 1, consists of the domain terminology, key metrics and their interpretation and describes a process in general.

Task-specific background knowledge deviates between tasks, e.g., the general median case duration serves as an example for the former category, while the dynamic assessment of the median case duration of a subprocess belongs to the latter category, depicted in Table 2.

We argue that the combination of statistical descriptive background knowledge and narrative rule translations of process clusters effectively support users, while covering all relevant cluster metrics and minimizing wrong entity representations.

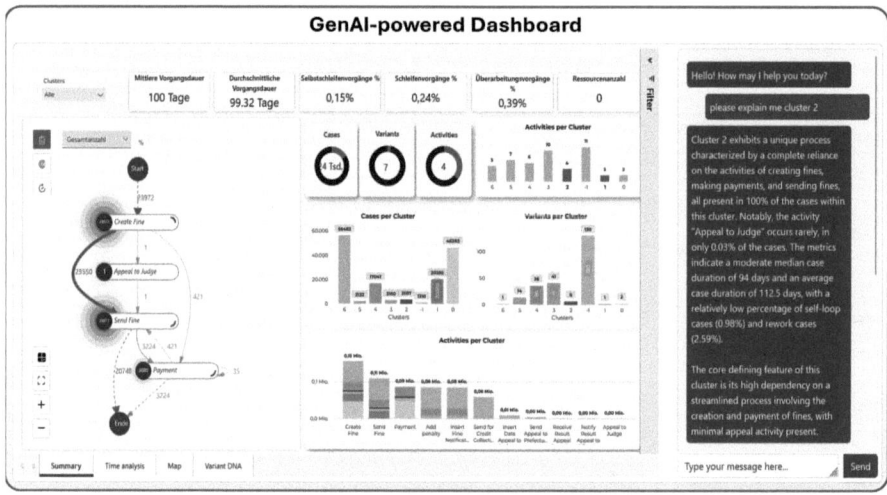

Fig. 3. Interactive process analysis dashboard with generative AI explanations.

Table 1. Essential Background Knowledge.

Name	Definition
Process mining concepts	
process	A sequence of activities to achieve a specific goal.
event log	Process data set: case identifiers, activities, and timestamps.
case	Activity sequence of one case identifier, also known as a trace.
...	...
Process model metrics	
median case duration	Medium duration of traces conditioned on case identifiers.
average case duration	Mean duration of traces conditioned on case identifiers.
self loop case ratio	Percentage of cases with repeating activities.
...	...

Precise instructions are supposed to minimize the risk of hallucinations while ensuring clear and concise responses. To maintain focus, our system prompt is tailored to four specific tasks, actively rejecting user requests beyond these predefined objectives. The utilized LLM is optimized for cluster descriptions, cluster comparisons, process overviews, and key metrics reports:

Describe Highlight what is special in cluster X compared to all other clusters. What insights can you generate from the rules? Finally, summarize in one sentence what is the core defining feature of this cluster. Keep it short!

Compare Is there a significant difference in activities? Is there a significant difference in any key metric or are they similar? How do the XAI rules differ? Finally, summarize in one sentence. Keep it short!

Overview What is this process about? Are there any special clusters? How much noise is there within the clustering?

Key Metrics You can explain all key metrics for which you have been provided a definition in the following background information.

Example 9. We present an explanatory dialogue between our XAI-based LLM and an analyst, based on Fig. 4. In this example, cluster 4 is described and compared to cluster 2, generating the following explanations:

User: Give a brief overview of the process.

Table 2. Task-specific Background Knowledge: Structured input data.

JSON tag	Description	Example
activities	Activity array of a cluster.	[{ "Activity": "Create Fine", "TotalActivityCount": 3587, "DistinctCasesWithActivity": 3587, "PercentageOfCasesWithActivity": 100.0 },...]
ClusterExplainRRule	Explanation for a cluster based on activity existence.	Send Fine is TRUE AND Add penalty is FALSE AND Payment is TRUE AND Insert Date Appeal to Prefecture is FALSE
DeclareExplainerRule	Explanation for a cluster based on temporal logic.	Absence(Insert Date Appeal To Prefecture) AND Absence(Insert Fine Notification) AND (ChainResponse(Send Fine,Payment) OR Response(Payment, Send Fine))
...	...	...

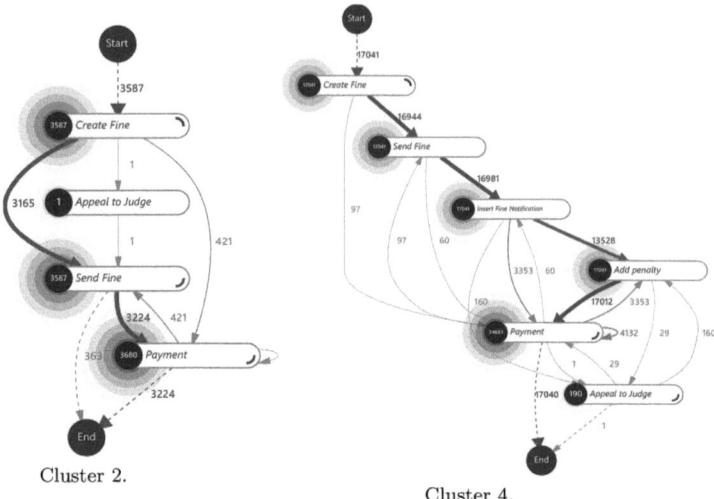

Cluster 2.   Cluster 4.

Fig. 4. Directly Follows Graphs, showing differing process complexities.

Model: The Road Traffic Fine Management Process involves handling the issuance, notification, payment, and enforcement of traffic violation fines. Analyzed through clustering, it reveals 150,000 cases with 231 variants and 11 unique activities, with noise represented in "Cluster -1," indicating diverse behaviors and some inconsistencies in the process.

User: Make a list of the most important clusters and give them a name.

Model:
1. Cluster 0: Efficient Fine Management
2. Cluster 2: Streamlined Payment Processing
3. Cluster 6: Common Fine Management Variant
4. Cluster 4: Complex Rework Instances

User: Describe cluster 4.

Model: Cluster 4 is defined by cases with high rework activity (42.2 %), the highest across all clusters. It focuses on a process that always includes "Create Fine," "Send Fine," "Insert Fine Notification," "Add Penalty," and "Payment."

While some appeals to a judge (1.11 %) exist, cases involving "Send for Credit Collection" are absent. The median case duration is 304 days, with a high complexity indicated by 36 variants and 6 unique activities. The process also emphasizes a temporal dependency where "Insert Fine Notification" leads to "Payment."

User: What is the difference between clusters 2 and 4?

Model: Cluster 2 is characterized by cases frequently following a straightforward progression of activities ("Create Fine → Send Fine → Payment") with no rework activity related to added penalties or notifications. It excludes "Insert Date Appeal to Prefecture" and "Insert Fine Notification." It also has a significantly smaller number of total cases (3587) and higher focus on payment sequencing.

Cluster 4, on the other hand, features a more complex process with extremely high rework activity (42.2%) primarily due to frequent self-loops involving "Add Penalty" and "Payment." It also contains rare discretionary activities, such as "Appeal to Judge" (1.11%), indicative of exceptional cases. Its variant structure includes more events (6 activities) and diverse internal activities like notifications.

User: Compare clusters 2 and 4 based on their key metrics.

Model: When comparing Clusters 2 and 4 based on their key metrics:

- **Case Volume**: Cluster 2: 3,587 cases vs. Cluster 4: 17,041 cases.
- **Median Case Duration**: Cluster 2: 94 days vs. Cluster 4: 304 days.
- **Rework Percentage**: Cluster 2: low rework percentage vs. Cluster 4: high rework rate of 42.2%.
- **Variants**: Cluster 2: 6 variants vs. Cluster 4: 36 variants.

In summary, Cluster 2 is more efficient with fewer cases, shorter durations, and low rework, while Cluster 4 is more complex with higher volumes, longer durations, and significant rework.

The next section will assess the verbalization quality. Users will rate the verbalization of various LLMs and rank the LLMs according to their verbalization capabilities.

5 Empirical Evaluation

Setup. We assess the verbalization capabilities of various LLMs for cluster explanations in the process mining context in a user study. Precisely, we compare the performance in the *description* and *comparison* tasks across the gpt-4o, gpt-4o-mini, LLama-70B, and LLama-8B[4] models with identical background

---

[4] gpt-4o: https://platform.openai.com/docs/models#gpt-4o,
gpt-4o-mini: https://platform.openai.com/docs/models#gpt-4o-mini LLama-70B: https://huggingface.co/meta-llama/Llama-3.3-70B-Instruct LLama-8B: https://huggingface.co/meta-llama/Llama-3.1-8B-Instruct all 28 January 2025.

knowledge (Table 1 and 2) on the state-of-the-art Road Traffic Fine Management (RTFM) data set[5], using HDBSCAN with a minimum cluster size of 1500 and a minimum sample size of 750.

Seven participants – data scientists and/or process mining experts – were asked to evaluate the soundness, fluency, completeness, context awareness, and length [45] of the explanations for three randomly chosen cases for each task: completeness and soundness refer to the integrity and correctness of the narrative output entities wrt. the rule entities; fluency quantifies to which extent the LLM output resembles *natural* language; context awareness assesses the degree to which the output entities are put into the correct semantic relation; the length reports the outputs' word counts. The users assessed the soundness, fluency, completeness, and context awareness with a three-point scale (low, medium. high) and additionally ranked the LLM outputs. All results are mean values of every participant and case conditioned on the model (and metric).

In each case, users were confronted with the raw cluster explainer rules (Definition 7) and DECLARE constraints to examine the verbalization of each LLM (Definition 8). DECLARE is the most commonly used constraint language in the context of declarative process mining [33]. It serves as an additional human evaluation baseline as it its capable of displaying temporal semantics, unlike our conjunctive rules [11].

Results. The results of our user study are organized as follows: First, we will provide evidence for each of the two tasks separately. Second, we will deduce general insights from the task results. We present our results in multiple formats: Tables present the user ratings wrt. each metric (Tables 3 and 4). Distribution plots further visualize the frequency of the user responses for each metric (Fig. 5) and heatmaps depict the user model preference ranking (Fig. 6).

Table 3. Single-cluster explanation results. Values represent mean user ratings or mean word count, averaged across participants and evaluated explanations.

model	soundness	fluency	completeness	context	length
Llama-70B	1.619	1.238	1.095	1.0	104.0 (±14.2)
Llama-8B	1.429	1.048	1.143	0.857	136.7 (±57.5)
gpt-4o	**1.714**	**1.429**	**1.286**	**1.048**	106.1 (±15.8)
gpt-4o-mini	1.667	1.333	1.095	0.952	**97.1** (±11.0)

Single-Cluster Explanation. GPT models and Llama-70B perform similarly in terms of the user attributed soundness on the single-cluster explanation task (Table 3). Llama-8B results are slightly lower. Comparable results arise for the reported fluency, even when generally on a lower performance level. Diverse

---
[5] https://data.4tu.nl/articles/dataset/Road_Traffic_Fine_Management_Process/12683249, 28 January 2025.

Table 4. Cluster comparison results. Values represent mean user ratings or mean word count, averaged across participants and evaluated explanations.

model	soundness	fluency	completeness	context	length
Llama-70B	1.571	1.048	0.810	0.619	**125.2** (±28.1)
Llama-8B	1.286	0.429	0.810	**0.905**	184.8 (±52.7)
gpt-4o	**1.619**	**1.238**	**1.143**	0.810	151.3 (±34.2)
gpt-4o-mini	1.571	1.000	0.905	0.857	148.6 (±34.9)

findings exist in terms of the completeness and context-awareness of the verbalizations with modest performance levels across LLMs. On average, Llama-8B verbalizations have a higher word count, hinting towards a negative correlation between output length and verbalization performance results. A graphical assessment provides one additional insight (Fig. 5a): All models except Llama-8B receive comparatively high soundness ratings, whereas the remaining metrics show diverse findings. Notably, users mostly agree on a mid-level completeness of gpt-4o-mini. In terms of model rankings, users, on average, tend to prefer gpt-4o verbalizations, while preferences among other models were less decisive, as illustrated by the heatmap (Fig. 6a).

Cluster Comparison. In terms of soundness and fluency of the verbalizations for the cluster comparison task, the GPT models and the larger Llama model are advantageous compared to LLama-8B (Table 4). The gpt-4o model is clearly beneficial regarding the verbalizations' completeness. The context awareness of all models is on a modest level. Interestingly, Llama-70B produces the briefest outputs, followed by the GPT models and LLama-8B, again having the top word count. The dispersion visualization of the user assessments revels a tendency to medium ratings with the GPT models performing sightly better in terms of soundness and a clear fluency drawback of LLama-8B (Fig. 5b). Regarding the users' model ranking (Fig. 6b), gpt-4o is superior and especially preferred over the Llama models.

General Findings. The user study results convey into three general findings:

(i) The `Llama-8B` model tends to underperform in the verbalization of explanations in the process mining domain across multiple tasks.
(ii) The flagship model `gpt-4o` yields the best-rated verbalizations and is ranked best among users.
(iii) Diverse findings arise for `Llama-70B` and `gpt-4o-mini`, illustrating that solid alternatives exist outside of the GPT model family and even current smaller models are capable of a profound performance.

6 Discussion

Summary and Conclusion. Our work demonstrates a GenAI-enhanced interactive process discovery framework that enhances cluster-based analysis with context-aware explanations. This approach showcases the synergy between modern LLMs and explainable clustering for process mining. In detail, we introduce an explainable clustering paradigm for event logs, bridging a gap between

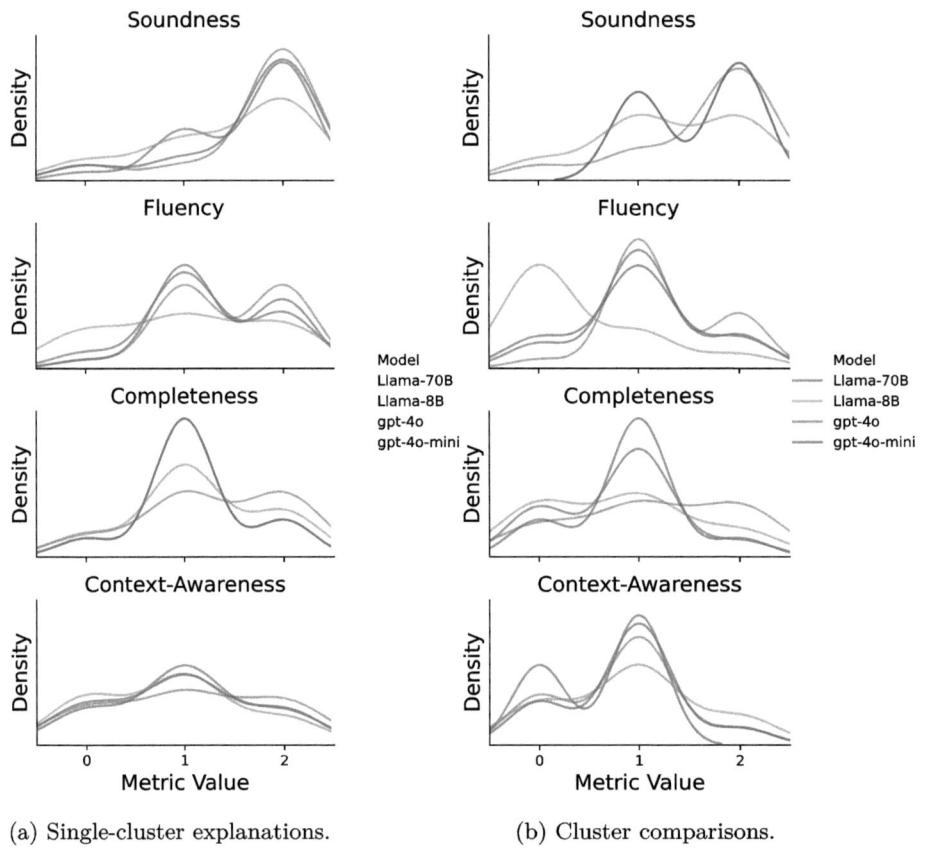

(a) Single-cluster explanations.   (b) Cluster comparisons.

Fig. 5. Densities for key evaluation metrics.

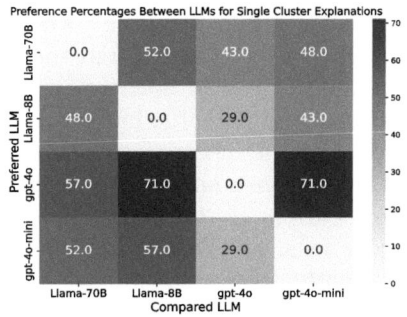
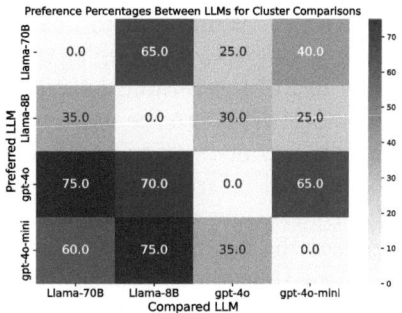

(a) Single-cluster explanations. (b) Cluster comparisons.

Fig. 6. User preference heatmaps, where each cell shows the percentage of user evaluations preferring the row model over the column model.

process mining and XAI (Algorithm 1). Additionally, we present a demonstrator that accounts for the target group shift from data scientists and ML experts to business analysts (Fig. 3). By combining descriptive statistics and natural language control flows, our front end empowers end users to dynamically investigate the underlying structures of process mining graphs. Finally, we evaluate the viability of LLM verbalizations of the derived cluster explanations in the process mining domain in a user study. The results indicate that some models, especially `gpt-4o`, are superior for explanation verbalizations compared to others (Figs. 6a and 6b). Notably, there exist well-performing, computationally cheaper alternatives, precisely `gpt-4o-mini`, hinting towards an optimal solution within the trade-off scale between computational costs and high-quality verbalizations (Tables 3 and 4).

Related Results. Our literature review (Sect. 2) leads us to the conclusion that this article presents the first method that accompanies XAI for clustering and LLM verbalizations in the process mining domain. To our knowledge, we present first approach with these properties explicitly aiming to be operated by users without ML expertise. Our work connects existing research, which all present significant advances in their respective fields: For instance, [16,21,39] all present promising solutions to reduce the complexity of process mining graphs. Other articles contain strategies to increase the expressiveness of XAI by transferring various explanation modalities into narrative explanations [29,37]. Our work provides insights into the performance of LLMs similar to research on diverse application domains. Examples include [35], who evaluate a prompt optimization strategy for news group analysis, or [44], who compare multiple multi-modal LLMs for downstream tasks such as image captioning.

Limitations. While our approach demonstrates a strong potential to deliver interactive and narrative explanations, several challenges remain: First, the verification of LLM-generated output is highly complex. Textual descriptions may not accurately capture the underlying explanations, and potential hallucinations could further contribute to misleading narratives. Second, incorporating substantial contextual information often entails high token consumption, which makes LLM verbalizations costly in practice. Third, our current clustering pipeline does not reflect the temporal semantics of the event logs, potentially missing critical information about process dynamics. Currently, we formalize background knowledge in structured JSON files; in the future, we plan to transition to formal ontologies, serving as a knowledge base in a RAG (Retrieval-Augmented Generation) approach alongside the LLM. Finally, our evaluation is restricted to a single event log, two tasks, seven participants, and the LLM verbalization's understandability rather than the base XAI rule quality, limiting the robustness of the quantitative results deduced from the user study.

Outlook. For future evaluations, we aim to expand our scope by exploring other event logs with all tasks and engaging a more diverse pool of participants. Furthermore, we plan to test other clustering algorithms and integrate additional explanation methods to enrich the toolkit and provide broader contextual insights for explaining cluster outcomes with LLMs. A key priority will be ensuring the reliability of LLM-generated text by verifying it against the original explainer outputs, thereby minimizing the risk of hallucinations and inaccuracies. Additionally, incorporating user domain knowledge could enhance contextual-awareness, when tailoring explanations to complex or specialized environments. Interactive clustering presents promising opportunities for users to refine clusters, filter out irrelevant instances, and iteratively adjust cluster boundaries. Relevant inspirations can be drawn from the supervised ML literature [23,38,40]. We anticipate that interactive workflows will enhance user engagement and contribute to more effective, context-aware, and explainable process mining. By integrating domain knowledge, interactivity, and diverse explanation modalities, we envision a more robust and flexible application of process mining in practice.

Acknowledgments. Funded by the Bavarian Ministry of Economic Affairs (BayVFP) under KIGA: DIK0313/02.

Ethical Considerations. Our study focuses on a methodological approach and does not involve the use of personal or sensitive data that would raise privacy or ethical concerns. As our analysis is centered on business processes, it remains purely technical and does not involve human subjects or personally identifiable information.

Disclosure of Interests. The authors have no competing interests to declare that are relevant to the content of this article.

References

1. van der Aalst, W.: Process Discovery: An Introduction, pp. 163–194. Springer, Heidelberg (2016). https://doi.org/10.1007/978-3-662-49851-4_6
2. van der Aalst, W.M.P.: On the pareto principle in process mining, task mining, and robotic process automation. In: Hammoudi, S., Quix, C., Bernardino, J. (eds.) Proceedings of the 9th International Conference on Data Science, Technology and Applications, DATA 2020, Lieusaint, Paris, France, 7–9 July 2020, pp. 5–12. SciTePress (2020)
3. van der Aalst, W.M.P.: Process mining: a 360 degree overview. In: van der Aalst, W.M.P., Carmona, J. (eds.) Process Mining Handbook. LNBIP, vol. 448, pp. 3–34. Springer (2022). https://doi.org/10.1007/978-3-031-08848-3_1
4. van der Aalst, W.M.P.: Object-centric process mining: unraveling the fabric of real processes. Mathematics **11**(12) (2023). https://doi.org/10.3390/math11122691
5. van der Aalst, W.M.P., Song, M.: Mining social networks: uncovering interaction patterns in business processes. In: Desel, J., Pernici, B., Weske, M. (eds.) Business Process Management: Second International Conference, BPM 2004, Potsdam, Germany, 17–18 June 2004. Proceedings. LNCS, vol. 3080, pp. 244–260. Springer (2004). https://doi.org/10.1007/978-3-540-25970-1_16
6. van der Aalst, W.M.P., Weijters, A.J.M.M.: Process mining: a research agenda. Comput. Ind. **53**(3), 231–244 (2004). https://doi.org/10.1016/J.COMPIND.2003.10.001
7. van der Aalst, W.M.P., Weijters, T., Maruster, L.: Workflow mining: discovering process models from event logs. IEEE Trans. Knowl. Data Eng. **16**(9), 1128–1142 (2004). https://doi.org/10.1109/TKDE.2004.47
8. van der Aalst, W.M.P., et al.: Process mining manifesto. In: Daniel, F., Barkaoui, K., Dustdar, S. (eds.) Business Process Management Workshops - BPM 2011 International Workshops, Clermont-Ferrand, France, 29 August 2011, Revised Selected Papers, Part I. LNBIP, vol. 99, pp. 169–194. Springer (2011). https://doi.org/10.1007/978-3-642-28108-2_19
9. van der Aalst, W.M.: Process mining: discovering and improving Spaghetti and Lasagna processes. In: 2011 IEEE Symposium on Computational Intelligence and Data Mining (CIDM), pp. 1–7 (2011). https://doi.org/10.1109/CIDM.2011.6129461
10. Adriansyah, A., Sidorova, N., van Dongen, B.F.: Cost-based fitness in conformance checking. In: Caillaud, B., Carmona, J., Hiraishi, K. (eds.) 11th International Conference on Application of Concurrency to System Design, ACSD 2011, Newcastle Upon Tyne, UK, 20–24 June 2011, pp. 57–66. IEEE Computer Society (2011). https://doi.org/10.1109/ACSD.2011.19
11. Amling, J., Scheele, S., Slany, E., Lang, M., Schmid, U.: Explainable AI for mixed data clustering. In: Longo, L., Lapuschkin, S., Seifert, C. (eds.) Explainable Artificial Intelligence - 2nd World Conference, xAI 2024, Valletta, Malta, 17–19 July 2024, Proceedings, Part II. CCIS, vol. 2154, pp. 42–62. Springer (2024). https://doi.org/10.1007/978-3-031-63797-1_3

12. Arya, V., et al.: One explanation does not fit all: a toolkit and taxonomy of AI explainability techniques (2019). https://doi.org/10.48550/arXiv.1909.03012
13. Berti, A., van Zelst, S.J., van der Aalst, W.M.P.: Process Mining for Python (PM4Py): bridging the gap between process- and data science (2019). http://arxiv.org/abs/1905.06169
14. Bertsimas, D., Orfanoudaki, A., Wiberg, H.M.: Interpretable clustering: an optimization approach. Mach. Learn. **110**(1), 89–138 (2021). https://doi.org/10.1007/S10994-020-05896-2
15. Bobek, S., Nalepa, G.J.: Local Universal Explainer (LUX) – a rule-based explainer with factual, counterfactual and visual explanations (2024). https://doi.org/10.48550/arXiv.2310.14894
16. Cadez, I.V., Heckerman, D., Meek, C., Smyth, P., White, S.: Model-based clustering and visualization of navigation patterns on a web site. Data Min. Knowl. Discov. **7**(4), 399–424 (2003). https://doi.org/10.1023/A:1024992613384
17. Cohen, J., Huan, X., Ni, J.: Shapley-based explainable AI for clustering applications in fault diagnosis and prognosis. J. Intell. Manuf. **35**(8), 4071–4086 (2024). https://doi.org/10.1007/S10845-024-02468-2
18. Evermann, J., Thaler, T., Fettke, P.: Clustering traces using sequence alignment. In: Reichert, M., Reijers, H.A. (eds.) Business Process Management Workshops - BPM 2015, 13th International Workshops, Innsbruck, Austria, 31 August–3 September 2015, Revised Papers. LNBIP, vol. 256, pp. 179–190. Springer (2015). https://doi.org/10.1007/978-3-319-42887-1_15
19. Gad-Elrab, M.H., Stepanova, D., Tran, T., Adel, H., Weikum, G.: ExCut: explainable embedding-based clustering over knowledge graphs. In: Pan, J.Z., et al. (eds.) The Semantic Web - ISWC 2020 - 19th International Semantic Web Conference, Athens, Greece, 2–6 November 2020, Proceedings, Part I. LNCS, vol. 12506, pp. 218–237. Springer (2020). https://doi.org/10.1007/978-3-030-62419-4_13
20. Ghahfarokhi, A.F., Akoochekian, F., Zandkarimi, F., van der Aalst, W.M.P.: Clustering object-centric event logs. In: Gusikhin, O., Hammoudi, S., Cuzzocrea, A. (eds.) Proceedings of the 12th International Conference on Data Science, Technology and Applications, DATA 2023, Rome, Italy, 11–13 July 2023, pp. 444–451. SCITEPRESS (2023). https://doi.org/10.5220/0012123900003541
21. Greco, G., Guzzo, A., Pontieri, L., Saccà, D.: Discovering expressive process models by clustering log traces. IEEE Trans. Knowl. Data Eng. **18**(8), 1010–1027 (2006). https://doi.org/10.1109/TKDE.2006.123
22. Guidotti, R., Monreale, A., Ruggieri, S., Pedreschi, D., Turini, F., Giannotti, F.: Local rule-based explanations of black box decision systems (2018). https://doi.org/10.48550/arXiv.1805.10820
23. Heidrich, L., Slany, E., Scheele, S., Schmid, U.: FairCaipi: a combination of explanatory interactive and fair machine learning for human and machine bias reduction. Mach. Learn. Knowl. Extr. **5**(4), 1519–1538 (2023). https://doi.org/10.3390/make5040076
24. Koschmider, A., et al.: Process mining for unstructured data: challenges and research directions. In: Michael, J., Weske, M. (eds.) Modellierung 2024, Potsdam, Germany, 12–15 March 2024. LNI, vol. P-348, pp. 119–136. Gesellschaft für Informatik e.V. (2024). https://doi.org/10.18420/MODELLIERUNG2024_012

25. Leemans, S.J.J., Fahland, D., van der Aalst, W.M.P.: Scalable process discovery with guarantees. In: Gaaloul, K., Schmidt, R., Nurcan, S., Guerreiro, S., Ma, Q. (eds.) Enterprise, Business-Process and Information Systems Modeling - 16th International Conference, BPMDS 2015, 20th International Conference, EMMSAD 2015, Held at CAiSE 2015, Stockholm, Sweden, 8–9 June 2015, Proceedings. LNBIP, vol. 214, pp. 85–101. Springer (2015). https://doi.org/10.1007/978-3-319-19237-6_6
26. MacKay, D.J.C.: Information Theory, Inference, and Learning Algorithms. Cambridge University Press (2003). https://doi.org/10.1017/s026357470426043x
27. Madhulatha, T.S.: An overview on clustering methods (2012). https://doi.org/10.48550/arXiv.1205.1117
28. Marin-Castro, H.M., Tello-Leal, E.: Event log preprocessing for process mining: a review. Appl. Sci. **11**(22) (2021). https://doi.org/10.3390/app112210556
29. Mavrepis, P., Makridis, G., Fatouros, G., Koukos, V., Separdani, M.M., Kyriazis, D.: XAI for all: can large language models simplify explainable AI? (2024). https://doi.org/10.48550/arXiv.2401.13110
30. McInnes, L., Healy, J., Astels, S.: hdbscan: hierarchical density based clustering. J. Open Source Softw. **2**(11), 205 (2017). https://doi.org/10.21105/JOSS.00205
31. Morichetta, A., Casas, P., Mellia, M.: EXPLAIN-IT: towards explainable AI for unsupervised network traffic analysis. In: Proceedings of the 3rd ACM CoNEXT Workshop on Big DAta, Machine Learning and Artificial Intelligence for Data Communication Networks, Big-DAMA@CoNEXT 2019, Orlando, FL, USA, 9 December 2019, pp. 22–28. ACM (2019). https://doi.org/10.1145/3359992.3366639
32. Nguyen, P., Slominski, A., Muthusamy, V., Ishakian, V., Nahrstedt, K.: Process trace clustering: a heterogeneous information network approach. In: Venkatasubramanian, S.C., Jr., Wagner, M., Jr. (eds.) Proceedings of the 2016 SIAM International Conference on Data Mining, Miami, Florida, USA, 5–7 May 2016, pp. 279–287. SIAM (2016). https://doi.org/10.1137/1.9781611974348.32
33. Pesic, M., Schonenberg, H., van der Aalst, W.M.P.: DECLARE: full support for loosely-structured processes. In: 11th IEEE International Enterprise Distributed Object Computing Conference, EDOC 2007, 15–19 October 2007, Annapolis, Maryland, USA, pp. 287–300. IEEE Computer Society (2007). https://doi.org/10.1109/EDOC.2007.14
34. Raedt, L.D., Blockeel, H.: Using logical decision trees for clustering. In: Lavrac, N., Dzeroski, S. (eds.) Inductive Logic Programming, 7th International Workshop, ILP-97, Prague, Czech Republic, 17–20 September 1997, Proceedings. LNCS, vol. 1297, pp. 133–140. Springer (1997). https://doi.org/10.1007/3540635149_41
35. Resendiz, Y.M., Klinger, R.: MOPO: multi-objective prompt optimization for affective text generation. In: Rambow, O., Wanner, L., Apidianaki, M., Al-Khalifa, H., Eugenio, B.D., Schockaert, S. (eds.) Proceedings of the 31st International Conference on Computational Linguistics, COLING 2025, Abu Dhabi, UAE, 19–24 January 2025, pp. 5588–5606. Association for Computational Linguistics (2025). https://aclanthology.org/2025.coling-main.375/
36. Schallner, L., Rabold, J., Scholz, O., Schmid, U.: Effect of superpixel aggregation on explanations in LIME - a case study with biological data. In: Cellier, P., Driessens, K. (eds.) Machine Learning and Knowledge Discovery in Databases - International Workshops of ECML PKDD 2019, Würzburg, Germany, 16–20 September 2019, Proceedings, Part I. CCIS, vol. 1167, pp. 147–158. Springer (2019). https://doi.org/10.1007/978-3-030-43823-4_13

37. Schneider, J.: Explainable generative AI (GenXAI): a survey, conceptualization, and research agenda. Artif. Intell. Rev. **57**(11), 289 (2024). https://doi.org/10.1007/S10462-024-10916-X
38. Slany, E., Scheele, S., Schmid, U.: Bayesian CAIPI: a probabilistic approach to explanatory and interactive machine learning. In: Nowaczyk, S., et al. (eds.) Artificial Intelligence, ECAI 2023 International Workshops, pp. 285–301. Springer, Cham (2024). https://doi.org/10.1007/978-3-031-50396-2_16
39. Song, M., Günther, C.W., van der Aalst, W.M.P.: Trace clustering in process mining. In: Ardagna, D., Mecella, M., Yang, J. (eds.) Business Process Management Workshops, BPM 2008 International Workshops, Milano, Italy, 1–4 September 2008. Revised Papers. LNBIP, vol. 17, pp. 109–120. Springer (2008). https://doi.org/10.1007/978-3-642-00328-8_11
40. Teso, S., Kersting, K.: Explanatory interactive machine learning. In: Conitzer, V., Hadfield, G.K., Vallor, S. (eds.) Proceedings of the 2019 AAAI/ACM Conference on AI, Ethics, and Society, AIES 2019, Honolulu, HI, USA, 27–28 January 2019, pp. 239–245. ACM (2019). https://doi.org/10.1145/3306618.3314293
41. Veiga, G.M., Ferreira, D.R.: Understanding spaghetti models with sequence clustering for ProM. In: Rinderle-Ma, S., Sadiq, S., Leymann, F. (eds.) Business Process Management Workshops, BPM 2009 International Workshops, Ulm, Germany, 7 September 2009. Revised Papers. LNBIP, vol. 43, pp. 92–103. Springer (2009). https://doi.org/10.1007/978-3-642-12186-9_10
42. Weerdt, J.D., vanden Broucke, S.K.L.M., Vanthienen, J., Baesens, B.: Active trace clustering for improved process discovery. IEEE Trans. Knowl. Data Eng. **25**(12), 2708–2720 (2013). https://doi.org/10.1109/TKDE.2013.64
43. van Zelst, S.J., Cao, Y.: A generic framework for attribute-driven hierarchical trace clustering. In: del-Río-Ortega, A., Leopold, H., Santoro, F.M. (eds.) Business Process Management Workshops - BPM 2020 International Workshops, Seville, Spain, 13–18 September 2020, Revised Selected Papers. LNBIP, vol. 397, pp. 308–320. Springer (2020). https://doi.org/10.1007/978-3-030-66498-5_23
44. Zhang, D., et al.: MM-LLMs: recent advances in multimodal large language models. In: Ku, L., Martins, A., Srikumar, V. (eds.) Findings of the Association for Computational Linguistics, ACL 2024, Bangkok, Thailand and virtual meeting, 11–16 August 2024, pp. 12401–12430. Association for Computational Linguistics (2024). https://doi.org/10.18653/V1/2024.FINDINGS-ACL.738
45. Zytek, A., Pidò, S., Veeramachaneni, K.: LLMs for XAI: future Directions for Explaining Explanations (2024). https://doi.org/10.48550/arXiv.2405.06064

Open Access This chapter is licensed under the terms of the Creative Commons Attribution 4.0 International License (http://creativecommons.org/licenses/by/4.0/), which permits use, sharing, adaptation, distribution and reproduction in any medium or format, as long as you give appropriate credit to the original author(s) and the source, provide a link to the Creative Commons license and indicate if changes were made.

The images or other third party material in this chapter are included in the chapter's Creative Commons license, unless indicated otherwise in a credit line to the material. If material is not included in the chapter's Creative Commons license and your intended use is not permitted by statutory regulation or exceeds the permitted use, you will need to obtain permission directly from the copyright holder.

Balancing Fairness and Interpretability in Clustering with FairParTree

Cristiano Landi[1(✉)] , Alessio Cascione[1] , Marta Marchiori Manerba[1] , and Riccardo Guidotti[1,2]

[1] University of Pisa, Pisa, Italy
{cristiano.landi,alessio.cascione,marchiori.manerba}@phd.unipi.it,
{cristiano.landi,alessio.cascione,marchiori.manerba}@di.unipi.it
[2] ISTI-CNR Pisa, Pisa, Italy
riccardo.guidotti@isti.cnr.it

Abstract. The revolution involving Machine Learning has transformed data analytics, making algorithms important in decision-making processes across various domains, even in sensitive scenarios. Indeed, traditional clustering algorithms often lack interpretability and exhibit biases, leading to discriminatory practices and opaque decision-making. To overcome these limitations, we introduce FairParTree, a fair and interpretable clustering algorithm that integrates fairness constraints directly into the clustering process, ensuring that the resulting clusters do not disproportionately disadvantage any particular group. By leveraging the structure of decision trees, FairParTree enhances the interpretability of clustering results by providing clear and understandable motivations for cluster assignments through rule-based explanations. We evaluate FairParTree against state-of-the-art competitors. Through extensive experiments, we show that it maintains strong performances w.r.t. fairness, interpretability, and clustering quality across different dataset sizes, thus positioning itself as a competitive, fair, and interpretable clustering algorithm.

Keywords: Ethical ML · Fair Clustering · Interpretable Clustering

1 Introduction

Recent advancements in Machine Learning (ML) have significantly transformed various domains, enabling algorithms to analyze complex data and playing a crucial role in high-stakes decision-making scenarios and, therefore, in our day-to-day lives [41]. However, concerns about fairness have emerged, particularly in applications where data-driven grouping can inadvertently reinforce biases [6,18]. When learning from biased data, clustering methods may lead to unfair partitions, disproportionately affecting certain groups and amplifying existing disparities. This issue is critical in sensitive real-world contexts such as resource allocation, hiring, recommendation systems, and medical research, where unintended biases in grouping have serious consequences that must be avoided [15].

Moreover, models' increasing complexity has rendered them less interpretable, devising black box systems where developers and end-users can not understand and, hence, trust the automated decisions returned [4]. Comprehending how choices are made is critical in evaluating ML from an ethical stance.

Most literature is focused and limited to supervised settings [33]. Recently, the ML community began addressing these concerns for unsupervised tasks like clustering algorithms [15]. Embedding fairness in clustering is crucial as these algorithms are employed in critical applications such as loan approvals, hiring processes, and personalized marketing. As biased classification algorithms, unfair clustering algorithms result in discrimination: biased clusters can mirror and reinforce existing societal inequalities, leading to systematic disparate treatment favoring individuals from certain demographics over others [8].

Another strong limitation of clustering algorithms is their lack of interpretability [26]. While the growing interest in eXplainable Artificial Intelligence (XAI) has led to the development of numerous methods to explain supervised learning approaches, the explainability of unsupervised learning algorithms remains an open challenge [16]. In particular, traditional clustering methods do not provide an intuitive understanding of the criteria used for data assignment and, therefore, the underlying logic behind their partitioning [26]. For instance, the centroids employed by k-Means to define different groups may become ineffective when dealing with many features or when centroid values are too similar. Likewise, dendrograms express the distance at which clusters were merged but do not explain the reasoning behind the joining [26]. Indeed, the difficulty in interpreting the obtained results reduces model transparency and decreases user trust in automated decisions. Moreover, a systematic integration of fairness and interpretability is still missing. This gap highlights the need for novel methodologies that ensure clustering models are both fair and interpretable, making them more reliable, transparent, and trustworthy.

Aiming to bridge the gap between fairness and interpretability in clustering, we present FairParTree (FPT), a fair and interpretable clustering algorithm. To ensure fairness, we incorporate the usage of fairness measures by design, i.e., directly into the clustering process, to guarantee that the resulting groups do not disproportionately disadvantage any protected attribute such as gender or age. In particular, we enforce fairness by constraining the goodness score of each split by adopting and adapting two well-established clustering fairness measures, namely *Balance* [17] and *Max Fairness Cost* [16]. Furthermore, drawing inspiration from privacy-preserving frameworks, we introduce a novel measure, (k, l, t)-*Fairness* [36]. Thus, FairParTree leverages one of the three previously mentioned fairness measures to evaluate the impact of a fairness penalty on decision splits. By making unfair splits more costly, it encourages the selection of fairer alternatives. Furthermore, FairParTree ensures interpretability by extending ParTree [26], a hierarchal partitioning tree-based clustering approach. As ParTree, FairParTree addresses the interpretability limitations of traditional fair clustering algorithms through the structure of decision trees, offering clear cluster assignments and providing users with a transparent view of the clustering process. Specifically, each decision node within the tree represents a logical and straightforward condition, allowing users to understand the rationale behind each decision.

Through extensive experiments on several datasets, FairParTree is compared against state-of-the-art algorithms adopting three evaluation profiles: clustering quality, interpretability, and fairness. Competitors with whom we compare our method reflect these three dimensions: traditional clustering algorithms, interpretable clustering algorithms, and fair clustering algorithms. Overall, FairParTree achieved state-of-the-art performance in all three evaluations, thus positioning itself as a competitive, interpretable, and fair clustering algorithm. Specifically, regarding fairness evaluation measures, FairParTree is on par and at times outperforms state-of-the-art competitors. Moreover, when analyzing the number of conditions required to describe all clusters, FairParTree is effective in terms of interpretability, generating comparatively easier-to-interpret results.

In summary, the contributions of this work are the following: *(i)* fairness-aware clustering integrating fairness penalties in the clustering process; *(ii)* novel measure to assess clustering process fairness based on insights from the privacy domain; *(i)* combination of fairness and interpretability through a practical solution that mitigates bias while ensuring transparency; *(iv)* comprehensive evaluation of FairParTree's performance across fairness, interpretability, and clustering quality against state-of-the-art methods.

The remainder of the paper is structured as follows. In Sect. 2, we report a critical review of state-of-the-art frameworks and solutions from the interpretable and fair clustering domain, specifically discussing interpretable tree-based methods, fairness measures, and approaches that incorporate fairness constraints into the clustering process. Section 3 frames the fair clustering problem and provides the necessary technical background describing ParTree, the building block of our framework. The main contribution, FairParTree, is detailed in Sect. 4, where we formalize the fairness measures, introduce the penalization term, and present how they are leveraged to achieve a fair and interpretable partitioning split. The experimental results, together with the technical setup and the datasets used, are reported in Sect. 5. Finally, Sect. 6 illiterates future research directions.

2 Related Work

Driven by the need to improve process equity and transparency, interpretable and fair clustering focuses on designing algorithms that offer insights into their decision-making processes, prioritizing fair and auditable outcomes without compromising the results' integrity. In the following, we present key developments in interpretable and fair clustering, discussing interpretability methods, fairness measures, and techniques that integrate fairness constraints into clustering.

Aiming to provide insights into how data is grouped, techniques such as DReaM [13], IMM [34], ExKMC [23], and TASC [14] increase transparency by employing decision trees or rule-based partitioning to visualize clustering rationale. Indeed, recent developments in tree-based clustering methods have introduced frameworks that balance efficiency and transparency. Among these approaches, the TIC algorithm [10] adopts specific distance measures as splitting criteria, while the CLTREE [30] leverages synthetic points to mimic data's natural distribution. Solutions like CUBT [22] focus instead on minimizing description length or using Mixed Integer Optimization [9] to produce optimal clustering trees. Moreover, ParTree is a tree-based clustering method that employs a recursive, top-down strategy and provides interpretable results. Indeed, we adopt ParTree as the building block of our proposal since it is the most performative algorithm among tree-based approaches, as demonstrated by experiments conducted in [26]. Unlike the previously mentioned approaches, our proposal contributes to the interpretable clustering field by simultaneously ensuring fairness and interpretability through its hierarchical tree structure. Notably, it stands out by directly integrating fairness penalties into its interpretable clustering process, ensuring equitable representation without compromising transparency.

Despite advancements in interpretable ML, the methods discussed largely overlook fairness constraints, which are crucial in many real-world applications. This gap motivates the exploration of fair clustering techniques, which we discuss in the following. In [24], the complexity of selecting appropriate fairness measures is emphasized, particularly regarding clustering algorithms due to the inherent trade-offs among these measures when base rates vary across groups. Indeed, no fairness measure is universally optimal for clustering, urging a balanced approach based on specific dataset characteristics and clustering goals. Moreover, how these measures are formalized varies greatly across the literature. For instance, fairness in clustering is discussed in [15] by examining group-level and individual-level fairness notions, categorizing approaches based on the timing of fairness consideration— whether before, during, or after the clustering process.

Given the diversity of fairness definitions and their implications in clustering, different algorithmic strategies have been proposed to embed fairness constraints at various stages of the clustering process. Following the framing proposed in [15], the techniques are categorized into pre-processing, in-processing, and post-processing, each targeting bias at different stages of the algorithmic life cycle to promote equitable treatment across diverse groups. Among these, in-processing techniques offer a direct means of balancing fairness and clustering objectives, as they modify the core clustering procedure to respect fairness constraints inherently. Since our proposal belongs to this category, in the following we focus the discussion on this specific family of strategies. Among widely adopted approaches, the Variational Fair Clustering (VFC) method [42] optimizes the trade-off between the clustering objective and a Kullback-Leibler fairness penalty term, which measures the divergence between the required and achieved proportions of the protected group within the clusters by tuning a specific hyperparameter λ. Differently, Fair Round-Robin Algorithm for Clustering (FRAC) [27] solves a fair assignment problem at each iteration of a standard clustering algorithm, rearranging the data points to ensure τ-ratio fairness. In this context, τ is a vector where each component represents the required fraction of data points from each protected attribute value in each cluster. In the experimental evaluation, we adopt VFC and FRAC as benchmarks for FairParTree. While both seek to balance fairness constraints within the clustering process, they do not account for interpretability aspects. In contrast, our proposal is designed to simultaneously ensure fairness by maintaining a fair distribution of instances and transparency by leveraging a hierarchical tree structure. This dual objective distinguishes it from other in-processing techniques.

Among other latest trends, the Fair Tree Classifier and the Splitting Criterion AUC for Fairness (SCAFF) were introduced in [2] and [7], respectively. The Fair Tree Classifier stands out for its novel integration of threshold-free demographic parity with ROC-AUC optimization, facilitating the inclusion of multiple, multicategorical, or intersectional protected attributes. FairKM consists of an adaptation of the K-MEANS algorithm that integrates a fairness term into the objective function of clustering, ensuring that protected attributes are represented fairly within each cluster [3]. Similarly, in [25], the focus is on mitigating potential biases in K-MEANS through Fair-Lloyd, a modified version of Lloyd's heuristic. Finally, in [1], fairness notions in classification, such as demographic parity and equal opportunity, are revisited.

In conclusion, unlike methods that adjust fairness post-hoc or preprocess data to mitigate bias, FairParTree enforces fairness constraints inherently within its clustering logic. By embedding these constraints into the tree construction through its penalty mechanism, FairParTree provides a novel, fair, and interpretable framework, setting itself apart from conventional approaches.

3 Setting the Stage

In the following, we first define the clustering and the fair clustering problems. Then, we provide an overview of ParTree (PT) [26], highlighting the key concepts and methodologies essential for understanding our proposal.

3.1 Fair Clustering Problem

Solving a clustering problem consists of partitioning a set of instances into subsets, or clusters, such that similar instances are grouped together. More formally:

Definition 1 (Clustering Problem). *Given a dataset X, the clustering problem consists in finding a partitioning function Ψ that assigns instances to a set of k disjoint subsets, or clusters, $\mathcal{C} = \{C_1, \ldots, C_k\}$, such that:*

$$X = \bigcup_{i=1}^{k} C_i, \quad \text{where} \quad C_i \cap C_j = \emptyset \quad \forall \, i \neq j.$$

Additionally, the resulting partition $\mathcal{C}$ should minimize a given clustering cost function $\mathcal{J}$, which quantifies the quality of the clustering in terms of compactness and separation. Formally, we would like to find a clustering function Ψ such that:

$$\arg\min_{\Psi} \mathcal{J}(\mathcal{C}).$$

The cost function $\mathcal{J}$ varies with the kind of clustering method used, and different approaches can be considered, as discussed in [20].

The fair clustering problem builds on the above problem by considering also the distribution of protected attributes within the instances grouped in the same clusters. Specifically, the clustering result is considered valid if the level of unfairness is minimized according to a fairness measure ϕ. More formally:

Definition 2 (Fair Clustering Problem). *Given a dataset X and a protected attribute $\mathcal{A}$ with possible values $\mathcal{A} = \{a_1, \ldots, a_q\}$, the objective is to find a partitioning function Ψ^* that assigns instances to a set of k clusters $\mathcal{C} = \{C_1, \ldots, C_k\}$, minimizing a clustering cost function $\mathcal{J}$ while simultaneously ensuring fairness in the distribution of protected attribute values across the clusters. Formally:*

$$\arg\min_{\Psi^*} \mathcal{J}(\mathcal{C}) + \lambda \sum_{i=1}^{k} \phi(C_i, \mathcal{A}),$$

where $\mathcal{J}$ is the chosen clustering cost function, quantifying the quality of the clustering, and $\phi(C_i, \mathcal{A})$ is a fairness violation function that quantifies the disparity in the distribution of protected attribute values within each cluster C_i. The fairness penalty measure is designed such that the resulting clusters exhibit a fair distribution of protected attribute values. The parameter λ controls the clustering quality and fairness trade-off.

After summarizing ParTree (PT), we present FairParTree, our proposed solution to the *Fair Clustering Problem* which instantiates the desired clustering function Ψ^* and can be combined with a variety of fairness penalty measures.

3.2 Interpretable Partitioning Tree Clustering Algorithm

Since our proposal builds upon ParTree (PT) [26], we provide a brief summary of the essential background to ensure the contribution is self-contained and easily understandable. PT is a tree-based clustering method solving the clustering problem that produces interpretable clustering results without accounting for fairness. It leverages a recursive, top-down strategy, starting from the entire dataset and progressively partitioning it into smaller clusters.

As illustrated in Algorithm 1, PT starts by initializing an empty set of clusters $\mathcal{C}$ (line 1) and creating the root of the tree $\mathscr{R}$ (line 2), which contains the entire dataset X. Then $\mathcal{C}$ and $\mathscr{R}$ are pushed into a priority queue $\mathcal{Q}$ (line 3), where the cluster size determines the priority of each element. The queue $\mathcal{Q}$ stores clusters that are candidates for further splitting. PT iteratively extracts the cluster with the highest priority C and its corresponding tree node $\mathscr{N}$ from the queue $\mathcal{Q}$ (line 4–5). If the current cluster C is too small or the node $\mathscr{N}$ has reached a specified maximum depth (line 6), the node is converted into a leaf (line 7), and the cluster C is added to the final clustering result $\mathcal{C}$. If the cluster does not meet any of the previous halting conditions, then the algorithm selects

Algorithm 1: PartitionTree(X, $max\_clusters$, max_depth, min_sample, ε)

Input : X - dataset, $max\_clusters$ - max number of clusters, max_depth - max tree depth, min_sample - min cluster size, ε - percentage of BIC parent discount
Param : qs - queue score function
Output: $\mathcal{C}$ - clustering, R - clustering tree

1 $\mathcal{C} \leftarrow \emptyset$;   // init. clustering result
2 $\mathscr{R} \leftarrow \text{make\_node}(X)$;   // init. tree root
3 $\mathcal{Q} \leftarrow push(\overline{\mathcal{Q}}, \text{qs}(X), \langle X, \mathscr{R} \rangle)$;   // init. priority queue
4 **while** $|\mathcal{Q}| > 0 \wedge |\mathcal{C}| + |\mathcal{Q}| < max\_clusters$ **do**
5 $\quad \langle C, \mathcal{N} \rangle \leftarrow pop(\mathcal{Q})$;   // extract tree node from queue
6 $\quad$ **if** $|C| < min\_sample \vee depth(\mathcal{N}) > max\_depth$ **then**
7 $\quad\quad \mathcal{C} \leftarrow \mathcal{C} \cup \{C\}$; $\mathscr{L} \leftarrow \text{make\_leaf}(\mathcal{N})$; // add cluster and make leaf
8 $\quad\quad$ **continue**;
9 $\quad f, C_1, C_2 \leftarrow \text{make\_split}(C)$ // make split
10 $\quad$ **if** $bic(C) < bic([\overline{C_1}, C_2]) - \varepsilon |bic(C)|$ **then**
11 $\quad\quad \mathcal{C} \leftarrow \mathcal{C} \cup \{C\}$; $\mathscr{L} \leftarrow \text{make\_leaf}(\mathcal{N})$; // add cluster and make leaf
12 $\quad\quad$ **continue**;
13 $\quad \mathcal{N}_l \leftarrow \text{make\_node}(C_1)$; $\mathcal{N}_r \leftarrow \text{make\_node}(C_2)$; // make left and right node
14 $\quad \mathcal{N} \leftarrow \text{update\_node}(f, \mathcal{N}_l, \mathcal{N}_r)$ // update tree
15 $\quad \mathcal{Q} \leftarrow push(\mathcal{Q}, \text{qs}(C_1), \langle C_1, \mathcal{N}_l \rangle)$; $\mathcal{Q} \leftarrow push(\mathcal{Q}, \text{qs}(C_2), \langle C_2, \mathcal{N}_r \rangle)$; // update queue
16 **while** $|\mathcal{Q}| > 0$ **do**
17 $\quad \langle C, \mathcal{N} \rangle \leftarrow pop(\mathcal{Q})$;   // extract tree node from queue
18 $\quad \mathcal{C} \leftarrow \mathcal{C} \cup \{C\}$; $\mathscr{L} \leftarrow \text{make\_leaf}(\mathcal{N})$; // add cluster and make leaf
19 **return** $\mathcal{C}, \mathscr{R}$;

the best univariate splitting threshold (line 9). The split quality is evaluated using the Bayesian Information Criterion (BIC) [37]. If the split improves the clustering, i.e., the BIC of the two resulting clusters is better than the original cluster minus a small adjustment factor ε, the split is accepted, and the two new clusters are added to the queue for further processing (lines 10–12). Otherwise, the cluster C is added to the final clustering result $\mathcal{C}$ (lines 13–15). The factor ε adjusts the sensibility to minor improvements. It continues partitioning until either the maximum number of clusters or the maximum depth is reached or no further beneficial splits can be made according to the BIC criterion. Then, the clusters remaining in the queue are transformed into leaves (lines 16–18). Finally, it returns the clustering $\mathcal{C}$ and the corresponding binary tree $\mathscr{R}$, which provides an interpretable representation of the data partitioning logic (line 19).

To find the best split (line 9), PT implements three splitting strategies [26]:

- *Center-based Split*: similar to K-MEANS algorithm [39], the best split is the one that minimizes the Mean Squared Error (MSE) relative to centroids;
- *Impurity-based Split*: it utilizes an impurity measure, like Entropy, to optimize impurity reduction across all features;
- *Principal Component-based Split*: it employs dimensionality reduction techniques to find the best axis-parallel split.

Among the three variants for finding the best split, in [26] is experimentally shown that principal component-based splitting achieves the best performance. Using the principal component methods is based on the intuition that the resulting principal components are orthogonal to each other and capture as much variance as possible through a dimensionality reduction algorithm. Furthermore, the principal component-based splitting can be easily adapted to different types

Algorithm 2: make_split_PC(X)

Input   : X - dataset
Param : $nbr\_components$ - number of components
Output: f - binary partitioning function, C_1, C_2 - cluster partitions

1 $j^* \leftarrow \infty; bs^* \leftarrow \infty;$ // init. split function and best score
2 $A \leftarrow get\_PCA(X, nbr\_components));$ // calculate PCA
3 **for** $j \in [\overline{1}, nbr\_components]$ **do**   // for every principal component
4      $f, bs \leftarrow train\_tree\_regressor(X, A^{(j)});$ // build data partitioner
5   **if** $bs < bs^*$ **then**   // if better partitioning
6          $j^* \leftarrow j; bs^* \leftarrow bs;$ // update split function and best score
7 $f, bs \leftarrow train\_tree\_regressor(X, A^{(j^*)});$ // build data partitioner
8 $C_1, C_2 \leftarrow split\_data(f, X);$ // make binary partition
9 **return** $f, C_1, \overline{C_2};$

of data using Principal Component Analysis (PCA) for continuous variables, Multiple Correspondence Analysis (MCA) for categorical variables, and Factor Analysis of Mixed Data (FAMD) for mixed data [26]. Consequently, we adopt this variant in our extension to include fairness.

Algorithm 2 outlines the principal component-based splitting process. It begins by applying a dimensionality reduction method – selected from the three aforementioned approaches based on the data type – to produce a reduced representation A (line 2). Then, for each principal component $A^{(j)}$ (line 3), the algorithm trains a shallow decision tree regressor f to identify the axis-parallel split along X that best predicts the principal component $A^{(j)}$ of analyzed data (line 4). If a score bs better than the current best score bs^* is found, the algorithm updates the best splitting function and the corresponding score (lines 5–6). Finally, it returns the optimal splitting function and the resulting partitioned clusters. Notably, while the original ParTree implementation uses the BIC score [26], we adopt a modified score – detailed in the next section – that considers both fairness and the quality of the principal component prediction used as the target variable.

In Algorithm 2, lines 4 and 7 are highlighted in blue to emphasize the primary modifications to the *train_tree_regressor* function introduced by the FairParTree extension. This function, further detailed in Algorithm 3, has been enhanced to select the optimal splitting feature for separating a given principal component while incorporating a fairness penalty to promote fair clustering. Additionally, it returns the score used, which simultaneously considers both information gain and the fairness penalty.

4 FairParTree

We now introduce FairParTree (FPT), a clustering algorithm that integrates fairness constraints into the (modified) ParTree framework presented previously. In the following, we first present the measures used to evaluate clustering algorithms' fairness. Then, we show how these measures can be incorporated into PARTREE to account for fairness when evaluating the best splitting condition.

4.1 Evaluating Fair Partitioning Splits

To implement FPT, we construct the fair and interpretable partitioning split on top of the principal component-based split, as this variant has been experimentally proven to be the most efficient and effective [26]. Once the principal components are computed, they are used as the target variable for a decision tree regressor to build a shallow tree with a single split on the dataset features, identifying the optimal split for their prediction. At each node of the decision tree, the best split is determined by the feature-threshold pair that maximizes information gain. The core idea behind FPT is to integrate fairness by penalizing the information gain of splits where the resulting child nodes exhibit bias with respect to the protected attribute. This approach discourages the formation of unfair clusters while allowing a balance between clustering quality and fairness.

In the following, we formalize and introduce three splitting penalties. We start the discussion by highlighting how the three measures are mutually exclusive. Indeed, fairness notions are often application-specific, and a particular definition might be preferable in certain settings compared to others. For instance, in some contexts, ensuring proportionality may be more effective than achieving balance, and vice-versa [16]. Most importantly, optimizing one definition often undermines the other, making adopting them simultaneously or in combination impractical. Therefore, since no single measure can universally apply across all scenarios, in FPT we let the user choose which measures to embed with respect to the current context while ruling out the others. Specifically, to constrain the goodness score of each split, we implement two well-known clustering fairness measures, namely *Balance* [17] and *Max Fairness Cost* [16]. Additionally, inspired by frameworks used in the privacy domain, we propose the *(k,l,t)-Fairness* penalization. This approach allows users to define fairness with finer granularity during clustering by adapting concepts from *k-anonymity* [38], *l-diversity* [31], and *t-closeness* [29].

Balance. Proposed in [17], given a dataset X, a set of clusters $\mathcal{C} = \{C_1, \ldots, C_k\}$, and a set of protected attribute values $\mathcal{A} = \{a_1, \ldots, a_m\}$, the *Balance* quantifies the fairness of the distribution of protected attribute values across clusters as:

$$Balance(\mathcal{C}, \mathcal{A}) = \min_{C \in \mathcal{C}, a_i \in \mathcal{A}} \min \left\{ \frac{Pr^{a_i}}{Pr^{a_i}_C}, \frac{Pr^{a_i}_C}{Pr^{a_i}} \right\}$$

where $Pr^{a_i}_C$ represents the proportion of protected attribute value a_i in cluster C, while Pr^{a_i} is the proportion of protected attribute value a_i in the dataset X. The balance lies between 0 and 1: the higher the value, the fairer the cluster. The penalization term is measured as *imbalance* and computed as $1 - Balance(\mathcal{C}, \mathcal{A})$.

Max Fairness Cost. The *Max Fairness Cost (MFC)* [16] measures the distance between the proportion of protected attribute values within each cluster and the ideal proportion provided as input by the user. The lower the *MFC* value, the fairer the clusters. Formally, given I^{a_i} as the ideal proportion of protected attribute value a_i within each cluster, MFC is computed as follows:

$$MFC(\mathcal{C}, \mathcal{A}) = \max_{C \in \mathcal{C}} \frac{1}{q} \sum_{a_i \in \mathcal{A}} |Pr_C^{a_i} - I^{a_i}|$$

For our purposes, for each value a_i of the protected attribute, the ideal proportion I^{a_i} is defined as the proportion of instances in the dataset X where the protected attribute takes the value a_i.

(k, l, t)-Fairness. In the following, we propose a novel penalization measure based on privacy framings. Within privacy, the research community formalizes various measures to assess the privacy properties of a set of data. We propose a new fairness penalization measure inspired by concepts of *k-anonymity*, *l-diversity*, and *t-closeness*. The first property, *k-anonymity*, measures how an individual's data can not be distinguished from at least $k - 1$ other individuals within the dataset, ensuring basic anonymity, primarily by transforming quasi-identifiers. *l-diversity* enhances this aspect by requiring that each group of indistinguishable records contains at least l well-represented, diverse, protected attributes, reducing the risk of attribute disclosure. Finally, *t-closeness* further strengthens privacy by ensuring that the distribution of protected attributes within any group is close to the distribution in the entire dataset, thus limiting information leakage even when diversity exists [36]. In the following, we detail our novel declination of these properties for the fairness clustering task.

k-Fairness. A dataset X respects the k-anonymity property if the information for each individual can not be distinguished from at least $k - 1$, where $k \in \mathbb{N}$, individuals whose information also appears in the dataset X. We reformulate this property for cluster fairness as follows: for each protected attribute value a_i, the k-Fairness requires that, for each cluster C, the number of records in C having a_i as protected attribute value should be equal or more than k. Additionally, we easily derive a penalization measure from this function:

$$k\text{-}Fairness(\mathcal{C}, \mathcal{A}) = \min_{C \in \mathcal{C},\, a_i \in \mathcal{A}} \begin{cases} 0, & \text{if } X_C^{a_i} \geq k \\ \frac{k - X_C^{a_i}}{k}, & \text{otherwise} \end{cases}$$

This penalization measure returns a value between $[0, 1]$ (the lower, the fairer). Intuitively, k-Fairness can constrain (or penalize) all the splits forming clusters with less than k individual for each protected group.

l-Fairness. An equivalence class respects *l*-diversity if at least l distinct values exist for the protected attribute. A dataset X features *l*-diversity if every equivalence class has *l*-diversity. This property can be easily translated into a fairness clustering context: clusters are *l*-Fairness if each cluster contains at least l different protected attribute values. Formally, given $\Gamma(X_C)$ as the set of distinct protected attributes in cluster C, we derive the penalization measure as follows:

$$l\text{-}Fairness(\mathcal{C}, \mathcal{A}) = \min_{C \in \mathcal{C}} \begin{cases} 0 & \text{if } |\Gamma(X_C)| \geq l \\ \frac{l - \Gamma(X_C)}{l} & \text{otherwise} \end{cases}$$

This measure penalizes all clusters with less than l different values in the protected attribute, i.e., it penalizes clusters that marginalize a subset of individuals. Additionally, when combined with k-Fairness, the two penalization measures impose, for each cluster, to have at least $l \leq m$ different protected attribute values where at least k instances represent each one.

t-Fairness. An equivalence class features t-closeness if the distance between the distribution of a protected attribute in this class and the distribution of the attribute in the whole dataset X is no more than a threshold t. A dataset X respects t-closeness if all its equivalence classes maintain t-closeness. To measure the distance between distributions, in [29] is used the Earth's Mover Distance (EMD, aka Wasserstein distance). Let $EMD_C^{a_i}$ represent the minimum EMD between the distributions of non-protected attributes for all records with the protected attribute value a_i compared against the distribution for every other protected attribute value. Since EMD involves binning the values, we leverage the number of bins to normalize the distance, ensuring it ranges between $[0, 1]$. We formulate the penalization as follows:

$$t\text{-}Fairness(\mathcal{C}, \mathcal{A}) = \min_{C \in \mathcal{C},\ a_i \in \mathcal{A}} \begin{cases} 0 & \text{if } EMD_C^{a_i} \leq t \\ EMD_C^{a_i} - t & \text{otherwise} \end{cases}$$

(k, l, t)-Fairness. To ensure that the most severely violated constraint among the three is not weakened in an average and does not affect other values through aggregation, we set the (k, l, t)-Fairness as the maximum value between k-Fairness, l-Fairness, and t-Fairness. To further clarify the underlying insight, the (k, l, t)-Fairness penalization measure pushes each cluster to hold a similar distribution of values between different protected attributes. Since clustering aims to group similar instances together, it could be argued that the algorithm optimizes this penalization measure intrinsically, i.e., by design. This argument can be applied to distance-based clustering approaches, and ParTree does not belong to such a family. Indeed, in ParTree, a cluster is defined by a set of axis-parallel rules, which are not chosen based on closeness to a certain position on the feature space, particularly for the principal component-based variant embraced in FPT. Therefore, in this setting, t-Fairness tends to drive the clustering algorithm to prefer clusters where instances with different values of protected attributes have similar distributions for all the other features.

4.2 Fair and Interpretable Partitioning Split

In the following, we formalize the training process of the tree splitting function as a decision tree regressor implemented by FPT. Specifically, we describe how the fairness penalty terms introduced in the previous section are integrated into the splitting criteria of PT. Algorithm 3 outlines the fitting procedure of the decision tree regressor, which identifies the feature-threshold pair yielding the highest information gain, adjusted by fairness penalties, to construct the tree-splitting function. This fair version replaces the *train_tree_regressor* function used in PT (line 4, in Algorithm 2, highlighted in blue).

Algorithm 3: $train\_fair\_tree\_regressor(X, A^{(j)}, sa, w, \alpha, \beta)$

Input : X - dataset with h features; $A^{(j)}$ - j-th principal component; sa - index of the protected attribute in $[0, m-1]$; w - penalization weight; α - upper bound on the proportion of sa values; β - lower bound on the proportion of sa values
Param : T - set of splitting thresholds for all features
Output: f^* - best fair tree splitting function using a feature-threshold pair with highest penalized information gain bs^* - best splitting score

1   $f^* \leftarrow \emptyset$; $bs^* \leftarrow -\infty$;   // initialize best splitting function, and score
2   **for** $i \in [0, m-1] \land i \neq sa$ **do**   // for each feature except the protected one
3   **for** $thr \in T^{(i)}$ **do**   // for each threshold of that feature
4       $f \leftarrow make\_partitioner(i, thr)$ // build binary tree splitter
5       $X_l, X_r \leftarrow \bar{f}(X)$;   // apply binary tree splitter
6       $s \leftarrow info\_gain(X, A^{(j)}, i, thr)$ // compute information gain
7   **if** $Pr_{X_l}^{sa_{max}} > \alpha \lor Pr_{X_r}^{sa_{max}} > \alpha$ **then**   // check upper bound violation
8   **continue**;   // check next feature-threshold
9   **if** $Pr_{X_l}^{sa_{min}} < \beta \lor Pr_{X_r}^{sa_{min}} < \beta$ **then**   // check lower bound violation
10   **continue**;   // check next feature-threshold
11       $\xi \leftarrow fair\_penalty(\{X_l, X_r\}, \{sa\})$;   // compute candidate's split penalty
12       $s \leftarrow 1/(1 + e^{-s})$ // normalize score to [0, 1]
13       $s \leftarrow s - s \cdot w \cdot \xi$ // apply fairness penalty
14   **if** $s > bs$ **then**   // update if better split
15         $f^* \leftarrow f$;   // update best tree partitioner
16         $bs^* \leftarrow s$;   // update best score
17 **return** f^*, bs^*

Compared to the classical algorithm for fitting decision trees in regression tasks, we introduce three additional hyperparameters: the weight of the fairness penalty w, and, inspired by [5], the upper and lower bounds α and β on the proportion of each protected group within a cluster. As in the classical approach, for each attribute i – excluding the protected one sa – and for each candidate threshold $T^{(i)}$ (lines 2–3), Algorithm 3 begins by constructing the candidate partitioning function f (line 4) and applying it to split the dataset into two disjoint subsets, X_l and X_r (line 5). The function $make\_partitioner$ generates f, which implements the logic "if $X^{(i)} \leq thr$ then X_l else X_r" to perform the partitioning. The quality of the split is then evaluated using the information gain $info\_gain$ computed as R^2 (line 6).

Next, Algorithm 3 deviates from its classical version by evaluating the split's fairness. First, it checks if the splitting is admissible in terms of fairness w.r.t. α and β (lines 7–10). We define $Pr_{X_l}^{sa_{max}}$ and $Pr_{X_r}^{sa_{max}}$ as the most frequent protected attribute value for the two partitions. Similarly, we define $Pr_{X_l}^{sa_{min}}$ and $Pr_{X_r}^{sa_{min}}$ as the least frequent protected attribute value. Under those definitions, a splitting function is considered admissible if $Pr_{X_l}^{sa_{max}}$ and $Pr_{X_r}^{sa_{max}}$ do not exceed α and $Pr_{X_l}^{sa_{min}}$ and $Pr_{X_r}^{sa_{min}}$ are greater than β (lines 7-10). This ensures that the distribution of protected attribute values remains balanced within the allowed range in both child nodes.

If the split is admissible, the function $fair\_penalty$ computes the fairness penalty ξ with respect to the two partitions, X_l and X_r, by analyzing the groups obtained based on the sensitive attribute sa (line 11). This function can be implemented using one of the measures previously introduced, i.e., *Balance*, *MFC*, or $(k,l,t)-Fairness$. It is important to note that these measures are applied greedily according to the algorithm's strategy, considering only the local binary split. However, the same measures can still be used to evaluate the overall clustering quality by analyzing all the resulting clusters. After that, we ensure that the quality of the split s, measured by information gain, is bounded within the range $[0,1]$ using a sigmoid function. This transformation emphasizes extreme values, rewarding good, and penalizing poor choices of splitting attributes and thresholds. The score s is then adjusted by subtracting the product of the fairness penalty ξ with the penalization weight w (line 13). If the current split achieves a better score than the best one found so far, i.e., $s > bs^*$, the algorithm updates both the best score bs^* and the corresponding best splitting function f^*. Finally, the procedure returns the best splitting function f^*, which maximizes the information gain penalized by the selected fairness measure (line 17).

Given n as the number of instances and m as the number of features in the dataset X such that $m \ll n$, the computational complexity of FPT can be computed as follows. For every node in the tree, i.e., $O(\log_2 n)$ for a balanced tree, FPT computes the PCA, $O(\min(m \cdot n^2, m^2 \cdot n)) = O(m^2 \cdot n)$ [32]. Then FPT fits the fair tree regressor, which requires $nbr\_components \cdot n \cdot m$ to scan every possible splitting threshold for each feature in the dataset. Except for t-Fairness, all the other metrics, i.e., Balance, Max Fairness Cost, k-Fairness, and l-Fairness, are computed only on the protected attribute in linear time. However, t-Fairness, requires computing the Earth's Mover Distance (EMD) [29]. Thus, the exact algorithm for t-Fairness has a complexity of $O(m \cdot n^3)$, where the $O(n^3)$ term comes from the EMD computation [11]. To improve efficiency, we compute the EMD on data binned into $\sqrt{n}$ bins, reducing the computational complexity to $O(n \cdot \sqrt{n})$. Assuming $nbr\_components \approx m$, the overall complexity of FPT is $O(\log_2 n \cdot m^4 \cdot n^2)$, and, since $m \ll n$, $O(n^2 \cdot \log_2 n)$. For the FPT-P, which uses the (k,l,t)-*Fairness* as penalization metric, and hence needs to compute t-*Farirness*, we have $O(n^3 \cdot \sqrt{n} \cdot \log_2 n)$.

5 Experiments

We evaluate here our proposal[1] in terms of clustering quality, interpretability, and fairness by benchmarking FairParTree (FPT) against established techniques over a variety of datasets. We aim to demonstrate that FPT achieves competitive clustering performance compared to state-of-the-art approaches while simultaneously providing an interpretable structure and fairer clusters.

---

[1] Code available on GitHub: https://github.com/fismimosa/FairTree.

Table 1. Datasets summary after preprocessing.

dataset	# records	# feat.	# cont.	# cat.	target	protected
titanic	891	6	5	1	passenger survival	sex
compas	7,214	36	27	9	recidivism within two years	sex, race, age_cat
credit	30,000	24	23	1	default payment	age_cat, marriage sex, education
bank	45,211	17	7	10	deposit subscription	marital, education age_cat, housing, default
diabetes	99,493	42	8	34	hospital readmission	race, gender, age

5.1 Datasets

We experiment with five datasets: titanic, compas, credit, bank, and diabetes[2]. Table 1 reports some datasets' basic characteristics before the preprocessing phase. Four datasets are commonly adopted to evaluate state-of-the-art fair clustering algorithms [15]. Additionally, we included the *titanic* dataset since the sex feature can be considered as a protected attribute. For our experiments, we applied the following preprocessing steps to all datasets. For datasets containing the *age* feature, we discretized it into intervals of 10 years to encode it as a protected categorical attribute. Moreover, we removed the original target variable from each dataset during the clustering phase. Categorical features with less than 10 unique values are one-hot encoded before applying any clustering methods to ensure compatibility with clustering approaches that rely on distance measures. Categorical features with more than 10 unique values are dropped to prevent excessive dimensionality after one-hot encoding[3]. Apart from the protected attribute under analysis, each feature is rescaled to a range of $[0, 1]$. Other minor dataset-specific preprocessing is applied and is detailed in the project repository.

5.2 Baseline and Competitors

We assess FPT's performance against diverse existing clustering strategies. First, we evaluate its ability to obtain well-separated clusters in comparison

---

[2] Datasets available at: https://www.kaggle.com/c/titanic/data, https://github.com/propublica/compas-analysis, https://archive.ics.uci.edu/dataset/350/default+of+credit+card+clients, https://archive.ics.uci.edu/dataset/222/bank+marketing, and https://archive.ics.uci.edu/dataset/296/diabetes+130-us+hospitals+for+years+1999-2008.

[3] Specifically, for the compas dataset we drop *type_of_assessment* and *v_type_of_assessment*; for the diabetes dataset we drop *discharge_disposition_id*, *admission_source_id*. For additional details, please refer to the GitHub Repository.

to standard algorithms that do not incorporate fairness constraints[4]: K-MEANS (KM) [39] and DBSCAN (DB) [19], i.e., the best-performing centroid-based and density-based competitors reported in [26]. Next, we compare FPT interpretability against other interpretable clustering methods. Specifically, we consider the original PT algorithm, as well as K-MEANS TREE (KMT) [40], which extends K-MEANS by learning clusters and iteratively refining their centroids based on the outputs of an optimal oblique decision tree[5]. Finally, we evaluate FPT's fairness by comparing it to established fair algorithms, namely Variational Fair Clustering (VFC) [42] and Fair Round-Robin Algorithm for Clustering (FRAC) [27], to assess the extent to which fairness is respected across clusters while maintaining high clustering quality. These competitors[6] are introduced in Sect. 2.

5.3 Evaluation Measures

Our evaluation is threefold. To assess clustering quality, we use the *Adjusted Rand Index* (*ARI*) [28], which measures the similarity between the predicted and true clusters while adjusting for chance, the *Fowlkes-Mallows Index* (*FM*) [21], which evaluates clustering quality based on the geometric mean of *Precision* and *Recall*, and the *Normalized Mutual Information* (*NMI*), which quantifies the mutual dependence between the predicted and true clusters.

Since some of the datasets under analysis lacks a predefined clustering ground truth, we use the target class as a reference to assess the quality of clustering measures. This approach assumes that the target class provides a meaningful structure, while not a perfect substitute for a true ground truth, it offers a practical way to asses clustering using metrics like *FM* and *NMI*. Although we also report the *silhouette score* [35] calculated using the Euclidean distance, we point out that silhouette scores may favor distance-based clustering methods, like KM and KMT, over other algorithms like DBSCAN, RT and FPT. Regarding interpretability, we adopt two measures as proxies for the complexity of local and global explanations by exploiting the tree structure of our methods and the competitors. Specifically, the *Maximum Rule Length (MRL)* represents the longest path from the root to a leaf node in the decision tree, reflecting the complexity of the most difficult clusters to interpret. The *Number of Conditions (NOC)* measures the total conditions required to describe all identified clusters, serving as a proxy for global explanation complexity. Lower *MRL* and *NOC* values indicate greater interpretability, as fewer conditions are needed to describe the method's results. Finally, concerning the fairness dimension, it is evaluated through *Balance* [17] and *Max Fairness Cost* [16], which are commonly used as fairness evaluation measures in the literature [12]. We underline again that

---
[4] For both algorithms, we leverage https://scikit-learn.org/stable/modules/clustering.html.
[5] Both methods are available within https://github.com/cri98li/ParTree.
[6] The methods are available at https://github.com/imtiazziko/Variational-Fair-Clustering and https://github.com/shivi98g/Fair-k-means-Clustering-via-Algorithmic-Fairness.

FPT does not gain an advantage from using *Balance* and *Max Fairness Cost* as evaluation measures. Indeed, while FPT applies these measures *locally* at each partitioning split to penalize the score, the evaluation of all algorithms is based on these scores calculated from the *global* clustering result $\mathcal{C}$. Also, we do not use the proposed *(k, l, t)-Fairness* measure since it is heavily affected by the chosen values of k, l, and t, making it less reliable for consistent comparisons.

5.4 Hyperparameter Selection and Experimental Setup

We evaluate each method across a diverse range of hyperparameters, selecting the optimal configuration for the final model assessment based on the evaluation measures adopted, the dataset, and the protected attribute under analysis.

For DBSCAN, we explore $\epsilon \in \{0.1, 0.25, 0.5, 0.75, 1\}$ while using *Euclidean Distance* as the distance measure. For centroid-based clustering methods such as K-MEANS and KMT, we vary the number of clusters $k \in \{2, 4, 8, 16\}$, ensuring alignment with the maximum number of leaves in a FPT tree of depth $1, 2, 3$, and 4, respectively. The same configuration is applied to the FRAC algorithm. We employ the *Squared Euclidean Distance* as the objective cost function to evaluate cluster compactness in centroid-based methods. For VFC, we tune the regularization parameter $\lambda \in [0, 10,000]$ in increments of $1,000$, resulting in $\lambda \in \{0, 1000, 2000, \ldots, 10,000\}$. For VFC, we set the required target distribution to match the proportion of each protected attribute value in the dataset, following the original experiments conducted in [42]. Similarly, for FRAC, we adopt the configuration proposed in the main experiments in [27], setting each component of τ to $\frac{1}{k}$, where k represents the number of clusters. Lastly, we set the maximum number of iterations for VFC to 100, while for FRAC, standard K-MEANS, and KMT, we use 300 iterations.

For FPT, we assess its performance for ϵ values in $\{0, 0.1, 0.2\}$, where ϵ indicates (in Algorithm 1) the adjustment factor used when comparing the BIC of the clusters resulting from a split with the BIC of the original cluster. We restrict the trees to a maximum of 2, 4, 8, or 16 clusters, ensuring alignment with the maximum number of leaves. The same configurations are tested for PT. Regarding fairness, we evaluate FPT with for *Balance* as the fairness measure, i.e., FPT-B, by considering $w \in \{0.1, 0.3, 0.5, 0.7, 0.9\}$. For FPT incorporating *MFC*, i.e., FPT-M, we explore values of $w \in \{0.2, 0.5, 0.8\}$. Lastly, in the case of (k, l, t)-Fairness, i.e., FPT-P, we experiment with $\hat{k} \in \{0.8, 0.9, 0.95\}$, $\hat{l} \in \{0.45, 0.7, 1.0\}$, and $t \in \{0.0, 0.1, 0.2, 0.5, 0.8\}$, with $w \in \{0.2, 0.5, 0.8\}$. Where $k = k\text{-}anonimity(X) * \hat{k}$ and $l = l\text{-}diversity(X) * \hat{l}$ We set the upper and lower bounds (α, β) in FPT to $+\infty$ and $-\infty$, respectively, as their values can be too specific to each dataset, chosen protected attribute, and application. We choose to focus on evaluating the effects of fairness penalization measures, leaving the analysis of their impact to future studies.

Each method is individually evaluated on each dataset and each protected attribute. Specifically, we assess the performance of each method by considering one protected attribute at a time while retaining the remaining protected attributes as features during the clustering process. This approach yields distinct

Table 2. Average performance of each method w.r.t each dataset ± standard deviation. For each evaluation measure, the best performer is in bold, and the best performer runner-up is in italics and blue.

Method	SIL ↑	ARI ↑	FM ↑	NMI ↑	Balance ↑	MFC ↓
FPT-B	.24 ± .31	.13 ± .13	.55 ± .19	.15 ± .18	.72 ± .25	.03 ± .03
FPT-M	.17 ± .31	.14 ± .15	.56 ± .18	.16 ± .20	.49 ± .36	.04 ± .03
FPT-P	.34 ± .29	.16 ± .13	.66 ± .12	**.17 ± .19**	**.77 ± .19**	**.02 ± .02**
FRAC	.42 ± .18	.07 ± .07	.61 ± .05	.07 ± .09	.67 ± .35	.03 ± .07
VFC	.68 ± .09	.09 ± .09	.70 ± .08	.07 ± .08	.62 ± .34	.04 ± .06
KMT	.67 ± .09	.12 ± .11	.68 ± .09	.08 ± .09	.63 ± .33	.04 ± .07
PT	.15 ± .34	.13 ± .14	.55 ± .19	.15 ± .20	.45 ± .34	.05 ± .03
KM	.57 ± .16	.09 ± 0.1	.59 ± .17	.07 ± .08	.48 ± .33	.06 ± .08
DB	**.88 ± .15**	**.18 ± .15**	**.81 ± .07**	.16 ± .16	.35 ± .44	.19 ± .14

evaluation results for each protected attribute. The same procedure is applied consistently across all datasets.

5.5 Results

In the following, we conduct a detailed analysis of the results, focusing on clustering quality, interpretability, and fairness. Table 2 summarizes the performance of the methods tested in terms of clustering quality and fairness, highlighting the best-performing approach for each evaluation measure. To improve readability, we average the results across all datasets. Regarding clustering quality, DB achieves the highest performance w.r.t *SIL*, *ARI*, and *FM*. This is likely due to its tendency to form an overly small number of very large clusters (typically one or two), which may be of limited practical use but favor these evaluation measures. VFC result to be the best method runner up w.r.t. *SIL* and *FM*. FPT-P, the FPT variant using the privacy-inspired penalization measure, emerges as the best method for *NMI* and the runner-up for *ARI*, despite the high standard deviations across all methods' scores. This suggests that, despite the fairness penalization and the constraints imposed by the interpretability requirement – enforced through the use of axis-parallel splits – it still guarantees remarkable clustering quality. In terms of *NMI*, FPT-P is followed by DB and FPT-M.

Figure 1 shows the Critical Difference (CD) diagrams for the clustering quality measures, depicting the rank of each method. Two methods are tied if the null hypothesis that their performances are equivalent can not be rejected using the Nemenyi test at $\alpha = 0.05$. Notably, in three out of four measures, one of the FPT variants is tied with one of the best-performing competitors. *SIL* is the measure where all variants of FPT perform the worst, though they still improve upon PT. For *ARI*, FPT-P emerges as the best-performing model. Additionally, all variants rank in the top half of the leaderboard and are tied together. For *FM*, only FPT-P is in the top half; while tied with VFC and KMT, it is not

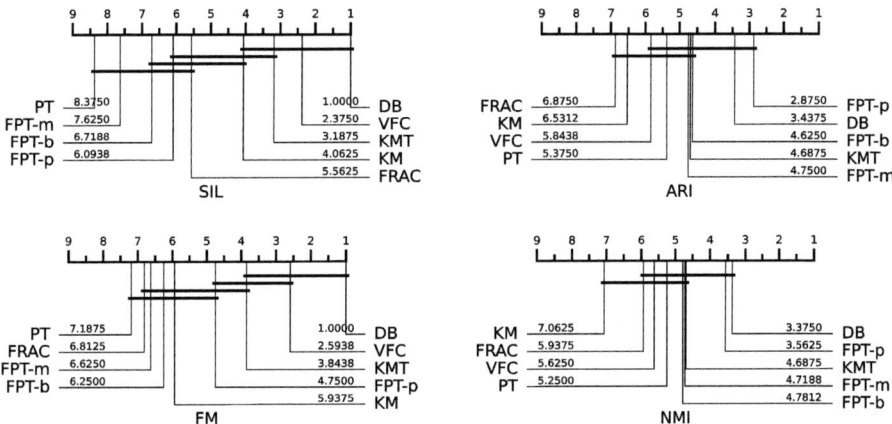

Fig. 1. Critical Difference plots with Nemenyi at 95% confidence comparing cluster quality scores among all datasets.

tied with the best-performing method, DB. Finally, for *NMI*, all FPT variants rank in the top half. Except for the worst-performing method, KM, all FPT variants are tied with the other competitors.

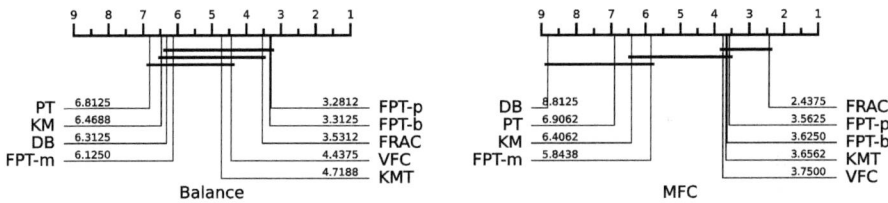

Fig. 2. Critical Difference plots with Nemenyi at 95% confidence comparing cluster fairness scores among all datasets.

Regarding fairness, still in Table 2, we can notice that FRT-P is the best-performing method for both *Balance* and *MFC*, highlighting the significance of our proposed penalization measure. FPT-P is also the method with the lowest standard deviation, highlighting high stability across different datasets. Additionally, the second-best performer in both measures is FPT-B, suggesting that fair clustering via penalization is fairer than classic clustering methods and can achieve better results w.r.t. fair competitors. By analyzing the CD diagrams in Fig. 2 we notice FPT-P being the best performer method, and FPT-B having nearly identical performance w.r.t. the *Balance* score. As expected, all the fair-aware methods rank in the top half, except for FPT-M, although still tied to the top-performing method. We notice a similar pattern regarding *MFC*: all the fair-aware methods rank in the top half, with FPT-M being the only exception.

Table 3. Average *MRL* and *NOC* of each method w.r.t each dataset ± standard deviation. For each evaluation measure, the best performer is in bold, and the best performer runner-up is in italics.

	FPT-B	FPT-M	FPT-P	PT	KMT
$MRL \downarrow$	3.88 ± 1.41	3.94 ± 1.18	*3.81 ± 1.56*	3.94 ± 1.06	**2.56 ± 1.21**
$NOC \downarrow$	4.00 ± 2.53	4.12 ± 2.42	**3.69 ± 2.50**	4.25 ± 2.29	*3.81 ± 3.92*

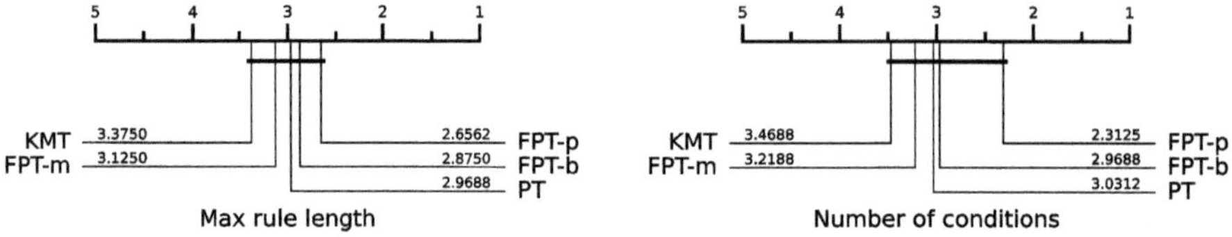

Fig. 3. Critical Difference plots with Nemenyi at 95% confidence comparing cluster interpretability among all datasets.

Concerning interpretability, Table 3 reports the average *MRL* and *NOC* of tree-based interpretable methods. The best-performing methods are FPT-P and KMT. While KMT generally uses simpler rules for the most complex clusters, FPT-P requires fewer conditions to describe all clusters. The CD diagrams in Fig. 3 show that each FPT variant is tied with all other interpretable competitors. Nonetheless, despite the ties, FPT-P ranks first for both measures.

To conclude, the experiments demonstrate that FPT enhances PT in terms of clustering quality and interpretability while also integrating the fairness constraint. Compared to its competitors, FPT exhibits a slightly lower but not statistically significant clustering quality relative to the classic algorithm. However, it is on par and, at times, outperforms the fair clustering competitors, highlighting its effectiveness in balancing multiple objectives simultaneously. Additionally, all FPT variants, particularly FPT-P, showcase strong performance for the interpretability and fairness dimensions, often ranking among the top methods when evaluated against interpretable and fair competitors. This finding suggests that FPT is a well-rounded approach capable of producing good-quality clusters while concurrently addressing the challenges of interpretability and fairness. By delivering competitive performance across multiple dimensions, FPT emerges as a valuable approach for scenarios where both interpretability and fairness are critical properties to be embedded in clustering tasks.

6 Conclusion

In this paper, we have introduced FairParTree, a fair and interpretable clustering algorithm that directly integrates fairness constraints into the clustering process while maintaining high quality and interpretability. Our approach leverages decision trees to provide interpretable cluster assignments while embedding fairness constraints to ensure that the resulting partitions do not disadvantage any protected group. Indeed, one of the key contributions of this work is the integration of different fairness measures - namely Balance, Max Fairness Cost, and a novel (k, l, t)-Fairness inspired by privacy - that provides a flexible framework for ensuring fair clustering across various application domains.

We demonstrated through extensive experimentation across multiple datasets that FairParTree effectively balances clustering quality, interpretability, and fairness, achieving state-of-the-art performance in all three evaluations. Specifically, findings showed that FairParTree achieved competitive performance in terms of clustering quality while significantly improving fairness compared to traditional algorithms. Our results reinforce the viability of FairParTree as a practical solution for real-world scenarios requiring both interpretability and fairness.

Future work could investigate integrating additional fairness measures within the clustering process. Indeed, while FairParTree allows flexibility in choosing fairness constraints, selecting the most suitable fairness measure for a given application remains a challenge. Future research could investigate automated techniques for dynamically selecting the most appropriate fairness constraint based on dataset characteristics and domain requirements. Additionally, conducting human evaluations to qualitatively assess FairParTree explanations' perceived fairness and comprehensibility would offer insights into their practical usability.

Acknowledgments. The authors would like to thank Federico Volpi, whose master's thesis project provided the basis for developing this contribution. This work has been partially supported by the Italian Project Fondo Italiano per la Scienza FIS00001966 "MIMOSA", by the PRIN 2022 framework project "PIANO" (Personalized Interventions Against Online Toxicity) under CUP B53D23013290006, by the European Community Horizon 2020 programme under the funding schemes ERC-2018-ADG G.A. 834756 "XAI", by the European Commission under the NextGeneration EU programme âĂŞ National Recovery and Resilience Plan (Piano Nazionale di Ripresa e Resilienza, PNRR) Project: "SoBigData.it âĂŞ Strengthening the Italian RI for Social Mining and Big Data Analytics" âĂŞ Prot. IR0000013 âĂŞ Av. n. 3264 del 28/12/2021, M4C2 - Investimento 1.3, Partenariato Esteso PE00000013 - "FAIR" - Future Artificial Intelligence Research" - Spoke 1 "Human-centered AI", and "FINDHR" that has received funding from the European Union's Horizon Europe research and innovation program under G.A. 101070212.

References

1. Abbasi, M., Bhaskara, A., Venkatasubramanian, S.: Fair clustering via equitable group representations. In: Elish, M.C., Isaac, W., Zemel, R.S. (eds.) FAccT '21: 2021 ACM Conference on Fairness, Accountability, and Transparency, Virtual Event/Toronto, Canada, March 3–10, 2021, pp. 504–514. ACM (2021). https://doi.org/10.1145/3442188.3445913, https://doi.org/10.1145/3442188.3445913
2. Abraham, S.S., P, D., Sundaram, S.S.: Fairness in clustering with multiple sensitive attributes. CoRR abs/1910.05113 (2019). http://arxiv.org/abs/1910.05113

3. Abraham, S.S., P, D., Sundaram, S.S.: Fairness in clustering with multiple sensitive attributes. In: Bonifati, A., et al. (eds.) Proceedings of the 23rd International Conference on Extending Database Technology, EDBT 2020, Copenhagen, Denmark, March 30 – April 02, 2020, pp. 287–298. OpenProceedings.org (2020). https://doi.org/10.5441/002/EDBT.2020.26
4. Abusitta, A., Li, M.Q., Fung, B.C.M.: Survey on explainable AI: techniques, challenges and open issues. Expert Syst. Appl. 255, 124710 (2024). https://doi.org/10.1016/J.ESWA.2024.124710
5. Ahmadian, S., Epasto, A., Kumar, R., Mahdian, M.: Clustering without overrepresentation. In: Teredesai, A., Kumar, V., Li, Y., Rosales, R., Terzi, E., Karypis, G. (eds.) Proceedings of the 25th ACM SIGKDD International Conference on Knowledge Discovery & Data Mining, KDD 2019, Anchorage, AK, USA, August 4–8, 2019, pp. 267–275. ACM (2019). https://doi.org/10.1145/3292500.3330987
6. Angwin, J., Larson, J., Mattu, S., Kirchner, L.: Machine bias: there's software used across the country to predict future criminals. and it's biased against blacks. ProPublica (2016). https://www.propublica.org/article/machine-bias-risk-assessments-in-criminal-sentencing
7. Barata, A.P., Takes, F.W., Herik, H., Veenman, C.J.: Fair tree classifier using strong demographic parity. arXiv preprint arXiv:2110.09295 (2021)
8. Bera, S.K., Chakrabarty, D., Flores, N., Negahbani, M.: Fair algorithms for clustering. In: Wallach, H.M., Larochelle, H., Beygelzimer, A., d'Alché-Buc, F., Fox, E.B., Garnett, R. (eds.) Advances in Neural Information Processing Systems 32: Annual Conference on Neural Information Processing Systems 2019, NeurIPS 2019, December 8–14, 2019, Vancouver, BC, Canada, pp. 4955–4966 (2019). https://proceedings.neurips.cc/paper/2019/hash/fc192b0c0d270dbf41870a63a8c76c2f-Abstract.html
9. Bertsimas, D., Orfanoudaki, A., Wiberg, H.M.: Interpretable clustering: an optimization approach. Mach. Learn. **110**(1), 89–138 (2021). https://doi.org/10.1007/S10994-020-05896-2
10. Blockeel, H., Raedt, L.D., Ramon, J.: Top-down induction of clustering trees. CoRR cs.LG/0011032 (2000). https://arxiv.org/abs/cs/0011032
11. Bringmann, K., Staals, F., Wegrzycki, K., van Wordragen, G.: Fine-grained complexity of earth mover's distance under translation. In: SoCG. LIPIcs, vol. 293, pp. 25:1–25:17. Schloss Dagstuhl - Leibniz-Zentrum für Informatik (2024)
12. Caton, S., Haas, C.: Fairness in machine learning: a survey. CoRR abs/2010.04053 (2020). https://arxiv.org/abs/2010.04053
13. Chen, J., et al.: Interpretable clustering via discriminative rectangle mixture model. In: Bonchi, F., Domingo-Ferrer, J., Baeza-Yates, R., Zhou, Z., Wu, X. (eds.) IEEE 16th International Conference on Data Mining, ICDM 2016, December 12–15, 2016, Barcelona, Spain, pp. 823–828. IEEE Computer Society (2016). https://doi.org/10.1109/ICDM.2016.0097
14. Chen, Y., Hsu, W., Lee, Y.: TASC: two-attribute-set clustering through decision tree construction. Eur. J. Oper. Res. **174**(2), 930–944 (2006). https://doi.org/10.1016/J.EJOR.2005.04.029
15. Chhabra, A., Masalkovaite, K., Mohapatra, P.: An overview of fairness in clustering. IEEE Access **9**, 130698–130720 (2021). https://doi.org/10.1109/ACCESS.2021.3114099

16. Chhabra, A., Mohapatra, P.: Fair algorithms for hierarchical agglomerative clustering. In: Wani, M.A., Kantardzic, M.M., Palade, V., Neagu, D., Yang, L., Chan, K.Y. (eds.) 21st IEEE International Conference on Machine Learning and Applications, ICMLA 2022, Nassau, Bahamas, December 12–14, 2022, pp. 206–211. IEEE (2022). https://doi.org/10.1109/ICMLA55696.2022.00036, https://doi.org/10.1109/ICMLA55696.2022.00036
17. Chierichetti, F., Kumar, R., Lattanzi, S., Vassilvitskii, S.: Fair clustering through fairlets. In: Guyon, I., et al. (eds.) Advances in Neural Information Processing Systems 30: Annual Conference on Neural Information Processing Systems 2017, December 4–9, 2017, Long Beach, CA, USA, pp. 5029–5037 (2017)
18. Dressel, J., Farid, H.: The accuracy, fairness, and limits of predicting recidivism. Sci. Adv. **4**(1), eaao5580 (2018). https://doi.org/10.1126/sciadv.aao5580
19. Ester, M., Kriegel, H., Sander, J., Xu, X.: A density-based algorithm for discovering clusters in large spatial databases with noise. In: Simoudis, E., Han, J., Fayyad, U.M. (eds.) Proceedings of the Second International Conference on Knowledge Discovery and Data Mining (KDD-96), Portland, Oregon, USA, pp. 226–231. AAAI Press (1996)
20. Ezugwu, A.E., et al.: A comprehensive survey of clustering algorithms: state-of-the-art machine learning applications, taxonomy, challenges, and future research prospects. Eng. Appl. Artif. Intell. **110**, 104743 (2022). https://doi.org/10.1016/J.ENGAPPAI.2022.104743
21. Fowlkes, E.B., Mallows, C.L.: A method for comparing two hierarchical clusterings. J. Am. Stat. Assoc. **78**(383), 553–569 (1983)
22. Fraiman, R., Ghattas, B., Svarc, M.: Interpretable clustering using unsupervised binary trees. Adv. Data Anal. Classif. **7**(2), 125–145 (2013). https://doi.org/10.1007/S11634-013-0129-3
23. Frost, N., Moshkovitz, M., Rashtchian, C.: EXKMC: expanding explainable k-means clustering. CoRR abs/2006.02399 (2020). https://arxiv.org/abs/2006.02399
24. Garg, P., Villasenor, J.D., Foggo, V.: Fairness metrics: a comparative analysis. In: Wu, X., et al. (eds.) 2020 IEEE International Conference on Big Data (IEEE BigData 2020), Atlanta, GA, USA, December 10-13, 2020, pp. 3662–3666. IEEE (2020). https://doi.org/10.1109/BIGDATA50022.2020.9378025
25. Ghadiri, M., Samadi, S., Vempala, S.S.: Socially fair k-means clustering. In: Elish, M.C., Isaac, W., Zemel, R.S. (eds.) FAccT '21: 2021 ACM Conference on Fairness, Accountability, and Transparency, Virtual Event / Toronto, Canada, March 3–10, 2021, pp. 438–448. ACM (2021). https://doi.org/10.1145/3442188.3445906
26. Guidotti, R., Landi, C., Beretta, A., Fadda, D., Nanni, M.: Interpretable data partitioning through tree-based clustering methods. In: Bifet, A., Lorena, A.C., Ribeiro, R.P., Gama, J., Abreu, P.H. (eds.) DS 2023. LNCS, vol. 14276, pp. 492–507. Springer, Cham (2023). https://doi.org/10.1007/978-3-031-45275-8_33
27. Gupta, S., Ghalme, G., Krishnan, N.C., Jain, S.: Efficient algorithms for fair clustering with a new notion of fairness. Data Min. Knowl. Discov. **37**(5), 1959–1997 (2023). https://doi.org/10.1007/S10618-023-00928-6
28. Hubert, L., Arabie, P.: Comparing partitions. J. Classif. **2**, 193–218 (1985)
29. Li, N., Li, T., Venkatasubramanian, S.: t-closeness: privacy beyond k-anonymity and l-diversity. In: Chirkova, R., Dogac, A., Özsu, M.T., Sellis, T.K. (eds.) Proceedings of the 23rd International Conference on Data Engineering, ICDE 2007, The Marmara Hotel, Istanbul, Turkey, April 15-20, 2007. pp. 106–115. IEEE Computer Society (2007). https://doi.org/10.1109/ICDE.2007.367856

30. Liu, B., Xia, Y., Yu, P.S.: Clustering through decision tree construction. In: Proceedings of the 2000 ACM CIKM International Conference on Information and Knowledge Management, McLean, VA, USA, November 6-11, 2000. pp. 20–29. ACM (2000). https://doi.org/10.1145/354756.354775
31. Machanavajjhala, A., Kifer, D., Gehrke, J., Venkitasubramaniam, M.: L-diversity: Privacy beyond k-anonymity. ACM Trans. Knowl. Discov. Data **1**(1), 3 (2007). https://doi.org/10.1145/1217299.1217302
32. Mamat, N.J.Z., Daniel, J.K.: Statistical analyses on time complexity and rank consistency between singular value decomposition and the duality approach in AHP: a case study of faculty member selection. Math. Comput. Model. **46**(7–8), 1099–1106 (2007)
33. Mehrabi, N., Morstatter, F., Saxena, N., Lerman, K., Galstyan, A.: A survey on bias and fairness in machine learning. ACM Comput. Surv. **54**(6), 115:1–115:35 (2021)
34. Moshkovitz, M., Dasgupta, S., Rashtchian, C., Frost, N.: Explainable k-means and k-medians clustering. In: Proceedings of the 37th International Conference on Machine Learning, ICML 2020, 13–18 July 2020, Virtual Event. Proceedings of Machine Learning Research, vol. 119, pp. 7055–7065. PMLR (2020). http://proceedings.mlr.press/v119/moshkovitz20a.html
35. Rousseeuw, P.J.: Silhouettes: a graphical aid to the interpretation and validation of cluster analysis. J. Comput. Appl. Math. **20**, 53–65 (1987)
36. Ruggieri, S.: Using t-closeness anonymity to control for non-discrimination. Trans. Data Priv. **7**(2), 99–129 (2014)
37. Schwarz, G.: Estimating the dimension of a model. Ann. Stat. **6**(2), 461–464 (1978). https://doi.org/10.1214/aos/1176344136
38. Sweeney, L.: k-anonymity: a model for protecting privacy. Int. J. Uncertain. Fuzziness Knowl. Based Syst. **10**(5), 557–570 (2002). https://doi.org/10.1142/S0218488502001648
39. Tan, P., Steinbach, M.S., Karpatne, A., Kumar, V.: Introduction to Data Mining, 2nd esn. Pearson (2019)
40. Tavallali, P., Tavallali, P., Singhal, M.: K-means tree: an optimal clustering tree for unsupervised learning. J. Supercomput. **77**(5), 5239–5266 (2021). https://doi.org/10.1007/S11227-020-03436-2
41. Tufail, S., Riggs, H., Tariq, M., Sarwat, A.I.: Advancements and challenges in machine learning: a comprehensive review of models, libraries, applications, and algorithms. Electronics **12**(8), 1789 (2023)
42. Ziko, I.M., Yuan, J., Granger, E., Ayed, I.B.: Variational fair clustering. In: Thirty-Fifth AAAI Conference on Artificial Intelligence, AAAI 2021, Thirty-Third Conference on Innovative Applications of Artificial Intelligence, IAAI 2021, The Eleventh Symposium on Educational Advances in Artificial Intelligence, EAAI 2021, Virtual Event, February 2–9, 2021, pp. 11202–11209. AAAI Press (2021). https://doi.org/10.1609/AAAI.V35I12.17336

Open Access This chapter is licensed under the terms of the Creative Commons Attribution 4.0 International License (http://creativecommons.org/licenses/by/4.0/), which permits use, sharing, adaptation, distribution and reproduction in any medium or format, as long as you give appropriate credit to the original author(s) and the source, provide a link to the Creative Commons license and indicate if changes were made.

The images or other third party material in this chapter are included in the chapter's Creative Commons license, unless indicated otherwise in a credit line to the material. If material is not included in the chapter's Creative Commons license and your intended use is not permitted by statutory regulation or exceeds the permitted use, you will need to obtain permission directly from the copyright holder.

Features Importance-Based XAI

Antithetic Sampling for Top-K Shapley Identification

Patrick Kolpaczki[1,2](✉), Tim Nielen[1], and Eyke Hüllermeier[1,2]

[1] LMU Munich, Munich, Germany
[2] Munich Center for Machine Learning, Munich, Germany
`patrick.kolpaczki@lmu.de`

Abstract. Additive feature explanations rely primarily on game-theoretic notions such as the Shapley value by viewing features as cooperating players. The Shapley value's popularity in and outside of explainable AI stems from its axiomatic uniqueness. However, its computational complexity severely limits practicability. Most works investigate the uniform approximation of all features' Shapley values, needlessly consuming samples for insignificant features. In contrast, identifying the k most important features can already be sufficiently insightful and yields the potential to leverage algorithmic opportunities connected to the field of multi-armed bandits. We propose *Comparable Marginal Contributions Sampling* (CMCS), a method for the *top-k identification problem* utilizing a new sampling scheme taking advantage of correlated observations. We conduct experiments to showcase the efficacy of our method compared to competitive baselines. Our empirical findings reveal that estimation quality for the *approximate-all problem* does not necessarily transfer to *top-k identification* and vice versa.

Keywords: Shapley Value · Game Theory · Explainable AI

1 Introduction

The fast-paced development of artificial intelligence poses a double-edged sword. Obviously on one hand, machine learning models have significantly improved in prediction performance, most famously demonstrated by deep learning models. But, on the other hand, their required complexity to exhibit these capabilities comes at a price. Human users face concerning challenges comprehending the decision-making of such models that appear to be increasingly opaque. The field of explainable AI [25, 34] offers a simple yet popular approach to regain understanding and shed light onto these black box models by means of *additive feature explanations* [11]. Probing a model's behavior to input, this explanation method assigns importance scores to the utilized features. Depending on the explanandum of interest, each score can be interpreted as the feature's impact on the models' prediction for a particular instance or its generalization performance.

The Shapley value [32] has emerged as a prominent mechanism to assign scores. Taking a game-theoretic perspective, each feature is viewed as a player in a *cooperative game* in which the players can form coalitions and reap a *collective benefit* by solving a task together. For instance, a coalition representing a feature subset can be rewarded with the generalization performance of the to be explained model using only that subset. Posing the omnipresent question of how to divide in equitable manner the collective benefit that all players jointly achieve, reduces the search for feature importance scores to a *fair-division problem*. The Shapley value is the unique solution to fulfill certain desiderata which arguably capture an intuitive notion of fairness [32]. The marginal contributions of a player to all coalitions, denoting the increase in collective benefit when joining a coalition, are taken into a weighted sum by the Shapley value.

It has been extensively applied for *local explanations*, dividing the prediction value [22], and *global explanations* that divide prediction performance [9]. In addition to providing understanding, other works proposed to utilize it for the selection of machine learning entities such as features [6,35], datapoints [13], neurons in deep neural networks [14], or base learners in ensembles [30]. We refer to [31] for an overview of its applications in machine learning. Unfortunately, the complexity of the Shapley value poses a serious limitation: its calculation encompasses all coalitions within the exponentially growing power set of players. Hence, the exact computation of the Shapley value is quickly doomed for even moderate feature numbers. Ergo, the research branch of estimating the Shapley value has sparked notable interest, in particular the challenge of precisely approximating the Shapley values of all players known as the *approximate-all problem*.

However, often the exact importance scores just serve as a means to find the most influential features, be it for explanation or preselection [6,35], and are not particularly relevant themselves. Hence, we advocate for the *top-k identification problem* [18] in which an approximation algorithm's goal is to identify the k players with highest Shapley values, without having to return precise estimates. This incentivizes to forego and sacrifice precision of players' estimates for whom reliable predictions of top-k membership already manifest during runtime. Instead, the available samples, reflecting finite computational power at disposal, are better spent on players on the verge of belonging to the top-k in order to speed up the segregation of top-k players from the rest.

Contribution. We propose with *Comparable Marginal Contributions Sampling* (CMCS), Greedy CMCS, and CMCS@K novel top-k identification algorithms for the Shapley value. More specifically, our contributions are:

- We present a new representation of the Shapley value based on an altered notion of marginal contribution and leverage it to develop CMCS. On the theoretical basis of antithetic sampling, we underpin the intuition behind utilizing correlated observations especially for top-k identification.
- Moreover, with Greedy CMCS and CMCS@K we propose multi-armed bandit-inspired enhancements. Our proposed algorithms are model-agnostic and applicable to any cooperative game independent of the domain of interest.
- Lastly, we observe how empirical performance does not directly translate from the approximate-all to the top-k identification problem. Depending on the task, different algorithms are favorable and a conscious choice is advisable.

2 Related Work

The problem of precisely approximating all players' Shapley values has been extensively investigated. Since the Shapley value is a weighted average of a player's marginal contributions, methods that conduct mean estimation form a popular class of approximation algorithms. Most of these sample marginal contributions as performed by *ApproShapley* [4]. Many variance reduction techniques, that increase the estimates' convergence speed, have been incorporated: stratification [2,3,23,27,28,33], antithetic sampling [16,24], and control variates [15]. Departing from the notion of marginal contributions, other methods view the Shapley value as a composition of coalition values and sample these instead for mean estimation [8,19,20]. A different class of methods does not approximate Shapley values directly, but fits a parametrized surrogate game via sampling. As the surrogate game represents the game of interest increasingly more faithful, its own Shapley values become better estimates. Due to the surrogate game's highly restrictive structure these can be obtained in polynomial time. *KernelSHAP* [22] is the most prominent member of this class with succeeding extensions [7,29]. See [5] for an overview of further methods for feature attribution and specific model classes.

First to consider the top-k identification problem for Shapley values were [26] by simply returning the players with the highest estimates effectively computed by *ApproShapley* [4]. This straightforward reduction of top-k identification to the approximate-all problem can be realized with any approximation algorithm.

[18] establish a connection to the field of multi-armed bandits [21] and thus open the door to further algorithmic opportunities that top-k identification has to offer. Here, pulling an arm of a slot machine metaphorically captures the draw of a sample from a distribution. Usually, one is interested in maximizing the cumulative random reward obtained from sequentially playing the multi-armed slot machine or finding the arm with highest mean reward. Modeling each player as an arm and its reward distribution to be the player's marginal contributions distributed according to their weights within the Shapley value [18], facilitates the usage of bandit algorithms to find the k distributions with highest mean values which represent the players' Shapely values. The inherent trade-off between constantly collecting information from all arms to avoid falling victim to the estimates' stochasticity and selecting only those players that promise the most information gain to correctly predict top-k membership, constitutes the well-known exploration-exploitation dilemma.

Bandit algorithms such as *Gap-E* [12] and *Border Uncertainty Sampling (BUS)* [18] tackle it by greedily selecting the next arm to pull as the one that maximizes a selection criterion which combines the uncertainty of top-k membership and its sample number. In contrast *Successive Accepts and Rejects (SAR)* [1] phase-wise eliminates arms whose top-k membership can be reliably predicted. *SHAP@K* [17] employs an alternative greedy selection criterion based on confidence intervals for the players' estimates. In each round, samples are taken from two players, one from the currently predicted top-k and one outside of them, with the highest overlap in confidence intervals. The overlap is interpreted as the likelihood that the pair is mistakenly partitioned and should be swapped instead.

3 The Top-k Identification Problem

We introduce cooperative games and the Shapley value formally in Sect. 3.1, and briefly after present the widely studied problem of approximating all players' Shapley values in a cooperative game Sect. 3.2. On that basis, we introduce the problem of identifying the top-k players with the highest Shapley values in Sect. 3.3 and distinguish it from the former by highlighting decisive differences in performance measures which will prepare our theoretical findings and arising methodological avenues alluded to in Sect. 4.

3.1 Cooperative Games and the Shapley Value

A cooperative game $(\mathcal{N}, \nu)$ consists of a *player set* $\mathcal{N} = \{1, \ldots, n\}$ and a *value function* $\nu : \mathcal{P}(\mathcal{N}) \to \mathbb{R}$ that maps each subset $S \subseteq \mathcal{N}$ to a real-valued worth. The players in $\mathcal{N}$ can cooperate by forming *coalitions* in order to achieve a goal. A coalition is represented by a subset S of $\mathcal{N}$ that includes exactly all players which join the coalition. The formation of a coalition resolves in the (partial) fulfillment of the goal and a collective benefit $\nu(S)$ disbursed to the coalition which we call the *worth* of that coalition. The empty set has no worth, i.e. $\nu(\emptyset) = 0$. The abstractness of this notion offers a certain versatility in modeling many cooperative scenarios. In the context of feature explanations for example, each player represents a feature and the formation of a coalition is interpreted to express that a model or learner uses only that feature subset and discards those features absent in the coalition. Depending on the desired explanation type, the prediction value for a datapoint of interest or an observed behavior of the model over multiple instances, for example generalization performance on a test set, is commonly taken as the worth of a feature subset.

A central problem revolving around cooperative games is the question of how to split the collective benefit that all players achieve together among them. More precisely, which share ϕ_i of the *grand coalition's* worth $\nu(\mathcal{N})$ should each player $i \in \mathcal{N}$ receive? A common demand is that these payouts ϕ are to be fair and reflect the contribution that each player provides to the fulfillment of the goal. Guided by this rationale, the Shapley value [32] offers a popular solution by assigning each player i the payoff

$$\phi_i = \sum_{S \subseteq \mathcal{N} \setminus \{i\}} \frac{1}{n \binom{n-1}{|S|}} \cdot [\nu(S \cup \{i\}) - \nu(S)]. \tag{1}$$

The difference in worth $\Delta_i(S) := \nu(S \cup \{i\}) - \nu(S)$ is known as *marginal contribution* and reflects the increase in collective benefit that i causes by joining the coalition S. The reason for the Shapley value's popularity lies within its axiomatic justification. It is the unique payoff distribution to simultaneously satisfy the four axioms, symmetry, linearity, efficiency, and dummy player [32], which capture an intuitive notion of fairness in light of the faced fair division problem. Despite this appeal, the Shapley value comes with a severe drawback. The number of coalition values contained in its summation grows exponentially w.r.t. the number of players n in the game. In fact, its exact calculation is provably NP-hard [10] if no further assumption on the structure of ν is made, and as a consequence, the Shapley value becomes practically intractable for datasets with even medium-sized feature numbers. This issue necessitates the precise estimation of Shapley values to provide accurate explanations.

3.2 Approximating All Shapley Values

Within the *approximate-all problem*, the objective of an approximation algorithm $\mathcal{A}$ is to precisely estimate the Shapley values $\phi = (\phi_1, \ldots, \phi_n)$ of all players by means of estimates $\hat{\phi} = (\hat{\phi}_1, \ldots, \hat{\phi}_n)$ for a given cooperative game $(\mathcal{N}, \nu)$. We consider the *fixed-budget* setting in which the number of times $\mathcal{A}$ can access ν to evaluate the worth $\nu(S)$ of a coalition S of its choice is limited by a budget $T \in \mathbb{N}$. Thus, $\mathcal{A}$ can sequentially retrieve the worth of T many, possibly duplicate, coalitions to construct its estimate $\hat{\phi}$. This captures the limitation in time, computational resources, or monetary units that a practical user is facing to avoid falling victim to the exact computation's complexity. Furthermore, it is motivated by the observation that the access to ν poses a common bottleneck, by performing inference of complex models or re-training on large data, instead of the negligible arithmetic operations of $\mathcal{A}$.

Since $\mathcal{A}$ potentially uses randomization, for instance by drawing samples and evaluating random coalitions, the comparison of $\hat{\phi}$ and ϕ needs to incorporate this randomness to judge the approximation quality. In light of this, the expected *mean squared error* is a wide-spread measure of approximation quality that is to be minimized by $\mathcal{A}$:

$$\mathbb{E}[\text{MSE}] := \frac{1}{n} \sum_{i \in \mathcal{N}} \mathbb{E}\left[\left(\phi_i - \hat{\phi}_i\right)^2\right]. \tag{2}$$

3.3 Identifying Top-k Players: A Subtle but Significant Difference

Instead of estimating the exact Shapley values of *all* players, of which many might be similar and insignificant, one could be interested in just finding the players that possess the highest Shapley values, with the particular values being incidental. More precisely, in the *top-k identification problem* (TkIP) an approximation algorithm $\mathcal{A}$ is confronted with the task of returning an estimate $\hat{\mathcal{K}} \subseteq \mathcal{N}$ of the coalition $\mathcal{K}^*$ with given size $k \in [n] := \{1, \ldots, n\}$ that contains the players with the highest Shapley values in the game $(\mathcal{N}, \nu)$. We consider again the fixed-budget setting with budget T.

However, $\mathcal{K}^*$ is not necessarily unique as players may share the same Shapley value. We restrain from any assumptions on the value function ν and will thus present notions and measures capable of handling the ambiguity of $\mathcal{K}^*$. We call a coalition $\mathcal{K} \subseteq \mathcal{N}$ of k many players *eligible* if the sum of Shapley values associated to the players in $\mathcal{K}$ is maximal:

$$\sum_{i \in \mathcal{K}} \phi_i = \max_{S \subseteq \mathcal{N}: |S|=k} \sum_{i \in S} \phi_i. \tag{3}$$

We denote by $\mathcal{E}_k \subseteq \mathcal{P}(\mathcal{N})$ the set of all eligible coalitions. Any eligible estimate $\hat{\mathcal{K}}$ is correct and $\mathcal{A}$ should not be punished for it. Note that for distinct Shapley values we have $\mathcal{E}_k = \{\mathcal{K}^*\}$. In the following, we give in a first step precision measures (to be maximized) and error measures (to be minimized) for $\hat{\mathcal{K}}$ given $\mathcal{E}_k$ and extend them in a second step to the randomness of $\mathcal{A}$. A straightforward way to judge the quality of an estimate $\mathcal{K}$ is the *binary precision* [18]

$$\psi_{\text{bin}}(\hat{\mathcal{K}}) := \begin{cases} 1 & \text{if } \hat{\mathcal{K}} \in \mathcal{E}_k \\ 0 & \text{otherwise} \end{cases} \tag{4}$$

that maximally punishes every wrongly included player in $\hat{\mathcal{K}}$. In order to further differentiate estimates that are close to being eligible from ones that have little overlap with an eligible coalition, we introduce the *ratio precision*

$$\psi_{\text{rat}}(\hat{\mathcal{K}}) := \frac{1}{k} \max_{\mathcal{K} \in \mathcal{E}_k} |\mathcal{K} \cap \hat{\mathcal{K}}| \tag{5}$$

which measures the percentage of correctly identified players in $\hat{\mathcal{K}}$ by counting how many players can remain in $\hat{\mathcal{K}}$ after swapping with players from $\mathcal{N} \setminus \hat{\mathcal{K}}$ to form an eligible coalition. It serves as a gradual but still discrete refinement of the binary precision with both measures assigning values in the unit interval $[0, 1]$. Let $\phi_{k^*} := \min_{\mathcal{K} \in \mathcal{E}_k} \min_{i \in \mathcal{K}} \phi_i$ be the minimal Shapley value in any eligible coalition. Obviously, it is the minimal value for all coalitions in $\mathcal{E}_k$. [17] propose the *inclusion-exclusion error* which is the smallest $\varepsilon > 0$ that fulfills

$$\underbrace{\phi_i \geq \phi_{k^*} - \varepsilon}_{\text{inclusion}} \quad \text{and} \quad \underbrace{\phi_j \leq \phi_{k^*} + \varepsilon}_{\text{exclusion}} \tag{6}$$

for all $i \in \hat{\mathcal{K}}$ and all $j \in \mathcal{N} \setminus \hat{\mathcal{K}}$:

$$\rho_{\text{inc+exc}} := \inf\{\varepsilon \in \mathbb{R}^{\geq 0} \mid \forall i \in \hat{\mathcal{K}} : \phi_i \geq \phi_{k^*} - \varepsilon, \forall j \in \mathcal{N} \setminus \hat{\mathcal{K}} : \phi_j \leq \phi_{k^*} + \varepsilon\}. \tag{7}$$

In simple terms, it measures how much the sum of Shapley values associated with $\hat{\mathcal{K}}$ can increase at least or that of $\mathcal{N} \setminus \hat{\mathcal{K}}$ can decrease by swapping a single player between them. To account for the randomness of $\mathcal{A}$, effectively turning $\hat{\mathcal{K}}$ into a random variable, the expectation of each measure poses a reasonable option just as in Sect. 3.2. Worth mentioning is that $\mathbb{E}[\psi_{\text{bin}}(\hat{\mathcal{K}})]$ turns out to be the probability that $\mathcal{A}$ flawlessly solves the top-k identification problem. [17] resort to probably approximate correct (PAC) learning. Specifically for the inclusion-exclusion error they call $\mathcal{A}$ for $\delta \in [0, 1]$ an (ϵ, δ)-PAC learner if

$$\mathbb{P}(\rho_{\text{inc+exc}}(\hat{\mathcal{K}}) \leq \varepsilon) \geq 1 - \delta \tag{8}$$

holds after $\mathcal{A}$ terminates on its own with unlimited budget at disposal. Obviously, any algorithm for the approximate-all problem can be translated to top-k identification by simply returning the k players with the highest estimates.

4 The Opportunity of Correlated Observations

The two problems of approximating all players and top-k identification differ in goal and quality measures, hence they also incentivize different sampling schemes. It is the aim of our work to emphasize and draw attention to our observation that the role of correlated samples between players plays a fundamental role for the top-k identification problem, whereas this is not the case for the approximate-all problem. We demonstrate this at the example of a simple and special class of approximation algorithms that can solve both problem statements. We call an algorithm $\mathcal{A}$ an *unbiased equifrequent player-wise independent sampler* if it samples marginal contributions for all players in M many rounds. In each round $m \in \{1, \ldots, M\}$ $\mathcal{A}$ draws n coalitions $S_1^{(m)}, \ldots, S_n^{(m)}$, one for each $i \in \mathcal{N}$, according to a fixed joint probability distribution over $\mathcal{P}(\mathcal{N} \setminus \{1\}) \times \ldots \times \mathcal{P}(\mathcal{N} \setminus \{n\})$ with marginal distribution

$$\mathbb{P}\left(S_i^{(m)} = S\right) = \frac{1}{n \cdot \binom{n-1}{|S|}} \qquad (9)$$

for each $i \in \mathcal{N}$. Note that this implies $\mathbb{E}[\Delta_i(S_i^{(m)})] = \phi_i$ for all players. Further, the samples are independent between rounds and $\mathcal{A}$ aggregates the samples of each player to an estimate of its Shapley value $\hat{\phi}_i$ by taking the mean of their resulting marginal contributions, i.e.

$$\hat{\phi}_i = \frac{1}{M} \sum_{m=1}^{M} \Delta_i\left(S_i^{(m)}\right), \qquad (10)$$

which is an unbiased estimate of ϕ_i. For the approximate-all problem $\mathcal{A}$ simply returns these estimates and for identifying the top-k players it returns the set of k players $\hat{\mathcal{K}}$ that yield the highest estimates $\hat{\phi}_i$. Ties can be solved arbitrarily. A well-known member of this class of approximation algorithms is *ApproShapley* proposed by [4]. For the approximate-all problem one can quickly derive the expected mean squared error of $\mathcal{A}$ to be

$$\mathbb{E}[\text{MSE}] = \frac{1}{nM} \sum_{i \in \mathcal{N}} \sigma_i^2, \qquad (11)$$

where $\sigma_i^2 := \mathbb{V}[\Delta_i(S_i^{(m)})]$ denotes the variance of player i's marginal contributions. The expected MSE decreases for a growing number of samples M and the sum of variances σ_i^2 can be seen as a constant property of the game $(\mathcal{N}, \nu)$ that is independent of $\mathcal{A}$. In contrast, turning to top-k identification, we show the emergence of another quantity in Theorem 1 if one considers the inclusion-exclusion error. Let $\mathbb{K}_\varepsilon := \{\mathcal{K} \subseteq \mathcal{N} \mid |\mathcal{K}| = k, \rho_{\text{inc+exc}}(\mathcal{K}) \leq \varepsilon\}$ for any $\varepsilon \in \mathbb{R}^{\geq 0}$.

The central limit theorem can be applied within our considered class and thus we assume each $\sqrt{M}((\hat{\phi}_i - \hat{\phi}_j) - (\phi_i - \phi_j))$ to be normally distributed.

Theorem 1. *Every unbiased equifrequent player-wise independent sampler $\mathcal{A}$ for the top-k identification problem returns for any cooperative game $(\mathcal{N}, \nu)$ an estimate $\hat{\mathcal{K}}$ with inclusion-exclusion error of at most $\varepsilon \geq 0$ with probability at least*

$$\mathbb{P}(\hat{\mathcal{K}} \in \mathbb{K}_\varepsilon) \geq \sum_{\mathcal{K} \in \mathbb{K}_\varepsilon} \left[1 - \sum_{\substack{i \in \mathcal{K} \\ j \in \mathcal{N} \setminus \mathcal{K}}} \Phi\left(\sqrt{M} \frac{\phi_j - \phi_i}{\sigma_{i,j}}\right) \right],$$

where $\sigma_{i,j}^2 := \mathbb{V}[\Delta_i(S_i^{(m)}) - \Delta_j(S_j^{(m)})]$ and Φ denotes the standard normal cumulative distribution function.

The proof is given in Appendix A.1. Notice the difference to Eq. (11) for approximating all Shapley values. The MSE directly reflects the change of each single player's estimate $\hat{\phi}_i$, but in contrast, for identifying top-k an estimate may change arbitrarily as long as the partitioning of the players into top-k and outside of top-k stays the same.

For most pairs i, j with $i \in \mathcal{K}$ and $j \in \mathcal{N} \setminus \mathcal{K}$ of a coalition $\mathcal{K} \in \mathbb{K}_\varepsilon$ with sufficiently small ε, it holds $\phi_i > \phi_j$. Thus, for a fixed game $(\mathcal{N}, \nu)$ and fixed budget T, the lower bound in Theorem 1 should favorably increase if $\sigma_{i,j}$ decreases which can be influenced by $\mathcal{A}$ due to the allowed flexibility in its sampling scheme. Note that $\mathcal{A}$ is only restricted in the marginal contribution of each $S_i^{(m)}$ but not in the joint distribution of $S_1^{(m)}, \ldots, S_n^{(m)}$. In fact, the variance of the difference between marginal contributions decomposes to

$$\sigma_{i,j}^2 = \sigma_i^2 + \sigma_j^2 - 2\text{Cov}\left(\Delta_i\left(S_i^{(m)}\right), \Delta_j\left(S_j^{(m)}\right)\right). \tag{12}$$

Consequently, an increased covariance between sampled marginal contributions of top-k players and bottom players improves our lower bound. Leveraging the impact of covariance shown by Eq. 12 in the sampling procedure is generally known as *antithetic sampling*, a variance reduction technique for Monte Carlo methods to which our class belongs. Our considered class of approximation algorithms does not impose any restrictions on the contained covariance between marginal contributions sampled within the same round m. We interpret this as degrees of freedom to shape the sampling distribution. Striving towards more reliable estimates $\hat{\mathcal{K}}$, we propose in Sect. 5 an approach based on the suspected improvement that positively correlated observations promise.

5 Antithetic Sampling Approach

Motivated by Sect. 4, we develop in Sect. 5.1 *Comparable Marginal Contributions Sampling* (CMCS), a budget-efficient antithetic sampling procedure that naturally yields correlated observations applicable for both problem statements. We take inspiration from [17,18] and extend CMCS with a greedy selection criterion in Sect. 5.2, deciding from which players to sample from, to exploit opportunities that top-k identification offers.

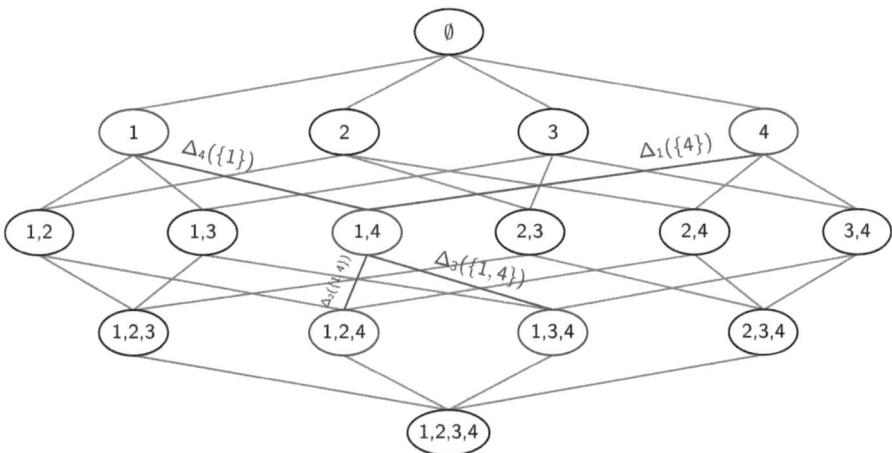

Fig. 1. A cooperative game spans a lattice with each coalition $S \subseteq \mathcal{N}$ forming a node and each marginal contribution $\Delta_i(S)$ being represented by an edge between S and $S \cup \{i\}$, exemplified here for $\mathcal{N} = \{1, 2, 3, 4\}$. CMCS draws a random coalition S and computes the extended marginal contributions $\Delta'_i(S) = \Delta_i(S \setminus \{i\})$ of all players $i \in \mathcal{N}$. For $n = 4$ it evaluates five coalitions and retrieves four marginal contributions.

5.1 Sampling Comparable Marginal Contributions

We start by observing that the sampling of marginal contributions can be designed to consume less than two evaluations of ν per sample. In fact, the budget restriction T is not coupled to the evaluation of marginal contributions as atomic units but single accesses to ν. Instead of separately evaluating $\nu(S)$ and $\nu(S \cup \{i\})$ for each $\Delta_i(S)$, the evaluations can be reused to form other marginal contributions and thus save budget. This idea can already be applied to the sampling of permutations of the player set. [4] evaluate for each drawn permutation π the marginal contribution $\Delta_i(\text{pre}_i(\pi))$ of each player i to the preceding players in π. Except for the last player in π, each evaluation $\nu(\text{pre}_i(\pi) \cup \{i\})$ can be reused for the marginal contribution of the succeeding player.

We further develop this paradigm of *sample reusage* by exploiting the fact that any coalition $S \subseteq \mathcal{N}$ appears in n many marginal contributions, one for each player, namely in $n - |S|$ many of the form $\Delta_i(S)$ for $i \notin S$ and $|S|$ many of the form $\Delta_i(S \setminus \{i\})$ for $i \in S$. We meaningfully unify both cases by establishing the notion of an *extended marginal contribution* in Definition 1.

Definition 1. *For any cooperative game $(\mathcal{N}, \nu)$, the extended marginal contribution of a player $i \in \mathcal{N}$ to a coalition $S \subseteq \mathcal{N}$ is given by*

$$\Delta_i'(S) := \nu(S \cup \{i\}) - \nu(S \setminus \{i\}).$$

Fittingly, this yields $\Delta_i'(S) = \Delta_i(S \setminus \{i\})$ for $i \in S$ and $\Delta_i'(S) = \Delta_i(S) = \Delta_i(S \setminus \{i\})$ for $i \notin S$. Thus, we circumvent the case of $\Delta_i(S) = 0$ for $i \in S$.

We aim to draw in each round m (of M many) a coalition $S^{(m)} \subseteq \mathcal{N}$, compute the extended marginal contributions $\Delta_i'(S^{(m)})$ of *all* players as illustrated in Fig. 1, and update each $\hat{\phi}_i$ as the average of the corresponding observations:

$$\hat{\phi}_i = \frac{1}{M} \sum_{m=1}^{M} \Delta_i'\left(S^{(m)}\right). \tag{13}$$

We reuse the coalition value $v_{S^{(m)}} = \nu(S^{(m)})$ to update all estimates by computing each extended marginal contribution as

$$\Delta_i'\left(S^{(m)}\right) = \begin{cases} v_{S^{(m)}} - \nu(S^{(m)} \setminus \{i\}) & \text{if } i \in S \\ \nu(S^{(m)} \cup \{i\}) - v_{S^{(m)}} & \text{otherwise} \end{cases}. \tag{14}$$

Consequently, updating all n estimates requires only $n+1$ calls to ν such that we obtain a *budget-efficiency* of $\frac{n}{n+1}$ sampled observations per call. In comparison, drawing marginal contributions separately yields a budget-efficiency of $1/2$. In order to make this approach effective, it is desirable to obtain unbiased estimates leading to the question whether there even exists a probability distribution over $\mathcal{P}(\mathcal{N})$ to sample $S^{(m)}$ from such that $\mathbb{E}[\Delta_i'(S^{(m)})] = \phi_i$ for all $i \in \mathcal{N}$. Indeed, we show its existence in Proposition 1 by means of a novel representation of the Shapley value based on extended marginal contributions.

Proposition 1. *For any cooperative game $(\mathcal{N}, \nu)$, the Shapley value of each player $i \in \mathcal{N}$ is a weighted average of its extended marginal contributions. In particular, it holds*

$$\phi_i = \sum_{S \subseteq \mathcal{N}} \frac{1}{(n+1)\binom{n}{|S|}} \cdot \Delta_i'(S).$$

See Appendix A.2 for a proof. The weighted average allows to view the Shapley value as the expected extended marginal contribution and thus drawing $S^{(m)}$ from the distribution

$$\mathbb{P}\left(S^{(m)} = S\right) = \frac{1}{(n+1)\binom{n}{|S|}} \quad \text{for all } S \subseteq \mathcal{N} \tag{15}$$

yields unbiased estimates. Note that this is indeed a well-defined probability distribution over $\mathcal{P}(\mathcal{N})$ as shown in Appendix A.2. The resulting algorithm *Comparable Marginal Contributions Sampling* (CMCS) is given by Algorithm 1. It requires the cooperative game (N, ν), the budget T, and the parameter k as input. The number of performed rounds M is bounded by $M = \lfloor \frac{T}{n+1} \rfloor$. We solve sampling from the exponentially large power set of $\mathcal{N}$ by first drawing a size ℓ ranging from 0 to n uniformly at random (line 3) and then drawing uniformly a coalition S of size ℓ (line 4). This results in the probability distribution of Eq. (15) since there are $n+1$ sizes and $\binom{n}{\ell}$ coalitions of size ℓ to choose from. For the top-k identification problem CMCS returns the set of k many players $\hat{\mathcal{K}}$ for which it maintains the highest estimates $\hat{\phi}_i$. Ties are solved arbitrarily.

Algorithm 1. Comparable Marginal Contributions Sampling (CMCS)

Input: $(\mathcal{N}, \nu)$, $T \in \mathbb{N}, k \in [n]$
1: $\hat{\phi}_i \leftarrow 0$ for all $i \in \mathcal{N}$
2: **for** $m = 1, \ldots, \lfloor \frac{T}{n+1} \rfloor$ **do**
3:      Draw $\ell \in \{0, \ldots, n\}$ uniformly at random
4:      Draw $S \subseteq \mathcal{N}$ with $|S| = \ell$ uniformly at random
5:      $v_S \leftarrow \nu(S)$
6:      **for** $i \in \mathcal{N}$ **do**
7:          $\Delta_i \leftarrow \begin{cases} v_S - \nu(S \setminus \{i\}) & \text{if } i \in S \\ \nu(S \cup \{i\}) - v_S & \text{otherwise} \end{cases}$
8:          $\hat{\phi}_i \leftarrow \frac{(m-1) \cdot \hat{\phi}_i + \Delta_i}{m}$
9:      **end for**
10: **end for**

Output: $\hat{\mathcal{K}}$ containing k players with highest estimate $\hat{\phi}_i$

CMCS can also be applied for the approximate-all problem by simply returning its estimates since its sampling procedure and computation of estimates is independent of k. Thus, it is also an unbiased equifrequent player-wise independent sampler (see Sect. 4) because the marginal contributions obtained in each round stem from a fixed joint distribution and the resulting marginal distributions coincide with Eq. (9) as implied by Proposition 1. Hence for T being a multiple of $n+1$, its expected MSE is according to Eq. 11:

$$\mathbb{E}[\text{MSE}] = \frac{n+1}{nT} \sum_{i \in \mathcal{N}} \sigma_i^2. \tag{16}$$

For the top-k identification the sampling scheme in CMCS yields an interesting property. All players share extended marginal contributions to the same reference coalitions $S^{(m)}$. Intuitively, this makes the estimates more comparable, as all have been updated using the same samples. Instead of estimating ϕ_i and ϕ_j precisely, CMCS answers the relevant question whether $\phi_i > \phi_j$ holds, by comparing the players marginal contributions to roughly the same coalitions, modulo the case of $i \in S$ and $j \notin S$ or vice versa. Instead, drawing marginal contributions separately, independently between the players, can, metaphorically speaking, be viewed as comparing apples with oranges.

Consequently, the estimates $\hat{\phi}_i$ and $\hat{\phi}_j$ are correlated and we further conjecture that the covariance $\text{Cov}(\Delta_i'(S^{(m)}), \Delta_j'(S^{(m)})) = \mathbb{E}[\Delta_i'(S^{(m)}) \Delta_j'(S^{(m)})] -$

$\mathbb{E}[\Delta'_i(S^{(m)})]\mathbb{E}[\Delta'_j(S^{(m)})]$ has a positive impact on the inclusion-exclusion error of CMCS in light of Theorem 1. For cooperative games in which the marginal contribution of a player is influenced by the coalitions size, our sampling scheme should yield positively correlated samples. In this case, if player i or j is added to the same coalition S, it is likely that both have a positive marginal contribution (or both share a negative) which in turn speaks for a positive covariance. For the general case, the covariance is stated in Proposition 2.

Proposition 2. *For any cooperative game $(\mathcal{N},\nu)$ the covariance between the extended marginal contributions of any players $i \neq j$ of the same round sampled by CMCS is given by*

$$Cov\left(\Delta'_i\left(S^{(m)}\right), \Delta'_j\left(S^{(m)}\right)\right) = \frac{1}{n+1} \sum_{S \subseteq \mathcal{N}\setminus\{i\}} \Delta_i(S) \left(\frac{\Delta'_j(S)}{\binom{n}{|S|}} + \frac{\Delta'_j(S\cup\{i\})}{\binom{n}{|S|+1}}\right) - \phi_i \phi_j.$$

The proof is given in Appendix A.2. The sum can be seen as the Shapley value ϕ_i in which each marginal contribution of i is additionally weighted by extended marginal contributions of j. To demonstrate the presumably positive covariance and give evidence to our conjecture, we consider a simple game of arbitrary size n with $\nu(\mathcal{N}) = 1$ and $\nu(S) = 0$ for all coalitions $S \neq \mathcal{N}$. Each player has a Shapley value of $\frac{1}{n}$ and the covariance in Proposition 2 given by $\frac{1}{n+1} - \frac{1}{n^2}$ is strictly positive for $n \geq 2$.

5.2 Relaxed Greedy Player Selection for Top-k Identification

Striving for budget-efficiency in the design of a sample procedure might be favorable, however, CMCS as proposed in Sect. 5.1 is forced to spend budget on the retrieval of marginal contributions for all players in order to maximize budget-efficiency. This comes with the disadvantage that evaluations of ν are performed to sample for a player i whose estimate $\hat{\phi}_i$ is possibly already reliable enough and does not need further updates compared to other players. This does not even require $\hat{\phi}_i$ to be precise in absolute terms. Instead, it is sufficient to predict with certainty whether i belongs to the top-k or not by comparing it to the other estimates. This observation calls for a more selective mechanism deciding which players to leave out in each round and thus save budget.

A radical approach is the greedy selection of a single player which maximizes a *selection criterion* based on the collected observations that incorporates incentives for exploration and exploitation. Gap-E [1,12] composes the selection criterion out of the uncertainty of a player's top-k (exploitation) membership and its number of observations (exploration). Similarly, BUS [18] selects the player i minimizing the product of its estimate's distance to the predicted top-k border $\frac{1}{2}(\min_{i\in\hat{\mathcal{K}}}\hat{\phi}_i - \max_{j\in\mathcal{N}\setminus\hat{\mathcal{K}}}\hat{\phi}_j)$ times its sample number M_i. In the same spirit but outside of the fixed-budget setting, SHAP@K [17] chooses for given $\delta \in (0,1)$ the two players $i \in \hat{\mathcal{K}}$ and $j \in \mathcal{N} \setminus \hat{\mathcal{K}}$ with the highest overlap in their δ/n-confidence intervals of their estimates $\hat{\phi}_i$ and $\hat{\phi}_j$. It applies a stopping condition and terminates when no overlaps between $\hat{\mathcal{K}}$ and $\mathcal{N} \setminus \hat{\mathcal{K}}$ larger then a specified error ε exist. Assuming normally distributed estimates $\hat{\phi}_i$ under the central limit theorem, it holds $\mathbb{P}(\rho_{\text{inc+exc}}(\hat{\mathcal{K}}) \leq \varepsilon) \geq 1 - \delta$ for its prediction $\hat{\mathcal{K}}$.

Given the core idea of CMCS to draw samples for multiple players at once in order to increase budget-efficiency and obtain correlated observations, the greedy selection of a single player as done in [12,18] or just a pair [17] is not suitable for our method. The phase-wise elimination performed by SAR [1] is not viable as it assumes all observations to be independent in order to analytically derive phase lengths. Instead, we relax the greediness by probabilistically selecting a set of players $P^{(m)} \subseteq \mathcal{N}$ in each round m, favoring those players who fulfill a selection criterion to higher degree. By doing so, we propose *Greedy CMCS* that intertwines the overcoming of the exploration-exploitation dilemma with the pursuit of budget-efficiency. We do not abandon exploration, since every player gets a chance to be picked, and the selection criterion incentivizes exploitation as it reflects how much the choice of a player benefits the prediction $\hat{\mathcal{K}}$.

Our selection criterion is based on the current knowledge of $\hat{\phi}_1, \ldots, \hat{\phi}_n$ and the presumably best players $\hat{\mathcal{K}}$. Inspired by Theorem 1, we approximate the probability of each pair of players $i \in \hat{\mathcal{K}}$ and $j \in \mathcal{N} \setminus \hat{\mathcal{K}}$ being incorrectly partitioned by Greedy CMCS as

$$\hat{p}_{i,j} := \Phi\left(\sqrt{M_{i,j}} \frac{\hat{\delta}_{i,j}}{\hat{\sigma}_{i,j}}\right). \tag{17}$$

For all pairs $(i,j) \in \mathcal{N}^2$ we track:

- the number of times $M_{i,j}$ that both i and j have been selected in a round,
- the mean difference $\hat{\delta}_{i,j} := \frac{1}{M_{i,j}} \sum_{m=1}^{M_{i,j}} \Delta'_j(S^{(f_{i,j}(m))}) - \Delta'_i(S^{(f_{i,j}(m))})$ of their sampled marginal contributions within these $M_{i,j}$ rounds, where $f_{i,j}(m)$ denotes the m-th round in which i and j are selected, and
- the estimate $\hat{\sigma}^2_{i,j}$ of the variance $\sigma^2_{i,j} := \mathbb{V}[\Delta'_i(S^{(m)}) - \Delta'_j(S^{(m)})]$ w.r.t. Eq. (15) derived from the sampled observations.

Important to note is that we may not simply use the difference $\hat{\phi}_j - \hat{\phi}_i$ of our Shapley estimates, including all rounds, instead of $\hat{\delta}_{i,j}$ because $\hat{\phi}_i$ and $\hat{\phi}_j$ may differ in their respective total amount of total samples M_i and M_j such that the central limit theorem used for Theorem 1 is not applicable anymore. We derive Eq. (17) in Appendix A.3.

For each pair $(i,j) \in \hat{\mathcal{K}} \times (\mathcal{N} \setminus \hat{\mathcal{K}})$ the estimate $\hat{p}_{i,j}$ quantifies how likely i and j are wrongly partitioned: Greedy CMCS estimates $\hat{\phi}_i \geq \hat{\phi}_j$ although $\phi_i < \phi_j$ holds. Since we want to minimize the probability of such a mistake, it comes natural to include the pair (i,j) with the highest estimate $\hat{p}_{i,j}$ in the next round of Greedy CMCS to draw marginal contributions from, i.e. $i,j \in P^{(m)}$. As a consequence, $\hat{\phi}_i$ and $\hat{\phi}_j$ should become more reliable causing the error probability to shrink. Let $Q^{(m)} \subseteq \hat{\mathcal{K}} \times (\mathcal{N} \setminus \hat{\mathcal{K}})$ be the set of selected pairs in round m from which the selected players are formed as $P^{(m)} = \{i \in \mathcal{N} \mid \exists (i,j) \in Q^{(m)} \vee \exists (j,i) \in Q^{(m)}\}$. In order to allow for more than two updated players in a round m, i.e.

$|Q^{(m)}| > 1$, but waive pairs that are more likely to be correctly classified, we probabilistically include pairs in $Q^{(m)}$ depending on their $\hat{p}$-value. Let $\hat{p}_{\max} = \max_{i \in \hat{\mathcal{K}}, j \notin \hat{\mathcal{K}}} \hat{p}_{i,j}$ be the currently highest and $\hat{p}_{\min} = \min_{i \in \hat{\mathcal{K}}, j \notin \hat{\mathcal{K}}} \hat{p}_{i,j}$ the currently lowest value. We select each pair (i,j) independently with probability

$$\mathbb{P}\left((i,j) \in Q^{(m)}\right) = \frac{\hat{p}_{i,j} - \hat{p}_{\min}}{\hat{p}_{\max} - \hat{p}_{\min}} \text{ for all } (i,j) \in \hat{\mathcal{K}} \times (\mathcal{N} \setminus \hat{\mathcal{K}}). \qquad (18)$$

This forces the pair with $\hat{p}_{\max}$ to be picked and that with $\hat{p}_{\min}$ to be left out. The probability of a pair beings elected increases monotonically with its $\hat{p}$-value.

Within an executed round we do not only collect marginal contributions for players in $P^{(m)}$ and update $M_{i,j}$, $\hat{\delta}_{i,j}$, and $\hat{\sigma}_{i,j}^2$ for all $(i,j) \in Q^{(m)}$. We use the collected information to its fullest by also updating the estimates of all pairs (i,j) with both players being present in $P^{(m)}$ despite $(i,j) \notin Q^{(m)}$. Visually speaking, we update the complete subgraph induced by $P^{(m)}$ with players being nodes and edges containing the pairwise estimates.

Since the assumption of normally distributed estimates motivated by the central limit theorem is not appropriate for a low number of samples, we initialize Greedy CMCS with a warm-up phase as proposed for SHAP@K [17]. During the warm-up $M_{\min}$ many rounds of CMCS are performed such that afterwards every player's Shapley estimate is based on $M_{\min}$ samples. This consumes a budget of $(n+1)M_{\min}$ many evaluations. $M_{\min}$ is provided to Greedy CMCS as a parameter. Subsequently, the above described round-wise greedy sampling is applied as the second phase until the depletion of the in total available budget T. The pseudocode of the resulting algorithm Greedy CMCS is given in Appendix B.

Instead of our proposed selection mechanism, one can sample in the second phase only from the two players $i \in \hat{\mathcal{K}}$ and $j \notin \hat{\mathcal{K}}$ with the biggest overlap in confidence intervals as performed by SHAP@K. Leaving the sampling of CMCS in the first phase untouched, we call this variant *CMCS@K*. This is feasible since the choice of the sampling procedure in SHAP@K is to some extent arbitrary, as long as it yields confidence intervals for the Shapley estimates.

6 Empirical Results

We conduct multiple experiments of different designs to assess the performance of sampling comparable marginal contributions at the example of explanation tasks on real-world datasets. First, we demonstrate in Sect. 6.1 the iterative improvements of our proposed algorithmic tricks ranging from the naive independent sampling to Greedy CMCS and CMCS@K. 6.2 investigates whether favorable MSE values of algorithms for the approximate-all problem translate on the same cooperative games to the inclusion-exclusion error for top-k identification. In Sect. 6.3 we compare our variants of CMCS against baselines and state-of-the-art competitors. Lastly, we investigate in Sect. 6.4 the required budget until the stopping criterion of [17] applied to CMCS guarantees an error of at most ε with probability at least $1 - \delta$. All performance measures are calculated by exhaustively computing the Shapley values in advance and averaging the results over 1000 runs. Standard errors are included as shaded bands. We compare against *ApproShapley* [4], *KernelSHAP* [22] (with reference implementation provided by the `shap` python package, the one to sample without replacement), *Stratified SVARM* [19], *BUS* [18], and *SamplingSHAP@K* [17] which is SHAP@K drawing samples according to ApproShapley. For both SamplingSHAP@K and CMCS@K, we use $M_{\min} = 30$ and confidence intervals of δ/n with $\delta = 0.001$. We drop *Gap-E* [12] and *SAR* [1] due to worse performances[1].

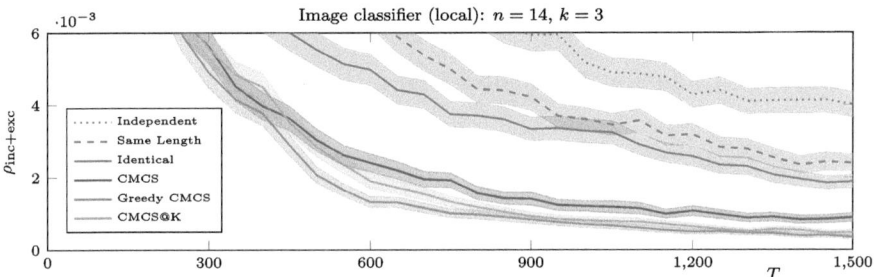

Fig. 2. Inclusion-exclusion error ε for increasingly comparable sampling variants (*Independent*, *Same Length*, *Identical*), incorporation of sample-reusage (CMCS), and greedy selection (Greedy CMCS, CMCS@K) depending on T.

Datasets and Games. Analogously to [19,20], we generate cooperative games from two types of explanation tasks in which the Shapley values represent feature importance scores. For global games, we construct the value function by training a *sklearn* random forest with 20 trees on each feature subset and taking its classification accuracy, or the R^2-metric for regression tasks, on a test set as the coalitions' worth. We employ the *Adult* ($n = 14$, classification), *Bank Marketing* ($n = 16$, classification), *Bike Sharing* ($n = 15$, regression), *Diabetes* ($n = 10$, regression), *German Credit* ($n = 20$, classification), *Titanic* ($n = 11$, classification), and *Wine* ($n = 13$, classification) dataset. For local games, we create a game by picking a random datapoint and taking a pretrained model's prediction value as each coalition's worth. Feature values are imputed by their mean, respectively mode. For this purpose we take the *Adult* ($n = 14$, XGBoost, classification), *ImageNet* ($n = 14$, ResNet18, classification), and *NLP Sentiment* ($n = 14$, DistilBERT transformer, regression, IMDB data) dataset.

6.1 Advantage of Comparable Sampling

Greedy CMCS builds upon multiple ideas whose effects onto the approximation quality is depicted in isolation by Fig. 2. As a baseline we consider the *independent* sampling of marginal contributions of each player with distribution given

---

[1] All code can be found at https://github.com/timnielen/top-k-shapley.

in Eq. (9). The comparability of the samples is stepwise increased by sampling in each round marginal contributions to coalitions of the *same length* for all players, and next using the *identical* coalition $S^{(m)}$ drawn according to Eq. (15). In compliance with our conjecture, the decreasing error from *independent* to *same length* and further to *identical* speaks in favor of the beneficial impact that comes with correlated observations. The biggest leap in performance is caused by reusing the evaluated worth $\nu(S^{(m)})$ appearing in each marginal contribution of the *independent* variant resulting in CMCS. The sample reusage alone almost doubles the budget-efficiency from $1/2$ to $n/n+1$. On top of that, incorporating (relaxed) greedy sampling gifts Greedy CMCS and CMCS@K a further advantage by halving the error for higher budget ranges.

6.2 MSE vs Inclusion-Exclusion Error

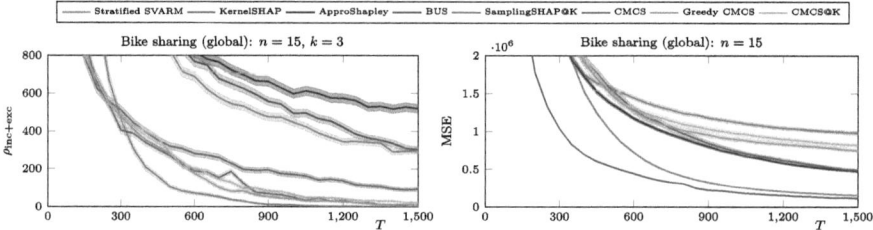

Fig. 3. Comparison of achieved inclusion-exclusion error of various algorithms for top-k identification (left) and approximate-all (right) depending on T.

Given the similarities between the problem statements of approximating all Shapley values (cf. Sect. 3.2) and that of top-k identification (cf. Sect. 3.3) at first sight, one might suspect that approximation algorithms performing well in the former, also do so in the latter and vice versa. However, Fig. 3 shows a different picture. The best performing methods Stratified SVARM and KernelSHAP remain consistent but change in order. The variants of CMCS are less favorable in terms of MSE but are barely outperformed in top-k identification. We interpret this as further evidence that top-k identification indeed rewards positively correlated samples supporting our intuition of comparability. Most striking is the difference between ApproShapley and CMCS. Assuming to know $\nu(\emptyset) = 0$, ApproShapley exhibits a budget-efficiency of 1 as it consumes in each sampled permutation n evaluations and retrieves n marginal contributions, which is only slightly better than that of CMCS with $n/n+1$. Thus, it should be only marginally better in approximation according to Eqs. (11) and (16). Our results in Fig. 3 confirm the precision of our theory. However, notice how CMCS significantly outperforms ApproShapley in terms of $\rho_{\text{inc+exc}}$ despite the almost identical budget usage. Hence, it is the stronger correlation of samples drawn by CMCS combined with the nature of top-k identification that causes the observed advantage of comparable sampling.

6.3 Comparison with Existing Methods

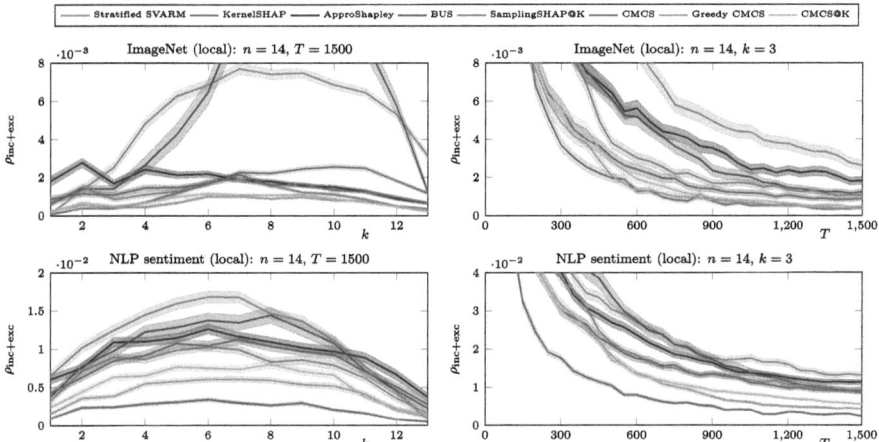

Fig. 4. Comparison of achieved inclusion-exclusion error with baselines for local explanations: fixed budget with varying k (left) and fixed k with increasing budget (right).

Figure 4 and 5 compare the performances of our methods against baselines for local and global games. For fixed $k = 3$, we observe the competitiveness of Greedy CMCS and CMCS@K being mostly on par with KernelSHAP, but getting beaten by Stratified SVARM for global games, which in turns subsides at local games. Greedy CMCS exhibits stable performance across both explanation types and the whole range of k. On the other hand, if instead the budget is fixed, Greedy CMCS has often the upper hand for values of k close to $n/2$ and is even with KernelSHAP for lower k.

6.4 Budget Consumption for PAC Solution

Assuming normally distributed Shapley estimates, SHAP@K is a (ε, δ)-PAC learner [17], i.e. upon self-induced termination it holds $\rho_{\text{inc}+\text{exc}}(\hat{\mathcal{K}}) \leq \varepsilon$ with probability at least $1 - \delta$. KernelSHAP is not applicable as it does not yield confidence bounds. For this reason [17] sample marginal contributions referred as *SamplingSHAP@K*. Its stopping condition is triggered as soon as no δ/n confidence intervals for the estimates $\hat{\phi}_i$ overlap between $\hat{\mathcal{K}}$ and $\mathcal{N} \setminus \hat{\mathcal{K}}$. We apply the stopping condition to our algorithms and compare to SamplingSHAP@K in the PAC-setting. Table 1 shows the average number of calls to ν until termination that is to be minimized. For some local games the number of calls is significantly higher due to the large variance in the difficulty of the respective games induced from each datapoint. CMCS@K shows the best results in nearly every game by some margin, which makes it the algorithm of choice for PAC-learning. Thus, CMCS@K is preferable when guarantees for approximation quality are required and improves upon SHAP@K due to its refined sampling mechanism.

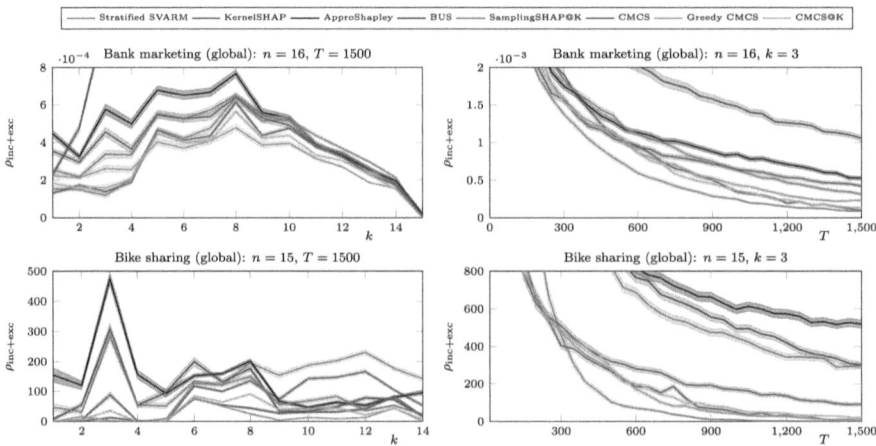

Fig. 5. Comparison of achieved inclusion-exclusion error with baselines for global explanations: fixed budget with varying k (left) and fixed k with increasing budget (right).

Table 1. Average number of calls to ν in the PAC-setting (see Eq. 8) across different datasets averaged over 200 runs using $\delta = 0.01$ and $\epsilon = 0.0005$ for $k = 5$.

Game	SamplingSHAP@K		CMCS		CMCS@K		Greedy CMCS	
	#samples	SE	#samples	SE	#samples	SE	#samples	SE
Adult (global)	38 998	1 247	137 861	2 517	**30 995**	673	39 071	738
German credit (global)	21 939	336	56 738	1 129	**16 437**	248	22 327	328
Bike sharing (global)	4 850	97	13 053	164	**3 982**	54	8 894	117
Bank marketing (glo.)	15 124	287	39 144	875	**12 000**	206	16 260	267
Diabetes (global)	3 723	94	7 793	143	**2 976**	55	4 593	85
Titanic (global)	4 852	113	11 036	237	**3 884**	72	5 782	124
Wine (global)	34 953	1 046	120 859	1 906	**29 913**	641	34 265	501
NLP sentiment (local)	626 346	188 125	3 351 274	764 663	568 261	156 674	**447 252**	77 149
ImageNet (local)	135 851	39 335	578 670	196 181	**108 267**	32 067	261 586	147 126
Adult (local)	18 464	4 391	55 779	17 954	**14 406**	3 645	16 160	3 765

7 Conclusion

We emphasized differences between the problem of approximating all Shapley values and that of identifying the k players with highest Shapley values. Analytically recognizing the advantage that correlated samples promise, we developed with CMCS an antithetic sampling algorithm that reuses evaluations to save budget. Our extensions Greedy CMCS and CMCS@K employ selective strategies for sampling. Both demonstrate competitive performances, with Greedy CMCS being better suited for fixed budgets, whereas CMCS@K is clearly favorable in the PAC-setting. Our proposed methods are not only model-agnostic, moreover, they can handle any cooperative game, facilitating their application for any explanation type and domain even outside of explainable AI. The difficulties that some algorithms face when translating their performance to top-k identification suggest that practitioner's being consciously interested in top-k explanations might have an advantage by applying tailored top-k algorithms instead of the trivial reduction to the approximate-all problem. Future work could investigate the sensible choice of the warm-up length in Greedy CMCS and CMCS@K which poses a trade-off between exploration and exploitation. Modifying our considered problem statement to identify the players with highest absolute Shapley values poses an intriguing variation for detecting the most impactful players and opens the door to new approaches. Finally, Shapley interactions enrich Shapley-based explanations. The number of pairwise interactions grows quadratically with n, hence top-k identification could play an even more significant role. Our work can be understood as a methodological precursor to such extensions.

Disclosure of Interests. The authors have no competing interests to declare that are relevant to the content of this article.

A Theoretical Analysis

A.1 Proof of Theorem 1

For the estimate $\hat{\mathcal{K}} \subseteq \mathcal{N}$ returned by an algorithm for the top-k identification problem we can obviously state

$$\mathbb{P}(\hat{\mathcal{K}} \in \mathbb{K}_\varepsilon) = \sum_{\mathcal{K} \in \mathbb{K}_\varepsilon} \mathbb{P}(\hat{\mathcal{K}} = \mathcal{K}).$$

Given the construction of $\hat{\mathcal{K}}$, $\mathcal{A}$ must choose any $i \in \mathcal{N}$ to be in $\hat{\mathcal{K}}$ if $\hat{\phi}_i > \hat{\phi}_j$ holds for at least $n - k$ many players $j \in \mathcal{N}$. Hence, for any $\mathcal{K} \in \mathbb{K}_\varepsilon$ we have:

$$\begin{aligned}
\mathbb{P}(\hat{\mathcal{K}} = \mathcal{K}) &\geq \mathbb{P}(\forall i \in \mathcal{K} \; \forall j \in \mathcal{N} \setminus \mathcal{K} : \hat{\phi}_i > \hat{\phi}_j) \\
&= 1 - \mathbb{P}(\exists i \in \mathcal{K} \; \exists j \in \mathcal{N} \setminus \mathcal{K} : \hat{\phi}_i \leq \hat{\phi}_j) \\
&\geq 1 - \sum_{\substack{i \in \mathcal{K} \\ j \in \mathcal{N} \setminus \mathcal{K}}} \mathbb{P}(\hat{\phi}_i \leq \hat{\phi}_j)
\end{aligned}$$

Given the assumptions on the sampling procedure and the aggregation to estimates $\hat{\phi}_1, \ldots, \hat{\phi}_n$, we can apply the central limit theorem (CLT) to state that for any $i \in \mathcal{K}$ and $j \in \mathcal{N} \setminus \mathcal{K}$ the distribution of $\sqrt{M}\left((\hat{\phi}_i - \hat{\phi}_j) - (\phi_i - \phi_j)\right)$ converges to a normal distribution with mean 0 and variance $\sigma_{i,j}^2$ as $M \to \infty$ since $\mathbb{E}[\hat{\phi}_i - \hat{\phi}_j] = \phi_i - \phi_j$. Although M is finite as it is limited by the budget T, we assume it to be normally distributed, to which it comes close to in practice for large M. Hence, for any $i \in \mathcal{K}$ and $j \in \mathcal{N} \setminus \mathcal{K}$ we derive:

$$\begin{aligned}
\mathbb{P}(\hat{\phi}_i \leq \hat{\phi}_j) &= \mathbb{P}(\hat{\phi}_i - \hat{\phi}_j \leq 0) \\
&= \mathbb{P}((\hat{\phi}_i - \hat{\phi}_j) - (\phi_i - \phi_j) \leq -(\phi_i - \phi_j)) \\
&= \mathbb{P}(\sqrt{M}((\hat{\phi}_i - \hat{\phi}_j) - (\phi_i - \phi_j)) \leq \sqrt{M}(\phi_j - \phi_i)) \\
&\stackrel{CLT}{=} \Phi\left(\sqrt{M}\frac{\phi_j - \phi_i}{\sigma_{i,j}}\right)
\end{aligned}$$

where Φ is the standard normal cumulative distribution function. Putting the intermediate results together, we obtain

$$\mathbb{P}(\hat{\mathcal{K}} \in \mathbb{K}_\varepsilon) \geq \sum_{\mathcal{K} \in \mathbb{K}_\varepsilon} \left[1 - \sum_{\substack{i \in \mathcal{K} \\ j \in \mathcal{N} \setminus \mathcal{K}}} \Phi\left(\sqrt{M} \frac{\phi_j - \phi_i}{\sigma_{i,j}}\right) \right].$$

A.2 Comparable Marginal Contributions Sampling

Proof that Eq. 15 induces a well-defined probability distribution:
Obviously it holds $\mathbb{P}(S) \geq 0$ and for the sum of probabilities we have:

$$\sum_{S \subseteq \mathcal{N}} \mathbb{P}(S) = \sum_{S \subseteq \mathcal{N}} \frac{1}{(n+1)\binom{n}{|S|}} = \sum_{\ell=0}^n \sum_{\substack{S \subseteq \mathcal{N} \\ |S|=\ell}} \frac{1}{(n+1)\binom{n}{\ell}} = \sum_{\ell=0}^n \frac{\binom{n}{\ell}}{(n+1)\binom{n}{\ell}} = 1.$$

Proof of Proposition 1:
For any $i \in \mathcal{N}$ we derive:

$$\sum_{S \subseteq \mathcal{N}} \frac{1}{(n+1)\binom{n}{|S|}} \Delta_i'(S) = \sum_{\substack{S \subseteq \mathcal{N} \\ i \in S}} \frac{1}{(n+1)\binom{n}{|S|}} \Delta_i(S \setminus \{i\}) + \sum_{\substack{S \subseteq \mathcal{N} \\ i \notin S}} \frac{1}{(n+1)\binom{n}{|S|}} \Delta_i(S)$$

$$= \sum_{S \subseteq \mathcal{N} \setminus \{i\}} \frac{1}{(n+1)\binom{n}{|S|+1}} \Delta_i(S) + \sum_{S \subseteq \mathcal{N} \setminus \{i\}} \frac{1}{(n+1)\binom{n}{|S|}} \Delta_i(S)$$

$$= \sum_{S \subseteq \mathcal{N} \setminus \{i\}} \frac{1}{n+1} \left(\frac{1}{\binom{n}{|S|+1}} + \frac{1}{\binom{n}{|S|}} \right) \Delta_i(S)$$

$$= \sum_{S \subseteq \mathcal{N} \setminus \{i\}} \frac{1}{n \cdot \binom{n-1}{|S|}} \Delta_i(S)$$

$$= \phi_i$$

Proof of Proposition 2:
Given the unbiasedness of the samples, i.e. $\mathbb{E}[\Delta_i'(S^{(m)})] = \phi_i$ for every $i \in \mathcal{N}$, the covariance is given by:

$$\text{Cov}\left(\Delta_i'(S^{(m)}), \Delta_j'(S^{(m)})\right) = \mathbb{E}\left[\Delta_i'(S^{(m)})\Delta_j'(S^{(m)})\right] - \mathbb{E}\left[\Delta_i'(S^{(m)})\right]\mathbb{E}\left[\Delta_j'(S^{(m)})\right]$$
$$= \mathbb{E}\left[\Delta_i'(S^{(m)})\Delta_j'(S^{(m)})\right] - \phi_i \phi_j$$

For the first term we derive:

$$\mathbb{E}\left[\Delta_i'(S^{(m)})\Delta_j'(S^{(m)})\right]$$
$$= \sum_{S \subseteq \mathcal{N}} \frac{1}{(n+1)\binom{n}{|S|}} \cdot \Delta_i'(S)\Delta_j'(S)$$
$$= \frac{1}{n+1} \sum_{S \subseteq \mathcal{N} \setminus \{i,j\}} \frac{\Delta_i(S)\Delta_j(S)}{\binom{n}{|S|}} + \frac{\Delta_i(S)\Delta_j(S \cup \{i\})}{\binom{n}{|S|+1}} + \frac{\Delta_i(S \cup \{j\})\Delta_j(S)}{\binom{n}{|S|+1}} + \frac{\Delta_i(S \cup \{j\})\Delta_j(S \cup \{i\})}{\binom{n}{|S|+2}}$$
$$= \frac{1}{n+1} \sum_{S \subseteq \mathcal{N} \setminus \{i,j\}} \Delta_i(S) \left(\frac{\Delta_j(S)}{\binom{n}{|S|}} + \frac{\Delta_j(S \cup \{i\})}{\binom{n}{|S|+1}} \right) + \Delta_i(S \cup \{j\}) \left(\frac{\Delta_j(S)}{\binom{n}{|S|+1}} + \frac{\Delta_j(S \cup \{i\})}{\binom{n}{|S|+2}} \right)$$
$$= \frac{1}{n+1} \sum_{S \subseteq \mathcal{N} \setminus \{i\}} \Delta_i(S) \left(\frac{\Delta_j'(S)}{\binom{n}{|S|}} + \frac{\Delta_j'(S \cup \{i\})}{\binom{n}{|S|+1}} \right)$$

A.3 Approximating Pairwise Probabilities for Greedy CMCS

Analogously to Appendix A.1, we derive for any pair $i, j \in \mathcal{N}$ and unbiased equifrequent player-wise independent sampler:

$$\begin{aligned}
\mathbb{P}(\phi_i < \phi_j) &= \mathbb{P}(\phi_i - \phi_j < 0) \\
&= \mathbb{P}((\hat{\phi}_i - \hat{\phi}_j) - (\phi_i - \phi_j) > \hat{\phi}_i - \hat{\phi}_j) \\
&= \mathbb{P}(\sqrt{M}((\hat{\phi}_i - \hat{\phi}_j) - (\phi_i - \phi_j)) > \sqrt{M}(\hat{\phi}_i - \hat{\phi}_j)) \\
&\stackrel{CLT}{=} \Phi\left(\sqrt{M}\frac{\hat{\phi}_j - \hat{\phi}_i}{\sigma_{i,j}}\right)
\end{aligned}$$

Since this statement does not require the knowledge of an eligible coalition $\mathcal{K}$, we can estimate the likelihood of $\phi_i < \phi_j$ during runtime of the approximation algorithm. For this purpose, we use the sample variance to estimate $\sigma_{i,j}$. Note that M is the number of drawn samples that both $\hat{\phi}_i$ and $\hat{\phi}_j$ share. Since the players' marginal contributions are selectively sampled, Greedy CMCS substitutes M by the true number of joint appearances $M_{i,j}$ and $\hat{\phi}_i - \hat{\phi}_j$ by $\hat{\delta}_{i,j}$ which only takes into account marginal contributions of i and j which have been acquired during rounds in which both players have been selected.

B Pseudocode of Greedy CMCS

In addition to the pseudocode in Algorithm 2, we provide further details regarding the tracking of estimates and probabilistic selection of players.

Algorithm 2. Greedy CMCS

Input: $(\mathcal{N}, \nu)$, $T \in \mathbb{N}, k \in [n], M_{\min}$
1: $\hat{\phi}_i, M_i \leftarrow 0$ for all $i \in \mathcal{N}$
2: $M_{i,j}, \Sigma_{i,j}, \Gamma_{i,j} \leftarrow 0$ for all $i, j \in \mathcal{N}$
3: $t \leftarrow 0$
4: **while** $t < T$ **do**
5:     Draw $\ell \in \{0, \ldots, n\}$ uniformly at random
6:     Draw $S \subseteq \mathcal{N}$ with $|S| = l$ uniformly at random
7:     $v_S \leftarrow \nu(S)$
8:     $t \leftarrow t + 1$
9:     $P \leftarrow \text{SelectPlayers}$
10:     **for** $i \in P$ **do**
11:         **if** $t = T$ **then**
12:             exit
13:         **end if**
14:         $\Delta_i \leftarrow \begin{cases} v_S - \nu(S \setminus \{i\}) & \text{if } i \in S \\ \nu(S \cup \{i\}) - v_S & \text{otherwise} \end{cases}$
15:         $\hat{\phi}_i \leftarrow \frac{(M_i - 1) \cdot \hat{\phi}_i + \Delta_i}{M_i}$
16:         $M_i \leftarrow M_i + 1$
17:         $t \leftarrow t + 1$
18:     **end for**
19:     $M_{i,j} \leftarrow M_{i,j} + 1$ for all $i, j \in P$
20:     $\Sigma_{i,j} \leftarrow \Sigma_{i,j} + (\Delta_i - \Delta_j)$ for all $i, j \in P$
21:     $\Gamma_{i,j} \leftarrow \Gamma_{i,j} + (\Delta_i - \Delta_j)^2$ for all $i, j \in P$
22: **end while**
Output: $\hat{\mathcal{K}}$ containing k players with highest estimate $\hat{\phi}_i$

Algorithm 3. SELECTPLAYERS

1: $P \leftarrow \mathcal{N}$
2: **if** $M_{i,j} \geq M_{\min}$ for all $i, j \in \mathcal{N}$ **then**
3: $\quad \hat{\mathcal{K}} \leftarrow k$ players of $\mathcal{N}$ with highest estimate $\hat{\phi}_i$, solve ties arbitrarily
4: $\quad \hat{\mathcal{K}}' \leftarrow \mathcal{N} \setminus \hat{\mathcal{K}}$
5: $\quad \hat{\sigma}_{i,j}^2 \leftarrow \frac{1}{M_{i,j}-1}\left(\Gamma_{i,j} - \frac{\Sigma_{i,j}^2}{M_{i,j}}\right)$ for all $i \in \hat{\mathcal{K}}, j \in \hat{\mathcal{K}}'$
6: $\quad \hat{p}_{i,j} \leftarrow \Phi\left(\sqrt{M_{i,j}}\frac{-\Sigma_{i,j}}{\sqrt{\hat{\sigma}_{i,j}^2}}\right)$ for all $i \in \hat{\mathcal{K}}, j \in \hat{\mathcal{K}}'$
7: $\quad$ **if** $\min_{i,j} \hat{p}_{i,j} \neq \max_{i,j} \hat{p}_{i,j}$ **then**
8: $\quad\quad P, Q \leftarrow \emptyset$
9: $\quad\quad$ **for** $(i,j) \in \hat{\mathcal{K}} \times \hat{\mathcal{K}}'$ **do**
10: $\quad\quad\quad$ Draw Bernoulli realization $B_{i,j}$ with $\mathbb{P}(B_{i,j}=1) = \frac{\hat{p}_{i,j}-\min_{i,j}\hat{p}_{i,j}}{\max_{i,j}\hat{p}_{i,j}-\min_{i,j}\hat{p}_{i,j}}$
11: $\quad\quad\quad$ **if** $B_{i,j}=1$ **then**
12: $\quad\quad\quad\quad Q \leftarrow Q \cup \{(i,j)\}$
13: $\quad\quad\quad\quad P \leftarrow P \cup \{i,j\}$
14: $\quad\quad\quad$ **end if**
15: $\quad\quad$ **end for**
16: $\quad$ **end if**
17: **end if**
Output: $\mathcal{P}$

- Initialize estimator $\hat{\phi}_i$ and individual counter of sampled marginal contributions M_i for each player.
- Initialize for each player pair: the counter for joint appearances in rounds $M_{i,j}$, the sum of differences of marginal contributions $\Sigma_{i,j}$, and the sum of squared differences of marginal contributions $\Gamma_{i,j}$.
- Given $d_m := \Delta_i(S_m \setminus \{i\}) - \Delta_j(S_m \setminus \{j\})$ the unbiased variance estimator is

$$\hat{\sigma}_{i,j}^2 := \frac{1}{M_{i,j}-1}\sum_{m=1}^{M_{i,j}}(d_m - \bar{d})^2 = \frac{1}{M_{i,j}-1}\left(\Gamma_{i,j} - \frac{\Sigma_{i,j}^2}{M_{i,j}}\right).$$

- In each round, select with SELECTPLAYERS players P for whom to form an extended marginal contribution:
  - First phase: select all players $M_{\min}$ times: $P = \mathcal{N}$.
  - Second phase: otherwise, partition the players into top-k players $\hat{\mathcal{K}}$ and the rest $\hat{\mathcal{K}}' = \mathcal{N} \setminus \hat{\mathcal{K}}$ based on the estimates $\hat{\phi}_1, \ldots, \hat{\phi}_n$.
  - Compute $\hat{p}_{i,j} \approx P(\phi_i < \phi_j)$ for all pairs $i \in \hat{\mathcal{K}}, j \in \hat{\mathcal{K}}'$.
  - If all pairs are equally probable, select all players as it is not reasonable to be selective.
  - Otherwise, sample a set of pairs Q based on $\hat{p}_{i,j}$.
  - Select all players as members of P that are in at least one pair in Q.
- Sample a coalition S and cache its value.
- Form for all selected players in P their extended marginal contribution $\Delta'_i(S)$ and update their estimator $\hat{\phi}_i$.
- Update the values $M_{i,j}$, $\Sigma_{i,j}$, and $\Gamma_{i,j}$ for all $i, j \in P$ required for computing the variance estimates $\hat{\sigma}_{i,j}^2$ and $\hat{p}_{i,j}$.

- In practice, we precompute and cache $\nu(\emptyset)$ and $\nu(\mathcal{N})$ in the beginning. We do that for **ALL** tested algorithms for a fair comparison.
- We modify Stratified SVARM to only precompute coalition values for sizes 0 and n, instead of including sizes 1 and $n-1$. Instead of integrating this optimization into all our algorithms, we remove it as it requires a budget of $2n$ which might be infeasible for games with large numbers of players.

References

1. Bubeck, S., Wang, T., Viswanathan, N.: Multiple identifications in multi-armed bandits. In: Proceedings of the 30th International Conference on Machine Learning (ICML), pp. 258–265 (2013)
2. Burgess, M.A., Chapman, A.C.: Approximating the shapley value using stratified empirical bernstein sampling. In: Proceedings of the Thirtieth International Joint Conference on Artificial Intelligence, IJCAI, pp. 73–81 (2021)
3. Castro, J., Gómez, D., Molina, E., Tejada, J.: Improving polynomial estimation of the shapley value by stratified random sampling with optimum allocation. Comput. Oper. Res. **82**, 180–188 (2017)
4. Castro, J., Gómez, D., Tejada, J.: Polynomial calculation of the shapley value based on sampling. Comput. Oper. Res. **36**(5), 1726–1730 (2009)
5. Chen, H., Covert, I.C., Lundberg, S.M., Lee, S.: Algorithms to estimate shapley value feature attributions. Nature Mach. Intell. **5**(6), 590–601 (2023)
6. Cohen, S.B., Dror, G., Ruppin, E.: Feature selection via coalitional game theory. Neural Comput. **19**(7), 1939–1961 (2007)
7. Covert, I., Lee, S.I.: Improving kernelshap: practical shapley value estimation using linear regression. In: The 24th International Conference on Artificial Intelligence and Statistics AISTATS. Proceedings of Machine Learning Research, vol. 130, pp. 3457–3465 (2021)
8. Covert, I., Lundberg, S., Lee, S.I.: Shapley feature utility. In: Machine Learning in Computational Biology (2019)
9. Covert, I., Lundberg, S.M., Lee, S.: Understanding global feature contributions with additive importance measures. In: Proceedings of Advances in Neural Information Processing Systems (NeurIPS) (2020)
10. Deng, X., Papadimitriou, C.H.: On the complexity of cooperative solution concepts. Math. Oper. Res. **19**(2), 257–266 (1994)
11. Doumard, E., Aligon, J., Escriva, E., Excoffier, J., Monsarrat, P., Soulé-Dupuy, C.: A comparative study of additive local explanation methods based on feature influences. In: Proceedings of the International Workshop on Design, Optimization, Languages and Analytical Processing of Big Data (DOLAP), pp. 31–40 (2022)
12. Gabillon, V., Ghavamzadeh, M., Lazaric, A., Bubeck, S.: Multi-bandit best arm identification. In: Proceedings in Advances in Neural Information Processing Systems (NeurIPS), pp. 2222–2230 (2011)
13. Ghorbani, A., Zou, J.Y.: Data shapley: equitable valuation of data for machine learning. In: Proceedings of the 36th International Conference on Machine Learning ICML, vol. 97, pp. 2242–2251 (2019)
14. Ghorbani, A., Zou, J.Y.: Neuron shapley: Discovering the responsible neurons. In: Proceedings of Advances in Neural Information Processing Systems (NeurIPS) (2020)

15. Goldwasser, J., Hooker, G.: Stabilizing estimates of shapley values with control variates. In: Proceedings of the Second World Conference on eXplainable Artificial Intelligence (xAI) pp. 416–439 (2024)
16. Illés, F., Kerényi, P.: Estimation of the shapley value by ergodic sampling. CoRR **abs/1906.05224** (2019)
17. Kariyappa, S., Tsepenekas, L., Lécué, F., Magazzeni, D.: Shap@k: Efficient and probably approximately correct (PAC) identification of top-k features. In: Proceedings of AAAI Conference on Artificial Intelligence (AAAI), pp. 13068–13075 (2024)
18. Kolpaczki, P., Bengs, V., Hüllermeier, E.: Identifying top-k players in cooperative games via shapley bandits. In: Proceedings of the LWDA 2021 Workshops: FGWM, KDML, FGWI-BIA, and FGIR, pp. 133–144 (2021)
19. Kolpaczki, P., Bengs, V., Muschalik, M., Hüllermeier, E.: Approximating the shapley value without marginal contributions. In: Proceedings of AAAI Conference on Artificial Intelligence (AAAI), pp. 13246–13255 (2024)
20. Kolpaczki, P., Haselbeck, G., Hüllermeier, E.: How much can stratification improve the approximation of shapley values? In: Proceedings of the Second World Conference on eXplainable Artificial Intelligence (xAI), pp. 489–512 (2024)
21. Lattimore, T., Szepesvári, C.: Bandit Algorithms. Cambridge University Press (2020)
22. Lundberg, S.M., Lee, S.I.: A unified approach to interpreting model predictions. In: Proceedings of Advances in Neural Information Processing Systems (NeurIPS) pp. 4768–4777 (2017)
23. Maleki, S., Tran-Thanh, L., Hines, G., Rahwan, T., Rogers, A.: Bounding the estimation error of sampling-based shapley value approximation with/without stratifying. CoRR **abs/1306.4265** (2013)
24. Mitchell, R., Cooper, J., Frank, E., Holmes, G.: Sampling permutations for shapley value estimation. J. Mach. Learn. Res. **23**(43), 1–46 (2022)
25. Molnar, C.: Interpretable Machine Learning. 2 edn. (2022). https://christophm.github.io/interpretable-ml-book
26. Narayanam, R., Narahari, Y.: Determining the top-k nodes in social networks using the shapley value. In: Proceedings of International Joint Conference on Autonomous Agents and Multiagent Systems (AAMAS), pp. 1509–1512 (2008)
27. O'Brien, G., Gamal, A.E., Rajagopal, R.: Shapley value estimation for compensation of participants in demand response programs. IEEE Trans. Smart Grid **6**(6), 2837–2844 (2015)
28. Okhrati, R., Lipani, A.: A multilinear sampling algorithm to estimate shapley values. In: 25th International Conference on Pattern Recognition ICPR, pp. 7992–7999 (2020)
29. Pelegrina, G.D., Kolpaczki, P., Hüllermeier, E.: Shapley value approximation based on k-additive games. CoRR **abs/2502.04763** (2025)
30. Rozemberczki, B., Sarkar, R.: The shapley value of classifiers in ensemble games. In: The 30th ACM International Conference on Information and Knowledge Management CIKM, pp. 1558–1567 (2021)
31. Rozemberczki, B., et al.: The shapley value in machine learning. In: Proceedings of the Thirty-First International Joint Conference on Artificial Intelligence IJCAI, pp. 5572–5579 (2022)
32. Shapley, L.S.: A value for n-person games. In: Contributions to the Theory of Games (AM-28), Volume II, pp. 307–318. Princeton University Press (1953)

33. van Campen, T., Hamers, H., Husslage, B., Lindelauf, R.: A new approximation method for the shapley value applied to the wtc 9/11 terrorist attack. Soc. Netw. Anal. Min. **8**(3), 1–12 (2018)
34. Vilone, G., Longo, L.: Notions of explainability and evaluation approaches for explainable artificial intelligence. Inform. Fusion **76**, 89–106 (2021)
35. Wang, H., Liang, Q., Hancock, J.T., Khoshgoftaar, T.M.: Feature selection strategies: a comparative analysis of shap-value and importance-based methods. J. Big Data **11**(1), 44 (2024)

Open Access This chapter is licensed under the terms of the Creative Commons Attribution 4.0 International License (http://creativecommons.org/licenses/by/4.0/), which permits use, sharing, adaptation, distribution and reproduction in any medium or format, as long as you give appropriate credit to the original author(s) and the source, provide a link to the Creative Commons license and indicate if changes were made.

The images or other third party material in this chapter are included in the chapter's Creative Commons license, unless indicated otherwise in a credit line to the material. If material is not included in the chapter's Creative Commons license and your intended use is not permitted by statutory regulation or exceeds the permitted use, you will need to obtain permission directly from the copyright holder.

Detecting Concept Drift with SHapley Additive ExPlanations for Intelligent Model Retraining in Energy Generation Forecasting

Brígida Teixeira[1], Tiago Pinto[2], and Zita Vale[1(✉)]

[1] GECAD–Research Group on Intelligent Engineering and Computing for Advanced Innovation and Development, LASI–Intelligent Systems Associate Laboratory, ISEP, Polytechnic of Porto, R. Dr. António Bernardino de Almeida, 431, 4249-015 Porto, Portugal
{bct,zav}@isep.ipp.pt

[2] Universidade de Trás-os-Montes e Alto Douro e INESC-TEC, Quinta de Prados, 5000-801 Vila Real, Portugal
tiagopinto@utad.pt

Abstract. Accurate energy generation forecasting is essential for effective energy management. However, it remains a complex task due to the influence of dynamic factors such as meteorological conditions, seasonal variations, and evolving grid operations. Ensuring model reliability over time requires continuous assessment to detect performance degradation. Traditional retraining strategies, including periodic updates and statistical drift detection techniques, often struggle to balance model accuracy with computational efficiency. This study introduces a novel approach that leverages SHapley Additive Explanations (SHAP) to dynamically detect concept drift by analyzing variations in feature importance. The methodology establishes a baseline SHAP distribution and identifies deviations that indicate drift, prompting model retraining when necessary. A comparative evaluation is conducted against conventional methods, including scheduled retraining, Adaptive Windowing (ADWIN), and the Kolmogorov-Smirnov (KS) test. Furthermore, a sensitivity analysis examines the impact of key configuration parameters on detection accuracy and computational cost. The results demonstrate that SHAP-based drift detection improves forecasting accuracy, achieving a 26.67% to 35.29% reduction in Mean Squared Error, while maintaining an adaptive retraining strategy. These findings underscore the potential of SHAP as an interpretable and efficient approach for managing concept drift in energy forecasting applications.

Keywords: Concept Drift · SHapley Additive exPlanations (SHAP) · Energy Forecasting · Intelligent Model Retraining · Explainable AI

1 Introduction

Machine learning (ML) models have become essential in various fields, including healthcare, finance, and energy systems. In energy generation forecasting, accurate predictions are crucial for balancing supply and demand, optimizing grid operations, and efficiently integrating renewable energy sources [1]. However, one of the most significant challenges in ML-based forecasting is ensuring that models maintain their accuracy in dynamic and evolving environments [2].

In this context, concept drift refers to changes in the statistical properties of the target variable, which can degrade predictive performance and lead to inefficient energy management [3]. These drifts can arise from evolving weather conditions, seasonal variations, grid stability changes, or shifts in consumer demand [4]. Consequently, ensuring that forecasting models remain robust and adaptive to these changes is fundamental for modern energy systems.

Concept drift detection has been widely explored in power and energy systems (PES), particularly in cybersecurity and fault detection. Recent studies have proposed frameworks to distinguish genuine grid disturbances from cyberattacks, leveraging dimensionality reduction techniques and deep learning [5]. Additionally, real-time data stream analysis models have been applied to detect anomalies in consumer energy behavior, differentiating deviations caused by genuine shifts in consumption patterns from fraudulent activities [6].

Retraining strategies are used to mitigate concept drift in energy forecasting. A recent study introduced an Extreme Learning Machine (ELM)-based framework to address concept drift in wind energy forecasting, allowing models to adjust dynamically to changing environmental conditions without frequent, computationally expensive reconfigurations [7]. Traditional statistical methods, such as the Kolmogorov-Smirnov (KS) test and the Page-Hinkley test, remain widely used for detecting drift in energy time series [8]. The KS test compares distributions over time to identify significant shifts in data behavior, while the Page-Hinkley test detects gradual changes in average values, making it effective for identifying slow-moving drifts in energy generation [9]. An alternative and widely adopted approach for concept drift detection is Adaptive Windowing (ADWIN) [10], which dynamically adjusts a sliding window based on detected changes in the data stream. ADWIN has been employed in power systems to identify abrupt and gradual shifts in load demand, weather conditions, and energy prices. These techniques rely on monitoring error rates or applying statistical bounds to detect distributional shifts. While effective and theoretically grounded, these statistical approaches are more suited for classification tasks and generally offer limited interpretability, making it difficult to identify the root causes of drift or determine which features contribute most to performance degradation [11].

Due to these limitations, Explainable AI (XAI) has gained prominence in energy forecasting [12]. Techniques such as SHapley Additive ExPlanations (SHAP) [13] provide insights into how individual features influence model predictions over time. In energy forecasting, SHAP can highlight which meteorological or grid-related variables drive prediction errors as drift occurs [14]. This level of interpretability is crucial for energy operators, as it enables them to identify and address the underlying causes of model degradation rather than relying solely on automated retraining. Integrating interpretability into drift detection represents a significant advancement in energy forecasting, enhancing the adaptability of predictive models while ensuring that energy generation forecasts remain accurate despite evolving patterns. Recent studies have demonstrated the benefits of SHAP in drift analysis, not only in energy forecasting but also in cybersecurity and complex time-series prediction tasks [14].

This work presents a SHAP-based approach for detecting concept drift in regression tasks by computing a drift score that quantifies the deviation of SHAP values from a dynamic reference distribution. The detection mechanism relies on a rolling baseline of SHAP value statistics and uses a dynamic thresholding function that adapts to recent drift score variability. Once drift is detected, the model is retrained using a buffered window of recent observations, and the SHAP baseline is updated incrementally using an Exponential Moving Average (EMA) to ensure smooth adaptation over time. This approach is applied to energy generation forecasting and is compared against conventional retraining strategies, including periodic updates, ADWIN, and the Kolmogorov–Smirnov test. A sensitivity analysis is also conducted to evaluate the influence of key configuration parameters on both detection accuracy and computational efficiency.

The remainder of this paper is structured as follows: Sect. 2 details the methodology. Section 3 describes the case study and experimental setup. Section 4 presents the results and discusses key findings. Finally, Sect. 5 concludes with an analysis of the proposed work and directions for future research.

2 Methodology

The proposed methodology introduces an intelligent retraining framework that leverages SHAP to detect concept drift in energy generation forecasting. The approach dynamically monitors variations in feature importance, triggering retraining when significant deviations from identified historical.

The framework consists of several interconnected components: data preprocessing, initial model training, SHAP-based drift detection, adaptive model retraining, and performance evaluation. Initially, the model is trained on historical data and establishes a baseline SHAP distribution. During real-time operation, SHAP values are continuously computed and compared against this baseline using a dynamic thresholding mechanism. When a drift is detected, the model is updated using an Exponential Moving Average (EMA) to refine the baseline and a buffered retraining process to incorporate new data. This ensures that the forecasting model remains accurate while minimizing unnecessary computational overhead. The workflow of the proposed methodology is illustrated in Fig. 1, and each component is detailed in the following subsections.

2.1 Data Preprocessing

A structured preprocessing pipeline is implemented to ensure an optimized dataset for predictive modeling, comprising feature selection, normalization, and data partitioning. The dataset contains historical energy generation records from 2023, collected from a photovoltaic (PV) system and a meteorological station

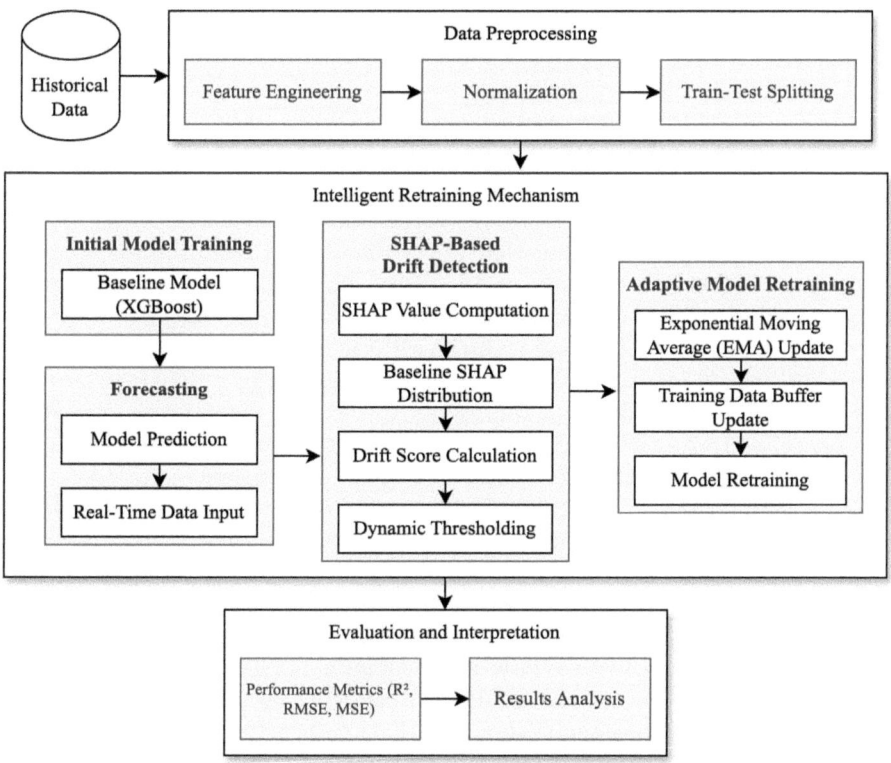

Fig. 1. Workflow of the proposed SHAP-based intelligent retraining framework.

at an office building. It includes key environmental variables such as outdoor temperature, humidity, solar radiation, wind speed, and atmospheric pressure, which influence power generation. A derived feature, the period of the day (ranging from 0 to 143), is added to capture daily cyclic patterns. Normalization is applied to rescale all features using Min-Max scaling to the range [0,1], ensuring numerical stability and preventing features with larger magnitudes from dominating the learning process. The target variable, representing energy generation, undergoes the same normalization to maintain consistency. Finally, the dataset is split into training and testing subsets to enable model evaluation.

2.2 Initial Model Training

Once the data has been preprocessed, an initial forecasting model is trained using a ML algorithm. During training, SHAP values are computed to establish a reference distribution of feature importance. These SHAP values provide insight into how different input features contribute to the model's predictions, forming

2.3 SHAP-Based Concept Drift Detection

To maintain the reliability of the forecasting model over time, it is essential to continuously monitor the evolution of relationships between input features and the target variable, ensuring that any shifts do not compromise predictive performance. This is achieved by continuously computing SHAP values for each new observation, which quantify the contribution of each feature at a given moment, allowing for direct comparison with past feature importance.

Concept drift is identified by measuring the deviation of SHAP values from a rolling baseline. This baseline represents the expected feature contributions over a predefined historical period and is constructed using a moving window of $n_{\text{days\_baseline}}$ past observations. The rolling mean and variance of SHAP values for each feature are computed as in Eq. 1, where N is the number of historical instances in the baseline window. Each ϕ_i denotes the SHAP value vector of the i-th instance, containing one value per input feature, which quantifies the contribution of each feature to the model's prediction. The mean vector μ_p thus represents the typical importance of each feature under stable conditions, while the variance vector σ_p^2 captures how much those contributions fluctuate across the baseline window. These statistics define a reference distribution used to assess whether new observations deviate significantly from previously observed patterns of feature relevance.

In Eq. 2, the SHAP Drift Score $D_{\text{SHAP}}(t)$ is computed as the Euclidean distance between the current SHAP value vector ϕ_t and the baseline mean vector μ_p. This score reflects how much the feature importance profile of the current observation diverges from the historically expected pattern, providing a quantitative signal for potential concept drift. A drift event is triggered when the SHAP Drift Score exceeds a dynamically computed threshold. Unlike traditional fixed thresholds, this approach adapts its sensitivity based on recent fluctuations in the observed drift scores. As defined in Eq. 3, the threshold at time t is calculated as the rolling mean $\mu_{D_{\text{SHAP}}}$ of past scores, plus a multiple of their rolling standard deviation $\sigma_{D_{\text{SHAP}}}$. The hyperparameter k controls how tolerant the method is to deviations: lower values make the detector more reactive, while higher values reduce sensitivity. This adaptive mechanism helps prevent false positives by accounting for natural variability in the data and reacting only to statistically significant changes.

$$\mu_p = \frac{1}{N}\sum_{i=1}^{N} \phi_i, \quad \sigma_p^2 = \frac{1}{N}\sum_{i=1}^{N} (\phi_i - \mu_p)^2 \tag{1}$$

$$D_{\text{SHAP}}(t) = ||\phi_t - \mu_p|| \tag{2}$$

$$\text{Threshold}(t) = \mu_{D_{\text{SHAP}}} + k \cdot \sigma_{D_{\text{SHAP}}} \tag{3}$$

It is important to note that the SHAP vectors ϕ_t retain the sign of each feature's contribution, allowing the detection mechanism to capture both increases and decreases in influence, including potential inversions in effect direction. This ensures that the Euclidean distance reflects not only the magnitude of change, but also meaningful directional shifts in feature behavior.

2.4 Adaptive Model Retraining

When a drift event is detected, the model undergoes adaptive retraining to incorporate the latest data distribution while minimizing unnecessary updates. The retraining mechanism consists of three key components.

First, to keep the SHAP baseline representative of recent patterns, it is updated incrementally using EMA rather than being recomputed from scratch. This ensures a smooth adaptation to gradual changes without abruptly discarding past information. As shown in Eq. 4, the new baseline mean μ_p^{new} and baseline deviation σ_p^{new} are updated by blending the previous baseline values with the current SHAP vector ϕ_t. The parameter $\alpha \in [0,1]$ controls the adaptation rate: higher values give more weight to recent observations, allowing faster adaptation, while lower values emphasize stability by retaining more influence from past data. Next, the training data buffer is updated, ensuring the retraining process incorporates the most recent observations while discarding outdated data beyond a set limit. This prevents excessive memory usage and ensures the model remains focused on relevant patterns. Finally, the model is retrained using the updated dataset, allowing it to learn from recent patterns while retaining the predictive knowledge acquired in previous iterations. This approach optimizes computational efficiency while maintaining high forecasting accuracy by restricting retraining to only those instances where drift has been detected.

Once the model has been retrained, it resumes forecasting, generating new predictions that are evaluated against actual energy generation values. The performance of the forecasting model is assessed using standard error metrics, including Mean Squared Error (MSE), Root Mean Squared Error (RMSE), and coefficient of determination (R^2).

$$\mu_p^{\text{new}} = (1-\alpha)\cdot\mu_p + \alpha\cdot\phi_t, \quad \sigma_p^{\text{new}} = (1-\alpha)\cdot\sigma_p + \alpha\cdot|\phi_t - \mu_p| \qquad (4)$$

3 Case Study

This section presents the experimental evaluation of the SHAP-based drift detection framework applied to energy generation forecasting. The objective is to assess its ability to maintain high predictive accuracy while adapting to evolving data distributions. The proposed method is compared against established drift detection strategies: scheduled retraining, ADWIN, the KS test, and a fixed baseline without retraining. Experiments were conducted using the XGBRegressor from the xgboost library [15], chosen for its robustness in time-series regression and ability to model nonlinear relationships. The model uses default settings: 100 boosting rounds (n_estimators=100), maximum depth 6, learning rate 0.3, full subsampling of instances and features, and squared error as the objective.

The dataset comprises 10-minute interval measurements from a photovoltaic (PV) system and a local meteorological station at the GECAD research center (Porto, Portugal), spanning January 1 to September 15, 2023. It includes 12 input features, such as solar radiation, UV index, wind speed, and outdoor temperature. The initial training set covers January 1 to July 31, while test observations arrive incrementally from August 1 onward. Upon drift detection, retraining is triggered using the original training data extended with all test samples up to the current time. This approach combines stability and adaptability by leveraging both historical and recent patterns.

A sensitivity analysis was first conducted over a constrained period (August 1âĂŞ10) to explore the impact of four key hyperparameters: threshold multiplier ($k\_threshold \in \{1.75, 2.0, 2.25, 2.5\}$), SHAP baseline window ($n\_days\_baseline \in \{5, 10\}$), range of adjacent periods ($range\_periods \in \{4, 6, 8\}$), and EMA learning rate ($\alpha_{ema} \in \{0.3, 0.5, 0.7\}$). A total of 72 configurations were evaluated to balance accuracy and computational cost. The best configuration was used in a full evaluation from August 1 to September 15, comparing the SHAP-based approach to the alternative methods. Feature importance evolution was also tracked to highlight the necessity of adaptive modeling.

4 Results and Discussion

This section presents the results of the SHAP-based drift detection methodology, analyzing its impact on forecasting performance. First, a sensitivity analysis identifies the optimal parameter configuration, balancing accuracy and retraining efficiency. Then, the full study evaluates the method's effectiveness in adapting to concept drift while maintaining reliable predictions.

4.1 Sensitivity Analysis

To determine the optimal parameter configuration for the SHAP-based concept drift detection methodology, a sensitivity analysis was conducted across various values of $k_{threshold}$, $n_{days\_baseline}$, range_period, and α_{ema}. This analysis aimed to identify a balance between predictive accuracy, measured through the RMSE and computational efficiency, quantified by the number of model retrainings. A composite score was formulated to evaluate the trade-off between these factors, where a lower RMSE and fewer retrainings contribute to a better performance.

To determine the optimal parameter configuration for the SHAP-based concept drift detection methodology, a sensitivity analysis was conducted across various values of $k_{threshold}$, $n_{days\_baseline}$, range_period, and α_{ema}. This analysis aimed to identify a balance between predictive accuracy, measured through the RMSE, and computational efficiency, quantified by the number of model retrainings. To combine both objectives into a unified metric, each was first normalized

Table 1. Top 5 Configurations Ranked by Composite Score

Parameter	1	2	3	4	5
$k_{threshold}$	2.0	2.0	2.0	2.0	2.0
$n_{days\_baseline}$	5	5	5	5	5
range_period	6	6	4	6	4
α_{ema}	0.5	0.3	0.7	0.7	0.5
RMSE	0.0969	0.0958	0.0946	0.0982	0.0948
Retrainings	115	130	149	121	152
Composite Score	-1.0486	-1.0392	-1.0305	-1.0177	-1.0070

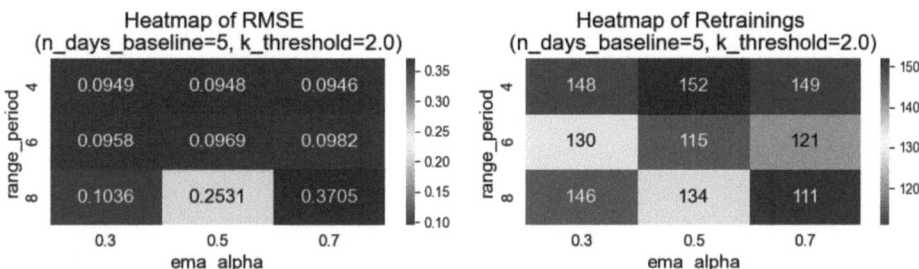

Fig. 2. Heatmaps of RMSE (left) and Retrainings (right) for $n_{days\_baseline} = 5$, $k_{threshold} = 2.0$.

to the range $[0, 1]$ using min-max normalization. The number of retrainings was inverted such that lower values contribute positively to the overall score. A composite score was then computed as a weighted average of the normalized metrics.

The top five configurations, ranked by this composite score, are presented in Table 1. The best-performing configuration was obtained with $k_{threshold} = 2.0$, $n_{days\_baseline} = 5$, range_period = 6, and $\alpha_{ema} = 0.5$, achieving an RMSE of 0.0969 with 115 retrainings. The second-best configuration retained the same parameters except for $\alpha_{ema} = 0.3$, resulting in a slightly lower RMSE of 0.0958 at the cost of 130 retrainings. A further reduction in RMSE was observed in the third-ranked configuration (range_period = 4, $\alpha_{ema} = 0.7$), reaching 0.0946 RMSE, but with 149 retrainings. These results confirm that lower RMSE values often correlate with more frequent retraining, but the performance gains are not always proportional. This reinforces the value of using a composite score to capture the trade-off between accuracy and efficiency in real-world deployments. To further illustrate the impact of range_period and α_{ema}, two heatmaps are presented in Fig. 2. The left panel displays RMSE values, while the right panel illustrates the corresponding number of retrainings. Both heatmaps consider $n_{days\_baseline} = 5$ and $k_{threshold} = 2.0$, as these values were identified as optimal based on the best-performing configurations in Table 1.

The heatmaps show that larger range_period values lead to fewer retrainings while maintaining acceptable RMSE, suggesting that a broader temporal context reduces sensitivity to noise and avoids overreacting to local changes. Lower α_{ema}

Table 2. Performance comparison of different retraining strategies.

Model	MSE	RMSE	R^2	Retrainings
SHAP	0.0077	0.0879	0.8741	717
Scheduled	0.0105	0.1023	0.8295	45
KS Test	0.0114	0.1069	0.8139	396
ADWIN	0.0116	0.1076	0.8113	26
Fixed	0.0119	0.1089	0.8068	0

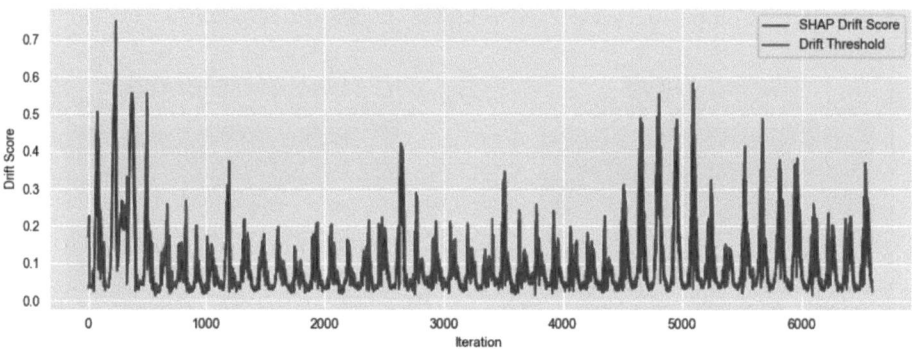

Fig. 3. SHAP Drift Score and Dynamic Threshold Over Time.

values (0.3 and 0.5) generally improve forecasting accuracy, while higher values introduce instability by overemphasizing recent SHAP changes, increasing false positives. Moderate α_{ema} values smooth updates, balancing responsiveness and stability. These results highlight the trade-off between sensitivity and robustness: overly reactive settings raise retraining frequency and noise amplification, while overly conservative ones delay drift detection. A balanced configuration offers reliable detection and efficient updates, emphasizing the importance of careful hyperparameter tuning in real-world use.

4.2 Study Results

Following the sensitivity analysis, the best-performing hyperparameter configurations ($n_{\text{days\_baseline}} = 5$, $k_{\text{threshold}} = 2.0$, range_period = 6, and $\alpha_{\text{ema}} = 0.5$) were used to evaluate the full forecasting study over an extended period from August 1 to September 15, 2023. This section presents the results of the SHAP-based retraining framework and compares its performance with alternative retraining strategies, including scheduled retraining, ADWIN, and the KS Test.

Table 2 presents the performance of forecasting strategies using XGBRegressor. The SHAP-based approach achieved the lowest RMSE (0.0879) and highest R^2 (0.8741), confirming its superior accuracy. In contrast, the fixed model performed worst, highlighting the need for dynamic updates to handle concept drift.

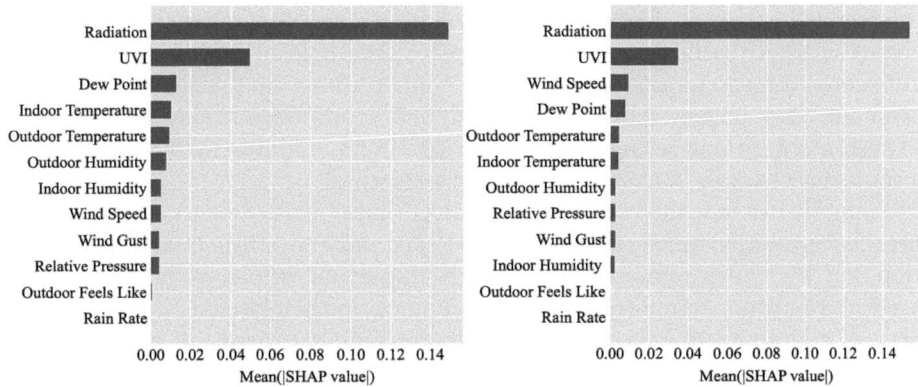

Fig. 4. SHAP Feature Importance: Baseline (left) vs. Final (right).

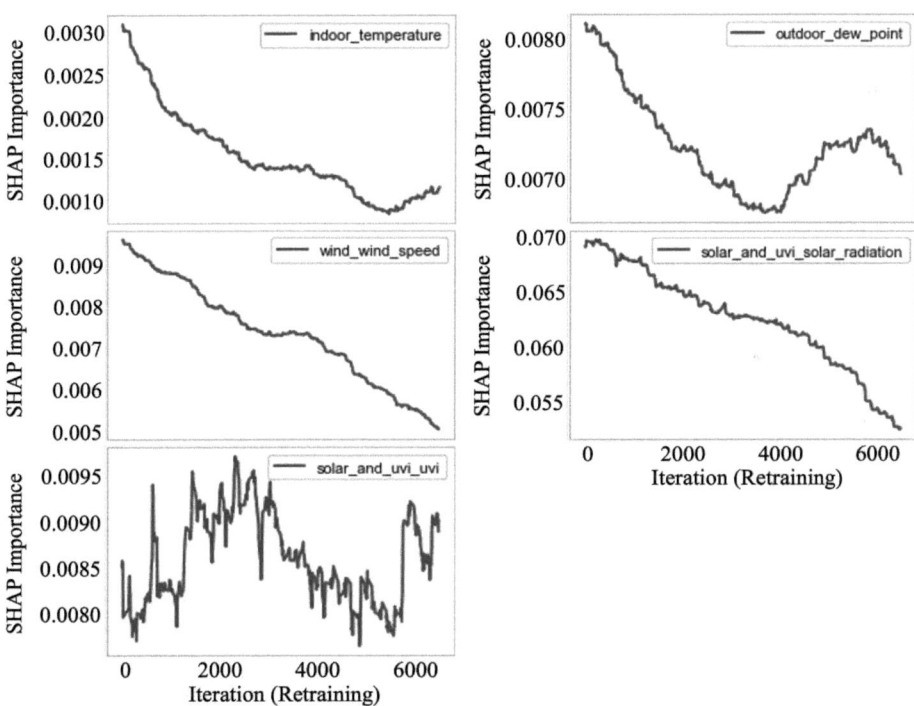

Fig. 5. Evolution of SHAP Feature Importance for the Top 5 Features Across Retraining Iterations.

The SHAP method triggered 717 retrainings over 46 d due to its sensitivity to subtle shifts in feature importance. While this ensures model alignment with evolving data, it may lead to excessive updates in dynamic settings. In resource-constrained scenarios, mechanisms like minimum retraining intervals or stability buffers may be needed. These trade-offs will be addressed in future work. Figure 3 shows the SHAP drift score and its adaptive threshold over time. Peaks in the drift score correspond to shifts in feature contributions, and when exceeding the threshold, they trigger retraining. This dynamic approach maintains a balance between stability and adaptability, ensuring timely updates without overfitting to transient changes in energy generation patterns.

To further assess the robustness of SHAP-based drift detection, Fig. 4 compares feature importance rankings at the start and end of the study. Solar radiation and UV index remained consistently important, while variables like wind speed and outdoor temperature showed changes in their predictive roles. These variations support the need for adaptive retraining to capture evolving data patterns. Figure 5 illustrates how SHAP values for the top five features changed across iterations, with a decline in relevance for some (e.g., wind speed, indoor temperature), while solar radiation remained a key predictor. The results confirm that the SHAP-based drift detection framework consistently outperforms baseline methods in maintaining forecasting accuracy while adapting to distribution shifts. Its retraining strategy offers a strong balance between performance and update frequency, reducing unnecessary model updates without sacrificing robustness. Observed shifts in feature importance reinforce the need for adaptive, explainable models. A preliminary evaluation of alternative SHAP explainers (KernelExplainer and LinearExplainer) showed promising results, though KernelExplainer's high computational cost limits real-time use. Future work will focus on optimizing these explainers and evaluating their performance across diverse forecasting scenarios.

5 Conclusion

This study proposed a SHAP-based drift detection framework for energy generation forecasting, using feature importance variations to dynamically detect distribution shifts. Results show that the SHAP-based method consistently outperforms alternatives, achieving lower forecasting errors and maintaining adaptability to changing data patterns. Temporal analysis of feature importance emphasized the need for adaptive, interpretable modeling, as key predictors fluctuated over time. Sensitivity analysis revealed that tuning hyperparameters, such as baseline window size, threshold multiplier, and EMA learning rate, can balance accuracy and computational efficiency. Although focused on energy forecasting, the approach is generalizable to other time-dependent regression tasks. Preliminary tests with alternative SHAP explainers, like KernelExplainer, showed promise but highlighted the need for efficiency improvements. Future work will explore optimizing these explainers and integrating feature ranking dynamics into drift detection.

Acknowledgments. This work has been developed in the frame of PRECISE project (PTDC/EEI-EEE/6277/2020), DOI: 10.54499/PTDC/EEI-EEE/6277/2020, that receiving funding from FEDER Funds through the COMPETE program and from

National Funds. The authors used the facilities and equipment provided by the GECAD research center (UIDB/00760/2020), DOI: 10.54499/UIDB/00760/2020. Brígida Teixeira is supported by national funds through FCT, Portugal government, with PhD grant reference 2020.08174.BD, DOI: 10.54499/2020.08174.BD.

References

1. Yao, Z., et al.: Machine learning for a sustainable energy future. Nat. Rev. Mater. **8**, 202–215 (2023)
2. Tolun, Ö., Zor, K., Tutsoy, O.: A comprehensive benchmark of machine learning-based algorithms for medium-term electric vehicle charging demand prediction. J. Supercomputing **81**, 475 (2025)
3. Samarajeewa, C., et al.: An artificial intelligence framework for explainable drift detection in energy forecasting. Energy AI **17**, 100403 (2024)
4. Shaer, I., Shami, A.: Thwarting cybersecurity attacks with explainable concept drift. In: 2024 International Wireless Communications and Mobile Computing (IWCMC), pp. 1785–1790 (2024)
5. Mehmood, T., et al.: DRIFTNET-EnVACK: adaptive drift detection in cloud data streams with ensemble variational auto-encoder featuring contextual network. IEEE Access **12**, 80020–80034 (2024)
6. Wang, J., Cao, H., et. al.: An adaptive deep learning method integrating transfer learning and concept drift detection for wind power forecasting. In: 2024 43rd Chinese Control Conference (CCC), pp. 6275–6280 (2024)
7. Lin, X., Chang, L., Nie, X., Dong, F.: Temporal attention for few-shot concept drift detection in streaming data. Electronics **13**, 2183 (2024)
8. Agrahari, S., Singh, A.: Concept drift detection in data stream mining: a literature review. J. King Saud Univ. Comput. Inf. Sci. **34**, 9523–9540 (2022)
9. Shahad, P., Raj, E.D.: Interpretability-based virtual drift detection and adaptation algorithm: a case study on Tetouan's energy data. In: 2024 International Conference On Intelligent Computing and Emerging Communication Technologies (ICEC), pp. 1–6 (2024,11)
10. Stojnev Ilić, A., Stojanović, D.: Concept drift detection and adaptation in IoT data stream analytics. In: 2023 16th International Conference On Advanced Technologies, Systems And Services In Telecommunications (TELSIKS), pp. 211–214 (2023)
11. Zhou, Y., Ge, Y., Jia, L.: Double robust federated digital twin modeling in smart grid (2024)
12. Machlev, R., et al.: Explainable Artificial Intelligence (XAI) techniques for energy and power systems: review, challenges and opportunities. Energy AI **9**, 100169 (2022)
13. Lundberg, S., Lee, S.: A unified approach to interpreting model predictions. In: Advances in Neural Information Processing Systems, 2017-December, pp. 4766-4775 (2017)
14. Abdulla, N., Demirci, M., Ozdemir, S.: Smart meter-based energy consumption forecasting for smart cities using adaptive federated learning. Sustain. Energy, Grids Networks **38**, 101342 (2024)
15. Chen, T., Guestrin, C.: XGBoost: a scalable tree boosting system. In: Proceedings of the 22nd ACM SIGKDD International Conference on Knowledge Discovery and Data Mining, pp. 785–794 (2016)

Open Access This chapter is licensed under the terms of the Creative Commons Attribution 4.0 International License (http://creativecommons.org/licenses/by/4.0/), which permits use, sharing, adaptation, distribution and reproduction in any medium or format, as long as you give appropriate credit to the original author(s) and the source, provide a link to the Creative Commons license and indicate if changes were made.

The images or other third party material in this chapter are included in the chapter's Creative Commons license, unless indicated otherwise in a credit line to the material. If material is not included in the chapter's Creative Commons license and your intended use is not permitted by statutory regulation or exceeds the permitted use, you will need to obtain permission directly from the copyright holder.

Counterfactual Shapley Values for Explaining Reinforcement Learning

Yiwei Shi[✉] and Weiru Liu

School of Engineering Mathematics and Technology, University of Bristol, Bristol, UK
{yiwei.shi,weiru.liu}@bristol.ac.uk

Abstract. This paper introduces an approach based on Counterfactual Shapley Values, which enhances explainability in reinforcement learning by integrating counterfactual analysis with Shapley Values. The approach aims to quantify and compare the contributions of different state dimensions to various action choices. To more accurately analyze the impacts of these contributions, we introduce new characteristic value functions, the *Counterfactual Difference based Characteristic Value functions* and the *Average Counterfactual Difference based Characteristic Value functions*. These functions help to evaluate the differences in contributions between optimal and non-optimal actions. Experiments across several RL domains, such as GridWorld, FrozenLake, and Taxi, demonstrate the effectiveness of the Counterfactual Shapley Values method. The results show that this method not only improves transparency in complex RL systems but also quantifies the differences across various decisions.

Keywords: Explainable Artificial Intelligence · Explainable Reinforcement Learning · Shapley Values

1 Introduction

Reinforcement learning (RL) has applications in autonomous navigation [1–3], healthcare [4], financial strategy optimization [5], and smart city management [6]. However, the key to achieving widespread adoption of these applications lies in overcoming the challenge of explainability [7] in RL models. The inability to adequately explain RL models could provoke ethical and regulatory issues and meet with resistance from potential users, collectively impeding the extensive application and further advancement of RL technology.

Research in explainable reinforcement learning is primarily focused on two approaches: *intrinsic interpretability* and *post-hoc interpretability*. Intrinsic interpretability strategies enhance model transparency by simplifying the model's structure, often at the expense of reducing the model's performance. For instance, decision tree models, which represent intrinsic interpretability, visually demonstrate decision pathways through their tree-like structure but may fail to capture more complex data patterns. In contrast, post-hoc interpretability methods treat the model as a black box and reveal the decision-making logic by analyzing the relationships between inputs and outputs, thus preserving the model's complexity. *Counterfactuals* and *Shapley Values* are both post-hoc explanation methods that provide insights without intervening in the internal structure of the model.

Shapley Value is a method for measuring the contribution of individuals to the total payoff in cooperative games. In an application of Shapley values to Explainable Artificial Intelligence (XAI), each feature is regarded as a *player*, while the model's predictive outcome is considered the "total payoff" [8]. The Shapley Value assesses the average contribution of each feature to the predictive outcome by considering all possible combinations of features.

Investigations employing Shapley Values are remarkably limited across both multi-agent reinforcement learning (MARL) and single-agent in RL. However, MARL research demonstrates a relatively richer engagement with Shapley value applications, which are principally concentrated across three aspects. Firstly, *Value Decomposition*, [9] integrates Shapley Value theory with multi-agent Q-learning (SHAQ) to address value decomposition in global reward games, where Shapley Values play a critical role in ensuring equitable distribution of rewards based on individual agent contributions. Secondly, *Credit Assignment*, [10] introduces the Shapley Q-value within MARL (SQDDPG) to reallocate global rewards among agents, leveraging Shapley Values to quantify and fairly distribute the rewards reflecting each agent's marginal contribution to the collective success. Lastly, *Model Explanation*, [11] uses Shapley Values to explain cooperative strategies and individual contributions in multi-agent reinforcement learning, approximating Shapley Values via Monte Carlo sampling to reduce computational costs. Shapley Values offer a way to interpret complex multi-agent interactions, making it clearer how each agent's decisions and actions contribute to the overall dynamics and results of the system.

To our knowledge, only the SVERL in [12], within the scope of RL research excluding MARL, utilizes Shapley Values to explain the decision-making process in reinforcement learning. Although SVERL provides a method for understanding and explaining the contribution of state features in the decision-making process of reinforcement learning agents, it has limitations in explaining specific action choices. The core of SVERL lies in analyzing the contribution of state features to the expected returns of an agent, rather than directly investigating why action a is chosen over action b in the same state, and it does not offer a mechanism to quantify the difference between these action choices. This means that while SVERL can help us indirectly understand how certain features influence an agent's decisions, it cannot directly answer why an agent prefers a specific action, nor can it compare the merits of different actions. This limitation is not unique to SVERL but is a challenge faced by all methods that rely on Shapley Values to explain the decision-making process in reinforcement learning.

Counterfactuals can effectively address some of the limitations associated with explaining specific action choices in RL. By comparing the utility (Long-Term Expected Return) of the actual action at a specific state with that of the counterfactual (alternative) action at that state, counterfactuals can help clarify why an agent prefers one action over another and quantify the impact of different actions.

In reinforcement learning, two main generative explanation methods by counterfactuals - one based on *deep generative models* and the other on *generating counterfactual states* - share a common limitation: the difficulty in quantifying differences between counterfactual instances. While methods based on deep generative models [13] can create realistic *what if* scenarios, comparing these instances in a high-dimensional latent space is challenging, as conventional distance metrics may not apply. On the other hand, methods that focus on minor state adjustments to guide different decisions also face challenges in quantifying the actual impact of these subtle changes on agent behavior, since even small modifications can have widespread effects in complex RL environments. Therefore, although these methods provide valuable insights into the decision-making process in RL, their difficulty in quantifying differences between counterfactual instances limits their application scope and the depth of their explanations.

To address the challenges of quantifying differences in reinforcement learning explanations, we develop an approach based on *Counterfactual Shapley Value* (CSV). Some previous research has explored the integration of counterfactual explanations with Shapley Values, such as addressing credit assignment problems in MARL in [14] or providing explanations in supervised learning [15]. The former develops a novel method to assign credits in multi-agent systems using counterfactual thinking and Shapley values, which quantifies each agent's contribution by considering what would happen if certain agents were absent, allowing for a fair and accurate assessment of each agent's impact on the collective outcome. The latter uses counterfactual scenarios to enhance Shapley value explanations, providing insights into how changes to input features could influence model predictions. It makes explanations more actionable by showing which features to adjust to achieve desired outcomes. Our work is fundamentally different. For the first time, we have applied the combination of counterfactual reasoning and Shapley Values to the domain of reinforcement learning, introducing the innovative Counterfactual Shapley Value approach. This method not only retains the benefits of traditional Shapley Values in quantitative analysis but also enhances the understanding of decision-making by examining specific hypothetical scenarios, such as "*What would happen if a specific action were not taken?*". Our approach brings a more transparent and interpretable perspective to decision-making in reinforcement learning, significantly alleviating the limitations of previous explanatory methods.

In this paper, our research contributions are threefold: (1) We have incorporated counterfactual mechanisms to calculate the differences in contributions between actions, thus providing new avenues for computing explanatory values within reinforcement learning. (2) We have designed two novel characteristic value functions—the *Counterfactual Difference based Characteristic Value Function* and the *Average Counterfactual Difference based Characteristic Value Function*—which incorporate counterfactual mechanisms for calculating Shapley Values. **Specifically, our approach utilizes these counterfactual differ-**

ence based characteristic value functions to derive the corresponding counterfactual difference Shapley Values, abbreviated as **Counterfactual Shapley Values**. This offers new avenues for computation and enhances the interpretability of agents' decision-making processes. (3) Lastly, we have tested and analyzed this method across multiple RL environments, where the quantified results from Counterfactual Shapley Value have allowed us to explain the behavior of agents, thereby demonstrating the effectiveness of our approach.

2 Counterfactual Differences in Reinforcement Learning

2.1 Markov Decision Process

In the domain of reinforcement learning, an agent's interaction with the environment is conceptualized as a Markov Decision Process (MDP), denoted by MDP $= (S, A, P, R, \gamma)$, where S is the set of all possible states, A is the set of actions, P is the state transition probabilities $P(s'|s, a) : S \times A \times S \to [0, 1]$, $R(s, a) : S \times A \to \mathbb{R}$ represents the reward function $R(s, a)$, $\gamma \in [0, 1]$ denotes the discount factor the cumulative reward and G_t represents the sum of discounted future rewards starting from time t. It is mathematically defined as $G_t = \sum_{k=0}^{\infty} \gamma^k R_{t+k+1}$, with R_{t+k+1} signifying the immediate reward received at time $t + k + 1$. The role of cumulative reward is fundamental, serving as a critical metric to assess and guide the agent's performance. The agent's objective is to discover a policy $\pi : S \times A \to [0, 1]$ that assigns probabilities to actions in each state, with the aim of optimizing the cumulative expected reward over time. The state-value function $V^\pi(s) = \mathbb{E}^\pi[G_t \mid S_t = s]$ computes the expected return from starting in state s under policy π, while the action-value function $Q^\pi(s, a) = \mathbb{E}^\pi[G_t \mid S_t = s, A_t = a]$ assesses the expected return after taking action a in state s under the same policy. The optimal policy, therefore, is defined by maximizing these functions, $V^*(s)$ and $Q^*(s, a)$, to achieve the highest possible expected returns from all states and actions.

2.2 Counterfactual Differences

From the perspective of explaining agent behavior, effectively comparing two distinct actions requires not only evaluating the immediate reward following action execution and the expected long-term return but also exploring counterfactual scenarios —"what would happen if a different action were chosen?" To facilitate this, we introduce the notion of counterfactual difference (CD), including both *action counterfactual differences* (ΔQ) and *state counterfactual differences* (ΔV), to thoroughly analyze the impacts of various actions. The action counterfactual differences examines the difference in Q values between the actual action taken and a hypothetical alternative action in a given state, while the state counterfactual differences focuses on the variance in V values for the new states resulting from these actions.

The action counterfactual differences, denoted as $\Delta Q^\pi(s, a^*, a)$, is calculated by the comparison between the expected return of taking an optimal action a^*

under the policy π in state s, against the expected return of taking another action a under the same policy π in the same state s. This comparison yields the differences value, revealing the potential utility deviation resulting from an alternative action choice. $\Delta Q^\pi(s, a^*, a)$ is calculated as follows:

$$\Delta Q^\pi(s, a^*, a) = Q^\pi(s, a^*) - Q^\pi(s, a) \tag{1}$$

where $Q^\pi(s, a^*)$ represents the expected return of executing the optimal action a^* in state s under the policy π, while $Q^\pi(s, a)$ signifies the expected return of executing the counterfactual action a under the same policy π in the same state. Although the policy usually prioritizes executing what is assessed as the optimal action, the reward of non-optimal actions is also recorded during training to maintain a balance between exploration and exploitation. This forms the basis for a counterfactual analysis scenario, through which we can compare the expected return of non-optimal actions to optimal actions, thereby evaluating how different state features contribute to these two types of decisions.

The policy π can be either a *fully learned policy* or a *partially learned policy*. Both types of policies aim to select actions with the highest Q values in each state, which are considered optimal. In a fully learned policy, the agent has converged to an optimal strategy and can execute the optimal choices with high accuracy. On the other hand, a partially learned policy refers to a policy that has not fully converged, where the agent has not yet completely learned the optimal Q values or strategy. Although such a policy theoretically aims to maximize rewards, it may not always choose the best actions in practice because it struggles to accurately calculate Q values and predict long-term returns. Additionally, the agent may still explore non-optimal actions due to incomplete training. Therefore, this study focuses on fully learned policies, which have reached convergence and can execute the optimal actions reliably.

The state counterfactual differences, denoted as $\Delta V^\pi(s^*, s')$, quantify the variation in expected return when transitioning from the current state s to an optimal state s^* under the policy π, compared to transitioning to a different state s' under the same policy π. This difference highlights the expected return change resulting from adopting the optimal action compared to an alternative action, both originating from the same starting state. The counterfactual difference $\Delta V^\pi(s^*, s')$ is calculated as follows:

$$\Delta V^\pi(s^*, s') = V^\pi(s^*) - V^\pi(s') \tag{2}$$

where s^* represents the optimal state that the agent aims to reach according to its fully learned policy. It is important to note that under a fully learned policy, the optimal state is unique given the current state, as the policy has converged to the most rewarding strategy. Thus, s^* is determined by the optimal action at state s, and s', which is a different state, may be reached only through suboptimal actions or due to randomness in the environment.

Although some states s' may only be reached through suboptimal actions a with very low probabilities under a fully learned policy, these states still have their own v-values from the value function, which represent the expected rewards that could be obtained starting from these states. Even if these states are not frequently visited under the optimal policy, counterfactual methods allow us to explore these less optimal states to analyze how suboptimal actions could have been chosen. However, it is essential to note that in the context of a fully learned policy, the agent will not generally explore these states unless they are part of the historical training data. The model's ability to analyze state transitions heavily relies on the data collected during the training process. As the model may not have explored all possible state-action combinations, this can limit its ability to handle highly complex environments. In contrast, Q-value methods are not dependent on the specific transition dynamics of the environment but rather evaluate the expected rewards for each state-action pair. This approach allows them to overcome the dependency on training data and makes them more applicable in complex and uncertain environments.

In RL, the main difference between the Q-value and the V-value is that the Q-value involves a combination of state and action, allowing direct quantification of the expected return for each action taken in a given state through Q(s, a). This makes the Q-value particularly well-suited for direct use in the decision-making process, as it provides clear guidance on action selection for each state. In contrast, the V-value is only related to the state and does not involve actions, reflecting the maximum expected return achievable from a state when following the optimal action. This characteristic of not being directly linked to specific actions makes the V-value less straightforward in establishing connections between states from a policy perspective, typically requiring the use of the value functions of subsequent states $V(s')$ or $V(s^*)$ to reflect the utility of actions.

2.3 Average Counterfactual Difference

To extend the analysis on agent behavior and the expected return (utility) impacts of varying policies, we investigate further into the counterfactual differences by introducing the concepts of Average Counterfactual differences (ACD) for $Q(s, a)$ and $V(s)$. These metrics offer a refined approach to evaluate and compare the efficacy of the optimal action against a spectrum of alternative actions.

For $Q(s, a)$, the *Average Action Counterfactual differences*, denoted as $\Delta \overline{Q}^\pi(s, a^*)$, provides a comprehensive measure by averaging the expected return differences between the optimal action a^* and all other possible actions within the action space. This metric is particularly useful for evaluating the relative advantage of the optimal action by considering its expected return gain over the average expected return of all alternative actions. The formula for $\Delta \overline{Q}^\pi$ is given by:

$$\Delta \overline{Q}^\pi(s, a^*) = \mathbb{E}_{a \sim A}\left[\Delta Q^\pi(s, a^*, a)\right]$$
$$= \frac{1}{|A|} \sum_{a \in A} \Delta Q^\pi(s, a^*, a) \quad (3)$$
$$= \frac{1}{|A|} \sum_{a \in A} \left[Q^\pi(s, a^*) - Q^\pi(s, a)\right]$$

Similarly, for $V(s)$, *the Average State Counterfactual Differences*, $\Delta\overline{V}^\pi(s)$, quantifies the average expected return change when transitioning from the current state s to an optimal state s^*, compared to transitions to all other potential states s' according to policy π. This metric aids in understanding the broader implications of policy choices on the agent's position and subsequent expected return. The computation of $\Delta\overline{V}^\pi$ is as follows:

$$\begin{aligned}
\Delta\overline{V}^\pi(s) &= \mathbb{E}_{s' \sim S'}[\Delta V^\pi(s^*, s')] \\
&= \frac{1}{|S'|} \sum_{s' \in S'} \Delta V^\pi(s^*, s') \\
&= \frac{1}{|S'|} \sum_{s' \in S'} \left[V^\pi(s^*) - V^\pi(s')\right],
\end{aligned} \quad (4)$$

where $S' = \{s' \mid P(s'|s, a) \geq 0, \forall a \in A\}$ which means that S' includes all states that may be reached by taking any action a in the action space A from the state s.

The comparison of $\Delta\overline{Q}$ with ΔQ, and $\Delta\overline{V}$ with ΔV, highlights their roles in providing analytical depth and breadth within reinforcement learning, crucial for both strategic planning and precise decision-making. More importantly, these models enhance the interpretability and transparency of decision-making processes. ACD offer a broad perspective on the impacts of different actions, aiding in policy clarity, while CD provide detailed insights into specific actions, enhancing operational transparency. Together, they ensure decisions are informed, accountable, and transparent, catering to both overarching polices and immediate actions.

3 Shapley Values for RL

3.1 Introduction to Shapley Values

Shapley Values, originally proposed by [16], are a fundamental concept in cooperative game theory. They provide a fair and mathematically grounded method for allocating the payoff among players in a cooperative setting, based on their individual contributions to the total outcome. The Shapley Value of a player is the average marginal contribution of that player to the payoff, taken over all possible coalitions that the player can be a part of.

Mathematically, the Shapley Value ϕ_i for player i in a game with players set N and a characteristic function v that assigns a value to each coalition of players is defined as:

$$\phi_i = \sum_{S \subseteq N \setminus \{i\}} \frac{|S|!(|N| - |S| - 1)!}{|N|!} \left(v(S \cup \{i\}) - v(S)\right),$$

where S is a subset of N excluding i, and $v(S)$ represents the characteristic function's value of coalition S. This formulation ensures that each player's contribution is systematically accounted for, considering all possible coalitions and appropriately weighting their impact.

Shapley Values satisfy four fundamental axioms: *Efficiency:* [17] The total value is distributed among all players. *Symmetry:* [18] Players with identical contributions receive equal values. *Dummy:* [19] If a player contributes nothing to any coalition, they receive a value of zero. *Additivity:* [20] The Shapley Values from separate cooperative games can be combined linearly. These properties make Shapley Values particularly appealing for scenarios where an equitable distribution of resources or credit is crucial.

3.2 Shapley Values in Reinforcement Learning and Characteristic Value Functions

In the context of Reinforcement Learning, Shapley Values offer a principled way to assess the individual contributions of state features to the decision-making efficacy of an RL agent. This is particularly valuable in *explainability and feature attribution*, where understanding how different state components influence the agent's policy is crucial.

Let $F = \{0, 1, \ldots, n-1\}$ denote the index set corresponding to the **state features** of the environment. The **state space** can be represented as:

$$S = S^{(0)} \times S^{(1)} \times \ldots \times S^{(n-1)},$$

where each $S^{(i)}$ represents the domain of a specific feature i. For any state s, a *partial state observation* over a subset of features $C \subseteq F$ is defined as:

$$s^C = < s^{(j)} \mid s^{(j)} \in S^{(j)}, j \in C >.$$

A crucial component in applying Shapley Values is the *Characteristic Value Function (CVF)*, denoted as $v(\cdot)$, which quantifies the expected contribution of state feature subsets to the agent's performance. Formally, for a subset of state features $C \subseteq F$, the CVF is defined as:

$$v(s^C) = \mathbb{E}\left[\sum_{t=0}^{\infty} \gamma^t r_t \mid s_t^C\right],$$

with the convention that when no features are known ($C = \emptyset$), the value is set to zero:

$$v(\emptyset) = 0.$$

This mirrors the assumption that without any observable state features, no meaningful value can be estimated.

The Shapley Value for a state feature i is given by:

$$\phi_i = \sum_{C \subseteq F \setminus \{i\}} \frac{|C|!(|F| - |C| - 1)!}{|F|!} \cdot \delta(i, C), \tag{5}$$

where the *marginal contribution* $\delta(i, C)$ is defined as:

$$\delta(i, C) = v(C \cup \{i\}) - v(C).$$

This formulation allows us to quantify the importance of each state feature by computing its **average marginal contribution** across all possible subsets.

Vanilla-CVF Approach: In Reinforcement Learning, the characteristic value functions, Q-values and V-values, are dependent on the chosen feature set C used to define the state representation. When the composition of C changes—such as by removing a specific feature—this necessitates an adaptation in the policy, which in turn results in different Q-values and V-values. For the state representation:

$$v_{\text{vani}}^{Q/V}(C) = Q^{\pi^C}(s,a) \quad \text{or} \quad V^{\pi^C}(s).$$

Since different feature subsets lead to different policy behaviors, the induced policy π^C (derived from an RL agent that perceives only the subset C of state features) is *not necessarily identical to* π^F, which is based on full observation of the entire state space. This variation in policies poses a significant challenge in accurately computing the *marginal contribution* of each feature to the agent's overall decision-making process.

4 Counterfactual Shapley Values

In the XRL, it is imperative to gain a comprehensive understanding of the fundamental motivations underlying the decision-making processes of agents. While Shapley Values do not clarify the policy significance of action choices directly, the incorporation of counterfactual analysis enhances the ability to assess the potential effects of various actions in hypothetical scenarios, thereby offering deep insights into the policy selections of agents.

It is noteworthy that the value functions $Q(s,a)$ and $V(s)$, while pivotal in guiding agents towards optimal decision-making, also serve as *utility functions* for computing Shapley Values, highlighting their significance in analyzing agent behavior. By employing these value functions as characteristic value function, a more precise quantitative analysis of the specific contributions of different dimensions in any given state can be achieved.

4.1 Counterfactual Difference Based Characteristic Value Function

In the Shapley Value calculations for reinforcement learning, selecting an appropriate characteristic value function is essential. Typically, these functions are derived from fundamental elements like the value function or the action-value function, which can be straightforwardly used to compute what are known as 'vanilla' characteristic values. Once the policy is learned, the agent's behavior becomes fixed. In any given state, it almost always chooses the best action, hardly considering other suboptimal options. In this way, choosing the optimal action versus not choosing it forms a counterfactual scenario, which represents theoretical possibilities that do not actually occur. However, to facilitate more detailed comparisons in counterfactuals, particularly between an optimal action and a suboptimal one within the same state, employing counterfactual characteristic value function becomes essential. This method thoroughly quantifies the expected return difference when choosing the optimal action instead of a suboptimal alternative, this counterfactual analysis significantly contributes to the transparency and explainability of decisions within reinforcement learning models, as it offers clear insights into the reasons behind preferring certain actions over others, thus making the decision-making process more understandable and justifiable. The Counterfactual Difference (CD) characteristic value functions are expressed as follows:

CD Characteristic Value Functions (for Single-Action Comparisons).

$$v_{CD}^Q(C) = \Delta Q^C(s^C, a^*, a), \tag{6}$$

$$v_{CD}^V(C) = \Delta V^C(s^{*C}, s'^C), \tag{7}$$

where $s^{*C} \sim P(\cdot|s^C, a^*)$ and $s'^C \sim P(\cdot|s^C, a)$ are the states reached from state s^C by executing the optimal action a^* and a suboptimal action a, respectively. Here, $\Delta Q^C(s^C, a^*, a)$ and $\Delta V^C(s^{*C}, s'^C)$ denote the differences in Q-values and V-values resulting from the policy trained within a subset C of the state space, compared to a full state space approach. The values, derived from a reduced set of features, offer a more focused interpretation, highlighting the difference in outcomes when considering specific state and action subsets, as opposed to the full state space used in earlier definitions of the Q and V functions.

The computation of the Shapley Value by CD approach is indispensable for highlighting the relative advantage and direct impact of the optimal action against a specific alternative, offering granular insights into the decision-making process. This method calculates the difference between two specific actions. Using the CD characteristic value function, we can obtain a Counterfactual Difference Shapley Value (CD-SPV), which directly reflects how each feature influences the difference in outcomes between these two actions.

Expanding the scope, the computation of the Shapley Value by ACD approach averages the expected return differences between the optimal action and all suboptimal actions A', providing a comprehensive evaluation of the action's efficacy across the entire action space. The ACD characteristic value functions are defined as:

ACD Characteristic Value Functions (for averaged comparisons).

$$v_{ACD}^Q(C) = \frac{1}{|A|} \sum_{a \in A} \Delta Q^C(s^C, a^*, a), \tag{8}$$

$$v_{ACD}^V(C) = \frac{1}{|S'^C|} \sum_{s'^C \in S'^C} \Delta V^C(s^{*C}, s'^C). \tag{9}$$

where $S'^C = \{s'^C \mid P(s'^C|s^C, a) \geq 0, \forall a \in A\}$ means that S'^C includes all possible states reachable from s^C by taking any action a within the reduced action space A from the state s^C in the limited subset C of the state space. In this case, S'^C captures the expected next states considering the full action space from a state in subset C, allowing for a broader evaluation of action effectiveness compared to the CD method.

The ACD computation approach excels by demonstrating the overall dominance of the optimal action and providing a comprehensive view of the policy's depth and robustness. Unlike the CD method, the ACD method calculates the average difference between all possible actions and a specific action (usually the optimal action). The ACD characteristic value function offers an evaluation of how a specific action generally compares to other available actions, helping to assess the policy's general utility across a range of possible states and actions, as opposed to focusing on a direct action-to-action comparison as with the CD approach.

Together, the CD and ACD computation approaches enrich the analysis of policy performance in reinforcement learning by offering both detailed and broad perspectives. While the CD method allows for focused evaluations of specific action dynamics, the ACD delivers a macroscopic understanding of the policy's general utility and resilience. This dual approach strengthens the analytical framework for policy interpretation, emphasizing policy insights over direct policy optimization.

4.2 Shapley Value Using Counterfactual Difference Characteristics Value Functions

Recall that in Sect. 3.2 we have introduced how Shapley Value can be integrated in RL for assessing feature importance using Eq. (5) and a characteristic value function $v(\cdot)$ that assigns a value to each subset (coalition) $C \subseteq N$, the Shapley Value ϕ_i of player i is computed via Eq. (5):

By substituting $v(\cdot)$ with, for example, $v_{CD}^V(\cdot)$ / $v_{CD}^Q(\cdot)$ or $v_{ACD}^V(\cdot)$ / $v_{ACD}^Q(\cdot)$ into Eq. (5), one obtains Shapley values that quantify how each dimension affects the difference in expected return between the optimal and suboptimal actions (or between an optimal action and *all* other actions on average). In this way, Eq. (5) underpins the Counterfactual Shapley Values framework, providing a

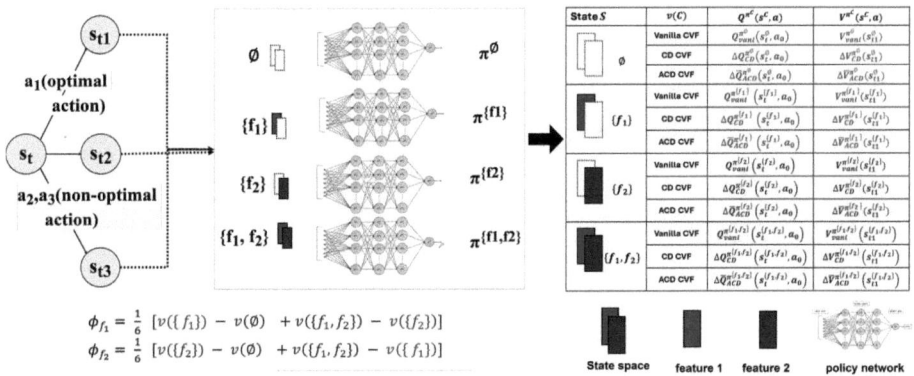

Fig. 1. Computation of Counterfactual Shapley Value using VANI-CVF, CD-CVF, and ACD-CVF.

rigorous, axiomatic foundation for allocating "contribution scores" among state features based on their importance in driving RL policy decisions.

An example of calculating Counterfactual Shapley Values using the *vani-CVF*, *CD-CVF*, and *ACD-CVF* approaches, assuming a state with two features, is shown in Fig. (1). This figure show the process of using the newly introduced characteristic value functions, CD-CVF and ACD-CVF, to compute Counterfactual Shapley Values. The approach involves training separate policy networks for different feature subsets, where the induced policies π^C are learned based on the optimal policy for each feature subset. By comparing the expected return differences between optimal and suboptimal actions, and computing the Shapley values using these functions, the method provides insight into how different state features contribute to the agent's decision-making process.

5 Experiments

We present experimental results from various domains in RL, applying Counterfactual Shapley Value analysis to understand the influence of optimal versus suboptimal actions on individual dimensions of the state space.

5.1 Explanation in Gridworld 1 and Gridworld 2

In **GridWord-1** on Fig. (2a), it is easily discovered that the optimal action for each non-target state is to move right →. However, relying solely on the value-table on Fig. (2c) generated by state-value functions or action-value functions can only explain the choice of the current action, without explaining the specific impact of that action on the state features. In other words, due to the state possessing multiple dimensions, it is not feasible to directly compare the influence of any dimension on the selection of optimal actions through the analysis of value functions and related techniques.

Using the *Counterfactual Difference Shapley Value* (CD-SPV) and *Average Counterfactual Difference Shapley Value* methods (ACD-SPV) for calculation of Shapley Value by state-value function (V-value), we can examine the differences between the optimal action and all non-optimal actions, as well as between the optimal action and specific non-optimal actions. This facilitates our comprehension of how these differences affect each dimension of the state. Throughout this process, we will utilize the Shapley Value method offered by the Vanilla characteristic value function (Vanilla-SPV) for thorough analysis.

The findings obtained from the analysis of the **GridWord-1** scenario using the *ACD-SPV*, *CD-SPV* and *Vanilla-SPV* methods are presented in Fig. (3). The functionalities of these three methods are introduced as follows:

Vanilla-SPV(i) or **Vani(i)**: The list results show the Shapley Values for each dimension (feature) of the state, which indicate the individual contributions of different dimensions (feature) to the choice of action i. In short, these Shapley Values allow us to see the importance and influence of each state dimension in the decision-making process. *Lower index i corresponds to better actions, with*

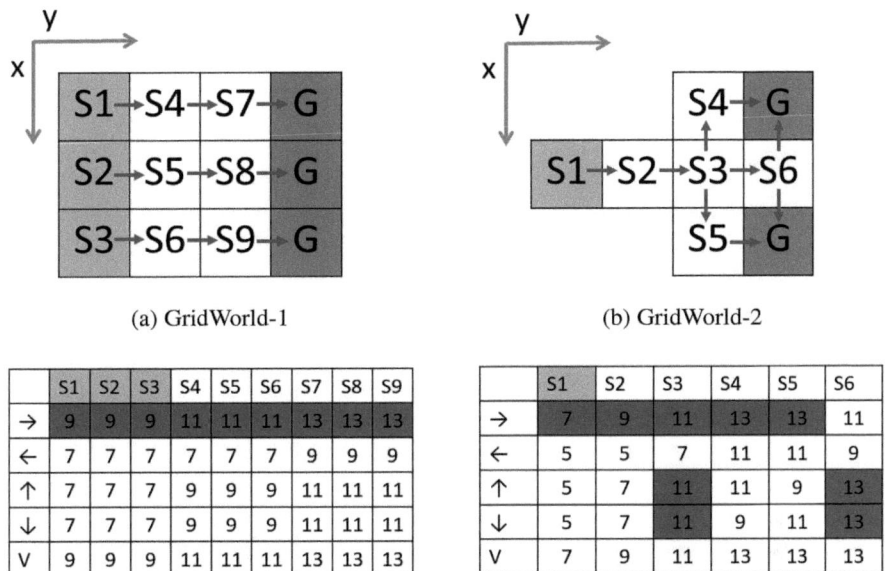

Fig. 2. Comparison of GridWorld-1 and GridWorld-2, including their corresponding values of $V(s)$, $Q(s,a)$ based on π^*.

action 0 corresponding to the optimal action, which has a Shapley Value for each feature denoted by Vani(0). The next best action corresponds to Vani(1), and subsequent actions are similarly denoted by Vani(2), Vani(3), etc.

CD-SPV(i, j) or CD(ij): By examining the differences in the contribution of each dimension of a certain state to the selection of different actions i and j, the list results show the relative importance of state dimensions (feature) by differences in Shapley Values under varying actions. Since we typically focus on the optimal action $i = 0$ compared to non-optimal action j, it can describe how the different dimensions of a state contribute differently to the optimal and non-optimal actions. This clarifies why, in certain scenarios, opting for action i over action j might be more advantageous. *CD(0,1) compares the optimal action 0 with the suboptimal action 1, revealing the relative differences in each dimension when action 0 is executed instead of action 1. Conversely, CD(1,0) indicates the comparison when action 1 is executed instead of action 0, and CD(0,1) is the negative of CD(1,0) in each dimension (feature), meaning CD(0,1) = -CD(1,0). The results show that a larger positive difference indicates that the dimension is more important for the decision-making; conversely, a larger negative difference indicates that the dimension has a negative impact on the decision; if the difference is close to zero, it means that this dimension contributes equally under both scenarios. Similarly, CD(0,2) and CD(0,3) compare the optimal action with the second and third suboptimal actions, respectively.* We consider all subopti-

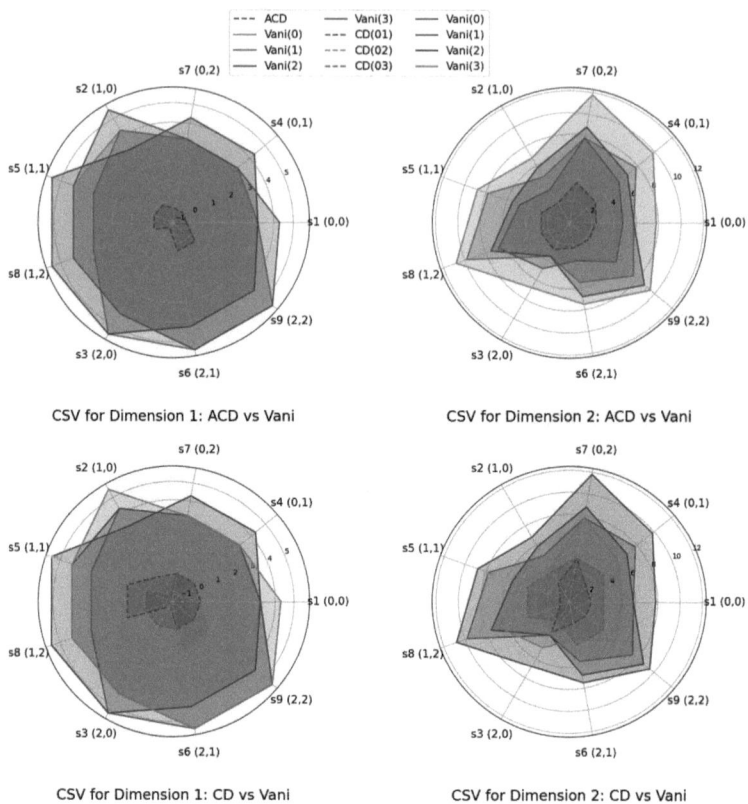

Fig. 3. Comparison of Shapley Values across Vanilla-SPV, CD-SPV, and ACD-SPV for each state dimension in GridWorld-1.

mal actions to be counterfactual actions because, once the policy is learned, the current policy will not execute these suboptimal actions. Of course, in the same state, there may be multiple optimal actions that are equally valid and executable. We choose one of these as the optimal action, and the rest are regarded as counterfactual actions, that is, suboptimal actions.

ACD-SPV or **ACD**: By examining the average differences in the contribution of each dimension of a certain state to the selection of the optimal action versus **all** non-optimal actions, the list results provide the benchmark of contribution for comparing the average difference between executing the optimal and all non-optimal actions. This clarifies the average differential impact across various dimensions on the decision outcomes when optimal actions are executed as opposed to suboptimal actions, analyzing both the quality (positive or negative) and the degree of the impacts.

The Shapley values, computed as the difference between the optimal action and the average of all non-optimal actions, reflect the comparitive value of the optimal action. Although these values may appear modest in comparison to the direct contributions of specific actions, the positive values still indicate the superiority of the optimal action over any other, given its positive contribution across all state dimensions. This explains why, in certain situations, selecting the optimal action as opposed to any other action is preferable.

In our analysis of the **GridWorld-1** environment, several interesting insights were made. When three states s_1, s_2, and s_3 have the same V and Q values after policy learning, we intuitively expect their contributions to deciding the optimal action in each dimension to be consistent. However, when we use the *Vanilla-SPV* method to evaluate the specific contributions of each dimension on optimal action, we find that the contributions vary among similar states. The contributions of the two dimensions (or features) in s_1 are 3.2, and 5.8, and 4.3 and 4.8 respectively in s_2, while 5.5 and 3.5 respectively in s_3. These results suggest that even though the optimal actions for these states all involve moving to the right (which primarily affects the y-axis coordinate), the *Vanilla-SPV* method shows that in some cases the contribution of the first dimension (x-axis) appears to be higher than the second dimension (y-axis), which opposes our intuitive expectations. This indicates that although the *Vanilla-SPV* method can provide specific contribution for each dimension, it may not accurately reflect which dimension plays a more critical role in decision-making.

However, when we use the CD-SPV and ACD-SPV methods to evaluate the differences between states when performing optimal and suboptimal actions, we gain deeper insights. Taking state s_1 as an example, its optimal action is to move right ($\rightarrow$) while its suboptimal action is to move up ($\uparrow$) (the other three actions have the same Q or V value, thus they are also considered suboptimal). In this scenario, the differences in dimensions for these two actions are [0, 2]. Similarly, for states s_2 and s_3, the differences in the same conditions are [0, 2] and [−1.2, 3.2] respectively. The reason these two values differ is that the state transition paths are different after executing optimal and suboptimal actions. For example, when executing the optimal action ($\rightarrow$), s_2 transitions to s_5 and s_3 transitions to s_6; whereas when executing the suboptimal action ($\uparrow$), s_2 transitions to s_1 and s_3 transitions to s_2. The differences in state transitions resulting from executing optimal and suboptimal actions lead to different Q- or V-value differences, which are then used as characteristic value functions to derive Shapley Values. These Shapley Values reflect how each feature contributes to the difference between the two actions, rather than to a single action itself. These results first reveal the differences in each dimension between optimal and suboptimal scenarios, indicating how much each dimension is improved or reduced, and also show that the second dimension contributes more significantly to decision-making. Despite the three suboptimal actions of state s_1 having the same value, their differences vary because performing the optimal action leads s_1 to state s_4, while performing the actions up ($\uparrow$) and left ($\rightarrow$) keeps it in state s_1, but performing the action down ($\downarrow$) moves it to state s_2, demonstrating that even if some actions have the same Q or V value, their utilities can be completely different. ACD-SPV provides a balanced view, showing the average expected difference between the optimal action and all suboptimal actions. If the counterfactual difference between optimal and a particular suboptimal actions is significantly greater than the average, it indicates a large expected difference generated by this actions. This can be a useful metric for evaluating similar states in abstract state tasks.

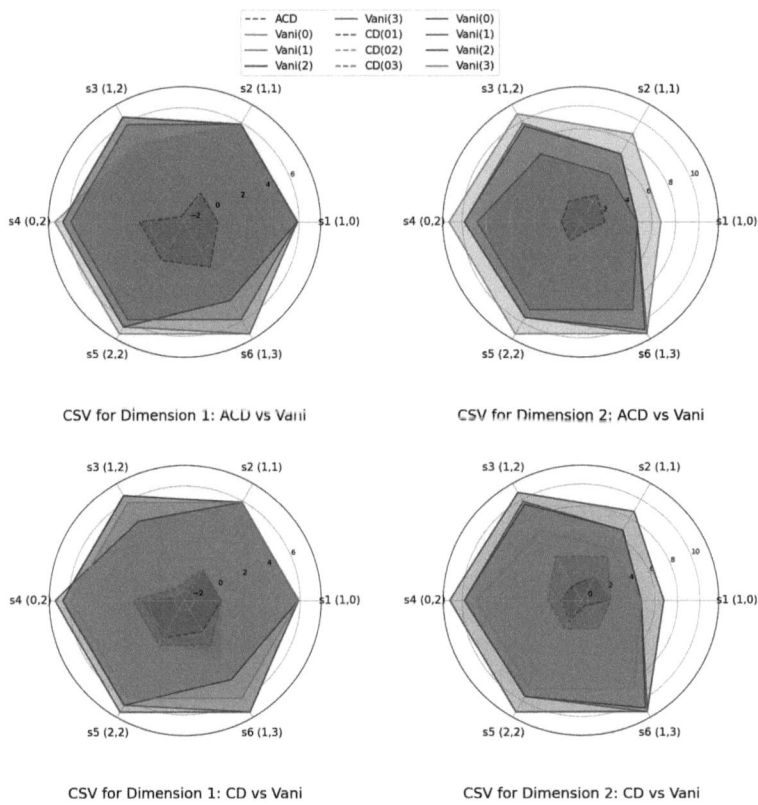

Fig. 4. Comparison of Shapley Values across Vanilla-SPV, CD-SPV, and ACD-SPV for each state dimension in GridWord-2.

Therefore, from Fig. (4), it is clear that the contribution of the second dimension significantly exceeds that of the first. The difference in contribution for the second dimension typically ranges between 2 and 3, while the first dimension has little to no positive contribution except in states s_6 and s_9. This situation occurs because, in these states, the CSV of the first dimension exceeds that of the second, resulting in a slight positive contribution for the first dimension in these specific states. However, this does not alter the fact that the overall contribution of the second dimension is greater than that of the first, clearly indicating that the second dimension contributes more to optimal decision-making than the first.

In **GridWord-2** on Fig. (2b), this environment has a starting position and multiple goal states. In states s_1 and s_2, by applying ACD-SPV and CD-SPV

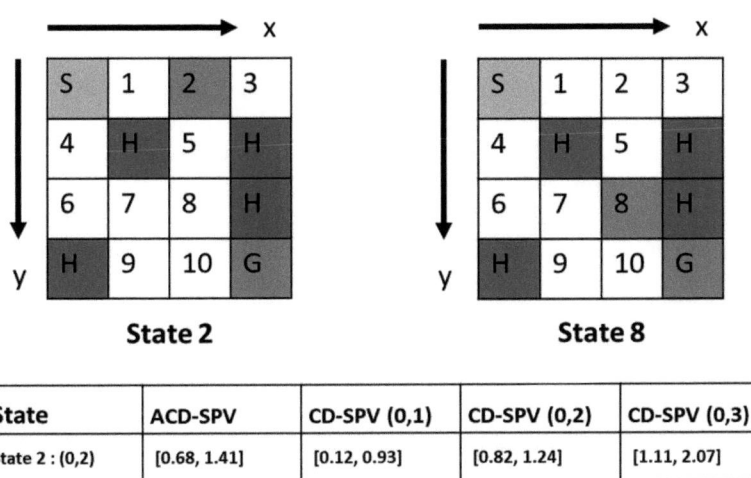

Fig. 5. State 2 and State 8 are respectively depicted on the upper left and upper right of the figure, representing the coordinates of the agent's current position. State 2 corresponds to (0,2), and State 8 corresponds to (2,2). Counterfactual Shapley Values for Each Dimension of States on FrozenLake are displayed in the table of the figure for these two states.

methods, it is clear that the impact of the second dimension on decision-making is significantly greater than that of the first dimension, which can almost be ignored. In states s_3 and s_6, there are multiple optimal actions. States s_4 and s_5 are completely symmetrical, and they are equidistant from two different goal states. From the ACD-SPV analysis, we understand that the optimal actions contribute in both the x and y dimensions, but the contribution of the y dimension is more significant, and both contributions are positive. In state s_6, the optimal actions primarily involve the first dimension because the optimal actions are to move up (↑) or down (↓), primarily changing the value of the first dimension, moving from (1,3) to either (0,3) or (2,3). In state s_3, compared to other actions, the optimal action's contribution in the first dimension is negative and similar in size to the second dimension. This indicates that in state s_3, when performing the optimal action, the impact of the first dimension is much less than other options. This is mainly because the forward action changes the y value, having almost no impact on the x-axis, while the right (→) and left (←) actions have a large difference in the contribution of the first dimension, with the former being 4.25 and the latter being 5.88, also explaining why in choosing the optimal action, the contribution of the first dimension is much lower than that of other actions.

5.2 Explanation in FrozenLake

FrozenLake is a reinforcement learning environment inspired by the challenge of traversing a frozen lake while avoiding treacherous holes, popularized by the OpenAI Gym framework [21]. This environment is depicted as a grid where each cell is marked as either safe ice (Squares with Digits) or a perilous hole (H), with designated starting (S) and goal (G) positions. The agent's objective is to navigate from the start to the goal without falling into any holes, guided solely by its position on the grid. The permissible actions are moving north, south, east, or west. The reward system is straightforward: falling into a hole incurs a -10 penalty, reaching the goal yields a $+10$ reward, and each move costs -1, incentivizing the agent to find the most efficient route to the goal. An episode begins with the agent at the start point and concludes successfully upon reaching the goal or unsuccessfully if the agent falls into a hole.

Table 1. Two states in Taxi for explanation

	State 1:[0, 4, 4, 1]	State 2:[0, 0, 0, 1]
ACD	$(-1.3, -0.4, -0.02, 0.2)$	$(-0.9, -0.4, 0.16, -0.0)$
CD(0,1)	$(-0.1, -0.0, -0.0, 0.2)$	$(-0.1, -0.0, 0.2, -0.0)$
CD(0,2)	$(-0.5, -0.1, 0.1, 0.1)$	$(-0.5, -0.1, 0.0, -0.0)$
CD(0,3)	$(-2.1, 0.0, 0.0, 0.2)$	$(-0.0, -0.0, 0.2, -0.1)$
CD(0,4)	$(-3.9, -1.9, -0.3, 0.2)$	$(-4.0, -1.9, 0.2, -0.0)$
CD(0,5)	$(0.1, 0.1, 0.1, 0.2)$	$(0.1, 0, 0.2, -0.3)$

In the **FrozenLake** environment, when considering the optimal action for State S_2 and State S_8 in Fig. (5), moving south ($\downarrow$) is identified as the best action for both two states. This is because moving south ($\downarrow$) brings one closer to the goal state, proving to be more effective than moving in other directions. For example, in State S_2, moving north ($\uparrow$) would result in staying in the same position (S_2), while moving south ($\downarrow$) would lead to reaching S_5. Although the southward move ($\downarrow$) only has a 0.12 higher contribution in the first dimension compared to moving north ($\uparrow$), it has a significantly higher contribution of 0.93 in the second dimension, demonstrating its clear advantage. In contrast, moving east ($\rightarrow$) or west ($\leftarrow$) results in lower contributions in both dimensions, indicating a substantial gap between these decisions and the optimal decision. In the case of State S_8, moving south ($\downarrow$) has a higher contribution towards reaching the goal, especially in the second dimension; moving east ($\rightarrow$), however, could result in falling into a hole, thereby creating a significant negative impact in the first dimension. Through such analysis, we can understand why some directions are not the best choices and how these decisions affect the overall policy.

5.3 Explanation in Taxi

The **Taxi** environment, a reinforcement learning benchmark by [22] and featured in OpenAI Gym [21], involves a taxi navigating a 5×5 grid to pick up and drop off a passenger at locations marked Red (R), Green (G), Blue (B), and Yellow (Y). The state captures the taxi's position and the passenger's status, either at a location or in the taxi. The taxi's tasks are to pick up the passenger and deliver them to their destination. It has six actions: move in four directions, pick up, and drop off. Rewards are set to encourage efficiency: -1 for each move, $+20$ for successful delivery, and -10 for failed pick-up or drop-off, guiding the taxi towards effective passenger transit.

In simple environments, we can easily use the state value function (V-value) to calculate the Shapley Value for interpretation, because in such environments, the transition from one state to another is usually straightforward and simple. This allows us to easily determine the next state and its corresponding value. However, in more complex environments, predicting the next state becomes more challenging, especially if we do not interact with the environment directly. In such cases, we recommend using the action value function (Q-value) to calculate the Shapley Value. Q-values help us assess the expected outcomes of specific actions without actually having to perform those actions. Therefore, Q-values are particularly suitable for use in environments where state transitions are complex or difficult to predict when providing post hoc explanations.

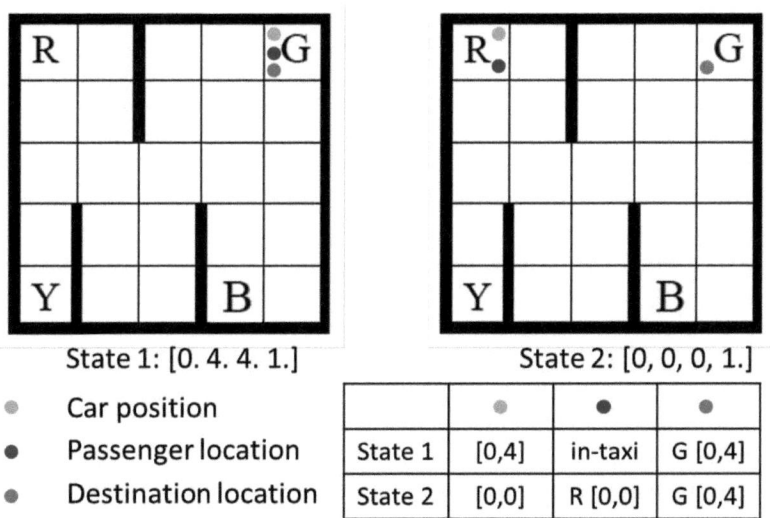

Fig. 6. State 1 and State 2 in Environment represent two different scenarios in the environment taxi.

In previous experiments, the primary focus was on actions related to the movement and how various state dimensions (features) influence decision-making, especially regarding movement in different directions. The current research expands the action space to include not only four movement actions but also two critical functions: *picking up* and *dropping off* passengers. This shift allows for an exploration of the decision-making process regarding when to pick up or drop off passengers based on the taxi's current state and its specific location in relation to the passenger and the destination. For example, in State 1, where the taxi and passenger are both at location [0,4], the optimal action is to *drop off* the passenger. Conversely, in State 2, where the taxi and the passenger are at [0,0] but the destination is [0,4], the optimal action is to *pick up* the passenger in Fig. (6). Note that in State 1, the taxi's current position is at [0,4], indicated by the yellow dot, and the passenger is also at position Green, which is [0,4], shown by the blue dot. At this moment, the passenger is inside the taxi, and their destination is also at position Green. Essentially, this state signifies that the passenger has reached the destination but remains in the taxi, and the optimal action for this state is to drop off. Similarly, State 2 is represented as [0,0,0,1], indicating that the taxi is at position [0,0], corresponding to the yellow dot. In this scenario, the passenger, located at position Red, is not inside the taxi, and their destination is at position Green, indicated by the green dot, which is different from the previous positions. In this case, the optimal action for the state is to pick up the passenger.

In two different states, Table (1) records the counterfactual Shapley Values for the optimal action and other suboptimal actions, reflecting the differences in contributions from different features within the same state to the optimal and suboptimal actions. In State 1, the optimal action is to drop off the passenger, while the worst choice is to pick up the passenger. The other four actions, which are related to movement, rank from second best action to fifth. In State 2, the best action is to pick up the passenger, while the worst choice is to drop off the passenger, with the remaining movement-related actions also ranking from second best action to fifth.

Through the calculation of CD-SPV, we observe that in State 1, the first two dimensions (i.e., the current position of the taxi) contribute less to the decision-making than the movement-related actions. This is because movement itself changes the position of the taxi. This means that in the current state, the dimensions related to location have a smaller impact on the choice of the best action compared to movement actions. From the ACD-SPV results, compared to other actions, only the last dimension (destination location) has a positive contribution, indicating that this dimension is crucial for decision-making in the current state.

Similarly, in State 2, the passenger's location dimension contributes more to the decision to pick up the passenger, the optimal action, than the other dimensions.

5.4 Explanation in Minesweeper

Minesweeper includes a 4×4 grid where each cell can display a value of 0, 1, 2, or remain unopened. Each number represents the count of mines adjacent to that cell. Initially, all cells are unopened, and players reveal cells to discover their contents. The game penalizes revealing a mine with a reward of −20, aiming to avoid mines and reveal all non-mine cells. The best possible outcome is a score of 0, achieved by successfully avoiding all mines, with no additional reward for speed or time efficiency. This setup is used for analyzing decision-making in machine learning.

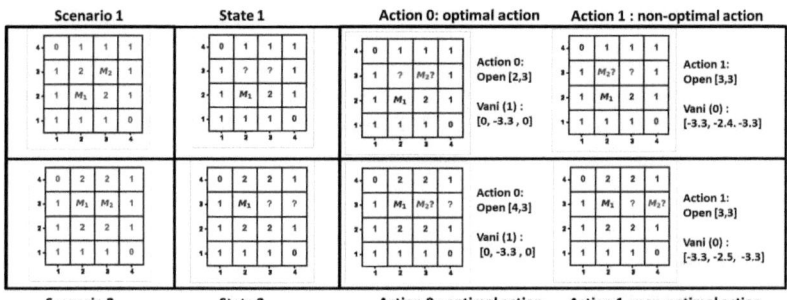

Fig. 7. The first column shows the actual arrangement of each position in the current game, which is unknown to the player. M_1 represents the location of the first mine, M_2 represents the location of the second mine, and other numbers indicate the number of mines adjacent to the current position. The second column shows a specific state of the game at the current progress, with blue characters indicating known or observable positions, and red question marks indicating unknown distributions, i.e., positions where mines may be present. The third column lists potential actions, such as M_2? indicating the player's assumption of the location of the second mine, i.e., opening another question mark position. (Color figure online)

This environment is different from previous ones because here, each selectable action directly corresponds to a specific dimension, and each square's selection is an independent decision in a given state. In Fig. 7, we demonstrate this with two completely different scenarios. In each scenario, the first cell displays the actual mine distribution, which is usually unknown, but for demonstration purposes, we place it at the forefront. The second cell shows the current state we are studying, and the third cell displays the potential actions, such as predicting the next mine-free location in unopened square. If the prediction is incorrect, resulting in a selection of a position with a mine, the game will end. Otherwise, the game continues or is won.

In State 1, if the mine's location is correctly predicted, the remaining position is safe no matter which one is chosen. However, if the prediction is incorrect, a position with a mine will be selected, leading to game failure. Therefore, the Shapley Values for the two actions are[0,-3,0], [-3.3,-2.4,-3.3], respectively, Here, the first dimension corresponds to the coordinates of positions [2,3], and the second dimension corresponds to the coordinates of positions [3,3]. All other known dimensions (features) are considered as one dimension (feature), and the overall contribution to the decision-making is combined in the third dimension in Shapley Values. By comparing the Shapley Values of different action, We find that the dimensions without mines and the observable dimensions contribute equally to selecting the optimal action, and if a position with a mine is chosen, both parts will provide a contribution of −3.3 to this decision. Similarly, in State 2, the optimal action can be determined by comparing the Shapley Values of different actions. The uniqueness of this environment lies in the fact that each action is directly linked to a specific dimension, allowing us to view them as comparing the effects of different actions. In this comparison, actions with higher Shapley Values indicate that their corresponding dimensions are more important in the current decision-making process. Moreover, the observable dimensions (features) also make significant contributions to the final decision and cannot be overlooked in the decision-making process.

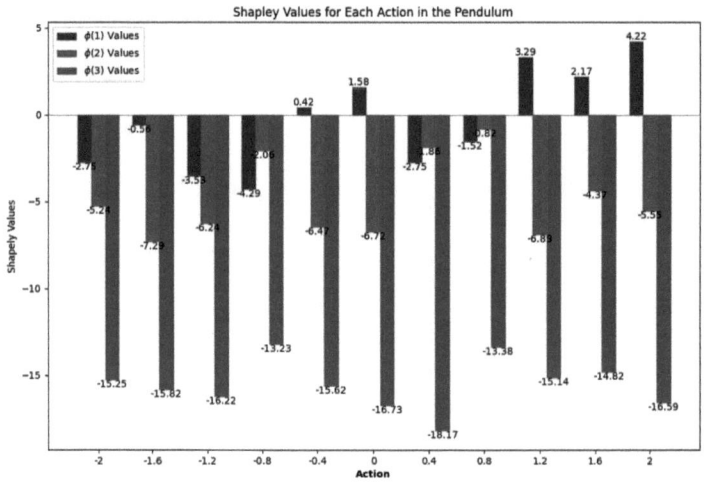

Fig. 8. Shapley Values for State Dimension Combinations of Pendulum.

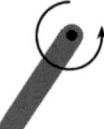

Fig. 9. State [-0.707, -0.707, 1] of Pendulum.

5.5 Explanation in Pendulum

The **Pendulum** environment simulates an inverted pendulum swingup problem from [23], where the goal is to apply torque to swing the pendulum into an upright position. The system starts with a pendulum at a random angle (θ) between $[-\pi, \pi]$ and a random angular velocity (torque) between $[-1, 1]$. The observation space consists of the pendulum's x-y coordinates at the free end and its angular velocity,state is $[cos(\theta), sin(\theta), torque]$, while the action space is a single-dimensional array between $[-2, 2]$ representing the applied torque. This setup challenges control algorithms to stabilize the pendulum with minimal effort in a continuous state and action space.

Due to the task involving a continuous action space, we first need to convert the continuous action space from $[-2, 2]$ into a discrete action space $-2, -1.6, -1.2, -0.8, -0.4, 0, 0.4, 0.8, 1.2, 1.6, 2$ for ease of training and explanation. Next, we choose the state $[-0.707, 0.707, 3]$ for analysis in Fig. 9. In this state, the pendulum is at a 225-degree angle with an angular velocity of 1, indicating that the pendulum has just fallen from the left side. We calculated the Shapley values for all possible actions in this state and recorded the results in Fig. 8. Due to the large action space, we do not show the complete CD-SPV results but directly provide the ACD-SPV results, which are [5.0, -0.76, -1.15]. Analysis shows that the best action is to apply the maximum positive torque. We also find that the first dimension of the state is the most critical for the current decision. Although the third dimension of the state has a significant negative impact (contribution) on the decision, this impact is common across other action choices and is not distinctive. Therefore, the first dimension of the state is the most important factor in the decision-making process.

6 Conclusion

In this research, we introduced a novel application of Counterfactual Shapley Values for enhancing the explainability of reinforcement learning models. Our method not only quantifies the contributions of different dimensions of the state to decision-making but also compares the differences between optimal and non-optimal actions across these dimensions. Simultaneously, it indicates which dimensions contribute positively to optimal actions, which ones negatively, and which ones are crucial features distinguishing optimal from non-optimal actions. Additionally, combining the Shapley Value calculated from the Counterfactual Difference Characteristic Value Function and the Average Counterfactual Difference Characteristic Value Function provides more comprehensive details on the contribution of each dimension. The efficacy of the CSV method was demonstrated across multiple RL scenarios, including applications in Grid-World, FrozenLake, and Taxi environments. Each case study provides additional perspectives to aid in understanding the variances in state contributions during the decision-making process and identifying the significant dimensions within the state, offering valuable insights for developers and interested parties seeking to build trust in autonomous systems.

References

1. Chen, J., Li, S.E., Tomizuka, M.: Interpretable end-to-end urban autonomous driving with latent deep reinforcement learning. IEEE Trans. Intell. Transp. Syst. **23**(6), 5068–5078 (2021)
2. Shi, Y., Wen, M., Zhang, Q., Zhang, W., Liu, C., Liu, W.: Autonomous goal detection and cessation in reinforcement learning: a case study on source term estimation. arXiv preprint arXiv:2409.09541 (2024)
3. Shi, Y., McAreavey, K., Liu, C., Liu, W.: Reinforcement learning for source location estimation: a multi-step approach. In: 2024 IEEE International Conference on Industrial Technology (ICIT), pp. 1–8. IEEE (2024)
4. Liu, S., Ngiam, K.Y., Feng, M.: Deep reinforcement learning for clinical decision support: a brief survey. arXiv preprint arXiv:1907.09475 (2019)
5. Jiang, Z., Xu, D., Liang, J.: A deep reinforcement learning framework for the financial portfolio management problem. arXiv preprint arXiv:1706.10059 (2017)
6. Kumar, N., Mittal, S., Garg, V., Kumar, N.: Deep reinforcement learning-based traffic light scheduling framework for SDN-enabled smart transportation system. IEEE Trans. Intell. Transp. Syst. **23**(3), 2411–2421 (2021)
7. Ma, H., McAreavey, K., Liu, W.: TSFeatLIME: an online user study in enhancing explainability in univariate time series forecasting. In: 2024 IEEE 36th International Conference on Tools with Artificial Intelligence (ICTAI), pp. 578–585. IEEE (2024)
8. Lundberg, S.M., Lee, S.-I.: A unified approach to interpreting model predictions. In: Advances in Neural Information Processing Systems, vol. 30 (2017)
9. Wang, J., Zhang, Y., Gu, Y., Kim, T.-K.: SHAQ: incorporating Shapley value theory into multi-agent Q-learning. In: Koyejo, S., Mohamed, S., Agarwal, A., Belgrave, D., Cho, K., Oh, A., Eds., Advances in Neural Information Processing Systems, vol. 35, pp. 5941–5954. Curran Associates, Inc. (2022). https://proceedings.neurips.cc/paper_files/paper/2022/file/27985d21f0b751b933d675930aa25022-Paper-Conference.pdf
10. Wang, J., Zhang, Y., Kim, T.-K., Gu, Y.: Shapley Q-value: a local reward approach to solve global reward games. Proc. AAAI Conf. Artif. Intell. **34**(05), 7285–7292 (2020)
11. Heuillet, A., Couthouis, F., Díaz-Rodríguez, N.: Collective explainable AI: explaining cooperative strategies and agent contribution in multiagent reinforcement learning with Shapley values. IEEE Comput. Intell. Mag. **17**(1), 59–71 (2022)
12. Beechey, D., Smith, T.M., Şimşek, Ö.: Explaining reinforcement learning with Shapley values. In: International Conference on Machine Learning, pp. 2003–2014. PMLR (2023)
13. Olson, M.L., Khanna, R., Neal, L., Li, F., Wong, W.-K.: Counterfactual state explanations for reinforcement learning agents via generative deep learning. ArXiv abs/2101.12446 (2021)
14. Li, J., Kuang, K., Wang, B., Liu, F., Chen, L., Wu, F., Xiao, J.: Shapley counterfactual credits for multi-agent reinforcement learning. In: Proceedings of the 27th ACM SIGKDD Conference on Knowledge Discovery & Data Mining, pp. 934–942 (2021)
15. Albini, E., Long, J., Dervovic, D., Magazzeni, D.: Counterfactual Shapley additive explanations. In: Proceedings of the 2022 ACM Conference on Fairness, Accountability, and Transparency, pp. 1054–1070 (2022)

16. Shapley, L.S.: A value for n-person games. In: Contributions to the Theory of Games. Princeton University Press, pp. 307–317 (1953)
17. Roth, A.E.: The Shapley Value: Essays in honor of Lloyd S. Cambridge University Press, Shapley (1988)
18. Shapley, L.S.: A value for n-person games. In: Contribution to the Theory of Games, vol. 2 (1953)
19. Winter, E.: The Shapley Value. In: Handbook of Game Theory with Economic Applications, vol. 3, pp. 2025–2054 (2002)
20. Peleg, B., Sudhölter, P.: Introduction to the Theory of Cooperative Games, vol. 34. Springer Science & Business Media (2007)
21. Brockman, G., et al.: OpenAI gym. arXiv preprint arXiv:1606.01540 (2016)
22. Dietterich, T.G.: The taxi problem: a case study in reinforcement learning. Five Open Problems in Reinforcement Learning (1998)
23. Towers, M.: Gymnasium (2023). https://zenodo.org/record/8127025

Open Access This chapter is licensed under the terms of the Creative Commons Attribution 4.0 International License (http://creativecommons.org/licenses/by/4.0/), which permits use, sharing, adaptation, distribution and reproduction in any medium or format, as long as you give appropriate credit to the original author(s) and the source, provide a link to the Creative Commons license and indicate if changes were made.

The images or other third party material in this chapter are included in the chapter's Creative Commons license, unless indicated otherwise in a credit line to the material. If material is not included in the chapter's Creative Commons license and your intended use is not permitted by statutory regulation or exceeds the permitted use, you will need to obtain permission directly from the copyright holder.

Improving the Weighting Strategy in KernelSHAP

Lars Henry Berge Olsen[1,2](✉) and Martin Jullum[2]

[1] Department of Mathematics, University of Oslo, Oslo, Norway
[2] Norwegian Computing Center, Oslo, Norway
{lhbolsen,jullum}@nr.no

Abstract. In Explainable AI (XAI), Shapley values are a popular model-agnostic framework for explaining predictions made by complex machine learning models. The computation of Shapley values requires estimating non-trivial *contribution functions* representing predictions with only a subset of the features present. As the number of these terms grows exponentially with the number of features, computational costs escalate rapidly, creating a pressing need for efficient and accurate approximation methods. For tabular data, the KernelSHAP framework is considered the state-of-the-art model-agnostic approximation framework. KernelSHAP approximates the Shapley values using a weighted sample of the contribution functions for different feature subsets. We propose a novel modification of KernelSHAP which replaces the stochastic weights with deterministic ones to reduce the variance of the resulting Shapley value approximations. This may also be combined with our simple, yet effective modification to the KernelSHAP variant implemented in the popular Python library SHAP. Additionally, we provide an overview of established methods. Numerical experiments demonstrate that our methods can reduce the required number of contribution function evaluations by 5% to 50% while preserving the same accuracy of the approximated Shapley values – essentially reducing the running time by up to 50%. These computational advancements push the boundaries of the feature dimensionality and number of predictions that can be accurately explained with Shapley values within a feasible runtime.

Keywords: Explainable artificial intelligence · Shapley values · model-agnostic explanation · prediction explanation · feature dependence

1 Introduction

The field of Explainable Artificial Intelligence (XAI) has developed various explanation frameworks to provide insights into the inner workings of complex models and to make their predictions more understandable to humans [2,13,30]. Developing and adopting XAI frameworks is crucial for bridging the gap between model complexity and transparency, trustworthiness, and explainability. One of the most used explanation frameworks is *Shapley values* [31,37].

Shapley values stem from cooperative game theory but are in the context of XAI, often used as a *local* feature attribution framework that explains how the features contribute to the prediction $f(x)$ made by a complex predictive model f. Local means that we explain the prediction of single observations x.

Computing Shapley values is generally an NP-hard problem [15,16], and directly calculating Shapley values for feature attribution has a computational complexity which is exponential in the number of features M. The reason for this is that the Shapley value formula requires evaluating a *contribution function* $v(\mathcal{S})$ for every subset (coalition) $\mathcal{S}$ of the set of features, which in total amounts to 2^M different feature subsets. Evaluation of $v(\mathcal{S})$ is typically costly, especially for *conditional* Shapley values, which is often preferable over *marginal* Shapley values for real life model explanations [9,13]. Reducing the number of evaluations of $v(\mathcal{S})$ for different coalitions $\mathcal{S}$ therefore directly reduces the computational cost, which is crucial for making (conditional) Shapley values a feasible model-agnostic explanation framework beyond low and medium dimensional feature spaces.

A variety of approximation strategies have been proposed in the literature [7]. In this paper, we consider the widely used, model-agnostic approximation method `KernelSHAP` [26], where model-agnostic means that it is applicable to any model f. `KernelSHAP` formulates the Shapley values as the solution to a certain weighted least squares problem, and then approximates that solution by using a weighted sample of the coalitions $\mathcal{S}$, instead of all the 2^M combinations. It is widely recognized as the state-of-the-art model-agnostic approximation framework for tabular data [7,23], largely due to its broad utilization of the $v(\mathcal{S})$ evaluations. In its original form, `KernelSHAP` sample coalitions $\mathcal{S}$ with replacement, and weigh the elements in the unique set of coalitions based on their sampling frequency. A drawback of this procedure is the random and undesirable variability in the weights of the sampled coalitions, which is caused by the stochastic sampling frequency.

The main contribution of the paper is three-fold. First, we provide an overview of established sampling and weighting strategies within `KernelSHAP`. Second, we propose a modification of the `KernelSHAP` procedure, where we for a given sample of coalitions, replace the stochastic weights with deterministic weights. This useful modification reduces the variance of the resulting Shapley value approximations. We incorporate our deterministic weighting procedure not only into the original `KernelSHAP` procedure, but also into various existing extensions and improvements of the original procedure, such as antithetic/paired sampling and semi-deterministic sampling. Additionally, we propose a simple yet effective modification to the variant of `KernelSHAP` implemented in the widely-used SHAP Python library [26]. Third, through simulation studies with tabular data, we compare the strategies and demonstrate that our `KernelSHAP` modifications consistently outperform existing methods. Specifically, we illustrate how our best-performing procedure reduces the required number of coalitions by $5-50\%$, potentially halving the running time, compared to the `KernelSHAP` method implemented in the SHAP Python library, while maintaining the same accuracy.

Finally, note that all our modified `KernelSHAP` procedures are perfectly applicable to other Shapley value applications within XAI, such as *global* feature attributions (i.e., the overall model performance) [14] and data valuation [19], and frankly any other application of Shapley values also outside of the XAI domain. Investigating the efficiency in such situations is, however, outside the scope of this paper.

Section 2 introduces the Shapley value explanation framework, and describe how to compute them exactly and approximately using the `KernelSHAP` framework. Section 3 outlines coalition sampling and weighting strategies within the `KernelSHAP` framework, encompassing both established methods and our novel approaches. Section 4 presents numerical simulation studies comparing the accuracy of the different approximation strategies, while Sect. 5 conducts experiments on real-world data. Finally, Sect. 6 provides conclusions and outlines further work.

2 Shapley Values

Originally, Shapley values were proposed as a solution concept for how to divide the payout of a cooperative game $v : \mathcal{P}(\mathcal{M}) \mapsto \mathbb{R}$ onto the players based on four axioms [37]. The game is played by M players where $\mathcal{M} = \{1, 2, \ldots, M\}$ denotes the set of all players and $\mathcal{P}(\mathcal{M})$ is the power set, that is, the set of all subsets of $\mathcal{M}$. We call $v(\mathcal{S})$ the *contribution function*[1] and it maps a subset of players $\mathcal{S} \in \mathcal{P}(\mathcal{M})$, also called a *coalition*, to a real number representing their contribution in the game v. The Shapley values $\phi_j = \phi_j(v)$ assigned to each player j, for $j = 1, \ldots, M$, uniquely satisfy the following properties:

Efficiency: They sum to the value of the grand coalition $\mathcal{M}$ minus the empty set $\emptyset$, that is, $\sum_{j=1}^{M} \phi_j = v(\mathcal{M}) - v(\emptyset)$.
Symmetry: Two equally contributing players j and k, that is, $v(\mathcal{S} \cup \{j\}) = v(\mathcal{S} \cup \{k\})$ for all $\mathcal{S}$, receive equal payouts $\phi_j = \phi_k$.
Dummy: A non-contributing player j, that is, $v(\mathcal{S}) = v(\mathcal{S} \cup \{j\})$ for all $\mathcal{S}$, receives $\phi_j = 0$.
Linearity: A linear combination of n games $\{v_1, \ldots, v_n\}$, that is, $v(\mathcal{S}) = \sum_{k=1}^{n} c_k v_k(\mathcal{S})$, has Shapley values given by $\phi_j(v) = \sum_{k=1}^{n} c_k \phi_j(v_k)$.

The values $\phi_j, j = 1, \ldots, M$, which uniquely satisfy these axioms, were shown by [37] to be given by the formula:

$$\phi_j = \sum_{\mathcal{S} \in \mathcal{P}(\mathcal{M} \setminus \{j\})} \frac{|\mathcal{S}|!(M - |\mathcal{S}| - 1)!}{M!} \left(v(\mathcal{S} \cup \{j\}) - v(\mathcal{S})\right), \tag{1}$$

---
[1] It is also called the *value*, *reward*, *lift*, and *characteristic* function in the literature.

where $|\mathcal{S}|$ is the number of players in coalition $\mathcal{S}$. The number of terms in (1) is 2^M, hence, the complexity grows exponentially with the number of players M.

When using Shapley values for local feature attributions of a prediction model, the cooperative game $v(\mathcal{S})$ is related to the predictive model f, the features represent the players, and the payout is the predicted response $f(\boldsymbol{x})$, for a specific explicand $\boldsymbol{x} = \boldsymbol{x}^*$. The Shapley value ϕ_j in (1) is then a weighted average of the jth feature's marginal contribution to each coalition $\mathcal{S}$ and describes the importance of the jth feature in the prediction $f(\boldsymbol{x}^*) = \phi_0 + \sum_{j=1}^{M} \phi_j^*$, where ϕ_0 denotes the value not assigned to any of the features, typically set to the mean prediction $\mathbb{E}\left[f(\boldsymbol{x})\right]$. That is, the Shapley values sums to the difference between the prediction $f(\boldsymbol{x}^*)$ and the global mean prediction.

In this paper, we consider the tabular data setting of supervised learning where the predictive model $f(\boldsymbol{x})$ is trained on $\mathcal{X} = \{\boldsymbol{x}^{[i]}, y^{[i]}\}_{i=1}^{N_{\text{train}}}$. Here $\boldsymbol{x}^{[i]}$ is an M-dimensional feature vector, $y^{[i]}$ is a univariate response, and N_{train} is the number of training observations. Additionally, we focus on *conditional Shapley values*, which is properly defined below. Conditional Shapley values incorporates feature dependencies into the explanations [1], contrasting *marginal Shapley values* where one omits the dependencies [8]. The two versions differ only in their definition of $v(\mathcal{S})$ and coincide when the features are independent. Conditional Shapley values, introduced below, may be preferable in many situations [1,9,13], and are consistent with standard probability axioms [13, Proposition 7]. However, they come at a higher computational cost due to the need to model dependencies across arbitrary feature subsets. This computational burden likely explains why most software implementations, and to some extent XAI-research, are oriented around the marginal approach, further limiting the practical adoption of conditional Shapley values. We focus on the conditional approach since that is where efficiency enhancements are most critical. However, all methods in this paper apply equally to marginal Shapley values, where computational efficiency is also a significant concern. Throughout this article, we refer to conditional Shapley values when discussing Shapley values unless otherwise specified.

For the conditional Shapley value explanation framework, the contribution function $v(\mathcal{S})$ in (1) is the expected response of $f(\boldsymbol{x})$ conditioned on the features in $\mathcal{S}$ taking on the values $\boldsymbol{x}_{\mathcal{S}}^*$ [26]. That is, for continuously distributed features,

$$v(\mathcal{S}) = \mathbb{E}[f(\underbrace{\boldsymbol{x}_{\bar{\mathcal{S}}}, \boldsymbol{x}_{\mathcal{S}}}_{x})|\boldsymbol{x}_{\mathcal{S}} = \boldsymbol{x}_{\mathcal{S}}^*] = \int f(\boldsymbol{x}_{\bar{\mathcal{S}}}, \boldsymbol{x}_{\mathcal{S}}^*) p(\boldsymbol{x}_{\bar{\mathcal{S}}}|\boldsymbol{x}_{\mathcal{S}} = \boldsymbol{x}_{\mathcal{S}}^*) \, d\boldsymbol{x}_{\bar{\mathcal{S}}}, \qquad (2)$$

with an equivalent formula using sums for discretely distributed features. Here, $\boldsymbol{x}_{\mathcal{S}} = \{x_j : j \in \mathcal{S}\}$ denotes the features in subset $\mathcal{S}$, $\boldsymbol{x}_{\bar{\mathcal{S}}} = \{x_j : j \in \bar{\mathcal{S}}\}$ denotes the features outside $\mathcal{S}$, that is, $\bar{\mathcal{S}} = \mathcal{M}\backslash\mathcal{S}$, and $p(\boldsymbol{x}_{\bar{\mathcal{S}}}|\boldsymbol{x}_{\mathcal{S}} = \boldsymbol{x}_{\mathcal{S}}^*)$ is the conditional density of $\boldsymbol{x}_{\bar{\mathcal{S}}}$ given $\boldsymbol{x}_{\mathcal{S}} = \boldsymbol{x}_{\mathcal{S}}^*$. To compute the Shapley values in (1), we need to compute (2) for all $\mathcal{S} \in \mathcal{P}(\mathcal{M})$, except for the edge cases $\mathcal{S} \in \{\emptyset, \mathcal{M}\}$. For $\mathcal{S} = \emptyset$, we have by definition that $\phi_0 = v(\emptyset) = \mathbb{E}[f(\boldsymbol{x})]$, where the average training response $\overline{y}_{\text{train}}$ is a commonly used estimate [1]. Moreover, for $\mathcal{S} = \mathcal{M}$, we have $\boldsymbol{x}_\mathcal{S} = \boldsymbol{x}^*$ and $v(\mathcal{M}) = f(\boldsymbol{x}^*)$. We denote the non-trivial coalitions by $\mathcal{P}^*(\mathcal{M}) = \mathcal{P}(\mathcal{M})\backslash\{\emptyset, \mathcal{M}\}$.

Computing (2) is not straightforward for a general data distribution and model. Assuming independent features, or having f be linear, simplifies the computations [1,26], but these assumptions do not generally hold. There is a wide range of methods used to estimate $v(\mathcal{S})$, using, e.g., Gaussian assumptions [1,9], conditional inference trees [36], or variational auto-encoders [34]. See [35] for an extensive overview.

2.1 Approximation Strategies

In this section, we highlight procedures that use approximations or model assumptions to reduce the computational complexity of the Shapley value explanation framework and make the computations tractable in higher dimensions. The approximative speed-up strategies can be divided into model-specific and model-agnostic strategies [8].

The model-specific strategies put assumptions on the predictive model f to improve the computational cost, but some of the strategies are restricted to marginal Shapley values. For conditional Shapley values, [1,9] derive explicit expressions for linear models to speed up the computations, and [25] proposes the path-dependent TreeSHAP algorithm for tree-based models. [43] improves the speed of the TreeSHAP algorithm by pre-computing expensive steps at the cost of a slightly higher memory consumption, and the Linear TreeSHAP [4] reduces the time complexity from polynomial to linear time. There are also speed-up strategies for deep neural network models, but they are limited to marginal Shapley values [3,40].

The model-agnostic strategies put no assumptions on the predictive model f and often use stochastic sampling-based estimators [1,5,26,29,32]. That is, to speed up the computations, they approximate the Shapley value explanations by a sampled subset of the coalitions instead of considering all of them. Thus, the strategies are stochastic, but converge to the exact solution. One of the most common model-agnostic strategies is the aforementioned KernelSHAP strategy [12,26], which we consider and introduce properly in Sect. 2.2.

There exist other approximation strategies linked to alternative Shapley formulations, such as the permutation sampling-based frameworks based on the random order value formulation [8,38,39]. We focus on improving the KernelSHAP framework as it has superior efficiency compared to permutation sampling-based frameworks. In the context of conditional Shapley values, the primary computational burden is related to the number of $v(\mathcal{S})$ values that need to be calculated. KernelSHAP leverages *all* computed $v(\mathcal{S})$ values to determine the Shapley values for *all* features. In contrast, permutation sampling only uses a portion of the evaluated $v(\mathcal{S})$ values to estimate each feature's Shapley value, resulting in less efficient utilization of these values. Examples of approximation strategies for the permutation sampling-based framework include orthogonal spherical codes [29], stratified sampling [5,28], and many others [12,21,29]. However, these strategies typically cannot be directly integrated into the KernelSHAP approximation framework and are thus considered outside the scope of this article. Another method by [23], based on splitting the summand in (1) into two components to be estimated separately, also utilizes all computed $v(\mathcal{S})$ for all Shapley value. In their simulation experiments for local model explanations, it performed similar or worse than an unpaired version of `KernelSHAP`. For a broad introduction to various model-agnostic and model-specific strategies approximation strategies for Shapley values in XAI, we refer to [8].

2.2 The `KernelSHAP` Framework

[26] shows that the Shapley value formula in (1) may also be conveniently expressed as the solution of the following weighted least squares problem:

$$\arg\min_{\phi \in \mathbb{R}^{M+1}} \sum_{\mathcal{S} \in \mathcal{P}(\mathcal{M})} k(M, |\mathcal{S}|) \left(\phi_0 + \sum_{j \in \mathcal{S}} \phi_j - v(\mathcal{S}) \right)^2, \quad (3)$$

where

$$k(M, |\mathcal{S}|) = \frac{M-1}{\binom{M}{|\mathcal{S}|} |\mathcal{S}| (M - |\mathcal{S}|)}, \quad (4)$$

for $|\mathcal{S}| = 0, 1, 2, \ldots, M$, are the *Shapley kernel weights* [6,26]. In practice, the infinite Shapley kernel weights $k(M, 0) = k(M, M) = \infty$ can be set to a large constant $C = 10^6$ [1]. The matrix solution of (3) is

$$\boldsymbol{\phi} = (\boldsymbol{Z}^T \boldsymbol{W} \boldsymbol{Z})^{-1} \boldsymbol{Z}^T \boldsymbol{W} \boldsymbol{v} = \boldsymbol{R} \boldsymbol{v}. \quad (5)$$

Here $\boldsymbol{Z}$ is a $2^M \times (M+1)$ matrix with 1s in the first column (to obtain ϕ_0) and the binary representations[2] of the coalitions $\mathcal{S} \subseteq \mathcal{M}$ in the remaining columns. While $\boldsymbol{W} = \mathrm{diag}(C, \boldsymbol{w}, C)$ is a $2^M \times 2^M$ diagonal matrix containing the Shapley kernel weights $k(M, |\mathcal{S}|)$. The $\boldsymbol{w}$ vector contains the $2^M - 2$ finite Shapley kernel weights, which we normalize to sum to one for numerical stability. Finally, $\boldsymbol{v}$ is a column vector of height 2^M containing the contribution function values $v(\mathcal{S})$. The $\mathcal{S}$ in $\boldsymbol{W}$ and $\boldsymbol{v}$ corresponds to the coalition of the corresponding row in $\boldsymbol{Z}$. The $\boldsymbol{R}$ matrix is independent of the explicands. When explaining N_{explain} predictions, we can replace $\boldsymbol{v}$ with a $2^M \times N_{\mathrm{explain}}$ matrix $\boldsymbol{V}$, where column i contains the contribution functions for the ith explicand.

The weighted least squares solution formulation naturally motivates approximate solutions by solving (3) using sampled subset of coalitions $\mathcal{D} \subseteq \mathcal{P}(\mathcal{M})$ (with replacement) instead of all coalitions $\mathcal{S} \in \mathcal{P}(\mathcal{M})$. This is the `KernelSHAP` approximation framework [26] and the corresponding approximation is

$$\boldsymbol{\phi}_{\mathcal{D}} = (\boldsymbol{Z}_{\mathcal{D}}^T \boldsymbol{W}_{\mathcal{D}} \boldsymbol{Z}_{\mathcal{D}})^{-1} \boldsymbol{Z}_{\mathcal{D}}^T \boldsymbol{W}_{\mathcal{D}} \boldsymbol{v}_{\mathcal{D}}, \quad (6)$$

---

[2] For example, the binary representation of $\mathcal{S} = \{1, 3\}$ when $M = 4$ is $[1, 0, 1, 0]$.

where only the $N_{\text{coal}} = |\mathcal{D}|$ unique coalitions in $\mathcal{D}$ are used. If a coalition $\mathcal{S}$ is sampled K times, then the corresponding weight in $\boldsymbol{W}_\mathcal{D} = \text{diag}(C, \boldsymbol{w}_\mathcal{D}, C)$, denoted by $w_\mathcal{S}$, is proportional to K, as we normalize the weights for numerical stability. The KernelSHAP framework is also useful in lower dimensions if $v(\mathcal{S})$ is expensive to compute. [41] shows that the KernelSHAP approximation framework is consistent and asymptotically unbiased, while [12] shows that it is empirically unbiased for even a modest number of coalitions. A particularly nice property of KernelSHAP is that the full $\boldsymbol{v}_\mathcal{D}$ is utilized to estimate *all* the M Shapley values, making it a sampling efficient approximation method.

3 Sampling and Weighting Strategies

In this section, we describe established (unique, paired, and PySHAP) and novel (paired c-kernel, PySHAP*and PySHAP* c-kernel) strategies for selecting the N_{coal} unique coalitions in $\mathcal{D}$ and how to weigh them in (6) when approximating Shapley value explanations. Table 1 gives an overview of all the strategies and their characteristic properties. The empty and grand coalitions are always included in the approximations; thus, they are excluded from the sampling procedure. Consequently, N_{coal} is an integer between (exclusive) 2 and 2^M, as the full set of coalitions yields exact Shapley values. To simplify our descriptions and derivations below, let $T_L(\mathcal{S})$ denote the number of times coalition $\mathcal{S}$ has been sampled, after drawing L coalitions (resulting in the $N_\mathcal{S}$ unique coalitions).

In Fig. 1, we illustrate the normalized weights $w_\mathcal{S}$ used in (6) by the different strategies introduced below for an $M = 10$-dimensional setting with $N_{\text{coal}} \in \{100, 250, 750, 1000\}$. We index the coalitions by first ordering them based on coalition size, i.e., $\{1\}$ precedes $\{1, 2\}$, and then by their elements for equal-sized coalitions, i.e., $\{1, 2\}$ precedes $\{1, 3\}$. This indexing ensures that coalitions with indices i and $2^M + 1 - i$ are complementary, for $i = 1, 2, \ldots, 2^M$, as seen by the paired strategies where the weights are symmetric around the dashed vertical lines in Fig. 1. The weights of the empty ($i = 1$) and grand ($i = 2^M = 1024$) coalitions are omitted as they are strategy-independent and infinite.

3.1 Unique

The unique strategy is the standard established method for obtaining N_{coal} unique coalitions, and uses them to estimate Shapley values through KernelSHAP. It starts by sampling a sequence of $L \geq N_{\text{coal}}$ coalitions with replacements from the Shapley kernel weight distribution

$$p_\mathcal{S} = p(\mathcal{S}) = \frac{k(M, |\mathcal{S}|)}{\sum_{\mathcal{S} \in \mathcal{P}^*(\mathcal{M})} k(M, |\mathcal{S}|)} = \frac{k(M, |\mathcal{S}|)}{\sum_{q=1}^{M-1} k(M, q)\binom{M}{q}}, \qquad (7)$$

where $k(M, |\mathcal{S}|)$ is the Shapley kernel weight given in (4). We determine the coalitions using a two-step procedure to avoid listing all $|\mathcal{P}^*(\mathcal{M})| = 2^M - 2$

Table 1. Overview of the sampling strategies along with the weight $w_\mathcal{S}$ they give to a coalition $\mathcal{S}$ in (6). Strategies in *italic* font are the new methods introduced in the present paper, while the black are existing methods. **Stochastic sampling**: all strategies use stochastic sampling with replacement to form the coalition set $\mathcal{D}$, except the PySHAP-based strategies, which deterministically include coalitions that are expected to be sampled before sampling the rest. **Paired sampling**: whether the strategy samples the paired coalitions $\mathcal{S}$ and $\bar{\mathcal{S}}$ together. **Equal weights within each coalition size**: whether coalitions of the same size have the same weight. **Weight $w_\mathcal{S}$ converges to $p_\mathcal{S}$**: whether the weight $w_\mathcal{S}$ converges to $p_\mathcal{S}$ in (7) when $N_{\text{coal}} \to 2^M$. The non-c-kernel strategies converge in theory, but the convergence is slow in practice due to large weight variability for the sampled coalitions; see Fig. 1. **Weight $w_\mathcal{S}$ is proportional to**: specifies the proportional weight $w_\mathcal{S}$ given to coalition $\mathcal{S}$ in (6). The $T_L(\mathcal{S})$ notation should be read as "the number of times $\mathcal{S}$ is sampled", while L is the total number of coalitions sampled such that $\mathcal{D}$ contains N_{coal} unique coalitions and $p_\mathcal{S} \propto k(M, |\mathcal{S}|)$ as defined in (7).

Strategy	Stochastic sampling	Paired sampling	Equal weights within each coalition size	Weight $w_\mathcal{S}$ converges to $p_\mathcal{S}$	Weight $w_\mathcal{S}$ is proportional to
Unique	✓	✗	✗	∼	$T_L(\mathcal{S})$
Paired	✓	✓	✗	∼	$T_L(\mathcal{S}) + T_L(\bar{\mathcal{S}})$
Paired c-kernel	✓	✓	✓	✓	$2p_\mathcal{S}/(1 - (1 - 2p_\mathcal{S})^{L/2})$
PySHAP	∼	∼	✗	∼	$\begin{cases} T_L(\mathcal{S}) & \text{if sampled and } |\mathcal{S}| = |\bar{\mathcal{S}}| \\ T_L(\mathcal{S}) + T_L(\bar{\mathcal{S}}) & \text{if sampled and } |\mathcal{S}| \neq |\bar{\mathcal{S}}| \\ p_\mathcal{S} & \text{otherwise} \end{cases}$
PySHAP*	∼	✓	✗	∼	$\begin{cases} T_L(\mathcal{S}) + T_L(\bar{\mathcal{S}}) & \text{if sampled} \\ p_\mathcal{S} & \text{otherwise} \end{cases}$
PySHAP* c-kernel	∼	✓	✓	✓	$\begin{cases} 2p_\mathcal{S}/(1 - (1 - 2p_\mathcal{S})^{L/2}) & \text{if sampled} \\ p_\mathcal{S} & \text{otherwise} \end{cases}$

coalitions. First, we sample the coalition sizes $|\mathcal{S}| \in \{1, \ldots, M-1\}$ using weighted sampling with replacement, where the weights are $k(M, |\mathcal{S}|)\binom{M}{|\mathcal{S}|}$. Second, we uniformly sample $|\mathcal{S}|$ of the M features without replacement. We repeat this procedure L times until we have N_{coal} unique coalitions, which will constitute $\mathcal{D}$. We use the sampling frequencies as the weights $w_\mathcal{S}$ in (6) since coalitions can been sampled multiple times. That is,

$$w_\mathcal{S} \propto T_L(\mathcal{S}), \tag{8}$$

meaning that $w_\mathcal{S}$ is proportional to the number of times coalition $\mathcal{S}$ is sampled. This strategy was outlined by [1,26].

3.2 Paired

The paired strategy is a simple, commonly used and established extension of the unique strategy, utilizing the variance reduction technique *paired sampling*[3] [24, Ch. 9] for improved approximation accuracy. [8,12] demonstrate that paired

---
[3] Also called *antithetic* and *halved* sampling in the literature.

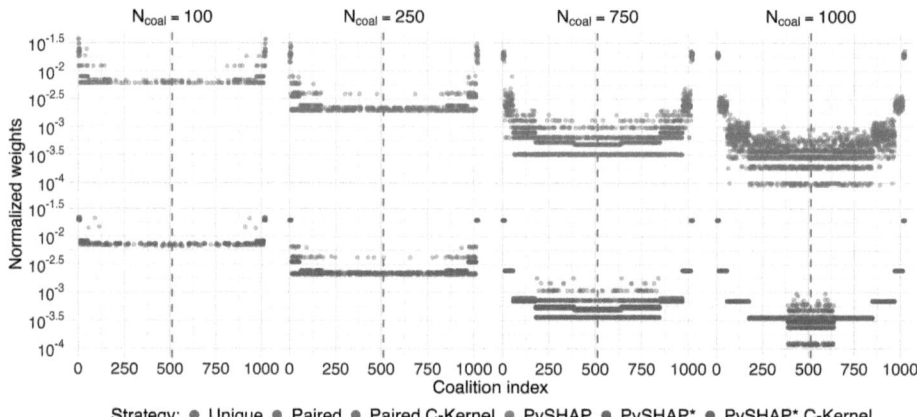

Fig. 1. The normalized weights $w_\mathcal{S}$ used in (6) by the strategies in Sect. 3 for different number of unique coalitions N_{coal} in an $M = 10$-dimensional setting. The **paired**-based strategies are symmetric around the vertical line. The **paired c-kernel** and **PySHAP* c-kernel** strategies both have identical weights within each coalition size, but their weights are slightly different from each other.

sampling reduces the variance of the Shapley value approximations compared to the **unique** strategy due to negative correlation between the $v(\mathcal{S})$ and $v(\bar{\mathcal{S}})$ values. The **paired** sampling strategy pairs each sampled coalition $\mathcal{S}$, determined by the **unique** strategy, with its complement/inverse $\bar{\mathcal{S}} = \mathcal{M}\setminus\mathcal{S}$. Note that inserting $\bar{\mathcal{S}}$ in (7) yields $p_{\bar{\mathcal{S}}} = p_\mathcal{S}$ as $k(M, |\mathcal{S}|) = k(M, M - |\mathcal{S}|)$ in (4). Without loss of generality, let $\mathcal{S}$ be the smaller set of $\mathcal{S}$ and $\bar{\mathcal{S}}$, and $\bar{\mathcal{S}}$ the larger. This will be useful in the remainder of the paper when we talk about coalition size as then $|\mathcal{S}| \leq \lfloor M/2 \rfloor$, where $\lfloor \cdot \rfloor$ denotes the floor function. Conceptually, we only sample coalitions $\mathcal{S}$ with coalition indices less than or equal to 2^{M-1} and then add their paired counterparts $\bar{\mathcal{S}}$ with coalition indices larger than 2^{M-1}. The probability of sampling $\mathcal{S}$ is then $p_\mathcal{S} + p_{\bar{\mathcal{S}}} = 2p_\mathcal{S}$, where $p_\mathcal{S}$ is given in (7). However, the doubling is redundant when normalizing the probabilities, as all coalitions have doubled their probability. Note that N_{coal} will always be an even number for the **paired** strategy. The **paired** strategy also stabilizes the sampling frequencies by ensuring that $\mathcal{S}$ and $\bar{\mathcal{S}}$ always obtain the same weights, as seen in Fig. 1. The weights are given by

$$w_\mathcal{S} \propto T_L(\mathcal{S}) + T_L(\bar{\mathcal{S}}), \tag{9}$$

i.e., proportional to the combined number of times $\mathcal{S}$ and $\bar{\mathcal{S}}$ is sampled.

3.3 Paired C-Kernel

A byproduct of using the sampling-based procedure for approximating the Shapley values in the **unique** and **paired** strategies, is that given the set of uniquely sampled coalitions, the weights $w_\mathcal{S}$ used in $\boldsymbol{W}_\mathcal{D}$ of (6) are still stochastic. This introduces undesirable variance in the approximation. Below we derive and present the novel **paired c-kernel** strategy which removes this stochasticity by using a new weighting scheme for the sampled coalitions.

Using the normalized Shapley kernel weights $p_\mathcal{S}$ for approximating Shapley values for all sampled coalitions might appear intuitive, as they correspond to the expected proportions of each coalition, and are used in the computations when all coalitions are present. However, this strategy results in biased weights because it fails to consider that we only use the sampled coalitions when approximating the Shapley values (the remaining coalitions technically have weight zero). Hence, we need to condition on $\mathcal{S}$ being among the N_{coal} uniquely sampled coalitions. Our **paired c-kernel** strategy addresses this issue, correcting the Shapley kernel weights by conditioning on the coalitions being sampled at least once.

For ease of understanding, we first explain the correction technique for the **unique** setting before we extend it to the **paired** setting, which is the one we consider in this article. The **unique** strategy samples a sequence of $L \geq N_{\text{coal}}$ coalitions with replacements until N_{coal} unique coalitions are obtained. The probability of sampling a coalition $\mathcal{S}$ with size $|\mathcal{S}|$ is $p_\mathcal{S}$ given by (7).

The stochasticity in the random weights $w_\mathcal{S} \propto T_L(\mathcal{S})$ will be removed by replacing them with their expected value, conditional on the coalitions being sampled. Since the weights $w_\mathcal{S}$ are normalized over the sampled coalitions for numerical stability, it suffices to find $E[T_L(\mathcal{S})|T_L(\mathcal{S}) \geq 1]$. These conditional expectations can then be normalized over the sampled coalitions as before. By the law of total expectation, we have that

$$E[T_L(\mathcal{S})] = E[T_L(\mathcal{S})|T_L(\mathcal{S}) \geq 1] \Pr(T_L(\mathcal{S}) \geq 1)$$
$$+ E[T_L(\mathcal{S})|T_L(\mathcal{S}) = 0] \Pr(T_L(\mathcal{S}) \geq 0)$$
$$= E[T_L(\mathcal{S})|T_L(\mathcal{S}) \geq 1] \Pr(T_L(\mathcal{S}) \geq 1),$$

where the latter equality follows since $E[T_L(\mathcal{S})|T_L(\mathcal{S}) = 0] = 0$. Moreover, since $E[T_L(\mathcal{S})] = Lp_\mathcal{S}$, and $\Pr(T_L(\mathcal{S}) \geq 1) = 1 - \Pr(T_L(\mathcal{S}) = 0) = 1 - (1 - p_\mathcal{S})^L$, we have that

$$E[T_L(\mathcal{S})|T_L(\mathcal{S}) \geq 1] = \frac{E[T_L(\mathcal{S})]}{\Pr(T_L(\mathcal{S}) \geq 1)} = \frac{Lp_\mathcal{S}}{1 - (1 - p_\mathcal{S})^L}. \qquad (10)$$

Thus, the corrected, Shapley kernel weights $w_\mathcal{S}$ for the **unpaired c-kernel** strategy is proportional to the expression in (10), i.e.

$$w_\mathcal{S} \propto \frac{p_\mathcal{S}}{1 - (1 - p_\mathcal{S})^L}, \qquad (11)$$

which are deterministic given the unique sampled coalitions.

In Sect. 3.2, we discussed that **paired** sampling conceptually only samples coalitions $\mathcal{S}$ with coalition indices less than or equal to 2^{M-1} and then adds the paired $\bar{\mathcal{S}}$. Thus, the number of sampling steps L is halved, $E[T_{L/2}(\mathcal{S})] = Lp_\mathcal{S}/2 + Lp_{\bar{\mathcal{S}}}/2 = Lp_{\bar{\mathcal{S}}} = Lp_\mathcal{S}$, i.e. as before, except that $\Pr(T_{L/2}(\mathcal{S}) \geq 1) =$

$1 - \Pr(T_{L/2}(\mathcal{S}) = 0) = 1 - (1 - p_\mathcal{S} - p_{\bar{\mathcal{S}}})^{L/2} = 1 - (1 - 2p_\mathcal{S})^{L/2}$ takes a slightly different form. The `paired c-kernel` strategy is therefore the `paired` equivalent of (11), which weigh the sampled coalitions by

$$w_\mathcal{S} \propto \frac{p_\mathcal{S}}{1 - (1 - 2p_\mathcal{S})^{L/2}}, \qquad (12)$$

where once again, $w_\mathcal{S}$ are normalized over the sampled coalitions.

The `paired c-kernel` strategy assigns equal weight to coalitions within the same coalition size and between paired coalition sizes $|\mathcal{S}|$ and $|\bar{\mathcal{S}}| = M - |\mathcal{S}|$, as illustrated in Fig. 1. Note that (12) is deterministic given the sampled coalitions obtained after L sampling trials. However, if L is not fixed up front, but considered a byproduct of a fixed number of *unique* coalitions N_{coal}, then there is still some stochasticity from L left in (12). Since sampling of a subset of coalitions is already required when approximating Shapley values, this is mainly of technical character. Note however that, when accounting also for the coalition sampling process, (12) is clearly stochastic, leading to different Shapley value estimates each time.

3.4 PySHAP

The `KernelSHAP` method implemented in the popular SHAP Python library [27] samples coalitions using a modification of the `paired` strategy. It splits the sampling procedure into a deterministic and sampling-based part based on the number of unique coalitions N_{coal}. Below we introduce this established strategy, which we will denote by `PySHAP`.

The `PySHAP` strategy deterministically includes all coalitions of size $|\mathcal{S}|$ and $M - |\mathcal{S}|$ if the number of remaining coalitions to sample N^*_{coal} exceeds the expected number of coalitions needed to sample all coalitions of these sizes, i.e., $2\binom{M}{|\mathcal{S}|}$. This process bears some resemblance to stratified sampling with strata defined by coalition size. The strategy begins with coalition size one and increments by one until the number of remaining coalitions N^*_{coal} becomes insufficient. Denote the coalition size at which the `PySHAP` strategy stops by $P \in \{1, 2, \ldots, \lceil (M+1)/2 \rceil\}$, where $\lceil \cdot \rceil$ is the ceiling function. All coalitions of size $|\mathcal{S}| < P$ and $|\mathcal{S}| > M - P$ are then included, and their corresponding weights are assigned according to the normalized Shapley kernel weight in (7). Figure 1 illustrates the deterministic inclusion of coalitions as a function of N_{coal}, showing that more coalition sizes are deterministically included as N_{coal} increases.

The remaining N^*_{coal} coalitions are sampled with replacements from the non-included coalition sizes, i.e., $|\mathcal{S}| \in [\![P, M - P]\!]$, following a two-step procedure similar to the one described in Sect. 3.1. Here, $[\![a, b]\!]$ denotes the inclusive integer interval between a and b. First, a coalition size $|\mathcal{S}| \in [\![P, M - P]\!]$ is selected with probability proportional to $p_\mathcal{S}\binom{M}{|\mathcal{S}|}$, where $p_\mathcal{S}$ is the normalized Shapley kernel weight for a coalition $\mathcal{S}$ of size $|\mathcal{S}|$ as given in (7). Second, a coalition $\mathcal{S}$ of size $|\mathcal{S}|$ is sampled among the $\binom{M}{|\mathcal{S}|}$ possible coalitions with uniform probability.

The paired coalition $\bar{\mathcal{S}}$ is also included, except when $|\mathcal{S}| = |\bar{\mathcal{S}}|$, a situation that occurs only when M is even. The sampling frequencies are used as weights $w_\mathcal{S}$, but scaled to sum to the remaining normalized Shapley kernel weights, i.e., $1 - 2\sum_{q=1}^{P-1} p_q \binom{M}{q}$.

For the sake of clarity, consider an example with $M = 10$ and $N_{\text{coal}} = 100$, as illustrated in Fig. 1. Then the normalized Shapley kernel weight for a coalition of size one is $p_1 = 0.0196$. This means PySHAP includes the $2\binom{10}{1} = 20$ coalitions of size one and nine when $N_{\text{coal}} \geq \frac{1}{0.0196} = 51.02$, which is the case in our example. The remaining number of coalitions is then $N^*_{\text{coal}} = 80$. The next step is to re-normalize the four remaining Shapley kernel weights, which we denoted by q_2, q_3, q_4, and q_5. This yields $q_2 = 0.00404$, $q_3 = 0.00116$, $q_4 = 0.00058$, and $q_5 = 0.00046$, which ensures that $\sum_{l=2}^{\lfloor M/2 \rfloor} q_l \binom{M}{l} = 1$. Thus, PySHAP includes all coalitions of size two and eight if $N^*_{\text{coal}} > \frac{1}{0.00404} = 247.5$, which it is not. This implies that N_{coal} must be greater than or equal to $20 + 248 = 268$ to include coalition sizes one, two, eight, and nine. Consequently, the remaining $N^*_{\text{coal}} = 80$ coalitions will be sampled by first selecting the coalition size $|\mathcal{S}|$ with probability $q_\mathcal{S} \binom{M}{|\mathcal{S}|}$, followed by uniformly sampling a coalition $\mathcal{S}$ among the $\binom{M}{|\mathcal{S}|}$ coalitions of size $|\mathcal{S}|$. This procedure is repeated until N^*_{coal} unique coalitions are sampled[4], and the corresponding sampling frequencies are used as weights. However, these weights are scaled such that they sum to $1 - 2\binom{M}{1}p_1 = 1 - 2 \times 10 \times 0.0196 = 0.608$.

3.5 PySHAP*

In our examination of the PySHAP implementation within version 0.46.0 of SHAP (the latest version as of February 2025), we found that the sampling strategy explicitly does *not* pair coalitions when the coalition size is $|\mathcal{S}| = |\bar{\mathcal{S}}|$, a condition which only applies when M is even. It remains unclear to us whether this is an intentional design choice or an oversight. However, based on our finding, we propose the new, very simple extension PySHAP* which always pair coalitions. Notably, PySHAP and PySHAP* are equivalent when M is odd.

3.6 PySHAP* c-kernel

The PySHAP* c-kernel strategy integrates the Shapley kernel weight correction technique described in Sect. 3.3 into PySHAP*'s stochastic sampling step in an attempt to achieve better and more stable weights for the sampled coalitions. Specifically, the sampled coalitions receive weights according to (12), but scaled to sum to the remaining normalized Shapley kernel weights, as outlined in Sect. 3.4.

---

[4] Originally, PySHAP stops sampling after reaching an upper limit of $4N^*_{\text{coal}}$ sampled coalitions, including duplicates, which means that the total number of unique coalitions can be less than N_{coal}. However, we disable this upper limit to ensure a fair comparison with the other strategies, which utilize N_{coal} unique coalitions.

3.7 Other Sampling Strategies

We explored several other sampling strategies, which generally performed worse, more erratically, or were more computationally intensive than the ones discussed above. For completeness, this section provides a brief overview of these strategies.

A strategy to stabilize the weights in the `paired` strategy is to average the sampling frequencies within each coalition size. Additionally, we also repeated the sampling step B times and used the empirical means of the averaged sampling frequencies to obtain even more stable weights. However, both strategies performed similarly, though slightly and uniformly worse than the `paired c-kernel` strategy. Applying these ideas to the `PySHAP*` strategy yielded improvements but they still fell short compared to the `PySHAP* c-kernel` strategy.

To remove the stochasticity of L in the `paired c-kernel` and `PySHAP* c-kernel` strategies, we replaced L in (12) with $\mathbb{E}[L]$, which is a quantity we can compute using results related to the *coupon collector's problem* [17]. Namely, $\mathbb{E}[L] = 2\sum_{q=0}^{\tilde{N}_S - 1}(-1)^{\tilde{N}_S - 1 - q}\binom{2^{M-1}-1-q-1}{2^{M-1}-1-\tilde{N}_S}\sum_{|\mathcal{T}|=q}\frac{1}{1-P_{\mathcal{T}}}$, where $\tilde{N}_S = N_{\text{coal}}/2$, $\sum_{|\mathcal{T}|=q}$ represents the sum over all sets of paired coalitions that contain q unique paired coalitions, and $P_{\mathcal{T}} = \sum_{\mathcal{S}\in\mathcal{T}} 2p_{\mathcal{S}}$. Computing this quantity is extremely computationally intensive as the number of terms in the inner sum is bounded by $\mathcal{O}(2^{2^M}/\sqrt{2^M})$. Additionally, the obtained improvements are negligible and unlikely to affect practical applications.

Directly using the uncorrected Shapley kernel weights performs poorly, except when $N_{\text{coal}} \approx 2^M$, where these weights are nearly correct. We also considered a modified version of `PySHAP*` that includes all coalitions of a given size immediately when N_{coal} exceeds the number of such coalitions, rather than when they are expected to be sampled. This modification yields good results when N_{coal} results in no sampling; however, its erratic behavior for other N_{coal} values makes it an unreliable sampling strategy.

4 Numerical Simulation Studies

A major problem in evaluating explanation frameworks is that real-world data has no true Shapley value explanations. In this section, we consider two setups where we simulate Gaussian data for which we can compute the true/exact Shapley values ϕ using all 2^M coalitions. We then compare how close the approximated Shapley values $\phi_{\mathcal{D}}$ are ϕ using the different strategies and based on the coalitions in $\mathcal{D} \subset \mathcal{P}(\mathcal{M})$. This paper does not focus on estimating the contribution functions $v(\mathcal{S})$ but on strategies for selecting the coalitions $\mathcal{S}$. Thus, we compute the $v(\mathcal{S})$ once using the `gaussian` approach in the `shapr` R-package [22] (or with partly analytical expression for the linear model case in Sect. 4.2), store them, and load the needed $v(\mathcal{S})$ values for the sampling strategies.

To elaborate, we generate the training observations and explicands from a multivariate Gaussian distribution $p(\boldsymbol{x}) = p(\boldsymbol{x}_{\mathcal{S}}, \boldsymbol{x}_{\bar{\mathcal{S}}}) = \mathcal{N}_M(\boldsymbol{\mu}, \boldsymbol{\Sigma})$, where $\boldsymbol{\mu} = [\boldsymbol{\mu}_{\mathcal{S}}, \boldsymbol{\mu}_{\bar{\mathcal{S}}}]^T$ and $\boldsymbol{\Sigma} = \begin{bmatrix} \boldsymbol{\Sigma}_{\mathcal{S}\mathcal{S}} & \boldsymbol{\Sigma}_{\mathcal{S}\bar{\mathcal{S}}} \\ \boldsymbol{\Sigma}_{\bar{\mathcal{S}}\mathcal{S}} & \boldsymbol{\Sigma}_{\bar{\mathcal{S}}\bar{\mathcal{S}}} \end{bmatrix}$. The conditional distribution is then $p(\boldsymbol{x}_{\bar{\mathcal{S}}}|\boldsymbol{x}_{\mathcal{S}} =$

$x_{\bar{S}}^*) = \mathcal{N}_{|\bar{S}|}(\boldsymbol{\mu}_{\bar{S}|S}, \boldsymbol{\Sigma}_{\bar{S}|S})$, where $\boldsymbol{\mu}_{\bar{S}|S} = \boldsymbol{\mu}_{\bar{S}} + \boldsymbol{\Sigma}_{\bar{S}S}\boldsymbol{\Sigma}_{SS}^{-1}(\boldsymbol{x}_S^* - \boldsymbol{\mu}_S)$ and $\boldsymbol{\Sigma}_{\bar{S}|S} = \boldsymbol{\Sigma}_{\bar{S}\bar{S}} - \boldsymbol{\Sigma}_{\bar{S}S}\boldsymbol{\Sigma}_{SS}^{-1}\boldsymbol{\Sigma}_{S\bar{S}}$. With an explicit formula for $p(\boldsymbol{x}_{\bar{S}}|\boldsymbol{x}_S = \boldsymbol{x}_S^*)$, we can estimate (2) by Monte Carlo integration

$$v(\mathcal{S}) = v(\mathcal{S}, \boldsymbol{x}^*) = \mathbb{E}\left[f(\boldsymbol{x}_{\bar{S}}, \boldsymbol{x}_S)|\boldsymbol{x}_S = \boldsymbol{x}_S^*\right] \approx \frac{1}{K} \sum_{k=1}^{K} f(\boldsymbol{x}_{\bar{S}}^{(k)}, \boldsymbol{x}_S^*) = \hat{v}(\mathcal{S}), \quad (13)$$

where $\boldsymbol{x}_{\bar{S}}^{(k)} \sim p(\boldsymbol{x}_{\bar{S}}|\boldsymbol{x}_S = \boldsymbol{x}_S^*)$, for $k = 1, 2, \ldots, K$, and K is the number of Monte Carlo samples. The `gaussian` approach in `shapr` generate conditional samples $\boldsymbol{x}_{\bar{S}}^{(k)}$ from $p(\boldsymbol{x}_{\bar{S}}|\boldsymbol{x}_S = \boldsymbol{x}_S^*)$, for $k = 1, 2, \ldots, K$ and $\mathcal{S} \in \mathcal{P}^*(\mathcal{M})$, and use them in (13) to accurately estimate $v(\mathcal{S})$. The parameters $\boldsymbol{\mu}$ and $\boldsymbol{\Sigma}$ are easily estimated using the sample mean and covariance matrix of the training data, respectively. However, in the present setup, we provide the true parameters to `shapr` to eliminate the uncertainty in estimating them and to obtain the true Shapley values.

We evaluate the performance of the sampling strategies by computing the averaged mean absolute error (MAE) between the exact ($\boldsymbol{\phi}$) and approximated ($\boldsymbol{\phi}_{\mathcal{D}}$) Shapley values, averaged over B repetitions (with different seeds), N_{explain} explicands, and M features. A similar criterion has been used in [1,33,34,36]. The MAE $= \overline{\text{MAE}}_B(\boldsymbol{\phi}, \boldsymbol{\phi}_{\mathcal{D}})$ is given by

$$\text{MAE} = \frac{1}{B}\sum_{b=1}^{B} \text{MAE}_b = \frac{1}{B}\sum_{b=1}^{B} \frac{1}{N_{\text{explain}}} \sum_{i=1}^{N_{\text{explain}}} \frac{1}{M}\sum_{j=1}^{M} |\phi_{i,j} - \phi_{\mathcal{D}_b, i, j}|. \quad (14)$$

Remark: The sampling step is more expensive for the first three strategies in Sect. 3 due to the repeated sampling with replacements. More precisely, the sampling procedure is time-consuming when $N_{\text{coal}} \approx 2^M$ and M is large as the probability of sampling one of the $N_{\text{coal}} - |\mathcal{D}|$ remaining unique coalitions is minuscule and takes many iterations. For the `paired` sampling procedure in the $M = 20$-dimensional setting in Sect. 4.2, we sample on average $L = 80\,738\,405$ coalitions before we have $2^M = 1\,048\,576$ unique coalitions. In contrast, the `PySHAP`, `PySHAP*`, and `PySHAP* c-kernel` sample only on average $L = 2\,306\,978$ coalitions. The drastic reduction results from deterministically including the most important coalitions, which reduces the pool of coalitions to sample from and aligns their sampling probabilities more closely. However, note that computing the contribution functions is typically the most computationally demanding part of Shapley value computations [35] and not the sampling of coalitions.

4.1 XGBoost Model

We let $M = 10$ and $N_{\text{train}} = N_{\text{explain}} = 1000$. We generate the data according to a multivariate Gaussian distribution $\boldsymbol{x} \sim \mathcal{N}_M(\boldsymbol{0}, \boldsymbol{\Sigma})$, where $\boldsymbol{\Sigma}$ is the equi-correlation matrix[5]. That is, 1 on the diagonal and $\rho \in \{0, 0.2, 0.5, 0.9\}$ off-diagonal, where one value of ρ is used in each experiment. We generate a response using the formula $y = 2 + 10X_1 + 0.25X_2 - 3X_3 - X_4 + 1.5X_5 - 0.5X_6 + 10X_7 + 1.25X_8 + 1.5X_9 - 2X_{10} + X_1X_2 - 2X_3X_5 + 2X_4X_8 - 3X_9X_{10} + 3X_1X_3X_7 - X_2X_6X_8 - 2X_3X_8X_{10} + 4X_1X_4X_7X_9$, which contains arbitrary coefficients and significant higher-order interactions effects.

We fit a cross-validated xgboost model [10] to this regression problem to act as the predictive model f. To obtain the true/exact Shapley values ϕ, we use Monte Carlo integration with $K = 5000$ Monte Carlo samples for each coalition and explicand. This is done using the gaussian approach in the shapr-package and we repeat the sampling strategies $B = 500$ times as they are stochastic.

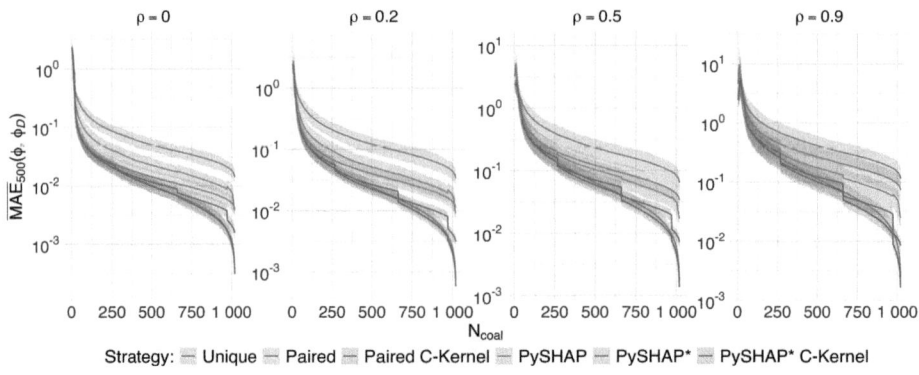

Fig. 2. XGBoost experiment: MAE = $\overline{\text{MAE}}_{500}(\phi, \phi_{\mathcal{D}})$ for different number of coalitions N_{coal} and dependencies levels ρ on log-scale together with 95% confidence bands.

In Fig. 2, we plot the MAE curves for the different strategies and dependence levels as a function of the number of unique coalitions N_{coal}. These plots include 95% empirical confidence bands to show the variation in MAE_b scores across 500 repeated experiments. The confidence bands become narrower as N_{coal} increases. While this may not be visually apparent in the figures, where the bands appear uniform, this is just an effect of the logarithmic scale of the y-axis. Note that some strategies do not converge to zero as $N_{\text{coal}} \to 2^M$. This is because we plot the MAE as a function of N_{coal} and do not include $N_{\text{coal}} = 2^M$, where we would naturally use the exact solution (5) instead of the approximate one (6). If we had plotted the MAE as a function of samples L and continued sampling new coalitions even when $N_{\text{coal}} = 2^M$, then the MAE curves for all strategies would eventually converge to zero.

Figure 2 reveals five key findings. First, a paired sampling procedure in essential as the non-paired unique strategy yields the worst performance. Second, fixing the inconsistent pairing in the PySHAP strategy results in distinct

---
[5] We obtain nearly identical results when $\Sigma_{i,j} = \rho^{|i-j|}$.

improvements with the PySHAP* strategy. Third, the MAE curves for the PySHAP-based strategies exhibit jumps at N_{coal} values where additional coalition sizes are deterministically included. Notably, there is a significant improvement at $N_{\text{coal}} = 268$, reflecting the deterministic inclusion of coalitions of sizes two and eight, as discussed in Sect. 3.4. A possible reason PySHAP* sees a larger drop in MAE than PySHAP at these points is that fewer coalitions are in the sampleable set after the jump. As a result, a greater share of the sampleable set is sampled and thereby paired in PySHAP* making the pairing more effective. Fourth, the increased performance of PySHAP* over paired and PySHAP* c-kernel over paired c-kernel suggests that the semi-deterministic sampling strategy outperforms the fully stochastic sampling procedure. Fifth, and most importantly, the paired c-kernel and PySHAP* c-kernel strategies, which leverage our Shapley kernel weight correction technique, significantly outperform the other strategies. For low dependence levels ρ and smaller N_{coal} values, the paired c-kernel and PySHAP* c-kernel strategies perform similarly, with the latter becoming more precise at higher ρ and N_{coal} values. However, their confidence bands overlap.

The MAE values should be interpreted together with f to better understand the scale of the errors. Recall the efficiency axiom which states that $f(\boldsymbol{x}^*) = \phi_0 + \sum_{j=1}^{M} \phi_j^*$. That is, the Shapley values explain the difference between ϕ_0 and the predicted response $f(\boldsymbol{x}^*)$ for different explicands $\boldsymbol{x}^*$. In Fig. 3, we plot histograms of the $f(\boldsymbol{x}^*)$ values together with the corresponding ϕ_0 values for the four dependence levels. If the difference between ϕ_0 and $f(\boldsymbol{x}^*)$ is small, then the Shapley values are often small too; we illustrate this for the real-world data set in Sect. 5. Thus, obtaining a low absolute error is easier for explicands with a predicted response closer to ϕ_0.

In the simulation studies, we have that $\frac{1}{N_{\text{explain}}} \sum_{i=1}^{N_{\text{explain}}} |\phi_0 - f(\boldsymbol{x}^*)|$ equals 11.54, 12.27, 13.02, 15.98 for the four dependence levels $\rho \in \{0, 0.2, 0.5, 0.9\}$, respectively. This means that, on average, each of the ten absolute Shapley values are 1.154, 1.227, 1.302, and 1.598, respectively. Thus, we consider an MAE between 10^{-1} and 10^{-2} to yield satisfactory accurate approximated Shapley values. This corresponds to an N_{coal} around 100 to 500 in the different setups for the paired c-kernel and PySHAP* c-kernel, while the unique and paired strategies need almost all coalitions to obtain the same accuracy for $\rho = 0.9$. In Fig. 4, we illustrate the reduction in N_{coal} when using the PySHAP* c-kernel strategy to achieve the same MAE scores as the other strategies. In practice, where we do not have access to $\boldsymbol{\phi}$, it is more applicable to gradually increase N_{coal} until $\boldsymbol{\phi}_{\mathcal{D}}$ obtains some convergence criterion; see [12].

4.2 Linear Regression Model

In the second simulation study, we investigate a higher dimensional setup. However, we are limited by the computational complexity of the true Shapley values growing exponentially with the number of features. Thus, we settle on an $M = 20$-dimensional Gaussian data setup with a linear model as the predictive

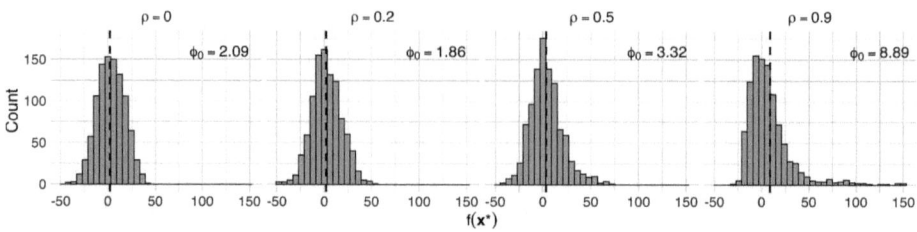

Fig. 3. XGBoost experiment: histograms of the predicted responses $f(\boldsymbol{x}^*)$ for the 1000 explicands together with $\phi_0 = \mathbb{E}[f(\boldsymbol{x})] = \overline{y}_{\text{train}}$ for each dependence level.

model f, as we can then obtain analytical expressions for the contribution function [1, Appendix B.2]. More precisely, the contribution function in (2) for linear models with dependent features simplifies to $v(\mathcal{S}) = f(\boldsymbol{x}_{\overline{\mathcal{S}}} = \boldsymbol{\mu}_{\overline{\mathcal{S}}|\mathcal{S}}, \boldsymbol{x}_{\mathcal{S}} = \boldsymbol{x}_{\mathcal{S}}^*)$, where $\boldsymbol{\mu}_{\overline{\mathcal{S}}|\mathcal{S}} = \mathbb{E}[\boldsymbol{x}_{\overline{\mathcal{S}}}|\boldsymbol{x}_{\mathcal{S}} = \boldsymbol{x}_{\mathcal{S}}^*] = \boldsymbol{\mu}_{\overline{\mathcal{S}}} + \boldsymbol{\Sigma}_{\overline{\mathcal{S}}\mathcal{S}}\boldsymbol{\Sigma}_{\mathcal{S}\mathcal{S}}^{-1}(\boldsymbol{x}_{\mathcal{S}}^* - \boldsymbol{\mu}_{\mathcal{S}})$ for Gaussian data. This allows us to avoid time-consuming simulations needed in the Monte Carlo integration procedure in (13) when computing the contribution function values $v(\mathcal{S})$ for the $2^M = 1\,048\,576$ different coalitions and N_{explain} explicands.

We generate $N_{\text{train}} = 1000$ training observations and $N_{\text{explain}} = 250$ explicands following a Gaussian distribution $\boldsymbol{x} \sim \mathcal{N}_M(\boldsymbol{0}, \boldsymbol{\Sigma}_\rho)$, where $\boldsymbol{\Sigma}_\rho = \text{diag}(B_3^\rho, B_4^\rho, B_3^\rho, B_5^\rho, B_2^\rho, B_2^\rho, B_1^\rho)$ is a block diagonal matrix. Here B_j^ρ is an equi-correlation matrix of dimension $j \times j$ and $\rho \in \{0, 0.2, 0.5, 0.9\}$. We generate the responses according to $\boldsymbol{y} = \boldsymbol{X}\boldsymbol{\beta}$, where arbitrarily $\boldsymbol{\beta} = [2, 1, 0.25, -3, -1, 1.5, -0.5, 0.75, 1.25, 1.5, -2, 3, -1, -5, 4, -10, 2, 5, -0.5, -1, -2]$ and the first value is the intercept. We fit a linear model to the data and repeat the strategies $B = 150$ times.

In Fig. 5, we plot the MAE curves for each strategy together with 95% empirical confidence bands for the different dependence levels as a function of N_{coal}. We do not focus on $\rho = 0$ as it is a trivial case where the Shapley values are explicitly given by $\phi_j = \beta_j(x_j^* - \mathbb{E}[x_j])$, for $j = 1, 2, \ldots, M$ [1, Appendix B.1]. For all dependence levels, we see that our strategies outperform the established unique, paired, and PySHAP strategies by a significant margin. For $\rho \geq 0$, the PySHAP* strategy performs much better than the three previous strategies, but there is still a notable gap to the paired c-kernel and PySHAP* c-kernel strategies. The latter two perform very similarly, with overlapping confidence bands, but the average performance of the PySHAP* c-kernel strategy is slightly better for all values of N_{coal}. Additionally, the PySHAP strategy exhibits erratic behavior when $N_{\text{coal}} \approx 2^M$, as it samples coalitions only from the innermost coalition size in an unpaired manner. This undesirable behavior is eliminated when we pair the sampled coalitions and use the corrected Shapley kernel weights. We obtain similar results to those in Fig. 5 for other linear simulation experiments not included in this paper with $M \in \{10, 12, 14, 17, 20\}$ and different coefficient values and correlation matrices.

In Fig. 6, we plot histograms of the $f(\boldsymbol{x}^*)$ values together with the corresponding ϕ_0 values for the four dependence levels. While the corresponding values of

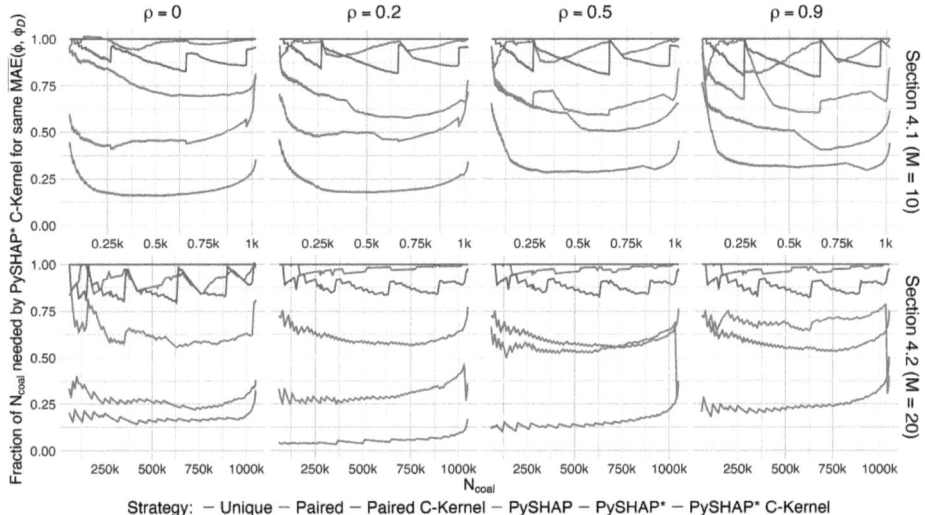

Fig. 4. The reduction in N_{coal} needed by the PySHAP* c-kernel strategy to obtain the same MAE as the other strategies. E.g., for the experiment in Sect. 4.1 with $\rho = 0.2$ and $N_{\text{coal}} = 500$, the PySHAP* c-kernel strategy obtains the same MAE score as the PySHAP strategy using only $0.5 \times 500 = 250$ coalitions, i.e., a 50% reduction. In general, we see similar curves for the different experiments, and all strategies perform significantly worse than the PySHAP* c-kernel strategy. The exception is the paired c-kernel strategy in a small region in the top left figure, where it has a fraction above one, indicating that PySHAP* c-kernel requires a larger N_{coal} than paired c-kernel.

$\frac{1}{N_{\text{explain}}} \sum_{i=1}^{N_{\text{explain}}} |\phi_0 - f(\boldsymbol{x}^*)|$ equals 15.23, 14.89, 14.56, and 14.62, respectively. Which yields an average of 0.76, 0.74, 0.73, and 0.73 per Shapley value. Thus, we consider an MAE between 10^{-2} and $10^{-2.5}$ to give satisfactory accurate approximated Shapley values. This corresponds to an N_{coal} around 2000 to 300 000 in the different setups for the paired c-kernel and PySHAP* c-kernel strategies. Note that the number of coalitions N_{coal} needed for this precision level increases when the dependence increases.

5 Real-World Data Experiments

As a real world example, we consider the Red Wine data set from the UCI Machine Learning Repository to evaluate the sampling strategies on real non-Gaussian data. We fit a cross-validated random forest model[6] to act as the predictive model. We compute the Shapley values $\boldsymbol{\phi}$ by estimating the contribution function (2) values via a random forest regression model approach[7] with default hyperparameter values: trees = 500, mtry = 3, and min.node.size = 5.

---

[6] A ranger model [42] with trees = 200, mtry = 4, and min.node.size = 3.
[7] See the regression approach vignette of the shapr R-package.

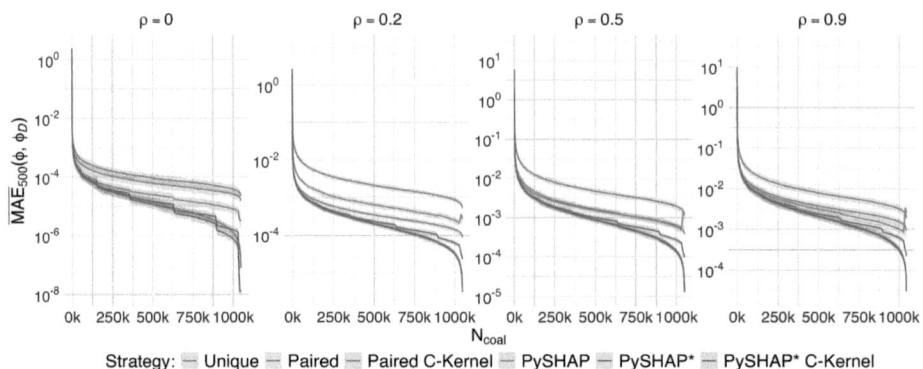

Fig. 5. Linear experiment: MAE = $\overline{\mathrm{MAE}}_{150}(\boldsymbol{\phi}, \boldsymbol{\phi}_\mathcal{D})$ curves for each strategy and dependence level ρ on log-scale together with 95% confidence bands, which are very narrow.

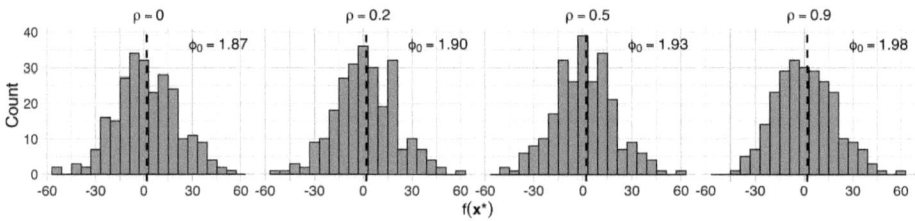

Fig. 6. Linear experiment: histograms of the predicted responses $f(\boldsymbol{x}^*)$ for the 250 explicands together with $\phi_0 = \mathbb{E}[f(\boldsymbol{x})] = \overline{y}_{\mathrm{train}}$ for each dependence level.

[35] determined this estimation approach to yield the most precise Shapley values for this data set and predictive model. We compare these Shapley values $\boldsymbol{\phi}$ using all 2^M coalitions with the approximated Shapley values $\boldsymbol{\phi}_\mathcal{D}$ obtained by using only $N_{\mathrm{coal}} = |\mathcal{D}|$ unique coalitions determined by the different sampling strategies.

The Red Wine data set contains information about variants of the Portuguese Vinho Verde wine [11]. The response is a `quality` value between 0 and 10, while the $M = 11$ continuous features are based on physicochemical tests: `fixed acidity`, `volatile acidity`, `citric acid`, `residual sugar`, `chlorides`, `free sulfur dioxide`, total `sulfur dioxide`, `density`, `pH`, `sulphates`, and `alcohol`. For the Red Wine data set, most scatter plots and marginal density functions display structures and marginals far from the Gaussian distribution, as most of the marginals are right-skewed. Many features have no to moderate correlation, with a mean absolute correlation of 0.20, while the largest absolute correlation is 0.683 (between `pH` and `fix_acid`). The data set contains 1599 observations, and we split it into a training (1500) and a test (99) data set.

In Fig. 7, we display the MAE = $\overline{\mathrm{MAE}}_{500}(\boldsymbol{\phi}, \boldsymbol{\phi}_\mathcal{D})$ values with 95% empirical confidence bands. The results are similar to those we obtained for the simulation studies in Sect. 4. The best strategy across all numbers of coalitions is the

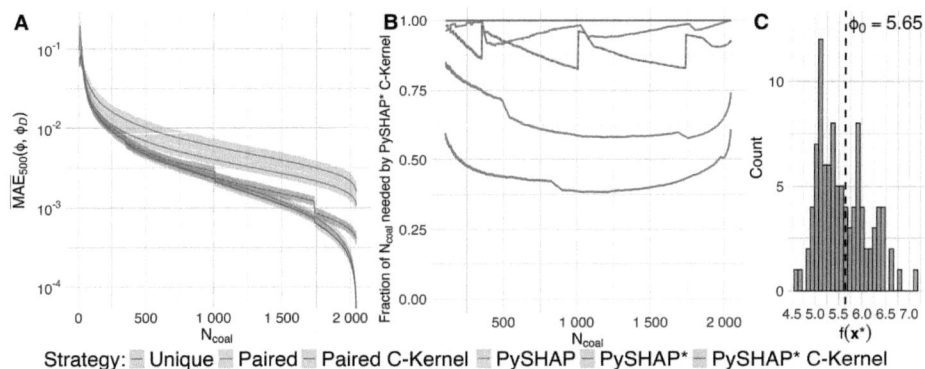

Fig. 7. Red Wine experiment: **A)** The MAE = $\overline{\text{MAE}}_{500}(\phi, \phi_\mathcal{D})$ values with 95% confidence bands for different values of N_{coal} on log-scale. **B)** Same type of figure as explained in Fig. 4. **C)** Histogram of the predicted responses $f(\boldsymbol{x}^*)$ for the 99 explicands together with $\phi_0 = \mathbb{E}[f(\boldsymbol{x})] = \overline{y}_{\text{train}}$.

PySHAP* c-kernel strategy, with the paired c-kernel a close second with partially overlapping confidence bands. The PySHAP and PySHAP* strategies perform identically as M is odd, but they are significantly outperformed by the two best methods, especially when N_{coal} increases. The unique and paired strategies are by far the worst performing methods for all values of N_{coal}.

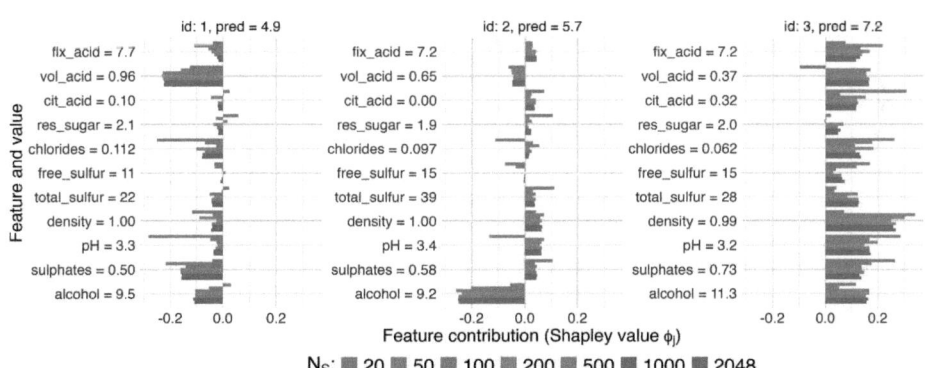

Fig. 8. Red Wine experiment: comparing the Shapley values ϕ, obtained using all 2048 coalitions, with the approximated Shapley values $\phi_\mathcal{D}$ obtained by the simple PySHAP* c-kernel strategy when increasing the number of unique coalitions N_{coal} in the subset $\mathcal{D}$. The approximated Shapley values are close to the exact values when N_{coal} larger than 100 to 200.

As stated in Sect. 4, the MAE should be interpreted together with the $f(\boldsymbol{x})$ to obtain a proper understanding of the scale of the errors. If the difference between $\phi_0 = 5.65$ and $f(\boldsymbol{x}^*)$ is small, then the Shapley values are often small too. See explicand two in Fig. 8 with $f(\boldsymbol{x}^*) = 5.7$, where all but one Shapley value is less than 0.05 in absolute value. Thus, obtaining a low absolute error is easier for explicands with a predicted response closer to ϕ_0. We have that $\frac{1}{N_{\text{explain}}} \sum_{i=1}^{N_{\text{explain}}} |\phi_0 - f(\boldsymbol{x}^*)| = 0.43947$, which means that the 11 Shapley values move the ϕ_0 value by 0.44, or 0.04 per Shapley value, on average. We consider an MAE of $10^{-2.5} \approx 0.0032$ and 10^{-3} to be low and very low, respectively. For the former, the `paired c-kernel` and `PySHAP*` c-kernel strategies archive this for $N_{\text{coal}} \approx 800$, while $N_{\text{coal}} \approx 1500$ for the very low MAE value, a precision level not archived by the `unique` and `paired` strategies.

In Fig. 8, we compare the approximated Shapley values $\phi_{\mathcal{D}}$ computed by the `PySHAP*` c-kernel strategy with the Shapley values ϕ using all coalitions for three arbitrarily selected explicands with increasing predicted responses. We see that the magnitude of the Shapley values is larger for predictions further away from ϕ_0, and the approximated Shapley values are close to the exact values for N_{coal} larger than 100 to 200. Hence, had this been known in advance, it would have sufficed to use 100 or 200 coalitions with the `PySHAP*` c-kernel strategy, providing large computational savings. Note that, by chance, the $\phi_{\mathcal{D}}$ estimates can be close to ϕ for low values of N_{coal} for some features and explicands.

6 Conclusion and Further Work

A major drawback of the Shapley value explanation framework is its computational complexity, which grows exponentially with the number of features. The `KernelSHAP` framework addresses this by approximating Shapley values through a weighted least squares solution, using a sampled subset $\mathcal{D}$ of the 2^M coalitions. However, the stochasticity in the weights used in `KernelSHAP` introduces additional, undesired variance into the approximate Shapley values. We propose the novel `paired c-kernel` strategy for weighing the N_{coal} unique elements in $\mathcal{D}$ which is deterministic rather than stochastic, given the unique coalitions. Moreover, our `PySHAP*` strategy makes a correction to the `PySHAP` strategy implemented in the `SHAP` Python library to ensure consistent pairing of sampled coalitions for all coalition sizes. Finally, the `PySHAP*` c-kernel strategy combines these two modifications.

Through simulation studies and real-world data examples, we show empirically that our strategies lead to *uniformly* more accurate approximation for conditional Shapley values, while using fewer coalitions than the existing strategies. Specifically, the established `unique`, `paired`, and `PySHAP` strategies are consistently outperformed by our modified `PySHAP*` strategy, which in turn is outperformed by our innovative `paired c-kernel` and `PySHAP*` c-kernel strategies. These latter two strategies perform very similarly, with overlapping confidence bands for the MAE score; however, the `PySHAP*` c-kernel strategy achieves a slightly lower average MAE.

We recommend the `PySHAP*` c-kernel strategy for its simplicity, consistent high accuracy, and reduced sampling time due to its semi-deterministic inclusion of coalitions. Notably, the `PySHAP*` `c-kernel` strategy shows improvement jumps when a new coalition size is deterministically incorporated. The values where these jumps occur can be precomputed, and the results indicate a significant performance boost by choosing a number of coalitions N_{coal} slightly higher than these values. This property can be leveraged to develop more effective convergence detection procedures for iterative Shapley value estimation [12].

Additionally, we identify three main areas for future research. First, even though this paper focus on conditional Shapley values, our strategies are also directly applicable for marginal Shapley values, and can be adapted to global Shapley values (e.g., `SAGE` [14]), Shapley interaction values (e.g., `KernelSHAP-IQ` [18]) and Data Shapley for data valuation [19]. Similar ideas may also be applied to the alternative approximation approaches of [23]. Finally, it would be interesting to investigate whether our strategies remain effective if we replace the initial random coalition sampling in `KernelSHAP` with stratified sampling based on coalition size. Although we have no reason to doubt that our `paired c-kernel` and `PySHAP*` `c-kernel` strategies is superior also in these domains, a thorough investigation is needed to confirm this. Shapley value applications where approximate solutions with `KernelSHAP` is relevant would also be interesting use cases for our `KernelSHAP` modification. Second, it would be interesting to explore whether our method could be extended and improved by guiding the initial coalition sampling toward more informative subsets for the given model and dataset. This may for instance be achieved by using pilot estimates of $v(\mathcal{S})$ to identify the most important coalitions and then assigning them greater weight in the sampling process. Taylor approximations as discussed in [20] may also serve as a viable alternative in this context. Third, it would be valuable to obtain theoretical insights into the weighting strategies and, if possible, derive theoretical guarantees. For instance, understanding whether the current schemes are optimal, or if better strategies can be found, could be beneficial.

The main computational burden of approximating Shapley values lies in estimating the contribution function values $v(\mathcal{S})$ rather than sampling and determining the weights of the coalitions $\mathcal{S}$. Thus, the running time is approximately proportional to the number of unique coalitions N_{coal} being used. Therefore, our proposed strategies, which reduce N_{coal} while maintaining the accuracy of the approximated Shapley values, are very computationally beneficial. Figures 4 and 7 show that, in our experiments, using the `PySHAP*` `c-kernel` strategy reduced the number of required coalitions by 50% to 95% compared to the `unique` strategy, 25% to 50% compared to the `paired` strategy, and 5% to 50% compared to the `PySHAP` strategy, depending on N_{coal} and the dependence level between the features. Importantly, these reductions significantly decrease the computational cost and time for Shapley value explanations, enhancing their feasibility in practical applications.

Acknowledgments. The Norwegian Research Council supported this research through the BigInsight Center for Research-driven Innovation, project number 237718, Integreat Center of Excellence, project number 332645, and EU's HORIZON Research and Innovation Programme, project ENFIELD, grant number 101120657.

Appendix

A Implementation Details

The main strategies are implemented in version 1.0.4 of the `shapr`-package [22] while the code for the simulation studies is available at the following GitHub repository: https://github.com/NorskRegnesentral/PaperShapleyValuesImprovingKernelSHAP. The implementation of the `PySHAP`-based strategies are based on the kernel.py file in version 0.46 of the SHAP Python library [27]. To generate the true contribution functions and Shapley values in Sect. 4.1, we have used the `gaussian` approach in `shapr` with $K = 5000$ Monte Carlo samples from the true Gaussian distribution. While we used explicit formulas for the contribution function in Sect. 4.2. In Sect. 5, we used the `random forest separate regression` approach introduced in [35] to compute $v(\mathcal{S})$.

References

1. Aas, K., Jullum, M., Løland, A.: Explaining individual predictions when features are dependent: more accurate approximations to Shapley values. Artif. Intell. **298**, 103502 (2021)
2. Adadi, A., Berrada, M.: Peeking inside the black-box: a survey on explainable artificial intelligence (xai). IEEE Access **6**, 52138–52160 (2018)
3. Ancona, M., Oztireli, C., Gross, M.: Explaining deep neural networks with a polynomial time algorithm for Shapley value approximation. In: ICML, pp. 272–281. PMLR (2019)
4. Bifet, A., Read, J., Xu, C., et al.: Linear tree Shap. Adv. Neural. Inf. Process. Syst. **35**, 25818–25828 (2022)
5. Castro, J., Gómez, D., Molina, E., Tejada, J.: Improving polynomial estimation of the Shapley value by stratified random sampling with optimum allocation. Comput. Oper. Res. **82**, 180–188 (2017)
6. Charnes, A., Golany, B., Keane, M., Rousseau, J.: Extremal principle solutions of games in characteristic function form: core, Chebychev and Shapley value generalizations. In: Econometrics of planning and efficiency, pp. 123–133. Springer (1988)
7. Chen, H., Covert, I.C., Lundberg, S.M., Lee, S.I.: Algorithms to estimate Shapley value feature attributions. arXiv preprint arXiv:2207.07605 (2022)
8. Chen, H., Covert, I.C., Lundberg, S.M., Lee, S.I.: Algorithms to estimate Shapley value feature attributions. Nature Mach. Intell. **5**(6), 590–601 (2023)
9. Chen, H., Janizek, J.D., Lundberg, S., Lee, S.I.: True to the model or true to the data? arXiv preprint arXiv:2006.16234 (2020)
10. Chen, T., He, T., Benesty, M., Khotilovich, V., Tang, Y., Cho, H., et al.: XGBoost: extreme gradient boosting. R package version 0.4-2 **1**(4), 1–4 (2015)
11. Cortez, P., Teixeira, J., Cerdeira, A., Almeida, F., Matos, T., Reis, J.: Using data mining for wine quality assessment. In: Gama, J., Costa, V.S., Jorge, A.M., Brazdil, P.B. (eds.) DS 2009. LNCS (LNAI), vol. 5808, pp. 66–79. Springer, Heidelberg (2009). https://doi.org/10.1007/978-3-642-04747-3_8
12. Covert, I., Lee, S.I.: Improving kernelshap: practical Shapley value estimation using linear regression. In: International Conference on Artificial Intelligence and Statistics, pp. 3457–3465. PMLR (2021)

13. Covert, I., Lundberg, S., Lee, S.I.: Explaining by removing: a unified framework for model explanation. J. Mach. Learn. Res. **22**(209), 1–90 (2021)
14. Covert, I., Lundberg, S.M., Lee, S.I.: Understanding global feature contributions with additive importance measures. In: Advances in Neural Information Processing Systems, vol. 33 (2020)
15. Deng, X., Papadimitriou, C.H.: On the complexity of cooperative solution concepts. Math. Oper. Res. **19**(2), 257–266 (1994)
16. Faigle, U., Kern, W.: The Shapley value for cooperative games under precedence constraints. Internat. J. Game Theory **21**, 249–266 (1992)
17. Flajolet, P., Gardy, D., Thimonier, L.: Birthday paradox, coupon collectors, caching algorithms and self-organizing search. Discret. Appl. Math. **39**(3), 207–229 (1992)
18. Fumagalli, F., Muschalik, M., Kolpaczki, P., Hüllermeier, E., Hammer, B.: KernelSHAP-IQ: weighted least square optimization for Shapley interactions. In: Proceedings of the 41st International Conference on Machine Learning, vol. 235, pp. 14308–14342. PMLR (2024)
19. Ghorbani, A., Zou, J.: Data Shapley: equitable valuation of data for machine learning. In: International Conference on Machine Learning, pp. 2242–2251. PMLR (2019)
20. Goldwasser, J., Hooker, G.: Stabilizing estimates of Shapley values with control variates. In: World Conference on XAI pp. 416–439. Springer (2024)
21. Illés, F., Kerényi, P.: Estimation of the Shapley value by ergodic sampling. arXiv preprint arXiv:1906.05224 (2019)
22. Jullum, M., Olsen, L.H.B., Lachmann, J., Redelmeier, A.: shapr: explaining machine learning models with conditional Shapley values in R and Python. arXiv preprint arXiv:2504.01842 (2025)
23. Kolpaczki, P., Bengs, V., Muschalik, M., Hüllermeier, E.: Approximating the Shapley value without marginal contributions. In: Proceedings of the AAAI Conference on Artificial Intelligence, vol. 38, pp. 13246–13255 (2024)
24. Kroese, D.P., Taimre, T., Botev, Z.I.: Handbook of Monte Carlo methods. John Wiley & Sons (2013)
25. Lundberg, S., et al.: From local explanations to global understanding with explainable AI for trees. Nature Mach. Intell. **2**(1), 56–67 (2020)
26. Lundberg, S.M., Lee, S.I.: A unified approach to interpreting model predictions. In: Advances in Neural Information Processing Systems, pp. 4765–4774 (2017)
27. Lundberg, S.M., Lee, S.I.: Shap (2024), https://pypi.org/project/shap/, python package version 0.46.0
28. Maleki, S.: Addressing the computational issues of the Shapley value with applications in the smart grid. Ph.D. thesis, University of Southampton (2015)
29. Mitchell, R., Cooper, J., Frank, E., Holmes, G.: Sampling permutations for Shapley value estimation. J. Mach. Learn. Res. **23**(43), 1–46 (2022)
30. Molnar, C.: Interpretable Machine Learning. 2 edn. (2022). https://christophm.github.io/interpretable-ml-book
31. Molnar, C.: Interpreting Machine Learning Models With SHAP. 1 edn. (2023). https://christophmolnar.com/books/shap/
32. Okhrati, R., Lipani, A.: A multilinear sampling algorithm to estimate Shapley values. In: 2020 25th International Conference on Pattern Recognition (ICPR), pp. 7992–7999. IEEE (2021)
33. Olsen, L.H.B.: Precision of individual Shapley value explanations. arXiv preprint arXiv:2312.03485 (2023)

34. Olsen, L.H.B., Glad, I.K., Jullum, M., Aas, K.: Using Shapley values and variational autoencoders to explain predictive models with dependent mixed features. J. Mach. Learn. Res. **23**(213), 1–51 (2022)
35. Olsen, L.H.B., Glad, I.K., Jullum, M., Aas, K.: A comparative study of methods for estimating model-agnostic Shapley value explanations. Data Mining Knowl. Discov. 1–48 (2024)
36. Redelmeier, A., Jullum, M., Aas, K.: Explaining predictive models with mixed features using Shapley values and conditional inference trees. In: ICross-Domain Conference for Machine Learning and Knowledge Extraction, pp. 117–137 (2020)
37. Shapley, L.S.: A value for n-person games. Contrib. Theory Games **2**(28), 307–317 (1953)
38. Strumbelj, E., Kononenko, I.: An efficient explanation of individual classifications using game theory. J. Mach. Learn. Res. **11**, 1–18 (2010)
39. Strumbelj, E., Kononenko, I.: Explaining prediction models and individual predictions with feature contributions. Knowl. Inf. Syst. **41**(3), 647–665 (2014)
40. Wang, R., Wang, X., Inouye, D.I.: Shapley explanation networks. In: ICLR (2020)
41. Williamson, B., Feng, J.: Efficient nonparametric statistical inference on population feature importance using Shapley values. In: ICML, pp. 10282–10291. PMLR (2020)
42. Wright, M., Ziegler, A.: ranger: a fast implementation of random forests for high dimensional data in C++ and R. J. Stat. Softw. **77**(1), 1–17 (2017)
43. Yang, J.: Fast treeshap: accelerating Shap value computation for trees. arXiv preprint arXiv:2109.09847 (2021)

Open Access This chapter is licensed under the terms of the Creative Commons Attribution 4.0 International License (http://creativecommons.org/licenses/by/4.0/), which permits use, sharing, adaptation, distribution and reproduction in any medium or format, as long as you give appropriate credit to the original author(s) and the source, provide a link to the Creative Commons license and indicate if changes were made.

The images or other third party material in this chapter are included in the chapter's Creative Commons license, unless indicated otherwise in a credit line to the material. If material is not included in the chapter's Creative Commons license and your intended use is not permitted by statutory regulation or exceeds the permitted use, you will need to obtain permission directly from the copyright holder.

POMELO: Black-Box Feature Attribution with Full-Input, In-Distribution Perturbations

Luan Ademi, Maximilian Noppel(✉), and Christian Wressnegger

KASTEL Security Research Labs, Karlsruhe Institute of Technology,
Karlsruhe, Germany
noppel@kit.edu

Abstract. Model-agnostic explanation methods provide importance scores per feature by analyzing a model's responses to perturbed versions of the sample to be explained. The explanation's quality therefore hinges on the made perturbations and, most importantly, suffers if these lead to out-of-distribution samples. Unfortunately, this is the case for the popular LIME explanation method. In this paper, we thus introduce POMELO, an extension to LIME leveraging generative AI for full-input, in-distribution sampling. We define key properties of such samplers: distribution alignment, diversity, and locality. Based on these, we discuss different neural samplers based on normalizing flows and diffusion models. Our results demonstrate that neural samplers outperform traditional perturbation strategies and yield explanations that are better aligned with human intuition. Supplementary material to our paper is available at https://intellisec.de/research/pomelo.

Keywords: LIME · Normalizing Flows · Diffusion Models

1 Introduction

In recent years, the community has proposed a plethora of techniques for explaining machine learning models [4,12,13,20,28,35,40,41,46,53]. One of the most popular and most widely used methods in practice [19] is LIME [35]. As a post-hoc, black-box explanation method LIME operates without access to the model's weights, gradients, or its neurons' activation. Instead, it generates explanations using only the model's input-output behavior.

To do so, LIME queries the model's soft-label probabilities for perturbed variants of the sample to be explained. Based on these soft-labels and the binary masks representing the made perturbations, LIME trains an interpretable surrogate model. Each perturbed sample "misses" certain segments of the original sample, that is, segments are replaced with a baseline, e.g., a constant value like gray or black, a blurred patch [11], or the mean value of the segment (cf. Fig. 1).

L. Ademi and M. Noppel—Both authors contributed equally to this research.

Fig. 1. Perturbed samples generated using different perturbation strategies.

Unfortunately, these strategies give rise to a fundamental limitation: the perturbations are out-of-distribution (o.o.d.), and thus, explanations may capture undefined and/or irrelevant model behavior [16,17,33].

To address this issue, we revise the perturbation strategies of LIME and propose our extension POMELO that can be thought of as a full-input variant of LIME. It leverages generative models to generate perturbed but in-distribution (i.d.) versions for an original sample. In contrast to related work, we allow changes on the full input, instead of random segments only. Our method thus grounds explanations on realistic changes, induced by the training distribution, and produces more interpretable insights into the model's decision-making process. As an example of our new, *full-input* perturbation strategies, Fig. 1 depicts perturbed samples from a normalizing flow and a diffusion model (cf. Sect. 2.4) on the right. The use of full-input perturbations has one crucial advantage over related work: the generative model "knows" the feature correlations and perturbs correlated feature together, independent of their spatial position in the image. With segment-wise replacement, as used in LIME, this is not possible. The probability that larger features or distributed correlations are replaced together is low if the segments are picked at random.

We are the first to show how generative AI with *full-input perturbations* can be used within the LIME-framework for the complex *image domain*. However, other extensions of LIME with similar motivations exist, though: For instance, Qiu et al. [33] use naive perturbation strategies and weighs the perturbed samples according to an inlier score when training the surrogate model. Others use in-painting strategies to fill in the "missing" segments in images [2,6], or for anomaly detection on tabular data [48]. Furthermore, one can use Variational Autoencoders (VAEs) to explain temperature time series forecasting in blast furnace [39] or Conditional Tabular GANs [52] to enhance LIME's robustness against attacks [38].

In summary, we make the following contributions:

- **Key Properties of Samplers.** We develop a framework that consists of three key properties of effective full-input samplers: *distribution alignment*, *diversity* and *locality*. We discuss the trade-offs and relations between the properties and propose metrics to assess different aspects of them.
- **Full-Input Perturbation Strategies for LIME.** We demonstrate how full-input perturbation strategies can be integrated into LIME, giving rise to our novel approach POMELO. Therefore, we examine two concrete strategies,

one based on normalizing flows and one based on denoising diffusion implicit models (DDIMs). Based on the key properties, we compare the resulting perturbed samples against the traditional LIME perturbation strategies.
- **Comprehensive Evaluation.** We compare the explanation performance of our approach against traditional LIME in terms of the explanation quality, diversity, locality, distribution alignment, and computational feasibility. We demonstrate that the descriptive accuracy metric is closely aligned with the used perturbation strategy in the explanation.

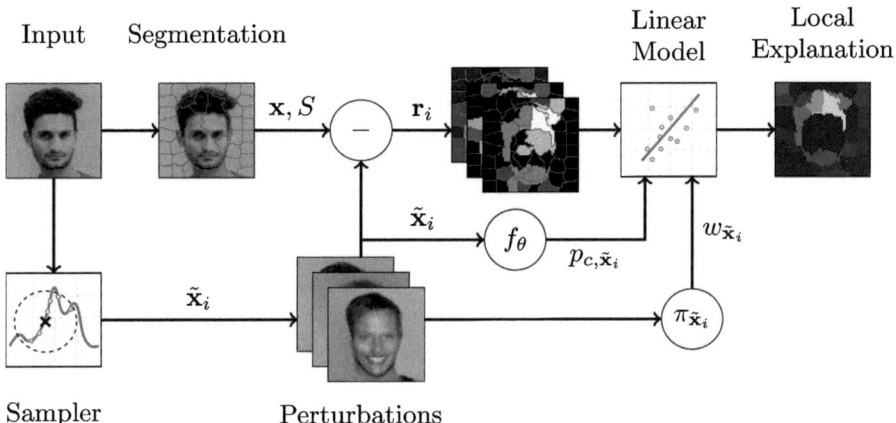

Fig. 2. Overview depiction of POMELO. We replace LIME's perturbation strategies with an in-distribution *full-input* sampler and employ a more concise interpretable representation based on the segment-wise ℓ_1 distance between the original sample and the perturbed samples.

2 POMELO

We extend the LIME explanation method as a remedy to the out-of-distribution (o.o.d.) problem. Our extension, POMELO, replaces the naive perturbation strategies with more powerful generative approaches, denoted as *neural samplers*. This change comes with peculiarities if the perturbations are not limited to specific segments, a problem we describe and solve in this section.

After introducing our basic notation, we first state the o.o.d. problem in Sect. 2.1, and its relation to meaningfulness in Sect. 2.2. In Sect. 2.3, we formalize three key properties a sampler should satisfy. Next, we describe three concrete perturbation strategies that adhere to these criteria in Sect. 2.4. We regard them as proof-of-concepts to demonstrate the benefits of our extension. In Sect. 2.5, we introduce our core contribution: how to generate interpretable representations from full-input perturbations. And lastly, Sect. 2.6 describes how we build explanations from all the above. In Fig. 2, we provide an overview on the methodology of POMELO.

Notation. Throughout the paper, we consider a classifier $\mathcal{F}_\theta : \mathcal{X} \to \mathcal{Y}$, that maps samples $\mathbf{x} \in \mathcal{X}$ to classes/labels $y \in \mathcal{Y}$ based on a soft-label $\mathcal{F}_\theta(\mathbf{x}) = \arg\max_c f_\theta(\mathbf{x})_c$. The model's parameters θ are learned on a training dataset $\mathcal{D}_{train}$ and eventually are validated on a separate dataset $\mathcal{D}_{val}$. A sampler $\mathcal{S} : \mathcal{X} \to P(\mathcal{X})$, where P is the powerset, produces a set of perturbed samples, and a segmentation algorithm Seg provides a segmentation, given a sample.

2.1 The Out-of-Distribution Problem

LIME employs relatively simple perturbation strategies, such as overwriting segments/super-pixels with constant values or blurring a segment. These perturbations are supposed to mimic the removal of the respective segment but also diverge heavily from the real-world distribution. Hence, LIME explanations are based on o.o.d. samples, not reflecting the model's real-world decision-making process in benign environments. A model's responses to black or gray patches simply express exactly this; how does the model react to black or gray patches. We argue, that explaining based on this results in misleading explanations [33]. In adversarial environments, in turn, the fact that LIME uses o.o.d. samples can even be exploited to bootstrap attacks on the explanation [15,42]. Training neural networks to make correct predictions on all samples remains a tricky problem [16,17,29,47], and thus, LIME explanations do not faithfully explain a model's decisions.

2.2 Relating In-Distribution Perturbations and Meaningfulness

Grounding explanations in the model's data distribution produces more reliable and interpretable insights. However, it is important to note, that i.d. perturbed samples are not always semantically meaningful variations of the original sample. Depending on the data distribution also meaningless but dominant features like copyright tags on horse images [3,23] or tags on images of skin cancer [36] are in-distribution, i.e., neural samplers might produce such features. Fortunately, the pure existence of such features does not influence the explanation much. Only, if they are (spuriously) correlated with the model's soft-labels, the explanation will pick them up, which is a desirable property. In other words, *POMELO explains the model* and *the underlying data distribution together*.

2.3 Key Properties of Perturbation Strategies

To achieve i.d. perturbed samples, we employ *samplers*. Given a sample $\mathbf{x}$, a sampler $\mathcal{S} : \mathcal{X} \to P(\mathcal{X})$ generates a set of perturbed samples. The perturbed samples should satisfy three key properties to ensure robust and meaningful explanations, which we discuss here. Later, in Sect. 4, we present metrics to measure to what extent the properties are achieved by our investigated samplers.

- **Distribution Alignment** (DA) . Given an i.d. sample $\mathbf{x}$, the perturbed samples $\tilde{\mathbf{x}}_i$ should also be i.d.. Formally, a sampler should satisfy $\mathbf{x} \sim \mathfrak{D} \Rightarrow \mathcal{S}(\mathbf{x}) =: \tilde{\mathbf{x}} \sim \mathfrak{D}$, where $\mathfrak{D}$ denotes the true distribution in deployment. For o.o.d. samples the samplers might generate o.o.d. perturbations. This scenario equals explaining o.o.d. samples and is left as future work, though.
- **Diversity** (D) . The set of perturbed samples should be diverse, exploring different classes and many facets of the decision surface. Explanations based on biased samples lead to a skewed view of the model's decision-making process, possibly missing influential directions. Therefore, the perturbed samples should spread in diverse directions and explore all nearby decision boundaries and the shape of the soft-label surface.
- **Locality** (L) . In addition to diversity, perturbed samples should be in the neighborhood of the original sample. Only so do they remain relevant to the explained prediction and preserve the semantic of a local explanation method.

Trade-Offs between the Key Properties. The three properties above restrict each other. Locality and distribution alignment can theoretically be satisfied simultaneously, e.g., via returning very close perturbed samples or even the orginal sample itself. In practice, distributions are seldom so spiky that insufficient variations can be found nearby. In other words, a very spiky distribution would be a distribution where one sample is absolutely in-distribution but moving it just an insignificant bit in any direction makes it out-of-distribution. Diversity, in turn, often requires larger changes and conflicts with locality. Depending on the shape of the distribution, the diversity could also conflict with the distribution alignment, e.g., if the distribution is so narrow (almost a line) that the sampler can only perturb in two directions, not allowing much diversity. Therefore, the sampler (or its parametrization) must balance the three properties.

While challenging to quantify, we propose to determine the parametrization by balancing locality with diversity. We provide details on this expensive process in Appendix B. The trade-offs with distribution alignment, on the other hand, are of theoretical nature, and depend more on the distribution than on the parametrization of the sampler.

2.4 Generating In-Distribution Samples

We present two full-input samplers based on normalizing flows [8,9,21,34] and diffusion models [18,43,45]. For comparison, we describe a third sampler utilizing diffusion-based in-painting similar to RePaint [27]. The training of each sampler requires access to the training dataset of the model being analyzed, or, at least, to a similar dataset with a comparable distribution. Note that this is an additional requirement compared to the naive perturbation strategies of LIME.

Normalizing Flows. Normalizing flows [8,9,21,34] are powerful density estimators with exact invertibility. Flows are composed out of a sequence of K *parameterized* bijective functions $flow = f_K \circ \cdots \circ f_1$. This sequence transforms a simple base distribution $p_{\mathcal{Z}}$ (often Gaussian) into a complex distribution $p_{\mathcal{X}}$, e.g., the distribution of realistic images of celebrities. The parameters of the flow are learned by minimizing the Kullback-Leibler (KL) divergence between the current distribution of images $p_{\mathcal{X}}$ and the desired distribution p_{train}, provided by the training data. Building on this foundation, architectures like Glow [21] achieve competitive results in image generation on datasets such as CelebA [24], but also in other applications like lattice field theory [31]. The core benefit of flows is their exact invertibility, which enables downstream tasks like interpolation and semantic manipulation, making flows a perfect candidate for POMELO.

By leveraging the latent space of a normalizing flow, we obtain the latent representation of $\mathbf{x} \in \mathcal{X}$ as $\mathbf{z} := flow^{-1}(\mathbf{x}) \in \mathcal{Z}$. This representation $\mathbf{z}$ is then perturbed to a new point $\tilde{\mathbf{z}}$ and mapped back to the input space of images $\tilde{\mathbf{x}} := flow(\tilde{\mathbf{z}})$. The perturbation in latent space equals an interpolation between $\mathbf{z}$ and a randomly sampled point $\mathbf{z}^* \sim p_{\mathcal{Z}}$ from the base distribution. Formally,

$$\tilde{\mathbf{z}} = (1 - \lambda) \odot \mathbf{z} + \lambda \odot \mathbf{z}^* \text{ with } \lambda \sim \mathcal{N}_{dim(\mathcal{Z})}(\mu, \sigma) ,$$

where μ and σ control the locality of the perturbed samples. In Appendix B, we provide further details on why we set μ to 0.5 and σ to 0.3. While picking the interpolation factors λ at random is a novel strategy, related work already suggests that interpolations in $\mathcal{Z}$ produce meaningful changes for CelebA [21].

Denoising Diffusion Implicit Models (DDIMs). Diffusion-based models show exceptional performance in image generation and data augmentation [7,18] and, therefore, are a second promising candidate for our aim. More specifically, we use denoising diffusion implicit models [44]. Compared to earlier denoising diffusion probabilistic models (DDPMs) [18], these implicit models provide fundamental benefits for our case.

But one step back. From a functional point of view, diffusion models generate realistic images from pure Gaussian noise. This capability is learned through reconstructing a sample $\mathbf{x}_0$, from a progressively corrupted version $\mathbf{x}_T$. By iteratively predicting and removing the noise over multiple time steps t, the model gradually refines its output, effectively reversing the corruption process. These two involved processes are the forward process ($\mathbf{x}_0 \to \mathbf{x}_T$) that introduces noise, and the reverse process ($\mathbf{x}_T \to \mathbf{x}_0$) that denoises the corrupted sample. In denoising diffusion implicit models (DDIMs), the reverse process can be *deterministic*, allowing for an accompanying deterministic forward process (cf. Appendix A). This configuration allows us to encode a sample as a noisy representation and reconstructing it with minimal error [7,44].

Our proposed sampling strategy exploits this advantage of DDIMs. It uses the deterministic forward process, eventually reaching a noisy but revertible representation of the sample. Afterward, it follows a slightly probabilistic reverse process that introduces deviations, eventually resulting in different perturbed

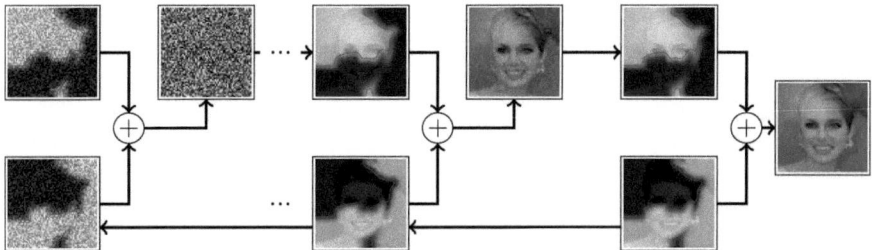

Fig. 3. Our in-painting methodology. In a multi-step process we combine the parts for the noisy original image for present patches(forward process from left to right) and pure noise for missing areas (reverse process, from left to right).

samples of the original sample. The involved randomness can be controlled with a noise scaling factor η, where $\eta = 1$ results in the DDIM reverse process equaling the probabilistic DDPM reverse process, and $\eta = 0$ yields in a fully deterministic reverse process.

Intuitively our approach generates perturbed samples by adding deterministic noise, resulting in a noisy version of the original sample that can be exactly reconstructed by the reverse process. However, by introducing noise in the reconstruction, we deviate from the original sample, creating a perturbed sample that is conditioned on the original sample.

In-Painting. An inherent "problem" of the aforementioned perturbation strategies is their tendency to change the entire image. *This "problem" is exactly what POMELO solves.* As a reference for our experiments we use diffusion-based in-painting as a localized but also neural alternative with changes in specific segments only. In-painting is performed by iteratively merging noisy versions of the original sample $\mathbf{x}_t^{\mathrm{orig}}$ into a diffusion process of an initially random masked intermediate $\mathbf{x}_t^{\mathrm{mask}}$. A schematic representation of this process is provided in Fig. 3. At each step, the merged sample $\mathbf{x}_t$ is calculated as follows:

$$\mathbf{x}_t = M \odot \mathbf{x}_t^{\mathrm{orig}} + (1 - M) \odot \mathbf{x}_t^{\mathrm{mask}},$$

where the in-painted sample $\mathbf{x}_t^{\mathrm{mask}}$ is derived using a denoising step of the previous merged sample $\mathbf{x}_{t-1}$ and the noisy sample $\mathbf{x}_t^{\mathrm{orig}}$ is generated by applying the forward process of the DDIM model on the original sample. For the mask M, we use the segmentation from LIME and create a random mask by selecting a subset of the segments, equivalent to LIME's methodology. To ensure smoother transitions, we apply a Gaussian blur to the mask, resulting in soft edges around the in-painted regions. Similarly to the DDIM-based strategy, the noise level can be controlled by the η parameter and the number of reverse steps.

This approach is closely resembles RePaint [27], but without the iterative resampling process. We omitted resampling because it is to computationally expensive when generating hundreds of images per explanation. While resampling could enhance the semantic consistency of perturbations, we are unable to perform an extensive evaluation with this method.

2.5 Interpretable Representations

In contrast to LIME, POMELO's full-input perturbation strategies produce global changes, unrestricted by the segmentation. Each segment is perturbed to some degree and the binary interpretable representation of LIME cannot be applied (removed/not removed). To maintain a low-dimensional interpretable feature space for the surrogate model, we quantify the full-input changes in a per-segment manner. More concretely, we use a *real-value interpretable space* based on a distance metric $D_\mathcal{X}$ in the input space $\mathcal{X}$. Given the segmentation of the original sample $S = \text{Seg}(\mathbf{x})$, we calculate the interpretable representation $\mathbf{r} \in [0,1]^{|S|}$ of a given perturbed sample $\tilde{\mathbf{x}}$ as follows: For each segment $\mathbf{s}_i \in S$ we assign a score:

$$r_i = 1 - \frac{D_\mathcal{X}(\mathbf{x}_{[\mathbf{s}_i]}, \tilde{\mathbf{x}}_{[\mathbf{s}_i]})}{\max_\mathbf{v} D_\mathcal{X}(\mathbf{x}_{[\mathbf{s}_i]}, \mathbf{v})} , \qquad (1)$$

where $\mathbf{x}_{[\mathbf{s}_i]}$ and $\tilde{\mathbf{x}}_{[\mathbf{s}_i]}$ are the pixel vectors of the segment $\mathbf{s}_i$ of the original and the perturbed sample, respectively. For our experiments, we employ the ℓ_1-norm as the distance metric $D_\mathcal{X}$. We denote this process of generating an interpretable representation from the original sample $\mathbf{x}$, a perturbed sample $\tilde{\mathbf{x}}$, and the segmentation S with a minus sign in Fig. 2.

2.6 Generation of Explanations

Based on the interpretable representations we craft an explanation via the LIME methodology. Given sample $\mathbf{x}$, its segmentation S, and a model θ, we create a set of perturbed samples and their corresponding representations, $\{(\tilde{\mathbf{x}}_1, \mathbf{r}_1), \ldots, (\tilde{\mathbf{x}}_n, \mathbf{r}_n)\}$. The perturbed samples are weighted using a kernel $\pi(\tilde{\mathbf{x}}_i, \mathbf{x})$, i.e., the cosine similarity between $\tilde{\mathbf{x}}_i$ and $\mathbf{x}$. Next, we collect the soft-labels $f_\theta(\tilde{\mathbf{x}}_i)_c$ of the winning class $c = \mathcal{F}_\theta(\mathbf{x})$ for each perturbed sample. This process results in a dataset consisting of $(\pi(\tilde{\mathbf{x}}_i, \mathbf{x}), \tilde{\mathbf{x}}_i, \mathbf{r}_i, f_\theta(\tilde{\mathbf{x}}_i)_c)$ tuples, which are then used to train a linear surrogate model as LIME does, but on the $[0,1]^{|S|}$ space instead of the binary $\{0,1\}^{|S|}$ space. The resulting surrogate model approximates the original model in a local neighborhood, and its learned coefficients represent the contribution of each feature of $\mathbf{r}$ (each segment) to the decision process.

3 Metrics

This section introduces the metrics to evaluate the perturbed samples' distribution alignment (Sect. 3.1), diversity (Sect. 3.2), and locality (Sect. 3.3). Thereafter follow the metrics for the explanation quality, which are reasonability (Sect. 3.4), fidelity (Sect. 3.5), and stability (Sect. 3.6).

3.1 Measuring Distribution Alignment DA

To evaluate distribution alignment, we embed perturbed samples in the penultimate layer of a pretrained model and apply two o.o.d. detection techniques:

- **Mahalanobis Score.** For each validation sample we generate n perturbed samples, which are embedded using the penultimate layer of a ResNet18 model trained on the CelebA dataset. We compute the Mahalanobis uncertainty scores $\mathcal{U}_{MD}$ over these embeddings, following Lee et al. [25]. The required class-conditional Gaussian distributions are estimated using 30,000 training samples from the CelebA dataset. As references for clearly o.o.d. samples (compared to CelebA) we use CIFAR-10 images [22] and Gaussian noise embedded in the same model. We omit to transform the uncertainty scores into binary decisions (i.d./o.o.d.), and report the raw scores instead.
- **UMAP.** To gain qualitative insights, we project the above embeddings into a 2D space using uniform manifold approximation and projection (UMAP) [30], allowing for visual assessment of their alignment with the original distribution. Following Rousseeuw [37], we use the silhouette score as a quantitative measure.

3.2 Measuring Diversity D

We measure the different aspects of diversity with the two entropy-based metrics.

- **Shannon Entropy.** First, we asses the hard-label diversity via the Shannon entropy of the distribution of winning classes induced by the perturbed samples. A good sampler would produce a uniform distribution, ensuring that the perturbed samples are diverse and not biased toward one class. Formally, we measure E_{hard} as $-\sum_{c \in C} p(c) \cdot \log p(c)$, where $p(c)$ is the probability that a perturbed sample is predicted as class c.
- **Differential Shannon Entropy.** In addition, we measure the differential Shannon entropy of the soft-labels. The reasoning behind this is that the interpretable model is trained on the soft-labels of the predicted class instead of the hard-labels. Theorically, the differential entropy of the soft-labels is defined as $E_{soft} := -\int_0^1 \text{pdf}(s) \log \text{pdf}(s) \, ds$, where $\text{pdf}(s)$ is the probability density function of the soft-labels. We approximate this formula with 20 bins via the trapezoidal rule for numerical integration from `scikit-learn`.

3.3 Measuring Locality L

The locality of the perturbed samples around the original sample is measured with two metrics: the ℓ_2 distance and the structural similarity index (SSIM) [49]. *Note that the second measure is specific for the image domain. One might use any application-specific measures of locality for the domain at hand.*

3.4 Measuring Reasonability ⓡ

We assess the reasonability of the generated explanations by comparing the relevant regions identified by the explanations with ground truth annotation masks from the CelebAMask-HQ dataset [24]. Therefore, we first scale the explanations to the $[0, 1]$ interval. Then we transform each 0-to-1-scaled explanation $\mathbf{r}$ into a binary mask of relevant and irrelevant pixels based on a threshold τ via $\mathbf{r}_{bin}^{\tau} := \mathbf{r} > \tau$. Based on the binary mask $\mathbf{r}_{bin}^{\tau}$ and the binary annotation mask $\mathbf{a}$ we define the intersection size as $IS^{\tau} := ||\mathbf{r}_{bin}^{\tau} \wedge \mathbf{a}||_1$ and construct three metrics:

- **Intersection over Union.** First, we measure the Intersection over Union as $IoU^{\tau} := \frac{IS^{\tau}}{||\mathbf{r}_{bin}^{\tau} \vee \mathbf{a}||_1}$, and the area under the curve as $\overline{IoU} := \int_0^1 IoU^{\tau} d\tau$.
- **Explanation Mask Recall.** Next, we compute the ratio of annotation pixels covered with relevant pixels and denote this metric as explanation mask recall and define it as $EMR^{\tau} := \frac{IS^{d}\tau}{||\mathbf{a}||_1}$ and $\overline{EMR} := \int_0^1 EMR^{\tau} d\tau$.
- **Explanation Mask Precision.** Lastly, we measure the explanation mask precision as $EMP^{\tau} := \frac{IS^{\tau}}{||\mathbf{r}_{bin}^{\tau}||_1}$, and $\overline{EMP}$ analog as the area under the curve.

3.5 Measuring Fidelity ⓕ

We assess the fidelity via the descriptive accuracy [50], originally termed as pixel flipping [4], and later as the deletion/insertion game [32] or very recently as most-influential first (MIF) [5]. In this work, we use the terms deletion and insertion game. In the deletion game we start with the original image and "remove" pixels in the order of descending importance scores in the explanation. In the insertion game, on the other hand, we start with a baseline image and add pixels from the original image in the same order. When multiple pixels share the same importance score, their deletion or insertion order is determined randomly. As LIME produces homogeneous importance scores within one segment this happens regularly. To compensate for this randomness we evaluate each explanation 10 times. At each insertion or deletion step the soft-label of the original prediction is recorded, leading to *deletion* and *insertion* graphs, respectively. Based on these graphs we calculate the bounded area under curve (AUC) at 50 % flipped pixels as $AUC_{del}^{50\%}$ and $AUC_{ins}^{50\%}$, respectively. For the calculation we apply the trapezoidal rule for numerical integration from `scikit-learn` and flip 1 pixel per step. Because of the computational effort involved in the in-painting baseline we flip 128 pixels at a time here.

3.6 Measuring Stability ⓢ

The stability of explanations assesses how consistent the explanations are in consecutive runs. Therefore, $\{\mathbf{r}_1, \mathbf{r}_2, \ldots, \mathbf{r}_m\}$ represents a set of m explanations extracted for a given sample. We compute the mean explanation, denoted as $\bar{\mathbf{r}}$ and then measure the mean distance from $\bar{\mathbf{r}}$:

$$\text{Stability} = \frac{1}{n}\sum_{i=1}^{n} D_{\mathcal{E}}(\mathbf{r}_i, \bar{\mathbf{r}}), \tag{2}$$

where $D_{\mathcal{E}}(\mathbf{r}_i, \bar{\mathbf{r}})$ is a distance metric in the explanation space, e.g., in our experiments it is the ℓ_2-distance.

4 Evaluation

In this section, we first present our experimental setup in Sect. 4.1. The following subsections contain our results for the sampler property distribution alignment (Sect. 4.2) and the diversity-locality trade-off (Sect. 4.3). Thereafter follow the explanation quality metrics reasonablility (Sect. 4.4), fidelity (Sect. 4.5), and stability (Sect. 4.6).

4.1 Experimental Setup

We evaluated all samplers on the CelebA dataset [26], which contains portrait images of celebrities. For the reasonability metric, we used the CelebAMask-HQ dataset [24], which provides annotation masks for a subset of CelebA. We focus on hair color classification and reduce the classes to *blond*, *black*, *gray*, *brown*, and *bald*, and ignoring samples with ambiguous classification[1] [51].

Classification Models. We generate explanations for a ResNet18 [14] classifier trained to predict the hair color by means of the `torchvision` library. The images are scaled to 64×64 pixel before training with a batch size of 4,096 and a learning rate of 0.001 for 12 epochs. The model achieves 91 % validation accuracy which is sufficient for our purpose of evaluating an explanation method.

Parametrization of LIME. We configure the LIME algorithm according to its original implementation, using a cosine similarity kernel with a width of 0.25, and $n = 800$ perturbations per sample. The segmentation is generated with simple linear iterative clustering (SLIC) [1] set to 65 segments, which is suitable for 64 × 64 images.

Generative Models. We use the pretrained Generative FLOW (GLOW) model by Dombrowski et al. [10], the implementation from the `diffusers` library, and the author's public GitHub repository. In addition, we train a DDIM model using the code provided by the `diffusers` library on the CelebA training data.

---

[1] Some samples in the CelebA dataset have two hair colors assigned. These samples are ignored in our study.

Table 1. Quantitative results of neural samplers (top) and naive samplers (bottom), evaluated on their distribution alignment (DA), diversity (D), and locality (L). Results are presented as the mean and standard deviations, where applicable.

Sampler	DA		D		L	
	D_M ($\downarrow$)	Sil. ($\uparrow$)	E_{hard} ($\uparrow$)	E_{soft} ($\uparrow$)	ℓ_2 ($\downarrow$)	SSIM ($\uparrow$)
Flow	**398.32**	0.013	1.07±0.43	2.73±0.64	17.13±4.38	0.655±0.064
Diffusion	415.33	**0.011**	**1.48**±0.34	2.56±0.56	17.88±4.13	0.552±0.091
In-painting	418.80	0.031	1.08±0.48	2.55±0.74	19.14±5.39	0.578±0.081
Black-Out	717.17	0.578	0.44±0.32	1.21±0.92	39.36±9.58	0.402±0.084
Gray-Out	611.63	0.216	1.20±0.52	**2.95**±0.87	22.40±4.29	0.564±0.071
Mean	423.31	0.019	0.42±0.48	1.92±1.49	**6.80**±1.81	**0.792**±0.048
Blur	496.39	0.055	0.89±0.53	2.61±1.06	13.02±3.00	0.644±0.065

Experiment Design. We analyze explanations for the winning class on 5,000 randomly selected samples from the CelebA dataset. Optimization techniques, such as reduced floating-point precision and graph compilation, minimize the computational overhead without compromising performance. The hyperparameters of all components of our work are displayed in Appendix B. If not mentioned differently, the number of perturbation n is 800 per sample and 5,000 randomly selected validation samples are evaluated due to resource restrictions. For some evaluations, the one or the other number is lowered because of computational restrictions. We always mention such limitations in the respective paragraph.

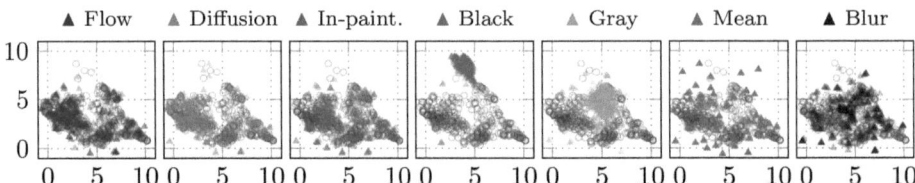

Fig. 4. *Distribution Alignment* (DA). The 2D UMAP projections of 500 randomly selected perturbed samples and 500 training samples (gray circles) based on their feature embeddings.

4.2 Distribution Alignment (DA)

At the core of this work we aim to generate i.d. perturbed samples to overcome the o.o.d. problem in LIME. Here, we evaluate the distributional alignment of the perturbed samples via the Mahalanobis uncertainty scores [25] of 20 perturbed samples for each selected validation samples. We compare the scores to other unperturbed validation samples and two sets of clearly o.o.d. samples: First CIFAR-10 images [22] and, second, Gaussian noise. In addition, we visualize the feature space using UMAP [30] to gain qualitative insights.

According to our results in Table 1 the neural samplers achieve uncertainty scores on par with the validation samples, which reach 413. The flow sampler performs best (398), followed closely by the diffusion sampler (415) and the in-painting sampler (418). The perturbations of all three can be considered i.d. according to these scores. Expectedly, the mean sampler and blur sampler exhibit slightly worse but comparable performance with 423 and 496, respectively. The black-out sampler and the gray-out sampler, in turn, generate o.o.d. samples and achieve scores of 717 and 611, respectively. Even the clearly o.o.d. CIFAR-10 images achieve an score of 640. The Gaussian noise sets the referenz with 1,388.

In Fig. 4, we provide a 2D UMAP projection of the embedded perturbed samples. The figure, supports our above finding visually. The flow sampler, the diffusion sampler, and the in-painting sampler exhibit a close overlap with the validation samples while the mean sampler and blur sampler show a slight deviation only. The black-out sampler shows a clear separation, indicating a strong o.o.d. behavior. Similarly, the gray-out sampler exhibits a vastly different spread, being more clustered. These results confirm the ability of neural samplers to produce in-distribution perturbed samples, while traditional samplers induce a clear out-of-distribution behavior.

4.3 Diversity D and Locality L

Robust, meaningful, and local explanations require a careful balance between diversity and locality of the perturbed samples. Our evaluation reveals that neural samplers generally achieve this balance better than traditional samplers. The diffusion sampler achieves the highest diversity score of 1.48. This superior performance can be attributed to the ability to induce *different* class changes. Traditional samplers may also induce class changes, but in shattered regions of the decision surface or toward specific classes (cf. next paragraph). The in-painting sampler exhibits weaker diversity due to its focus on localized perturbations, hindering consistent full-input changes. Perturbations on the basis of segments may not expose interactions between segments, e.g., the probability of changing all hair segments at once is rather low. Among the traditional samplers, the gray-out sampler performs best. The black-out sampler performs poorly in both, the locality and the diversity property.

In Fig. 5, we depict the diversity-locality trade-off. The arrows represent the desired direction. While the mean samplers consistently excels in one property, it also fails in the other one. Neural samplers make a good trade-off together with the in-painting, blur, and gray-out sampler. The black-out sampler is worst.

Analysis of the Label Distributions. We analyze the label distribution induced by the perturbed samples and compare them to the label distribution of

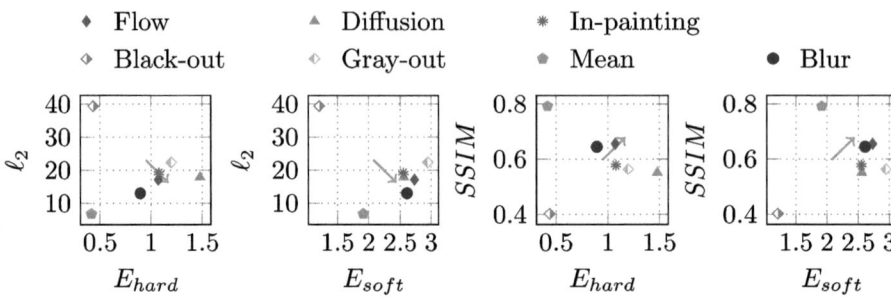

Fig. 5. The trade-offs between the diversity D and the locality L . The gray arrows indicate the desired direction.

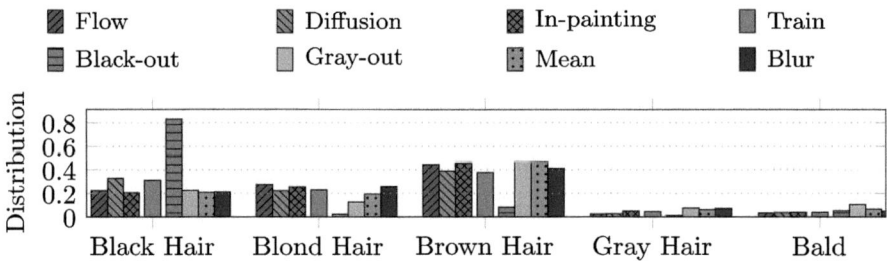

Fig. 6. The hard-label distributions of the perturbed samples as a proxy for diversity D . The black-out sampler shows a strong bias toward black hair. Neural samplers are depicted in left chunk, the training data in the middle, and naive samplers on the right.

the training data (cf. Fig. 6). In contrast to diversity, which examines variability in the perturbed samples at the individual instance level, we take a global perspective here by evaluating a random subset of all perturbed samples, uncovering broader patterns. Interestingly, the black-out sampler, in fact, has a bias toward the *black hair* class. This bias limits the representational effectiveness of the perturbations, as it skews them toward a specific label. Such biases can hinder a sampler's ability to provide meaningful explanations for certain classes, because it cannot generate sufficiently diverse or representative perturbed samples for all classes. This observation aligns with and explains the diversity and locality results of the black-out sampler.

4.4 Reasonability R

We assess the reasonability of our method POMELO on the basis of annotation masks from the CelebAMask-HQ dataset. The overlap between these human-provided annotations and the explanations indicates how well the explanations

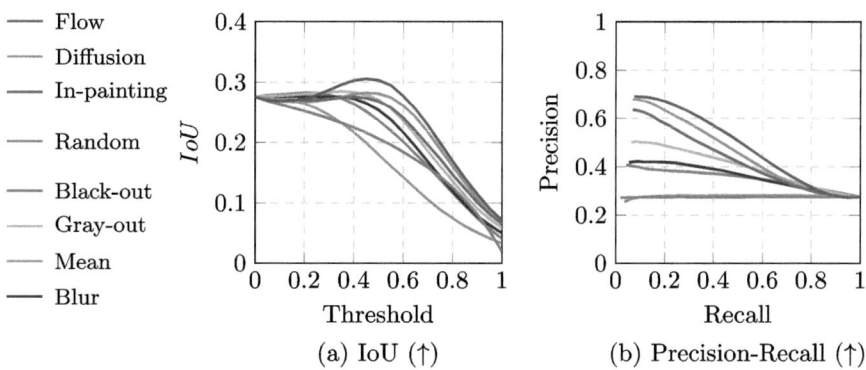

Fig. 7. Reasonability ⓡ results for all samplers and a baseline of random explanations. Find the intersection-over-union curve on the left (a), and the precision-recall curve on the right (b).

Table 2. Quantitative results of the explanation methods for properties reasonability ⓡ, stability ⓢ, and fidelity ⓕ. The fidelity is measured as the AUC with the in-painting replacement strategy for 50% replaced pixels. Results are presented as the mean with standard deviations, where applicable.

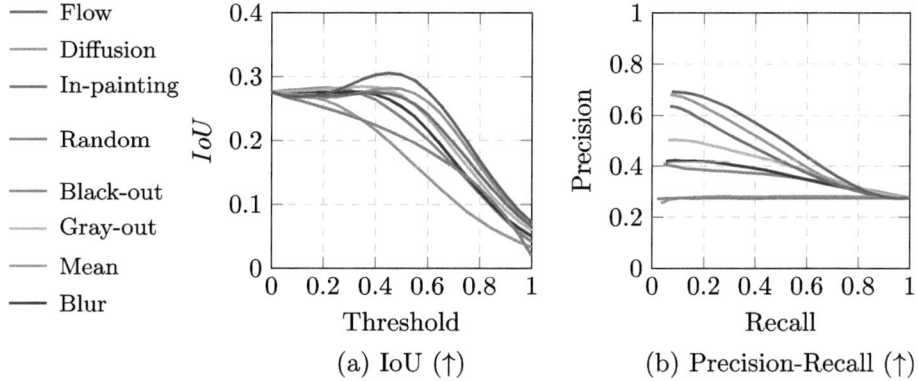

align with the human understanding of the problem (Table 2). We measure this overlap with three metrics and display the results in Fig. 7. Explanations based on neural samplers, in particular based on the flow sampler, outperform traditional LIME explanations in all three metrics, indicating a stronger alignment with the human-provided masks. In particular, for the intersection over union and the precision POMELO excels.

This performance might stem from the fact that neural samplers modify dominant features, such as hair color, eye color, or facial structure, and that reasonable correlations dominate the training data. Hence, the perturbations are often consistent with the human-ontological understanding of the data.

Reasonability does not assess, however, how well the explanations capture a model's actual decision process (cf. Fidelity). For instance, a model might base its decisions on a-typical patterns and artifacts that are not captured by human-defined ontology but still are present in the training data, e.g., a copyright tag on many images of horses [3]. By training the neural sampler on the same training data, such patterns would also be captured and be highlighted at their spatial position. Based on the high alignment with the annotation masks and through the manual investigation of various explanation, we assume that no such dominate spurious correlations are present in CelebA.

To make this more clear; If every blond celebrity would have blue eyes, the neural sampler would only perturb both features together. But, the difference between the perturbed samples and the original sample would then also be at the spatial position of the eyes and the hair. Thus, both areas would be hightlighted as relevant. Our method therefore serves as a helpful debugging tool to find such spurios correlations with spatial constraints.

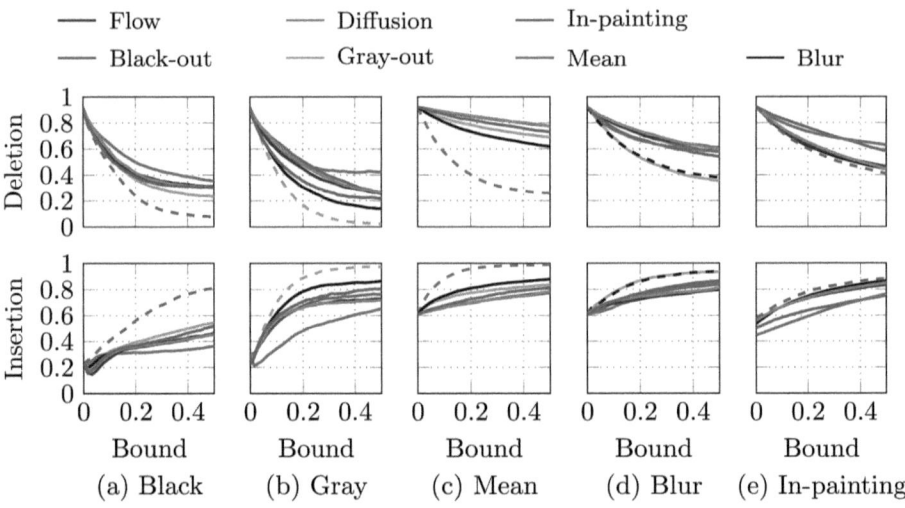

Fig. 8. Results for the deletion game (↓) in the top row and the insertion game (↑) in the bottom row. The fidelity F depends on the replacement strategy in the sense that samplers perform best when paired with their corresponding replacement strategy, highlighted as dashed lines. In the insertion game with an in-painting replacement strategy the starting point is uncertain as almost the whole image is generated by the in-painter.

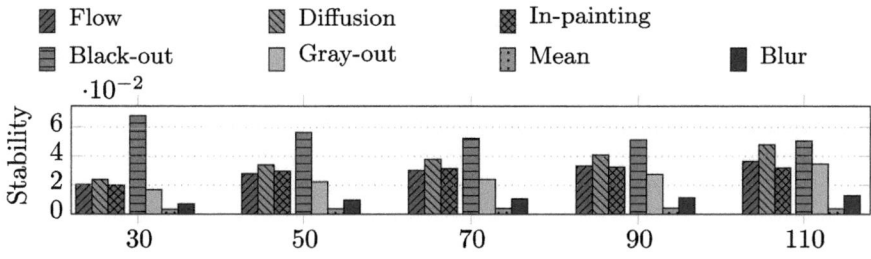

Fig. 9. The stability ⓢ (↓) evaluated for a varying number of segments between 30 and 110, with neural samplers on the left and naive samplers on the right.

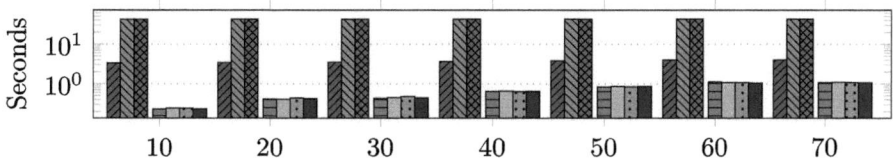

Fig. 10. The computational costs ⓒ (↓) for generating 1,000 samples in seconds of wall time across a varying amount of segments between 10 and 70. Neural samplers are in the left and naive samplers in the right chunk.

4.5 Fidelity ⒡

With fidelity we measure how well the explanation method captures the model's decision process, independently from the human-understanding of the problem. Therefore, we evaluate the descriptive accuracy in the deletion and insertion game for different base images. Concretely, our base images are black, gray, the segment-wise mean of the original image, and the blurred original image (Fig. 10). In addition, we use the in-painting sampler to fill in the deleted parts for the image based on the remaining information, as already suggested by related work [5].

Figure 8 depicts the deletion graph (top) and the insertion graph (bottom) for the respective base images from left to right. In the deletion game a lower curve represents a better explanation quality, while in the insertion game a higher curve represents a better explanation quality. Not surprisingly, the perturbation strategies perform best when paired with their corresponding replacement strategies. This outcome is likely because fidelity aligns directly with the samplers' objectives: Capturing the model's behavior when pixels are replaced with the respective base. The fidelity evaluation effectively tests the explanations with the same perturbations used in their creation, and consequently inherently favors the corresponding perturbation strategy.

Due to these limitations of the metric we are hesitate to draw definitive conclusions from it (Fig. 11). Instead, we consider our findings as a strong indication of the need for different fidelity metrics. These novel metric should more appropriately assess the performance of various explanation strategies without being biased toward certain replacement strategies. We argue that the in-painting replacement strategy is in line with our methodology and captures interactions between feature, while the other strategies do not. Interactions are the reasons why we use complex black-box models in the first place and should therefore definetely be considered in the explanation method as well.

4.6 Stability Ⓢ

A stable explanation method facilitates trust in the generated explanations. Neural samplers can produce a wide variety of perturbed samples, potentially reducing the stability of explanations. To investigate this, we assess the stability across 80 test sample, each with 5 explanations generated using $n = 800$ perturbations. We conduct this analysis across three segmentation counts (30, 70, and 110 segments) and add randomly generated explanations as a baseline.

Figure 9 presents the results of our stability study. All samplers outperform the random baseline by $\sim$1.5 orders of magnitude. The mean sampler and the blur sampler dominate the field and generate $\sim$1, respectively $\sim$0.5 orders of magnitude more stable explanation than the other 5 samplers. The commonly used black-out sampler generates the most instable explanations. Also, while subtle, we observe a decrease in stability with an increasing number of segments. In summary, neural sampling achieves competitive stability compared to traditional approaches within the evaluated context.

4.7 Computational Cost Ⓒ

Here, we compare the feasibility of generative perturbation strategies based on the mean wall time for generating 1,000 perturbed samples. The evaluation is conducted on a compute node with 24 CPU cores (AMD Ryzen 9 5900X) and a single NVIDIA RTX 3090 Ti GPU. LIME's default perturbations leverage multi-threading on all CPU cores, and neural samplers utilize GPU acceleration.

Not surprisingly, neural sampler require more time. However, the flow sampler demonstrated acceptable performance by taking around 2.5× longer (5 seconds versus 2 seconds). The DDIM-based strategy, in turn, takes around 35 seconds. Fortunately, the runtime of neural samplers remains unaffected by the number of segments used during the perturbation process, while the runtime of naive sampler increases with the number of segments. This makes POMELO a feasible solution for large and very segmented input domains. In addition, this property offers a practical benefit: It allows us to generate explanations with different segmentations using the same set of generatively-perturbed samples.

5 Conclusion

We address a major limitation of LIME: The used samplers are restricted to per-segment perturbations, resulting in out-of-distribution (o.o.d.) inputs, and unavoidably, in misleading explanations. Our extension POMELO uses *full-input* perturbations instead, allowing to capture large, complex, or even distributed correlations. We show that our samplers based on normalizing flows and denoising diffusion implicit models (DDIMs) exhibit a larger overlap with human-provided annotation masks. Our method's ability to utilize full-input, and in-distribution (i.d.) perturbations benefits explanation quality decisively.

Acknowledgment. We thank Christopher Anders for his feedback on our work and Klaus-Robert Müller for his support during the project. The authors gratefully acknowledge funding from the Helmholtz Association (HGF) within the topic "46.23 Engineering Secure Systems", and by the state of Baden-Württemberg through bwHPC.

A Details on the DDIM-Based Sampler

The reverse process of a DDIM is given by:

$$x_{t-1} = \sqrt{\alpha_{t-1}} \left(\frac{x_t - \sqrt{1-\alpha_t}\epsilon_\theta(x_t,t)}{\sqrt{\alpha_t}} \right) + \sqrt{1-\alpha_t-\sigma_t^2}\epsilon_\theta(x_t,t) + \sigma_t\epsilon_t \quad (3)$$

where σ_t controls the noise added in the reverse process, α_t represents the cumulative product of noise schedule coefficients, and $\epsilon_\theta(x_t,t)$ is the predicted noise at timestep t [44]. The noise schedule $\sigma_t(\eta)$ is defined as:

$$\sigma_t(\eta) = \eta \sqrt{\frac{1-\alpha_{t-1}}{1-\alpha_t}} \sqrt{1-\frac{\alpha_t}{\alpha_{t-1}}} \quad (4)$$

where $\eta = 1$ results in the DDIM reverse process equaling the DDPM reverse process, and $\eta = 0$ results in a deterministic reverse process.

Leveraging DDIM for Perturbation Generation. Assuming a deterministic reverse process ($\eta = 0$), the DDIM reverse process equation can be rearranged to derive the iterative definition of the forward process [7]:

$$\mathbf{x}_{t+1} = \sqrt{\alpha_{t+1}} \left(\frac{\mathbf{x}_t - \sqrt{1-\alpha_t}\epsilon_\theta(\mathbf{x}_t,t)}{\sqrt{\alpha_t}} \right) + \sqrt{1-\alpha_{t+1}}\epsilon_\theta(\mathbf{x}_t,t) \quad (5)$$

With many forward and reverse steps, this deterministic diffusion process can faithfully reconstruct $\mathbf{x}_0$ with minimal error [44]. To generate an in-distribution perturbation $\mathbf{x}'$ we first perform n forward-steps and collect the noisy intermediates $\tilde{\mathbf{x}}_i$ at each timestep. Next perform $m = n - i$ probabilistic ($\eta > 0$) reverse steps starting from the i-th intermediate. This probabilistic nature introduces

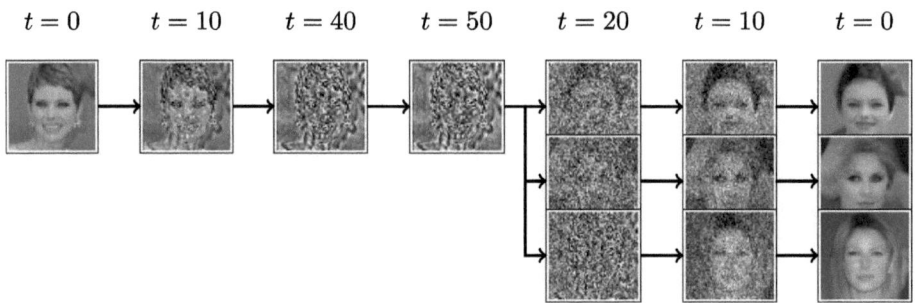

Fig. 11. Schematic of the proposed perturbation pipeline, which utilizes a deterministic forward process to generate noisy intermediates, followed by a probabilistic reverse process to introduce controlled randomness into the reconstruction.

randomness into the denoising process, which alters the trajectory at each reverse step, producing different perturbations even when starting from the same intermediate. In our experiments we always use $i = 0$, meaning we start the reverse process from the initial noisy intermediate.

B Hyperparameters

In Table 3, we present the hyperparameters we use in our experiment.

While an extensive grid search was computationally infeasible, we performed a manual search to find the best hyperparameters for each sampler. We generated perturbed samples for different samples with different values for the listed hyperparameters and selected the best in terms of locality and diversity by inspecting the resulting perturbed samples.

Table 3. Hyperparameter settings for our experiments.

Method	Hyperparameters
LIME	Kernel width = 0.25, Number of perturbations = 800
SLIC	Number of segments = 35, Compactness = 10
Traditional Samplers	Segment turn off rate = 0.5
Flow Sampler	$\mu = 0.5$, $\sigma = 0.3$
Diffusion Sampler	$\eta = 0.4$, $n = 50$, $i = 0$, $m = 50$
Inpainting	$\eta = 0.8$, $n = 50$, $i = 0$, $m = 50$, Segment turn off rate = 0.75

C Examples

In Fig. 12, we present examples of perturbed samples for the three samplers.

FlowSampler:
Lower quality perturbations, fast inference

DiffusionSampler:
High-quality perturbations, slow inference

InpaintingSampler:
High-quality *local* perturbations, slow.

Fig. 12. In-distribution perturbations generated using the three proposed in-distribution sampling strategies.

D Additional Reasonability Results

In addition to the *IoU* and the precision-recall plots in Sect. 4.4, we present the plots for the explanation mask recall and the explanation mask precision in Fig. 13. Generative samplers show au par results with the other baselines in the precision measure. In the recall measure they outperform traditional samplers.

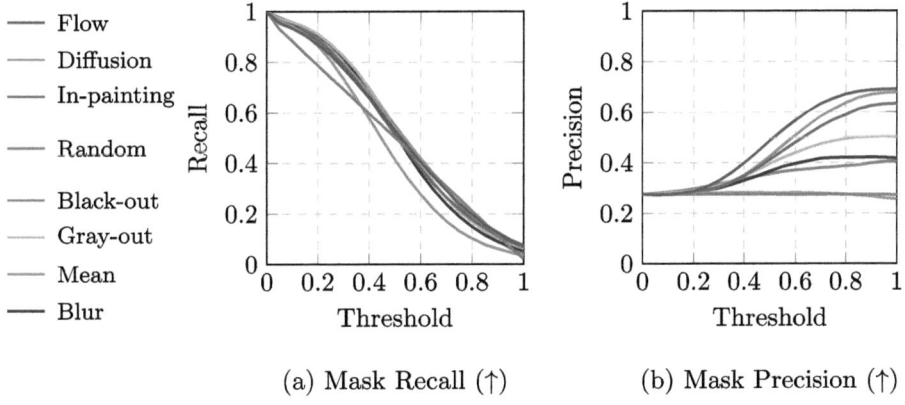

(a) Mask Recall (↑)   (b) Mask Precision (↑)

Fig. 13. Additional results of the explanation mask recall and precision.

References

1. Achanta, R., Shaji, A., Smith, K., Lucchi, A., Fua, P., Süsstrunk, S.: SLIC superpixels compared to state-of-the-art superpixel methods. IEEE Trans. Pattern Anal. Mach. Intell. **34**(11), 2274–2282 (2012)
2. Agarwal, C., Nguyen, A.: Explaining image classifiers by removing input features using generative models. In: Computer Vision - ACCV 2020 - 15th Asian Conference on Computer Vision, Kyoto, Japan, November 30 - December 4, 2020,

Revised Selected Papers, Part VI, Lecture Notes in Computer Science, vol. 12627, pp. 101–118 (2020)
3. Anders, C.J., Weber, L., Neumann, D., Samek, W., Müller, K.R., Lapuschkin, S.: Finding and removing clever Hans: using explanation methods to debug and improve deep models. Info. Fusion **77**, 261–295 (2022)
4. Bach, S., Binder, A., Montavon, G., Klauschen, F., Müller, K.R., Samek, W.: On pixel-wise explanations for non-linear classifier decisions by Layer-Wise Relevance Propagation. PLOS ONE **77**, 46 (2015)
5. Bluecher, S., Vielhaben, J., Strodthoff, N.: Decoupling pixel flipping and occlusion strategy for consistent XAI benchmarks. Trans. Mach .Learn. Res. **2024** (2024)
6. Chang, C.H., Creager, E., Goldenberg, A., Duvenaud, D.: Explaining image classifiers by counterfactual generation. In: Proc. of the International Conference on Learning Representations (ICLR) (2019)
7. Dhariwal, P., Nichol, A.: Diffusion Models Beat GANs on Image Synthesis (2021)
8. Dinh, L., Krueger, D., Bengio, Y.: NICE: Non-linear independent components estimation. In: Proc. of the International Conference on Learning Representations (ICLR) (2015)
9. Dinh, L., Sohl-Dickstein, J., Bengio, S.: Density estimation using Real NVP. In: Proc. of the International Conference on Learning Representations (ICLR) (2017)
10. Dombrowski, A.K., Gerken, J.E., Müller, K.R., Kessel, P.: Diffeomorphic counterfactuals with generative models. IEEE Trans. Pattern Anal. Mach. Intell. **46**(5), 3257–3274 (2024)
11. Fong, R., Vedaldi, A.: Interpretable explanations of black boxes by meaningful perturbation. In: Proc. of the IEEE/CVF International Conference on Computer Vision (ICCV), pp. 3449–3457 (2017)
12. Goyal, Y., Feder, A., Shalit, U., Kim, B.: Explaining Classifiers with Causal Concept Effect (CaCE). CoRR **abs/1907.07165** (2020)
13. Guo, W., Mu, D., Xu, J., Su, P., Wang, G., Xing, X.: LEMNA: Explaining deep learning based security applications. In: Proc. of the ACM Conference on Computer and Communications Security (CCS), pp. 364–379 (2018)
14. He, K., Zhang, X., Ren, S., Sun, J.: Deep residual learning for image recognition. In: Proc. of the IEEE Conference on Computer Vision and Pattern Recognition (CVPR), pp. 770–778 (2016)
15. Hegde, A., Noppel, M., Wressnegger, C.: Model-manipulation attacks against black-box explanations. In: Proc. of the Annual Computer Security Applications Conference (ACSAC) (2024)
16. Hendrycks, D., Dietterich, T.G.: Benchmarking neural network robustness to common corruptions and perturbations. In: Proc. of the International Conference on Learning Representations (ICLR) (2019)
17. Hendrycks, D., Mu, N., Cubuk, E.D., Zoph, B., Gilmer, J., Lakshminarayanan, B.: AugMix: a simple data processing method to improve robustness and uncertainty. In: Proc. of the International Conference on Learning Representations (ICLR) (2020)
18. Ho, J., Jain, A., Abbeel, P.: Denoising diffusion probabilistic models. In: Proc. of the Annual Conference on Neural Information Processing Systems (NeurIPS) (2020)
19. Holzinger, A., Saranti, A., Molnar, C., Biecek, P., Samek, W.: Explainable AI methods - a brief overview. In: Proc. of the International Workshop, beyond Explainable AI (xxAI), Lecture Notes in Computer Science, vol. 13200, pp. 13–38 (2020)

20. Kim, B., et al.: Interpretability beyond feature attribution: quantitative testing with concept activation vectors (TCAV). In: Proc. of the International Conference on Machine Learning (ICML), Proceedings of Machine Learning Research, vol. 80, pp. 2673–2682 (2018)
21. Kingma, D.P., Dhariwal, P.: Glow: generative flow with invertible 1×1 convolutions. In: Proc. of the Annual Conference on Neural Information Processing Systems (NeurIPS), pp. 10236–10245 (2018)
22. Krizhevsky, A., et al.: Learning multiple layers of features from tiny images. Citeseer (2009)
23. Lapuschkin, S., Wäldchen, S., Binder, A., Montavon, G., Samek, W., Müller, K.R.: Unmasking clever Hans predictors and assessing what machines really learn. Nat. Commun. **10**(1), 1096 (2019)
24. Lee, C.H., Liu, Z., Wu, L., Luo, P.: MaskGAN: towards diverse and interactive facial image manipulation. In: Proc. of the IEEE Conference on Computer Vision and Pattern Recognition (CVPR), pp. 5548–5557 (2020)
25. Lee, K., Lee, H., Lee, J., Shin: A simple unified framework for detecting out-of-distribution samples and adversarial attacks (2018)
26. Liu, Z., Luo, P., Wang, X., Tang, X.: Deep learning face attributes in the wild. In: Proc. of the IEEE/CVF International Conference on Computer Vision (ICCV) (2015)
27. Lugmayr, A., Danelljan, M., Romero, A., Yu, F., Timofte, R., Gool, L.V.: RePaint: inpainting using denoising diffusion probabilistic models. In: Proc. of the IEEE Conference on Computer Vision and Pattern Recognition (CVPR), pp. 11451–11461 (2022)
28. Lundberg, S.M., Lee, S.I.: A unified approach to interpreting model predictions. In: Proc. of the Annual Conference on Neural Information Processing Systems (NIPS), p. 10 (2017)
29. Madry, A., Makelov, A., Schmidt, L., Tsipras, D., Vladu, A.: Towards deep learning models resistant to adversarial attacks. In: Proc. of the International Conference on Learning Representations (ICLR) (2018)
30. McInnes, L., Healy, J., Saul, N., Großberger, L.: UMAP: uniform manifold approximation and projection. J. Open Source Softw. **3**(29), 861 (2018)
31. Nicoli, K.A., Nakajima, S., Strodthoff, N., Samek, W., Müller, K.R., Kessel, P.: Asymptotically unbiased estimation of physical observables with neural samplers. Phys. Rev. E: Stat. Phys., Plasmas, Fluids **101**(2), 023304 (2020)
32. Petsiuk, V., Das, A., Saenko, K.: RISE: Randomized input sampling for explanation of black-box models. CoRR **abs/1806.07421** (2018)
33. Qiu, L., et al.: Generating perturbation-based explanations with robustness to out-of-distribution data. In: Proc. of the International World Wide Web Conference (WWW), pp. 3594–3605 (2022)
34. Rezende, D.J., Mohamed, S.: Variational inference with normalizing flows. In: Proc. of the International Conference on Machine Learning (ICML), JMLR Workshop and Conference Proceedings, vol. 37, pp. 1530–1538 (2015)
35. Ribeiro, M.T., Singh, S., Guestrin, C.: "Why Should I Trust You?": explaining the predictions of any classifier. In: Proc. of the ACM SIGKDD International Conference on Knowledge Discovery and Data Mining (KDD) (2016)
36. Rieger, L., Singh, C., Murdoch, W.J., Yu, B.: Interpretations are useful: penalizing explanations to align neural networks with prior knowledge. In: Proc. of the International Conference on Machine Learning (ICML), vol. 119 (2020)
37. Rousseeuw, P.J.: Silhouettes: a graphical aid to the interpretation and validation of cluster analysis. J. Comput. Appl. Math. **20**, 53–65 (1987)

38. Saito, S., Chua, E., Capel, N., Hu, R.: Improving LIME robustness with smarter locality sampling. CoRR **abs/2006.12302** (2020)
39. Schockaert, C., Macher, V., Schmitz, A.: VAE-LIME: deep generative model based approach for local data-driven model interpretability applied to the ironmaking industry. CoRR **abs/2007.10256** (2020)
40. Selvaraju, R.R., Cogswell, M., Das, A., Vedantam, R., Parikh, D., Batra, D.: Grad-CAM: visual explanations from deep networks via gradient-based localization. Int. J. Comput. Vision **128**(2), 336–359 (2020)
41. Simonyan, K., Vedaldi, A., Zisserman, A.: Deep inside convolutional networks: visualising image classification models and saliency maps. In: Proc. of the International Conference on Learning Representations (ICLR) Workshop Track Proceedings (2014)
42. Slack, D., Hilgard, S., Jia, E., Singh, S., Lakkaraju, H.: Fooling LIME and SHAP: adversarial attacks on post hoc explanation methods. In: Proc. of the AAAI/ACM Conference AI, Ethics, and Society (AIES), pp. 180–186 (2020)
43. Sohl-Dickstein, J., Weiss, E.A., Maheswaranathan, N., Ganguli, S.: Deep unsupervised learning using nonequilibrium thermodynamics. In: Proc. of the International Conference on Machine Learning (ICML), pp. 2256–2265 (2015)
44. Song, J., Meng, C., Ermon, S.: Denoising diffusion implicit models. In: Proc. of the International Conference on Learning Representations (ICLR) (2021)
45. Song, Y., Ermon, S.: Generative modeling by estimating gradients of the data distribution. In: Proc. of the Annual Conference on Neural Information Processing Systems (NeurIPS) (2019)
46. Sundararajan, M., Taly, A., Yan, Q.: Axiomatic attribution for deep networks. CoRR **abs/1703.01365** (2017)
47. Szegedy, C., et al.: Intriguing properties of neural networks. In: Proc. of the International Conference on Learning Representations (ICLR) (2014)
48. Tritscher, J., Lissmann, P., Wolf, M., Krause, A., Hotho, A., Schlör, D.: Generative inpainting for shapley-value-based anomaly explanation. In: Proc. of the World Conference on eXplainable Artificial Intelligence (XAI), Communications in Computer and Information Science, vol. 2153, pp. 230–243 (2024)
49. Wang, Z., Bovik, A., Sheikh, H., Simoncelli, E.: Image quality assessment: from error visibility to structural similarity. Proc. of the IEEE Trans. Image Process. **13**(4), 600–612 (2004)
50. Warnecke, A., Arp, D., Wressnegger, C., Rieck, K.: Evaluating explanation methods for deep learning in security. In: Proc. of the IEEE European Symposium on Security and Privacy (EuroS&P) (2020)
51. Wu, H., Bezold, G., Günther, M., Boult, T.E., King, M.C., Bowyer, K.W.: Consistency and accuracy of CelebA attribute values. In: Proc. of the IEEE Conference on Computer Vision and Pattern Recognition (CVPR), pp. 3258–3266 (2023)
52. Xu, L., Skoularidou, M., Cuesta-Infante, A., Veeramachaneni, K.: Modeling tabular data using conditional GAN. In: Advances in Neural Information Processing Systems 32: Annual Conference on Neural Information Processing Systems 2019, NeurIPS 2019, December 8-14, 2019, Vancouver, BC, Canada, pp. 7333–7343 (2019)
53. Ying, R., Bourgeois, D., You, J., Zitnik, M., Leskovec, J.: GNNExplainer: generating explanations for graph neural networks. In: Proc. of the Annual Conference on Neural Information Processing Systems (NeurIPS), pp. 9240–9251 (2019)

Open Access This chapter is licensed under the terms of the Creative Commons Attribution 4.0 International License (http://creativecommons.org/licenses/by/4.0/), which permits use, sharing, adaptation, distribution and reproduction in any medium or format, as long as you give appropriate credit to the original author(s) and the source, provide a link to the Creative Commons license and indicate if changes were made.

The images or other third party material in this chapter are included in the chapter's Creative Commons license, unless indicated otherwise in a credit line to the material. If material is not included in the chapter's Creative Commons license and your intended use is not permitted by statutory regulation or exceeds the permitted use, you will need to obtain permission directly from the copyright holder.

Novel Post-hoc and Ante-hoc XAI Approaches

Explain to Gain: Introspective Reinforcement Learning for Enhanced Performance

Santiago Quintana-Amate[1(✉)], Delaney Stevens[1], Varniethan Ketheeswaran[1,2], Patrick Capaldo[1], Dylan Sheldon[1,3], and Mark Hall[1]

[1] Airbus AI Research, Filton, UK
santiago.quintana-amate@airbus.com
[2] University of Bath, Bath, UK
[3] University of Gloucestershire, Cheltenham, UK

Abstract. This article presents a new method for leveraging explainable reinforcement learning (XRL) knowledge to enhance the performance of reinforcement learning (RL) agents. Although current XRL approaches are mainly focused on improving interpretability and user trust by providing explanations for agent actions, their ability to guide and optimise RL agent's training is under-explored. To address this gap, we extend an existing introspective analysis framework by integrating XRL metrics directly into the training pipelines of model-free RL algorithms. This integration allows dynamic adjustments of algorithm-specific parameters based on real-time feedback from XRL metrics. The proposed methodology is validated across diverse OpenAI Gym environments (CartPole and Taxi). By evaluating both on-policy and off-policy approaches, we demonstrate that incorporating XRL insights leads to significant improvements in agent performance. The analysis of the results highlights the benefits regarding enhanced explainability and optimised decision-making. This work contributes in XRL research area by aligning interpretability with actionable performance gains, paving the way for more reliable and transparent RL systems in complex, real-world applications.

Keywords: Explainable Reinforcement Learning (XRL) · Introspective Reinforcement Learning (IxDRL) · Explainability Metrics · Dynamic Algorithm Adjustment · Exploration-Exploitation Trade-off · Explainable autonomous agents

1 Introduction

Reinforcement learning (RL) is a process through which agents learn sequential decisions by interacting with their environment and trying to maximise cumulative rewards over time [1]. By maximising cumulative rewards, RL has achieved successes in applications from gaming, robotics, to control systems, with many of these successes exceeding human capabilities in making complicated decisions [2,3]. RL also has serious challenges to overcome, such as data inefficiency, computational expense, and the uninterpretable nature of its decisions. These limit its application in real-world problems where safety, reliability, and interpretability are crucial [4]. Explainability has become an important need for RL systems in this scenario to overcome the "black-box" nature of deep reinforcement learning (DRL) models. Traditional RL models are not particularly revealing about the decision-making process, and it is difficult for users to trust or debug these systems [4,5]. Explainable reinforcement learning (XRL) aims to bridge this gap by making the reasoning of an agent's actions and policies more understandable to humans. This explainability is required in applications in certain fields, such as healthcare or autonomous systems, where insight into the reason for decisions can prevent costly errors and increase the acceptance of AI [6]. XRL not only enhances end-user trust in the AI system but also facilitates the identification of undesired behavior in RL agents. By providing actionable insight into an agent's decision-making, XRL enables developers to tune models more effectively, and consequently, improve performance and reliability [4,7]. Most efforts in XRL involve providing explanations of an agent's behavior to understand why it took some actions or followed some policies. These explanations generally aim to enhance interpretability and user trust in RL systems. However, there is a noticeable lack of research that examines how to effectively utilise the knowledge provided by XRL methods to improve the performance and stability of RL agents. While XRL methods can diagnose issues such as low confidence, dangerous actions, or bad policy execution, little work has tried to turn such insights into actionable recommendations that enhance training processes or correct agent deficiencies [8,9]. Recent work has started to explore this possible dual role of XRL. For example, it has been suggested that explainability metrics in the form of confidence levels or risk estimates can be leveraged to detect flaws in an agent's decision-making process, guiding targeted intervention during training (e.g., environmental redesign or additional training in problematic states) [7]. Yet, integration of XRL insights into the RL training pipeline remains underdeveloped [10]. This gap limits the scope of XRL to not only interpret but also enhance agent performance and adaptability in different scenarios. To overcome this challenge this work extends the research in [7]. While the original paper focuses on the study of RL agent capability by metrics derived from agent data gathered during the training process, this work extends it by applying the insights gained through these metrics—e.g., agent confidence and riskiness—towards model improvement. Specifically, we integrate the insights into the training process of model-free RL algorithms like Proximal Policy Optimisation (PPO) and Deep Q-Networks (DQN). This approach bridges the gap in the original research where explainability was largely used for post-hoc analysis and not actively guiding training processes. By incorporating these insights into training loops, we are expecting to generate agents that not only have high performance but they are also interpretable and reliable.

This work makes the following contributions:

1. **Framework Development:** Presenting a methodology for integrating XRL metrics into the training pipelines of model-free RL algorithms.
2. **Performance Improvement:** We demonstrate via empirical validation how insights from explainability analyses can be used to refine policies and improve agent performance across different tasks.

By aligning explainability with performance enhancement, this paper contributes to the growing body of research advocating for interpretable and high-performing RL systems.

2 Background

2.1 Explainable RL Methods

Explainable reinforcement learning methods are divided into three categories as described in [11]: feature importance, policy-level and learning process. **Feature importance** methods aim to find influential input features that affect the agent's decision. [12] accomplishes this balancing *specificity* (impact on the chosen action) and *relevance* (avoiding features affecting different actions) through harmonic means of softmax-normalised Q-value alterations and Kullback–ŞLeibler (KL) divergence measures, which eliminate noise. Similarly, [13] leverages the advantage function for action-specific measurement of feature significance by perturbing it to emphasise correctly alignment of the paddle in *Breakout* or enemy aggregations in *Space Invaders*. While such techniques are revealing agent stratcgy, there are some research cautions given that the saliency maps are observationally correlated values and not cause-effect, which requires complementary techniques to determine the hypotheses [14]. **Policy-level algorithms** focus on compressing an agent's long-term policy to a shorter form to better understand the model. These processes translate complex policies into abstract objects such as Markov chains of abstraction states or graphs, with landmarks marking significant points of decision making and expected next-step transitions [15–17]. For instance, techniques like TLdR described in [18], identify chief "landmarks" (propositions required to achieve goals) and follow their interconnectedness to capture an agent's plan over time. Therefore these methods can build trust on RL methods by making policies more explainable to allow researchers to be in a better position to analyse and decide top-level decision-making patterns [11]. The aim of **learning process** methods is to explain how agents acquire knowledge over time by dissecting training steps, meaningful experiences, and developing decision patterns. Such methods use tools like contrastive explanations, "what-if" scenarios (counterfactual explanations), and introspective analysis logs to spot weaknesses, experiment with hypotheses, and track how policies change [11]. In this context, **contrastive explanations** attempt to account for why an agent prefers one action over another, by contrasting predicted outcomes or detailing alternative situations. An example of this is demonstrated in [19] where they offer contrastive explanations for RL agents by decomposing action preferences into human-understandable future feature predictions using generalised value functions (GVFs). While performing equally well as baseline RL agents, it needs to have pre-defined features and does not have means to correct policies based on insights. By contrast, **methods for counterfactual explanations** generate modified game states to check whether agent choices differ. This reveals broken logic, such as agents not taking into account their ship position in Space Invaders [20]. Lastly, the area of **introspective analysis** has progressed with substantial work by several researchers. [7] introduced the IxDRL framework that applies "Interestingness" dimensions to quantify RL agent competence and investigate competency-controlling conditions. Building upon this, [21] investigated global and local interestingness analysis through clustering techniques and SHAP values to identify task components affecting agent action. [22] generalised introspection XRL to episodic and non-episodic tasks and gained insight into agent decision-making with normalised Q-values. [23] applied XRL to robotics to highlight goal-directed behavior and human-understandable explanations, whereas [24] demonstrated introspection in non-episodic tasks by using Q-values to estimate the probability of success for better interpretability. Further, [25] advanced the field by introducing outcome-guided counterfactuals, enabling an increased understanding of agent strategies via generative latent spaces. Together, these are steps towards a better understanding of RL agents' strengths and weaknesses. However, there is still a lack of research offering a way to leverage these insights in order to improve model performance and robustness.

2.2 XRL for Model Improvement

A primary challenge to the use of explainability in boosting the performance of reinforcement learning (RL) models is the difficulty of taking action upon the insights obtained by explainable methods. A number of works have sought to tackle this challenge by leveraging explainability as a means of performance enhancement [26–28].

Reward shaping has been extensively researched as a means to improving performance by modifying the reward function to facilitate learning. Within this framework, [26] proposed a potential-based reward shaping method, which provides policy invariance and accelerates the learning process. In this context, [27,29] dynamically adjust potential-based rewards to enhance sample efficiency. Other methods emphasise leveraging external guidance or previous knowledge. The Lazy-MDP method [30] proposes a "lazy" version that postpones decision-making to a stationary policy in order to enable agents to concentrate on important decisions, enhancing interpretability and efficiency.

Integration of explainability approaches for improving learning process has been successively applied in the context of classical training of transformers. For instance, [31] proposed a hybrid transformer with domain adaptation using interpretability techniques to detect risky situations. A similar case is presented in [32] where authors present an Explain to Improve Streaming Learning (ESL) framework for transformers that provides explanations that enhance model performance during training.

Similarly, self-imitation learning gives agents the motivation to reproduce previously successful actions, in effect reinforcing the good behaviors and improving exploration. Externally guided methods, learning from pre-trained agents [28] or humans [33], have also shown promise in assisting RL agents to solve complex tasks by providing external guidance during learning. In addition, [34] explored the use of data obtained during the learning process. This study used generated scoring maps to guide the agent's focus during training, thus improving the policy quality and learning efficiency.

In spite of these developments, the majority of current approaches draw upon prior knowledge or external information instead of investigating exhaustively the underlying causes of an agent's policy breakdowns or enabling targeted improvements in its decision-making processes [35]. These kinds of aspects are needed for explaining the reasons behind an agent's behavior when executing its policy and for leading to targeted improvements in its decision-making processes. The purpose of this paper is to fill this gap by introducing a new methodology that builds upon the findings presented in [7] to allow agents to respond to their own limitations and uncertainties. This methodology is not just applied to improve performance, but also to create more transparent, robust, and adaptive reinforcement learning systems that excel at solving complex real-world problems.

3 Methods

This section outlines the methodological approach used in this research to boost the performance of reinforcement learning (RL) agents using explainable reinforcement learning (XRL) metrics. We begin with an overview of basic RL principles, including its mathematical foundations and the two main classes of algorithms: policy gradient methods and value-based methods (Sect. 3.1). We then explain the use of XRL metrics to provide meaningful insights along the training process, explaining their relevance, computational complexity, and contribution to final performance (Sect. 3.2).

Based on these fundamental ideas, this paper investigates the use of XRL metrics in solving the exploration-exploitation trade-off, a crucial problem in the field of RL. This goal is achieved by novel adjustment mechanisms that utilise explainability feedback to boost exploration methods in real-time (Sect. 3.3). We then outline the mathematical equations required for enabling these adjustments, providing two different approaches for the dynamic adjustment of exploration coefficients based on metric values (Sect. 3.4). Together, these form a complete framework for the integration of explainability into RL training, enabling more reliable and efficient learning.

3.1 Reinforcement Learning

Reinforcement learning (RL) is a machine learning area where agents learn to make decisions through trial-and-error interactions with environments. RL problems are formalised as Markov decision processes (MDPs), defined by the tuple $M = (S, A, P, R, \gamma, \rho_0)$, where:

- S: Environment states.
- A: Agent actions.
- $P(s'|s,a)$: Transition probability to state s' after action a in state s.
- $R(s,a) \in R$: Reward function for action a in state s.
- $\gamma \in [0,1)$: Discount factor for future rewards.
- $\rho 0$: Initial state distribution.

The goal is to learn a policy $\pi(a|s)$ that maximizes the cumulative expected reward.

$$\pi^* = \mathrm{argmax}_\pi \mathbb{E}\left[\sum_{t=0}^{\infty} \gamma^t R_t\right] \tag{1}$$

where π^* is the optimal policy.

RL algorithms can be generally classified into two main categories: policy gradient and value-based methods. Policy gradient approaches directly optimise policy parameters to maximise expected returns, employing methods like REINFORCE or actor-critic methods. Examples include PPO and SAC, both working well in discrete and continuous action spaces.

Value-based methods learn value functions (V(s) or Q(s,a)) to guide decision-making. Deep Q-Networks (DQN) exemplifies this approach, with enhancements like prioritised experience replay that helps improving efficiency. These methods have demonstrated to work well in problems with bounded action spaces or well-defined value systems.

3.2 Explainable RL Metrics

In this study, to enhance agent performance, four explainability metrics proposed in the IxDRL framework [7] were selected. These metrics—*confidence, incongruity, goal conduciveness*, and *riskiness*—were chosen based on their actionability (capacity to directly inform interventions) [36] and computational efficiency (low overhead for real-time analysis) [37]. Below is a brief description of each metric and its relevance to performance optimisation:

Execution Certainty or Confidence: Quantifies the agent's certainty in its action selections by measuring the entropy of its policy distribution. For discrete actions, this is computed using evenness index applied to action probabilities as done in this study [38]. Low execution certainty indicates uncertain decision-making, signaling opportunities for targeted retraining or human guidance. Its computational simplicity enables real-time monitoring of policy stability.

Incongruity: Captures deviations between expected and observed outcomes using the temporal difference (TD) error. High incongruity values highlight unexpected transitions or reward anomalies, enabling fast detection of environmental stochasticity or model inaccuracies. This metric is critical for identifying scenarios requiring policy adaptation or environment recalibration. For the case of value-based approaches, such as DQN, the incongruity was calculated using softmax q values as described in [39].

Goal Conduciveness: Measures the agent's progress toward task objectives by analysing the first derivative of its value function over time. Positive values indicate states where the agent is advancing toward goals, while negative values suggest suboptimal trajectories. This metric guides exploration strategies to prioritise high-value states.

Riskiness: Evaluates the potential consequence of suboptimal actions by comparing the difference between the highest and lowest valued actions (in value-based methods) or the gap between primary and secondary action probabilities (in policy gradients). High riskiness flags critical decision points where small errors may lead to significant performance drops enabling proactive safeguards.

These metrics are derived directly from the agent's learned models, ensuring computational efficiency while providing actionable insights. In order to compute these metrics some information needs to be captured such as rewards, policy distributions (action probabilities), value function estimates (e.g., state and action values), and precomputed interaction trajectories. Metrics like incongruity additionally rely on temporal difference errors or deviations between predicted and observed outcomes.

3.3 Utilising XRL Metrics to Boost Agent Performance

A number of approaches have been suggested in the literature to improve the performance of agents, such as dynamic adjustment of the reward function [26] and utilising self-imitation learning [28], which incentivises agents to imitate previously successful actions. This research is specifically focused on tackling a key issue in reinforcement learning (RL): effective balancing of the exploration-exploitation dilemma, as identified in [40].

To solve this issue, we derive two equations (refer to Sect. 3.4) that utilise the main variable governing exploration-exploitation trade-offs in the given RL algorithm being used, along with explainability metrics. These equations compute new values for the variable, dynamically adjusting the exploration of the agent. To obtain results that are reproducible, robust, and generalisable, we test our approach by implementing two various reinforcement learning algorithms—Proximal Policy Optimization (PPO) and Deep Q-Networks (DQN)—in two varied environments provided by OpenAI Gym. This allows us to examine the utility of inserting explainability measurements into the training process for enhancing the performance of agents. The process to adaptively tune the trade-off between exploration and exploitation for all algorithms is described as follows (refer to Fig. 1):

1. **Data Capture:** At each training iteration, record action probabilities (policy), value estimates, rewards, and TD errors.

2. **Metric Computation:** Calculate *execution certainty*, *riskiness*, *goal conduciveness*, and *incongruity* using agent-environment interaction data.
3. **Parameter Update:** Apply one of the two equations (see Sect. 3.4) to adjust entropy (PPO) or ε (DQN) based on metric values and using previous exploration coefficient value.
4. **Clipping:** Restrict the updated exploration coefficient within bounds (e.g., $\varepsilon \in [0.01, 0.5]$) to maintain training stability.

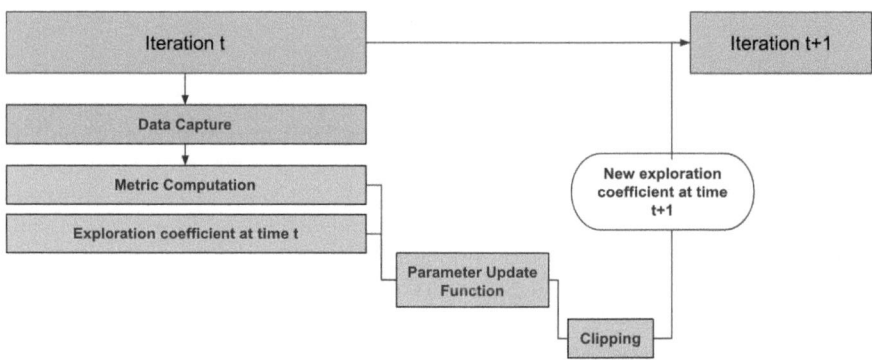

Fig. 1. Method to dynamically adjust agent exploration.

This strategy compromises between performance and explainability, converting XRL knowledge into policy changes that can be implemented. By aligning exploration strategies to the capabilities of the agent, we hope to quantify gains in cumulative rewards on various benchmarks, as described in Sect. 4.

3.4 Equations to Dynamically Adjust Agent Exploration

In the current study, two primary functions have been defined for dynamically adjusting the exploration-exploitation trade-off throughout the agent's training. For clarity and simplicity, we call the primary variable that controls this trade-off the *exploration coefficient*. The particular application of this coefficient varies depending on the algorithm used. For example, for the Proximal Policy Optimisation (PPO) algorithm, the exploration coefficient is equivalent to the entropy coefficient, which controls the stochasticity of the action selection. Conversely, in the Deep Q-Network (DQN) algorithm, the epsilon value represents the exploration parameter that determines the probability of selecting a random action compared to using the current policy.

Function 1: Compounded Threshold Approach. For Function 1, the exploration coefficient is calculated as presented in Eq. 2.

$$\text{EC}_{\text{new}} = \text{softclip}\left(\text{EC} \prod_m \begin{cases} \alpha_m & \text{if } v_m > \tau_m \\ \beta_m & \text{otherwise} \end{cases}, [\min, \max], \delta\right) \qquad (2)$$

where:

- EC_{new}: Updated exploration coefficient.
- softclip(): Constrains value to [min, max] with soft boundaries.
- δ: Soft zone for the clipping function.
- EC: Original exploration coefficient.
- m: Metric.
- α_m: Above-threshold multiplier for metric m.
- v_m: Value of metric m.
- τ_m: Threshold for metric m.
- β_m: Below-threshold multiplier for metric m.

This method entails dynamic adjustment of the exploration coefficient by evaluating whether metric values are above or below a specified threshold. For each metric, if its value is above the threshold, the exploration coefficient is reduced by multiplying it by a factor obtained from *above_thresh_factor_dict* in order to reduce the exploration coefficient and predispose towards exploitation. If the metric value is less than the threshold, the coefficient is boosted by using a factor from *below_thresh_factor_dict* to increase the exploration coefficient and encourage exploration.

Following these corrections, the new exploration coefficient is then clipped by using the *gradual_clip_positive* method to keep it within predetermined ranges set by [min max], and *soft_zone*, which preserves training stability. The approach was selected as it provides immediate control of how metrics influence exploration or exploitation. For instance, when in a situation a measure of "riskiness" is too high, the level of entropy can be decreased to prefer safer actions. Conversely, when "goal conduciveness" (GC) is low, entropy can be increased to promote exploratory behavior. Furthermore, this approach enables the definition of distinct thresholds and adjustment parameters for each measure, which makes it fit well into different situations and particularly valuable in cases where distinct thresholds for measures define appropriate moments to favor exploration over exploitation.

Function 2: Compounded Combination Approach. - in this case the exploration coefficient is computed as shown in Eq. (3).

$$EC_{new} = \text{softclip}\left(EC \prod_m \frac{\max_{norm\_range} - \min_{norm\_range}}{\max_m - \min_m}(v_m - \min_m), [\min, \max], \delta\right) \quad (3)$$

where:

- EC_{new}, softclip(), δ, EC, m, v_m: Same as in Function 1.
- norm_range: Range of values that the metric value will be normalised to be within.

This method normalises the value of every metric to a specified range defined by minimum and maximum values achieved during training. Following normalisation, metrics are tuned in relation to their proximity to the exploration coefficient. Metrics like goal conduciveness and execution certainty have an inverse relation with the exploration coefficient; i.e., high values of these metrics cause it to decrease allowing for exploitation. In contrary, measures like incongruity and riskiness display direct proportionality whereby higher values increase it facilitating exploration.

Then normalised values of metrics are scaled with current exploration coefficients. The resulting value is clipped by using *gradual_clip_positive* function to maintain it within desired ranges. Clipping provides stability and control during training by preventing extreme changes that could destabilise learning processes. The adjustment in real time guarantees that agents can balance exploration and exploitation well according to feedback from explainability metrics in real time.

This approach provides fewer fine-grained controls over how each individual explainability metric influencing agent's exploration behavior; however, it offers significant advantages when there is a need to dynamically combine multiple metrics without relying on predetermined thresholds. This feature makes it particularly useful in scenarios requiring constant adjustment of exploration coefficients based on different metrics. Furthermore, this method suits environments where metrics have large variations in scale or importance; scaling all metrics ensures equal contribution from each metric preventing domination by one metric. This inherent flexibility and scalability make it a good choice for achieving balance between exploration and exploitation in complicated reinforcement learning tasks.

4 Experiments

This section presents the environments and experimental setup designed to evaluate how explainability metrics impact reinforcement learning performance. We benchmarked two algorithms—Proximal Policy Optimisation (PPO) and Deep Q-Networks (DQN)—across two distinct environments: CartPole and Taxi. Our experiments were structured to address the following research questions:

1. How do individual and combined XRL metrics affect (i) sample efficiency, and (ii) overall performance? (see Sect. 5.1)
2. How do the two exploration coefficient adjustment functions compare in terms of performance? (see Sect. 5.2)
3. Are the improvements consistent across experiments (functions and metrics), RL algorithms and environments? (see Sect. 5.3)

4.1 Benchmarking Environments

The OpenAI Gym [41] environments used in this study represent a range of challenges in terms of state and action spaces, reward structures, and termination conditions while being computationally efficient. Table 1 summarises the key characteristics and sample efficiency thresholds for each environment.

To ensure comparability with prior work, we utilised the standard OpenAI Gym reward functions without modification. For the CartPole environment, early termination was enabled to assess the robustness of agents to abrupt episode endings.

Table 1. Environment characteristics

Environment	State Dim.	Action Dim.	Max. Reward	Sample Efficiency Threshold	Termination Conditions
CartPole	4	2 (Discrete)	2002	Mean reward ≥ 195 over 50 episodes	Pole angle > 12° or cart out of bounds
Taxi	500	6 (Discrete)	10	Mean reward ≥ 8 over 50 episodes	Passenger delivered

4.2 Experimental Setup

Explainability-driven metrics (*execution certainty, incongruity, goal conduciveness*, and *riskiness*) were computed in real time during training from per-timestep values. These metrics were experimented systematically across all combinatorial settings: first single (single-metric), then in pairs, then triplets, and then all four together, before being paired with two distinct functions (see Sect. 3.4) to enable dynamic exploration coefficient adjustments. For analysing performance, we evaluated training results with two metrics:

- **Smoothed episodic returns:** computed as a 100-episode rolling average of raw returns and cross-seed variability plotted with shaded ±1 standard deviation bands to assess consistency.
- **Sample efficiency:** in terms of number of training iterations to reach 90% maximum reward. We do this by conducting a test every 20 iterations for 100 episodes.

To test for robustness, we used five seeds per configuration in the evaluation phase. Policies were evaluated during training every 20 iterations, with each checkpoint being evaluated on 100 deterministic episodes ($\epsilon = 0$ for DQN, no entropy for PPO). Key metrics included:

- Within-Seed Stability: Standard deviation of returns within episodes for individual seeds.
- Cross-Seed Stability: Standard deviation of mean returns calculated across all seeds.

Furthermore, we conducted Welch's t-test ($\alpha = 0.05$) to measure the magnitude of performance differences between baseline and their XRL-enhanced counterparts. The test supports unequal variances present in RL reward distributions, offering a robust validation of cumulative reward gains. The baselines used in this study are the default implementations of PPO and DQN algorithms from the Ray RLlib library, which provide default hyperparameter settings for learning rates, discount factors, and network structures. Similarly, the exploration adjusted experiments also utilize these default hyperparameter settings to ensure a fair comparison.

Within the functions, the clipping interval varied by algorithm. For PPO, the clipping range was set to [0.001, 0.011]. Since RLlib's default baseline for the entropy coefficient is 0.01, the upper bound of 0.011 was selected to maintain a small margin above the baseline, ensuring sufficient exploration early in training. The lower bound of 0.001 was chosen to preserve minimal stochasticity, preventing premature convergence to suboptimal policies, and this value was preliminarily evaluated to confirm that it produced stable and reasonable results during training.

For DQN, the clipping range was defined as [0.05, 0.5]. The baseline DQN's epsilon follows a decay schedule, beginning at 1 and decreasing to 0.05 over 10,000 steps. The upper bound of 0.5 was selected to align with an initial exploration rate of 50% $\epsilon = 0.5$, allowing for substantial exploration at the beginning of training. This ensures the agent has sufficient opportunity to explore the state space and discover effective actions. The decay schedule is then dynamically adjusted based on explainability-driven metrics, enabling the agent to fine-tune the exploration-exploitation tradeoff in response to its performance, allowing for more targeted exploitation as the agent's behavior becomes more refined.

To establish appropriate threshold values for modifying the entropy coefficient (PPO) and epsilon decay (DQN), we conducted an analysis of the baseline training curves for four explainability driven metrics over 200 iterations across three random seeds (5, 42, and 123) on the two environments. Threshold values were derived by examining the points at which these metrics exhibited convergence toward the end of training, averaging their values only when they demonstrated consistency across seeds. The final selected thresholds are detailed in Table 2 and 3.

Table 2. DQN Function 1 Metric Thresholds for Epsilon

Environment	IC Threshold	GC Threshold	EC Threshold	Riskiness Threshold
Cartpole	0.5	0	8	0.13
Taxi	0.2	0	0.4	6.7

Table 3. PPO Function 1 Metric Thresholds for the Entropy Coefficient

Environment	IC Threshold	GC Threshold	EC Threshold	Riskiness Threshold
Cartpole	0.98	0	0.4	0.6
Taxi	−0.4	0	0.75	0.23

An exception to this pattern was observed in the Taxi PPO environment with seed 5, where the riskiness metric diverged to 0.45 instead of stabilizing around 0.23, as seen in the other seeds. In this case, the agent's performance was significantly degraded compared to the baseline, failing to meet the performance criterion of achieving zero total reward per episode. Due to the lack of convergence and substantial deviation from expected behavior, this instance was classified as an outlier and excluded when defining the riskiness threshold for Taxi PPO.

5 Results and Discussion

5.1 XRL Metric Synergy Analysis

Our comprehensive evaluation across environments reveals distinctive patterns in the performance of individual and pairs of explainability metrics. Based on training performance evaluation and analysing plots of smoothed episodic returns (Figs. 2, 3, 4 and 5), goal conduciveness (GC) was consistently the best performant individual metric, outperforming baseline versions for PPO and DQN in CartPole and Taxi environments.

When pairing metrics, we observed environment and algorithm-dependent synergies. DQN on CartPole performed best with the execution certainty (EC) and incongruity (IC) pair, where incongruity's ability to detect unexpected transitions was complementary to EC policy stabilisation gains. PPO, however, performed best with the EC, GC and riskiness (Risk) trio, where each of the metrics contributed distinct benefits to the learning process.

Another relevant observation is the apparent correlation between GC and Risk. In all of our top-performing configurations when looking at training results and more specifically the 100 episode smoothed plot, riskiness was always coupled with GC. This was especially pronounced in the Taxi environment, where pairs of GC-Risk outperformed the baseline and experiments involving riskiness by itself.

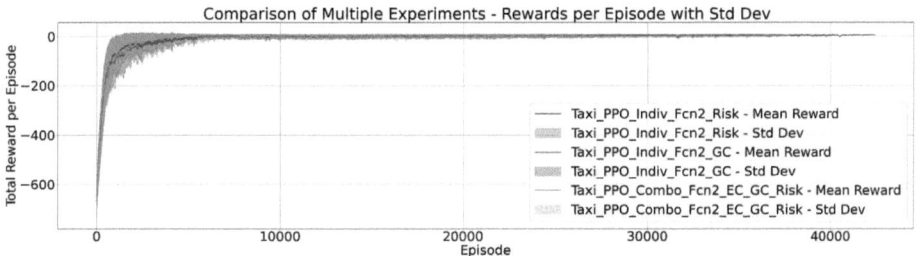

Fig. 2. Taxi PPO experiments, measured by total rewards per episode, comparing the following configurations: Function 2 with Riskiness; Function 2 with Goal Conduciveness; Function 2 with Execution Certainty, Goal Conduciveness, and Riskiness; and baseline.

The natural reason for this synergy is in the way these metrics complement each other. Riskiness measures the potential impact of suboptimal actions by calculating the difference between highest and lowest-valued actions. When an

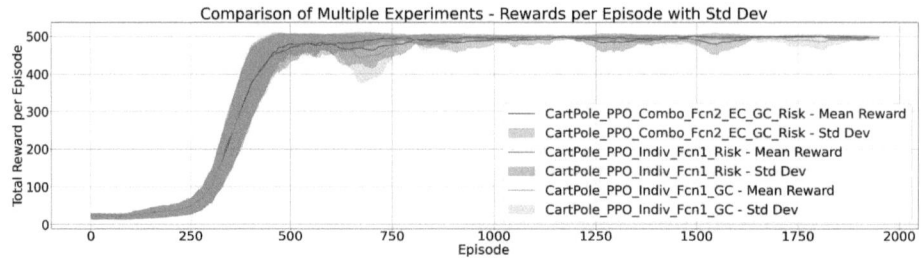

Fig. 3. CartPole PPO experiments, measured by total rewards per episode, comparing the following configurations: Function 2 with Execution Certainty, Goal Conducivness, and Riskiness; Function 1 with Riskiness; Function 1 with Goal Conduciveness; and baseline.

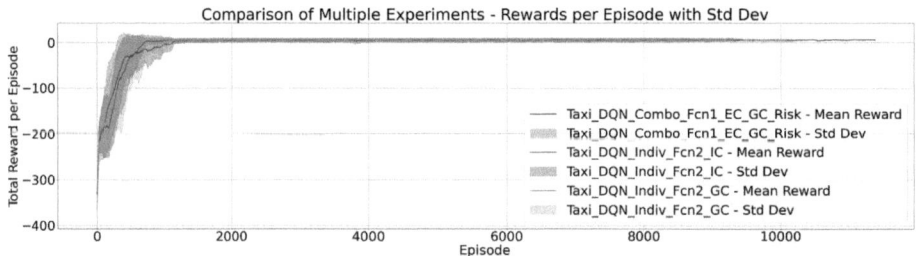

Fig. 4. Taxi DQN experiments, measured by total rewards per episode, comparing the following configurations: Function 1 with Execution Certainty, Goal Conducivness, and Riskiness; Function 2 with Incongruity; Function 2 with Goal Conduciveness; and baseline.

agent experiences high riskiness states (critical decision points), it becomes cautious and selective in taking actions. This selective action-taking seems to create a feedback process that positively affects GC, which monitors progress toward goals through value function trends.

In particular, by recognising and avoiding high-risk states, the agent prevents disastrous failures that otherwise lead to bad goal conduciveness. The agent learns to effectively identify critical points of decision at which errors would have a long-term performance-degrading effect. This risk-avoiding action results in stable value function increments over time, which is what GC quantifies.

We also observed trade-offs among measures. In particular, EC and Riskiness sometimes had opposing influences, with EC promoting exploitation (by decreasing exploration coefficient) and riskiness insisting on more exploration in critical states. The optimal balance between these measures was found to be environment-dependent, with CartPole favoring EC-dominant configurations and Taxi benefiting from more evenly balanced EC-Riskiness interactions. The results indicate that the selection of metrics must be environment-specific and algorithm-category-specific instead of having a one-size-fits-all approach. The effect when combination certain metrics, such as the riskiness-GC combination,

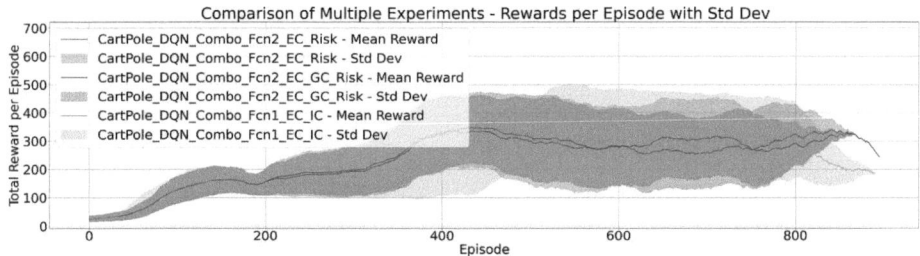

Fig. 5. CartPole DQN experiments, measured by total rewards per episode, comparing the following configurations: Function 2 with Execution Certainty and Riskiness; Function 2 with Execution Certainty, Goal Conducivness, and Riskiness; and Function 1 with Execution Certainty and Incongruity.

provides interesting prospects for designing more robust and efficient reinforcement learning systems.

5.2 Exploration Strategy Comparison

As observed by the entropy values corresponding to the execution of the PPO algorithm, our XRL metrics seem to lead the agent into following cyclic sequences of exploration and exploitation rather than enabling a smooth switch between both regimes (Figs. 6 and 7). The oscillating phenomenon can be described as a pendulum swinging between two discrete states, with periods of increased exploration followed by periods of increased exploitation.

The reactive "pendulum swings" point to a key consideration in the adaptation of dynamic exploration. Although our method is able to enhance performance across a variety of environments, the optimal pattern of exploration would more likely demonstrate a smoother evolution from exploration-dominant to exploitation-dominant behavior as training unfolds and reward milestones are achieved. Instead, we find that agents employing XRL-driven exploration have a tendency to vacillate between exploration and exploitation phases.

The cyclical pattern observed indicates that the present deployment is perhaps too sensitive to temporary shifts in metric values. As an example, when conduciveness of goals temporarily declines, the agent quickly shifts towards exploration and only comes back towards exploitation when performance improves. Although this sensitivity helps the agent to avoid falling in local optima it can introduce undesired variance into the learning process.

In the case of DQN, we also observe that using our approach leads to greater exploitation resulting in an epsilon of 0.05 (the minimum value) in fewer timesteps compared to the baseline. This means that our metrics can recognise when the agent has learned enough about the world and reduce random exploration to focus on exploiting learned policies. This is aligned with standard Deep Q-Network (DQN) training practices, where epsilon is usually decreased from a similarly high starting point (exploration-favorable) to a pre-set minimum value

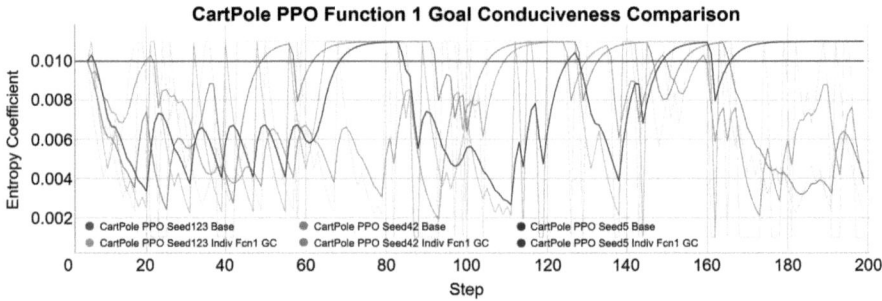

Fig. 6. Goal conduciveness inducing cyclic patterns in the PPO entropy coefficient.

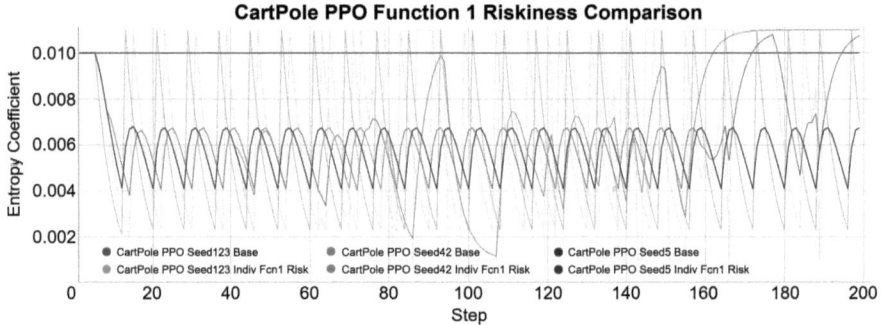

Fig. 7. Riskiness inducing cyclic patterns in the PPO entropy coefficient.

(exploitation-favored). The conventional approach uses constant decay schedules while our approach dynamically adjusts the decay rate according to real-time evaluations of XRL metrics.

This adaptive method seems especially useful in spaces of varying complexity for different states so that the agent can visit more in novel or difficult regions while rapidly taking advantage of familiarity in areas where it is already well known. When the agent finds regions of high complexity, these metrics increase exploration globally, influencing states with uncertain values where exploration has higher impact. As the agent learns how to behave better in complex areas, the metrics decrease exploration, what leads to an effective oscillation between exploration and exploitation.Comparison of these two strategies for decaying epsilon is shown in Fig. 8.

In order to assess the impact of using different functions to manage the dynamic agent exploration (refer to Sect. 3.4) we have compared some of the top experiments for the algorithms tested, which in this instance was when utilising the goal conduciveness XRL metric to change the exploration coefficient after each training iteration. Figures 9, 10, 11, and 12 show the difference for Function 1 and 2 when run across five different seeds.

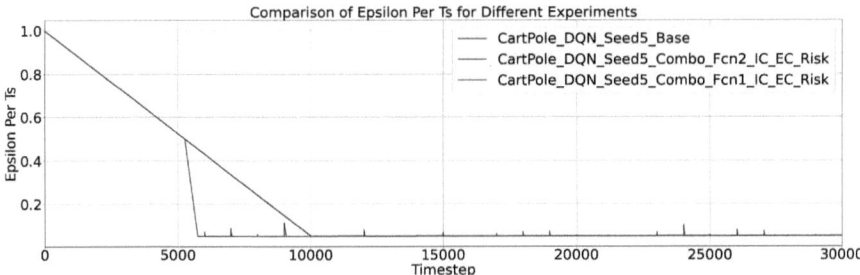

Fig. 8. Comparison of epsilon values per timestep for CartPole DQN baseline, and for the combination of Incongruity, Execution Certainty, and Riskiness for Functions 1 and 2.

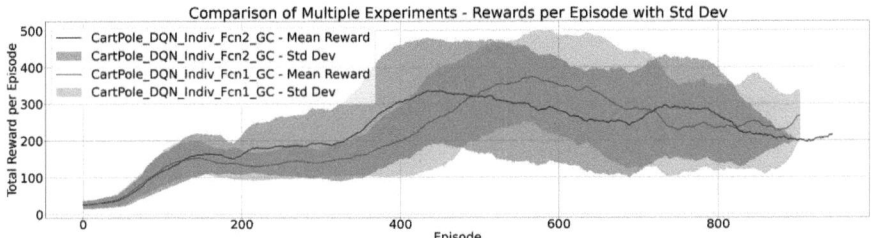

Fig. 9. CartPole DQN experiments, measured by total rewards per episode, comparing Functions 1 and 2 with the metric of Goal Conduciveness.

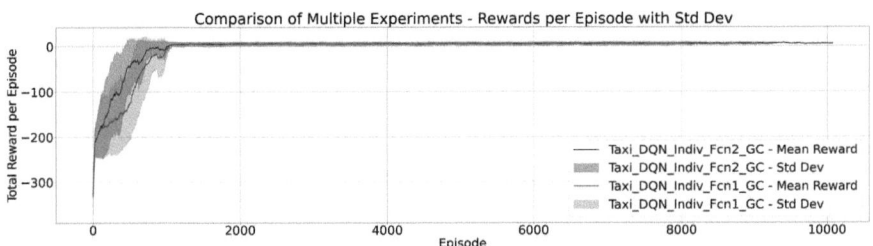

Fig. 10. Taxi DQN experiments, measured by total rewards per episode, comparing Functions 1 and 2 with the metric of Goal Conduciveness.

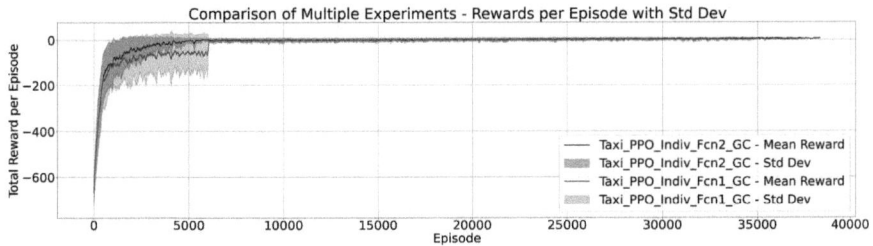

Fig. 11. Taxi PPO experiments, measured by total rewards per episode, comparing Functions 1 and 2 with the metric of Goal Conduciveness.

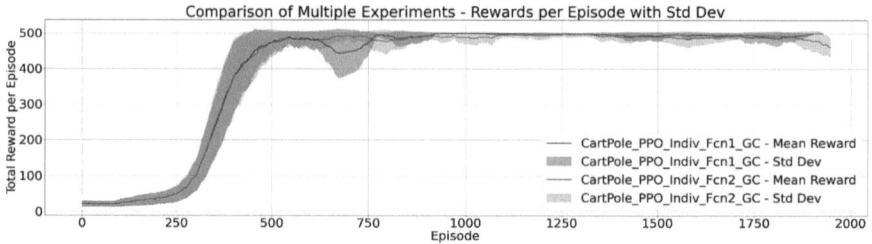

Fig. 12. CartPole PPO experiments, measured by total rewards per episode, comparing Functions 1 and 2 with the metric of Goal Conduciveness.

We observed that using Function 2, which normalises each metric's value to a specific range based on the minimum and maximum observed values, generally provides better results across environments. In particular, there is a clear performance advantage in the Taxi environment where Function 2 significantly outperforms Function 1 for both PPO and DQN implementations. For the CartPole environment, while Function 2 still yields better results, the performance margin between the two functions is notably smaller.

5.3 Cross-Algorithm Generalisation

The incorporation of XRL metrics into reinforcement learning algorithms has shown strong performance gains across various environments and algorithms. Table 4 presents the evaluation results for the CartPole and Taxi environments, illustrating the superior performance of XRL-augmented setups over their corresponding baselines.

Table 4. XRL-augmented and baseline experiment evaluation results for the CartPole/Taxi environments and DQN/PPO algorithms.

Env	Experiment	Alg	Mean	Stability	Std Dev	Steps to Threshold
Cartpole	Baseline	DQN	378.86	151.67	3.37	120
Cartpole	Baseline	PPO	375.57	95.21	4.47	20
Cartpole	Combo_Fcn2_GC_IC_Risk	DQN	434.33	46.73	9.72	60
Cartpole	Combo_Fcn2_GC_IC_Risk	PPO	463.49	25.53	11.52	20
Cartpole	Combo_Fcn2_GC_Risk	DQN	414.10	23.12	6.51	80
Cartpole	Combo_Fcn2_GC_Risk	PPO	451.43	63.27	13.44	20
Taxi	Baseline	DQN	4.25	1.37	6.71	100
Taxi	Baseline	PPO	−19.29	26.81	12.49	180
Taxi	Combo_Fcn2_GC_IC_Risk	DQN	5.13	0.19	0.12	60
Taxi	Combo_Fcn2_GC_IC_Risk	PPO	-2.25	8.08	10.85	180
Taxi	Combo_Fcn2_GC_Risk	DQN	4.23	1.67	6.50	120
Taxi	Combo_Fcn2_GC_Risk	PPO	−2.17	5.82	1.77	140

On CartPole environment, PPO algorithm obtained best result with GC-IC-Risk (Goal Conduciveness, Incongruity, and Riskiness) metric combination achieving an average reward of 463.49 whereas the baseline value was 375.57. DQN with the same metric combination also showed an improvement over its baseline. The stability measures also saw drastic enhancement, as the standard deviation dropped from 95.21 to 25.53 for PPO and from 151.67 to 46.73 for DQN using the GC-IC-Risk combination.

For the Taxi environment, where the task is more difficult as indicated by the negative baseline PPO performance, the improvements are even more pronounced. The PPO algorithm with GC-IC-Risk metrics improved from a baseline average reward of -19.29 to -2.25, indicating a dramatic decrease in negative rewards. As a comparison, the DQN algorithm using the same set of metrics improved from 4.25 to 5.13. Importantly, the stability metrics of DQN with GC-IC-Risk improved substantially, as indicated by a decrease in standard deviation from 1.37 to 0.19. The "Steps to threshold" column in Table 4 indicates the number of training iterations that each algorithm required to reach a performance benchmark of 90% of the maximum reward. This measure is used to evaluate sample efficiency, where lower values indicate faster convergence. XRL-augmented algorithms consistently demonstrated higher sample efficiency in a number of environments. In the CartPole environment, DQN with GC-IC-Risk reached the performance threshold in 60 iterations whereas the baseline reached it in 120 iterations, a 50% decrease in training steps needed. Similarly, in the Taxi environment, GC-IC-Risk enabled DQN to reach the performance threshold in 60 iterations compared to 100 for the baseline.

These enhancements highlight the capacity of XRL metrics to properly inform exploration strategies, resulting in more efficient policy learning and convergence to optimal solutions at a quicker pace. Statistical significance testing using Welch's t-test ($\alpha = 0.05$) confirmed that all these performance improvements were statistically significant in all CartPole and Taxi environments when using PPO, with very low p-values (much lower than the threshold for significance, Table 5). However, for the Taxi environment with DQN, the improvements seen did not translate to statistical significance. This means that XRL measure improvements can vary in relation to both the type and complexity of the environment.

Table 5. Welch's t-test results comparing XRL-augmented experiments against baselines for the CartPole/Taxi environments and DQN/PPO algorithms.

Environment	Algorithm Comparison	t-statistic	p-value	Significant ($\alpha= 0.05$)
CartPole	Baseline_DQN vs Combo_Fcn2_GC_IC_Risk_DQN	−17.0507	0.0001	Yes
CartPole	Baseline_DQN vs Combo_Fcn2_GC_Risk_DQN	−15.2019	0.0001	Yes
CartPole	Baseline_PPO vs Combo_Fcn2_GC_IC_Risk_PPO	−22.4999	0.0001	Yes
CartPole	Baseline_PPO vs Combo_Fcn2_GC_Risk_PPO	−16.9368	0.0001	Yes
Taxi	Baseline_DQN vs Combo_Fcn2_GC_IC_Risk_DQN	−0.4147	0.6881	No
Taxi	Baseline_DQN vs Combo_Fcn2_GC_Risk_DQN	0.0068	0.9947	No
Taxi	Baseline_PPO vs Combo_Fcn2_GC_IC_Risk_PPO	−3.2567	0.0045	Yes
Taxi	Baseline_PPO vs Combo_Fcn2_GC_Risk_PPO	−4.2910	0.0018	Yes

An interesting trend that was noticed during the training process was the correlation between the metrics of Goal Conduciveness (GC) and Riskiness. In experiments in which Riskiness was employed as a guiding metric, a consistent pattern of high values of Goal Conduciveness relative to the baseline was observed, despite Riskiness not following a clear pattern. This indicates that by considering the possible outcomes of actions (Riskiness), agents learn more effective strategies to navigate towards their goals (Goal Conduciveness). The overall performance results for every experimental setup, both individual metrics and combinations, are given in the Appendix. The results shown in Tables 2 and 3 pertain to the best configurations discovered in this study.

6 Conclusion

In this paper, we have presented the experimental exploration of a novel approach to leveraging explainable reinforcement learning insights for enhancing the performance of reinforcement learning agents. Our findings demonstrate that in some cases, this agent introspective approach does indeed provide benefits in performance.

There are of course limitations with the study that are important to acknowledge. For example, the environments selected in this study only have discrete action spaces, which is limiting to understand the full impact. Also, generation of the metrics requires additional computation to the baseline training, so there needs to be a clear benefit to justify the additional computational cost, which is not always the case.

Overall, our research contributes to the growing body of knowledge in actionable explainable RL for agent improvement. The study provides insights into this introspective approach, which opens up a variety of opportunities for future research, which are listed below:

- Extend the experimentation to include additional:
  - RL algorithms, such as IMPALA.
  - Environments with different characteristics and increased complexity.
- Experiment with various combinations of metrics, including when and how to use them during training.
- Explore and evaluate further explainability metrics that may improve performance.
- Formally evaluate the effectiveness of the metrics for RL explainability and trustability, beyond their benefit to improving performance.

Additionally, only a single value for each metric threshold τ_m, above and below threshold multipliers (α_m and β_m), and softclip intervals was selected to limit the scope of experiments, as testing multiple values would have exponentially increased the experimental load. However, future research could benefit from treating these parameters as hyperparameters to explore how varying values impact performance.

Appendix

Taxi and CartPole Results Summary

Experiment Name	Algorithm	CartPole			Taxi		
		Mean	Stability	Std. Dev.	Mean	Stability	Std. Dev.
Baseline	DQN	378.86	151.67	3.37	4.25	1.37	6.71
Baseline	PPO	375.57	95.21	4.47	-19.29	26.81	12.492
Ind_Fcn1_EC	DQN	338.43	146.72	6.59	4.96	0.28	1.04
Ind_Fcn1_EC	PPO	382.32	68.52	3.17	-37.18	57.06	10.37
Ind_Fcn1_GC	DQN	353.08	137.96	3.76	4.98	0.53	2.8
Ind_Fcn1_GC	PPO	378.88	7.8	4.79	-271.41	261.3	11.06
Ind_Fcn1_IC	DQN	361.53	88.29	12.9	5.12	0.29	0.51
Ind_Fcn1_IC	PPO	379.85	63.15	3.34	-22.15	34.25	2.02
Ind_Fcn1_Risk	DQN	447.51	23.14	4.32	-11.14	23.36	1.23
Ind_Fcn1_Risk	PPO	428.25	47.27	4.69	-2.25	8.16	3.27
Ind_Fcn2_EC	DQN	303.96	133.06	3.39	4.15	1.62	6.48
Ind_Fcn2_EC	PPO	464.4	19.07	3.53	1.33	5.16	0.47
Ind_Fcn2_GC	DQN	301.69	131.69	1.76	4.15	1.62	6.48
Ind_Fcn2_GC	PPO	403.89	72.51	7.03	3.31	1.06	1.76
Ind_Fcn2_IC	DQN	461.45	27.76	10.27	4.46	0.42	1.31
Ind_Fcn2_IC	PPO	392.41	60.78	5.05	-22.75	37.07	7.23
Ind_Fcn2_Risk	DQN	297.45	128.85	3.69	4.15	1.62	6.48
Ind_Fcn2_Risk	PPO	402.0	70.16	4.33	-21.53	32.41	15.45
Combo_Fcn1_EC_GC	DQN	359.77	171.44	10.76	5.29	0.22	0.1
Combo_Fcn1_EC_GC	PPO	387.45	70.51	17.67	-51.57	76.14	3.38
Combo_Fcn1_EC_GC_IC	DQN	331.58	113.28	8.3	-15.44	29.36	2.72
Combo_Fcn1_EC_GC_IC	PPO	456.03	29.82	7.73	-28.18	44.76	5.31
Combo_Fcn1_EC_GC_IC_Risk	DQN	417.22	112.09	10.25	3.09	2.6	2.26
Combo_Fcn1_EC_GC_IC_Risk	PPO	382.87	78.5	9.46	-236.23	324.48	4.08
Combo_Fcn1_EC_GC_Risk	DQN	218.75	131.42	2.85	5.44	0.19	0.23
Combo_Fcn1_EC_GC_Risk	PPO	429.94	43.74	4.08	-4.96	6.98	3.26
Combo_Fcn1_EC_IC	DQN	479.71	7.3	4.54	4.84	0.54	3.71
Combo_Fcn1_EC_IC	PPO	446.29	38.34	2.81	-28.98	46.85	10.28
Combo_Fcn1_EC_Risk	DQN	484.7	7.54	12.13	3.83	1.18	5.36
Combo_Fcn1_EC_Risk	PPO	406.1	64.84	6.8	-39.92	60.33	3.96
Combo_Fcn1_GC_IC	DQN	494.7	3.27	8.28	5.01	0.25	1.15
Combo_Fcn1_GC_IC	PPO	390.72	71.76	1.39	50.73	70.74	1.68
Combo_Fcn1_GC_IC_Risk	DQN	363.18	174.89	7.88	4.57	0.78	4.39
Combo_Fcn1_GC_IC_Risk	PPO	422.27	46.0	2.37	0.55	0.91	2.07
Combo_Fcn1_GC_Risk	DQN	480.33	9.7	7.53	4.83	0.6	5.83
Combo_Fcn1_GC_Risk	PPO	445.14	50.17	7.18	-43.98	64.78	5.87
Combo_Fcn1_IC_EC_Risk	DQN	359.27	174.09	2.96	5.06	0.45	2.53
Combo_Fcn1_IC_EC_Risk	PPO	452.11	31.52	5.67	-29.4	43.11	12.12
Combo_Fcn1_IC_Risk	DQN	469.64	19.38	11.16	-29.51	45.14	1.2
Combo_Fcn1_IC_Risk	PPO	405.86	66.95	2.1	-37.67	57.4	3.33
Combo_Fcn2EC_GC	DQN	414.18	26.99	14.13	4.23	1.67	6.5
Combo_Fcn2_EC_GC	PPO	389.04	50.09	3.74	-0.95	2.45	0.33
Combo_Fcn2_EC_GC_IC	DQN	378.52	123.0	9.12	4.31	1.69	3.83
Combo_Fcn2_EC_GC_IC	PPO	463.68	22.55	2.32	-25.12	41.54	8.82
Combo_Fcn2_EC_GC_IC_Risk	DQN	304.2	162.72	6.17	5.22	0.05	0.07
Combo_Fcn2_EC_GC_IC_Risk	PPO	467.09	23.82	4.65	-78.43	101.66	10.25
Combo_Fcn2_EC_GC_Risk	DQN	331.49	117.84	36.98	4.23	1.67	6.5
Combo_Fcn2_EC_GC_Risk	PPO	405.37	82.61	4.75	-1.29	4.44	2.46
Combo_Fcn2_EC_IC	DQN	323.91	133.95	8.94	2.45	3.39	1.45
Combo_Fcn2_EC_IC	PPO	453.48	24.98	13.67	-2.25	8.08	10.85
Combo_Fcn2_EC_Risk	DQN	345.9	128.87	6.0	4.23	1.67	6.5
Combo_Fcn2_EC_Risk	PPO	457.64	8.41	3.26	-3.21	2.05	1.66
Combo_Fcn2_GC_IC	DQN	394.06	128.51	17.4	3.75	2.29	5.91
Combo_Fcn2_GC_IC	PPO	457.06	29.19	4.97	-22.19	37.46	6.74
Combo_Fcn2_GC_IC_Risk	DQN	434.33	46.73	9.72	5.13	0.19	0.12
Combo_Fcn2_GC_IC_Risk	PPO	463.49	25.53	11.52	-2.25	8.08	10.85
Combo_Fcn2_GC_Risk	DQN	414.1	23.12	6.51	4.23	1.67	6.5
Combo_Fcn2_GC_Risk	PPO	451.43	63.27	13.44	-2.17	5.82	1.77
Combo_Fcn2_IC_EC_Risk	DQN	329.37	151.73	5.51	4.97	0.07	0.83
Combo_Fcn2_IC_EC_Risk	PPO	464.05	26.22	9.09	-22.22	37.44	7.44
Combo_Fcn2_IC_Risk	DQN	334.03	67.37	3.49	3.48	1.82	6.02
Combo_Fcn2_IC_Risk	PPO	453.59	32.32	2.58	-23.71	37.49	8.32

References

1. Sutton, R.S., Barto, A.G.: Reinforcement Learning: An Introduction. MIT Press, 2nd edn (2018)
2. Silver, D., et al.: A general reinforcement learning algorithm that masters chess, shogi, and go through self-play. Science **362**(6419), 1140–1144 (2018)
3. Vinyals, O., et al.: Grandmaster level in StarCraft II using multi-agent reinforcement learning. Nature **575**(7782), 350–354 (2019)
4. Puiutta, E., Veith, E.M.S.P.: Explainable reinforcement learning: A survey. In: Holzinger, A., Kieseberg, P., Tjoa, A.M., Weippl, E. (eds.) Machine Learning and Knowledge Extraction. LNCS, vol. 12279, pp. 77–95. Springer, Cham (2020)
5. Heuillet, A., Couthouis, F., Daz-Rodriguez, N.: Explainability in deep reinforcement learning. Knowl. Based Syst. **226**, 107152 (2021)
6. Jia, Y., Mcdermid, J., Lawton, T., Habli, I.: The role of explainability in assuring safety of machine learning in healthcare. IEEE Trans. Emerg. Top. Comput. **10**, 1746–1760 (2021)
7. Sequeira, P., Gervasio, M.: IxDRL: A novel explainable deep reinforcement learning toolkit based on analyses of interestingness. In: Ras, Z.W., Kak, S., Pizzi, N. (eds.) Explainable Artificial Intelligence. LNAI, vol. 14221, pp. 373–396. Springer, Cham (2023)
8. Lu, W., Zhao, X., Fryen, T., Lee, J.H., Li, M., Magg, S., Wermter, S.: Causal state distillation for explainable reinforcement learning. In: Proceedings of the 3rd Conference on Causal Learning and Reasoning, vol. 236, pp. 106–142. PMLR (2024)
9. Finkelstein, M., et al.: Explainable Reinforcement Learning via Model Transforms. In: Advances in Neural Information Processing Systems, vol. 35, pp. 12345–12358 (2022)
10. Guan, L., Verma, M., Guo, S., Zhang, R., Kambhampati, S.: Widening the pipeline in human-guided reinforcement learning with explanation and context-aware data augmentation. In: Advances in Neural Information Processing Systems, vol. 34, pp. 20047–20059 (2021)
11. Milani, S., Topin, N., Veloso, M., Fang, F.: Explainable reinforcement learning: a survey and comparative review. ACM Comput. Surv. **56**(7), 1–36, Article 168 (2024)
12. Puri, N., et al.: Explain your move: understanding agent actions using specific and relevant feature attribution. In: International Conference on Learning Representations (2020)
13. Yan, D.: Research on reinforcement learning explainable strategies based on advantage saliency. Front. omput. Intel. Syst. **3**(1), 124–129 (2022)
14. Atrey, A., Clary, K., Jensen, D.: Exploratory not explanatory: counterfactual analysis of saliency maps for deep reinforcement learning. In: International Conference on Learning Representations (2020)
15. Topin, N., Veloso, M.: Generation of policy-level explanations for reinforcement learning. In: Proceedings of the AAAI Conference on Artificial Intelligence, vol. 33, pp. 2514–2521 (2019)
16. Koul, A., Greydanus, S., Fern, A.: Learning finite state representations of recurrent policy networks. In: International Conference on Learning Representations (2019)
17. Amir, D., Amir, O.: Highlights: summarizing agent behavior to people. In: Proceedings of the 17th International Conference on Autonomous Agents and Multiagent Systems, pp. 1168–1176. IFAAMAS, Richland (2018)

18. Sreedharan, S., Srivastava, S., Kambhampati, S.: TLdR: Policy summarization for factored SSP problems using temporal abstractions. In: Proceedings of the International Conference on Automated Planning and Scheduling, vol. 30, pp. 272–280 (2020)
19. Lin, Z., Lam, K.H., Fern, A.: Contrastive explanations for reinforcement learning via embedded self predictions. In: International Conference on Learning Representations (2021)
20. Olson, M.L., Khanna, R., Neal, L., Li, F., Wong, W.K.: Counterfactual state explanations for reinforcement learning agents via generative deep learning. In: Proceedings of the AAAI Conference on Artificial Intelligence, vol. 35, pp. 8839–8847 (2021)
21. Sequeira, P., Hostetler, J., Gervasio, M.: Global and local analysis of interestingness for competency-aware deep reinforcement learning. In: Proceedings of the AAAI Conference on Artificial Intelligence, vol. 37, pp. 6126–6134 (2023)
22. Schroeter, N., Cruz, F., Wermter, S.: Introspection-based explainable reinforcement learning in episodic and non-episodic scenarios. IEEE Access **11**, 37615–37628 (2023)
23. Cruz, F., Dazeley, R., Vamplew, P., Moreira, I.: Explainable robotic systems: understanding goal-driven actions in a reinforcement learning scenario. Neural Comput. Appl. **33**, 11527–11546 (2021)
24. Ayala, A., Cruz, F., Dazeley, R., Vamplew, P., Fernandes, B.: Explainable deep reinforcement learning using introspection in a non-episodic task. IEEE Access **9**, 152419–152432 (2021)
25. Sequeira, P., Hostetler, J., Gervasio, M., Yeh, E.: Outcome-guided counterfactuals for reinforcement learning agents from a jointly trained generative latent space. In: Proceedings of the AAAI Conference on Artificial Intelligence, vol. 37, pp. 6135–6143 (2023)
26. Ng, A.Y., Harada, D., Russell, S.J.: Policy invariance under reward transformations: theory and application to reward shaping. In: Proceedings of the 16th International Conference on Machine Learning, pp. 278–287. Morgan Kaufmann, San Francisco (1999)
27. Devlin, S.M., Kudenko, D.: Dynamic potential-based reward shaping. In: Proceedings of the 11th International Conference on Autonomous Agents and Multiagent Systems, pp. 433–440. IFAAMAS, Richland (2012)
28. Wang, Z., Taylor, M.E.: Improving reinforcement learning with confidence-based demonstrations. In: Proceedings of the 26th International Joint Conference on Artificial Intelligence, pp. 3027–3033 (2017)
29. Ma, H., Luo, Z., Vo, T.V., Sima, K., Leong, T.Y.: Highly efficient self-adaptive reward shaping for reinforcement Learning. arXiv preprint arXiv:2401.00989 (2024)
30. Jacq, A., Ferret, J., Pietquin, O., Geist, M.: Lazy-MDPs: towards interpretable RL by learning when to act. In: Proceedings of the 21st International Conference on Autonomous Agents and Multiagent Systems, pp. 669–677. IFAAMAS, Richland (2022)
31. Mallick, R., et al.: A hybrid transformer with domain adaptation using interpretability techniques for the application to the detection of risk situations. Multimedia Tools Appl. **83**(35), 83339–83356 (2024)
32. Ayyar, M.P., Benois-Pineau, J., Zemmari, A.: ESL: explain to improve streaming learning for transformers. In: Pattern Recognition. LNCS, vol. 14995, pp. 160–175. Springer, Cham (2024)

33. Taylor, M.E., Yun, S., Hollinger, G.A., Borowczak, M., Nguyen, V., Osoba, O.A.: Improving reinforcement learning with human assistance: an argument for human subject studies with HippoGym. Neural Comput. Appl. **35**(32), 23429–23439 (2023)
34. Liu, Y., Wang, X., Chang, Y., Jiang, C.: Towards explainable reinforcement learning using scoring mechanism augmented agents. In: Knowledge Science, Engineering and Management. LNCS, vol. 13463, pp. 547–558. Springer, Cham (2022)
35. Sequeira, P., Gervasio, M.: Interestingness elements for explainable reinforcement learning: understanding agents' capabilities and limitations. Artif. Intell. **288**, 103367 (2020)
36. Finkelstein, M., et al.: Explainable Reinforcement Learning via Model Transforms. In: Advances in Neural Information Processing Systems, vol. 35, pp. 12345–12358 (2022)
37. Madumal, P., Miller, T., Sonenberg, L., Vetere, F.: Explainable reinforcement learning through a causal lens. In: Proceedings of the AAAI Conference on Artificial Intelligence, vol. 34, pp. 2493–2500 (2020)
38. Mulder, C.P.H., Bazeley-White, E., Dimitrakopoulos, P.G., Hector, A., Scherer-Lorenzen, M., Schmid, B.: Species evenness and productivity in experimental plant communities. Oikos **107**(1), 50–63 (2004)
39. Xu, M., Chen, X., Wang, J.: Policy correction and state-conditioned action evaluation for few-shot lifelong deep reinforcement learning. IEEE Trans. Neural Netw. Learn. Syst. **36**(4), 6843–6857 (2025)
40. Retzlaff, C., et al.: Human-in-the-loop reinforcement learning: a survey and position on requirements, challenges, and opportunities. J. Artif. Intell. Res. **79**, 359–415 (2024)
41. Brockman, G., et al.: OpenAI Gym. arXiv preprint arXiv:1606.01540 (2016)

Open Access This chapter is licensed under the terms of the Creative Commons Attribution 4.0 International License (http://creativecommons.org/licenses/by/4.0/), which permits use, sharing, adaptation, distribution and reproduction in any medium or format, as long as you give appropriate credit to the original author(s) and the source, provide a link to the Creative Commons license and indicate if changes were made.

The images or other third party material in this chapter are included in the chapter's Creative Commons license, unless indicated otherwise in a credit line to the material. If material is not included in the chapter's Creative Commons license and your intended use is not permitted by statutory regulation or exceeds the permitted use, you will need to obtain permission directly from the copyright holder.

Extending Decision Predicate Graphs for Comprehensive Explanation of Isolation Forest

Matteo Ceschin[1], Leonardo Arrighi[2](✉), Luca Longo[3], and Sylvio Barbon Junior[1]

[1] Department of Engineering and Architecture, University of Trieste, Trieste, Italy
sylvio.barbonjunior@units.it
[2] Department of Mathematics and Geosciences, University of Trieste, Trieste, Italy
leonardo.arrighi@phd.units.it
[3] Centre of Explainable Artificial Intelligence, Artificial Intelligence and Cognitive Load Rresearch Lab. Technological University Dublin, Dublin, Ireland
luca.longo@tudublin.ie

Abstract. The need to explain predictive models is well-established in modern machine learning. However, beyond model interpretability, understanding pre-processing methods is equally essential. Understanding how data modifications impact model performance improvements and potential biases and promoting a reliable pipeline is mandatory for developing robust machine learning solutions. Isolation Forest (iForest) is a widely used technique for outlier detection that performs well. Its effectiveness increases with the number of tree-based learners. However, this also complicates the explanation of outlier selection and the decision boundaries for inliers. This research introduces a novel Explainable AI (XAI) method, tackling the problem of global explainability. In detail, it aims to offer a global explanation for outlier detection to address its opaque nature. Our approach is based on the Decision Predicate Graph (DPG), which clarifies the logic of ensemble methods and provides both insights and a graph-based metric to explain how samples are identified as outliers using the proposed Inlier-Outlier Propagation Score (IOP-Score). Our proposal enhances iForest's explainability and provides a comprehensive view of the decision-making process, detailing which features contribute to outlier identification and how the model utilizes them. This method advances the state-of-the-art by providing insights into decision boundaries and a comprehensive view of holistic feature usage in outlier identification.—thus promoting a fully explainable machine learning pipeline.

Keywords: Ensemble Learning · Outliers · Explainable Artificial Intelligence · Interpretability · Anomalies · Tree-based Ensemble Model

1 Introduction

Most current Explainable AI (XAI) techniques predominantly focus on elucidating predictive models, often overlooking the necessity of addressing the entire data processing pipeline. This partial focus can result in incomplete explanations regarding the context, potentially leaving critical aspects of data handling and pre-processing—such as feature selection and outlier removal—obscured. As Lipton [9] argues, a holistic approach to explainability is essential for the credibility and utility of machine learning solutions. Similarly, authors advocate for a shift towards transparent machine learning ecosystems, where every pipeline component, from data preprocessing to model decision-making, is made transparent [7,21]. More robust, trustworthy explanations can be constructed by ensuring XAI techniques encompass the entire pipeline. Data preparation and transformation models before training a predictive model demand clarity equal to the last one for several reasons, including transparency, reliability, and regulatory requirements [18]. Firstly, transparency in pre-processing enhances the understandability of the data manipulations that occur before model training [20]. By understanding how data is cleaned, normalized, and selected during pre-processing, users can identify potential sources of bias or errors that might affect the model's performance. Furthermore, this process enables the detection and mitigation of data acquisition issues, such as systematic errors or noise, and supports enhancements to the overall system pipeline. Finally, clear documentation and explanation of all stages of data handling, including pre-processing, ensure compliance with these regulations and promote trust and reliability [22].

Among many pre-processing algorithms, Isolation Forest (iForest) [10] stands out due to its straightforward approach and effectiveness in swiftly handling outliers in high-dimensional data. However, the core mechanism of iForest, which relies on a random selection of features and split points to isolate anomalies, introduces stochasticity that can sometimes lead to ambiguous or non-intuitive results [8]. Consequently, providing explanations for the decisions made by iForest is essential, as it allows users to understand and trust the logic behind the identification of outliers, mainly when dealing with complex datasets. These explanations not only help validate the anomalies detected by iForest but also aid in fine-tuning the model by revealing potential biases or errors introduced by the randomness in the selection process [14]. Shapley Additive exPlanations (SHAP) [12] is currently used to explain the behaviour of the iForest model by providing insights into how features influence its predictions. In contrast, the Depth-based Isolation Forest Feature Importance (DIFFI) [4] method employs a tailored approach that leverages the internal structure of iForest to compute feature importances. However, both methods provide a local explanation that uses a feature importance vector to illustrate the model's decision-making process for identifying individual samples. While effective, these approaches mainly focus on feature-level contributions without exploring the structural or logical complexities of the iForest ensemble.

To overcome the limitation of providing only a vector of feature importances, we propose a method based on Decision Predicate Graphs (DPG) [2] to elucidate the logic and intrinsic aspects of the iForest ensemble. Building on the principles of the DPG technique, our method converts the iForest model into a graph, allowing us to exploit its structural properties and leverage established mathematical theories to elucidate the outlier detection process. According to Speith [19], the proposed method is global, as it explains the entire decision-making process of the iForest model, revealing general patterns and the feature interactions that drive the whole model's logic. This approach provides a mixed-type explanation, as done in other research [13,17], by integrating a visual representation of the model's decision-making process with a new quantitative metric, the Inlier-Outlier Propagation Score (IOP-Score), which assesses each feature's contribution to outlier detection. By extracting relationships and decision paths within the ensemble, our method enhances model transparency and delivers actionable insights into its internal mechanisms, surpassing traditional explanation techniques. Our work contributes in the following ways:

- Comprehensive global explanation of iForest: we propose a method to explain the iForest model, including details on feature boundaries for both inliers and outliers samples.
- The IOP-Score: a novel metric that quantifies a node's tendency to propagate toward either the inliers or outliers to enhance interpretability by distinguishing discriminative from neutral predicates in the iForest.
- Graph-based interpretability: by integrating DPG, we introduce a graph-based structure that models the isolation logic, such as feature influence on isolation depth and decision paths, enabling a detailed understanding of the detection process.

The results are derived from synthetic and well-established datasets to demonstrate the method's potential. However, we emphasize that the approach is generalizable, indicating its broad applicability across various related scenarios.

The remainder of this manuscript is structured as follows: Sect. 1 introduces the need for transparency in predictive models and pre-processing methods such as outlier detection with iForest. Section 2 provides a background on iForest, existing explanation techniques, and the DPG approach. Section 3 presents the DPG-based explanation framework for iForest, detailing the graph construction process and introducing the IOP-Score. Section 4 describes the experimental setup. Section 5 discusses the approach's limitations and potential extensions, addressing scalability and further improvements. Finally, Sect. 6 concludes the study, summarizing key contributions and outlining future research directions.

2 Background and Related Work

Our background and related work section presents the foundations of the iForest algorithm, the current research on explaining iForest, and finally a subsection about how DPG works and why we proposed a solution based on this approach.

2.1 Isolation Forest

One of the most widely used algorithms for anomaly detection is Isolation Forest, also known as iForest, a tree-based method introduced by Liu [10]. iForest is designed to efficiently identify outliers, data points that deviate significantly from other instances of the dataset, instead of inliers, representing most of the data and conforming to expected patterns. Among the various techniques available, iForest stands out for its efficiency and scalability, thanks to its linear time complexity and low memory consumption. Another key advantage is that iForest is an unsupervised learning method that does not require labeled data for training. Moreover, through an effective subsampling procedure, iForest mitigates the swamp effect, where regular points are wrongly identified as anomalies, and addresses the masking issue, which occurs when multiple anomalies conceal each other. iForest identifies outliers by recursively partitioning the data. Its core idea is that anomalies are rare and distinct from normal instances, requiring fewer random splits to isolate in the problem space. This characteristic enables the algorithm to separate anomalous data points from the majority of inliers efficiently.

Given a dataset X, where d features characterize each instance, the iForest consists of multiple binary trees, called Isolation Trees (iTrees), that form the forest. Each tree is built by randomly selecting a feature d_i and a random value v within the range $[\min(v_{d_i}), \max(v_{d_i})]$, where v_{d_i} are the values of the samples of X associated to the feature d_i. If an instance's selected feature value v_{d_i} is less than v, the instance is directed to the left branch; otherwise, it is directed to the right branch of the iTree. After each split, the dataset is partitioned so each branch contains a subset of X. This process is recursively applied to the resulting subsets until one of the following stopping conditions is met:

- The iTree reaches its maximum depth, which is defined as:

$$\lceil \log_2(\min(256, |X|)) \rceil,$$

  where $|X|$ is the number of samples of the dataset. This ensures that the tree does not grow indefinitely.
- A single instance has been completely isolated in a leaf node.
- Two or more identical instances have been grouped into a single leaf node, making further splits impossible.

Once an iTree is fully grown, each instance x in X is assigned to a leaf node. Its path length $h(x)$ is the number of edges traversed from the root to that leaf. This recursive process is repeated n times to build n trees in the forest. The final step of the iForest algorithm is the calculation of the *anomaly score* for each instance in the dataset. This score allows the model to determine whether a sample is an outlier (anomaly) or an inlier. The anomaly score is computed as follows:

$$s(x, n) = 2^{-\frac{\mathbb{E}(h(x))}{c(n)}},$$

where $\mathbb{E}(h(x))$ is the average path length of x across all trees in the forest, and $c(n)$ is a normalization factor that estimates the average path length required to isolate a data point in a binary search tree containing n instances and is given by:

$$c(n) = 2H(n-1) - \frac{2(n-1)}{n}$$

where $H(i)$ is the harmonic number, and it can be estimated by $ln(i) + 0.5772$ (Euler's constant). If $s(x,n) < 0.5$, then x is likely to be a typical instance (inlier). Conversely, if $s(x,n)$ is close to 1, then x is highly likely to be an outlier. The core idea behind the iForest algorithm is that outliers require fewer partitions to be isolated, resulting in shorter path lengths than inliers.

2.2 Explaining Isolation Forest Model

The literature presents several post-hoc XAI methods designed to interpret the iForest model. Post-hoc XAI methods are applied after training to provide interpretability without altering the model's internal structure, thereby preserving its performance. According to Speith [19], we can distinguish the model-agnostic XAI methods, such as SHapley Additive exPlanations (SHAP) [12], which can be applied independently of the underlying model, from the model-specific method, tailored for specific models or model classes. Considering proposals using SHAP, Rachwał et al. [16] proposed an improved iForest algorithm that dynamically excludes attributes based on SHAP indices, resulting in enhanced prediction accuracy and better feature selection. In their approach, SHAP values are used to quantify the importance of each feature, and models are iteratively trained with one feature excluded at a time. The final anomaly score of iForest is computed as a weighted average of these models' anomaly scores, where the weights are derived from the absolute SHAP values, prioritizing features with higher SHAP values and reducing the influence of less relevant ones. Liu and Aldrich [11] introduced the iForest-RF-SHAP framework, a novel approach for anomaly detection and explanation in coal data, which combines iForest, Random Forest, and SHAP. This framework outperformed traditional methods, such as principal component analysis, while offering detailed insights into variable contributions. In contrast, the main model-specific proposals specifically tailored to explain iForest models include the methods introduced in [1,4,8]. Kartha et al. [8] developed a method specifically designed to explain iForest anomaly predictions by assigning a vector of feature importance weights to each attribute, indicating its contribution to the anomaly detection process. These weights are computed by analyzing how much each attribute contributes to isolating a data point within the iForest trees, with higher weights associated with shorter path lengths. The result is an explanation vector that reflects the relative importance of each feature in determining the anomaly score. Arcudi et al. [1] introduced Extended Isolation Forest Feature Importance (ExIFFI), a method designed to deliver global and local explanations for iForest. ExIFFI uses feature importance metrics to explain anomaly detection comprehensively, offering a detailed perspective on how individual features contribute to the model's predictions. The feature importance metrics are computed by analyzing the projections of the hyperplane's normal vector at each node in the isolation trees and weighting them based on the degree of imbalance in the data split, favoring nodes where the sample falls into the smaller partition, thus attributing greater importance to features that isolate anomalies more effectively. Carletti et al. [4] presented Depth-based Isolation Forest Feature Importance (DIFFI), a method tailored for iForest. DIFFI provides global and local interpretability by analyzing how features influence the depth at which anomalies are isolated in the decision trees. This method explains the anomaly detection process and enables unsupervised feature selection, a valuable tool for handling high-dimensional data in anomaly detection problems. Despite the advancements in explaining iForest models using methods like SHAP, ExIFFI, and DIFFI, a significant gap remains in providing detailed interpretability regarding the values, intervals, and specific characteristics of inliers alongside outliers. This lack of explanation motivates the development of the DPG-based method, which aims to address these limitations.

2.3 Decision Predicate Graph

Decision Predicate Graph (DPG) is a post-hoc, model-specific XAI technique for interpreting tree-based ensemble models. The DPG method transforms the ensemble model into a weighted directed graph representing the entire decision-making process underlying the model. It then introduces graph-theoretic metrics that highlight key features of the ensemble model. After training the tree-based ensemble model, the internal nodes of each base learner, which contain the dataset's split rules, are used to construct predicates—feature-value associations expressed as logical statements (e.g., "$f_i > v$", where f_i is a generic feature and v is the associated value in the split). The predicates are the graph nodes, as Fig. 1 depicts.

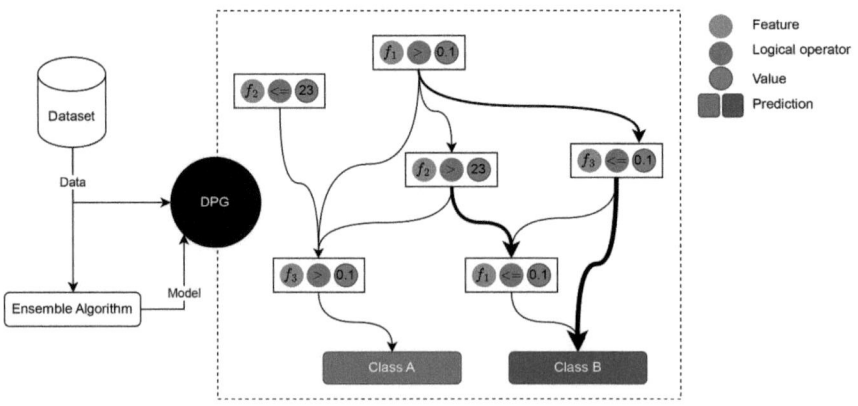

Fig. 1. Schematic demonstration of how DPG works.

Then, each training sample traverses the decision trees again. A node is connected to another if, during traversal, a data sample first satisfies the predicate of the initial node and then subsequently satisfies the predicate of the next node. The graph's edges represent the frequency predicates consecutively satisfied by the training samples during the model's training phase. The result is a global explanation of the model, comprising two main components: a visual representation of the decision-making process as a graph illustrating the entire structure.

The visual representation of iForest through DPG highlights how outliers and inliers are treated within the model. Unlike traditional feature importance methods, which provide a vector-based ranking, DPG could leverage graph structures to uncover decision paths, feature interactions, and hierarchical dependencies. This approach enhances interpretability by identifying which features contribute to an anomaly and explaining how and why those features lead to an outlier classification.

3 DPG-Based Explanation for Isolation Forest

We propose a novel post-hoc method based on DPG, a model-specific XAI technique designed to understand the decision-making process of the iForest model. An overview of our proposed approach can be seen in Fig. 2. Subsection 3.1 provides an in-depth explanation of each step.

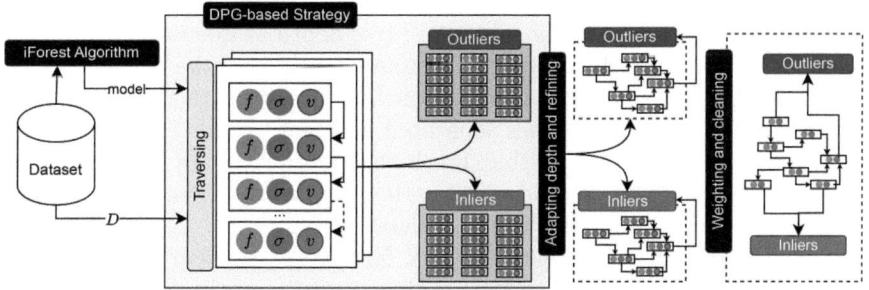

Fig. 2. Overview of the proposed approach: iForest DPG representation. Predicates are represented as triples (f, σ, v) and are color-coded (green, blue, and pink). (Color figure online)

This technique builds upon the construction method of the DPG, transforming the iForest into a graph structure. The method captures the inner logic of the iForest model, emphasizing the key decisions and the most frequently used features for identifying outliers. It provides a comprehensive global mixed-type explanation by combining a visual representation of the model's entire decision-making process, depicted as a graph, with a metric that quantifies the importance of each feature in detecting outliers. In this section, we detail the construction of our technique and present an in-depth explanation of its components. Additionally, we discuss the necessity of this technique, its advantages, and the key insights it offers into the model's behavior.

3.1 Proposed Global Explainability

Applying iForest: To construct the explanation, we begin with the iForest model trained on the dataset. The objective is to comprehend the model's decision-making process and identify features differentiating inliers from outliers. The model's output consists of the observations classified as outliers. These observations are assigned labels: "Outlier" if the model classifies them as such, and "Inlier" otherwise.

DPG-Based Strategy: Following the DPG proposal, we examine the internal nodes of each tree-based learner in iForest, which contain the dataset's split rules used to construct the predicates defined in DPG. These predicates are represented as triples (f, σ, v), where the sign (σ) can be either $>$ or $\leq$. Subsequently, each training sample traverses each tree. We identify all predicate lists satisfied by the samples in each tree-based learner. Each list is then extended by appending the label previously assigned to the observations: "Outlier" if the list results from an outlier's traversal of the tree, and "Inlier" otherwise. As a result, each observation is associated with a set of predicate lists.

Adapting to an iForest DPG: To align with the principles of iForest, which classifies observations that reach the maximum tree depth as inliers, we eliminate all predicate lists that exceed the trees' maximum depth from the outlier sets. This step is crucial because iForest identifies outliers based on their early isolation, i.e., when an observation becomes separated in a leaf before reaching the maximum depth. Since observations that reach this depth may not be truly isolated or may not exhibit outlier characteristics, their removal prevents ambiguity that could lead to their misclassification as inliers.

After generating the predicate lists, we further refine them by removing the values (v) from each predicate triple, resulting in pairs of the form (f, σ). From now on, we will refer to these pairs as predicates.

This abstraction is necessary because iForest selects the split value (v) randomly at each node and for each tree. As a result, the exact triples (f, σ, v) are typically unique to individual trees and are not shared or reused across trees. Aggregating predicates at the level of (f, σ, v) would therefore hinder cross-tree analysis and reduce the generalizability of the method. By focusing on the feature and direction of the split only, we retain a meaningful and aggregable representation of the isolation patterns across trees.

Weighting iForest DPG: Using the predicate lists, we construct a weighted directed graph that represents the entire model. The predicates serve as the nodes of the graph. A node is connected to another if, within the predicate lists, the predicate in the first node is immediately followed by the predicate in the second node. This ensures that the connection represents the sequential order in which the predicates are satisfied during a decision tree's traversal. The graph's edges represent the frequency with which the pair of predicates stored in the connected nodes appears consecutively in the predicate lists, with the order preserved. The resulting graph shows two classes: "Outlier" and "Inlier", with their respective predicates distinguished by their frequency and position within the model logic.

Cleaning iForest DPG: We can observe that when there is a significant imbalance between the number of outliers and inliers, adjusting the frequency calculation becomes necessary to ensure a fair comparison between the two classes. Predicates satisfied by outliers appear considerably less frequently than those satisfied by inliers. Consequently, identifying the distinctive predicates of each class becomes particularly challenging due to the low frequency of those associated with outliers. We, therefore, introduce a weighting system for the frequencies. For each dataset instance that traverses the model, the transition between two consecutive predicates contributes differently depending on the class assigned to the data point. If the instance is classified as an outlier, its contribution to the frequency is multiplied by a weight w_o. Otherwise, its contribution is multiplied by a weight w_i. The weights are defined as:

$$w_o = \frac{N_o + N_i}{N_o}, \quad w_i = \frac{N_o + N_i}{N_i}, \qquad (1)$$

where N_o and N_i denote the number of outliers and inliers in the dataset, respectively. We can, therefore, state that the transition between two consecutive predicates satisfied by an outlier has a weighted frequency equal to w_o, while that satisfied by an inlier has a weighted frequency equal to w_i. The weight of an edge is calculated as the sum of these weighted frequencies; for brevity, we refer to this sum as the *weighted frequency of the edge*.

Towards Explanation. Once the graph is constructed, we define a new metric called the *Inlier-Outlier Propagation Score* (IOP-Score), quantifying a node's tendency to lead toward either the "Outlier" or "Inlier" class. This score is calculated as the difference between the frequency of data transitions from a node toward the "Inlier" class and those toward the "Outlier" class, normalized by the total frequency of data transitions entering the node. This normalization ensures the score accounts for the node's overall context, providing a balanced measure of its tendency to propagate toward either class. So, the IOP-Score for a generic node v is defined as:

$$\text{IOP-Score}(v) = \frac{f_i(v) - f_o(v)}{f_{in}(v)}, \qquad (2)$$

where $f_i(v)$ is the frequency of the edge connecting node v to the "Inlier" class, $f_o(v)$ is the frequency of the edge connecting node to the "Outlier" class, and $f_{in}(v)$ is the sum of the frequencies of all edges entering node v.

- If IOP-Score(v) = 1, the node is fully associated with the "Inlier" class, meaning its frequency results exclusively from transitions toward the "Inlier" class. In other words, the predicate appears only in predicate lists generated by inliers traversing the model.
- If IOP-Score(v) = −1, the node is entirely associated with the "Outlier" class, with its frequency stemming solely from transitions toward the "Outlier" class, indicating that the predicate appears only in predicate lists generated by outliers.
- If IOP-Score(v) = 0, the node is considered neutral, as there is an equal frequency of transitions toward both the "Inlier" and "Outlier" classes.

In summary, an IOP-Score close to 0 indicates that the node is non-discriminative, while values near 1 or −1 signify predicates that strongly characterize one of the two classes.

Outlined in Algorithm 1, the proposed approach is presented in pseudocode to enhance clarity and understanding.

Algorithm 1: iForest as a graph for DPG-based Explanation

Input: Trained Isolation Forest model IF, Dataset D, maximum depth of trees $dmax$
Output: iForest DPG

1 Initialize empty graph G;
2 **foreach** base learner iTree (iT) in IF **do**
3   Extract split rules defining predicates (f, σ, v);
4   **foreach** training sample s traversing iT **do**
5   Record satisfied predicate lists;
6   **if** s classified as outlier **then**
7   Label list as "Outlier";
8   **else**
9   Label list as "Inlier";
10 Remove paths of predicates exceeding tree $dmax$ for outliers;
11 Transform predicate lists to pairs (f, σ);
12 **foreach** predicate pair (p_i, p_j) appearing consecutively **do**
13   Create directed edge $(p_i \rightarrow p_j)$ with frequency weight;
14 Apply class-based frequency weighting using `ComputeFrequencyWeights()`.
15 **return** G;

3.2 Understanding the Explanation Process

The proposed technique is designed to capture the key concept underlying iForest. In iForest, outliers are isolated more rapidly than inliers, requiring fewer splits to separate them from the rest of the dataset. Although selecting features and associated values at each split is random, outliers differ from inliers for certain features. These key features play a role in the splits that lead to the isolation of outliers. Our XAI method's purpose is to identify the features that differentiate outliers from inliers and understand their role in IF's decision-making process. Representing the process as a graph enables visualization of predicate sequences leading to each class, highlighting the typical paths of outliers. By incorporating information about the sign of the predicates, the method enables the interpretation of the direction of the constraints imposed by the model—that is, whether a feature contributes to the isolation of outliers by surpassing a certain threshold. Moreover, using the IOP-Score—calculated for each node of the graph—quantifies the relative contribution of features in distinguishing between the two classes. A low value of this metric indicates that the corresponding predicate is essential for isolating outliers, emphasizing that the outlier nature of observations depends on specific features. This aspect underscores the importance of correctly interpreting these features within the context of the application domain and the need to consider potential data errors that may affect the identification of outliers. Furthermore, the weight of the edges connecting the nodes—proportional to frequencies—indicates whether the predicates are immediately effective at distinguishing outliers, such as when outliers are easily separated along a feature, or whether they contribute indirectly by forming decision paths that require additional splits to isolate an outlier. By combining the graph structure with IOP-Score, the proposed technique provides a global and interpretable explanation of the model. It illustrates not only which features are used but also how and with what frequency they contribute to isolating outliers.

Table 1 summarizes how to interpret the DPG structure to understand its implications for outlier and inlier classification.

Table 1. DPG and their Implications for Outlier/Inlier interpretation

Component	Implication for Outlier/Inlier Detection
Node (Predicate)	Represent a decision made to identify a sample as an inlier or outlier pathway based on feature and condition
Weighted Edge	Indicates how frequently a decision path is used. Thicker edges leading to outliers highlight important anomaly detection features.
Node (Terminal)	Base on classified samples as inliers or outliers, helping identify critical predicates for anomaly separation.
IOP-Score	Predicates with negative IOP-Scores correspond to features that play a major role in isolating outliers, while positive values indicate features that help define inlier boundaries.

4 Experiments

This section demonstrates the novelty and contributions of our DPG-based approach to explaining the iForest. We utilized a synthetic dataset to construct challenging anomalies featuring multiple attributes across various scales. Additionally, we employed a benchmark dataset to facilitate a fair comparison with other techniques. This benchmark dataset was also used in the original iForest study. We conducted a comprehensive analysis, utilizing both visualizations and interpretations provided by our method.

Our implementation was developed in Python, leveraging a suite of libraries to facilitate anomaly detection, visualization, and data processing. The scikit-learn library [15] was utilized for the implementation of the iForest algorithm, while Graphviz enabled the visualization of the DPG[1], enhancing the interpretability of the decision-making process. To promote reproducibility and facilitate further research, the complete source code is publicly available on GitHub[2].

4.1 Synthetic Datasets

To analyze our XAI methods, we generated two synthetic datasets. Each dataset contains 200 data points characterized by six numerical features (denoted as F_i, where i ranges from 1 to 6), all forming a single-cluster distribution. We introduced outliers by randomly selecting samples and modifying specific feature values according to predefined rules. Each outlier is generated by altering two and four feature values from a randomly selected sample among the available ones. Each alteration is performed by rescaling the original value by a factor of 4 or 5 times the standard deviation of that feature computed over the entire dataset. The resulting dataset exhibits clearly defined anomalies, distinct feature variations, and a balanced level of complexity, making it well-suited for assessing explanation techniques in anomaly detection. We trained an iForest model with 200 trees for each study case to identify outliers. Since our focus is on XAI—where the primary objective is to explain the model's decisions rather than optimize predictive accuracy—the exact number of trees is not relevant to our scope. Therefore, we chose 200 trees to ensure robust and stable predictions.

Synthetic Dataset with One Outlier. The first dataset was generated by modifying four features of one sample, as reported in the Table 2, thereby producing a single outlier among 200 samples. In Fig. 3, we present a pair plot of the first synthetic dataset, where we can observe that the single outline stands apart from the clustered inliers.

The modified sample was correctly identified as an outlier by the iForest model. Then, applying our technique, we obtained iForest DPG, as shown in Fig. 4, where the classes outliers and inliers are distinguished by different colors. For each node, the IOP-Score was computed and represented by its color —these scores are summarized in Table 3.

Table 2. Sample 0 is the outlier in the first synthetic dataset. The table presents both the initial and final values of the modified features for this sample, along with the specific modifications applied to introduce the outlier.

Outliers	Feature	Initial Value	Final Value	Alteration
Sample 0	F_0	−2.12	2.29	+4.41
	F_3	4.05	−0.76	−4.81
	F_4	−6.01	−0.93	+5.08
	F_5	−7.21	−1.88	+5.33

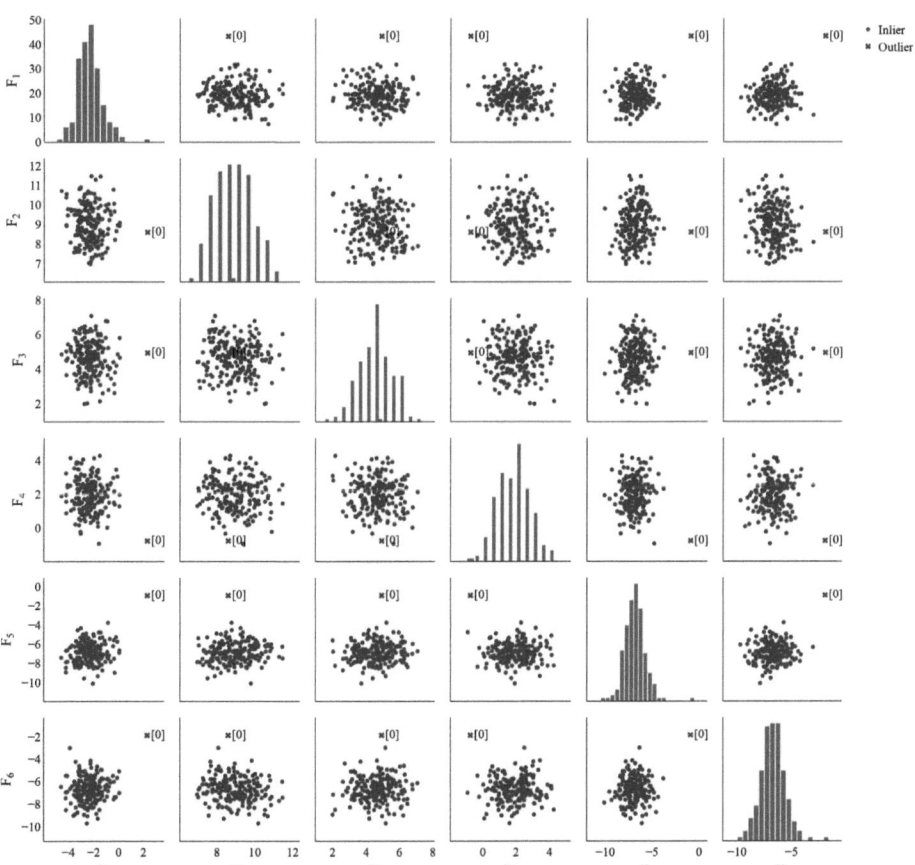

Fig. 3. Pairplot of the first synthetic dataset. The dataset comprises 200 samples with six numerical features and one outlier.

---

[1] Implementation available at: https://github.com/LeonardoArrighi/DPG.
[2] Implementation available at: https://github.com/Math0097/DPG-iForest.

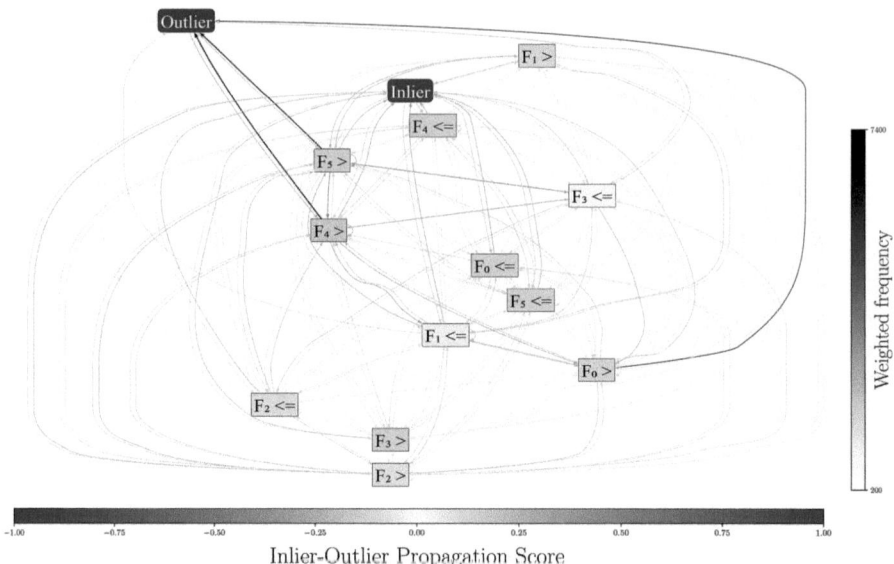

Fig. 4. Global representation of the iForest model as a DPG produced by our method for the first synthetic dataset. The vertical bar on the right indicates the edge weights, while the horizontal bar at the bottom displays the IOP-Score of the nodes.

Table 3. IOP-Score values assigned to each predicate (node) extracted from the DPG graph of the iForest model for the first synthetic dataset. The scores quantify a node's propensity to distinguish data toward the inliers (positive values) or outliers (negative values) class.

Predicate	IOP-Score
$F_4 <=$	0.1427
$F_0 <=$	0.1406
$F_5 <=$	0.1336
$F_3 >$	0.1304
$F_1 >$	0.1129
$F_2 <=$	0.0985
$F_2 >$	0.0807
$F_1 <=$	0.0426
$F_3 <=$	0.0091
$F_0 >$	-0.1202
$F_5 >$	-0.1362
$F_4 >$	-0.1580

By examining an in-depth view of the iForest model's internal process, we can observe that some nodes exhibit IOP-Score values below 0, indicating an association with the "Outliers" class. The nodes with the lowest scores contain particularly meaningful predicates—namely, $F_4 >$, $F_5 >$, and $F_0 >$—which correspond to the features altered to create the anomaly. The $>$ sign indicates that, for the outlier, these feature values exceed those of inliers, a fact further supported by the Fig. 3. Moreover, the edges connecting these nodes to the "Outlier" class are thicker, reflecting higher weighted frequencies; this suggests that the model consistently employs splits based on these predicates as final decision points to isolate outliers. In contrast, nodes involving predicates on F_3, despite it being one of the modified features, do not have low IOP-Score values and are not closely associated with the "Outlier" class. This indicates that F_3 does not consistently separate the anomalous sample from inliers, though it does contribute to the isolation process on several occasions. Finally, the remaining nodes with IOP-Score values above 0 are predominantly involved in splits that classify points as inliers.

Synthetic Dataset with Four Outliers. The second dataset is created by modifying four randomly selected samples according to the previously described rule, as detailed in Table 4. Figure 5 presents an overview of the entire dataset, highlighting four outliers. Unlike the previous dataset, this one is more complex because each outlier is generated by modifying different features. As a result, each outlier can be individually distinguished by a specific set of features, meaning that no single split can separate all outliers from the inliers.

Table 4. The first column lists the outliers in the second synthetic dataset. The table shows the initial and final values of the modified features for these samples, along with the specific modifications applied to introduce the outliers.

Outliers	Feature	Initial Value	Final Value	Alteration
Sample 0	F_0	−1.86	1.67	+3.53
	F_1	8.92	12.84	+3.93
Sample 1	F_0	−2.19	1.34	+3.53
	F_2	4.74	0.78	−3.95
Sample 2	F_0	−2.12	2.29	+4.41
	F_3	4.05	−0.76	−4.81
	F_5	−7.21	−1.88	+5.33
	F_4	−6.01	−0.93	+5.08
Sample 3	F_1	9.21	13.13	+3.93
	F_3	0.95	−2.90	−3.84

The trained iForest model successfully distinguished the modified samples as outliers. Moreover, features exhibiting consistent directional changes, such as

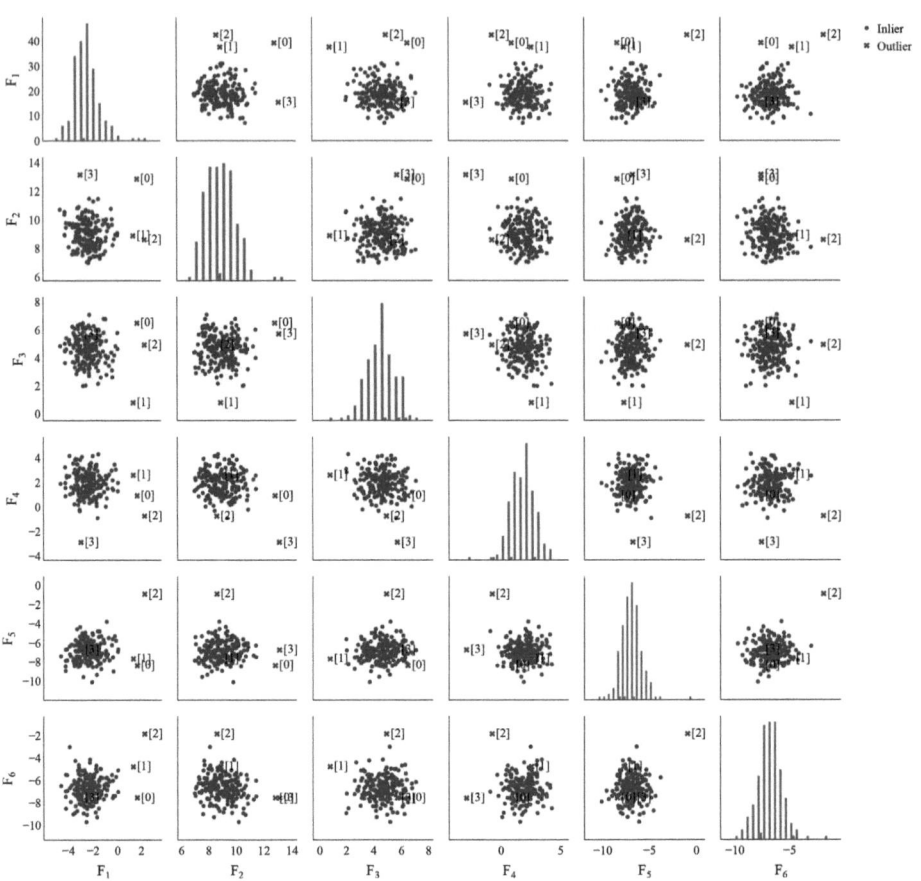

Fig. 5. Pairplot of the second synthetic dataset. The dataset comprises 200 samples with six numerical features, and four samples have been modified by altering between two to four.

increases in F_0 and F_1 or decreases in F_3, are more readily distinguishable than others. Similarly, as for the previous dataset, we applied our technique to explain the iForest process. The model is converted into the DPG shown in Fig. 6, where the classes "Outlier" and "Inlier" are distinguished by different colors. For each node, the IOP-Score is computed and represented by its color—these scores are summarized in Table 5.

Our technique helps interpret the inner logical process of the iForest model. In this scenario, outliers are less distinct from inliers and require the combined influence of multiple features to be isolated, making the model's structure more challenging to interpret than the previous case. Nevertheless, our representation and the IOP-Score provide valuable insights. We can observe that some predicates have an IOP-Score below 0, so they are strongly connected with the "Outlier" class. In particular, the nodes with the lowest IOP-Score are $F0 >$,

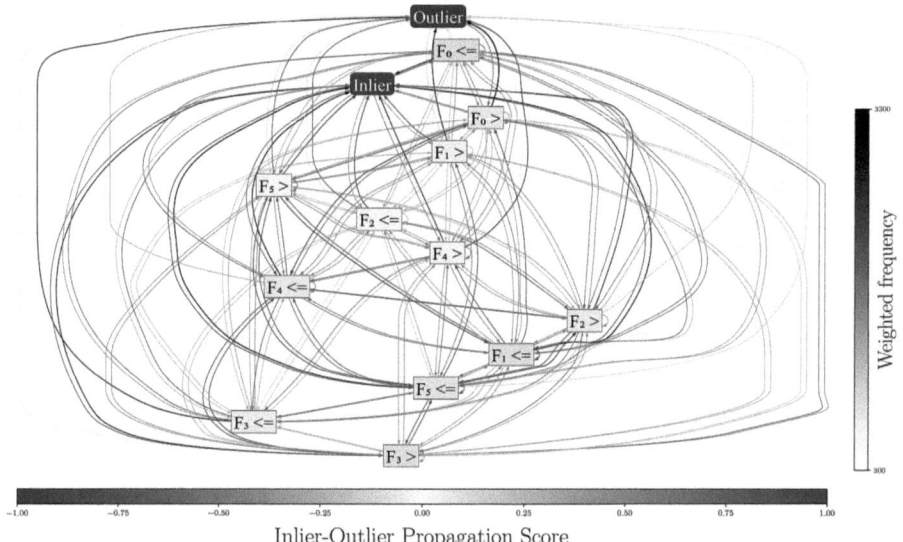

Fig. 6. Global representation of the iForest model as a DPG produced by our method for the second synthetic dataset. The vertical bar on the right indicates the edge weights, while the horizontal bar at the bottom displays the IOP-Score of the nodes.

Table 5. IOP-Score assigned to each predicate (node) extracted from the DPG graph of the iForest model for the second synthetic dataset. The scores quantify a node's propensity to channel data toward the inliers (positive values) or outliers (negative values) class.

Predicate	IOP-Score
$F_1 <=$	0.0884
$F_3 >$	0.0881
$F_0 <=$	0.0872
$F_5 <=$	0.0710
$F_4 <=$	0.0553
$F_2 >$	0.0542
$F_5 >$	0.0112
$F_2 <=$	0.0112
$F_4 >$	0.0084
$F_1 >$	−0.0257
$F_3 <=$	−0.0316
$F_0 >$	−0.0494

$F3 <=$, and $F1 >$, which comprehend the features deliberately altered to create the anomalies; these predicates are critical for the model to distinguish outliers. The thicker edges connecting these nodes to the "Outlier" class further underscore their frequent use in splits that isolate anomalous data points. Moreover, the directional signs in these predicates reveal how the model leverages the features—Figure 5 clearly shows that multiple outliers are isolated using these key splits. In addition, although F_4, F_2, and F_5 are also modified, their IOP-Scores are slightly above 0, indicating that splits involving these features do not consistently lead to outlier isolation. Finally, the remaining nodes, with IOP-Score values above 0, are primarily involved in splits that classify points as inliers.

4.2 Annthyroid Dataset

To evaluate the performance of our XAI methods in a real-world scenario, we used the *Annthyroid dataset*, which is widely adopted in the literature on outlier detection as a benchmark ([5,6]). The dataset represents thyroid function measurements, including hormone levels, biochemical indicators, and patient demographics. Each row corresponds to a patient sample, with multiple attributes capturing relevant physiological parameters. It consists of six numerical features (excluding the binary features) and 6916 samples. The features explored include *Age*, which provides demographic context; Thyroid-Stimulating Hormone (*TSH*), a critical regulator of thyroid function; *T3*, *TT4* (Total Thyroxine), and Free Thyroxine Index (*FTI*), which measure hormone concentrations in the blood; Thyroxine Uptake (*T4U*), which helps assess hormone-binding activity. The dataset consists of two classes: *normal* (inliers) and *anomalous* (outliers), where anomalies correspond to thyroid disorders. The class distribution is highly imbalanced, with normal cases forming the majority and anomalous instances accounting for only 3.61 % of the total samples. The Annthyroid dataset is available in the UCI machine learning repository in the medical domain ([3]).

We applied our proposal to obtain an iForest model (using 200 iTrees) into a DPG and obtained results similar to the literature [6]. The explanation can be appreciated in Fig. 7, where nodes represent predicate-based decision points while edges indicate the flow of decisions through these conditions. Thicker, darker edges correspond to frequently used decision paths, highlighting influential features, whereas lighter edges represent less significant decisions. *TSH* feature serves as a strong predicate point, with a high *TSH* value (*TSH* >) directing the flow toward the outlier node (red box). This indicates that high *TSH* levels are a significant factor in identifying thyroid anomalies with a superior limit. Similarly, a low *TSH* value (*TSH* <=) redirects the flow through additional feature-based decisions before reaching a final classification. The thin edges entering the *TSH* > node also imply that this feature alone is usually sufficient to separate outliers from the rest of the dataset. In contrast, the *T3* > feature necessitates further subdivision.

The IOP-Score, in Fig. 7, represented by the color scale at the bottom, provides further insight into how strongly each predicate affects outlier and inlier identification. Red-shaded paths and nodes indicate a high probability of leading to an outlier classification, while blue-shaded paths and nodes suggest a strong inlier association. *TSH >* is once again revealed as a highly important factor in anomaly detection. The other predicates make a slight contribution, primarily serving to delineate the boundaries of inlier behavior. More details about the obtained IOP-Score is available in Table 6.

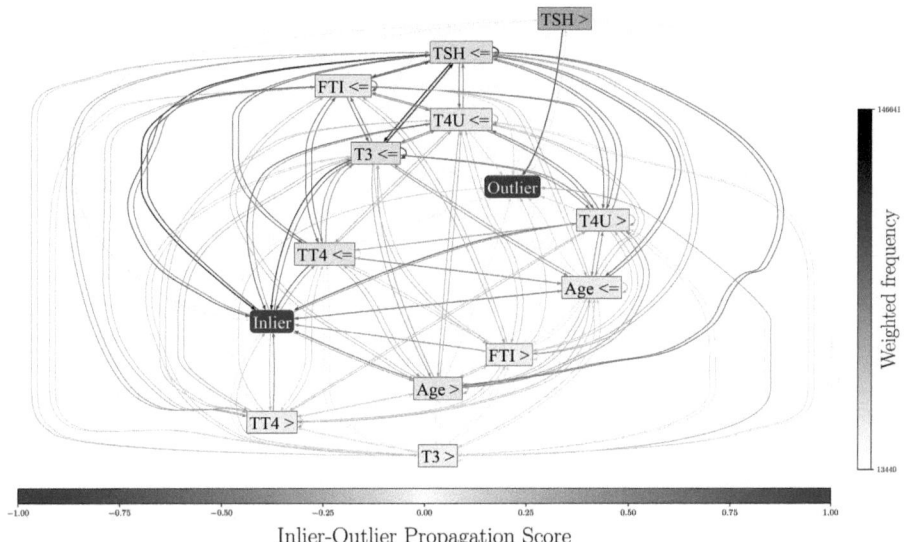

Fig. 7. Global representation of the iForest model as a DPG structure produced by our method for the Annthyroid dataset. The vertical bar on the right indicates the edge weights, while the horizontal bar at the bottom displays the IOP-Score of the nodes.

Notably, as observed in Table 6, the node with the lowest score corresponds to the predicate *TSH >*. This is particularly significant, as its highly negative score, along with the thick edge connecting it to the "Outliers" class, suggests that the model frequently relies on this feature to isolate anomalies. Similarly, the node containing the predicate *T3 >* also has a negative score, though closer to zero, indicating that while it contributes to outlier detection, it often requires additional splits to effectively isolate anomalies. Finally, the remaining nodes, with IOP-Score values above 0, are primarily involved in splits that classify data points as inliers.

5 Limitations and Extensions

While the proposed approach comprehensively explains the iForest model using DPG, some limitations must be acknowledged. The transformation of iForest into a graph structure introduces additional computational complexity, mainly when dealing with high-dimensional datasets containing many trees. This complexity also leads to scalability issues, as constructing and analyzing the DPG

Table 6. IOP-Score assigned to each predicate (node) extracted from the DPG of the iForest model for the Annthyroid dataset. The scores quantify a node's propensity to channel data toward the "Inlier" (positive values) or "Outlier" (negative values) class.

Predicate	IOP-Score
TSH <=	0.0965
T3 <=	0.0846
TT4 <=	0.0776
Age >	0.0683
T4U <=	0.0573
FTI <=	0.0556
T4U >	0.0551
Age <=	0.0515
TT4 >	0.0354
FTI >	0.0323
T3 >	−0.0282
TSH >	−0.2429

for large-scale iForest models can be memory-intensive, necessitating optimization techniques for practical deployment. Furthermore, although DPG provides a structured representation of the model, interpreting the graph structure in highly complex datasets requires complementary visualization techniques to enhance clarity. Additionally, while existing XAI methods, such as SHAP and DIFFI provide alternative explanations for iForest, a more in-depth comparison with these techniques is necessary to establish the specific advantages and trade-offs of DPG. Another important consideration is that the method relies on predicates extracted from iForest's split rules, which may not always capture subtle feature interactions.

To address these challenges, future work will focus on optimizing graph construction techniques, improving scalability, and integrating additional interpretability metrics to enhance the usability of DPG-based explanations. The method aims to identify key features that differentiate outliers from inliers by visualizing decision paths in a graph. The incorporation of predicate signs allows for an interpretation of whether a feature contributes to outlier isolation by surpassing a threshold. Combining the graph structure with the IOP-Score enables a global understanding of the model's decision-making process, shedding light on important features and their role in detecting anomalies.

6 Conclusion

In this work, we introduced a novel approach for explaining the iForest model using DPG. The DPG-based explanation provides a structured and interpretable representation of the outlier detection process. It offers a global perspective on the model's behavior and logic. Our approach addresses a gap in the explainability of tree-based ensemble models by extending the capabilities of traditional feature importance methods, such as SHAP and DIFFI, which primarily focus on local or vector-based explanations. The DPG allows for comprehensive visualization of decision paths, enabling users to interpret the isolation logic of iForest with greater clarity. Additionally, introducing the IOP-Score ensures that critical predicates contributing to outlier detection are effectively distinguished from those relevant to inliers. This paper contributes to the field of XAI by providing a transparent and interpretable method for understanding anomaly detection models, offering a highly extensible approach for accurately identifying outlier behavior.

Disclosure of Interests. The authors have no competing interests to declare that are relevant to the content of this article.

References

1. Arcudi, A., Frizzo, D., Masiero, C., Susto, G.A.: Enhancing interpretability and generalizability in extended isolation forests. Eng. Appl. Artif. Intell. **138**, 109409 (2024). https://doi.org/10.1016/j.engappai.2024.109409
2. Arrighi, L., Pennella, L., Marques Tavares, G., Barbon Junior, S.: Decision predicate graphs: enhancing interpretability in tree ensembles. In: World Conference on Explainable Artificial Intelligence, pp. 311–332. Springer Nature Switzerland (2024). https://doi.org/10.1007/978-3-031-63797-1_16
3. Bache, K., Lichman, M.: UCI machine learning repository. http://archive.ics.uci.edu/ml
4. Carletti, M., Terzi, M., Susto, G.A.: Interpretable anomaly detection with diffi: depth-based feature importance of isolation forest. Eng. Appl. Artif. Intell. **119**, 105730 (2023). https://doi.org/10.1016/j.engappai.2022.105730
5. Goldstein, M.: Unsupervised Anomaly Detection Benchmark (2015). https://doi.org/10.7910/DVN/OPQMVF
6. Goldstein, M., Uchida, S.: A comparative evaluation of unsupervised anomaly detection algorithms for multivariate data. PLoS ONE **11**(4), e0152173 (2016). https://doi.org/10.1371/journal.pone.0152173
7. Holzinger, A., Carrington, A., Müller, H.: Measuring the quality of explanations: the System Causability Scale (SCS). KI - Künstliche Intelligenz **34**(2), 193–198 (2020). https://doi.org/10.1007/s13218-020-00636-z
8. Kartha, N.S., Gautrais, C., Vercruyssen, V.: Why are you weird? infusing interpretability in isolation forest for anomaly detection. arXiv preprint arXiv:2112.06858 (2021). https://doi.org/10.48550/arXiv.2112.06858
9. Lipton, Z.C.: The mythos of model interpretability: in machine learning, the concept of interpretability is both important and slippery. Queue **16**(3), 31–57 (2018). https://doi.org/10.1145/3236386.3241340
10. Liu, F.T., Ting, K.M., Zhou, Z.H.: Isolation forest. In: 2008 Eighth IEEE International Conference on Data Mining, pp. 413–422. IEEE (2008). https://doi.org/10.1109/ICDM.2008.17

11. Liu, Y., Aldrich, C.: Anomaly detection and explanation in coal data using isolation forest, random forest, and shap. Int. J. Coal Geol. **250**, 103921 (2023). https://doi.org/10.1016/j.coal.2023.103921
12. Lundberg, S.M., Lee, S.I.: A unified approach to interpreting model predictions. In: Proceedings of the 31st International Conference on Neural Information Processing Systems, pp. 4768–4777. NIPS'17 (2017)
13. Makridis, G., Koukos, V., Fatouros, G., Separdani, M.M., Kyriazis, D.: Enhancing explainability in mobility data science through a combination of methods. In: Intelligent Computing, pp. 45–60. Springer (2024). https://doi.org/10.1007/978-3-031-62269-4_4
14. Ndao, M.L., Youness, G., Niang, N., Saporta, G.: Enhancing explainability in predictive maintenance: investigating the impact of data preprocessing techniques on xai effectiveness. In: The 37th International Conference of the Florida Artificial Intelligence Research Society. Florida, United States (2024). https://doi.org/10.32473/flairs.37.1.135526
15. Pedregosa, F., et al.: Scikit-learn: machine learning in Python. J. Mach. Learn. Res. **12**, 2825–2830 (2011)
16. Rachwał, Ł., Krawczyk, B., Woźniak, M.: Isolation forest with exclusion of attributes based on shapley index. IEEE Trans. Neural Netw. Learn. Syst. **34**(8), 4011–4022 (2023). https://doi.org/10.1109/ACCESS.2024.3432174
17. Rizzo, L., Longo, L.: A qualitative investigation of the explainability of defeasible argumentation and non-monotonic fuzzy reasoning. In: Proceedings for the 26th AIAI Irish Conference on Artificial Intelligence and Cognitive Science Trinity College Dublin, Dublin, Ireland, December 6-7th, 2018, pp. 138–149 (2018). https://doi.org/10.21427/tby8-8z04
18. Sipple, J., Youssef, A.: A general-purpose method for applying explainable AI for anomaly detection. In: International Symposium on Methodologies for Intelligent Systems, pp. 162–174. Springer (2022). https://doi.org/10.1007/978-3-031-16564-1_16
19. Speith, T.: A review of taxonomies of explainable artificial intelligence (XAI) methods. In: Proceedings of the 2022 ACM Conference on Fairness, Accountability, and Transparency, pp. 2239–2250. FAccT '22, Association for Computing Machinery (2022). https://doi.org/10.1145/3531146.3534639
20. Strasser, S., Klettke, M.: Transparent data preprocessing for machine learning. In: Proceedings of the 2024 Workshop on Human-In-the-Loop Data Analytics. pp. 1–6. Association for Computing Machinery, New York, NY, USA (2024). https://doi.org/10.1145/3665939.3665960
21. Vilone, G., Longo, L.: Development of a human-centred psychometric test for the evaluation of explanations produced by XAI methods. In: Explainable Artificial Intelligence, pp. 205–232. Springer Nature Switzerland (2023). https://doi.org/10.1007/978-3-031-44070-0_11
22. Zelaya, C.V.G.: Towards explaining the effects of data preprocessing on machine learning. In: 2019 IEEE 35th International Conference on Data Engineering (ICDE), pp. 2086–2090. IEEE (2019). https://doi.org/10.1109/ICDE.2019.00245

Open Access This chapter is licensed under the terms of the Creative Commons Attribution 4.0 International License (http://creativecommons.org/licenses/by/4.0/), which permits use, sharing, adaptation, distribution and reproduction in any medium or format, as long as you give appropriate credit to the original author(s) and the source, provide a link to the Creative Commons license and indicate if changes were made.

The images or other third party material in this chapter are included in the chapter's Creative Commons license, unless indicated otherwise in a credit line to the material. If material is not included in the chapter's Creative Commons license and your intended use is not permitted by statutory regulation or exceeds the permitted use, you will need to obtain permission directly from the copyright holder.

Mathematical Foundation of Interpretable Equivariant Surrogate Models

Jacopo Joy Colombini[1]($^{\boxtimes}$), Filippo Bonchi[2], Francesco Giannini[1], Fosca Giannotti[1], Roberto Pellungrini[1], and Patrizio Frosini[2]

[1] Scuola Normale Superiore, Pisa, Italy
{Filippo.Bonchi,Patrizio.Frosini}@sns.it
[2] Università di Pisa, Pisa, Italy
{JacopoJoy.Colombini,Francesco.Giannini,Fosca.Giannotti,
Roberto.Pellungrini}@unipi.it

Abstract. This paper introduces a rigorous mathematical framework for neural network explainability, and more broadly for the explainability of equivariant operators called Group Equivariant Operators (GEOs), based on Group Equivariant Non-Expansive Operators (GENEOs) transformations. The central concept involves quantifying the distance between GEOs by measuring the non-commutativity of specific diagrams. Additionally, the paper proposes a definition of interpretability of GEOs according to a complexity measure that can be defined according to each user's preferences. Moreover, we explore the formal properties of this framework and show how it can be applied in classical machine learning scenarios, like image classification with convolutional neural networks.

Keywords: Mathematical Foundation of XAI · XAI metrics · Equivariant Neural Networks

1 Introduction

What is an *"explanation"*? An explanation can be seen as a combination of elementary blocks, much like a sentence is formed by words, a formula by symbols, or a proof by axioms and lemmas. The key question is when such a combination effectively explains a phenomenon. Notably, the quality of an explanation is observer-dependent—what is clear to a scientist may be incomprehensible to a philosopher or a child. In our approach, an explanation of a phenomenon P is convenient for an observer $\mathbb{O}$ if (i) $\mathbb{O}$ finds it comfortable, meaning the building blocks are easy to manipulate, and (ii) it is convincing, meaning $\mathbb{O}$ perceives P and the explanation as sufficiently close. We contextualize this perspective by assuming that the phenomenon is an AI agent, viewed as an operator, thus saying that the action of an agent $\mathbb{A}$ is explained by another agent $\mathbb{B}$ from the perspective of an observer $\mathbb{O}$ if:

1. $\mathbb{O}$ perceives $\mathbb{B}$ as close to $\mathbb{A}$;
2. $\mathbb{O}$ perceives $\mathbb{B}$ as less complex than $\mathbb{A}$.

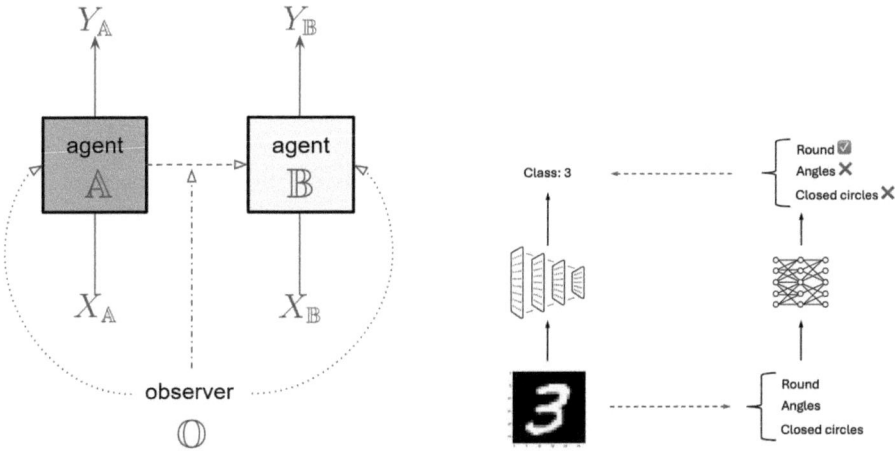

(a) An agent $\mathbb{B}$ explains an agent $\mathbb{A}$ for an observer $\mathbb{O}$: $\mathbb{O}$ perceives $\mathbb{B}$ as close to $\mathbb{A}$, and $\mathbb{B}$ as less complex than $\mathbb{A}$

(b) A practical example: an image classification task can be surrogated by a model based on textual concepts

Fig. 1. Representation of interpretable surrogate models exemplified on MNIST.

This is represented in Fig. 1 where we show this concept with an example. Notwithstanding the fact that observer $\mathbb{O}$ has the right to choose subjective criteria to measure how good $\mathbb{B}$ is to approximate $\mathbb{A}$ and their complexities, this paper introduces a mathematical framework for these measurements.

The growing use of complex neural networks in critical applications demands both high performance and transparency in decision-making. While AI interpretability and explainability have advanced, a rigorous mathematical framework for defining and comparing explanations is still lacking [33]. Recent efforts to formalize explanations [21] and interpretable models [29] do not provide practical guidelines for designing or training explainable models, nor do they incorporate the notion of an observer within the theory. Moreover, researchers emphasize the importance of Group Equivariant Operators (GEOs) in machine learning [3,14,19,41], as they integrate prior knowledge and enhance neural network design control [5]. While standard neural networks are universal approximators [17], this typically increases complexity. However, no existing XAI technique addresses explaining an equivariant model using another equivariant model.

This paper addresses this gap by introducing a framework for learning interpretable surrogate models of a black-box and defining a measure of interpretability based on an observer's subjective preferences. Given the importance of equivariant operators, our XAI framework is built on the theory of GEOs and Group Equivariant Non-Expansive Operators (GENEOs) [18]. GEOs, a broader class than standard neural networks, are well-suited for processing data with inherent symmetries. Indeed, equivariant networks, such as convolutional [20] and graph neural networks [36], have proven effective across different tasks [35]. Using GENEO-based transformations, we develop a theory for learning surrogate models of a given GEO by minimizing algebraic diagram commutation errors. The learned surrogate model can either perform a task or approximate a black-box model's predictions while optimizing interpretability based on an observer's perception of complexity, while allowing different observers to have distinct interpretability preferences for the same model architecture.

Contributions. Our contributions can be summarized as follows.

- Introduction of a mathematical framework to define interpretable surrogate models, where interpretability depends on a specific observer.
- Definition of a distance between GEOs using diagram non-commutativity, providing a quantitative method for model comparison and training.
- Formal definition of GEOs' complexity to assess model interpretability.
- We show empirically that these metrics enable training of more interpretable models, usable for direct task-solving or as surrogates for black-box models.

The paper is organized as follows. Section 2 recalls basics from different Mathematics areas that we use to define our metrics in Sect. 3. Section 4 shows how these metrics are used in practice to define a learning problem for an interpretable surrogate model. We show how the proposed framework can be used via an experimental evaluation in Sect. 5. Finally, Sect. 6 comments on related work and Sect. 7 draws conclusions and remarks on future work. The Appendix contains additional material and all proofs.

2 Mathematical Preliminaries

The framework proposed in this paper is founded on mathematical structures studied in various fields, such as geometry and category theory. Metric spaces and groups are used to define GE(NE)Os, while categories to compose them.

2.1 Perception Spaces and GE(NE)Os

Recall that a *pseudo-metric space* is a pair (X, d) where X is a set and $d\colon X \times X \to [0, \infty]$ is a pseudo-metric, namely a function such that, for all $x, y, z \in X$,

$$(R)\ d(x,x) = 0, \qquad (S)\ d(x,y) = d(y,x), \qquad (T)\ d(x,z) \leq d(x,y) + d(y,z).$$

A *metric* d is a pseudo-metric that additionally satisfies $d(x,y) = 0 \implies x = y$. $d\colon X \times X \to [0, \infty]$ is a *hemi-metric* if it only satisfies (R) and (T). We use the informal term distance to refer to either metrics, pseudo-metrics or hemi-metrics.

A *group* $\mathbf{G} = (G, \circ, \mathrm{id}_G)$ consists of a set G, an associative operation $\circ\colon G \times G \to G$ having a unit element $\mathrm{id}_G \in G$ such that, for all $g \in G$, there exists $g^{-1} \in G$ satisfying $g \circ g^{-1} = g^{-1} \circ g = \mathrm{id}_G$. A *group homomorphism* $T\colon (G, \circ_G, \mathrm{id}_G) \to$

$(K, \circ_K, \mathrm{id}_K)$ is a function $T\colon G \to K$ such that, for all $g_1, g_2 \in G$, $T(g_1 \circ_G g_2) = T(g_1) \circ_K T(g_2)$. Given a group $(G, \circ, \mathrm{id}_G)$ and a set X, a *group left action* is a function $*\colon G \times X \to X$ such that, for all $x \in X$ and $g_1, g_2 \in G$,

$$\mathrm{id}_G * x = x \quad \text{and} \quad (g_1 \circ g_2) * x = g_1 * (g_2 * x).$$

With these ingredients, we can now illustrate the notions of perception space GEO and GENEO. We refer the interested reader to [6,18] and [1,8,10] for a more extensive description of GENEOs and their applications.

Definition 1. *An (extended) perception space $(X, d_X, \mathbf{G}, *)$, shortly $(X, \mathbf{G})$, consists of a pseudo-metric space (X, d_X), a group $\mathbf{G}$, a left group action $*\colon G \times X \to X$ such that, for all $x_1, x_2 \in X$ and every $g \in G$,*

$$d_X(g * x_1, g * x_2) = d_X(x_1, x_2).$$

Example 1. $(X, \mathbf{G})$, with $\mathbf{G}$ the group of rotations of $0°, 90°, 180°, 270°$, and X a set of images closed under the actions of $\mathbf{G}$, is a perception space.

Notice that in any perception space, one can define a pseudo-metric over the group $\mathbf{G}$ by fixing $d_G(g_1, g_2) := \sup_{x \in X} d_X(g_1 * x, g_2 * x)$ for any $g_1, g_2 \in G$. With this definition, one can easily show that $\mathbf{G}$ is a topological group and that the action $*$ is continuous (see Proposition 2 in Appendix).

Definition 2. *Let $(X, G), (Y, K)$ be two (extended) perception spaces, $f\colon X \to Y$ and $t\colon G \to K$ a group homomorphism. We say that (f, t) is an (extended) group equivariant operator (GEO) if $g(g * x) = t(g) * f(x)$ for every $x \in X$, $g \in G$. (f, t) is said an (extended) group equivariant non-expansive operator (GENEO) in case it is a GEO and it is also non-expansive, i.e.,*

1. *$d_Y(f(x_1), f(x_2)) \leq d_X(x_1, x_2)$ for every $x_1, x_2 \in X$,*
2. *$d_K(t(g_1), t(g_2)) \leq d_G(g_1, g_2)$ for every $g_1, g_2 \in G$.*

The previous extended definitions generalize original perception pairs, GEOs, and GENEOs beyond data represented as functions. We simply refer to them as perception space, GEO, and GENEO. With slight abuse of notation, we use d_{dt} for the metric d_X on the set of data, and d_{gr} for the metric d_G on the group G, relying on context to specify the perception space (X, G) under consideration.

Example 2 (Neural Networks as GEOs). Neural networks are a special case of GEOs, with different architectures equivariant to specific groups. Convolutional Neural Networks (CNNs) are equivariant to translations, while Graph Neural Networks (GNNs) respect graph permutations. Although standard Multi-Layer Perceptrons are not typically equivariant, they can be viewed as GEOs on the trivial group $\mathbf{1}$, containing only the neutral element.

Example 3. Let X_α be the set of all subsets $\mathbb{R}^3$ and the group $\mathbf{G}_\alpha$ the group of all translations in $\mathbb{R}^3$, and let $\tau_{(x,y,z)}$ represent the translations by (x, y, z). Similarly define X_β and $\mathbf{G}_\beta$ in $\mathbb{R}^2$ with $\tau_{(x,y)}$ translating by (x, y). A GENEO (f, t) can be defined where $f(x)$ gives the shadow (orthogonal projection) of x in X_β and the homomorphism $t\colon \mathbf{G}_\alpha \to \mathbf{G}_\beta$ is given by $t(\tau_{(x,y,z)}) = \tau_{(x,y)}$ for projections onto the xy-plane. Similarly, defining $t(\tau_{(x,y,z)}) = \tau_{(y,z)}$ gives a GENEO for projections onto the yz-plane.

2.2 A Categorical Algebra of GEOs

We introduce a simple language to specify combinations of GEOs. Our proposal relies on the algebra of monoidal categories (CD-categories [12]) that enjoy an intuitive –but formal– graphical representation by means of string diagrams [38].

Syntax. We fix a set $\mathcal{S}$ of basic sorts and we consider the set $\mathcal{S}^*$ of words over $\mathcal{S}$: we write 1 for the empty word and $U \otimes V$, or just UV, for the concatenation of any two words $U, V \in \mathcal{S}^*$. Moreover, we fix a set Γ of operator symbols and two functions $ar, coar \colon \Gamma \to \mathcal{S}^*$. For an operator symbol $g \in \Gamma$, $ar(g)$ represents its arity, intuitively the types of its input and $coar(g)$ its coarity, intuitively its output. The tuple $(\mathcal{S}, \Gamma, ar, coar)$, shortly Γ, is what is called in categorical jargon a *monoidal signature*.

We consider terms generated by the following context-free grammar

$$c ::= \begin{array}{c} A_1 \\ \vdots \\ A_n \end{array}\!\!\boxed{g}\!\!\begin{array}{c} B_1 \\ \vdots \\ B_m \end{array} \;\bigg|\; \begin{array}{c}\lceil\;\;\rceil\\\lfloor\_\_\rfloor\end{array} \;\bigg|\; A\!\!-\!\!\!-\!\!A \;\bigg|\; \begin{array}{c}A\diagdown\;\;\diagup B\\ \times\\ B\diagup\;\;\diagdown A\end{array} \;\bigg|\; A\!-\!\!\!\!\!\triangleleft\!\!\begin{array}{c}A\\A\end{array} \;\bigg|\; A\!-\!\!\bullet \;\bigg|$$

$$c_1 \circ c_2 \quad | \quad c_1 \otimes c_2$$

where A, B, A_i, B_i are sorts in $\mathcal{S}$ and g is a symbol in Γ with arity $A_1 \otimes \cdots \otimes A_n$ and coarity $B_1 \otimes \cdots \otimes B_m$. Terms of our grammar can be thought of as circuits where information flows from left to right: the wires on the left represent the input ports, those on the right the outputs; the labels on the wires specify the types of the ports. The input type of a term is the word in $\mathcal{S}^*$ obtained by reading from top to bottom the labels on the input ports; Similarly for the outpus. The circuit $\begin{smallmatrix}A_1\\ \vdots \\ A_n\end{smallmatrix}\!\boxed{g}\!\begin{smallmatrix}B_1\\ \vdots \\ B_m\end{smallmatrix}$ takes n inputs of type $A_1, \ldots, A_n$ and produce m outputs of type $B_1, \ldots, B_m$; $\lceil\;\rceil$ is the empty circuit with no inputs and no output; $A\!-\!\!-\!A$ is the wire where information of type A flows from left to right; $\begin{smallmatrix}A\diagdown\;\diagup B\\\times\\B\diagup\;\diagdown A\end{smallmatrix}$ allows for crossing of wires; $A\!-\!\!\triangleleft\!\begin{smallmatrix}A\\A\end{smallmatrix}$ receives some information of type A and emit two copies as outputs; $A\!-\!\bullet$ receives an information of type A and discards it. For arbitrary circuits c_1 and c_2, $c_1 \circ c_2$ and $c_1 \otimes c_2$ represent, respectively their sequential and parallel composition drawn as

$$\begin{array}{c}A_1\\ \vdots \\ A_n\end{array}\!\boxed{c_2}\!\begin{array}{c}B_1\\ \vdots \\ B_m\end{array}\!\boxed{c_1}\!\begin{array}{c}C_1\\ \vdots \\ C_o\end{array} \quad \text{and} \quad \begin{array}{c}\begin{array}{c}A_1\\ \vdots \\ A_n\end{array}\!\boxed{c_1}\!\begin{array}{c}B_1\\ \vdots \\ B_m\end{array}\\ \begin{array}{c}C_1\\ \vdots \\ C_j\end{array}\!\boxed{c_2}\!\begin{array}{c}D_1\\ \vdots \\ D_k\end{array}\end{array}.$$

As expected, the sequential composition of c_1 and c_2 is possible only when the outputs of c_2 coincides with the inputs of c_1.

Remark 1. The reader may have noticed that different syntactic terms are rendered equal by the diagrammatic representation. For instance both $c_1 \circ (c_2 \circ c_3)$ and $(c_1 \circ c_2) \circ c_3$ are drawn as

$$\begin{array}{c}A_1\\ \vdots \\ A_n\end{array}\!\boxed{c_3}\!\begin{array}{c}B_1\\ \vdots \\ B_m\end{array}\!\boxed{c_2}\!\begin{array}{c}C_1\\ \vdots \\ C_o\end{array}\!\boxed{c_1}\!\begin{array}{c}D_1\\ \vdots \\ D_p\end{array}$$

This is not an issue since the two terms represent the same GEO via the semantics that we illustrate here below, after a minimal background on categories.

Categories. Diagrams are arrows of the (strict) CD category freely generated by the monoidal signature Γ. The reader who is *not* an expert in category theory may safely ignore this fact and only know that a *category* **C** consists of (1) a collection of objects denoted by $Ob(\mathbf{C})$; (2) for all objects $A, B \in Ob(\mathbf{C})$, a collection of arrows $f: A \to B$ with source object A and target object B; (3) for all objects A, an identity arrow $id_A: A \to A$ and (4) for all arrows $f: A \to B$ and $g: B \to C$, a composite arrow $g \circ f: A \to C$ satisfying

$$f \circ (g \circ h) = (f \circ g) \circ h \qquad f \circ id_A = f = id_B \circ f$$

for all $f: A \to B$, $g: B \to C$ and $h: D \to E$.

Three categories will be particularly relevant for our work: the category **Diag**$_\Gamma$ having words in $\mathcal{S}^*$ as objects and diagrams as arrows, the category **GEO** having perception spaces as objects and GEOs as arrows and the category **GENEO** having perception spaces as objects and GENEOs as arrows.

Semantics. As mentioned at the beginning of this section, our diagrammatic language allows one to express combinations of GEOs. Intuitively, the symbols in Γ are basic *building blocks* that can be composed in sequence and in parallel with the aid of some wiring technology. The building blocks have to be thought of as atomic GEOs, while diagrams as composite ones.

To formally provide semantics to diagrams in terms of GEOs, the key ingredient is an *interpretation* $\mathcal{I}$ of the monoidal signature Γ within the (monoidal) category **GEO**, shortly, a function assigning to each symbol $g \in \Gamma$ a corresponding GEO. Then, by means of a universal property (or, depending on one's perspective, abstract mumbo jumbo), one obtains a function (actually a functor) $[\![-]\!]_\mathcal{I}: \mathbf{Diag}_\Gamma \to \mathbf{GEO}$ assigning to each diagram the denoted GEOs (see Table 5 in the Appendix for a simple inductive definition).

Note that $[\![-]\!]_\mathcal{I}$ may not be surjective, in the sense that not all GEOs are denoted by some diagrams: we call $\mathcal{G}_\mathcal{I}^\Gamma$ the image of **Diag**$_\Gamma$ through $[\![-]\!]_\mathcal{I}$, i.e.,

$$\mathcal{G}_\mathcal{I}^\Gamma := \{(f,t) \mid \exists c \in \mathbf{Diag}_\Gamma \text{ s.t. } [\![c]\!]_\mathcal{I} = (f,t)\}.$$

Hereafter, we fix a monoidal signature Γ and an interpretation $\mathcal{I}$ and we write $\mathcal{G}_\mathcal{I}^\Gamma$ simply as $\mathcal{G}$. This represents the universe of GEOs that are interesting for the observer, which we are going to introduce in the next section.

3 Observers-Based Approximation and Complexity

This paper aims at developing an applicable mathematical theory of interpretable models, which is based on the following intuition: an agent $\mathbb{A}$ can be interpreted via another agent $\mathbb{B}$ from the perspective of an observer $\mathbb{O}$ if: i) $\mathbb{O}$ perceives $\mathbb{B}$ as similar to $\mathbb{A}$ and ii) $\mathbb{O}$ perceives $\mathbb{B}$ as less complex than $\mathbb{A}$. This perspective motivates us to build a framework allowing the modeling of distance measures for GEOs (Sect. 3.1) and their degree of complexity (opaqueness/not interpretability, Sect. 3.2), w.r.t. the specification of a certain observer.

Definition 3. *An observer $\mathbb{O}$ interested in $\mathcal{G}$ is a couple $(\mathbf{T}, \mathcal{C})$ where:*

- **T** *is a category of* translations GENEOs, *namely a category having as objects $Ob(\mathbf{T})$ those perception spaces that are sources and targets of GEOs in $\mathcal{G}$ and as arrows $Hom(\mathbf{T})$ a selected set of GENEOs.*
- $\mathcal{C}$ *is a* complexity assignment, *namely a function $\mathcal{C} \colon \Gamma \to \mathbb{R}^+$.*

The *translation GENEOs* in **T** describe all the possible ways that the observer can "translate" data belonging to one perception space into data belonging to another perception space. Requiring these to be GENEOs, i.e., non-expansive, ensures that such translations performed by the observer cannot enlarge distances between data. For example, the observer may admit only isometries as morphisms in **T**, or the observer may not admit any translation at all, meaning that **T** only contains identities (note that this is the smallest possible **T**).

The *complexity assignment* $\mathcal{C} \colon \Gamma \to \mathbb{R}^+$ maps any building block g from Γ into a positive real number, a quantity that represent how *complex* is perceived g by the observer. Here complexity does not refer to the usual computational complexity but rather to the degree of *stress* that the observer perceives in dealing with g. Note that such assignment is completely arbitrary and thus, different observers may assign different complexities to the same building block. Any observer can specify what are the types of functions that they deem interpretable and/or more informative, from their perspective, for a given problem.

3.1 Surrogate Distance of GEOs

To formalize the notion of a surrogate model for an observer $\mathbb{O}$, we introduce a new hemi-metric $h_{\mathbb{O}}$, which we call the *surrogate distance* of a GEO for another GEO. To proceed, it is fundamental the notion of *crossed translation pair*.

Definition 4. *Let $(f_\alpha, t_\alpha) \colon (X_\alpha, G_\alpha) \to (Y_\alpha, K_\alpha)$ and $(f_\beta, t_\beta) \colon (X_\beta, G_\beta) \to (Y_\beta, K_\beta)$ be two GEOs in $\mathcal{G}$. A crossed pair of translation π from (f_α, t_α) to (f_β, t_β), written $\pi \colon (f_\alpha, t_\alpha) \leftrightharpoons_{\mathbf{T}} (f_\beta, t_\beta)$, is a couple $\Big((l_{\alpha,\beta}, p_{\alpha,\beta}), (m_{\beta,\alpha}, q_{\beta,\alpha})\Big)$ where*

- $(l_{\alpha,\beta}, p_{\alpha,\beta}) \colon (X_\alpha, G_\alpha) \to (X_\beta, G_\beta)$ *is a GENEO in* **T**,
- $(m_{\beta,\alpha}, q_{\beta,\alpha}) \colon (Y_\beta, K_\beta) \to (Y_\alpha, K_\alpha)$ *is a GENEO in* **T**.

Figure 2 provides an intuitive visualization of a crossed pair of translation GENEOs. Note that the two GENEOs have opposite directions.

Next, we define the cost of a crossed translation pair.

Definition 5. *Let $\pi = \Big((l_{\alpha,\beta}, p_{\alpha,\beta}), (m_{\beta,\alpha}, q_{\beta,\alpha})\Big)$ be a crossed translation pair from $(f_\alpha, t_\alpha) \colon (X_\alpha, G_\alpha) \to (Y_\alpha, K_\alpha)$ to $(f_\beta, t_\beta) \colon (X_\beta, G_\beta) \to (Y_\beta, K_\beta)$. The* functional cost *of π, written $\mathrm{cost}(\pi)$, is defined as follows.*

$$\mathrm{cost}(\pi) := \frac{1}{|X_\alpha|} \sum_{x \in X_\alpha} d_{\mathrm{dt}}\Big((m_{\beta,\alpha} \circ f_\beta \circ l_{\alpha,\beta})(x), f_\alpha(x)\Big) \tag{1}$$

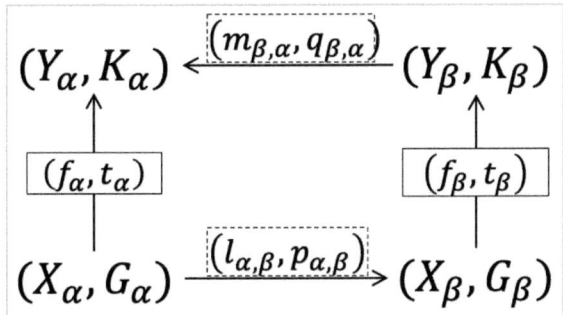

Fig. 2. Example of a crossed translation pair $\pi\colon (f_\alpha, t_\alpha) \leftrightharpoons_{\mathbf{T}} (f_\beta, t_\beta)$. We distinguish by solid and dashed blocks the GEOs in $\mathcal{G}$ from the GENEOs in $Hom(\mathbf{T})$.

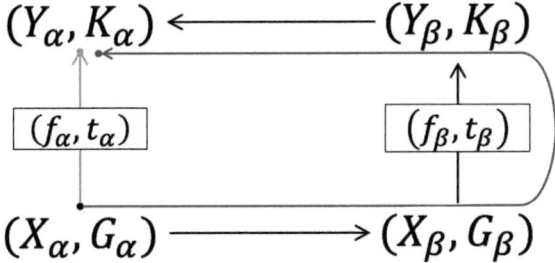

Fig. 3. The surrogate distance measures how far the diagram is to commute.

Remark 2. Note that in Eq. (1), $|X_\alpha|$ denotes the cardinality of the set X_α. Whenever such set is infinite the cost is not defined. Although this never happens in practical cases, one can easily generalize (1) to deal with infinite sets by enriching X_α with a Borel probability measure: see (4) in the Appendix.

Intuitively, the value $\mathrm{cost}(\pi)$ measures the distance of the two paths in the diagram in Fig. 3. With this, one can easily define a distance between GEOs.

Definition 6. *Let (f_α, t_α) and (f_β, t_β) be two GEOs in $\mathcal{G}$. The surrogate distance of (f_β, t_β) from (f_α, t_α), written $h_\mathbb{O}\bigl((f_\alpha, t_\alpha), (f_\beta, t_\beta)\bigr)$, is defined as*

$$\inf\{\mathrm{cost}(\pi) \mid \pi\colon (f_\alpha, t_\alpha) \leftrightharpoons_{\mathbf{T}} (f_\beta, t_\beta)\} \tag{2}$$

We emphasize that all considered GENEOs to define crossed pairs of translations must be in $\mathbf{T}$. The possibility of choosing $\mathbf{T}$ in different ways reflects the various approaches an observer can use to judge the similarity between data.

Example 4. Consider the smallest possible $\mathbf{T}$ (that is, no arrows between different perception spaces and only the identity between equal spaces) representing an observer who cannot translate the data. In this case, $h_\mathbb{O}\bigl((f_\alpha, t_\alpha), (f_\beta, t_\beta)\bigr) = \infty$

whenever (f_α, t_α) and (f_β, t_β) act on different perception spaces, since there is no translation pair $\pi\colon (f_\alpha, t_\alpha) \leftrightharpoons_\mathbf{T} (f_\beta, t_\beta)$. Whenever the perception spaces are the same, there is only one translation pair, formed by two identity GENEOs. Thus the surrogate distance of (f_β, t_β) from (f_α, t_α) collapses to the cost of such translation pair, that is,

$$\frac{1}{|X_\alpha|} \sum_{x \in X_\alpha} d_{\mathrm{dt}}\Big(f_\beta(x), f_\alpha(x)\Big)$$

Note that whenever d_{dt} assigns 0 to equal elements and 1 to different ones, this coincides with the standard notion of *fidelity* [32].

Theorem 1. *The function $h_\mathbb{O}$ is a hemi-metric on $\mathcal{G}$.*

Notice that while $h_\mathbb{O}$ is a hemi-metric, one can easily get a pseudo-metric by making it symmetric: $d_\mathbb{O} := \max\Big(h_\mathbb{O}\big((f_\alpha, t_\alpha), (f_\beta, t_\beta)\big), h_\mathbb{O}\big((f_\beta, t_\beta), (f_\alpha, t_\alpha)\big)\Big)$. We choose to stay with the non-symmetric distance $h_\mathbb{O}$ since it should measures how far the observer $\mathbb{O}$ perceives the surrogate (f_β, t_β) from the GEO to interpret (f_α, t_α). We believe that for this kind of measurement, it is more natural to drop symmetry, like, for instance, in the case of fidelity (Example 4).

3.2 Measures of Complexity

In Sect. 2.2 we have introduced string diagrams allowing for combining several building blocks taken from a given set of symbols Γ and we have illustrated how the semantics assigns to each diagram a GEO. Here, we establish a way to measure the *comfort* that an observer $\mathbb{B}$ has in dealing with a certain diagram. We call such measure the *complexity* of a diagram relative to $\mathbb{O}$.

To give a complexity to each diagram, we exploit the complexity assignment $\mathcal{C}\colon \Gamma \to \mathbb{R}^+$ of the observer $\mathbb{O}$ that provides a complexity to each building block.

Definition 7. *Let c be a diagram in $\mathbf{Diag}_\Gamma$. The complexity of a diagram c (relative to the observer $\mathbb{O}$), written $,c$, is inductively as follows:*

$$, \boxed{g} := \mathcal{C}(g) \qquad ,\ \Box\ := 0 \quad, c_1 \otimes c_2 := , c_1 +, c_2$$
$$, A\!\!\rightarrow\!\!{}_A^A := 0 \qquad ,\ {}_B^A\!\!\bowtie\!\!{}_A^B := 0 \quad, c_1 \circ c_2 := , c_1 +, c_2$$
$$, A\!\!-\!\!A := 0 \qquad ,\ A\!\!-\!\!\bullet := 0$$

Shortly, the complexity of a diagram c is the sum of all the complexities of the basic blocks occurring in c.

Example 5 (Number of Parameters). The set of basic blocks Γ may contain several generators that depend on one or more parameters whose value is usually learned during the training process. A common way to measure the complexity of a model is simply by counting the number of its parameter. This can be easily accommodated in our theory by fixing the function $\mathcal{C}\colon \Gamma \to \mathbb{R}^+$ to be the one mapping each generator $g \in \Gamma$ into its number of parameters. It is thus trivial to see that for all circuit c, $,c$ is exactly the total number of parameters of c.

Example 6 (Number of Nonlinearities). Let us assume that Γ contains as building blocks the functions computing the linear combinations of n given inputs, for every $n \in \mathbb{N}$ and for each tuple of real valued coefficients. Moreover, Γ contains as building blocks some classic activation functions in machine learning, such as the Sigmoid and the ReLu activation function. For instance, in our theory an observer may define the complexity $\mathcal{C}\colon \Gamma \to \mathbb{R}^+$ to assign to each linear function the complexity of 0 and to each nonlinear function the complexity of 1. Then the complexity of each circuit c, $,c$ is exactly the number of nonlinear functions applied in the circuit, e.g. the number of neurons in a multi-layer perceptrons with ReLu activation functions in the hidden layers and Sigmoid activation function in the output layer.

We notice that we defined the complexity function on syntactic diagrams and not on semantic objects. Indeed, an operator, like e.g. a GEO, can be realized by possibly several different diagrams, however the complexity of the different diagrams should be different. To understand this choice, imagine one has to define the complexity of a function that, given a certain array of integers, returns the array in ascending order. Clearly the complexity of this function should depend on the specific algorithm that is used to produce the output given a certain input, and not on the function itself.

4 Learning and Explaining via GE(NE)Os Diagrams

Section 3 introduces the basic definitions that can be operatively used to instantiate our framework. Indeed, Eq. (2) defines a hemi-metric that can be used as a loss function to train a surrogate GEO to approximate another GEO, whereas Definition 7 establishes a way to measure their interpretability in terms of elementary blocks. This section first shows how the learning of surrogate models is defined (Sect. 4.1), and then how we can easily extract explanations from the learned surrogate models (Sect. 4.2). For the following we assume to have fixed an observer $\mathbb{O} = (\mathbf{T}, \mathcal{C})$ interested in a set of GEOs $\mathcal{G}$.

4.1 Learning via GENEOs' Diagrams

Given two GEOs $\alpha, \beta \in \mathcal{G}$, with $\alpha = (f_\alpha, t_\alpha) : (X_\alpha, G_\alpha) \to (Y_\alpha, K_\alpha)$ and $\beta = (f_\beta, t_\beta) : (X_\beta, G_\beta) \to (Y_\beta, K_\beta)$, and the category $\mathbf{T}$ of translation GENEOs, the hemi-metric $h_\mathbb{O}$ as defined in Eq. (1) expresses the cost of approximating α with β via the available translation pairs, as illustrated in Fig. 3. In order to apply our framework to the problem of learning interpretable surrogate functions of a certain model on a certain dataset, from now on we assume that α is given, β is learnable by depending on a set of parameters $\theta \in \mathbb{R}^n$, and X_{dt} denotes the training set collecting the available input data. Therefore, learning f_β can be cast as the problem of finding the parameters θ, such that $h_\mathbb{O}(\alpha,\beta)$ is minimized on X_{dt}, i.e. that provide the lowest $cost(\pi)$ amongst the $\pi = \left((l^\pi_{\alpha,\beta}, p^\pi_{\alpha,\beta}), (m^\pi_{\beta,\alpha}, q^\pi_{\beta,\alpha})\right): \alpha \leftrightarrows_\mathbf{T} \beta$:

$$\theta^* = \arg\min_\theta \left(\inf_\pi \frac{1}{|X_{dt}|} \sum_{x \in X_{dt}} d_{dt}\left(m^\pi_{\beta,\alpha}(f_\beta(l^\pi_{\alpha,\beta}(x);\theta)), f_\alpha(x)\right)\right). \quad (3)$$

From our definition, the two perception spaces may be different. However, most frequently when learning surrogate functions, we have $W_\alpha = W_\beta = W$, for $W \in \{X, Y, \mathbf{G}, \mathbf{K}\}$, and there is only the translation pair $\pi = \left((id_X, id_G)(id_Y, id_K)\right)$. Thus, Eq. (3) simplifies in $\arg\min_\theta \frac{1}{|X_{dt}|} \sum_{x \in X_{dt}} d_{dt}\left(f_\beta(x;\theta), f_\alpha(x)\right)$, which corresponds to the fidelity measure between f_α and f_β, commonly used in XAI.

Example 7 (Classifier Explanations). Consider a classifier f_α equivariant w.r.t. the groups $\mathbf{G}_\alpha$ and $\mathbf{K}_\alpha = \mathbf{1}$, being $\mathbf{1}$ the trivial group. As an example, Fig. 4 illustrates two different GEOs f_β and f_γ that can be used to explain f_α. Notice that if the observer $\mathbb{O}$ has no access to f_α, i.e. $\mathbb{O}$ does not know how f_α is built (i.e. f_α is a black-box for $\mathbb{O}$), then f_α should be an atomic block in Γ. In this case, the observer $\mathbb{O}$ assigns to f_α the complexity $\mathcal{C}(f_\alpha) = \infty$.

Example 8 (Supervised Learning). Wether f_α denotes the function associating to each training input its label (i.e. the *supervisor*), then f_β and f_γ from Fig. 4 are simply two models trained via supervised learning, and their distance to f_α is the accuracy (that can be thought of as the fidelity w.r.t. the ground-truth).

f_β and f_γ differ in Example 7 only from the fact that f_β is equivariant on the same group $\mathbf{G}_\alpha$ than f_α, whereas f_γ might not. In fact, in case f_γ is not equivariant on $\mathbf{G}_\alpha$ we may prove that f_γ will be surely a non-optimal approximation.

Proposition 1. *Let $\mathbf{T}$, (f_α, t_α), (f_β, t_β) as in Example 4 and let NE be the set $\{(g, x) \in G_\alpha \times X \mid f_\beta(x) \neq f_\beta(g * x)\}$, i.e., the set containing all those couples falsifying equivariance of f_β w.r.t. $\mathbf{G}_\alpha$. Then*

$$h_\mathbb{O}((f_\alpha, t_\alpha), (f_\beta, t_\beta)) \geq \frac{|NE|}{2 \cdot |G_\alpha|}$$

Remark 3. As stated in the introduction, single-hidden-layer neural networks are universal approximators but may require a large number of hidden neurons, increasing complexity. If we cap the model's complexity, a neural network may not always approximate a given model accurately. Proposition 1 further establishes a fidelity lower bound based on non-equivariant datapoints.

4.2 Suitable Surrogate GEOs

We say that a GEO (f_α, t_α) is *explained* by another GEO (f_β, t_β) at the level ε for an observer $\mathbb{O} = (\mathbf{T}, \mathcal{C})$ if:

1. $h_\mathbb{O}\left((f_\alpha, t_\alpha), (f_\beta, t_\beta)\right) \leq \varepsilon;$ 2. $(f_\beta, t_\beta) \leq (f_\alpha, t_\alpha).$

The second condition means that the complexity of the surrogate explaining model (f_β, t_β) should be lower than the complexity of the given model (f_α, t_α). While not guaranteed, this requisite can be ensured by designing f_β with a suitable strategy. Recall that a model's complexity is defined by atomic building blocks in Γ, which are combined to form the model. Using the simplest possible blocks helps limit complexity, though their selection depends on the observer's knowledge and interpretability. Moreover, different studies [6] have shown how a proper domain-informed selection of GE(NE)Os, may strongly decrease the number of parameters necessary to solve a certain task w.r.t. a standard neural networks (as also shown by our experiments cf. Table 1).

Example 9. Given a set of GEOs $(f_i, t_i) \in \Gamma$, with complexity $k_i = \mathcal{C}((f_i, t_i))$, we can define f_β as a linear combination of $(f_1, t_1), \ldots, (f_n, t_n)$. According to Definition 7, the complexity, f_β would be $k_1 + \ldots + k_n$, plus eventually the complexities of the scalar multiplications.

5 Experiments

In order to validate experimentally our theory, we build a classification task on MNIST dataset and rely on our framework to appropriately define an interpretable surrogate model. With our experiments we aim to answer two main research questions: wether personalized complexity measures are able to properly formalize an observer subjectivity, and if knowledge of the domain and of the complexity measured by an observer can lead to ad-hoc surrogate models with a better trade-off between complexity and accuracy. Thus for all the reported results, we assume to have fixed one (or more) given observers.[1]

5.1 Data

MNIST contains $70,000$ grayscale (values from 0 to 255) images of handwritten digits (0–9), each image being 28×28 pixels. We linearly rescale the images so that the values lay in $[0, 1]$. The images rescaled belong to $\{0, \frac{1}{255}, \ldots, 1\}^{28 \times 28}$ We split our dataset into three stratified random disjoint subsets: training, validation, and test set, of 60%, 20% and 20% of images respectively.

5.2 Models

As opaque model, we employ a standard CNN, with the Tiny-Vgg architecture, that is composed by two convolutional layers as tail and a linear classifier head. To realize our GEOs surrogate approximation, we use two different architectures. From the MNIST training set, we extract randomly a set of patterns p_i. These patterns are square cutouts of train images, with height (H) and width (W)

---

[1] Our code is available at https://github.com/jacopojoy98/GENEO.

of choice and with a center point chosen with probability proportional to the intensity of the image x:

$$p_i = x|_{Q_i}, \quad (c_{x_i}, c_{y_i}) \sim x$$

$$Q_i = \{c_{x_i} - \frac{W}{2}, \ldots, c_{x_i} + \frac{W}{2}\} \times \{c_{y_i} - \frac{H}{2}, \ldots, c_{y_i} + \frac{H}{2}\}$$

For each image x we identify the presence of a pattern p_i in position (i, j) with the following function:

$$f(x)_{p_i} : \{0, \frac{1}{255}, \ldots, 1\}^{28 \times 28} \to \{0, \frac{1}{199920}, \ldots, 1\}^{28 \times 28}$$

$$f_{p_i}(x)_{n,m} = 1 - \frac{\sum_{(i,j) \in Q_i} |x((i,j) + (n,m)) - p_i((i,j))|}{\text{vol } Q_i}$$

The choice of these specific patterns can be motivated by a domain knowledge or by the preferences that an observer can inject through a thoughtful design of theirs GEOs' building blocks for the classification task.

The first GEO then performs a Image-Wide-Maxpool to create a flat vector with as many entries as are the patterns, and whose i^{th} entry indicates the intensity with which the pattern was identified within the image

$$L_i = \max_{n,m}(f_{p_i}(x)_{n,m})$$

These intensities are then linearly combined with an activation function to identify the correct digit

$$\text{OUT}^k = \sigma\left(\sum_j \gamma_j^k L_j + b^k\right)$$

The second GEO instead, after the identification of patterns, selects for each pattern the position with the maximum activation through the Channel-Wise-Max (CWM)

$$CWM(f_{p_i}(x))_{n,m} = \begin{cases} s & \text{if } s = \max(f_{p_i}(x)) \\ 0 & \text{otherwise} \end{cases}$$

These matrices of activations are then linearly combined with a downstream nonlinear activation function

$$L_{n,m} = \sigma\left(\left(\sum_i w_i \cdot CWM(f_{p_i}(x))_{n,m}\right) + b_i\right)$$

The entries of this matrix are then linearly combined with a final sigmoidal activation function to produce the output of the model

$$\text{OUT}^k = \sigma\left(\left(\sum_{ij} w_{ji}^k \cdot L_{ji}\right) + b^k\right)$$

Table 1. The different models utilized with the relative hyperparameters, chosen on the validation set.

Model	Params	Epochs	LR	Model	Params	Epochs	LR	PATTERNS
CNN	228010	3	$3e-3$	GEO_1	5010	296	$3e-3$	500
MLP	31810	57	$2e-4$	GEO_1	3510	148	$7e-3$	350
MLP	15910	57	$1e-4$	GEO_1	1710	456	$2e-2$	170
MLP	7850	5	$2e-3$	GEO_1	1510	564	$1e-2$	150
MLP	5575	58	$2e-4$	GEO_1	1210	496	$2e-2$	120
MLP	3985	58	$2e-4$	GEO_1	990	198	$5e-2$	98
MLP	3190	9	$2e-3$	GEO_2	8101	39	$1e-3$	250
				GEO_2	8051	496	$1e-3$	200
				GEO_2	8001	483	$1e-3$	150
				GEO_2	7951	335	$1e-3$	100
				GEO_2	7901	451	$1e-3$	50

To compare results, we chose a series of simple Multi-Layer Perceptrons, trained directly on the MNIST dataset. In particular, we used MLPs with the following configurations: with no hidden layers, with one hidden layer of dimension 5, 7, 20 and 40. The two models with hidden layers of dimension 5 and 7 are chosen to create MLPs with number of parameters similar to our GEOs. In Table 1 we report the most relevant characteristics of all the models we compare in our experiments.

5.3 Experiment Setup

We performed the experiments training all models over the ground truth.

We employed early stopping on the validation set to determine the optimal number of training epochs. The accuracy was then evaluated on a separate test set. We also trained a portion of our models on a rescaled version of MNIST for which every separate group of 2×2 points was substituted with the max of the four pixels, effectively reshaping the images to 14×14 and allowing us to compare also models which start from different perception spaces.

5.4 Results

We first follow our theoretical framework to define the translation diagram of our experimental setup. Indeed, we are in a classical classification scenario, that can be easily represented by the graph in Fig. 4.

We start from the basic perception space (X, G_α) that is, our image dataset X and the group of admissible transformations G_α. Here, we have translations as admissible group actions in G_α and f_α is the opaque CNN. Our first GEO model f_β operates on the same perception space (X, G_α), as it works on the thorus of the images, preserving translations. Therefore, the translation GENEO is composed given by the couple (id_X, id_{G_α}). Both the second GEO and the MLP, represented by f_γ instead do not preserve any transformation in the group. Therefore the perception space becomes $(X, \mathbf{1})$ where $\mathbf{1}$ denotes the trivial group. Being ! the annihilator homomorphism from any group to the trivial group, the translation GENEO for this GEO is given by the couple $(id_X, !)$. All models have $(Y, \mathbf{1})$ as their output, since they all work on the space of output classes.

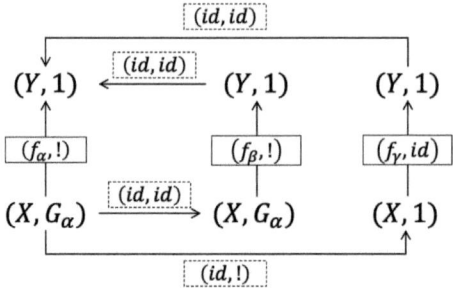

Fig. 4. Diagrams of two GEOs explaining a given GEO, where ! represents the annihilator homomorphism from any group to the trivial group **1**.

Table 2. Models with relative complexities, accuracies and fidelities w.r.t CNN.

Model	C_1	C_2	Acc	Fid
CNN	228010	37578	97.8%	
MLP	31810	50	96.3%	93.6%
MLP	15910	30	94.1%	93.5%
MLP	7850	10	91.8%	90.9%
MLP	5575	17	90.3%	89.6%
MLP	3985	15	85.4%	86.1%
MLP	3190	14	85.1%	80.3%

Model	C_1	C_2	Acc	Fid
GEO_1	5010	510	96.6%	92.5%
GEO_1	3510	360	95.4%	91.9%
GEO_1	1710	180	95.3%	92.4%
GEO_1	1510	160	93.7%	90.7%
GEO_1	1210	130	93.4%	91.5%
GEO_1	990	100	92.2%	89.3%
GEO_2	8101	511	92.9%	92.5%
GEO_2	8051	411	92.0%	91.8%
GEO_2	8001	311	92.6%	91.6%
GEO_2	7951	211	91.3%	91.1%
GEO_2	7901	111	88.5%	91.4%

Table 3. The output of some of the models trained on a rescaled version of the starting perception space. The hyperparameters have been kept the same as the non rescaled experiments

Model	C_1	C_2	Acc
MLP	8290	50	96.3%
MLP	1970	10	91.8%
MLP	1459	17	90.3%
MLP	1045	15	86.3%

Model	C_1	C_2	Acc
GEO_1	5010	510	95.9%
GEO_1	3510	360	95.5%
GEO_1	1710	180	93.6%
GEO_1	990	100	91.1%
GEO_2	2221	511	93.1%
GEO_2	2121	411	92.5%
GEO_2	2021	111	89.5%

To show how the subjectivity of an observer may influence the results in practice, we measure complexity using two measures: Firstly we assign complexity 1 to each parameter of the model and we sum over all the parameters. Then we assign complexity 1 to all the non-linearities of the model, summing over all the non linearities. We report the performances obtained by the different models in Table 2 and we also compare the results with a different perception space in Table 3 where we present the results for resized images.

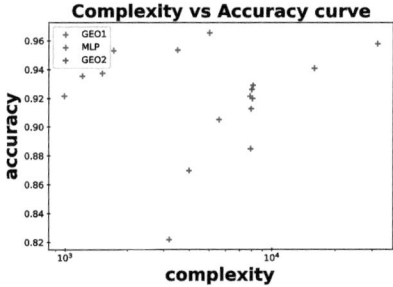
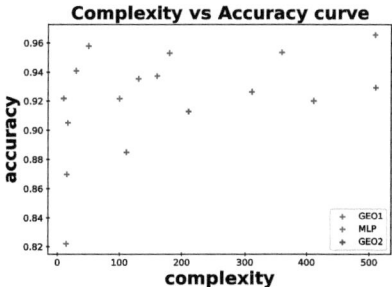

(a) The proposed GEOs can outperform, at similar complexity, model-agnostic MLPs. Notice that the translational equivariant GEO is able to perform much better at minor complexity.

(b) A second observer, who ascribes complexity only to the non-linearities, can have a different complexity vs accuracy curve.

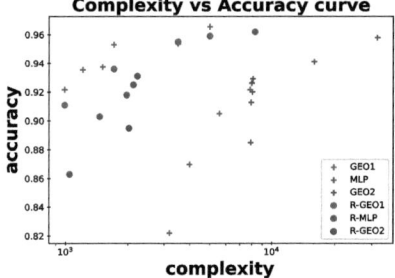
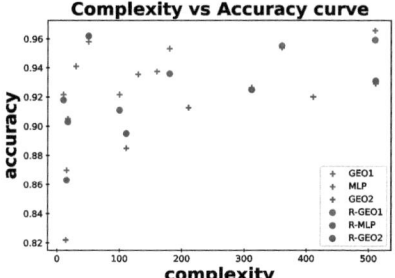

(c) Changing the starting perception space does not affect significantly the performances, whereas the first observer sees GEO_1 with unchanging complexities and GEO_2 and the MLP with much smaller complexity.

(d) The different observer is not affected by any change in the measured complexity.

Fig. 5. Accuracy vs complexity comparisons.

The results show that the models built via thoughtful GEOs' building blocks can approximate quite well the original task, providing models that are less complex for both the measure specified by the observer. The complexity vs accuracy curves reprensenting the experiments are shown in Fig. 5.

6 Related Work

Explainable AI has become a fundamental field in AI that covers methodologies designed to provide understandable explanations of the inner workings of a ML model to a human being [27]. Roughly, XAI methods can be categorized into post-hoc methods, i.e., methods aiming to explain another trained opaque ML models, and interpretable-by-design methods, i.e., ML models that provide explanations to the users inherently, by virtue of their intrinsic transparency [9,42]. One of the most well-known techniques for post-hoc explnations is to train a surrogate interpretable model to reproduce the same output as an opaque model [15,24,28]. In this regard, our paper provides a solid mathematical framework that subsumes both these two paradigms in the same theory.

A key point in XAI is the way the quality of the provided explanations can be measured. For instance, explanations and interpretability can be evaluated qualitatively (user studies) or quantitatively (direct model metrics) [2,30,32,43]. Qualitative measures include user performance, engagement, and explanation clarity [4,16,34,37]. Quantitative measures include explanation completeness [40], fidelity [22], classification accuracy [23], and faithfulness [31]. Complexity measure of explanations is often used for logic-based explainers [13], but it is generally limited to be a count on the number of propositional variables in a formula. While this can easily be accomodated in our framework, up to the author knowledge, no other methods consider complexity measures from the perspective of an observer, offering flexibility in choosing suitable metrics for the task and models.

While there is a large agreement on the needs for XAI models, there are very few works that try to provide a formal mathematical theory of explanations and/or interpretability for ML models. For instance, in [39] the authors propose a new class of "compositionally-interpretable" models, which extend beyond intrinsically interpretable models to include causal models, conceptual space models, and more, by using category theory. [21] proposes a framework based on Category Theory and Institution Theory to define explanations and (explainable) learning agents mathematically. However, these works do not provide a practical measure for the interpretability of the models, completely omit the formalization of an observer, and do not take into account the notion of group equivariant operators. Another seminal work is [25,26], which provides a more general foundation framework based on properties and desiderata for interpretable ML. However, it does not make any specific mention to a proper mathematical framework.

Finally, our framework is based on the theory of GE(NE)Os, which has been already used to bridge Topological Data Analysis (TDA) and ML. For instance, GENEOs originates from persistent homology with G-invariant non-expansive operators and have been succesfully applied for 1D-signal comparisons and image recognition based on topological features [18]. Moreover, GENEOs have been applied to protein pocket detection [6,8] and graph comparison [7]. While as observed in [8] GENEOs are more inherently interpretable due to a limited dependency on parameters, the theory we present in this paper significantly extend the previous applications, by aiming at the formalization of a more sound XAI theory evaluable quantitatively and based on observers' preferences.

7 Conclusions and Future Work

This work explores the theoretical properties of GE(NE)Os to build a theoretical framework to build surrogate interpretable models, and measure in a rigorous way the trade-off between complexity and performance. By formally proving the properties of our framework and with the experiments that we provide, we lay the groundwork for future research and opening avenues for practical applications in analyzing and interpreting complex data transformations. Our proposal highlights how it is possible to frame the theory of interpretable models through GE(NE)Os and opens new interesting research directions for Explainable AI. One such direction will be to formally describe existing machine learning models in terms of GE(NE)Os, to study the best interpretable approximations for typical tasks. Moreover, an interesting possible research could be to realize interpretable latent space compression through the use of GE(NE)Os.

Acknowledgments. This work has been partially supported by the Partnership Extended PE00000013 - "FAIR - Future Artificial Intelligence Research" - Spoke 1 "Human-centered AI" and ERC-2018-ADG G.A. 834756 "XAI: Science and technology for the eXplanation of AI decision making". This research was partly funded by the Advanced Research + Invention Agency (ARIA) Safeguarded AI Programme and carried out within the National Centre on HPC, Big Data and Quantum Computing - SPOKE 10 (Quantum Computing) and by the European Union NextGenerationEU - National Recovery and Resilience Plan (NRRP) M.4 C.2, I.N.1.4 CUP N. I53C22000690001. Bonchi is supported by the Ministero dell'Universitá e della Ricerca of Italy grant PRIN 2022 PNRR No. P2022HXNSC - RAP (Resource Awareness in Programming). P.F. conducted a portion of his research within the framework of the CNIT WiLab National Laboratory and the WiLab-Huawei Joint Innovation Center. His work received partial support from INdAM-GNSAGA, the COST Action CaLISTA, and the HORIZON Research and Innovation Action PANDORA. This work was also funded by the European Union under Grant Agreement no. 101120763 - TANGO. Views and opinions expressed are however those of the author(s) only and do not necessarily reflect those of the European Union or the European Health and Digital Executive Agency (HaDEA). Neither the European Union nor the granting authority can be held responsible for them.

Disclosure of Interests. The authors have no competing interests.

Appendix

Proposition 2. Let $(X, d_X, \mathbf{G}, *)$ be a perception pair. The followings hold.

(a) $(\mathbf{G}, \circ)$ *is a topological group.*
(b) The action of $\mathbf{G}$ *on* X *is continuous.*

Proof. To prove (a) it is sufficient to prove that the maps $(g', g'') \mapsto g' \circ g''$ and $g \mapsto g^{-1}$ are continuous. First of all, we have to prove that if a sequence (g'_i) converges to g' and a sequence (g''_i) converges to g'' in G, then the sequence

$(g'_i \circ g''_i)$ converges to $g' \circ g''$ in G. We observe that, for every $x \in X$,

$$\begin{aligned}
d_X((g'_i \circ g''_i) * x, (g' \circ g'') * x) &= d_X(g'_i * (g''_i * x), g' * (g'' * x)) \\
&\leq d_X(g'_i * (g''_i * x), g'_i * (g'' * x)) \\
&\quad + d_X(g'_i * (g'' * x), g' * (g'' * x)) \\
&= d_X(g''_i * x, g'' * x) \\
&\quad + d_X(g'_i * (g'' * x), g' * (g'' * x)) \\
&\leq d_G(g''_i, g'') + d_G(g'_i, g').
\end{aligned}$$

Thus, $d_G(g'_i \circ g''_i, g' \circ g'') \leq d_G(g''_i, g'') + d_G(g'_i, g')$. This proves the first property. Then, we have to prove that if a sequence (g_i) converges to g in G, then the sequence (g_i^{-1}) converges to g^{-1} in G. We have that

$$\begin{aligned}
d_X(g_i^{-1} * x, g^{-1} * x) &= d_X(g_i * (g_i^{-1} * x), g_i * (g^{-1} * x)) \\
&= d_X((g_i \circ g_i^{-1}) * x, (g_i \circ g^{-1}) * x) \\
&= d_X(x, (g_i \circ g^{-1}) * x) \\
&= d_X((g \circ g^{-1}) * x, (g_i \circ g^{-1}) * x) \\
&= d_X(g * (g^{-1} * x), g_i * (g^{-1} * x)) \\
&\leq d_G(g, g_i).
\end{aligned}$$

Therefore, $d_G(g_i^{-1}, g^{-1}) \leq d_G(g, g_i)$. This proves our second property.

Now we prove (b). We have to prove that if a sequence (x_i) converges to x in X and a sequence (g_i) converges to g in G, then the sequence $(g_i * x_i)$ converges to $g*x$ in X. Since $\lim_{i\to\infty} x_i = x$ and $\lim_{i\to\infty} g_i = g$, then $\lim_{i\to\infty} d_X(x_i, x) = 0$ and $\lim_{i\to\infty} d_X(g_i * x, g * x) = 0$. We have that, for every $x \in X$,

$$\begin{aligned}
d_X(g_i * x_i, g * x) &\leq d_X(g_i * x_i, g_i * x) + d_X(g_i * x, g * x) \\
&= d_X(x_i, x) + d_X(g_i * x, g * x) \\
&\leq d_X(x_i, x) + d_G(g_i, g).
\end{aligned}$$

Semantics of Diagrams. It is convenient to first fix some notation.

Remark 4 (Notation). Given two sets X and Y, we write $X \times Y$ for their Cartesian product and $\sigma_{X,Y} \colon X \times Y \to Y \times X$ for the symmetry function mapping $(x,y) \in X \times Y$ into $(y,x) \in Y \times X$; given two functions $f_1 \colon X_1 \to Y_1$ and $f_2 \colon X_2 \to Y_2$, we write $f_1 \times f_2 \colon X_1 \times X_2 \to Y_1 \times Y_2$ for the function mapping $(x_1, x_2) \in X_1 \times X_2$ into $(f(x_1), f(x_2)) \in Y_1 \times Y_2$; Given $f \colon X \to Y$ and $g \colon Y \to Z$, we write $g \circ f \colon X \to Z$ for their composition. For an arbitrary set X, we write $\mathrm{id}_X \colon X \to X$ for the identity function, and $\Delta_X \colon X \to X \times X$ for the copier function mapping $x \in X$ into $(x,x) \in X \times X$; We write 1 for a singleton set that we fix to be $\{\star\}$ and $!_X \colon X \to 1$ for the function mapping any $x \in X$ into $\star$.

Given two perception spaces (X, G) and (Y, K), their direct product written $(X, G) \otimes (Y, K)$ is the perception space $(X \times Y, G \times K)$, where the distance on $X \times Y$ is defined as $d_{X \times Y}((x_1, y_1), (x_2, y_2)) := \max\{d_X(x_1, x_2), d_Y(y_1, y_2)\}$ while the group action is defined pointwise, that is $(g, k) * (x, y) = (g * x, k * y)$. We write $\sigma_{(X,G),(Y,K)} \colon (X, G) \otimes (Y, K) \to (Y, K) \otimes (X, G)$ as $(\sigma_{X,Y}, \sigma_{G,K})$.

Table 4. The CD category of GEOs. Above $(f,t)\colon (X,G) \to (Y,K)$, $(f',t')\colon (Y,K) \to (Z,L)$ and $(f_1,t_1)\colon (X_1,G_1) \to (Y_1,K_1)$, $(f_2,t_2)\colon (X_2,G_2) \to (Y_2,K_2)$ are GEOs. The notation on the right hand side is in Remark 4.

$$\mathrm{id}_{X,G} := (\mathrm{id}_X, \mathrm{id}_G) \colon (X,G) \to (X,G)$$
$$\Delta_{X,G} := (\Delta_X, \Delta_G) \colon (X,G) \to (X,G) \otimes (X,G)$$
$$!_{X,G} := (!_X, !_G) \colon (X,G) \to (1,1)$$
$$\sigma_{(X,G),(Y,K)} := (\sigma_{X,Y}, \sigma_{G,K}) \colon (X,G) \otimes (Y,K) \to (Y,K) \otimes (X,G)$$
$$(f,t) \circ (f',t') := (f' \circ f, t' \circ t) \colon (X,G) \to (Z,L)$$
$$(f_1,t_1) \otimes (f_2,t_2) := (f_1 \times f_2, t_1 \times t_2) \colon (X_1,G_1) \otimes (X_2,G_2) \to (Y_1,K_1) \otimes (Y_2,K_2)$$

Table 5. The semantics $[\![-]\!]_\mathcal{I}\colon \mathbf{Diag} \to \mathbf{GEO}$ for an interpretation $\mathcal{I}$. Operations and constants occurring on the right hand side of the above equations are those in (4). Above $\mathcal{I}_\mathcal{S}$ is a function mapping each $A \in \mathcal{S}$ in a perception space such that, for all $g \in \Gamma$ with arity $A_1 \otimes \cdots \otimes A_n$ and coarity $B_1 \otimes \cdots \otimes B_m$, the source of $\mathcal{I}(g)$ is $\bigotimes_{i=1}^n \mathcal{I}_\mathcal{S}(A_i)$ and its target is $\bigotimes_{j=1}^m \mathcal{I}_\mathcal{S}(B_j)$.

$$[\![\;g\;]\!]_\mathcal{I} := \mathcal{I}(g) \qquad [\![\;]\!]_\mathcal{I} := \mathrm{id}_{1,1} \qquad [\![c_1 \otimes c_2]\!]_\mathcal{I} := [\![c_1]\!]_\mathcal{I} \otimes [\![c_2]\!]_\mathcal{I}$$
$$[\![A \multimap]\!]_\mathcal{I} := \Delta_{\mathcal{I}_\mathcal{S}(A)} \qquad [\![\;\times\;]\!]_\mathcal{I} := \sigma_{\mathcal{I}_\mathcal{S}(A), \mathcal{I}_\mathcal{S}(B)} \qquad [\![c_1 \circ c_2]\!]_\mathcal{I} := [\![c_1]\!]_\mathcal{I} \circ [\![c_2]\!]_\mathcal{I}$$
$$[\![A \longrightarrow A]\!]_\mathcal{I} := \mathrm{id}_{\mathcal{I}_\mathcal{S}(A)} \qquad [\![A \multimap\bullet]\!]_\mathcal{I} := !_{\mathcal{I}_\mathcal{S}(A)}$$

With this notation one can extend the above structures of sets and functions to perception spaces and GEOs as illustrated in Table 4. By simply checking that the definitions in Table 4 provide GEOs, one can prove the following result.

Lemma 1. *$\mathbf{GEO}$ is a CD category in the sense of [12].*

From this fact, and the observation that $\mathbf{Diag}_\Gamma$ is the (strict) CD category freely generated from the monoidal signature Γ, one obtains that, for each interpretation $\mathcal{I}$, there exists a unique CD functor $[\![-]\!]_\mathcal{I}\colon \mathbf{Diag} \to \mathbf{GEO}$ extending $\mathcal{I}$. Its inductive definition is illustrated in Table 5

Cost of Translation Pairs for Infinite Perception Spaces. Here we explain how the cost of translation pairs defined in (1) can be defined for arbitrary sets X_α.

To proceed, we need to equip each metric space X_α with a Borel probability measure μ_α, in the spirit of [11]. In simple terms, the measure μ_α represents the probability of each data point in X_α appearing in our experiments. We will assume that all GENEOs in $\mathbf{T}$ are not just distance-decreasing (i.e., non-expansive) but also *measure-decreasing*, i.e., if $(l_{\alpha,\beta}, p_{\alpha,\beta}) : (X_\alpha, G_\alpha) \to (X_\beta, G_\beta)$ belongs to $\mathbf{T}$ and the set $A \subseteq X_\alpha$ is measurable for μ_α, then $l_{\alpha,\beta}(A)$ is measurable for μ_β, and $\mu_\beta(l_{\alpha,\beta}(A)) \leq \mu_\alpha(A)$. Moreover, we assume that the function $f_{\alpha,\beta} : X_\alpha \to \mathbb{R}$, defined for every $x \in X_\alpha$ as $f_{\alpha,\beta}(x) := d_{\mathrm{dt}}\Big((m_{\beta,\alpha} \circ f_\beta \circ l_{\alpha,\beta})(x), f_\alpha(x)\Big)$, is integrable with respect to μ_α.

Definition 8. Let $\pi = \Big((l_{\alpha,\beta}, p_{\alpha,\beta}), (m_{\beta,\alpha}, q_{\beta,\alpha})\Big)$ be a crossed translation pair from $(f_\alpha, t_\alpha) \colon (X_\alpha, G_\alpha) \to (Y_\alpha, K_\alpha)$ to $(f_\beta, t_\beta) \colon (X_\beta, G_\beta) \to (Y_\beta, K_\beta)$. The functional cost of π, written $\mathrm{cost}(\pi)$, is defined as follows.

$$\mathrm{cost}(\pi) = \int_{X_\alpha} d_{\mathrm{dt}}\Big((m_{\beta,\alpha} \circ f_\beta \circ l_{\alpha,\beta})(x), f_\alpha(x)\Big)\, d\mu_\alpha \tag{4}$$

Proof of Theorem 1. For sake of generality, we illustrate the proof for the case where $\mathrm{cost}(\pi)$ is defined as in (4). The case of $\mathrm{cost}(\pi)$ as in (1) follows by fixing μ_α as uniform Borel measure. Let us prove that $h_{\mathbb{O}}$ enjoys the triangle inequality, i.e., $h_{\mathbb{O}}(\alpha, \gamma) \leq h_{\mathbb{O}}(\alpha, \beta) + h_{\mathbb{O}}(\beta, \gamma)$, where α, β and γ are three GEOs in $\mathcal{G}$ illustrated on the right. We consider three translation pairs:

$\alpha := (f_\alpha, t_\alpha) \colon (X_\alpha, G_\alpha) \to (Y_\alpha, K_\alpha)$
$\beta := (f_\beta, t_\beta) \colon (X_\beta, G_\beta) \to (Y_\beta, K_\beta)$
$\gamma := (f_\gamma, t_\gamma) \colon (X_\gamma, G_\gamma) \to (Y_\gamma, K_\gamma)$

$\pi_1 := \Big((l_{\alpha,\beta}, p_{\alpha,\beta}), (m_{\beta,\alpha}, q_{\beta,\alpha})\Big) \colon \alpha \rightleftharpoons_{\mathbf{T}} \beta$
$\pi_2 := \Big((l_{\beta,\gamma}, p_{\beta,\gamma}), (m_{\gamma,\beta}, q_{\gamma,\beta})\Big) \colon \beta \rightleftharpoons_{\mathbf{T}} \gamma$
$\pi_3 := \pi_2 \circ \pi_1 = \Big((l_{\beta,\gamma} \circ l_{\alpha,\beta}, p_{\beta,\gamma} \circ p_{\alpha,\beta}), (m_{\beta,\alpha} \circ m_{\gamma,\beta}, q_{\beta,\alpha} \circ q_{\gamma,\beta})\Big) \colon \beta \rightleftharpoons_{\mathbf{T}} \gamma$

Please note that if no crossed pair like π_1 or π_2 exists, then $h_{\mathbb{O}}(\alpha, \beta) + h_{\mathbb{O}}(\beta, \gamma) = \infty$, and hence the triangle inequality trivially holds. By definition their costs are

$\mathrm{cost}(\pi_1) = \int_{X_\alpha} d_{\mathrm{dt}}\Big((m_{\beta,\alpha} \circ f_\beta \circ l_{\alpha,\beta})(x), f_\alpha(x)\Big)\, d\mu_\alpha$
$\mathrm{cost}(\pi_2) = \int_{X_\beta} d_{\mathrm{dt}}\Big((m_{\gamma,\beta} \circ f_\gamma \circ l_{\beta,\gamma})(y), f_\beta(y)\Big)\, d\mu_\beta$
$\mathrm{cost}(\pi_3) = \int_{X_\alpha} d_{\mathrm{dt}}\Big((m_{\beta,\alpha} \circ m_{\gamma,\beta} \circ f_\gamma \circ l_{\beta,\gamma} \circ l_{\alpha,\beta})(x), f_\alpha(x)\Big)\, d\mu_\alpha$

Since $(m_{\beta,\alpha}, q_{\beta,\alpha})$ is a GENEO, we have that for every $y \in X_\beta$,

$$d_{\mathrm{dt}}\Big((m_{\gamma,\beta} \circ f_\gamma \circ l_{\beta,\gamma})(y), f_\beta(y)\Big) \geq d_{\mathrm{dt}}\Big((m_{\beta,\alpha} \circ m_{\gamma,\beta} \circ f_\gamma \circ l_{\beta,\gamma})(y), (m_{\beta,\alpha} \circ f_\beta)(y)\Big)$$

and hence, setting $y := l_{\alpha,\beta}(x)$ and recalling that $l_{\alpha,\beta}$ is measure-decreasing,

$$\int_{X_\beta} d_{\mathrm{dt}}\Big((m_{\gamma,\beta} \circ f_\gamma \circ l_{\beta,\gamma})(y), f_\beta(y)\Big)\, d\mu_\beta$$
$$\geq \int_{X_\alpha} d_{\mathrm{dt}}\Big((m_{\beta,\alpha} \circ m_{\gamma,\beta} \circ f_\gamma \circ l_{\beta,\gamma} \circ l_{\alpha,\beta})(x), (m_{\beta,\alpha} \circ f_\beta(y) \circ l_{\alpha,\beta})(x)\Big)\, d\mu_\alpha.$$

Therefore, we have that $\text{cost}(\pi_1) + \text{cost}(\pi_2) =$

$$= \int_{X_\alpha} d_{\text{dt}}\Big((m_{\beta,\alpha} \circ f_\beta \circ l_{\alpha,\beta})(x), f_\alpha(x)\Big) d\mu_\alpha + \int_{X_\beta} d_{\text{dt}}\Big((m_{\gamma,\beta} \circ f_\gamma \circ l_{\beta,\gamma})(y), f_\beta(y)\Big) d\mu_\beta$$
$$\geq \int_{X_\alpha} d_{\text{dt}}\Big((m_{\beta,\alpha} \circ f_\beta \circ l_{\alpha,\beta})(x), f_\alpha(x)\Big) d\mu_\alpha$$
$$+ \int_{X_\alpha} d_{\text{dt}}\Big((m_{\beta,\alpha} \circ m_{\gamma,\beta} \circ f_\gamma \circ l_{\beta,\gamma} \circ l_{\alpha,\beta})(x), (m_{\beta,\alpha} \circ f_\beta \circ l_{\alpha,\beta})(x)\Big) d\mu_\alpha$$
$$\geq \int_{X_\alpha} d_{\text{dt}}\Big((m_{\beta,\alpha} \circ m_{\gamma,\beta} \circ f_\gamma \circ l_{\beta,\gamma} \circ l_{\alpha,\beta})(x), f_\alpha(x)\Big) d\mu_\alpha = \text{cost}(\pi_2 \circ \pi_1)$$

where the second to last inequality follows from the triangle inequality for d_{dt}. Therefore, $\text{cost}(\pi_1) + \text{cost}(\pi_2) \geq \text{cost}(\pi_2 \circ \pi_1)$. It follows that

$$\inf\{\text{cost}(\pi') \mid \pi' \colon \alpha \rightleftharpoons_\mathbf{T} \beta\} + \inf\{\text{cost}(\pi'') \mid \pi'' \colon \beta \rightleftharpoons_\mathbf{T} \gamma\}$$
$$= \inf\{\text{cost}(\pi') + \text{cost}(\pi'') \mid \pi' \colon \alpha \rightleftharpoons_\mathbf{T} \beta, \pi'' \colon \beta \rightleftharpoons_\mathbf{T} \gamma\}$$
$$\geq \inf\{\text{cost}(\pi'' \circ \pi') \mid \pi' \colon \alpha \rightleftharpoons_\mathbf{T} \beta, \pi'' \colon \beta \rightleftharpoons_\mathbf{T} \gamma\}$$
$$\geq \inf\{\text{cost}(\pi) \mid \pi \colon \alpha \rightleftharpoons_\mathbf{T} \gamma\}$$

and thus $h_\mathbb{O}(\alpha, \beta) + h_\mathbb{O}(\beta, \gamma) \geq h_\mathbb{O}(\alpha, \gamma)$. In other words, (T) holds.

To prove (R) i.e., that for all GEOs $(f_\alpha, t_\alpha) \colon (X_\alpha, G_\alpha) \to (Y_\alpha, K_\alpha)$, it holds that $h_\mathbb{O}\Big((f_\alpha, t_\alpha), (f_\alpha, t_\alpha)\Big) = 0$, observe that, since $\mathbf{T}$ is a category there exists the crossed pair of translation $\iota := \Big((\text{id}_{X_\alpha}, \text{id}_{G_\alpha}), (\text{id}_{Y_\alpha}, \text{id}_{K_\alpha})\Big)$ given by the identity morphisms. One can easily check that $\text{cost}(\iota) = 0$ and thus

$$\inf\{\text{cost}(\pi) \mid \pi \colon (f_\alpha, t_\alpha) \rightleftharpoons_\mathbf{T} (f_\alpha, t_\alpha)\} = 0.$$

Proof of Proposition 1. Fix $A := \{(g, x) \mid f_\alpha(x) = f_\beta(x)\}$, $B := \{(g, x) \mid f_\alpha(g * x) = f_\beta(g * x)\}$ and $C := \{(g, x) \mid f_\beta(x) = f_\beta(g * x)\}$ and observe that $A \cap B \subseteq C$. Thus, by denoting with $\overline{X}$, the complement of a set X, it holds that $\overline{A} \cup \overline{B} \supseteq \overline{C}$ and thus

$$|\overline{A}| + |\overline{B}| \geq |\overline{C}|. \tag{5}$$

We now use the hypothesis that G_α is a group, to show the bijection of $\overline{A}$ and $\overline{B}$: define $\iota \colon \overline{B} \to \overline{A}$ as $\iota(g, x) := (g, g * x)$ and $\kappa \colon \overline{A} \to \overline{B}$ as $\kappa(g, x) := (g, g^{-1} * x)$. Observe that the functions are well defined and that they are inverse to each other. Thus $|\overline{A}| = |\overline{B}|$ that, thanks to (5) gives us

$$2 \cdot |\overline{A}| \geq |\overline{C}|.$$

To conclude observe that $\overline{C}$ is NE and that $|\overline{A}|$ is $|G_\alpha| \cdot h_\mathbb{O}((f_\alpha, t_\alpha), (f_\beta, t_\beta))$.

References

1. Ahmad, F., Ferri, M., Frosini, P.: Generalized permutants and graph GENEOs. Mach. Learn. Knowl. Extract. **5**(4), 1905–1920 (2023). https://doi.org/10.3390/make5040092
2. Alangari, N., Menai, M.E.B., Mathkour, H., Almosallam, I.: Exploring evaluation methods for interpretable machine learning: a survey. Information **14**(8), 469 (2023)
3. Anselmi, F., Rosasco, L., Poggio, T.: On invariance and selectivity in representation learning. Inf. Infer. J. IMA **5**(2), 134–158 (2016). https://doi.org/10.1093/imaiai/iaw009
4. Arora, S., Pruthi, D., Sadeh, N.M., Cohen, W.W., Lipton, Z.C., Neubig, G.: Explain, edit, and understand: rethinking user study design for evaluating model explanations. In: AAAI, pp. 5277–5285. AAAI Press (2022)
5. Bengio, Y., Courville, A., Vincent, P.: Representation learning: a review and new perspectives. IEEE Trans. Pattern Anal. Mach. Intell. **35**(8), 1798–1828 (2013)
6. Bergomi, M.G., Frosini, P., Giorgi, D., Quercioli, N.: Towards a topological-geometrical theory of group equivariant non-expansive operators for data analysis and machine learning. Nat. Mach. Intell. **1**(9), 423–433 (2019). https://doi.org/10.1038/s42256-019-0087-3
7. Bocchi, G., Ferri, M., Frosini, P.: A novel approach to graph distinction through geneos and permutants. Sci. Rep. **15**(1), 6259 (2025). https://doi.org/10.1038/s41598-025-90152-7
8. Bocchi, G., et al.: A geometric XAI approach to protein pocket detection. In: xAI-2024 Late-breaking Work, Demos and Doctoral Consortium Joint Proceedings - The 2nd World Conference on eXplainable Artificial Intelligence, vol. 3793, pp. 217–224 (2024). https://ceur-ws.org/Vol-3793/paper_28.pdf
9. Bodria, F., Giannotti, F., Guidotti, R., Naretto, F., Pedreschi, D., Rinzivillo, S.: Benchmarking and survey of explanation methods for black box models. Data Min. Knowl. Disc. **37**(5), 1719–1778 (2023)
10. Camporesi, F., Frosini, P., Quercioli, N.: On a new method to build group equivariant operators by means of permutants. In: Holzinger, A., Kieseberg, P., Tjoa, A.M., Weippl, E. (eds.) CD-MAKE 2018. LNCS, vol. 11015, pp. 265–272. Springer, Cham (2018). https://doi.org/10.1007/978-3-319-99740-7_18
11. Cascarano, P., Frosini, P., Quercioli, N., Saki, A.: On the geometric and riemannian structure of the spaces of group equivariant non-expansive operators (2023). https://arxiv.org/abs/2103.02543
12. Cho, K., Jacobs, B.: Disintegration and bayesian inversion via string diagrams. Math. Struct. Comput. Sci. **29**(7), 938–971 (2019)
13. Ciravegna, G., et al.: Logic explained networks. Artif. Intell. **314**, 103822 (2023)
14. Cohen, T., Welling, M.: Group equivariant convolutional networks. In: International Conference on Machine Learning, pp. 2990–2999 (2016)
15. Collaris, D., Gajane, P., Jorritsma, J., van Wijk, J.J., Pechenizkiy, M.: LEMON: alternative sampling for more faithful explanation through local surrogate models. In: IDA. Lecture Notes in Computer Science, vol. 13876, pp. 77–90. Springer, Heidelberg (2023). https://doi.org/10.1007/978-3-031-30047-9_7
16. Colley, A., Kalving, M., Häkkilä, J., Väänänen, K.: Exploring tangible explainable AI (tangxai): a user study of two XAI approaches. In: OZCHI, pp. 679–683. ACM (2023)

17. Cybenko, G.: Approximation by superpositions of a sigmoidal function. Math. Control Signals Syst. **2**(4), 303–314 (1989)
18. Frosini, P., Jabłoński, G.: Combining persistent homology and invariance groups for shape comparison. Disc. Comput. Geom. **55**(2), 373–409 (2016). https://doi.org/10.1007/s00454-016-9761-y
19. Gerken, J.E., et al.: Geometric deep learning and equivariant neural networks. Artif. Intell. Rev. (2023)
20. Gerken, J.E., et al.: Geometric deep learning and equivariant neural networks. Artif. Intell. Rev. **56**(12), 14605–14662 (2023)
21. Giannini, F., Fioravanti, S., Barbiero, P., Tonda, A., Liò, P., Di Lavore, E.: Categorical foundation of explainable AI: a unifying theory. In: World Conference on Explainable Artificial Intelligence, pp. 185–206. Springer, Heidelberg (2024). https://doi.org/10.1007/978-3-031-63800-8_10
22. Guidotti, R., Monreale, A., Ruggieri, S., Turini, F., Giannotti, F., Pedreschi, D.: A survey of methods for explaining black box models. ACM Comput. Surv. **51**(5), 93:1–93:42 (2019)
23. Harder, F., Bauer, M., Park, M.: Interpretable and differentially private predictions. In: AAAI, pp. 4083–4090. AAAI Press (2020)
24. Heidari, F., Taslakian, P., Rabusseau, G.: Explaining graph neural networks using interpretable local surrogates. In: TAG-ML. Proceedings of Machine Learning Research, vol. 221, pp. 146–155. PMLR (2023)
25. Hoffman, R.R., Klein, G.: Explaining explanation, part 1: theoretical foundations. IEEE Intell. Syst. **32**(3), 68–73 (2017)
26. Hoffman, R.R., Mueller, S.T., Klein, G.: Explaining explanation, part 2: empirical foundations. IEEE Intell. Syst. **32**(4), 78–86 (2017)
27. Kay, J.: Foundations for human-AI teaming for self-regulated learning with explainable AI (XAI). Comput. Hum. Behav. **147**, 107848 (2023)
28. Lualdi, P., Sturm, R., Siefkes, T.: Exploration-oriented sampling strategies for global surrogate modeling: a comparison between one-stage and adaptive methods. J. Comput. Sci. **60**, 101603 (2022)
29. Marconato, E., Passerini, A., Teso, S.: Interpretability is in the mind of the beholder: a causal framework for human-interpretable representation learning. Entropy **25**(12), 1574 (2023)
30. Mirzaei, S., Mao, H., Al-Nima, R.R.O., Woo, W.L.: Explainable AI evaluation: a top-down approach for selecting optimal explanations for black box models. Inf. **15**(1), 4 (2024)
31. Murdoch, W.J., Singh, C., Kumbier, K., Abbasi-Asl, R., Yu, B.: Definitions, methods, and applications in interpretable machine learning. Proc. Natl. Acad. Sci. 22071–22080 (2019). https://doi.org/10.1073/pnas.1900654116
32. Nauta, M., et al.: From anecdotal evidence to quantitative evaluation methods: a systematic review on evaluating explainable AI. ACM Comput. Surv. **55**(13s), 295:1–295:42 (2023)
33. Palacio, S., Lucieri, A., Munir, M., Ahmed, S., Hees, J., Dengel, A.: Xai handbook: towards a unified framework for explainable ai. In: Proceedings of the IEEE/CVF International Conference on Computer Vision, pp. 3766–3775 (2021)
34. Panigutti, C., et al.: Co-design of human-centered, explainable AI for clinical decision support. ACM Trans. Interact. Intell. Syst. **13**(4), 21:1–21:35 (2023)
35. Ruhe, D., Brandstetter, J., Forré, P.: Clifford group equivariant neural networks. Adv. Neural. Inf. Process. Syst. **36**, 62922–62990 (2023)

36. Satorras, V.G., Hoogeboom, E., Welling, M.: E (n) equivariant graph neural networks. In: International Conference on Machine Learning, pp. 9323–9332. PMLR (2021)
37. Schulze-Weddige, S., Zylowski, T.: User study on the effects explainable AI visualizations on non-experts. In: ArtsIT. Lecture Notes of the Institute for Computer Sciences, Social Informatics and Telecommunications Engineering, vol. 422, pp. 457–467. Springer, Heidelberg (2021). https://doi.org/10.1007/978-3-030-95531-1_31
38. Selinger, P.: A survey of graphical languages for monoidal categories. In: New Structures for Physics, pp. 289–355. Springer, Heidelberg (2010). https://doi.org/10.1007/978-3-642-12821-9_4
39. Tull, S., Lorenz, R., Clark, S., Khan, I., Coecke, B.: Towards compositional interpretability for xai. arXiv preprint arXiv:2406.17583 (2024)
40. Wagner, J., Köhler, J.M., Gindele, T., Hetzel, L., Wiedemer, J.T., Behnke, S.: Interpretable and fine-grained visual explanations for convolutional neural networks. In: CVPR, pp. 9097–9107. Computer Vision Foundation/IEEE (2019)
41. Worrall, D.E., Garbin, S.J., Turmukhambetov, D., Brostow, G.J.: Harmonic networks: deep translation and rotation equivariance. In: Proceedings of IEEE Conference on Computer Vision and Pattern Recognition (CVPR), vol. 2, pp. 7168–7177 (2017)
42. Yang, W., et al.: Survey on explainable AI: from approaches, limitations and applications aspects. Hum. Centric Intell. Syst. **3**(3), 161–188 (2023)
43. Zhukov, A., Benois-Pineau, J., Giot, R.: Evaluation of explanation methods of AI - cnns in image classification tasks with reference-based and no-reference metrics. Adv. Artif. Intell. Mach. Learn. **3**(1), 620–646 (2023)

Open Access This chapter is licensed under the terms of the Creative Commons Attribution 4.0 International License (http://creativecommons.org/licenses/by/4.0/), which permits use, sharing, adaptation, distribution and reproduction in any medium or format, as long as you give appropriate credit to the original author(s) and the source, provide a link to the Creative Commons license and indicate if changes were made.

The images or other third party material in this chapter are included in the chapter's Creative Commons license, unless indicated otherwise in a credit line to the material. If material is not included in the chapter's Creative Commons license and your intended use is not permitted by statutory regulation or exceeds the permitted use, you will need to obtain permission directly from the copyright holder.

Interpretable Link Prediction via Neural-Symbolic Reasoning

Rodrigo Castellano Ontiveros[1](✉), Ehsan Bonabi Mobaraki[2], Francesco Giannini[3], Pietro Barbiero[4], Marco Gori[1], and Michelangelo Diligenti[1]

[1] University of Siena, Siena, Italy
{rodrigo.castellano,michelangelo.diligenti}@unisi.it
[2] Aalborg Universitet, Aalborg, Denmark
ebmo@cs.aau.dk
[3] Scuola Normale Superiore, Pisa, Italy
francesco.giannini@sns.it
[4] Università della Svizzera Italiana, Lugano, Switzerland
pietro.barbiero@usi.ch

Abstract. Knowledge Graph Embedding models have shown remarkable performances in different tasks like knowledge completion. However, they inherently lack interpretability, making it difficult to understand the reasoning behind their predictions. While different Neural-Symbolic (NeSy) models have been proposed to achieve interpretable reasoning through logic rules, existing evaluations primarily focus on accuracy, overlooking the critical assessment of explanation quality. This paper addresses this gap by introducing fully "interpretable-by-design" NeSy approaches for link prediction inspired by recently proposed models. Our framework employs reasoners that generate explicit logic proofs, utilizing either predefined or learned logic rules, ensuring transparent and explainable predictions. We go beyond traditional accuracy assessments, evaluating the quality of these explanations using established XAI metrics, including coherence. By quantitatively assessing the interpretability of our model, we aim to advance the development of trustworthy and understandable link prediction systems for Knowledge Graphs.

Keywords: Knowledge Graphs · Explainable AI · First-Order Logic

1 Introduction

Knowledge Graphs (KGs) are collections of incomplete factual knowledge represented as triplets (subject, predicate, object). Link prediction on KGs aims to infer these missing relationships by predicting the validity of new triplets based on the existing structure of the graph. Knowledge Graph Embedding (KGE) models have achieved remarkable success in link prediction tasks, effectively capturing complex relationships within knowledge graphs [19,23]. However, a significant drawback of these models from the eXplainable AI (XAI) perspective is their lack of transparency. The reasoning process behind their predictions is based on opaque latent representations, making it difficult to understand why a particular link is predicted [14]. While KGEs may implicitly encode certain relational or logic properties, such as transitivity or symmetry rules, it often remains unclear whether these properties are genuinely utilized in the prediction process [12,17]. Moreover, the reasoning performed by these methods can be prone to biases or impose overly rigid constraints, limiting their adaptability to diverse KGs.

XAI Methods over KGs. The majority of explainability methods for KGEs are symbolic based, where a rule miner is applied first and then logic reasoning can be applied on the extracted rule set. For instance, AMIE+ [10] mines rules by measuring the correlations over groups of atoms in the KG, and reports the most frequent rules according to different metrics such as the confidence or coverage. AnyBURL [16] and GenI [1] also exploit KG embeddings to learn the rules, but rely on ad hoc heuristics, generating tens of thousands of possible rules. These methods often rely on simple heuristic-based reasoners and, even if it is well known that they would benefit from using a fully fledge reasoner like ProbLog [7], scalability to even medium sized KGs would be hindered. To address the challenge of obscure reasoning in KGEs, various NeSy methods have also been proposed, with the aim of integrating symbolic logic rules into the reasoning process [25]. For instance, DRUM [20] and RNNLogic [18] exploit Recurrent Neural Networks to learn rules over KG embeddings, while similarly NCRL [6] adopts a recurrent attention unit. While these models improve reasoning capabilities compared to standard KGEs, they are often limited to simple composition rules and lack a comprehensive evaluation of the interpretability of their outputs. Since the predictions in these models often emerge as a join application of a large number of rules within a complex and non-linear decision process, the methods do not provide inspection capabilities to determine which rule is used to answer a query, therefore limiting their explainability. Indeed, the reported evaluations of these NeSy models primarily focus on predictive accuracy, neglecting the critical assessment of explanation quality. Recently, Relational Concept Bottleneck Models (R-CBMs) [3,15] have been proposed as a class of NeSy models capable of providing explanations on relational domains. We believe that R-CBMs represent a promising direction, utilizing logic rules to provide more interpretable query answering over KGs. However, the explanations generated by R-CBMs have been evaluated only qualitatively, lacking quantitative assessments of classic XAI metrics, like accuracy, coherence, and coverage. Moreover, R-CBMs predictions depend on an initial KGE score of a fact, thus not guaranteeing the rules are applied to answer the queries. In addition, the explanations were often limited to one-hop reasoning, failing to capture more intricate, multi-step logical proofs.

Our Contribution. In this paper, we address these limitations by defining a fully interpretable-by-design NeSy model over KGs, inspired by the message-passing scheme of R-CBMs. Furthermore, we enhance the explanation capabilities of different NeSy models that can be considered as special R-CBMs. In particular, we make the following key contributions.

- We define a class of fully interpretable-by-design R-CBMs.
- We perform a thorough evaluation of the explanations generated by our framework, employing established XAI metrics such as accuracy and coherence. This allows us to quantify the interpretability of our model and provide a more rigorous assessment of the reasoning process.
- We extend the capabilities of models to generate more complex explanations in the form of deeper logic proofs, moving beyond simple one-hop reasoning. This enables the model to capture more nuanced and intricate relationships within the KG, providing more comprehensive and insightful explanations.

By quantifying the interpretability of our model and enabling the extraction of complex logic proofs, we aim to advance the development of trustworthy and understandable link prediction systems for KGs. We believe that this research contributes to a deeper understanding of the reasoning processes within NeSy models, paving the way for more transparent and reliable KG analysis.

The paper is organized as follows. Section 2 introduces the background on which our model (Sect. 3) is built. Section 4 reports our experimental analysis, and finally Sect. 5 draws some conclusions and future directions.

2 Preliminaries

Relational Languages. A relational setting can be formalized using a function-free First-Order Logic (FOL) language composed of constants (entities) $\mathcal{C}$, variables $\mathcal{X}$, and predicates (relations) $\mathcal{P}$. Atoms, such as *locIn(Paris, France)* or *nation(x)*, are expressions of predicates (e.g. *locIn* and *nation*) applied to entities (e.g. *Paris* and *France*) or variables (e.g. *x*). Standard logic connectives $\{\neg, \wedge, \vee, \rightarrow\}$ and quantifiers $\{\forall, \exists\}$ are used to build literals (an atom or its negation) and more complex logic formulas from these atoms, such as $\forall x\, nation(x) \rightarrow \exists y\, locIn(x, y)$, expressing that "Each nation is in a continent". In this paper, we focus on logic theories, i.e. sets of formulas composed of Horn clauses, i.e. disjunctions of literals with a single positive literal. A Horn clause is equivalent to a rule $b_1 \wedge \ldots \wedge b_n \rightarrow h$, where $b_1, \ldots, b_n$ are called *body* atoms and h is called the *head* atom.

Grounding FOL Theories. Grounding converts formulas with variables into ground formulas, containing only constants, by substituting variables with specific constants. For example, grounding $nation(x) \rightarrow locIn(x, y)$ with the substitution $\{x/France, y/Europe\}$ yields $nation(France) \rightarrow locIn(France, Europe)$. The Herbrand Universe (HU) is the set of all possible ground formulas derived from a given FOL theory. Full grounding constructs the entire HU, while grounding often refers to creating only a subset. Methods like Markov Logic Networks use a Grounded Markov Network (GMN), a graph representation of the HU, where nodes are ground atoms and edges connect atoms that appear together in a grounded formula. For instance, given the GMN [*nation(France)* → *locIn(France, Europe)*], we get nodes for *nation(France)* and *locIn(France, Europe)*, and an edge connecting them. In the considered models, we rely on the GMN of a FOL theory to build a dependency graph.

Knowledge Graph Embeddings. Knowledge graphs (KGs) represent relational knowledge as graphs, where entities are nodes, relations are edges, and facts are triples of two entities and a relation. These graphs are generally incomplete, and Knowledge Graph Embeddings (KGEs) address the task of knowledge graph completion by mapping entities and relations to a latent space, thus predicting of missing facts. KGEs learn embeddings by optimizing scoring functions that align with observed data. For example, RotatE [21] models relations as rotations in the complex embedding space, where each relation p corresponds to a rotation from the subject entity a to the object entity b. RotatE assigns each entity and relation an embedding vector e_a, e_b, and e_p, respectively, and calculates the score of the fact $p(a,b)$ by the distance between $e_a \circ e_p$ and e_b, being $\circ$ the Hadamard product. Other KGEs are ComplEx [22] or TransE [4].

Relational Concept Bottleneck Models. Relational Concept Bottleneck Models (R-CBMs) [3] merge concept-based XAI [13] and Graph Neural Networks (GNNs) [24] for relational domains. They process atoms via an encoder, predict with a scoring function, and aggregate predictions using a GNN-like dependency graph. The pipeline includes: (i) atom encoding and prediction, (ii) message-passing on the atom dependency graph, and (iii) prediction aggregation.

(i) A ground atom $A = p(a,b)$ is initially encoded as $h^0(A) = g_p(\mathbf{e}_a, \mathbf{e}_b) \in \mathbb{R}^H$, where a,b are entities and $\mathbf{e}_a, \mathbf{e}_b \in \mathbb{R}^H$ are their embeddings, p is a relation, g_p is the atom encoder, and H denotes the embedding size. The initial prediction is calculated as $y^0(A) = s(h^0(A))$, $s : \mathbb{R}^H \to [0,1]$ being a learnable predictor, such as an MLP with a sigmoid activation function or a kge scoring function.

(ii)-(iii) Update of the embeddings and predictions of the atoms is expressed as a message-passing GNNs scheme [11] over the GMN of a FOL theory R. For every atom $A = p(a,b)$, we denote by $\mathcal{N}_r(A)$ the set of nodes connected to A via the rule $r \in R$ in the GMN, and by $\mathcal{R}(A)$ the set of rules containing the atom A. Then for T steps, the message-passing of R-CBMs is defined as:

$$h_r^t(A) = u_{l(r)}\left(h^{t-1}(A), \left[h^{t-1}(B)\right]_{B \in \mathcal{N}_r(A)}\right) \quad (1)$$

$$y_r^t(A) = f_{l(r)}\left(y^{t-1}(A), \left[h_r^t(B), y^{t-1}(B)\right]_{B \in \mathcal{N}_r(A)}\right) \quad (2)$$

$$h^t(A) = \sum_{r \in \mathcal{R}(A)} h_r^t(A) \quad (3)$$

$$y^t(A) = \bigoplus_{r \in \mathcal{R}(A)} y_r^t(A) \quad (4)$$

where $u_{l(r)}$ and $f_{l(r)}$ represent edge-type dependent functions. Specifically, $u_{l(r)}$ performs a combine/update step, yielding an improved latent representation $h_r^t(A)$, while $f_{l(r)}$ executes a local readout, producing a prediction based solely on the neighborhood $\mathcal{N}_r(A)$. The symbol $\bigoplus$ denotes an aggregation operation, such as maximum or summation, applied to the predictions across all neighborhoods r belonging to the set $\mathcal{R}(A)$.

3 Methods

R-CBMs are not fully interpretable because the final prediction aggregates the predictions per-rule $y_r^t(A)$ for an atom A using a generic aggregator, which is generally opaque and complex. Furthermore, the dependency of the per-rule output $y_r^t(A)$ directly depends on the output of latent representations h_r^t, which are black boxes for a human operator. In this section, we propose a sequence of modifications to define a class of R-CBMs, where the decision process corresponds to a logic reasoning process, which can be unwound and traced back to provide a human interpretable explanation. In all the proposed algorithms, the basic idea is to structure the computation into a logic rule generation stage, which can depend on latent representations, and a rule execution stage, which is fully interpretable and understandable.

Depending on the different design decisions, we propose different models, providing different trade-offs between expressivity and interpretability, relying on the FOL theory of Horn clauses R.

3.1 Interpretable Semantic Based Regularization (I-SBR)

Semantic Based Regularization (SBR) [9] conjuncts the predictions of the body atoms to compute the prediction of the head atom in every rule r, using a selected t-norm. These methods were originally limited to unary predicates and a single reasoning propagation step. Here, we propose a relational recursive extension based on message-passing:

$$y_r^t(A) = t-norm\left([y^{t-1}(B)]_{B \in \mathcal{N}_r(A)}\right) \quad (5)$$

$$y^t(A) = \max_{r \in \mathcal{R}(A)} y_r^t(A), \quad (6)$$

where the y_r are initialized using $y_r^0(\alpha) = kge(\alpha)$, where α is the head node. There are t reasoning hops by applying the rules in R, with $0 \le t \le T$. The idea of the proposed architecture is to derive new facts by recursively executing the rules, which is equivalent to performing forward chaining starting from the kge predictions. Forward chaining in I-SBR relies on t-norms for the logic execution step, which guarantee differentiability and the possibility to train the kge end-to-end within a single computation graph. Thanks to the use of maximum aggregation in the computation of the prediction $y^t(\alpha)$, the score can be traced back from α to the body nodes, and this process can be recursively repeated providing a proof tree which can be provided as an explanation. In the experimental section, we show different examples of proof trees extracted using this methodology.

3.2 Interpretable Deep Concept Reasoners (I-DCR)

DCR [2] learns a formula for each head atom, given a set of candidate body atoms, then computes the output by using a t-norm:

$$y_r^t(A) = t\text{-}norm\left(\Phi_r(h^0(B), y^{t-1}(B))\right) \tag{7}$$

$$y^t(A) = \max_{r \in \mathcal{R}(A)} y_r^t(A) \tag{8}$$

where the y_r are initialized using $y_r^0(\alpha) = kge(\alpha)$, and $\Phi_r : \mathbb{R}^{H+1} \to [0,1]$ represents a logic formula processing the embedding representation and prediction of each atom in each rule r, to get a learned Horn Clause. In the original formulation, DCR was defined for a single step of propagation, however, we extend DCR to multiple iterations t, with $0 \le t \le T$, to enable multi-hop reasoning and restrict it to a max aggregation operator to merge the information from different rules. The resulting architecture, called I-DCR, can take advantage of latent representations to discover the rules to apply in a given context, unlike I-SBR, which assumes all rules to be predefined. I-DCR also preserves full human interpretability, as the generated rules are executed symbolically. Like in I-SBR, the use of t-norms to perform the logic reasoning step allows an end-to-end optimization of the KGE layer.

4 Experiments

4.1 Experimental Setup

We conducted a comprehensive series of experiments on diverse benchmark datasets to evaluate our proposed approach from different points of view.

The three benchmark datasets used for evaluation are: Countries [5], Family [6], and WN18RR [8]. The Countries dataset consists of three tasks (S1, S2, S3) that increase in difficulty, predicting locations based on neighborhood relations and locations. Family encodes familial relationships. WN18RR, derived from WordNet, ensures no inverse relation leakage.

The countries dataset follows predefined logical rules:
R_1: $LocIn(x, w) \land LocIn(w, z) \to LocIn(x, z)$
R_2: $NeighOf(x, y) \land LocIn(y, z) \to LocIn(x, z)$
R_3: $NeighOf(x, y) \land NeighOf(y, k) \land LocIn(k, z) \to LocIn(x, z)$
Rules for other datasets are extracted using AMIE [10], selecting them based on standard confidence. Dataset statistics are shown in Table 1.

Baseline Models. We compare two Neural-Symbolic (NeSy) models, I-SBR and I-DCR, against the KGE ComplEx.

Hyperparameter Settings. All models use 100-dimensional embeddings, Adam optimizer (10^{-2} learning rate), and are trained for 100 epochs.

Table 1. Detailed statistics of the datasets employed in our experiments.

Dataset	#Entities	#Relations	#Facts	Avg. Degree	#Rules
Countries S1	272	3	1,110	4.28	1
Countries S2	272	4	1,062	4.35	2
Countries S3	272	4	978	4.35	3
Family	3007	12	19,845	6.47	48
WN18RR	40,559	11	86,835	2.14	28

4.2 Evaluation Metrics

Mean Reciprocal Rank (MRR) measures the average reciprocal rank of the first correct answer in a ranked list:

$$\text{MRR} = \frac{1}{|Q|} \sum_{q \in Q} \frac{1}{\text{rank}_q} \qquad (9)$$

where Q is the set of queries, and rank_q is the position of the first correct answer.

Hits@N computes the proportion of queries where a correct answer appears within the top-N predictions:

$$\text{Hits@N} = \frac{1}{|Q|} \sum_{q \in Q} I(\exists \text{ correct answer in top-}N) \qquad (10)$$

where $I(\cdot)$ is an indicator function. In neural-symbolic models, explanations depend on the accuracy of predictions. Thus, high MRR and Hits@N are not just performance metrics but necessary conditions for generating faithful and trustworthy explanations, reinforcing their central role in evaluating explainability.

Coherence measures the agreement between two models by computing the ratio of queries for which both models produce the same top-ranked prediction:

$$\text{Coherence} = \frac{1}{|Q|} \sum_{q \in Q} I(\text{top prediction}_{\text{model}_1} = \text{top prediction}_{\text{model}_2}) \qquad (11)$$

where $I(\cdot)$ is an indicator function [2,13].

Together, these metrics capture both the predictive performance of the model (MRR, Hits @ N) and the transparency of its reasoning (coherence, proof traces).

4.3 Results

The primary objective of our experimental evaluation is to assess the performance of our proposed reasoners, namely I-SBR and I-DCR, in comparison with a baseline approach across multiple datasets. The baseline model used for this evaluation is ComplEx, which serves both as a direct benchmark and as the knowledge graph embedding method for the reasoners. By analyzing different

Table 2. Results for the metrics MRR and Hits (H) for the Countries Dataset.

Countries S2

Model	MRR	H@1	H@3	H@10
ComplEx	0.976	0.954	0.996	1.0
I-DCR	0.969	0.958	0.967	1.0
I-SBR	0.969	0.958	0.962	1.0

Countries S3

Model	MRR	H@1	H@3	H@10
ComplEx	0.866	0.808	0.879	1.0
I-DCR	0.979	0.962	0.996	1.0
I-SBR	0.983	0.967	1.0	1.0

Table 3. Results for the metrics MRR and Hits (H) for the Family and WN18RR datasets. For each method M, we indicate with $M^\star$ the results obtained when restricting the training set to the set of queries which are provable in the logic theory defined by the considered set of rules.

Family

Model	MRR	H@1	H@3	H@10
ComplEx	0.787	0.653	0.916	0.951
I-DCR	0.764	0.764	0.764	0.764
I-SBR	0.764	0.763	0.764	0.764
I-DCR*	1.0	1.0	1.0	1.0
I-SBR*	1.0	1.0	1.0	1.0

WN18RR

Model	MRR	H@1	H@3	H@10
AMIE+		0.358	-	0.388
AnyBurl	~0.47	~0.44	-	~0.55
ComplEx	0.384	0.376	0.387	0.397
I-DCR	0.380	0.350	0.370	0.381
I-SBR	0.382	0.340	0.369	0.385
I-DCR*	0.938	0.899	0.956	0.985
I-SBR*	0.931	0.906	0.965	0.987

evaluation metrics, we aim to provide insights into how well the reasoners perform in terms of ranking quality and coherence of predictions[1]

In the Countries dataset, the results for the S1 benchmark have been omitted due to the saturation of the evaluation metrics, which reach the optimal maximum value across all tested methods. In the S2 benchmark, ComplEx achieves an MRR score of 0.976 MRR. Both I-SBR and I-DCR exhibit very similar performance to the baseline when evaluated using MRR and Hits metrics, yielding a score of 0.969. Coherence of the I-SBR and I-DCR with the ComplEx model providing the initial embedded representations of the atoms is high, largely due to the overall strong performance of all models across the other metrics. However, in scenario S3, the performance difference becomes more pronounced. The reasoners outperform ComplEx significantly, with over a 10% increase in MRR and a 15% increase in Hits metrics. This substantial improvement corresponds to a lower coherence score with ComplEx, which is recorded at 0.80 for I-SBR and 0.81 for I-DCR. These results are detailed in Table 2 and 4.

For the Family and WN18RR datasets, the reasoners perform closely to the baseline as shown in Table 3. In the case of Family, the reasoners outperform ComplEx significantly for Hits@1. For WN18RR, the performance remains close to ComplEx, in spite of the inherent explainability of our reasoners. In the case of WN18RR, coherence is relatively low due to the generally lower scores across

---

[1] The code is available at https://github.com/rodrigo-castellano/Interpretable-NeSy.

Table 4. Coherence values for I-SBR and I-DCR against the ComplEx model providing the initial embedded representations of the atoms.

Model	Countries S2	Countries S3	Family	WN18RR
I-DCR	0.934	0.812	0.654	0.362
I-SBR	0.942	0.800	0.654	0.365

Table 5. Examples of local explanations as proof trees obtained for the Kinship Family and Countries datasets.

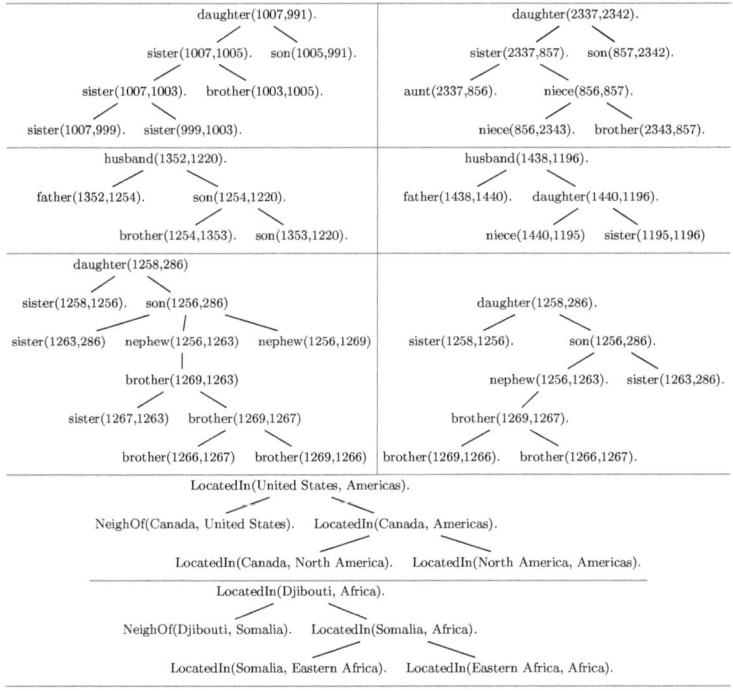

all methods, making it difficult to obtain an identical top-ranked prediction. When comparing against existing symbolic reasoners, AMIE+ achieves similar performance to our models, whereas AnyBurl outperforms them. It is essential to highlight that our methods rely on a small and controlled set of human-understandable logical rules. On the other hand, AnyBurl/AMIE move the complexity in the rule extraction phase, which returns a set of complex and not-human understandable rules which are at least two orders of magnitude larger than the set that we consider. For example, AnyBurl considers more than 75000 automatically mined rules for WN18RR, which are mostly applied in a shallow fashion. This distinction makes our models more interpretable as the generated proofs closely resemble the step-by-step reasoning process of humans, unlike the single application of not intuitive and hard to understand complex rules used by the competitors [2,13].

Table 6. Sample of the global explanations obtained by aggregating the local explanations over a dataset.

Dataset	Rule
Countries S1	$\forall a, b \exists c\, locIn(a,c) \wedge locIn(c,b) \rightarrow locIn(a,b)$
Countries S2	$\forall a, b \exists c\, neighOf(a,c) \wedge locIn(c,b) \rightarrow locIn(a,b)$
Countries S3	$\forall a, b \exists c, d\, neighOf(a,c) \wedge neighOf(c,d) \wedge locIn(d,b) \rightarrow locIn(a,b)$
	$\forall a, b \exists c\, neighOf(a,c) \wedge locIn(c,b) \rightarrow locIn(a,b)$
Family	$\forall a, b \exists c\, aunt(a,c) \wedge sister(b,c) \rightarrow aunt(a,b)$
	$\forall a, b \exists c\, aunt(a,c) \wedge brother(b,c) \rightarrow aunt(a,b)$
	$\forall a, b \exists c\, sister(a,c) \wedge father(c,b) \rightarrow aunt(a,b)$
	$\forall a, b \exists c\, sister(a,c) \wedge son(b,c) \rightarrow aunt(a,b)$
	$\forall a, b \exists c\, sister(a,c) \wedge mother(c,b) \rightarrow aunt(a,b)$
	$\forall a, b \exists c\, sister(a,c) \wedge daughter(b,c) \rightarrow aunt(a,b)$
WN18RR	$\forall a, b \exists c\, also\_see(b,a) \rightarrow also\_see(a,b)$
	$\forall a, b \exists c\, also\_see(a,c) \wedge also\_see(c,b) \rightarrow also\_see(a,b)$
	$\forall a, b\, deriv\_related\_form(b,a) \rightarrow deriv\_related\_form(a,b)$
	$\forall a, b \exists c\, has\_part(a,c) \wedge hypernym(c,b) \rightarrow hypernym(a,b)$
	$\forall a, b \exists c\, verb\_group(a,c) \wedge hypernym(c,b) \rightarrow hypernym(a,b)$

Due to the simplicity and compactness of the rule set used by our reasoners, not all test queries are provable within the logical framework. This is reflected in the rule coverage values of the datasets: 1.0 for Countries, 0.77 for Family, and 0.40 for WN18RR. For that reason, we decided to evaluate the models only on the test queries that can be proven with our rules. Under these conditions, both the baseline and the reasoners exhibit improved performance. This improvement is particularly striking for Family, where all metrics reach their maximum possible values. Similarly, in the case of WN18RR, the baseline and reasoner achieve MRR scores of 0.933 and 0.938, respectively.

4.4 Explanations

Global Explanations. Global explanations provide insight into the overall reasoning process by integrating local explanations across multiple test cases. This integration allows us to identify patterns in how the NeSy method classifies triplets, highlighting the logical rules most frequently used. Table 6 presents several representative examples from different datasets, showcasing the key logical patterns discovered by our model.

Local Explanations. The extracted local explanations take advantage of the deep logical reasoning used by the models. These proofs are not just chains, but are proof trees of arbitrary depth obtained thanks to the first-order logic formulas. This leads to a richer set of explanations that cover more queries. Using simple rules like those in Table 6 to build a proof tree is more intuitive and easier to understand than relying on long, flat rules. In contrast, applying such extended rules, often produced in large numbers by systems such as AnyBurl [16], can obscure the reasoning process and diminish explanation clarity [2,16].

Table 5 presents examples of local explanations as proof trees obtained for the Family dataset. These proof trees demonstrate how multiple reasoning steps contribute to deriving conclusions. These structured explanations reinforce the transparency of our model and highlight the advantage of incorporating first-order logic into knowledge-graph reasoning.

5 Conclusions and Future Work

This paper presents a class of neural-symbolic methods, which integrate latent representations and logic reasoning. The main advantage of this methodology is in the fact that, once the latent representations have instantiated the reasoning process, the final decision can be explained with high interpretability to a human operator. We presented an application in the domain of link prediction for knowledge graphs. Unlike most symbolic approaches for link prediction, our methodology is designed to allow a full retracing of the reasoning steps, resulting in explanations in the form of deep logical proofs, instead of the shallow rules typically used by symbolic KG methods. Results have shown that the methods perform well for the selected datasets when compared to the baseline, improving results in some cases due to multi-hop reasoning.

As future work, we plan to expand the set of methods defined within the framework, as well as to consider more complex rule sets. Finally, we plan to apply the same methodology for post-hoc explainers, by distilling a black-box model into its interpretable neural-symbolic counterpart.

Acknowledgments. This work has been partially supported by the Partnership Extended PE00000013 - "FAIR - Future Artificial Intelligence Research" - Spoke 1 "Human-centered AI". This work was also supported by the EU Framework Program for Research and Innovation Horizon under the Grant Agreement No 101073307 (MSCA-DN LeMuR).

Disclosure of Interests. The authors have no competing interests.

References

1. Amador-Domínguez, E., Serrano, E., Manrique, D.: GEnI: a framework for the generation of explanations and insights of knowledge graph embedding predictions. Neurocomputing **521**, 199–212 (2023)
2. Barbiero, P., et al.: Interpretable neural-symbolic concept reasoning. In: ICML, pp. 1801–1825 (2023)
3. Barbiero, P., Giannini, F., Ciravegna, G., Diligenti, M., Marra, G.: Relational concept bottleneck models. In: NeurIPS (2024)
4. Bordes, A., Usunier, N., Garcia-Duran, A., Weston, J., Yakhnenko, O.: Translating embeddings for modeling multi-relational data. In: NeurIPS, vol. 26, pp. 2787–2795 (2013)

5. Bouchard, G., Singh, S., Trouillon, T.: On approximate reasoning capabilities of low-rank vector spaces. In: AAAI Spring Symposia (2015)
6. Cheng, K., Amed, N.K., Sun, Y.: Neural compositional rule learning for knowledge graph reasoning. In: ICLR (ICLR) (2023)
7. De Raedt, L., Kimmig, A., Toivonen, H.: Problog: a probabilistic prolog and its application in link discovery. In: IJCAI (2007)
8. Dettmers, T., Minervini, P., Stenetorp, P., Riedel, S.: Convolutional 2D knowledge graph embeddings. In: Proceedings of the AAAI Conference (2018)
9. Diligenti, M., Gori, M., Sacca, C.: Semantic-based regularization for learning and inference. Artif. Intell. **244**, 143–165 (2017)
10. Galárraga, L., Teflioudi, C., Hose, K., Suchanek, F.M.: Fast rule mining in ontological knowledge bases with AMIE+. VLDB J. **24**(6), 707–730 (2015)
11. Gilmer, J., Schoenholz, S.S., Riley, P.F., Vinyals, O., Dahl, G.E.: Message passing neural networks. In: Machine Learning Meets Quantum Physics, pp. 199–214. Springer (2020)
12. Gutierrez Basulto, V., Schockaert, S.: From knowledge graph embedding to ontology embedding? An analysis of the compatibility between vector space representations and rules (2018)
13. Koh, P.W., et al.: Concept bottleneck models. In: ICML, pp. 5338–5348. PMLR (2020)
14. Lecue, F.: On the role of knowledge graphs in explainable AI. Semantic Web **11**(1), 41–51 (2020)
15. Marra, G., Diligenti, M., Giannini, F.: Relational reasoning networks. Knowl.-Based Syst. 112822 (2025)
16. Meilicke, C., Chekol, M.W., Betz, P., Fink, M., Stuckeschmidt, H.: Anytime bottom-up rule learning for large-scale knowledge graph completion. VLDB J. **33**(1), 131–161 (2024)
17. Pavlović, A., Sallinger, E.: Building bridges: knowledge graph embeddings respecting logical rules. In: 15th Alberto Mendelzon International Workshop on Foundations of Data Management (2023)
18. Qu, M., Chen, J., Xhonneux, L.P., Bengio, Y., Tang, J.: RNNLogic: learning logic rules for reasoning on knowledge graphs. In: ICLR (2020)
19. Rossi, A., Barbosa, D., Firmani, D., Matinata, A., Merialdo, P.: Knowledge graph embedding for link prediction: a comparative analysis. ACM TKDD **15**(2), 1–49 (2021)
20. Sadeghian, A., Armandpour, M., Ding, P., Wang, D.Z.: Drum: end-to-end differentiable rule mining on knowledge graphs. NeurIPS **32** (2019)
21. Sun, Z., Deng, Z.H., Nie, J.Y., Tang, J.: Rotate: knowledge graph embedding by relational rotation in complex space. In: ICLR (2019)
22. Trouillon, T., Welbl, J., Riedel, S., Gaussier, É., Bouchard, G.: Complex embeddings for simple link prediction. In: ICML, pp. 2071–2080. PMLR (2016)
23. Wang, M., Qiu, L., Wang, X.: A survey on knowledge graph embeddings for link prediction. Symmetry **13**(3), 485 (2021)
24. Wu, Z., Pan, S., Chen, F., Long, G., Zhang, C., Philip, S.Y.: A comprehensive survey on graph neural networks. IEEE Trans. Neural Netw. Learn. Syst. **32**(1), 4–24 (2020)
25. Zhang, W., Chen, J., Li, J., Xu, Z., Pan, J.Z., Chen, H.: Knowledge graph reasoning with logics and embeddings: survey and perspective. In: 2024 IEEE International Conference on Knowledge Graph (ICKG), pp. 492–499. IEEE (2024)

Open Access This chapter is licensed under the terms of the Creative Commons Attribution 4.0 International License (http://creativecommons.org/licenses/by/4.0/), which permits use, sharing, adaptation, distribution and reproduction in any medium or format, as long as you give appropriate credit to the original author(s) and the source, provide a link to the Creative Commons license and indicate if changes were made.

The images or other third party material in this chapter are included in the chapter's Creative Commons license, unless indicated otherwise in a credit line to the material. If material is not included in the chapter's Creative Commons license and your intended use is not permitted by statutory regulation or exceeds the permitted use, you will need to obtain permission directly from the copyright holder.

CausalAIME: Leveraging Peter-Clark Algorithms and Inverse Modeling for Unified Global Feature Explanation in Healthcare

Takafumi Nakanishi[✉][iD]

Tokyo University of Technology, 1404- 1 Katakuramachi, Hachioji City, Tokyo 192-0982, Japan
nakanishitf@stf.teu.ac.jp
https://www.transmedia-tech-lab.jp/

Abstract. In medical applications of machine learning, it is essential to interpret model behavior and explore the true association between features and clinical outcomes. Conventional Explainable AI approaches typically focus on "model-dependent" global feature importance from trained models, which may not guarantee "data-driven" causal relationships or medical consistency. To address this, we propose CausalAIME, a new framework that combines approximate inverse model explanations (AIME) with the Peter-Clark algorithm for causal discovery. This integration suppresses multicollinearity while enabling global visualization of both feature signs (positive or negative) and class-specific contributions. Furthermore, by choosing either the model's output $\hat{Y}$ or the true label Y as input, CausalAIME unifies both model-dependent and data-driven global feature importance within the same framework. Our experiments using breast cancer diagnostic data compared CausalAIME with existing methods such as Random Forest and SHAP, highlighting the advantages of CausalAIME in offering sign-based interpretability and causal perspectives, both critical in clinical settings. We anticipate that CausalAIME will contribute to enhanced explainability across various domains, including healthcare, by accommodating the needs for both true association analysis and model behavior interpretation.

Keywords: global feature importance · approximate inverse model explanations (AIME) · Peter-Clark (PC) algorithm · Causal and correlational relationships of explanatory variables

1 Introduction

In recent years, machine learning and deep learning have rapidly gained adoption in the medical field, finding wide-ranging applications such as image-based diagnosis and outcome prediction. However, in clinical settings, building high-accuracy models is not enough; it is also essential to *explain why* a given prediction is made to establish trust in real-world practice. To meet this need, various approaches have been proposed to interpret a model's decision rationale (e.g., SHapley Additive exPlanations (SHAP) [1] and LIME [2]), as well as feature-importance methods for Random Forests (Gini importance) [3]. Nonetheless, most of these methods offer "model-dependent" global feature importance by relying on the behavior of a trained model and do not guarantee any causal or statistical relationship with the true label.

This study highlights the importance of providing two types of global feature importance: *model-dependent global feature importance*, which identifies explanatory variables contributing to the target variable under a specific black-box machine learning model, and *model-independent (data-driven) global feature importance*, which uncovers the explanatory variables that genuinely contribute to the target variable. The former is useful when domain experts wish to adjust a machine learning model by examining its overall behavior, while the latter is important for users without domain knowledge or those analyzing entirely novel phenomena, as it indicates a "pure" relationship free from model bias. However, LIME only yields local feature importance, and the feature importance of both SHAP and Random Forest remain model-dependent; thus, they do not guarantee any causal or statistical relationship between the true target variable and its explanatory variables. This has caused confusion among explainable AI (XAI) users in other fields, particularly in medicine. Therefore, *defining and disseminating* these two types of global feature importance is necessary.

In practice, medical settings often demand the latter type of *model-independent global feature importance*. To address this, approximate inverse model explanations (AIME) [4] were proposed, which compute a near-inverse operator of a black-box model to derive both global and local feature importance algebraically. The original AIME study [4] focused on using X (the explanatory variables in machine learning) and $\hat{Y}$ (the outputs of the black-box model) to obtain an approximate inverse operator $A^\dagger$. However, $\hat{Y}$ can be replaced with the true label Y used in training. This enables AIME to derive both model-dependent (former) and data-driven (latter) types of global feature importance within a single framework.

Moreover, in medical practice, the causal and correlational structures among features are critically important. Hence, it is desirable to produce global feature importance with positive/negative coefficients, while *controlling for multicollinearity and accounting for causal perspectives*. Therefore, our study combines AIME with the Peter-Clark (PC) algorithm [5] to form a framework called *CausalAIME*, which derives global feature importance based on causal/correlational relationships among features. By switching between $\hat{Y}$ and Y as the label input, CausalAIME can yield both "model-dependent" and "data-driven" global feature importance under a single system; this paper emphasizes the "data-driven" aspect.

In this study, we conducted comparative experiments using a breast cancer diagnostic dataset [6] to evaluate AIME and CausalAIME against existing methods such as Random Forest and SHAP.

Reconciling the causal structure discovered by the PC algorithm with the approximate inverse operator in AIME under highly correlated feature spaces is difficult. Simply penalizing the magnitude of coefficients or applying standard regularization methods does not directly handle scenarios where multiple features exhibit strong dependencies or partial causal relationships. We introduce a novel difference-penalty term to address the difficulty in reconciling the causal structure discovered by the PC algorithm with the approximate inverse operator in AIME under highly correlated feature spaces. This term dynamically enforces consistency with the directed or undirected edges inferred by the PC algorithm, thereby suppressing multicollinearity and ensuring that each feature's contribution aligns with the causal or correlational constraints.

The main contributions of this study are as follows:

- We employ AIME to propose and implement a unified framework that handles two kinds of global feature importance (model-dependent and data-driven).
- By fusing the PC algorithm for causal discovery with AIME's approximate inverse operator, we introduce CausalAIME, which manages multicollinearity and offers interpretability through positive/negative signs.
- Through medical experiments comparing SHAP, Random Forest, and other existing methods, we show that CausalAIME meets the need for global feature importance and the structural (causal/correlational) perspective sought by medical professionals.

The remainder of this paper is organized as follows: Sect. 2 discusses the related studies. Section 3 outlines the proposed PC algorithm and AIME. Section 4 details the mathematical formulation of CausalAIME, incorporating the PC algorithm. Section 5 presents the experimental settings and results, followed by a discussion in Sect. 6. Finally, Sect. 7 concludes the study and discusses future research.

2 Related Works

In recent years, several XAI methods that incorporate causal relationships have been proposed. This section provides an overview of representative previous studies and clarifies how the proposed CausalAIME framework differs.

2.1 Introduction of Causality in Existing Studies

Counterfactual explanations using causal discovery [7] leverage causal discovery to estimate an unknown causal graph, and then use counterfactual probabilities to explain a black-box model behavior. Applications such as credit ratings explore the counterfactual values of explanatory variables based on the estimated causal graph. However, the main focus is on estimating the causal graph and performing counterfactual reasoning, not deriving the global feature importance.

The total causal effect calculation for fuzzy cognitive maps (TCEC-FCM) [8] algorithm was proposed for efficiently computing causal effects in large-scale fuzzy Cognitive Maps. It enhances AI model interpretability by performing a binary search and uses graph traversal to explore causal paths. However, this research specifically targeted fuzzy cognitive maps and did not address applying such methods to general black-box models or visualizing global feature importance using positive and negative coefficients.

Cinquini and Guidotti [9] proposed causality-aware locally interpretable model-agnostic explanations to integrate causal knowledge into data to produce stable local explanations. It extends the conventional LIME by building a localized approximate model that accounts for causal structures, aiming to achieve higher-fidelity explanations. This approach focuses on local explanations rather than addressing global-level feature importance, which considers causal factors and multicollinearity.

Termine et al. [10] proposed machine-learning explanations by surrogate causal models (MaLESCaMo) to learn surrogate causal models in local neighborhoods and generate causal counterfactual explanations. This method attempts to justify counterfactual-based explanations in a causal manner by inferring interactions among features from an actual causal structure. However, it is focused on local-neighborhood analysis rather than global feature importance or data-driven analysis, independent of the model's output.

Structural causal interpretations [11] uses Pearl's structural causal models to align the output of a learned model with human causal thinking. This highlights the importance of maintaining causal consistency between a machine learning model and its task; however, it mainly focuses on the coherence between a human mental model and the Pearlian framework. It does not emphasize the methods for presenting global feature importance with positive/negative signs or class-specific details.

Shapley flow [12] attempts to visualize feature interdependencies that conventional Shapley-based explanation methods may ignore by assigning credit to edges rather than to nodes in a causal graph. Specifically, it calculates the edge-level contributions across the entire graph to capture how input influences propagate to the output. However, Shapley flow focuses on how the model processes input features alongside a causal graph and does not directly provide data-driven global importance using the true label.

Finally, Breuer et al. [13] introduced causality-aware Shapley value for global explanations (CAGE), a novel framework that incorporates causal models into Shapley values, to offer more causally valid global explanations by applying causal interventions (do-operators) and reflecting the causal structure among the features in the sampling process. This approach assumes that the existing causal graph is known and does not automatically learn causal relationships. It primarily modifies Shapley value computation in a causal manner but does not comprehensively address a data-driven mode using the true label or suppress multicollinearity.

2.2 Positioning of This Research and the Characteristics of CausalAIME

Previous studies have contributed to integrating causality with XAI; however, many of them concentrate on local interpretations, such as counterfactuals or neighborhood-level analysis; assume an existing causal structure without fully exploring global feature importance that captures positive or negative contributions and class-specific information; or do not explicitly offer a framework to switch between model-dependent and data-driven modes. By contrast, CausalAIME incorporates the PC algorithm into AIME's approximate inverse operator framework, thereby estimating causal structures among features and obtaining coefficients that suppress multicollinearity, while providing global feature importance with signed and class-specific interpretations. Furthermore, it can switch between using the true label Y for the data-driven mode and the model output $\widehat{Y}$ for the model-dependent mode within the same framework. This study emphasizes the importance of data-driven global features required in medical settings. By delivering functionality that earlier methods have not fully covered, namely global feature importance with signed coefficients, causal-structure estimation addressing multicollinearity, and the coexistence of data-driven and model-dependent modes, we aimed to facilitate clinically meaningful explanations.

3 Overview of Peter-Clark Algorithm and Approximate InverseExlanations

3.1 Peter-Clark Algorithm Overview [5]

The PC algorithm [5] is a widely used causal discovery method for estimating both the skeleton and edge orientations of directed acyclic graphs (DAGs) based on conditional independence testing. In this section, we outline the basic PC procedure using the notation $X \in \mathbb{R}^{n \times N}$, where n is the number of feature dimensions, and N is the number of samples.

Basic Setup and Goal. Let

$$X = \begin{bmatrix} \mathbf{x}_1 \ \mathbf{x}_2 \ \dots \ \mathbf{x}_N \end{bmatrix} \in \mathbb{R}^{n \times N}, \tag{1}$$

where each column $\mathbf{x}_j \in \mathbb{R}^n$ represents the j-th sample of the n-dimensional features. The goal of the PC algorithm is to find a DAG whose nodes correspond to the n features (i.e., each row in X can be considered a single "feature dimension"), and whose edges indicate causal relationships or correlation among these features. In other words, we aim to determine which rows (features) are conditionally independent when other features are conditioned upon, thereby inferring the DAG structure.

Skeleton Construction via Conditional Independence Testing. The first step of the PC algorithm is *skeleton construction*, where we initially assume a fully connected undirected graph among the n feature nodes and systematically remove edges whenever we detect conditional independence. Specifically, for two distinct features i and k (where $i, k \in \{1, \ldots, n\}$ and $i \neq k$), the algorithm tries to find a conditioning set $S \subseteq \{1, \ldots, n\} \setminus \{i, k\}$ such that

$$P(\mathbf{x}_i, \mathbf{x}_k \mid S) = P(\mathbf{x}_i \mid S) P(\mathbf{x}_k \mid S). \qquad (2)$$

Here, "$\mathbf{x}_i$" represents the i-th row of X (i.e., the i-th feature across all N samples), and S is a subset of other features (rows). If $\mathbf{x}_i$ and $\mathbf{x}_k$ are conditionally independent given S, we remove the undirected edge between i and k. The PC algorithm gradually increases the size of S by removing edges that indicate conditional independence. Once the skeleton construction is completed, we obtain an undirected graph among the n feature nodes with certain edges removed.

Orientation of V-Structures. Next, the PC algorithm searches for *V-structures* in the undirected skeleton. A V-structure occurs when three distinct features i, j, k form an undirected chain $i - j - k$ in the skeleton, where i and k are not directly connected *and* j does not appear in the separating set for (i, k). In such cases,

$$i \rightarrow j \leftarrow k$$

is established as a V-structure (i.e., node j is a common child of i and k), yielding a partial orientation of the edges.

Further Orientation Rules and Iteration. After identifying V-structures, the PC algorithm applies additional orientation rules to propagate directions across the graph, ensuring that no directed cycles form and that the conditional independences discovered in the previous steps are preserved. Through these repeated rules, as many edges as possible in the skeleton are oriented, ultimately producing a DAG over the n features. This DAG represents the **causal structure** that aligns with the conditional independences observed in X.

Advantages and Limitations. An advantage of the PC algorithm is its relative simplicity and recognition as a general-purpose **causal discovery method**. By focusing on conditional independence testing among the n features, it systematically prunes and orients the edges using V-structures and additional rules. However, the number of independence tests can grow rapidly for large n; nevertheless, limiting the size of the conditioning sets helps manage computational costs. Furthermore, finite samples and measurement noise can introduce uncertainty into independence judgments.

In this study (Sect. 4), we utilize the PC algorithm's DAG estimation in *CausalAIME* to incorporate sign information for global feature importance, while addressing multicollinearity. Specifically, after obtaining a DAG (or partially oriented structure), we introduce penalty terms for directed or undirected edges in the approximate inverse operator $A^\dagger$ from AIME, thereby enforcing causal constraints on feature importance.

3.2 Approximate Inverse Model Explanations Overview [4]

This section describes the core concepts of the AIME model. Figure 1 shows an overview of AIME. Let $n, m \in \mathbb{N}$ represent the input and output dimensions, respectively, and N the sample size. We consider a function $f : \mathbb{R}^n \to \mathbb{R}^m$ such that $\mathbf{y}_i = f(\mathbf{x}_i)$ for each dataset $\{(\mathbf{x}_i, \mathbf{y}_i)\}_{i=1}^N$. Here, f is a black-box AI or machine learning model. The AIME framework derives global feature importance by constructing an approximate inverse operator: $\hat{f}^{-1} : \mathbb{R}^m \to \mathbb{R}^n$ for f.

For each dataset, we define

$$X = \begin{bmatrix} \mathbf{x}_1 & \mathbf{x}_2 & \cdots & \mathbf{x}_N \end{bmatrix} \in \mathbb{R}^{n \times N}, \quad Y = \begin{bmatrix} \mathbf{y}_1 & \mathbf{y}_2 & \cdots & \mathbf{y}_N \end{bmatrix} \in \mathbb{R}^{m \times N}. \quad (3)$$

The AIME method then defines a linear approximation of the inverse, $A^\dagger \in \mathbb{R}^{n \times m}$, by solving the following optimization:

$$A^\dagger = \arg\min_{M \in \mathbb{R}^{n \times m}} \|X - MY\|_F^2 = \arg\min_{M \in \mathbb{R}^{n \times m}} \sum_{i=1}^N \|\mathbf{x}_i - M\mathbf{y}_i\|_2^2, \quad (4)$$

where $\|\cdot\|_F$ denotes the Frobenius norm and $\|\cdot\|_2$ the Euclidean (L_2) norm.

In the above optimization, $M \in \mathbb{R}^{n \times m}$ represents a linear operator that maps each output vector $\mathbf{y}_i \in \mathbb{R}^m$ back to an approximation of the original input vector $\mathbf{x}_i \in \mathbb{R}^n$. We then solve for the particular matrix M that minimizes the reconstruction error $\|X - MY\|_F^2$ over all samples. After conducting this minimization, the optimal solution is denoted by $A^\dagger$. Strictly speaking, f^{-1} may not exist if f is not bijective or the input and output dimensions differ. Thus, $A^\dagger$ is best viewed as an *approximate* or "pseudo-inverse" of f. Conceptually, if an exact inverse f^{-1} did exist (for instance, in a strictly linear or otherwise perfectly invertible scenario), we would have $X = f^{-1}(Y)$. However, even when f is non-linear, the same least-squares principle still applies, where $A^\dagger$ can be regarded as a global linear approximation to the (potentially non-linear) inverse mapping of f. Under suitable conditions where YY^T is invertible, $A^\dagger$ takes a closed-form akin to the Moore–Penrose pseudoinverse, serving as a concise way to "invert" f in the least-squares sense. In practice, $A^\dagger$ serves as the global least-squares operator satisfying $\mathbf{x}_i \approx A^\dagger \mathbf{y}_i$. Under suitable conditions where YY^T is invertible, $A^\dagger$ can be written in a closed-form expression akin to the Moore–Penrose pseudoinverse, making it a direct linear approximation to "inverting" f in a least-squares sense.

Thus, AIME assumes the following approximate relationship:

$$X \approx A^\dagger Y. \quad (5)$$

Multiplying both sides of (5) by Y^T yields

$$XY^T \approx A^\dagger (YY^T).$$

If YY^T is invertible, then

$$A^\dagger \approx XY^T\left(YY^T\right)^{-1}. \quad (6)$$

Hence, $A^\dagger$ serves as a global linear approximation of f, where each entry $A^\dagger_{j,k}$ indicates how the k-th output dimension influences the j-th input dimension under this approximation.

The operators $A^\dagger$ in (5) and (6) are formally linear; however, it has been demonstrated that even for nonlinear or piecewise-differentiable functions f, $A^\dagger$ can serve as a weighted approximation of the Jacobian over the dataset, enabling AIME to capture relevant aspects of f^{-1}. AIME provides a more interpretable feature importance than LIME [2] or SHAP [1] when applied to certain convolutional neural networks [4].

A key point of AIME is the definition of Y in (3). If Y consists of outputs from the black-box model f in Fig. 1, then $A^\dagger$ yields the *model-dependent* global feature importance, reflecting how the learned model transforms inputs into outputs. However, if Y contains the true label vectors used for training (i.e., the ground-truth outputs), then $A^\dagger$ yields *model-independent* (data-driven) global feature importance, which many existing XAI methods do not offer. In medical or scientific contexts, where the underlying causal or statistical relationship are crucial, the latter perspective helps interpret which features truly affect the target variables, independent of any particular model bias. Thus, AIME's ability to handle both modes is a major strength, setting it apart from conventional XAI methods, which focus exclusively on model-dependent explanations.

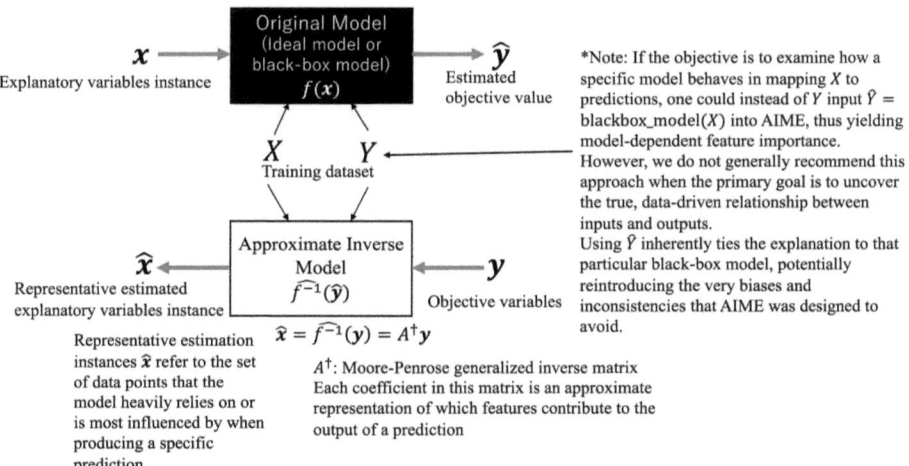

Fig. 1. Overview of AIME [4].

4 Formulation of CausalAIME

This section presents the formulation of **CausalAIME**, which combines the approximate inverse operator of AIME [4] with the causal structure inferred by the PC algorithm [5] to suppress multicollinearity and incorporate a causal perspective.

4.1 Summary of Variables and Parameters

- $X \in \mathbb{R}^{n \times N}$: Input feature matrix ($n$-dimensional, N samples).
- $\hat{Y} \in \mathbb{R}^{m \times N}$: Black-box model output matrix (m-dimensional, N samples).
- $A^{\dagger} \in \mathbb{R}^{n \times m}$: The approximate inverse operator matrix in AIME.
- E_{directed}: Set of directed edges determined by the PC algorithm.
- $E_{\text{undirected}}$: Set of undirected edges determined by the PC algorithm.
- λ: Hyperparameter controlling penalty strength.
- α: Scalar controlling the ratio at which child nodes refer to their parents.
- $a_{i,k}$: Element of $A^{\dagger}$, corresponding to feature i and output dimension k.

4.2 Causal Structure Estimation and Edge Classification

By applying the PC algorithm [5], we approximate a DAG over a set of features (nodes). In the final DAG, we classify the edges into two types:

- $E_{\text{directed}} \subseteq \{(i \to j)\}$: the set of directed edges, where node i is the "parent" of node j.
- $E_{\text{undirected}} \subseteq \{(u - v)\}$: the set of undirected edges denoting pairs of features u and v that exhibit strong dependency without a determined direction.

Here, $i \to j$ indicates that feature i influences feature j (parent-child relationship), while $u - v$ signals a high correlation between u and v but without a definitive direction. We leverage this information as a penalty term in the learning of the approximate inverse operator $A^{\dagger}$.

We begin by combining AIME's **least-squares reconstruction term** with *difference penalties* for directed and undirected edges derived from the PC algorithm [5]. Let $\hat{Y} \in \mathbb{R}^{m \times N}$ be the black-box model outputs (m-dimensional) for N samples and let $X \in \mathbb{R}^{n \times N}$ be the input features (n-dimensional). The approximate inverse operator $A^{\dagger} \in \mathbb{R}^{n \times m}$ in AIME typically solves

$$\min_{A^{\dagger}} \| X - A^{\dagger} \hat{Y} \|_F^2, \tag{7}$$

where $\|\cdot\|_F$ represents the Frobenius norm.

In CausalAIME, we incorporate the edge information from the PC algorithm into AIME's objective function through additional penalty terms. Specifically, we consider the objective function

$$\min_{A^{\dagger}} \| X - \hat{Y} A^{\top} \|^2 + \lambda \times P(A^{\dagger}, E_{\text{dir}}, E_{\text{undir}}), \tag{8}$$

E_{dir} and E_{undir} denote the sets of *directed edges* and *undirected edges*, respectively, as discovered by the PC algorithm. In other words, E_{dir} contains all edges with a direction $(i \to j)$, while E_{undir} consists of edges $(u-v)$ for which the PC algorithm has not determined an orientation. The term $P(A^\dagger, E_{\text{dir}}, E_{\text{undir}})$ imposes penalties based on these edges to reflect the causal/correlational constraints in the optimization. λ is a penalty coefficient, and $P(A^\dagger, E_{\text{dir}}, E_{\text{undir}})$ is the penalty term defined based on the edges. The following sections describe the penalty terms.

4.3 Difference Penalty (First Proposal)

A key motivation for introducing difference penalties based on the PC algorithm is to suppress multicollinearity and control how the contributions of the child nodes relate to their parents. A possible approach is

$$\min_{A^\dagger} \| X - A^\dagger \hat{Y} \|^2 + \lambda \Bigg(\sum_{(i \to j) \in E_{\text{directed}}} \sum_{k=1}^{m} \max\big(0,\, a_{j,k} - \alpha\, a_{i,k}\big)^2$$

$$+ \sum_{(u-v) \in E_{\text{undirected}}} \sum_{k=1}^{m} \Big\{ \max\big(0,\, a_{v,k} - \alpha\, a_{u,k}\big)^2 + \max\big(0,\, a_{u,k} - \alpha\, a_{v,k}\big)^2 \Big\} \Bigg),$$

(9)

where $a_{i,k}$ is the element of $A^\dagger$ (corresponding to feature i and output dimension k) and $\alpha > 0$ adjusts how much the child's contribution should refer to its parent.

Here, $A^\dagger \in \mathbb{R}^{n \times m}$ denotes the linear operator that maps each column of $\hat{Y} \in \mathbb{R}^{m \times N}$ back into the space of $X \in \mathbb{R}^{n \times N}$. Each element $a_{i,k}$ in $A^\dagger$ thus represents how strongly the k-th output dimension contributes to the i-th input dimension. As before, we seek to minimize the reconstruction error while introducing penalties based on the directed and undirected edges from the PC algorithm.

Intuition for Directed Edges $(i \to j)$. In (9),

$$\max\big(0,\, a_{j,k} - \alpha\, a_{i,k}\big)^2$$

penalizes cases where the child node j's contribution $a_{j,k}$ becomes excessively larger than $\alpha\, a_{i,k}$ for the parent node i.

Intuition for Undirected Edges $(u-v)$. For an undirected edge, we use

$$\max\big(0,\, a_{v,k} - \alpha\, a_{u,k}\big)^2 + \max\big(0,\, a_{u,k} - \alpha\, a_{v,k}\big)^2,$$

which indicates that the two highly correlated features u and v do not diverge significantly.

Issue. In preliminary experiments, (9) sometimes failed to effectively penalize when the term inside $\max(\cdot)$ remained negative, causing the penalty to remain zero. Consequently, even with a large λ, the penalty was not triggered, and **multicollinearity was not effectively suppressed** in some cases.

4.4 Revised Difference Penalty (Second Proposal)

To address this limitation, we replaced $\max(0, \cdot)$ with a formulation that squares the entire difference regardless of the sign. Specifically,

$$\min_{A^\dagger} \| X - A^\dagger \hat{Y} \|^2 + \lambda \Bigg(\sum_{(i \rightarrow j) \in E_{\text{directed}}} \sum_{k=1}^{m} (a_{j,k} - \alpha\, a_{i,k})^2 \\ + \sum_{(u-v) \in E_{\text{undirected}}} \sum_{k=1}^{m} \Big[(a_{v,k} - \alpha\, a_{u,k})^2 + (a_{u,k} - \alpha\, a_{v,k})^2 \Big] \Bigg). \tag{10}$$

Here, the **entire difference** is squared, penalizing divergence, whether positive or negative.

Advantages. By ignoring the sign, the penalty remains active across the entire optimization space. With a large λ, strongly correlated features avoid extremes on either side, leading to more stable suppression of multicollinearity.

We adopted (10) in the implementation of CausalAIME, enabling better control over cases wherein a child node's contribution diverges excessively from that of its parent node, as well as for pairs of features connected by undirected edges.

One fundamental distinction between AIME and CausalAIME lies in the treatment of inter-feature relationships. While AIME independently derives feature importance from the inverse mapping without considering relationships among features, CausalAIME explicitly incorporates both causal (directed) and correlational (undirected) dependencies between features, as identified by the PC algorithm. These dependencies are used to constrain the optimization process, penalizing inconsistencies between causally or strongly correlated features. As a result, CausalAIME not only suppresses multicollinearity but also produces feature importance values that are more coherent with the underlying data structure.

4.5 Significance of CausalAIME

As outlined above, by adding difference penalties to AIME's approximate inverse operator using directed/undirected edges from the PC algorithm, we simultaneously addressed both multicollinearity suppression and causal perspective. In particular, we combined the following:

1. AIME's flexibility to switch between model-dependent ($\hat{Y}$) and model-independent (true Y) modes
2. The introduction of difference penalties based on parent-child and high-correlation relationships inferred by the PC algorithm
3. Stability improvements gained by moving from a $\max(0, \cdot)$-based penalty to one that squares the entire difference, ignoring the sign

This enables a more interpretable and reliable global feature importance, particularly relevant in fields like healthcare. In practice, we minimize (10) for CausalAIME using gradient-based methods [14] to solve for $A^\dagger$. Other generic optimizers such as L-BFGS [15], SGD [16], Adam [17], and RMSProp [18] can also be used.

CausalAIME assumes some method for obtaining "directed or undirected dependencies among features." While the PC algorithm is one example, other causal inference methods (GES [19], fast causal inference (FCI) [20], LiNGAM [21], Bayesian structure learning [22], etc.) may be used to achieve similar results. Specifically, directed edges can be placed into E_{directed}, while undirected or unresolved edges in that direction can be included in $E_{\text{undirected}}$. These edges can be incorporated into CausalAIME. Under certain assumptions (as in LiNGAM, which assumes a *linear, non-Gaussian, acyclic model with no latent confounders*), if all edges are directed, CausalAIME could be implemented without undirected penalties, yielding a simpler formulation. Conversely, for approaches like FCI, which is a method designed to handle potential latent confounders and selection bias, or those considering latent variables, some edges may remain directionally uncertain, making CausalAIME's undirected penalty framework particularly useful.

Therefore, CausalAIME is not confined to the PC algorithms. For example, if a DAG or completed partially directed acyclic graph (CPDAG) can be obtained through other causal inference techniques, one can define analogous directed and undirected penalty terms in the same manner. However, it should be noted that each causal inference method operates under distinct assumptions (linearity, non-Gaussianity, the presence or absence of latent variables, etc.), which may influence the final causal structure.

5 Experiment

5.1 Experimental Environment

We compared the global feature importance results of Random Forest [3], SHAP [1], AIME [4], and CausalAIME using the Breast Cancer Wisconsin (Diagnostic) dataset [6]. Random Forest was implemented using scikit-learn 1.6.0, while SHAP was implemented using the publicly available library SHAP 0.46.0 [23,24]. AIME was deployed through the publicly released library aime-xai 0.1 [25,26], and CausalAIME was developed using NumPy 1.26.4, Panda 2.2.2, Networkx 3.4.2, matplotlib 3.10.0, and seaborn 0.13.2. All the experiments were conducted using Google Colaboratory Pro+, and the results are shown below.

We used the default Random Forest implementation from scikit-learn for feature importance analysis and as the underlying model for SHAP. Specifically, we used the RandomForestClassifier with default hyperparameters (100 estimators, Gini impurity, no maximum depth).

5.2 Qualitative Evaluation of Random Forest, SHAP, AIME, and CausalAIME

In this section, we compare and discuss the global feature importance results obtained by applying Random Forest [3], SHAP [1], AIME [4], and CausalAIME on the Breast Cancer Wisconsin (diagnostic) dataset [6]. Figures 2, 3, 5, and 6 show the results for Random Forest, SHAP, AIME, and CausalAIME, respectively.

Global Feature Importance by Random Forest. Fig. 2 shows the feature importances (Gini-based importance) from the Random Forest model. As summarized in Fig. 2, for instance, in the mean data, the *mean concave points* were the highest (approximately 0.768), followed by the *mean perimeter* (approximately 0.488) and *mean concavity* (approximately 0.4801). By contrast, *mean fractal dimension* was as low as approximately 0.0187, indicating that the model "barely used it."

This measure aggregates the frequency of splits and the degree of purity improvement for each feature. However, it is important to note that it **does not indicate the positive/negative direction of the contribution or differences between classes (benign vs. malignant)**. Hence, it cannot directly answer the clinically relevant question, "Which feature increases (or decreases) the risk of malignancy?" or decompose the contribution per class. Moreover, because these values depend on the internal structure of a specific Random Forest, they represent the importance of model-dependent global features. Consequently, while Random Forest global feature importance is useful for quick approximate assessments and identifying top features, it is **insufficient for a more detailed interpretation** (e.g., sign or class-specific information).

Global Feature Importance by SHAP. Figure 3 shows the global feature importance obtained using SHAP [1]. As evident from Fig. 3, in the mean data, *mean concave points*, *mean concavity*, and *mean area*, among others, exhibited high importance, similar to the Random Forest results, focusing on shape- and size-related features. Notably, SHAP can **output positive/negative values per class** (benign vs. malignant), which is a key feature. In this experiment, however, postprocessing and visualization steps aggregated the absolute values; thus, the benign and malignant rows appeared to be the same. This merging of positive and negative contributions into absolute values does not imply that SHAP is incapable of providing class-specific differences. Rather, the loss of sign information arises from the chosen visualization technique, which aggregates all contributions in absolute form, thereby obscuring any positive/negative distinctions in the final global measure.

SHAP is model-dependent, **theoretically computes how each feature either increases or decreases the malignant probability per instance**, and then aggregates these effects. Therefore, it generally provides a richer class-level interpretation than Random Forest's Gini-based importance. However, if

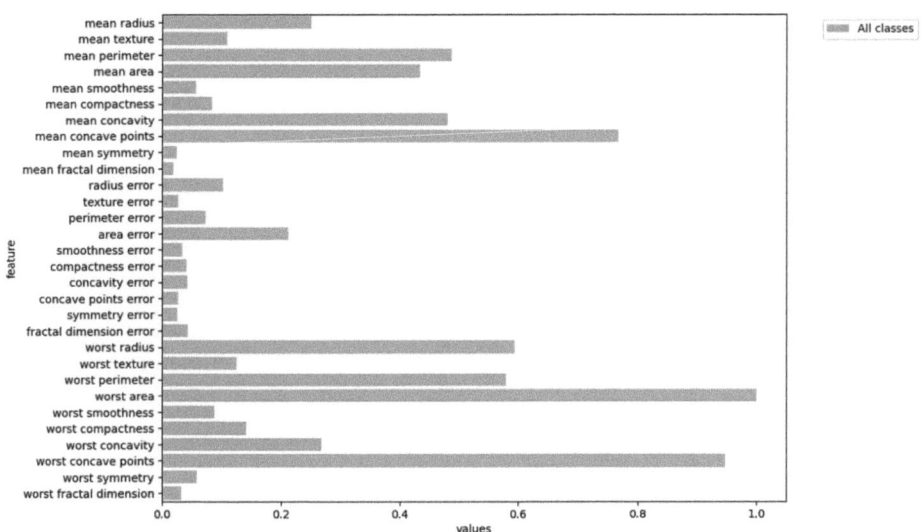

Fig. 2. Global feature importance results using Random Forest.

the model does not rely on features such as the textitmean fractal dimension, SHAP assigns them low contribution regardless of their potential medical interest.

Because the visualization likely aggregates results at the visualization stage, we further illustrate an example summary plot in Fig. 4, where the coloring or arrangement may differ. In this study, the positive/negative aspects were not clearly depicted, leading to medically relevant features receiving low importance if not actively exploited by the model.

Global Feature Importance by AIME. Figure 5 shows the global feature importance computed using AIME [4]. AIME allows switching between the model-dependent mode using black-box outputs $\hat{Y}$ and the data-driven mode using ground-truth labels Y. Here, we illustrate the "data-driven" mode. For each feature, AIME provides a signed coefficient for both benign and malignant classes.

For instance, in the mean data, *mean radius*, *mean perimeter*, and *mean concavity* had large negative coefficients for benign and large positive coefficients for malignancy, indicating that "the larger these values, the more likely the malignancy." This result aligns with several medical studies [27,28], which indicates that larger tumor size and more irregular shape correlate with malignancy. Conversely, *mean fractal dimension* shows a contradictory sign, likely due to multicollinearity, normalization, or other complex interactions [29]. The main advantage of AIME is that it **consistently presents class-specific signs and magnitudes** , an ability not offered by Random Forest's Gini-based importance or the standard SHAP absolute-values approach.

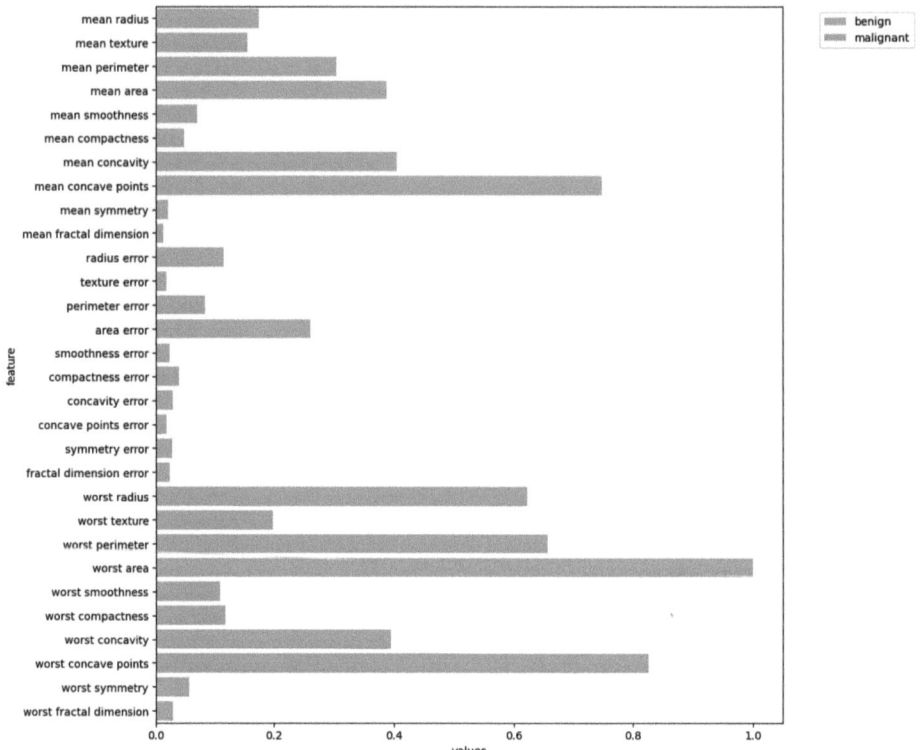

Fig. 3. Global feature importance results using SHAP.

Global Feature Importance by CausalAIME. Figure 6 shows the results of **CausalAIME**, which combines AIME with the PC algorithm [5] for causal structure estimation with $\lambda = 2.5, \alpha = 0.8$. Here, λ controls the overall strength of the penalty terms that enforce consistency among correlated or causally linked features, while α dictates the degree to which a child's coefficient is constrained relative to its parent's coefficient. The basic sign patterns (size and shape features yielding positive values for malignancy) are similar to AIME; however, the *mean fractal dimension* may show clearer positive/negative or larger absolute values. We infer that applying penalty terms based on high-correlation edges from the PC algorithm **strongly suppresses multicollinearity in the reconstruction process**.

Shape-related features, such as *mean concavity* and *mean compactness*, often show strong correlations and are prone to overlapping contributions in AIME. In CausalAIME, the introduced penalties distribute the contributions more evenly. Consequently, features that were considered "oddly signed" in AIME, such as *mean fractal dimension*, can become more medically consistent (e.g., showing a positive sign for malignancy). Even when the PC algorithm fails to identify directed edges, undirected edges with high correlation can still inform the

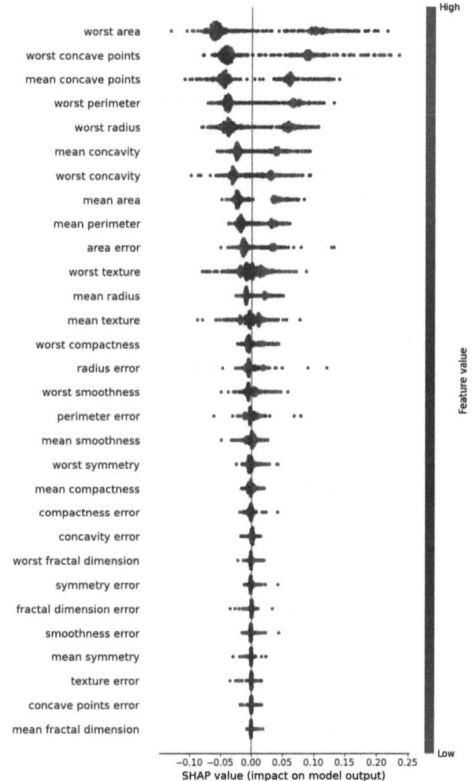

Fig. 4. SHAP-based global feature importance by summary plot (example).

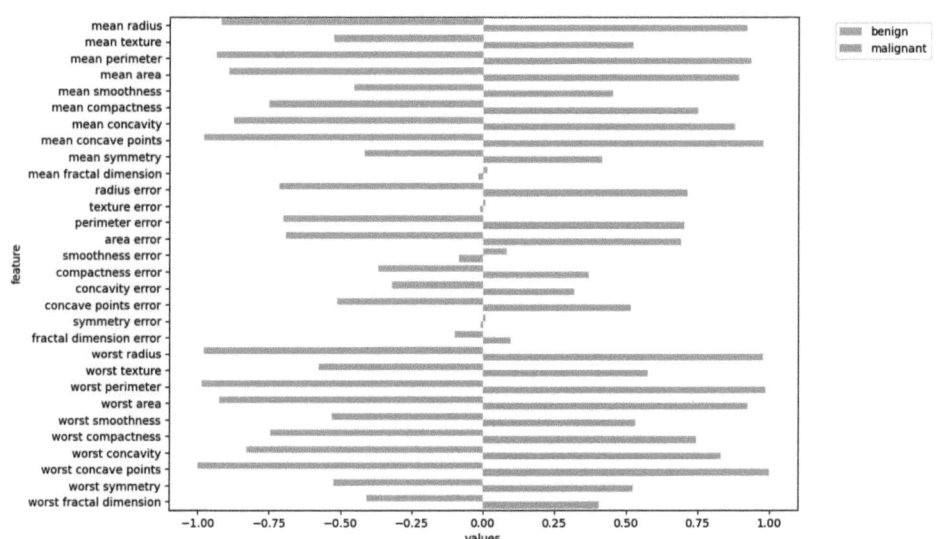

Fig. 5. Global feature importance results using AIME.

CausalAIME penalty, resulting in a more stable interpretation with lower multicollinearity. For instance, if two features are strongly correlated while the statistical tests used by the PC algorithm cannot decisively determine a direction (e.g., due to Markov equivalence or insufficient sample size), the edge remains undirected. In such cases, CausalAIME still leverages the high-correlation edge to penalize excessively divergent coefficients, thereby yielding a more stable interpretation despite the lack of a fully directed causal path.

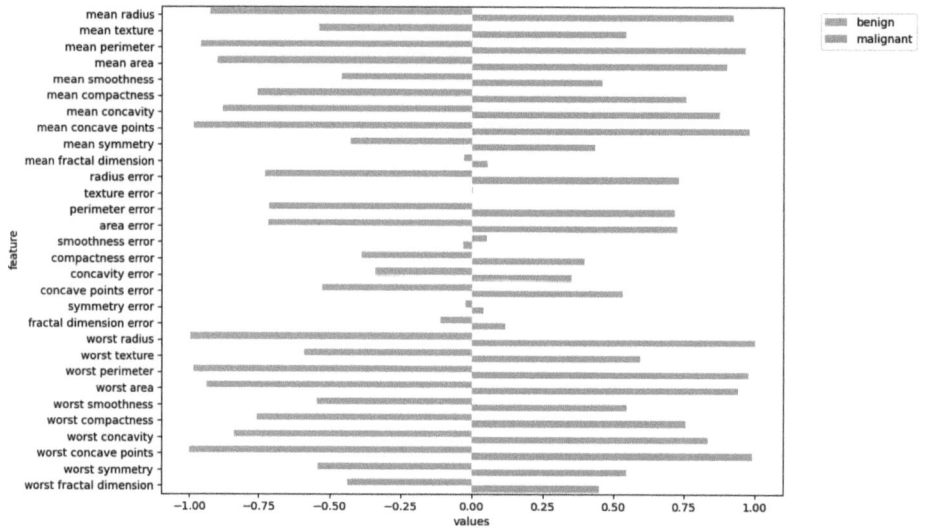

Fig. 6. Global feature importance results using CausalAIME.

Figure 7 illustrates the causal and correlational relationships among features derived from the PC algorithm. Although only a small number of edges show causality, incorporating these relationships aids in understanding medical knowledge and, by introducing them as penalty terms into AIME, enables CausalAIME to derive more accurate global feature importance.

Overall Comparison and Medical Consistency. These findings show that the Gini-based feature importance in Random Forest (Fig. 2) is computationally inexpensive and suitable for a rough overview of key features but **lacks sign or class-specific details**. Conversely, SHAP (Fig. 3) is model-dependent but can provide per-class or per-instance contributions, offering a richer explanation than raw Gini-based feature importance scores from a Random Forest (RF) model, often abbreviated as "RF Gini scores" for convenience. However, its global visualization typically involves absolute-value averaging, which may mask sign differences or unify class distinctions, depending on the pipeline.

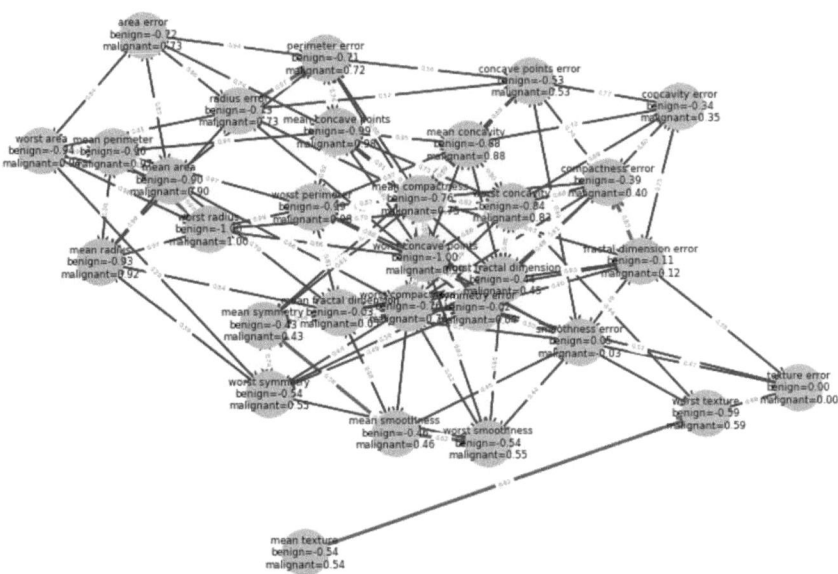

Fig. 7. CausalAIME's graph showing causal and correlational relationships. Each node in the figure represents a feature along with its importance, while the edges are colored: red indicates a directed edge (causal relationship) and blue indicates an undirected edge (correlational relationship).

AIME (Fig. 5) offers a flexible framework to switch between "model-dependent" (using $\hat{Y}$) and "data-driven" (using Y) modes, delivering **class-specific signed global importance**. This is promising for fields like medicine, where the true label's causal or statistical relationship is paramount. Finally, CausalAIME (Fig. 6) extends AIME by incorporating PC algorithm–based correlation or partial-correlation edges, enabling **more robust handling of highly correlated features**. In our experiments, size features and shape irregularities often emerged as strong indicators of malignancy, consistent with findings from various medical studies [27–29]. In AIME, some features (e.g., *mean fractal dimension*) might flip signs under different parameter settings or penalty strengths, reflecting complex interactions; however, in CausalAIME, the importance of these features is correct.

Overall, one must weigh model dependence, data-driven concerns, and multicollinearity or causal structures to select the appropriate method. In medical scenarios emphasizing **"true associations"** rather than purely model-oriented explanations, **CausalAIME's data-driven mode** appears especially advantageous, as it suppresses correlated feature redundancy and is not restricted by model biases, which may omit clinically relevant features.

5.3 Quantitative Evaluation of SHAP, AIME, and CausalAIME

Following the multi-faceted XAI framework proposed by Arreche et al. [30], we evaluated SHAP, AIME, and CausalAIME using six key metrics: *descriptive accuracy*, *sparsity*, *stability*, *efficiency*, *robustness*, and *completeness*. Following the E-XAI framework [30],, we computed:

- Descriptive accuracy as the correlation between the predicted outputs and those reconstructed using selected important features,
- Sparsity as the proportion of zero or near-zero importance features,
- Stability as the average cosine similarity of importance vectors under different training splits,
- Efficiency as the average computation time to obtain global importance,
- Robustness as the standard deviation of feature ranks under perturbations, and
- Completeness as the proportion of output variance explained by the top-k important features.

Additionally, we performed a Wilcoxon signed-rank test to check whether the differences in global feature importance among these methods were statistically significant.

Table 1 shows that AIME achieves the highest *descriptive accuracy* (avg. 0.91), closely followed by CausalAIME (avg. 0.88), whereas SHAP (avg. 0.75) ranks lower. For *sparsity*, SHAP yields a value of 0.95, indicating that it concentrates importance on very few features, whereas AIME and CausalAIME are distributed more evenly (around 0.40). All methods exhibit perfect *stability* (1.0000), indicating that their top-ranked features remain the same under repeated tests.

AIME is by far the fastest in *efficiency* (0.01 s), while SHAP is the slowest (42.19 s), and CausalAIME (7.57 s) lies in between. Regarding *robustness*, SHAP appears highly susceptible under both biased and adversarial conditions (1.00/1.00). AIME is very resistant to bias (0.00) but partially vulnerable to adversarial settings (0.50). CausalAIME exhibits moderate robustness against both threats (0.50/0.50). Finally, all methods show a *completeness* of 0.0000, suggesting that modifying only the top features often fails to alter the final prediction, leaving room for more comprehensive explanations.

Table 2 summarizes the Wilcoxon signed-rank test results, which indicate that none of the pairwise differences in global feature importance among SHAP, AIME, and CausalAIME are statistically significant at the 5% level. This does not imply that the three methods are identical; rather, the sample size and inherent variability of the dataset may limit the detection of subtle differences. In practice, however, AIME may be selected for its high accuracy and speed, SHAP for its strong sparsity (focusing on a very small set of key features), or CausalAIME to achieve a balanced trade-off, benefiting from partial causal-structure awareness and moderate computational cost.

Table 1. Comparison of SHAP, AIME, and CausalAIME on the Breast Cancer Wisconsin Dataset. Min–max ranges are shown with the average value in parentheses. Robustness is evaluated under Bias/Adv conditions. Completeness is the proportion of instances where altering top features fails to change the prediction.

XAI	Desc. Acc.	Sparsity	Stability	Time (s)	Rob. (B/A)	Compl.
SHAP	0.62–1.0 (0.75)	0.95–0.95 (0.95)	1.00	42.2	1.00 / 1.00	0.00
AIME	0.81–1.0 (0.91)	0.41–0.41 (0.41)	1.00	0.01	0.00 / 0.50	0.00
CausalAIME	0.64–1.0 (0.88)	0.40–0.41 (0.40)	1.00	7.6	0.50 / 0.50	0.00

Table 2. Wilcoxon signed-rank test results for pairwise comparisons of global feature importance.

Comparison	W-stat	p-value	Significance (5%)
SHAP vs. AIME	873.0	0.757179	not significant
SHAP vs. CausalAIME	885.0	0.825211	not significant
AIME vs. CausalAIME	741.0	0.277077	not significant

6 Discussion

The Gini-based feature importances from Random Forest is computationally inexpensive and provides a quick approximation of the extent to which each feature is used by the model. However, as shown in Sect. 5, only a single scalar is reported for the overall contribution, even in the binary classification setting (benign vs. malignant). Consequently, this study does not directly clarify the features that strengthen or weaken each class. Furthermore, it cannot indicate whether a feature increases malignancy or instead decreases it (i.e., promotes benign characteristics). Because this metric depends on the splitting frequency and purity improvements specific to Random Forests, a different model might yield entirely different rankings. Hence, while Random Forest's global feature importance is convenient for rapidly identifying key features, it falls short for medical interpretation or detailed class-specific analysis.

SHAP, despite being model dependent, can theoretically compute the contribution of each feature for each instance in terms of increasing or decreasing a prediction, offering a richer perspective than Random Forest-based Gini scores. However, when absolute values are used in a global visualization, they obscure class-specific or positive and negative information. Furthermore, if the model barely utilizes a certain feature—one that might be medically important—SHAP could assign it a low value, creating a false impression that "this feature does not matter." In these experiments, features like *mean fractal dimension* or *mean symmetry* often have low SHAP importance, even though they might be of particular interest to medical practitioners. Thus, although SHAP can provide richer explanations than Random Forest, it merely reflects the model's inherent biases and feature selection and therefore does not necessarily capture the true association between features and medical outcomes.

AIME can operate in the model-dependent mode using the trained model outputs $\hat{Y}$ or in the data-driven (model-independent) mode using the ground-truth labels Y. In the data-driven setting, clinically supported features such as "large tumor size correlates with malignancy" or "high shape irregularity aligns with malignancy" appear as positively signed coefficients in the malignant column (and negatively signed in the benign column). This offers a straightforward method for clinicians to identify the features that strongly enhance malignancy. However, AIME does not specifically address multicollinearity. Therefore, strong correlations among features can result in overly large coefficients in the same direction. Unexpected signs (such as those observed for the *fractal dimension*) may arise from these interactions.

Conversely, CausalAIME incorporates penalty terms derived from causal or correlational relationships estimated using the PC algorithm. This suppresses multicollinearity by penalizing pairs of strongly correlated features. Consequently, even if features such as *mean radius*, *mean area*, and *mean perimeter* share very high correlations, their contributions are not disproportionately large for only one of them. In cases where AIME alone might have produced sign reversals or minimal influences on certain features (e.g., *fractal dimension*), the PC algorithm's structural information adjusts them to more medically consistent values. By using the true labels Y, medical researchers can pursue a "true association" independent of any one model's bias, facilitating easier alignment with clinical reasoning.

These advantages persist even when the PC algorithm yields mostly undirected edges rather than any explicit causal direction. Correlated feature pairs can still trigger penalty constraints, enabling CausalAIME to effectively manage multicollinearity in both scenarios. Size-related features (radius, perimeter, and area) and shape irregularities (concavity, concave points, and compactness) often show large positive coefficients for malignancy, consistent with multiple prior studies [27–29], thus validating the experimental results. Intuitively, larger tumor sizes often correlate with more advanced disease progression, making such tumors more likely to be malignant. Similarly, shape irregularities (e.g., concavity, uneven borders) often arise when cancerous cells grow in disorganized patterns, as opposed to the smoother, more orderly shapes usually associated with benign growths. Consequently, features capturing these size- and shape-related properties naturally exhibit larger positive coefficients for malignancy, aligning with clinical observations and previous studies [27–29]. Although several features (e.g., *fractal dimension* [29]) may exhibit "unexpected" signs, we attribute this to dataset-specific interactions and the conditional independence tests of the PC algorithm.

Nevertheless, the outcomes of CausalAIME depend on parameters such as those governing the PC algorithm and the penalty strength λ or ratio α. No established automated procedure exists for selecting these hyperparameters. Our dataset's dimensionality is sufficiently small to allow manual tuning; however, larger datasets with hundreds or thousands of features may encounter computational challenges when running the PC algorithm and repeatedly applying different penalties.

From these experiments, the distinction between the "model-dependent" approaches (Random Forest and SHAP) and the "data-driven" approaches (AIME and CausalAIME) became clear. CausalAIME, in particular, appears promising in medical contexts where controlling multicollinearity is crucial and where class-specific signed global feature importance is needed. Nonetheless, further research is necessary to fine-tune parameters and refine causal direction estimates. CausalAIME's data-driven mode is particularly compelling for identifying clinically significant associations independent of model biases; however, researchers can also switch to the model-dependent mode ($\hat{Y}$) to capture the perspective of the learned model.

Further, we also conducted a quantitative comparison of SHAP, AIME, and CausalAIME based on six XAI metrics (descriptive accuracy, sparsity, stability, efficiency, robustness, and completeness), along with a Wilcoxon signed-rank test. While the Wilcoxon test did not reveal statistically significant differences among the three methods (i.e., all p-values > 0.05), the additional metrics highlighted distinct trade-offs. Specifically, AIME achieved the highest descriptive accuracy and the fastest execution time, whereas SHAP exhibited strong sparsity but incurred a high computational cost and was less robust. CausalAIME delivered a balanced performance, standing between AIME and SHAP in terms of accuracy, speed, and robustness. The absence of a statistically significant difference likely reflects the relatively small dataset, which may limit detection power, rather than indicating true equivalence among the methods. In practical scenarios, the choice of method can thus hinge on which metrics matter most—speed, interpretability, or robustness to adversarial or biased conditions. These multi-faceted results further affirm that CausalAIME provides a viable compromise while incorporating causal-structure information into feature-importance analysis.

In conclusion, this flexibility suggests great potential for CausalAIME in clinical applications and in scaling to larger datasets in future studies.

7 Conclusion

In this study, we developed CausalAIME, a novel framework that combines the approximate inverse operator of AIME [4] with the PC algorithm [5]. Specifically, in addition to the conventional model-dependent and model-independent modes inherent in AIME, we introduced penalty terms based on causal and correlational structures estimated by the PC algorithm [5]. This approach offers a way to derive global feature importance that accounts for both true associations and model behavior, which is critical in medical contexts and similar fields. It also demonstrates the advantages of simultaneously suppressing multicollinearity and providing signed coefficients for each class.

While CausalAIME demonstrates promising results in unifying model-dependent and data-driven global feature importance, it also has several limitations. First, the PC algorithm can be sensitive to sample size and model assumptions, potentially yielding incomplete or partially oriented graphs if the data do not meet its conditional-independence requirements. Second, hyperparameter tuning (e.g., λ, α) remains largely manual, and the penalty design might need fine-tuning for different domains or larger datasets. Third, in highly nonlinear or high-dimensional settings, the PC-based edge discoveries might become computationally expensive or prone to errors, and straightforward extensions of CausalAIME may not always scale efficiently. Furthermore, multicollinearity and unobserved confounders can affect both the causal structure estimation and the stability of the approximate inverse operator. These limitations underscore the need for further research, such as developing more robust causal discovery techniques under limited data, automating penalty tuning, and investigating how advanced nonparametric or deep-learning–based causal inference methods could be integrated to enhance the reliability of CausalAIME in large-scale applications.

Overall, CausalAIME is a valuable approach for applications that require investigation of both model behavior and true associations. By advancing this framework, we anticipate further improvements in the reliability of machine learning explanations and decision support.

Acknowledgments. In the preparation of this manuscript, we used language proofing and translation tools, including ChatGPT, Open PaperPal, and DeepL, to improve the clarity and readability of English text. These tools assisted in refining the language. The full responsibility for the accuracy and integrity of the final content remains solely with the authors. Any errors, oversights, or misinterpretations were entirely the responsibility of the authors.

Disclosure of Interests. The authors have no competing interests to declare that are relevant to the content of this article. All aspects of the research, including data collection, analysis, and presentation of the results, were conducted independently and impartially without external influence or financial support that could affect the integrity of the findings.

References

1. Lundberg, S. M., Lee, S. I.: A unified approach to interpreting model predictions. In: Proceedigs of the 31st International Conference on Neural Information Processing Systems, pp. 4768–4777 (2017). https://doi.org/10.5555/3295222.3295230
2. Ribeiro, M.T., Singh, S., Guestrin, C.: "Why should I trust you?": explaining the predictions of any classifier. In: Proceedings of the 22nd ACM SIGKDD International Conference on Knowledge Discovery and Data Mining, pp. 1135—1144 (2016). https://doi.org/10.1145/2939672.2939778
3. Breiman, L.: Random forests. Mach. Learn. **45**(1), 5–32 (2001). https://doi.org/10.1023/A:1010933404324

4. Nakanishi, T.: Approximate inverse model explanations (AIME): unveiling local and global insights in machine learning models. IEEE Access **11**, 101020–101044 (2023). https://doi.org/10.1109/ACCESS.2023.3314336
5. Spirtes, P., Glymour, C.: An algorithm for fast recovery of sparse causal graphs. Soc. Sci. Comput. Rev. **9**(1), 62–72 (1991). https://doi.org/10.1177/089443939100900106
6. Wolberg, W., Mangasarian, O., Street, N., Street, W.: Breast cancer wisconsin (diagnostic) [dataset]. UCI Machine Learning Repository (1993). https://doi.org/10.24432/C5DW2B. Accessed 16 Jan 2024
7. Takahashi, D., Shimizu, S., Tanaka, T.: Counterfactual explanations of black-box machine learning models using causal discovery with applications to credit rating. In: 2024 International Joint Conference on Neural Networks (IJCNN), pp. 1–8 (2024). https://doi.org/10.1109/IJCNN60899.2024.10650130
8. Tyrovolas, M., Kallimanis, N., Stylios, C.: Advancing explainable AI with causal analysis in large-scale fuzzy cognitive maps. ArXiv, abs/2405.09190 (2024). https://doi.org/10.48550/arXiv.2405.09190
9. Cinquini, M., Guidotti, R.: CALIME: causality-aware local interpretable model-agnostic explanations. In: Proceedings of Explainable Artificial Intelligence. xAI 2024. Communications in Computer and Information Science, vol. 2155. Springer, Cham, (2024). https://doi.org/10.1007/978-3-031-63800-8_6
10. Termine, A., Antonucci, A., Facchini, A.: Machine learning explanations by surrogate causal models (MaLESCaMo). In: Proceedings of xAI (Late-breaking Work, Demos, Doctoral Consortium), pp. 59–64 (2023)
11. Zecevic, M., Dhami, D., Rothkopf, C., Kersting, K. XAI establishes a common ground between machine learning and causality. In: Proceedings of xAI (Late-breaking Work, Demos, Doctoral Consortium) (2022)
12. Wang, J., Wiens, J., Lundberg, S.: Shapley flow: a graph-based approach to interpreting model predictions. In: Proceedings of The 24th International Conference on Artificial Intelligence and Statistics, PMLR, 130, pp. 721–729 (2021)
13. Breuer, N.O., Sauter, A., Mohammadi, M., Acar, E.: CAGE: causality-aware Shapley value for global explanations. In: Proceedings of Explainable Artificial Intelligence, xAI 2024, Communications in Computer and Information Science, vol. 2155. Springer, Cham5. Springer, Cham (2024). https://doi.org/10.1007/978-3-031-63800-8_8
14. Polak, E.: Optimization: Algorithms and Consistent Approximations., Applied Mathematical Sciences, Vol. 124. Springer, New York (1997). https://doi.org/10.1007/978-1-4612-0663-7
15. Nocedal, J.: Updating quasi-newton matrices with limited storage. Math. Comput. **35**(151), 773–782 (1980). https://doi.org/10.1090/S0025-5718-1980-0572855-7
16. Robbins, H., Monro, S.: A stochastic approximation method. Ann. Math. Stat. **22**(3), 400–407 (1951). https://doi.org/10.1214/aoms/1177729586
17. Kingma, D.P., Ba, J.: Adam: a method for stochastic optimization. In: Proceedings of the 3rd International Conference on Learning Representations (ICLR) (2015). https://arxiv.org/abs/1412.6980, last accessed 2024/1/16
18. Tieleman, T., Hinton, G.: Lecture 6.5—RMSProp: divide the gradient by a running average of its recent magnitude. COURSERA: Neural Networks for Machine Learning (2012). https://www.cs.toronto.edu/~tijmen/csc321/slides/lecture_slides_lec6.pdf, last accessed 2024/1/16
19. Chickering, D.M.: Optimal structure identification with greedy search. J. Mach. Learn. Res. **3**, 507–554 (2002)

20. Spirtes, P., Meek, C., Richardson, T.: Causal inference in the presence of latent variables and selection bias. In: Proceedings of the Eleventh Conference on Uncertainty in Artificial Intelligence, pp. 499–506 (1995)
21. Shimizu, S., Hoyer, P.O., Hyvärinen, A., Kerminen, A.: A linear non-gaussian acyclic model for causal discovery. J. Mach. Learn. Res. **7**, 2003–2030 (2006)
22. Koller, D., Friedman, N.: Probabilistic Graphical Models: Principles and Techniques. MIT Press (2009)
23. SHAP. https://github.com/shap/shap. Accessed 16 Jan 2024
24. SHAP. https://pypi.org/project/shap/. Accessed 16 Jan 2024
25. AIME: Approximate Inverse Model Explanations. https://github.com/ntakafumi/aime/. Accessed 16 Jan 2024
26. AIME: Approximate Inverse Model Explanations. https://pypi.org/project/aime-xai/. Accessed 16 Jan 2024
27. Narod, S.A.: Tumour size predicts long-term survival among women with lymph node-positive breast cancer. Curr. Oncol. **19**(5), 249–253 (2012). https://doi.org/10.3747/co.19.1043
28. Chitalia, R.D., Kontos, D.: Role of texture analysis in breast MRI as a cancer biomarker: a review. J. Magn. Reson. Imaging **49**(4), 927–938 (2019). https://doi.org/10.1002/jmri.26556
29. Elkington, L., Adhikari, P., Pradhan, P.: Fractal dimension analysis to detect the progress of cancer using transmission optical microscopy. Biophysica **2**(1), 59–69 (2022). https://doi.org/10.3390/biophysica2010005
30. Arreche, O., Guntur, T.R., Roberts, J.W., Abdallah, M.: E-XAI: evaluating blackbox explainable AI frameworks for network intrusion detection. In: IEEE Access, vol. 12, pp. 23954—23988 (2024). https://doi.org/10.1109/ACCESS.2024.3365140

Open Access This chapter is licensed under the terms of the Creative Commons Attribution 4.0 International License (http://creativecommons.org/licenses/by/4.0/), which permits use, sharing, adaptation, distribution and reproduction in any medium or format, as long as you give appropriate credit to the original author(s) and the source, provide a link to the Creative Commons license and indicate if changes were made.

The images or other third party material in this chapter are included in the chapter's Creative Commons license, unless indicated otherwise in a credit line to the material. If material is not included in the chapter's Creative Commons license and your intended use is not permitted by statutory regulation or exceeds the permitted use, you will need to obtain permission directly from the copyright holder.

XAI for Scientific Discovery

Interpreting the Structure of Multi-object Representations in Vision Encoders

Tarun Khajuria(✉), Braian Olmiro Dias, Marharyta Domnich, and Jaan Aru

Institute of Computer Science, University of Tartu, Tartu, Estonia
tarun.khajuria@ut.ee

Abstract. In this work, we interpret the representations of multi-object scenes in vision encoders through the lens of structured representations. Structured representations allow modeling of individual objects distinctly and their flexible use based on the task context for both scene-level and object-specific tasks. These capabilities play a central role in human reasoning and generalization, allowing us to abstract away irrelevant details and focus on relevant information in a compact and usable form. We define structured representations as those that adhere to two specific properties: binding specific object information into discrete representation units and segregating object representations into separate sets of tokens to minimize cross-object entanglement. Based on these properties, we evaluated and compared image encoders pre-trained on classification (ViT), large vision-language models (CLIP, BLIP, FLAVA), and self-supervised methods (DINO, DINOv2). We examine the token representations by creating object-decoding tasks that measure the ability of specific tokens to capture individual objects in multi-object scenes from the COCO dataset. This analysis provides insights into how object-wise representations are distributed across tokens and layers within these vision encoders. Our findings highlight significant differences in the representation of objects depending on their relevance to the pre-training objective, with this effect particularly pronounced in the CLS token (often used for downstream tasks). Meanwhile, networks and layers that exhibit more structured representations retain better information about individual objects. To guide practical applications, we propose formal measures to quantify the two properties of structured representations, aiding in selecting and adapting vision encoders for downstream tasks. Overall, we aim to advance the understanding of object-wise structured representations in vision encoders, thus enhancing their transparency and interpretability. By clarifying how these models bind and segregate object-level information, we enable better-informed decisions for optimal downstream task adaptation, ultimately aligning their behaviour more closely with human reasoning.

Keywords: Vision Encoders · Interpretability · Structured Representations · Transparency · Token Analysis · Explainable AI · Transformers

1 Introduction

Vision encoders are foundation models for complex visual inputs in AI, including applications where decisions must be transparent and justifiable, such as healthcare, autonomous vehicles, etc. However, the opacity of these models limits their trustworthiness and applicability in real-world scenarios [23]. Recognizing the necessity of increasing direct transparency of vision encoders that cannot be guaranteed by post-hoc methods [33], it becomes essential to focus on the structural representations within the vision encoders themselves. Vision encoders are trained under various objective functions to learn suitable representations of visual inputs, and a *good representation* is the one that contains the correct details for its downstream task [5]. Humans flexibly use structured mental representations for reasoning, where the exact aspect of the representation is generated according to the task context [17,31]. For instance, in a multi-object scene, we usually focus on only the main objects and infer their relationship to make inferences about the overall situation. However, we also have the ability to focus on individual objects in the scene if the task requires such richer representation abstracted from the scene; e.g., questions about the colour of a chair should be answered irrespective of what scene or surrounding one sees the chair.

In computer vision, especially for practical applications like robotics, vision encoders trained on large datasets are also expected to be useful for both the scene and the object-level encoding [34]. To understand to what extent the representations of pre-trained vision encoders allow for such ability, this study investigates if structured object-wise representations exist in the token space of vision encoders. As previous works [12,25,28] discuss how such abilities are dependent on having structured representations in a representation system, we build upon this notion of symbols and binding of representation described in these studies to propose two properties specific for an image encoder's representation to be more structured in token space:

1. (M_1) The model should be able to **bind** information specific to objects in the image into specific representation units, i.e. a fewer number of tokens can represent the object better than its input token representation;
2. (M_2) The model **segregates** representation of various objects of the input image in separate sets of tokens, i.e., there should be object-wise information disentanglement in the token space.

We expected these two properties for structured representation to promote better generalisation for the following reasons. First, binding object information into discrete units allows beneficial representation properties to be fully available for novel scenarios in solving downstream tasks. Second, disentanglement of these representation units ensures that one object's presence in the scene does not affect others' representation. This is important for extreme cases where the objects are present out-of-the-scene statistics of the trained distribution. Such spurious correlations in representations of object presence may cause failure for the downstream task.

As we analyse the spatial representations in the vision transformers' token space, our primary questions testing the above properties are the following: *Do transformers represent and maintain object-wise representations? Are these representations disentangled,* i.e. does a particular set of tokens only represent a particular object? We use the COCO dataset [22] with its instance object masks to characterise the token representations in relation to their input patch information. We set up decoding experiments in a two-object setting (at a time, within a multi-object scene) to determine how the encoders manage the representations of the two objects. We test encoders of three VLMs (CLIP [30], BLIP [21] and FLAVA [35]) and compare them with the larger versions (CLIP-L, BLIP-L), and also check the representations against a CLIP (Resnet X4) with a CNN backbone. We further compare against other pre-training objectives such as VIT (trained for image classification), DINO [8] and DINOv2 [27] (encoders pre-trained by image self-supervision).

To systematically evaluate these two properties, we design complementary tasks: (1) a paired-object decoding setup focusing on two objects at a time from the scene, and (2) a broader 20-object decoding task testing generalization to unrelated categories. In this way, we validate the inferences made by the original task and illustrate the usefulness of our proposed measure to predict the general object encoding ability of the structured representations.

In the literature, some experimental results were given alongside the release of the original models, which already provide partial inferences about their representations. For example, in CLIP [30], an experiment shows how learning linear decoder on the CLS token representation performs better than their proposed zero-shot classification. In DINO [8], we can see how different attention heads from the CLS token attend to prominent objects in the scene. While in DINOv2 [27], each token from the last layer can be classified using a linear layer to perform semantic segmentation to some satisfactory detail, showing the object-wise information expressed in the token space of the last layer.

In our analysis, motivated by these prior indications, we conduct a more systematic investigation into how object-specific representations arise across various encoders. We also test their generality, aiming to provide a more comprehensive understanding of the structure of information expressed in the token space of vision transformers that explains such observations. Our results show that the CLS tokens best models image-level information but, as an effect, prefer to represent the main objects in the scene. Still, object-specific areas in the tokens of the higher layers model hold the most discriminating features about the individual objects. Yet, the object-wise token representations are not disentangled since they can decode other objects in the scene with accuracy far above random guesses. We observe that the VLMs trained on objectives requiring the modeling of multiple objects have better multi-object representations in CLS token than VIT encoders trained for image classification. On the other hand, all VIT-based encoders have less segregated and more entangled object representations than CNN-based CLIP (Resnet X4). We highlight the CLS token's inability to model background objects in all models (except CLIP-L) as a possible failure mode when using this token for downstream tasks on multi-object images. Moreover, we show that our two measures of structured representations in the token space of the networks correlate highly with the retention of object-specific information for (less important) background objects. Hence, it illustrates the usefulness of these structured representations in representing multi-object scenarios in the token space and provides a measure to make decisions about appropriate layers to train decoders or adaptors for an appropriate downstream task.

Our main contributions are:

1. We identify two properties to evaluate structured representations in the token space of image encoders. We design experiments and create a relevant dataset using COCO's multi-object images to evaluate these properties and propose a measure related to each property.
2. Our method lets us understand the nature of information encoding through the lens of structured representations in vision encoders in the token space (about the encoded objects) at different encoder layers.
3. The results from this analysis led us to identify a failure in generalising over multiple objects in the scene. Further, our proposed measures of structured representation (M_1, M_2) help against the problem by indicating which tokes/layers and the kind of models can be used to obtain the best representations for the (less represented) background objects.

2 Related Work

Our investigation into structured representations in vision encoders relates to a greater problem of any model's ability to generalise across different scenarios. This overall problem with generalisation in deep learning (DL) methods has been comprehensively discussed [12] in light of the need for explicit inductive biases that allow for discrete yet flexible information binding. Discrete symbolic representations are considered a prerequisite for robust compositionality and reasoning [28], and new studies propose that such discrete information binding may originate from training existing models on large datasets [25,28]. Beyond discrete symbolic approaches, this issue carries over to the field of meta-learning with its aim to introduce and compositionally utilise modularity in neural networks to improve generalisation [17]. Concept bottleneck models are a series of models that try to explicitly learn human-interpretable intermediate outputs to be composed into final output labels [10,38]. However, this interpretability usually comes at the cost of downstream task performance. [15] introduced an extra loss in the intermediate layer on the networks for units to align to the interpretable concepts while preserving task performance. Many other works do not bind representations to any explicit intermediate concept but still have explicit discrete bottlenecks in their networks [24,26]. It has been shown that these networks learn better representations, which further help generalisation on downstream tasks [24,26,36].

2.1 Evaluating a Trained Model's Capabilities

In the case of evaluation of pre-existing networks, many works do not try to estimate the mechanisms or representation structure that lead to particular performance of networks on tasks but rather propose benchmarks to estimate the reasoning capabilities of the ANN models. [3] proposed a visual question-answering benchmark to evaluate the reasoning skills on images, with open-ended and free-form questions and expected solutions in free-form natural language. Visual genome [16] provided content-rich images with explicit annotation of object position and relationships, promoting models that exploit such information. Datasets such as CLEVR [14] were designed to correct for biases the models would utilise in the existing benchmarks to perform well without explicit reasoning. The ARO (Attribute, Relation, Order) dataset [39] has been proposed to test the correct binding of information when compositionally representing multi-object scenarios. Particularly in VLMs such as BLIP and CLIP, they find that the model outputs do not bind the compositional properties well and attribute the wrong order and features to objects when describing them. Though these benchmarks reveal model shortcomings at the final output, they do not clarify how (or if) the internal representations disentangle multiple objects.

2.2 Interpreting Model's Representations

In terms of analysis of model representations for concepts, early work by [2] showed the layer-wise progression of decoding accuracy for concepts in CNNs. [9] reveals the inner workings of transformers by showing how trained transformers can implement convolutions and, in the initial layers, form grid-like local attention patterns like a convolution filter. [32] shows that vision transformers differ from CNNs because of their ability to encode both local and global information in the initial layer. In contrast, CNNs exhibit a multi-scale feature representation hierarchy going from lower-scale local information captured in the initial layers to higher-scale global information captured in the higher layers [6].

Particularly for vision-language models, [7] analysed various models trained using cross-model attention, providing insights into the attention patterns between the two modality streams and the relative contribution of each modality towards downstream tasks. Further, they found function-specific attention heads in the pre-trained models. VL Interpret [1] was designed as a visualisation tool to interpret the vision-language model's instance-specific and aggregate statistics over attention distribution. Further, the tool helps visualise token representation as it passes through various network layers.

In contrast to these generic visualisation tools that look into the model's functioning or attention-based approaches, other studies inspect model representations, evaluating a specific computational functionality. [18] finds modular sub-networks in trained ANN models functionally responsible for separate tasks. Multiple studies further look into the notion of concepts in trained vision-language model representations. A study by [40] designed a test to check if primitive concepts emerge in the network's representations, which are used compositionally for downstream tasks. [25] defines tests for concepts in visual representations according to Fodor's criteria [11] and tests these criteria using a controlled synthetic dataset. Building on these insights, our work formulates explicit hypothesis about structured representations regarding object-wise binding and disentanglement in a well-defined scope of layer-wise distribution of representations in visual encoders. We explore natural scenes rather than heavily controlled settings, thus complementing the more synthetic or attention-centered studies above.

3 Methods

We train probes and use similarity measures to evaluate the network's representational structure. In the following section, we formally define measures related to our proposed properties of structured representations and describe the details of the experimental setup, data, and the networks analysed.

3.1 Formal Definition

Our method quantifies the information structure in layers of an image encoder by measuring two properties. Given an image I, containing at least two objects, denoted as a primary object O_p and a secondary object O_s, we denote the tokens originating from the primary object as T_p and those originating from secondary objects as T_s. Across a test set, the accuracy of a probe trained and evaluated using representation from T_p to decode object O_s is given by A_{ps}. Similarly, A_{pp}, A_{sp} and A_{ss} refer to the other token-object combinations.

In this study, for the first property (binding), we measure the ability of a localised region to decode the individual object. More precisely, we focus on tokens T_s's ability to decode object O_s linearly. Hence, we measure this over a set of images by A_{ss}. Thus,

$$M_1 = A_{ss}$$

The second property (segregation) estimates the mixing of information between the tokens from other objects. We estimate if representations from tokens T_s can decode object O_p. Over a set of images, we use the decoding accuracy A_{sp} to estimate this entanglement between token representations, which is the opposite of segregation. For better comparison among layers, we scale this value by the decoding accuracy of that object for from own token representation, i.e. A_{pp}. Hence, the final measure for entanglement of information is given by $\frac{A_{sp}}{A_{pp}}$.

$$M_2 = \frac{A_{sp}}{A_{pp}}$$

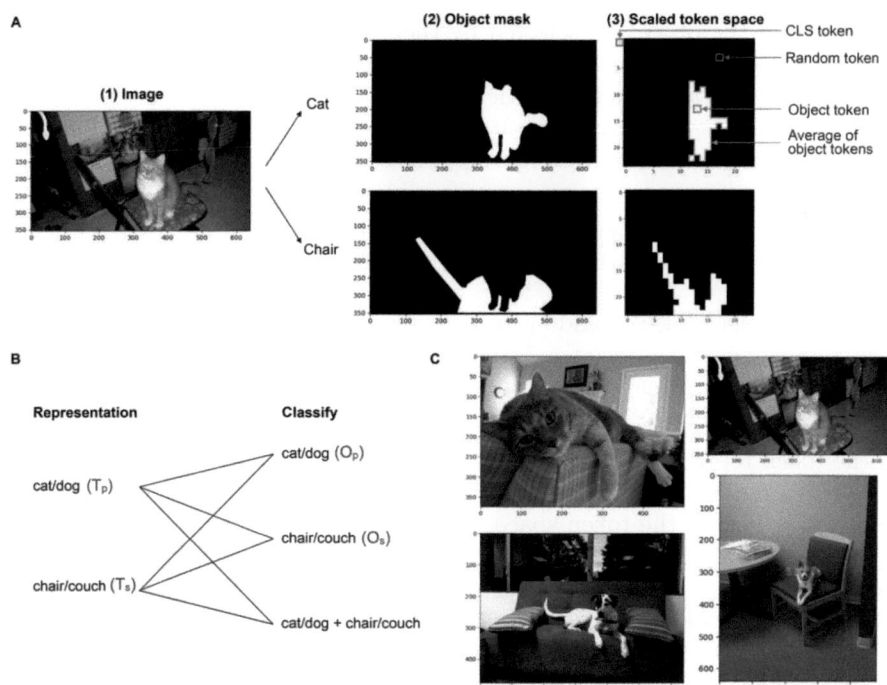

Fig. 1. A. Explanation of how the token representations are obtained. We analyse four kinds of tokens in this study: 1) CLS token: The special token usually used in models for downstream tasks; 2) Avg_obj(Object-specific token): obtained by averaging the token representations of the object-masked tokens as shown in the figure. 3) Random_obj (Object-specific token): Rather than averaging, we sample one of the tokens from the masked token space of the object 4) Random: Obtained by sampling any random token from the token space other than the CLS token **B.** Describes the experimental setup in which we perform decoding in paired object tasks; each object-specific representation decodes 1) the object itself, 2) the other object in the image, and 3) the combination of both objects. **C.** Shows a sample paired object decoding task; given an image, the task is to decode if it contains object1 (cat/dog), object2 (chair/couch) or a combination of both.

3.2 Experimental Setup: Paired Object Task

The main experiment for assessing how token space encodes multi-object information is the *paired object task*. The objective of this experimental setup is to have images that contain only one of the two primary objects and one of the four secondary objects. The basic inference we make is that *given a particular token representation of the image from the encoder, can we reliably infer both the primary and the secondary object?*

We try to infer the multi-object relations in a pairwise manner as the objects vary in location, size and occur in different scene context. We select a total of 6 object sets that help generalise over different object types. The particular importance of the objects is selected by their relative importance to the scene, which is further formalised in later experiments by quantifying their mention in the COCO captions for the particular image. We decode the combination of objects in the image from a single token or an average of tokens obtained from various parts of the image (see Fig. 1A). The tokens we are interested in include are:

1. CLS token: the token used and trained for the encoder's downstream task,
2. Average token (avg_obj): the average of token representation obtained from the object,
3. Random object token (random_obj): a single token randomly sampled from the object,
4. Random token (Random): a randomly sampled token from the image that served as a baseline.

The token representation is obtained at the output of each layer. To identify the tokens originating from an object, we scale the segmentation mask of the object to the size of the token space.

The paired-object probing task is designed as a classification task with the following settings: we use the tokens originating from 1) Primary object (T_p), 2) Secondary object (T_s) and use it to decode 1) Primary object (O_p) category, 2) Secondary object (O_s) category, 3) Combination of primary and secondary object categories (see Fig. 1B). We train and evaluate the probes with a train/val/test setup with 80/10/10 percent data splits. The reported accuracies are all final test set accuracies. All probes are linear and use the Scikit-learn [29]'s perceptron implementation, with its default parameters.

3.3 Experimental Setup: Global Probe

The global decoding task is proposed to test the generalisation of the numbers obtained by the paired-object task on completely different categories of objects. It also allows us to verify using a more complex multi-class (20 class) probe that the trends in the paired object task are not a result of a simple 2 class or 4 class decoding (as in the paired-object task). Finally, in this analysis, we formalise another notion of object importance in the test set data split between objects mentioned in the caption as 'in the caption' and objects not mentioned in the caption as 'not in the caption'. This further helps test the difference between main and secondary objects apart from the category level classification as primary and secondary objects used in the paired object task.

In this task, object-specific probes are trained, i.e. using Random_Obj and Avg_obj tokens to decode the object category from which those tokens are taken. These probes utilise the first 40000 images from the MSCOCO train set to train a probe for the layer and each token type. The 5000 images in the validation set are used for testing. As we are testing for generalisation, we exclude the object categories used in the six object sets used to calculate our structured representation measures given in Table 1 and randomly choose 20 object categories (given in Global section of Table 1) in the COCO dataset for this evaluation.

3.4 Dataset

We needed instance segmentation masks to associate the tokens with the object in the image. Hence, we used the COCO dataset and created subsets combining object categories. We then excluded images with more than one object category of primary or secondary type. We also sub-sample to balance the co-occurrence of all object combinations between the primary and secondary categories. This balancing step is important to measure entanglement correctly, as otherwise, the difference in the co-occurrence of primary and secondary objects allows the decoder to learn the presence of one from the other. While choosing the objects across primary and secondary class we preferred objects more likely to interact in the scene. Within the primary and secondary categories, we preferred objects that are similar to each other, so their embedded representations are not naturally distinct, increasing our probe's sensitivity. We obtain six task sets with a total of 16,288 images. For example, the first task contains a combination of objects from two sets, i.e. a primary object: animal (cat/dog) and a secondary object: furniture (chair/bench/bed/couch). The dataset and its object sets are detailed in Table 1. We call this set of tasks 'object pair decoding tasks'.

For the generalisation task, global probes were trained and tested on a larger dataset of 20 random classes (given in Table 1) beyond the ones used in the main analysis and measures. We selected the first 40000 images in COCO's training set for training and the 5000 images in the validation set for testing.

Table 1. For paired object decoding, we use 6 object sets with different numbers of images in each set. Each set contains images with different variations of objects. For the global object decoding task, we tested generalisation on 20 randomly chosen objects.

Paired-Object Probe	Set 1	Set 2	Set 3	Set 4	Set 5	Set 6
# Images	2414	5042	1953	2143	938	3738
Primary Object	cat, dog	dining table, person	train, bus	tv, laptop	microwave, oven	motorcycle, car
Secondary Object	bench, chair, couch, bed	pizza, knife, cup, cake	traffic light, bench, backpack, handbag	mouse, remote, keyboard, cellphone	bottle, spoon, knife, cup	traffic light, handbag, backpack, bicycle
Global Probe	sheep, bear, banana, potted plant, bowl, toilet, horse, apple, fire, parking meter, handbag, snowboard, broccoli, giraffe, stop sign,hydrant, cow, tie, hot dog, truck, wine glass					

3.5 Linear Probing

We probe the representations in pre-trained networks for our analysis. Probing an information system involves obtaining a representation, usually in the form of a vector from the system in response to an image. Then, we estimate if that particular vector can classify information about the stimuli correctly. The kind of information the probe can learn to classify, and the complexity of the probe (i.e. is it just a linear classifier or a complex multilayer NN) indicates the nature of information present in that layer's representation. We do not use a more complex probe because it is difficult to verify if the classification performance for them is a function of better representation or due to the learnt complex relationship in the probe [2,13]. Hence, we obtain representations from various parts (layers and spatial sections, i.e., tokens) of the network and use them to understand the network by looking at the ability of a linear probe to classify it.

3.6 Analysed Models and Their Configuration

We analysed the image encoders of the nine pre-trained models.

- **Vision-Language Models:** BLIP (ViT-B/16 and ViT-L/14) for image captioning, CLIP (ViT-B/16 and ViT-L/14) for image-text matching, and FLAVA with an additional multimodal encoder on top of vision and language encoders.
- **Baseline ViT-B/16:** trained on ImageNet21k for image classification.
- **CNN-based CLIP (ResNet X4):** an alternative architecture compared to ViT-based CLIP.
- **Self-Supervised Methods:** DINO and DINOv2, each trained on images without labels.

In CNN analysis, we obtained feature cells instead of tokens, i.e., we used the vector representation of a cell in the feature map by accumulating all the filter outputs at the cell location. In both transformers and CNNs, the place on the feature map representing the object is computed by scaling the object segmentation map to the size of the feature map at the layer. The images are pre-processed with the standard pre-processing function and setting provided along with the pre-trained network instances.

4 Results

In this section, we will discuss the results and observations made while looking at the vision encoders through the lens of structured representations. In Subsect. 1) we see how the images from the paired-object task allow us to see an aggregate and instance-specific view of the representation of various objects in different types of tokens and layers. Subsection 2) shows how the object representations are spread across object-specific tokens and CLS tokens with the example of BLIP. 3) We further discuss the results for all networks, discussing the key variations in the distribution of representations based on the type of network and the training objective. 4) Following up on the result of object-specific tokens having better representations than CLS tokens, we illustrate this effect by relating it to downstream tasks. 5) Finally, we correlate the results obtained till now to unrelated objects in the global decoding task. We see how the measures of structured representation can be used to estimate the layer and network better at retaining object-specific representations in multi-object scenes.

4.1 A Snapshot of Network's Global and Image-Specific Representation

Decoding the objects in a multi-object scene using the trained model's representations gives us a picture of how the information about the scene is organised in the network. In our study, we have used two kinds of decoding tasks (paired object and global decoding tasks) to estimate the architecture-level organisation of these representations over a set of images. We also generate representation similarity maps to analyse the representation of a single image in a particular model.

Using the paired object decoding tasks, in Fig. 2a, you can see the detailed results for decoding accuracies for the four types of token representation used in our analysis for the paired object decoding tasks. This provides a more detailed global picture of the model's representations of object pairs from the images. For an instance-wise image-level analysis of representations, we generate similarity maps of the object representations that show how a particular token's relation to other tokens changes across layers in the model for a particular image. Figure 2b shows the representation similarity map (visualising cosine similarity) for all tokens to two tokens (marked with yellow and blue squares in the original images) in an image 1) to the primary object 2) to the secondary object. One can notice how the representations of tokens originating from the same token start having similar representations as we move toward the upper layers. The tokens from the primary object (dog) acquire similar representation, but for the secondary object (pillow), many tokens outside the object also have high cosine similarity in the last layer.

Finally, we can see that the objects in the network can be linearly decoded considerably above random accuracy by using either a single token representation originating from the object or by using an average of token representations from the object. The general trend followed by these decoding accuracies can be seen in Fig. 3. The global object decoding probes, with their 20 class classification setting with larger train and test sets (40000 and 5000 respectively), provide a solid baseline of the ability of the token's representations to decode between multiple objects. This setup also tests on completely different sets of objects compared to the paired-object task (Objects in Table 1). The high correlation of these accuracies for each network (see Fig. 5) with paired-object classification tasks' results (i.e., M_1 as it uses Avg_Obj accuracy from the paired object decoding task) shows that the accuracies are not obtained due to an easy 2-way or 4-way classification task setup in the paired object tasks, nor by overfitting to a particular set of objects.

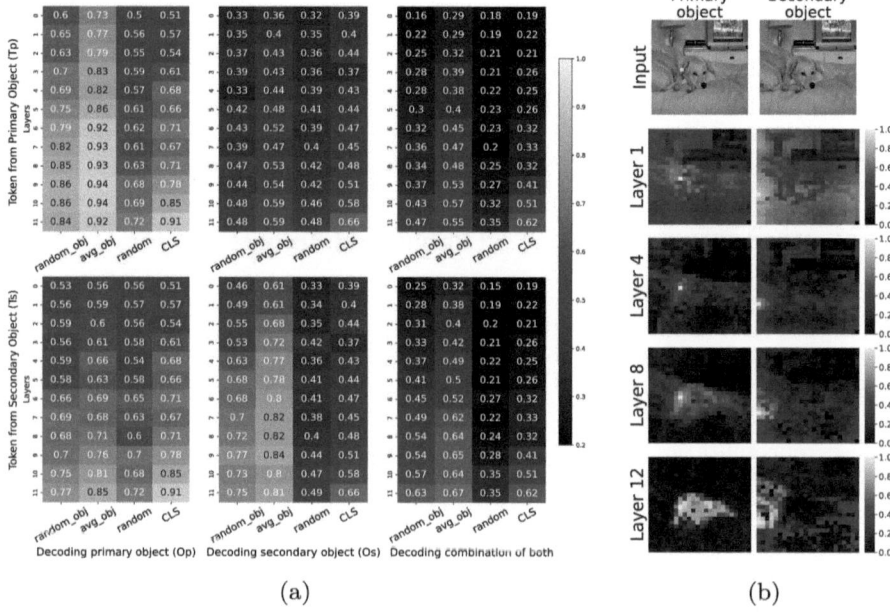

Fig. 2. a. Paired object decoding task results for BLIP across layers: Average decoding performance for different layers (y-axis) and token types (x-axis) over 6 tasks for BLIP. In the subfigures, the y-axis contains variations of where the object-specific tokens (random_obj and avg_obj) are obtained. The different columns show results for 1) decoding the primary object 2) the secondary object 3) the combination of both objects in the image. The decoding pattern remains after averaging, with the tokens from the objects modelling the most useful information for categorising the objects. The object-specific tokens are much better than the CLS token, which has to capture the larger scene context. **b.** Visualisation of cosine similarity of highlighted token to other tokens for a token from primary and secondary objects at various layers of BLIP model.

4.2 How Different Token Representations Encode Objects, Their Interaction, and Their Importance

In the paired-object tasks, the images consist of a primary object and a secondary object. We see the representation of these two object combinations in each image in four types of token representations from the models. Based on the results from the BLIP model shown in Fig. 2, we now discuss the general trend of representations across models. Specific differences are discussed in Subsect. 4.3.

In our results (see Fig. 4), in all pre-trained models, the primary objects are decoded equally well by the CLS token as the average token representation of the object. There is a decrease in decoding accuracy from primary to secondary object categories, partially due to the added complexity of a 4-way classification for the secondary object. However, the CLS token decodes the secondary objects with notably lower accuracy than both the object-specific tokens (avg_obj and random_obj). The CLS tokens, optimised for the downstream tasks in each network, are expected to model the best information about the scene. Yet this also means that not all objects are linearly decodable by the CLS token. We observe that the object-specific tokens have better object decoding accuracy compared to the CLS token (in BLIP, Fig. 2, the primary object has CLS: 0.91 vs Avg_Obj: 0.92 and the secondary object has CLS: 0.66 vs Avg_Obj: 0.81). There is a particular degradation in decoding performance using the CLS token for secondary objects, where its accuracy is far below the decoding accuracy of object-specific tokens (avg_obj and random_obj).

Previous analyses showed that object-specific tokens have the highest accuracy for decoding the particular object from which they originated. Still, they also have high decoding accuracy for the other objects in the image. This accuracy is far above random guess and allows these tokens to decode a combination of objects in the current image (see Fig. 2, for BLIP results). For example, the final decoding accuracy for the combination is 0.57, when using the primary (avg_obj) object token and 0.65 when using the secondary one. In Fig. 2, one can notice that the primary avg_obj token is much worse at representing the secondary objects than the other way around. These findings have implications for the disentanglement in object-specific tokens. Further, the CLS token still shows a decent decoding accuracy as it is optimised to capture more global information from the image. However, it remains lower than the object-specific secondary tokens, due to its weaker capturing of information about these secondary objects in the scene (CLS token decoding accuracy for the secondary object is 0.66 compared to 0.91 for the primary object, as seen in Fig. 2).

4.3 Variation of Representations Across Models with Different Training Objectives and Architectures: Key Insights

In this section, we compare the representations of the models with each other. Overall, across the models, the decoding accuracy of the object-specific tokens of the paired-object decoding tasks correlates with their global decoding task performance (see Fig. 5). The relative accuracy trends for various tokens are similar across most VLM models. A notable observation is the higher overall decoding performance of FLAVA, BLIP and BLIP-Large models, which also shows a higher segregation of object-wise representations (i.e., the random token accuracy is fairly lower in the last layer compared to object-specific tokens). These models also score high on our object binding measure and relatively low on entanglement (except BLIP-L and CLIP-L). The two self-supervised models, DINO and DINOv2, show a slightly lower score on object binding for secondary objects, yet their representations are more disentangled, which allows them to model the background objects relatively better. Interestingly, we observe in Fig. 3 that in DINOv2, the decoding accuracy of random_obj is higher than other models, aligning with its reported performance on use for semantic segmentation tasks using token-level classification.

We observe a difference in representations' structure due to architecture (Transformer vs CNN) and specific training on multi-object tasks (i.e., ViT vs other models). Consequently, there is a significant decrease in decoding accuracy

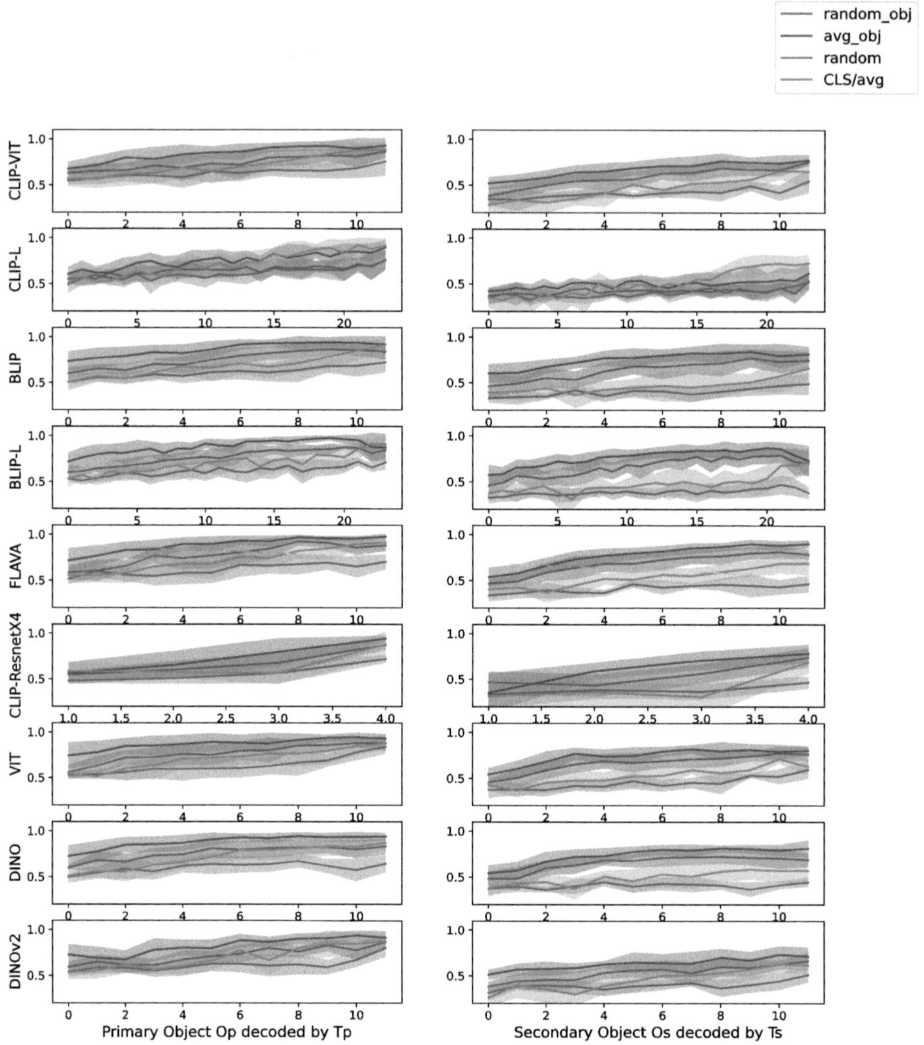

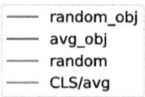

Fig. 3. Layer-wise test set decoding accuracy for primary and secondary objects for pre-trained models in the study. Results for all models are shown in the appendix. The accuracies are averaged over the six object sets. In each sub-graph, the y-axis denotes the decoding accuracy, and the x-axis denotes the layer at which the accuracy was observed. We observe consistent decoding trends across models with a few variations reported in Sect. 4.3.

using the random CNN unit representation compared to random ViT tokens (in the last layers, primary object: ViT 0.84 vs CNN 0.72; secondary object: ViT 0.54 vs CNN 0.45; see Fig. 3). Further, the object-specific tokens in CNNs have lower accuracy while decoding the other objects in the scene than their ViT counterpart (in the last layers, primary object: ViT 0.88 vs CNN 0.8; secondary object: ViT 0.6 vs CNN 0.59). This indicates that CNN has less entanglement of object-specific information across objects than the ViT counterpart in CLIP. We attribute these results to CNNs not having the ability for the information to travel across units in each layer; hence, the object information remains more localised. ViT trained on ImageNet21k shows the least differentiation between object-specific (Random_Obj: 0.88) and other tokens (Random: 0.84) compared to the other Transformer models. Here, a random token decodes the object with almost similar accuracy as the CLS token (CLS: 0.88; see Fig. 3), and tokens from one object can similarly decode the category of other objects in the scene. Hence, the scene-level information appears more uniformly dispersed in the representations of ViT tokens trained only on single object classification tasks. We note that this difference can be because the other models have been trained on objectives that require correct modelling and representation of multiple objects for downstream tasks like text matching, captioning, etc. Hence, the differentiation of object-specific tokens from random tokens and, consequently, the segregation of information is more explicit in the last layer in many of these networks than in ViT(trained for single object classification).

Turning to the *global decoding task*, we see that the newer VLMs like FLAVA and BLIP have higher accuracy for their object-specific representations than counterparts like CLIP (see Fig. 5). A larger model (BLIP-L) performs better than its base version. However, the layer-wise analysis (see Fig. 3) indicates that the CLS token outperforms object-specific tokens for CLIP-L. This points to a different binding mechanism, where the object-specific tokens have low classification accuracy across object categories, but the CLS token effectively binds both primary and secondary objects in the higher layers. Consequently, one can note that CLIP-L has the best scene-level decoding accuracy (0.66) when using the CLS token to decode the combination of primary and secondary objects. On the other hand, ViT trained on single object classification has the poorest accuracy in decoding a combination of objects using the CLS token (0.49). However, its object-specific regions maintain fairly good representations for individual objects (Avg_Obj $A_{pp} = 0.93$ and $A_{ss} = 0.80$).

Lastly, the decoding accuracy for object-specific tokens degrades the most on secondary objects, which is also correlated with its lower accuracy on objects 'not mentioned in the caption' in Fig. 5. Our layer-wise analysis in Fig. 3 also shows that in BLIP-L and many networks like ViT, DINOv2, CLIP, and BLIP, the secondary object accuracy starts decreasing in the final few layers, showing the effect of the training objective. We explore that effect further in the next two sections.

4.4 Special Token May Not Be Special for Your Downstream Task with Multi-object Images

Following up on the observations about the lower decoding accuracy of secondary objects for CLS tokens, we wanted to check if the low accuracy results are related to the object's importance in the downstream task (captioning in the

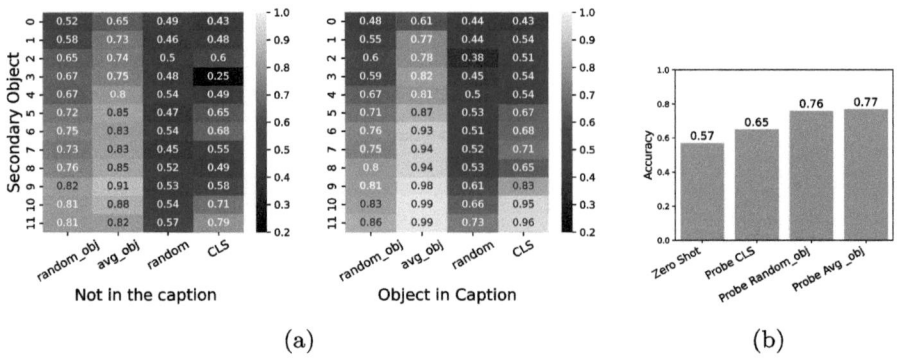

Fig. 4. a. Variation in decoding accuracy between instances of objects 'in caption' and 'not in caption'. Each subplot represents the decoding of the object by its object-specific representation. **b.** Object detection accuracy on the secondary objects in paired using probes trained on three different token representations from CLIP and zero-shot CLIP accuracy.

case of BLIP). Hence, we analysed the decoding accuracy for two sets of data. We divided the data based on whether the object was directly mentioned in the caption generated by the model. Due to this split, we rejected object sets with less than 400 samples in either of the new sets. Therefore, we are left with 3 object sets whose average results are reported in Fig. 4a. From Fig. 4a, one can see a decrease in decoding accuracy of the objects not mentioned in captions using all kinds of tokens considered in our analysis (average final layer accuracy for primary object, which was 'Object in caption': CLS: 1 and avg_token: 0.99, dropping to CLS: 0.87 and avg_obj 0.93 when the object is 'not in caption'. In the secondary object, the drop is from 'Object in caption': CLS: 0.96 and avg_obj: 0.99 to 'not in caption': CLS: 0.79 and avg_obj: 0.82). This means the network pays more attention to certain objects, and its learning of discriminative features deteriorates for objects not mentioned in the captions. We note that the decrease in decoding accuracy is most pronounced for the CLS token, showing the direct effect of the downstream task on the representation.

Using CLIP in a multi-object setting, we further use this understanding to check for failure in zero-shot object detection tasks. We use the classification task setting of the secondary objects in the paired-object probe. Specifically, the object-specific representation (random_token and avg_obj token) is used to learn probes to classify the secondary objects in images. We also evaluate the CLIP zero-shot performance to detect objects in the image with the prompt "An image containing a 'category'", where the category was replaced with 4 object categories of the set. We finally evaluate the accuracy of detecting the objects. The results confirm the original CLIP paper by showing that learning a probe gives better accuracy than zero-shot accuracy in CLIP (Probe CLS: 0.65 vs Zero Shot: 57; see Fig. 4b). Further, we also note that the object-specific regions in the token space achieve far better representations than the CLS token

(Random_Obj: 0.76 and Avg_Obj: 0.77). This emphasises that even though the CLS token is used to classify the objects in practice, comparing it to representations from the token space, we find that the object-specific regions perform much better in classification for CLIP.

4.5 Structured Representations in the Network Are Better to Retain the Representation of Objects in the Background

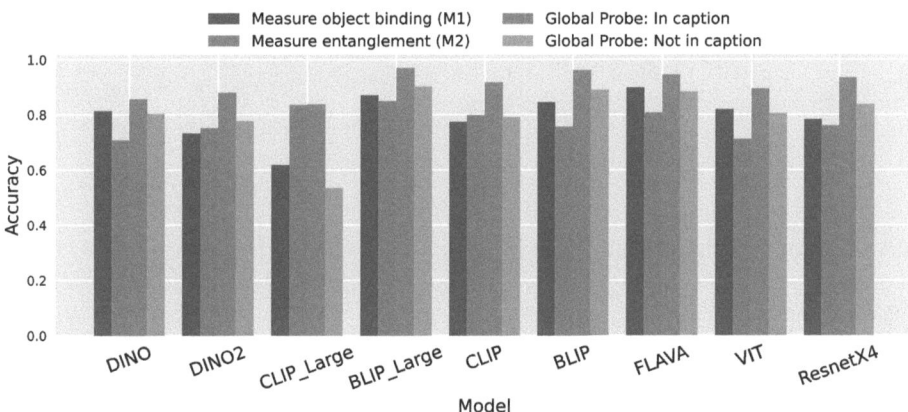

Fig. 5. The figure shows both measures of modularity evaluated for all vision encoders. Along with this, the figure has the accuracy of global probing task for avg_obj token evaluated for 'In caption': Objects mentioned in the caption and 'Not in caption': Objects not mentioned in the caption. The results for each network are from the layer with the best M_1 across the layers. We see how the first measure of modularity M_1 correlates highly with the accuracy of decoding background tokens across networks (Pearson's correlation coefficient = 0.94, p = 0.001). This also shows that the measures from the paired object task are highly predictive of general representation of objects in the network. The second measure of modularity (Measure of entanglement) M_2 correlates (Pearson's coefficient = 0.74, p = 0.02) with the drop in accuracy for objects 'not in the caption' compared to the objects mentioned 'in the caption'. Hence, more modular representations favour better representation of individual background objects.

As discussed in the previous section, the object-specific tokens in the main token space of the network have better ability to retain and model object-specific information for most objects than the CLS token. This makes them especially useful for tasks requiring information about objects that may not be the scene's focus

Table 2. Table showing the predicted layer with maximum object binding measure (M_1) and the actual layer with the best representation of background objects, i.e. Global Probe:'not in the caption' in the global decoding task.

Model	Layer Predicted	Best layer
DINO	8	7
DINO2	10	10
CLIP_Large	23	23
BLIP_Large	20	21
CLIP	10	9
BLIP	9	9
FLAVA	9	8
VIT	7	10
CLIP ResnetX4	3	3

(according to the training distribution). However, a key question remains: how do we quantify this ability of object-specific tokens across layers and networks? Our proposed measures of structured representations address this by evaluating the degree to which networks model and maintain separate object-wise information in the token space. In Fig. 5, we show these measures across all networks using the Avg_Obj tokens. Specifically, M_1 measures the decoding accuracy of the secondary object O_s using secondary object token T_s. We find (see Fig. 5) that when networks exhibit strong modular representations of secondary objects, they also decode other 20 "background" objects more effectively if those objects are not mentioned in the COCO captions. Indeed, there is a strong Pearson's correlation of +0.94 with the object binding measure M_1 and a moderate inverse correlation of −0.53 (p-value = 0.13) with the entanglement measure M_2. The role of structured representations becomes clearer when comparing 'not in caption' objects to 'in caption' objects: the token entanglement measure M_2 correlates 0.74 (p-value = 0.02) with the drop in accuracy for 'not in caption' objects. This indicates that the more segregated the information in the tokens, the better a network's object-specific representation can be in equally retaining and decoding objects not mentioned in the caption (background objects). Hence, this shows that more modular representations in vision encoders, i.e. representation agreeing to our two properties of 1) binding and 2) segregation, are signs of better retention of object-specific representation of even less important 'objects not in the caption'.

Our analysis also shows that in most encoders, the last layer is not the best choice for decoding the objects using the object-specific tokens from the networks; in models such as BLIP-L, object-wise representation degrades in the last two layers (0.87 in layer 20 to 0.73 in layer 23 for secondary objects), possibly due to the pressure of the objective function. In Table 2, we compare the estimated choice of the layer using the object binding measure M_1 and the layer with the best accuracy on background objects ('not mentioned in the caption').

Further, a lower entanglement score helped guide the choice when object binding measures are similar across layers. We see a good relative match between the estimated best layers using measures of modularity obtained using paired-object tasks and the best layers for the larger 20-class global decoding task. Hence, our measures of structured representations can be helpful in ascertaining which network and particular layers are useful to train decoders for tasks requiring information about background objects in multi-object scenarios.

5 Discussion

In this work, we identify two properties required in representations of image encoders for them to be more structured: 1) The model should be able to bind information specific to particular objects in the image into specific representation units, i.e. a limited number of tokens can represent the object better than its input representation. 2) The model should segregate various objects of the input image in separate sets of tokens, i.e., there should be object-wise information disentanglement in the token space.

Most vision encoders fulfill the first criterion, as they aggregate information from the image into smaller representation spaces functional for the downstream task. In particular, the decoding accuracy for all objects is higher than that of their raw input representation. However, our results demonstrated that the bottleneck at the CLS token does not represent all objects well.

We were interested in understanding whether separate representational units specialise in representing the image's constituent parts (objects). Our analysis shows that the object-specific (avg_obj, random_obj) tokens show decent decoding accuracy across the models. Each object-wise token's accuracy for classifying itself is our estimate for fulfilling this criterion. This accuracy is better than for the CLS token for all models except CLIP-L.

For the second characteristic, we looked at the network's capability to form disentangled representations of objects in the token space. We saw evidence that information about other objects also leaks into the object-wise representations. Ideally, each object representation can only decode that particular object, and other objects in the scene cannot be decoded by that representation. As the other objects can be decoded in our object representations (with accuracies of 0.89 by secondary object representations and 0.65 by primary object representations), their representations are already affected by the context, i.e. other objects. In addition, the higher the decoding accuracy of other objects in the scene, the higher the entanglement in the representation.

Our comparative analysis of the BLIP model's performance showed a notable degradation in decoding efficacy across all representations when objects were omitted from its captions. We replicate this result using the object-wise tokens for all models examined in the global probe study. This observation underscores the significant influence of the model's downstream objective on its representational capabilities. Most research predominantly assesses these networks' capabilities based on their final outputs, which rely on representations like a CLS token (for example, in [19,39]). Our findings show a loss in representing multiple objects while funnelling information into the CLS token. Further, the downstream objective's effect is the most extreme on the nature of the CLS representations.

We show that this causes suboptimal performance of these networks in simple tasks such as identifying objects in the multi-object setting, especially for background objects. We show that the networks have some structured information in token space i.e. they preserve object-specific information localised in the token space. Our analysis finally shows that the measures of structured information in the token space of models correlate with the ability of the models to generalise on background objects using a 20-class experiment. This way, our measures of structured information evaluate the models' ability to represent individual objects in a multi-object scene. These measures show which model's representations and at what layer are most structured for representing individual objects separately. They achieve this by not combining object representations in the token space (other than CLS token) under the influence of objective functions that can lead to abstracting the background objects while modelling the image. Access to this structured representation helps with tasks requiring access to detailed representations of individual objects in the scene.

The natural next step of this work is to verify the usefulness of the two representation measures on specific datasets (object categories) for the choice of the best layer and network on actual downstream tasks like semantic segmentation or object localisation. This way, one can estimate if the best-predicted layers for the networks give the best results, or in the case of the use of deep decoders for segmentation like in [4,20,37], it will show how much less data is needed to train a decoder as opposed to using the default final layer (especially for good performance on less prominent background objects).

6 Limitations

The probing and representation analysis methods we used have some limitations, and the results must be carefully interpreted. High decoding accuracy in a decoding task with two or four objects may be due to the easy decoding task (if the object classes are naturally distinct and it is only a 2/4 way classification). Further, the fact that one can classify a particular object from a few other classes may depend on representing a single or a few features distinguishing between the classes. This representation may not model many other aspects of the object. We controlled for this limitation by training global probes for 20-class classification using the same representations, showing reasonably high accuracy. Likewise, a lower decoding accuracy does not mean that the model does not have information about the particular object; the information is just not encoded with linear distinction at that layer/token. Overall, we are averaging over six object sets with many object categories. Hence, even though the exact numbers may not reflect the model's exact state, we can safely rely on the relative numbers to make inferences about the model and its representations.

7 Conclusion

In this work, we first formulated two characteristics for structured representations in an image encoder. We then analysed the representations of transformer-based image encoders in VIT, BLIP, CLIP, FLAVA, DINO, DINOv2 and CLIP (Resnet X4) image encoders. Through object decoding tasks, we create a view of the representation structure of these pre-trained models. We observed that object-specific areas hold the most discriminative features about the objects. Their discriminative ability decreased when the objects were not important for the downstream task but was still reasonably maintained. The token representations are not disentangled since they can decode other objects in the scene with accuracy far above random guesses. We found that the aggregate image representation, i.e. CLS token for transformers, does not represent all objects, and its discriminative ability degrades the most when the object is not useful for the trained downstream task. Our work thus characterises and measures the extent to which the representations of these image encoders are structured in the token space, that the individual objects are represented separately in the token space, but their representations are entangled. We also calculated the layerwise measures of representation and entanglement by object importance (estimated using captions), which provides insights into the failures and optimal adaptation of these networks to downstream tasks that utilise these individual object features.

Supplementary Materials The code to obtain data splits from the COCO dataset, experimental setup, and data analysis can be found in the repository linked below. Further detailed plots for the paired object task showing the decoding accuracy of objects across the layers of the network have been given in the notebooks in the supplementary material for all models.

https://github.com/tarunkhajuria42/Structured-representations

Acknowledgments. We thank Raul Vicente, and Meelis Kull for the valuable discussions and inputs on the paper. This work was supported by the Estonian Research Council grant PSG728, the Estonian Centre of Excellence in Artificial Intelligence (EXAI), funded by the Estonian Ministry of Education and Research and the European Union's Horizon 2020 Research and Innovation Programme under Grant Agreement No. 952060 (Trust AI).

Disclosure of Interests. The authors declare that they have no competing interests.

References

1. Aflalo, E., et al.: VL-interpret: an interactive visualization tool for interpreting vision-language transformers. In: Proceedings of the IEEE/CVF Conference on Computer Vision and Pattern Recognition, pp. 21406–21415 (2022)
2. Alain, G., Bengio, Y.: Understanding intermediate layers using linear classifier probes. arXiv preprint arXiv:1610.01644 (2016)
3. Antol, S., et al.: VQA: visual question answering. In: Proceedings of the IEEE International Conference on Computer Vision, pp. 2425–2433 (2015)
4. Ayzenberg, L., Giryes, R., Greenspan, H.: DINOv2 based self supervised learning for few shot medical image segmentation. In: 2024 IEEE International Symposium on Biomedical Imaging (ISBI), pp. 1–5. IEEE (2024)
5. Bengio, Y., Courville, A., Vincent, P.: Representation learning: a review and new perspectives. arxiv 2012. arXiv preprint arXiv:1206.5538 (2012)
6. Bronstein, M.M., Bruna, J., Cohen, T., Veličković, P.: Geometric deep learning: Grids, groups, graphs, geodesics, and gauges. arXiv preprint arXiv:2104.13478 (2021)
7. Cao, J., Gan, Z., Cheng, Yu., Yu, L., Chen, Y.-C., Liu, J.: Behind the scene: revealing the secrets of pre-trained vision-and-language models. In: Vedaldi, A., Bischof, H., Brox, T., Frahm, J.-M. (eds.) ECCV 2020. LNCS, vol. 12351, pp. 565–580. Springer, Cham (2020). https://doi.org/10.1007/978-3-030-58539-6_34
8. Caron, M., et al.: Emerging properties in self-supervised vision transformers. In: Proceedings of the IEEE/CVF International Conference on Computer Vision, pp. 9650–9660 (2021)
9. Cordonnier, J.B., Loukas, A., Jaggi, M.: On the relationship between self-attention and convolutional layers. arXiv preprint arXiv:1911.03584 (2019)
10. Fauw, J., et al.: Clinically applicable deep learning for diagnosis and referral in retinal disease. Nat. Med. **24**(9), 1342–1350 (2018)
11. Fodor, J.A.: Concepts: Where Cognitive Science Went Wrong. Oxford University Press (1998)
12. Greff, K., Van Steenkiste, S., Schmidhuber, J.: On the binding problem in artificial neural networks. arXiv preprint arXiv:2012.05208 (2020)
13. Hewitt, J., Liang, P.: Designing and interpreting probes with control tasks. arXiv preprint arXiv:1909.03368 (2019)
14. Johnson, J., Hariharan, B., Van Der Maaten, L., Fei-Fei, L., Lawrence Zitnick, C., Girshick, R.: CLEVR: a diagnostic dataset for compositional language and elementary visual reasoning. In: Proceedings of the IEEE Conference on Computer Vision and Pattern Recognition, pp. 2901–2910 (2017)
15. Koh, P.W., et al.: Concept bottleneck models. In: International Conference on Machine Learning, pp. 5338–5348. PMLR (2020)
16. Krishna, R., et al.: Visual genome: connecting language and vision using crowd-sourced dense image annotations. Int. J. Comput. Vis. **123**, 32–73 (2017)
17. Lake, B.M., Baroni, M.: Human-like systematic generalization through a meta-learning neural network. Nature **623**, 1–7 (2023)
18. Lepori, M.A., Serre, T., Pavlick, E.: Break it down: evidence for structural compositionality in neural networks. arXiv preprint arXiv:2301.10884 (2023)
19. Lewis, M., Yu, Q., Merullo, J., Pavlick, E.: Does clip bind concepts? Probing compositionality in large image models. arXiv preprint arXiv:2212.10537 (2022)
20. Li, F., et al.: Mask DINO: towards a unified transformer-based framework for object detection and segmentation. In: Proceedings of the IEEE/CVF Conference on Computer Vision and Pattern Recognition, pp. 3041–3050 (2023)

21. Li, J., Li, D., Xiong, C., Hoi, S.: Blip: bootstrapping language-image pre-training for unified vision-language understanding and generation. In: International Conference on Machine Learning, pp. 12888–12900. PMLR (2022)
22. Lin, T.-Y., et al.: Microsoft coco: common objects in context. In: Fleet, D., Pajdla, T., Schiele, B., Tuytelaars, T. (eds.) ECCV 2014. LNCS, vol. 8693, pp. 740–755. Springer, Cham (2014). https://doi.org/10.1007/978-3-319-10602-1_48
23. Lipton, Z.C.: The mythos of model interpretability: in machine learning, the concept of interpretability is both important and slippery. Queue **16**(3), 31–57 (2018)
24. Locatello, F., et al.: Object-centric learning with slot attention. Adv. Neural. Inf. Process. Syst. **33**, 11525–11538 (2020)
25. Lovering, C., Pavlick, E.: Unit testing for concepts in neural networks. Trans. Assoc. Comput. Linguist. **10**, 1193–1208 (2022)
26. Oord, A.v.d., Vinyals, O., Kavukcuoglu, K.: Neural discrete representation learning. arXiv preprint arXiv:1711.00937 (2017)
27. Oquab, M., et al.: DINOv2: learning robust visual features without supervision. arXiv preprint arXiv:2304.07193 (2023)
28. Pavlick, E.: Symbols and grounding in large language models. Phil. Trans. R. Soc. A **381**(2251), 20220041 (2023)
29. Pedregosa, F., et al.: Scikit-learn: machine learning in Python. J. Mach. Learn. Res. **12**, 2825–2830 (2011)
30. Radford, A., et al.: Learning transferable visual models from natural language supervision. In: International Conference on Machine Learning, pp. 8748–8763. PMLR (2021)
31. Radulescu, A., Shin, Y.S., Niv, Y.: Human representation learning. Annu. Rev. Neurosci. **44**(1), 253–273 (2021)
32. Raghu, M., Unterthiner, T., Kornblith, S., Zhang, C., Dosovitskiy, A.: Do vision transformers see like convolutional neural networks? Adv. Neural. Inf. Process. Syst. **34**, 12116–12128 (2021)
33. Rudin, C.: Stop explaining black box machine learning models for high stakes decisions and use interpretable models instead. Nat. Mach. Intell. **1**(5), 206–215 (2019)
34. Shridhar, M., Manuelli, L., Fox, D.: Cliport: what and where pathways for robotic 569 manipulation. In: Conference on Robot Learning, pp. 894–906 (2021)
35. Singh, A., et al.: FLAVA: a foundational language and vision alignment model. In: Proceedings of the IEEE/CVF Conference on Computer Vision and Pattern Recognition, pp. 15638–15650 (2022)
36. Träuble, F., et al.: Discrete key-value bottleneck. In: International Conference on Machine Learning, pp. 34431–34455. PMLR (2023)
37. Vobecky, A., Hurych, D., Siméoni, O., Gidaris, S., Bursuc, A., Pérez, P., Sivic, J.: Unsupervised semantic segmentation of urban scenes via cross-modal distillation. Int. J. Comput. Vis. **133**, 1–23 (2025)
38. Yi, K., Wu, J., Gan, C., Torralba, A., Kohli, P., Tenenbaum, J.: Neural-symbolic VQA: disentangling reasoning from vision and language understanding. In: Advances in Neural Information Processing Systems, vol. 31 (2018)
39. Yuksekgonul, M., Bianchi, F., Kalluri, P., Jurafsky, D., Zou, J.: When and why vision-language models behave like bags-of-words, and what to do about it? In: The Eleventh International Conference on Learning Representations (2022)
40. Yun, T., Bhalla, U., Pavlick, E., Sun, C.: Do vision-language pretrained models learn composable primitive concepts? arXiv preprint arXiv:2203.17271 (2022)

Open Access This chapter is licensed under the terms of the Creative Commons Attribution 4.0 International License (http://creativecommons.org/licenses/by/4.0/), which permits use, sharing, adaptation, distribution and reproduction in any medium or format, as long as you give appropriate credit to the original author(s) and the source, provide a link to the Creative Commons license and indicate if changes were made.

The images or other third party material in this chapter are included in the chapter's Creative Commons license, unless indicated otherwise in a credit line to the material. If material is not included in the chapter's Creative Commons license and your intended use is not permitted by statutory regulation or exceeds the permitted use, you will need to obtain permission directly from the copyright holder.

Leveraging Influence Functions for Resampling Data in Physics-Informed Neural Networks

Jonas R. Naujoks[1], Aleksander Krasowski[1], Moritz Weckbecker[1], Galip Ümit Yolcu[1], Thomas Wiegand[1,2,3], Sebastian Lapuschkin[1,4(✉)], Wojciech Samek[1,2,3(✉)], and René P. Klausen[1(✉)]

[1] Department of Artificial Intelligence, Fraunhofer Heinrich Hertz Institute, Berlin, Germany
{sebastian.lapuschkin,wojciech.samek,
rene.pascal.klausen}@hhi.fraunhofer.de
[2] Department of Electrical Engineering and Computer Science, Technische Universität Berlin, Berlin, Germany
[3] BIFOLD – Berlin Institute for the Foundations of Learning and Data, Berlin, Germany
[4] Centre of eXplainable Artificial Intelligence, Technological University Dublin, Dublin, Ireland

Abstract. Physics-informed neural networks (PINNs) offer a powerful approach to solving partial differential equations (PDEs), which are ubiquitous in the quantitative sciences. Applied to both forward and inverse problems across various scientific domains, PINNs have recently emerged as a valuable tool in the field of scientific machine learning. A key aspect of their training is that the data—spatio-temporal points sampled from the PDE's input domain—are readily available. Influence functions, a tool from the field of explainable AI (XAI), approximate the effect of individual training points on the model, enhancing interpretability. In the present work, we explore the application of influence function-based sampling approaches for the training data. Our results indicate that such targeted resampling based on data attribution methods has the potential to enhance prediction accuracy in physics-informed neural networks, demonstrating a practical application of an XAI method in PINN training.

Keywords: Physics-Informed Neural Networks · Data Attribution · Resampling · Explainable Artificial Intelligence

1 Introduction

The success of machine learning, particularly deep learning approaches, in recent years has led to significant breakthroughs and rapid growth in both research and

---

J. R. Naujoks and A. Krasowski—Equal contribution.

practical applications across diverse fields. In the natural sciences, deep learning applications come with the promise of providing efficient and performant solutions to otherwise classically intractable problems, such as protein structure prediction [1] or molecular dynamics [28]. Within the broader context of scientific machine learning, physics-informed neural networks (PINNs) [22] recently emerged as a promising avenue of research aimed at modeling partial differential equations (PDEs) by embedding physical constraints directly into neural network training. Here, PINNs incorporate prior domain knowledge through the use of PDE constraints. To date, they have been applied to a plethora of forward and inverse problems across diverse fields such as electromagnetics [2], fluid mechanics [29], medical imaging [26], and geophysics [23]. However, despite their potential, these methods often suffer from optimization challenges due to the composite and intricate loss functions inherent to PINNs. This encompasses gradient pathologies [32], ill-conditioned loss terms [15,24,33], pathological local minima [25], and irregularities in information propagation [5,36], all leading to suboptimal performance. The literature proposes several ways to tackle these issues, such as improving the optimization algorithm, architectural modifications, loss function curation, and training data refinement [10,31].

In this work, we approach training data refinement through the lens of explainable artificial intelligence (XAI). Specifically, we leverage techniques originating from the field of training data attribution (TDA) to guide training data selection for PINNs. TDA quantifies the influence of individual training points by answering crucial questions such as "Which training data points are particularly influential for a given prediction?" or "How would the model parameters change if a specific data point were added to or removed from the training set?". Such methods have been widely applied in computer vision and large language models, proving useful for model debugging, identifying memorization [21], reweighting noisy data [3], identifying vulnerabilities to adversarial attacks [12], and, in general, understanding model behavior through the lens of training data [9].

Given their ability to assess the importance of individual training points, TDA methods naturally extend to studying PINNs, where training data consists of coordinate points sampled from the PDE's input domain. Notably, PINNs offer a straightforward setting for applying TDA methods, as their training data can be efficiently generated. While standard PINN training typically makes use of random or structured grid-based sampling, there is an emerging body of research showing how adaptive sampling can substantially improve PINN training efficiency and solution accuracy [6,7,14,16,19,35]. Building on this, we investigate the promise of using XAI-based TDA techniques, specifically PINNfluence [20], to adaptively select PINN training points. More precisely, we explore the hypothesis that training points identified as *influential* via TDA methods provide informative supervision, thus improving the performance of PINNs.

Our Contributions can be summarized as follows:

- We propose a novel XAI-driven adaptive resampling approach to enhance PINN training.

- We empirically analyze and compare our PINNfluence-based resampling approach with alternative adaptive sampling strategies.
- We demonstrate that TDA approaches succeed in improving performance on par with state-of-the-art methods, highlighting their potential in PINN settings.

2 Theoretical Background and Methods

2.1 Physics-Informed Neural Networks

PINNs [22] are a widely used machine learning approach for solving partial differential equations. Let $\Omega \subset \mathbb{R}^n$ be an open and bounded domain, $\partial\Omega$ denote its boundary and $\overline{\Omega} = \Omega \cup \partial\Omega$ correspond to its closure. We consider the initial boundary value problem, defined by

$$\mathcal{N}[u](\boldsymbol{x}) = 0, \quad \boldsymbol{x} \in \Omega \qquad (1)$$
$$\mathcal{B}_k[u](\boldsymbol{x}) = 0, \quad \boldsymbol{x} \in \Gamma_k \subseteq \partial\Omega \text{ for } k = 1,...,K \quad . \qquad (2)$$

where $\mathcal{N}$ and $\mathcal{B}_k$ denote differential operators acting on the solution $u : \overline{\Omega} \to \mathbb{R}^d$ of Eqs. (1) and (2) with K initial or boundary conditions; $\boldsymbol{x}$ encompasses spatio-temporal coordinates.[1] Eq. (2) is formulated to include, among other types, both Dirichlet and Neumann boundary conditions.

PINNs approximate a solution u of Eqs. (1) and (2) with a neural network $\phi(\boldsymbol{x}; \theta)$ with trainable network parameters $\theta \in \Theta$. The training process minimizes the empirical risk, defined by a composite loss function $\mathcal{L} = \mathcal{L}_{\text{pde}} + \mathcal{L}_{\text{bc}}$, with $\mathcal{L}_{\text{pde}}(\boldsymbol{x}; \theta) := \mathbb{1}_\Omega(\boldsymbol{x}) \|\mathcal{N}[\phi(\boldsymbol{x}; \theta)]\|_2^2$ and $\mathcal{L}_{\text{bc}}(\boldsymbol{x}; \theta) := \sum_{k=1}^{K} \mathbb{1}_{\Gamma_k}(\boldsymbol{x}) \|\mathcal{B}_k[\phi(\boldsymbol{x}; \theta)]\|_2^2$, where $\mathbb{1}_A(\boldsymbol{x}) = 1$ for $x \in A$ and 0 otherwise. A further data-driven regression term can be included in the loss function, but is omitted here for clarity. For the training loss $\mathcal{L}_{\text{train}}(\theta) = \sum_{\boldsymbol{x} \in \mathcal{X}_{\text{train}}} \mathcal{L}(\boldsymbol{x}; \theta)$, we consider in general N_{pde} collocation points $\mathcal{X}_{\text{pde}} \subset \Omega$ sampled from the domain and N_{bc} points $\mathcal{X}_{\text{bc}} \subseteq \partial\Omega$ from its boundary, which together constitute the training set $\mathcal{X}_{\text{train}}$.

This study focuses on the resampling of these spatio-temporal training points and proposes an influence function-based method for adaptive selection during training. In all of our experiments, we enforce boundary and initial conditions through the use of hard constraints [18]. As a result, the loss $\mathcal{L}$ reduces to $\mathcal{L}_{\text{pde}}$. Consequently, the training data is sampled from Ω only.

2.2 PINNfluence

Introduced in [20], PINNfluence uses influence functions [12] for PINNs to measure the effect of individual training points on the model's behavior to validate

---

[1] Depending on the PDE, these coordinates may be purely spatial, purely temporal, both, or even any other physical quantity the PDE depends on.

its prediction. This is achieved by approximating how the loss (or any other function of the model output) would change if a specific training point were to be added to or removed from the training set and the model were retrained. The effect of adding a point $\boldsymbol{x}^+$ to the training dataset on the total test loss can be approximated as [20]

$$\text{Inf}_{\mathcal{L}_{\text{test}}(\hat{\theta})}(\boldsymbol{x}^+) := \nabla_\theta \mathcal{L}_{\text{test}}(\hat{\theta})^\top \mathcal{H}_{\hat{\theta}}^{-1} \nabla_\theta \mathcal{L}(\boldsymbol{x}^+; \hat{\theta}), \tag{3}$$

where $\hat{\theta}$ denotes the model parameters optimized on the training loss, $\mathcal{L}_{\text{test}}(\hat{\theta}) = \sum_{\boldsymbol{x} \in \mathcal{X}_{\text{test}}} \mathcal{L}(\boldsymbol{x}; \hat{\theta})$ is the total test loss and $\mathcal{H}_{\hat{\theta}} = \nabla_\theta^2 \sum_{\boldsymbol{x} \in \mathcal{X}_{\text{train}}} \mathcal{L}(\boldsymbol{x}; \hat{\theta})$ is the Hessian of the training loss with respect to θ. Due to the linearity of Eq. (3), the effect of adding multiple training points is simply given by the sum of individual effects. Recent work by [34] recontextualises such training data attributions methods as an approximation of not retraining the model on a disturbed dataset but of continued fine-tuning of the already trained model on this dataset. Therefore, PINNfluence can help us assess the counterfactual effect of adding new points to a fine-tuning set.

2.3 Resampling Approaches for PINNs

The training data of PINNs $\mathcal{X}_{\text{train}}$ consists of collocation points sampled from $\overline{\Omega}$. Usually, the data is sampled once before training and kept constant during the optimization procedure. The most straightforward sampling approaches include drawing points from a uniform distribution or an equidistant grid over $\overline{\Omega}$. Due to the complex nature of loss functions in PINNs, the distribution of $\mathcal{X}_{\text{train}}$ is paramount for effective training and high performance, and is generally problem-specific. One way of tackling this problem is adapting or constraining the weights of individual loss terms or individual data points [15,30]. Another effective strategy to improve the training of PINNs is to adaptively resample the collocation points. Resampling strategies such as residual-based adaptive refinement (RAR) [17] or variations of importance-based resampling [6,16,35], distribution-based approaches [7,19,35] and neural tangent kernel-based point selection [14] have demonstrated their ability to further improve performance. Another line of research has incorporated principles such as temporal causality in the sampling process itself [5]. In essence, these methods can be subsumed as adding or replacing collocation points based on a metric that reflects the PDE residual or gradients at collocation points of interest with the goal of increasing PINN performance.

Our work aligns with the aforementioned body of research: we employ a score-based metric for gauging the importance of potential collocation points. In contrast to these prior approaches, we utilize an XAI-guided metric obtained via PINNfluence.

2.4 PINNfluence-Based Resampling

In this subsection, we introduce our approach. Let $\mathcal{X}_{\text{cand}} \subset \overline{\Omega}$ denote a finite set of randomly sampled candidate points and let $\mathcal{S} : \overline{\Omega} \to \mathbb{R}_{\geq 0}$ be a scoring function. The choice of the scoring function will define the different resampling methods.

Scoring Training Data Based on PINNfluence. Recall the influence given by Eq. (3). This expression gives us a way to estimate the effect of adding a potential candidate training sample x^+ on the loss of a representative test set $\mathcal{X}_{\text{test}} \subseteq \overline{\Omega}$. Our PINNfluence-based scoring metric is thus defined by taking the absolute value of the influence function:

$$\mathcal{S}_{\text{Inf}}(x^+) := |\text{Inf}_{\mathcal{L}_{\text{test}}(\hat{\theta})}(x^+)|. \tag{4}$$

A positive influence indicates a reduction in the loss and vice versa. Intuitively, candidate training points x^+ have large absolute influences when they have a large effect on changing the output of the loss function through the approximated change in model parameters $\hat{\theta}$. Consequently, this formulation effectively prioritizes the most impactful candidates for refinement. Our choice of using the absolute value is motivated by the observation that PINNs often become trapped in local minima as stated before. By incorporating points that also potentially increase the loss, we introduce perturbations that may help the model break free from undesirable minima.

Distribution-Based Resampling. Scores retrieved through PINNfluence are often densely concentrated in a small area and therefore non-representative, which is undesirable if we wish to sample multiple points at once. Motivated by [19], the authors of [35] propose to sample from a probability density function proportional to the residual, which in practice can be implemented as a probability mass function. Given a set of candidate points $\mathcal{X}_{\text{cand}}$ and associated importance scores $\mathcal{S}(x)$ for all $x \in \mathcal{X}_{\text{cand}}$, we can define a discrete probability mass function over $\mathcal{X}_{\text{cand}}$ as

$$p(x) = \frac{\mathcal{S}(x)^\alpha + c}{\sum_{x' \in \mathcal{X}_{\text{cand}}} (\mathcal{S}(x')^\alpha + c)} \tag{5}$$

for each $x \in \mathcal{X}_{\text{cand}}$, where $\alpha, c \in \mathbb{R}_{\geq 0}$ are hyperparameters. Increasing the exponent α amplifies the difference between low and high scores, emphasizing high scores. A larger value of c smooths the distribution towards a uniform one, thus boosting the probability of adding low-scoring points. The new training set $\mathcal{X}_{\text{new}}$ is constructed by generating independent samples from $\mathcal{X}_{\text{cand}}$ according to p without replacement.

2.5 Resampling Based on Alternative Scoring Functions

We compare our proposed method with four alternative scoring functions $\mathcal{S}(x)$: Residual-based adaptive refinement, a standard PINN approach, an additional TDA method based on the gradient dot product and two derivative-based ones.

Residual-Based Adaptive Refinement (RAR) [17]. RAR scores, given by

$$\mathcal{S}_{\text{RAR}} = \|\mathcal{N}[\phi(\boldsymbol{x};\hat{\theta})]\|^2, \tag{6}$$

are assigned based on the PDE residual of the PINN output. This method prioritizes points where the model's prediction deviates the most from satisfying the PDE. Note that in [35], different residual-based sampling approaches are referred to as RAR-D (iteratively adding new samples) and RAD (resampling the entire set). In our work, we use both adding and replacing strategies but refer to the method simply as RAR, focusing on the scoring of importance rather than the sampling process.

Grad-Dot [4]. Grad-Dot approximates PINNfluence by replacing the Hessian with an identity matrix, which yields

$$\mathcal{S}_{\text{grad-dot}}(\boldsymbol{x}) = \left|\nabla_\theta \mathcal{L}_{\text{test}}(\hat{\theta})^\top \nabla_\theta \mathcal{L}(\boldsymbol{x};\hat{\theta})\right|. \tag{7}$$

Derivatives of the PINN Output. To complete our studies on different scoring functions, we introduce two heuristically motivated gradient-based measures:

- The L^2 norm of the prediction gradient with respect to its input:

$$\mathcal{S}_{\text{output-grad}}(\boldsymbol{x}) = \left\|\nabla_{\boldsymbol{x}} \phi(\boldsymbol{x};\hat{\theta})\right\|_2. \tag{8}$$

In a recent study [6], an alternative scoring function is proposed based on the second derivative of the neural network's output with respect to its inputs. Similarly, we consider the gradients of the network $\nabla_{\boldsymbol{x}} \phi(\boldsymbol{x};\theta)$. Given that PINNs approximate the true solution with some accuracy, we hypothesize that sampling points in regions where the function exhibits high sensitivity to input perturbations may identify informative training locations.

- The L^2 norm of the loss gradient with respect to model parameters:

$$\mathcal{S}_{\text{loss-grad}}(\boldsymbol{x}) = \left\|\nabla_\theta \mathcal{L}(\boldsymbol{x};\hat{\theta})\right\|_2. \tag{9}$$

This metric captures how strongly a given training point influences model updates, with higher values indicating points that drive larger parameter adjustments during optimization. This is different from influence function-based scores, which assess the change in the test loss or potentially any other function of the PINN output.

3 Experiments

Model Setup. To compare the methods introduced in Sect. 2, we evaluate them on four different PDEs, namely the diffusion, Burgers', Allen-Cahn and wave equations. Their mathematical descriptions and selected hyperparameters,

Algorithm 1. Resampling for PINNs

Require: Initial PINN model $\phi(\boldsymbol{x};\theta)$, PDE $\mathcal{N}[u](\boldsymbol{x}) = 0$, initial training dataset $\mathcal{X}_{\text{train}}$, number of training epochs $T_{\text{tr}} \geq 0$, number of fine-tuning epochs $T_{\text{ft}} > 0$, number of candidate points N_{cand}, number of points to sample k, resampling method, perturbation method (add or replace).

1: **Pretrain** $\phi(\boldsymbol{x};\theta)$ on $\mathcal{X}_{\text{train}}$ for T_{tr} epochs (*optional*).
2: **Sample** candidate collocation points uniformly:

$$\mathcal{X}_{\text{cand}} \sim \mathcal{U}(\overline{\Omega}), \quad |\mathcal{X}_{\text{cand}}| = N_{\text{cand}}.$$

3: **Compute** importance scores $\mathcal{S}(\boldsymbol{x})$ for all $\boldsymbol{x} \in \mathcal{X}_{\text{cand}}$.
4: **Select** training points by sampling from a distribution over their scores Eq. (5).
5: **Perturb** training dataset (*choose one*):
   – **Add:** $\mathcal{X}\text{train} \leftarrow \mathcal{X}\text{train} \cup \mathcal{X}_{\text{new}}$
   – **Replace:** $\mathcal{X}_{\text{train}} \leftarrow \mathcal{X}_{\text{new}}$.
6: **Fine-tune** $\phi(\boldsymbol{x};\theta)$ on the updated $\mathcal{X}_{\text{train}}$ for T_{ft} epochs.
7: **Repeat** steps 2–7 until a stopping criterion is met.

---

including the architecture of the used fully connected neural networks, are provided in the Appendix A.1. We employ distinct numbers of hidden layers and neurons tailored to each specific problem, using tanh activations throughout all experiments. All boundary and initial conditions are enforced via hard constraints, enabling sampling exclusively from the open domain Ω. All models use the `Adam` optimizer [11] with a learning rate of 10^{-3}. To calculate PINN-fluence, we utilize a modified `ArnoldiInfluenceFunction` implementation [27] from `captum` [13].

Evaluation Protocol. For evaluation, we consider a ground truth dataset $\mathcal{D}_{\text{gt}} = \{(\boldsymbol{x}_m, u(\boldsymbol{x}_m)) \mid m = 1, \ldots, N_{\text{gt}}\}$ consisting of input-output pairs. In the case of the diffusion and wave equations, where the analytical solution u is known, we randomly sample $\boldsymbol{x}_m$ uniformly from Ω. In contrast, for the Allen-Cahn and Burgers' equations, the input points $\boldsymbol{x}_m$ are sampled from an equidistant grid over Ω, with $u(\boldsymbol{x}_m)$ corresponding to a numerically obtained solution [35]. To evaluate the accuracy of the PINN solution, we compute the L^2 relative error over $\mathcal{D}_{\text{gt}}$:

$$\sqrt{\frac{\sum_{m=1}^{N_{\text{gt}}} [\phi(\boldsymbol{x}_m;\theta) - u(\boldsymbol{x}_m)]^2}{\sum_{m=1}^{N_{\text{gt}}} u(\boldsymbol{x}_m)^2}}. \tag{10}$$

Resampling Strategies. For each PDE, we conduct two experiments, differing in the perturbation strategy specified in Algorithm 1: **Adding** new samples to the training data ($\mathcal{X}_{\text{train}} \leftarrow \mathcal{X}_{\text{train}} \cup \mathcal{X}_{\text{new}}$) or **Replacing** ($\mathcal{X}_{\text{train}} \leftarrow \mathcal{X}_{\text{new}}$) the entire training set with newly sampled data based on the different scoring functions. In order to obtain a comparative baseline, we also include randomly resampling data points in our experiments. The number of candidate points from which we add or replace is set to 10 000 across all experiments. We fine-tune for a total of 100 000 iterations and resample every 1 000 steps. In the additive setting, models are pretrained for 5 000 iterations with $\mathcal{X}_{\text{train}}$ consisting of points drawn from a Hammersley sequence [8] and we sample from the distribution (Eq. (5)) with $\alpha = 2$ and $c = 0$, while the replacement-based setting starts with randomly initialized parameters and we sample with $\alpha = 1$ and $c = 1$. Each setting is evaluated over 10 runs. The respective numbers of samples for each PDE and setting are listed in Table 1 and Table 2, respectively.

3.1 Results

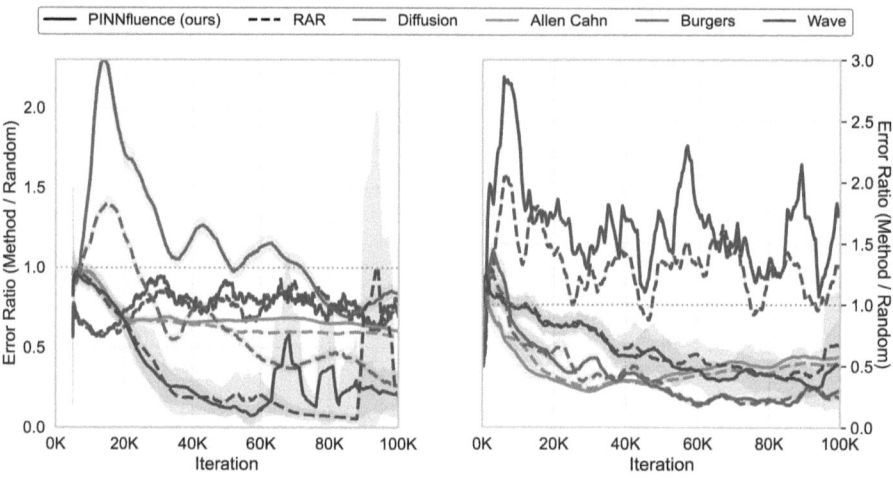

(a) Adding points: $\mathcal{X}_{\text{train}} \leftarrow \mathcal{X}_{\text{train}} \cup \mathcal{X}_{\text{new}}$ (b) Replacing points: $\mathcal{X}_{\text{train}} \leftarrow \mathcal{X}_{\text{new}}$

Fig. 1. Performance comparison between PINNfluence (*solid lines*) and RAR (*dashed lines*) resampling strategies across four PDEs (*different colors*), with results normalized to uniform random sampling. Lines represent the ratio of L^2 relative error (method to random sampling) averaged over 10 runs, with shaded regions indicating standard deviation. Lower values indicate better performance relative to random sampling. All curves are smoothed using a rolling average.

Figure 1 compares PINNfluence and RAR, relative to random sampling as a baseline. We omit the other methods here for clarity, since they generally underperform. Across all studied PDEs, these two methods display similar performance, with the exception of Burgers' equation in the addition setting, highlighting the usefulness of our XAI-driven approach.

Tables 1 and 2 summarize the relative errors for the addition- and replacement-based perturbation strategies, respectively. In both settings, for most PDEs, PINNfluence was competitive with RAR, whereas other methods lagged behind. Solely for the diffusion equation did all methods perform similarly, likely due to the problem's simplicity.

Table 1. Mean L^2 relative error (%) and standard deviation for sampling strategies when adding train points ($\mathcal{X}_{\text{train}} \leftarrow \mathcal{X}_{\text{train}} \cup \mathcal{X}_{\text{new}}$). The best model was chosen based on the iteration with lowest validation loss.

	Diffusion Eq.	Allen-Cahn Eq.	Burgers' Eq.	Wave Eq.
$|\mathcal{X}_{\text{train}}|$	30	1000	1000	1000
$|\mathcal{X}_{\text{new}}|$	1	10	10	10
PINNfluence (ours)	0.01 ± 0.004	2.0 ± 0.6	3.7 ± 2.2	0.7 ± 0.3
RAR	0.01 ± 0.003	1.8 ± 0.4	1.4 ± 0.9	0.7 ± 0.6
Grad-Dot	0.02 ± 0.007	4.1 ± 0.8	5.3 ± 3.4	0.9 ± 0.3
$||\nabla_x u||_2$	0.03 ± 0.011	4.2 ± 1.0	8.2 ± 7.5	14.9 ± 13.3
$||\nabla_\theta \mathcal{L}||_2$	0.02 ± 0.005	3.7 ± 0.4	5.7 ± 2.5	0.8 ± 0.2
Random	0.02 ± 0.006	3.4 ± 0.8	8.0 ± 4.6	29.7 ± 14.5

Table 2. Mean L^2 relative error (%) and standard deviation for sampling strategies when replacing the whole training set ($\mathcal{X}_{\text{train}} \leftarrow \mathcal{X}_{\text{new}}$). The best model was chosen based on the iteration with lowest validation loss.

	Diffusion Eq.	Allen-Cahn Eq.	Burgers' Eq.	Wave Eq.
$|\mathcal{X}_{\text{train}}|$	30	1000	1000	1000
PINNfluence (ours)	0.06 ± 0.02	3.0 ± 0.3	1.9 ± 0.8	8.1 ± 7.8
RAR	0.06 ± 0.02	2.8 ± 0.4	2.0 ± 1.4	11.1 ± 8.8
Grad-Dot	0.05 ± 0.01	4.5 ± 0.9	2.0 ± 0.7	17.7 ± 13.1
$||\nabla_x u||_2$	0.05 ± 0.01	13.0 ± 5.0	3.1 ± 1.2	46.1 ± 5.6
$||\nabla_\theta \mathcal{L}||_2$	0.06 ± 0.02	4.5 ± 0.6	1.5 ± 0.7	16.0 ± 9.6
Random	0.05 ± 0.02	5.3 ± 1.7	9.6 ± 9.9	44.3 ± 1.7

4 Discussion

We hypothesized that sampling training points based on their influence via an XAI-based training data attribution method would enhance the performance of PINNs. Our experimental results demonstrate that PINNfluence is able to accurately detect influential samples and improve prediction accuracy through fine-tuning, thereby validating the applicability of TDA methods in PINNs. Using PINNfluence as a scoring function, we matched the performance of RAR and outperformed the other investigated approaches. This constitutes the first time, to our knowledge, that training data attribution methods from explainable AI have been applied to guide the training and improve the accuracy of physics-informed neural networks. Furthermore, compared to another influence-based method, Grad-Dot, the additional Hessian computation in PINNfluence generally proved beneficial to the performance.

The primary limitation of our resampling approach is its computational cost. Residual-based resampling methods [17,35] evaluate the loss directly, requiring only a single forward pass through the PINN, with the exception of applying the PDE operator. The computation of PINNfluence as given in Eq. (3) presupposes the approximation of the Hessian of the loss function, the gradients of the loss of the test set and the candidate point to be added. All of these operations require (repeated) backward-passes through the network and thus require considerably more computational effort – in addition to computing their inner product. Thus, while PINNfluence provides a more theoretically motivated selection of training points, its scalability remains a challenge. Further, our experiments were limited to a small set of forward problems, restricting generalizability. We also focused solely on hard-constrained problems, omitting soft constraints. Finally, we excluded L-BFGS, a common second-order optimizer in PINN training, to reduce hyperparameters and maintain focus on point selection.

5 Conclusions

In this work, we have explored the application of influence function-based resampling in the training of PINNs, demonstrating that our XAI-guided PINNfluence method effectively identifies influential training points. Notably, its performance matches that of residual-based adaptive refinement (RAR). This showcases the potential of XAI-driven techniques in scientific machine learning, as such tailored sampling strategies can help address challenges in PINN training and enhance performance. Future work could focus on exploring more efficient computations of influence functions to enhance their practicality. Additionally, combining influence functions with the neural tangent kernel framework presents itself as a promising direction, as such approaches have successfully been applied to improve PINN performance [24,33].

Acknowledgments. This work was supported by the Fraunhofer Internal Programs under Grant No. PREPARE 40-08394.

Disclosure of Interests. The authors declare that they have no competing interests.

Code Availability. The code is available at https://github.com/aleks-krasowski/PINNfluence_resampling.

A Appendix

A.1 Partial Differential Equations

We consider the following PDEs with corresponding initial and boundary conditions, as well as the neural network architectures (note that the input and output dimensions depend on the PDE) used for each case:

– **Burgers'**: $\frac{\partial u}{\partial t} + u\frac{\partial u}{\partial x} = \nu\frac{\partial^2 u}{\partial x^2}$, $\nu = \frac{\pi}{100}$, with $u(x,0) = -\sin(\pi x)$ and $u(-1,t) = u(1,t) = 0$. Neural network: 3 hidden layers with 32 neurons each.

- **Allen-Cahn:** $\frac{\partial u}{\partial t} = D\frac{\partial^2 u}{\partial x^2} + 5(u - u^3)$, with $u(x,0) = x^2\cos(\pi x)$ and $u(-1,t) = u(1,t) = -1$. Neural network: 3 hidden layers with 64 neurons each.
- **Wave:** $\frac{\partial^2 u}{\partial t^2} - 4\frac{\partial^2 u}{\partial x^2} = 0$, with $u(x,0) = \sin(\pi x) + \frac{1}{2}\sin(4\pi x)$, $\frac{\partial u}{\partial t}(x,0) = 0$, and $u(0,t) = u(1,t) = 0$. Neural network: 5 hidden layers with 100 neurons each.
- **Diffusion:** $\frac{\partial u}{\partial t} = \frac{\partial^2 u}{\partial x^2} + e^{-t}(-\sin(\pi x) + \pi^2\sin(\pi x))$, with $u(x,0) = \sin(\pi x)$ and $u(-1,t) = u(1,t) = 0$. Neural network: 3 hidden layers with 32 neurons each.

References

1. Abramson, J., Adler, J., Dunger, J., Evans, R., et al.: Accurate structure prediction of biomolecular interactions with AlphaFold 3. Nature **630**(8016), 493–500 (2024)
2. Beltrán-Pulido, A., Bilionis, I., Aliprantis, D.: Physics-informed neural networks for solving parametric magnetostatic problems. IEEE Trans. Energy Convers. **37**(4), 2678–2689 (2022)
3. Braun, J., Kornreich, M., Park, J., Pawar, J., et al.: Influence based re-weighing for labeling noise in medical imaging. In: 2022 IEEE 19th International Symposium on Biomedical Imaging (ISBI), pp. 1–5 (2022)
4. Charpiat, G., Girard, N., Felardos, L., Tarabalka, Y.: Input similarity from the neural network perspective. In: Advances in Neural Information Processing Systems, vol. 32. Curran Associates, Inc. (2019)
5. Daw, A., Bu, J., Wang, S., Perdikaris, P. et al.: Mitigating propagation failures in physics-informed neural networks using retain-resample-release (R3) sampling. In: Proceedings of the 40th International Conference on Machine Learning, pp. 7264–7302. PMLR (2023)
6. Florido, J., Wang, H., Khan, A., Jimack, P.K.: Investigating guiding information for adaptive collocation point sampling in PINNs. In: Franco, L., de Mulatier, C., Paszynski, M., Krzhizhanovskaya, V.V., et al. (eds.) Computational Science – ICCS 2024, pp. 323–337. Springer Nature Switzerland, Cham (2024). https://doi.org/10.1007/978-3-031-63759-9_36
7. Gao, W., Wang, C.: Active learning based sampling for high-dimensional nonlinear partial differential equations. J. Comput. Phys. **475**, 111848 (2023)
8. Hammersley, J.M., Handscomb, D.C.: Monte Carlo Methods. Springer, Netherlands, Dordrecht (1964). https://doi.org/10.1007/978-981-13-2971-5
9. Hammoudeh, Z., Lowd, D.: Training data influence analysis and estimation: a survey. Mach. Learn. **113**(5), 2351–2403 (2024)
10. Hao, Z., Liu, S., Zhang, Y., Ying, C., et al.: Physics-informed machine learning: a survey on problems, methods and applications (2023). arXiv:2211.08064 [cs]
11. Kingma, D.P., Ba, J.: Adam: a method for stochastic optimization (2017). arXiv:1412.6980 [cs]
12. Koh, P.W., Liang, P.: Understanding black-box predictions via influence functions (2017). arXiv:1703.04730 [cs, stat]
13. Kokhlikyan, N., Miglani, V., Martin, M., Wang, E., et al.: Captum: a unified and generic model interpretability library for PyTorch (2020)
14. Lau, G.K.R., Hemachandra, A., Ng, S.K., Low, B.K.H.: PINNACLE: PINN Adaptive ColLocation and Experimental points selection (2024). arXiv:2404.07662

15. Liu, Q., Chu, M., Thuerey, N.: ConFIG: towards conflict-free training of physics informed neural networks (2025). arXiv:2408.11104 [cs]
16. Liu, Y., Chen, L., Ding, J.: Grad-RAR: an adaptive sampling method based on residual gradient for physical-informed neural networks. In: 2022 International Conference on Automation, Robotics and Computer Engineering (ICARCE), pp. 1–5 (2022)
17. Lu, L., Meng, X., Mao, Z., Karniadakis, G.E.: DeepXDE: a deep learning library for solving differential equations. SIAM Rev. **63**(1), 208–228 (2021)
18. Lu, L., Pestourie, R., Yao, W., Wang, Z., et al.: Physics-informed neural networks with hard constraints for inverse design. SIAM J. Sci. Comput. **43**(6), B1105–B1132 (2021)
19. Nabian, M.A., Gladstone, R.J., Meidani, H.: Efficient training of physics-informed neural networks via importance sampling. Comput.-Aid. Civil Infrastruct. Eng. **36**(8), 962–977 (2021)
20. Naujoks, J.R., Krasowski, A., Weckbecker, M., Wiegand, T., et al.: PINNfluence: influence functions for physics-informed neural networks (2024). arXiv:2409.08958 [cs]
21. Pruthi, G., Liu, F., Kale, S., Sundararajan, M.: Estimating training data influence by tracing gradient descent. In: Advances in Neural Information Processing Systems, vol. 33, pp. 19920–19930. Curran Associates, Inc. (2020)
22. Raissi, M., Perdikaris, P., Karniadakis, G.E.: Physics-informed neural networks: a deep learning framework for solving forward and inverse problems involving nonlinear partial differential equations. J. Comput. Phys. **378**, 686–707 (2019)
23. Rasht-Behesht, M., Huber, C., Shukla, K., Karniadakis, G.E.: Physics-Informed Neural Networks (PINNs) for wave propagation and full waveform inversions. J. Geophys. Res. Solid Earth **127**(5), e2021JB023120 (2022)
24. Rathore, P., Lei, W., Frangella, Z., Lu, L. et al.: Challenges in Training PINNs: a loss landscape perspective (2024)
25. Rohrhofer, F.M., Posch, S., Gößnitzer, C., Geiger, B.C.: On the role of fixed points of dynamical systems in training physics-informed neural networks (2023). arXiv:2203.13648 [cs]
26. Sahli Costabal, F., Yang, Y., Perdikaris, P., Hurtado, D.E., et al.: Physics-informed neural networks for cardiac activation mapping. Front. Phys. **8** (2020)
27. Schioppa, A., Zablotskaia, P., Vilar, D., Sokolov, A.: Scaling up influence functions (2021). arXiv:2112.03052 [cs]
28. Schütt, K.T., Sauceda, H.E., Kindermans, P.J., Tkatchenko, A., et al.: SchNet - a deep learning architecture for molecules and materials. J. Chem. Phys. **148**(24), 241722 (2018)
29. Sharma, P., Chung, W.T., Akoush, B., Ihme, M.: A review of physics-informed machine learning in fluid mechanics. Energies **16**(5), 2343 (2023)
30. Wang, S., Sankaran, S., Perdikaris, P.: Respecting causality for training physics-informed neural networks. Comput. Methods Appl. Mech. Eng. **421**, 116813 (2024)
31. Wang, S., Sankaran, S., Wang, H., Perdikaris, P.: An expert's guide to training physics-informed neural networks (2023). arXiv:2308.08468 [physics]
32. Wang, S., Teng, Y., Perdikaris, P.: Understanding and mitigating gradient pathologies in physics-informed neural networks (2020). arXiv:2001.04536 [cs, math, stat]
33. Wang, S., Yu, X., Perdikaris, P.: When and why PINNs fail to train: a neural tangent kernel perspective. J. Comput. Phys. **449**, 110768 (2022)
34. Wei, D., Padhi, I., Ghosh, S., Dhurandhar, A., et al.: Final-model-only data attribution with a unifying view of gradient-based methods (2024). arXiv:2412.03906 [cs]

35. Wu, C., Zhu, M., Tan, Q., Kartha, Y., et al.: A comprehensive study of non-adaptive and residual-based adaptive sampling for physics-informed neural networks. Comput. Methods Appl. Mech. Eng. **403**, 115671 (2023)
36. Wu, H., Ma, Y., Zhou, H., Weng, H., et al.: ProPINN: demystifying propagation failures in physics-informed neural networks (2025). arXiv:2502.00803 [cs]

Open Access This chapter is licensed under the terms of the Creative Commons Attribution 4.0 International License (http://creativecommons.org/licenses/by/4.0/), which permits use, sharing, adaptation, distribution and reproduction in any medium or format, as long as you give appropriate credit to the original author(s) and the source, provide a link to the Creative Commons license and indicate if changes were made.

The images or other third party material in this chapter are included in the chapter's Creative Commons license, unless indicated otherwise in a credit line to the material. If material is not included in the chapter's Creative Commons license and your intended use is not permitted by statutory regulation or exceeds the permitted use, you will need to obtain permission directly from the copyright holder.

Safe and Efficient Social Navigation Through Explainable Safety Regions Based on Topological Features

Victor Toscano-Duran[1](✉)[iD], Sara Narteni[2][iD], Alberto Carlevaro[2][iD], Jérôme Guzzi[3][iD], Rocio Gonzalez-Diaz[1][iD], and Maurizio Mongelli[2][iD]

[1] Department of Applied Mathematics I, University of Seville, Seville, Spain
{vtoscano,rogodi}@us.es
[2] CNR-IEIIT, Corso F.M. Perrone 24, 16152 Genoa, Italy
{sara.narteni,albertocarlevaro,maurizio.mongelli}@cnr.it
[3] SUPSI, IDSIA, Lugano, Switzerland
jerome.guzzi@supsi.ch

Abstract. The recent adoption of artificial intelligence (AI) in robotics has driven the development of algorithms that enable autonomous systems to adapt to complex social environments. In particular, safe and efficient social navigation is a key challenge, requiring AI not only to avoid collisions and deadlocks but also to interact intuitively and predictably with its surroundings. To date, methods based on probabilistic models and the generation of conformal safety regions have shown promising results in defining safety regions with a controlled margin of error, primarily relying on classification approaches and explicit rules to describe collision-free navigation conditions.

This work extends the existing perspective by investigating how topological features can contribute to the creation of explainable safety regions in social navigation scenarios, enabling the classification and characterization of different simulation behaviors. Rather than relying on behaviors parameters to generate safety regions, we leverage topological features through topological data analysis. We first utilize global rule-based classification to provide interpretable characterizations of different simulation behaviors, distinguishing between safe (free of collisions) and unsafe scenarios based on topological properties. Next, we define safety regions, S_ε, representing zones in the topological feature space where collisions are avoided with a maximum classification error of ε. These regions are constructed using adjustable SVM classifiers and order statistics, ensuring a robust and scalable decision boundary. To enhance interpretability, we extract local rules from these safety regions, ensuring that the decision-making process remains transparent and comprehensible.

Initially, we generate safety regions that separate simulations with and without collisions, achieving higher accuracy than methods that do not incorporate topological features. This approach also provides a deeper and more intuitive understanding of robot interactions within a navigable space. We then extend our methodology to design safety regions that ensure efficient simulations (i.e., free of deadlocks). Finally, we integrate both aspects to obtain comprehensive safety regions that guarantee both collision-free and deadlock-free simulations, defining an overall compliant simulation space.

Keywords: Safe navigation · Explainable artificial intelligence · Safety regions · Topological data analysis · Interpretability

1 Introduction

Nowadays, machine learning (ML) and deep learning (DL) play a fundamental role in a wide range of fields [32], with robotics standing out as a domain where autonomous decision-making finds fertile ground. Artificial intelligence (AI) supports a wide range of robotics applications [39], from object detection and recognition to healthcare, manufacturing, and agriculture. One of the most impactful applications of AI in robotics is assistive robotics, where social robots are designed to support everyday tasks, ensuring safe indoor and outdoor navigation while interacting effectively with humans and their surroundings.

However, as autonomous systems become more prevalent in social spaces, ensuring their safety and reliability remains a critical challenge [22]. AI models must operate as intended without harming users or the surrounding environment. To address this, many researchers in safe and explainable AI (XAI) [23] have focused on simulation and validation techniques to assess model reliability.

In particular, topological data analysis (TDA) has emerged as a promising tool in this context, offering new ways to characterize interactions and structures within the navigation space [13,19]. Within TDA, persistent entropy [36] stands out for its ability to efficiently track the evolution of topological features over time, and can be a robust measure for defining safe and efficient navigation regions and analyzing robot-agent interactions.

In this work, we address a simulated social navigation scenario inspired by human movement, where robots navigate between pairs of opposing targets, facing potential risks of collision and deadlock. These challenges compromise both the safety and efficiency of mobile navigation. To tackle this issue, we leverage topological features, specifically from persistent entropy, as input data to classify and characterize different simulation behaviors.

In a fleet of robots, topological features provide a quantifiable representation of the spatial structures that emerge during navigation, capturing patterns such as clustering, dispersion, and movement coordination. This allows us to systematically distinguish between safe (collision-free) and unsafe scenarios. By utilizing global rule-based classification, adjustable SVM classifiers, and order statistics, we construct safety regions that not only prevent collisions but also enhance navigation efficiency by avoiding deadlocks. Finally, we integrate these aspects to define a compliant navigation space, ensuring both collision-free and deadlock-free simulations. This approach supports the development of robust and explainable AI models, where topological insights can enhance transparency and performance in defining safe (without collisions), efficient (without deadlocks), and compliant (free of collisions and deadlocks) navigation strategies.

The remainder of the article is organized as follows: first, in Sect. 2, we present the state of the art and existing literature in the field. Section 3 introduces the preliminary concepts relevant to this study, including topology, confidence regions, and rule-based models, as well as the simulation-based robotic navigation environment. Section 4 details the proposed methodology for constructing safety regions regarding the topological feature space. Section 5 provides a comprehensive explanation of the experiments conducted, along with the results obtained. Finally, conclusions and future work are discussed in Sect. 6.

2 Related Work

The integration of machine learning (ML) and deep learning (DL) into robotics [28] has accelerated the capabilities of autonomous systems across various fields. Particularly within assistive and social robotics, the objective has evolved from simple navigation to enabling safe and interpretable decision-making around people. Early works on ML for robotics primarily focused on object detection and recognition [26,31], yet more recent efforts leverage DL algorithms to enhance contextual understanding and adaptive navigation. These advancements have led to behavioral AI models capable of dynamically adjusting to complex, changing environments, such as crowded indoor spaces while ensuring user safety.

The concept of explainable AI (XAI) [10,23,37] has emerged as a necessary framework to improve AI transparency and trustworthiness [21], particularly in safety-critical applications like social robotics. In this context, several studies propose the use of simulation and validation techniques to evaluate ML models before deployment in real-world scenarios, emphasizing safety and reliability in decision-making [1,2]. Additionally, explainability and interpretability enhance user trust, as evidenced in approaches like rule-based reinforcement learning and fuzzy logic systems for robotic risk mitigation, which incorporate predefined standards and probabilistic safety regions to guide exploration while minimizing risk and redundant actions [5,29].

To address this, topological data analysis (TDA) provides novel tools for examining complex data structures, making it possible to extract and interpret information about the underlying structure of navigational spaces. TDA techniques, such as persistent homology [7,11,17], have been applied to analyze spatial connectivity and the evolving structures within navigation environments [12,18,30], offering a quantifiable approach to characterize spatial and behavioral patterns over time. Persistent entropy [8], a summarization of persistent homology, quantifies the complexity of topological features over time, and is especially useful in scenarios where robots may need to navigate shared spaces while avoiding collisions and deadlocks to ensure safe and efficient navigations.

Moreover, persistent entropy has demonstrated its effectiveness in a variety of other applications such as characterizing idiotypic immune networks [35], analyzing similarities in piecewise linear functions and time series [36], and separating topological features from noise in Vietoris-Rips complexes [3]. These successful applications underscore its versatility and potential to provide robust insights across diverse domains. Due to its simplicity (providing a single scalar value at each time step making it computationally efficient while still capturing essential topological features), interpretability, stability [4], and proven success in other applications, as previously mentioned, make it an ideal choice for our work.

To the best of our knowledge, there are no previous works that utilize TDA-based methods specifically for defining safety regions in robot navigation. We have reviewed the state of the art and found that TDA has indeed been explored in various aspects of robot navigation, particularly for characterizing interactions and spatial structures (e.g., [12, 13, 18, 19, 30]). However, none of these works explicitly address the definition of safety regions using TDA.

The integration of TDA into the analysis of robotic systems marks a step forward in developing explainable models for safe navigation. This approach allows us to detect, quantify, and analyze safety regions, focusing on spatial structures formed by robots in motion [24]. By combining TDA with simulated environments, we contribute to the growing field of XAI for robotics by facilitating a more interpretable approach to parameter tuning within navigation models. This directly contributes to improving safety and reliability in socially aware robotic systems, offering the potential for broader applications in real-world, and human-centric environments [16].

3 Background

This section presents all preliminary concepts that are used throughout the paper. It begins by introducing topological foundations (Sect. 3.1), including an exploration of topological spaces and simplicial complexes as fundamental structures. Persistent homology and persistent entropy are also discussed, as they provide insights into the geometry and connectivity of data. Subsequently, the focus shifts to confidence regions (Sect. 3.2), defining safety regions based on probabilistic scaling and conformal prediction methods. These techniques ensure robust predictions with statistical guarantees. It continues explaining rule-based models (Sect. 3.3), emphasizing interpretability through global and local rule-extraction techniques, such as Anchors. However, these techniques often struggle to capture the underlying geometric and topological structure of data, limiting their ability to generalize across complex decision boundaries. To address this, the proposed methodology in Sect. 4 leverages topological features as inputs to enhance model interpretability and robustness. This subsection also highlights evaluation metrics like coverage and error for assessing rule-based classifiers' performance. To apply these concepts, as well as the methodology proposed in this paper, which is explained in Sect. 4, to the field of robotic navigation, a social robotics navigation simulator is employed, called Navground (described in Sect. 3.4). This simulator allows for testing navigation algorithms within multi-agent systems and evaluating their performance in diverse scenarios.

3.1 Topology Background

Topology and Topological Space. A topological space is a powerful mathematical concept for describing the connectivity of a space. Informally, a topological space is a set of points, each of them equipped with the notion of neighbourhood.

One way to represent a topological space is by decomposing it into simple pieces such that their common intersections are lower-dimensional pieces of the same kind. In this paper, we use simplicial complexes as the data structure to represent topological spaces.

Simplicial Complex. An *abstract simplicial complex* $\mathcal{K}$ is given by:

- A set V of 0-simplices (also called vertices);
- For each $k \geq 1$, a set of k-simplices $\sigma = \{v_0, v_1, \ldots, v_k\}$, where $v_i \in V$;
- Each k-simplex has $k + 1$ faces obtained by removing one of the vertices;
- If σ belongs to $\mathcal{K}$, then all the faces of σ must belong to $\mathcal{K}$.

A *simplicial complex* K is a geometric realization of an abstract simplicial complex $\mathcal{K}$ [20]. It is constructed as a nested family of simplices, where each simplex is a generalization of geometric shapes of various dimensions. Specifically, a 0-simplex corresponds to a point in a given Euclidean space $\mathbb{R}^n$, a 1-simplex represents an edge, a 2-simplex is a filled triangle, a 3-simplex is a filled tetrahedron, and so on. This hierarchical structure allows the simplicial complex to model higher-dimensional relationships between points in a mathematically rigorous way.

Homology groups are algebraic structures that describe features of a topological space $\mathcal{C}$. The k-th Betti number represents the rank of the k-dimensional homology group. Informally, for a fixed k, the k-th Betti number β_k counts the number of k-dimensional holes characterizing $\mathcal{C}$: β_0 is the number of connected components, β_1 counts the number of holes in $2D$ or tunnels in $3D$[1], β_2 can be thought of as the number of voids in geometric solids. In this work, we use simplicial homology, which consists of computing homology groups of simplicial complexes.

See [17,27] for an introduction to algebraic topology.

Persistent Homology. Topological data analysis, particularly persistent homology, has emerged as a valuable approach for studying the geometry and connectivity of datasets that evolve over time or space [24]. The primary objective of employing topological data analysis tools, like persistent homology and persistent entropy, in the context of fleet behavior modeling is to achieve a more nuanced understanding of system dynamics.

Persistent homology is a method for computing k-dimensional holes at different spatial resolutions. In this section, we briefly explain how this method works. For a more formal description, we refer the reader to [11].

---
[1] dD refers to the d - dimensional space $\mathbb{R}^d$.

In order to compute persistent homology, we need a nested sequence of increasing subcomplexes. More formally, a *filtered simplicial complex* or, for short, a *filtration* is a collection of subcomplexes $\{K(t) \mid t \in \mathbb{R}\}$ of a simplicial complex K such that $K(t) \subseteq K(s)$ for $t < s$ and there exists $t_{\max} \in \mathbb{R}$ such that $K(t_{\max}) = K$. The *filtration time* (or filter value) of a simplex $\sigma \in K$ is the smallest t such that $\sigma \in K(t)$. An example of a filtered simplicial complex is depicted in Fig. 1.

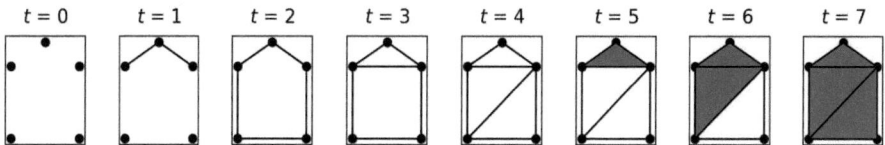

Fig. 1. A filtration for $t = 0, 1, 2, 3, 4, 5, 6, 7$ (from left to right).

Persistent homology describes how the homology of K changes along a filtration $\{K(t) \mid t \in \mathbb{R}\}$. A k-dimensional *Betti interval*, with endpoints $[t_{\text{start}}, t_{\text{end}})$, corresponds to a k-dimensional hole that appears at filtration time t_{start} and remains until time t_{end}.

To visualize the persistence of topological features, persistence diagrams are commonly used. **Persistence diagrams** are visual representations used in the study of persistent homology to illustrate the birth and death of topological features (such as connected components, loops, and voids) as the scale of observation changes. It consists in a set of points $(b_i, d_i) \in \mathbb{R}^2$ (with $b_i \leq d_i$). Each point represents the birth (b_i) and death (d_i) of a topological feature in a filtered space. Instead of points, we sometimes draw intervals representing the birth and death times of homology classes. This method, also known as **persistence barcodes** [14], provides an alternative visualization of the same information contained in persistence diagrams, plotting this data in bars. Each bar in the barcode corresponds to a topological feature and is represented by an interval $[b_i, d_i)$. An illustrative example of a persistence diagram and a persistence barcode is in Fig. 2.

Persistent Entropy. In order to measure how much the construction of a filtered simplicial complex is ordered, an entropy measure, called persistent entropy, was defined in [36]. A precursor of this definition was given in [8] to measure how different bars of a persistence barcode are in length. In other words, persistent entropy is a measure of the complexity of a topological space based on its persistence diagram.

Given a filtered simplicial complex $\{K(t) : t \in \mathbb{R}\}$, and the corresponding persistence diagram $D = \{(b_i, d_i) : i \in I\}$, where $b_i \leq d_i$ for all $i \in I$, and I is the index set that identifies the pairs (b_i, d_i) in D. As commented previously, each pair (b_i, d_i) corresponds to a topological feature that "appears" at time b_i (birth)

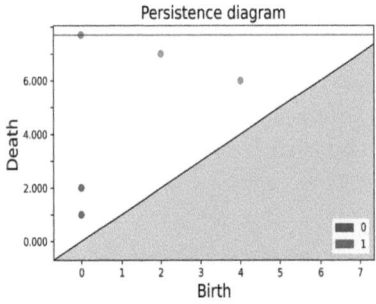
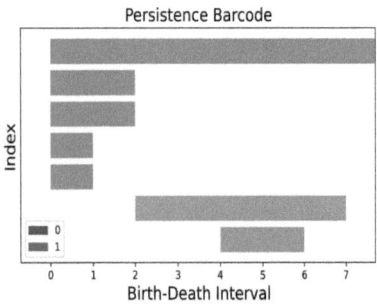

(a) Persistence diagram for filtration in Fig.1.

(b) Persistence barcodes for 0-dim and 1-dim for filtration in Fig.1.

Fig. 2. Persistence diagram and persistence barcode example.

and "disappears" at time d_i (death) as the filtration progresses. The *persistent entropy* PE of a filtered simplicial complex K is calculated as follows:

$$\text{PE} = -\sum_{i \in I} p_i \ln p_i \qquad (1)$$

where $p_i = \frac{\ell_i}{L}$, $\ell_i = d_i - b_i$, and $L = \sum_{i \in I} \ell_i$.

It is important to note that this formulation considers only the duration ℓ_i of each topological feature (bar), rather than its starting time b_i. This is because persistent entropy aims to capture the distribution of topological feature lifetimes rather than their birth times. Ignoring starting times ensures that the measure remains invariant under time shifts in the filtration, making it more robust for comparing different persistence barcodes. In particular, we focus on dimension 0, which is characterized by the fact that all features in this dimension are born at the same instant but have different durations, meaning some persist longer than others.

The maximum persistent entropy corresponds to the situation in which all the intervals in the barcode are of equal length. In that case, $\text{PE} = \ln n$, where n is the number of elements of I (i.e., the number of bars in the persistence diagram D). In contrast, the value of the persistent entropy decreases as more intervals of different lengths are present. A potential point of confusion arises because persistent entropy does not measure the entropy of the distribution of bar lengths directly. Instead, it measures the entropy of the probability distribution induced by the relative contributions of each bar to the total barcode length. If all bars had the same length, their contributions would be equal, maximizing entropy. Conversely, when some bars dominate the total length, entropy decreases. Thus, persistent entropy should be interpreted as the entropy of the distribution of bar indices weighted by their respective lifetimes, rather than the entropy of the length distribution itself.

For example, for the persistence barcode of dimension 0 in Fig. 2b, we have 5 bars (red bars correspond to 0 dimension topological features) with the following lengths l_i: $1, 1, 2, 2, 8$, obtaining a total length L of 14. Thus, the probabilities (p_i) in this case are: $\frac{1}{14}, \frac{1}{14}, \frac{2}{14}, \frac{2}{14}$, and $\frac{8}{14}$, resulting in a persistent entropy of 1.25.

The stability insights derived from persistence diagrams [9] and persistent entropy [4,36] offer a solid foundation for measuring the stability of topological features in response to minor changes. In particular, they guarantee that small perturbations in the input lead to short bars in the persistence barcode and result in minimal, bounded shifts in the persistent entropy. This property is especially useful in contexts like robot navigation, where slight variations in the robot's position—such as those occurring between two time instances with minimal displacement—can otherwise lead to significant uncertainties in the system's analysis.

3.2 Background on Confidence Regions

Here, the concept of *probabilistic safety region* is introduced, which we define as the subset of the input space where probabilistic guarantees for the prediction of a target (safe) class are provided. This approach begins with a discussion of adjustable classifiers, a specialized class of classifiers whose boundaries can be adjusted by a scalar parameter. This adjustability facilitates the construction of safety regions that offer reliability in classification by adjusting boundaries to meet specific performance metrics, such as minimizing false positives.

Following this, we integrate adjustable classifiers with two statistical approaches: probabilistic scaling and conformal prediction. These methods construct the desired safety regions with probabilistic assurances, which can be applied to machine learning classifiers without specific assumptions on the underlying data distribution.

Adjustable Classifiers. Consider an input space $X \subseteq \mathbb{R}^d$ and an output space $Y = \{-1, +1\}$, where a binary adjustable classifier is defined as:

$$\phi_\theta(x, \rho) = \begin{cases} +1, & \text{if } f_\theta(x, \rho) < 0, \\ -1, & \text{otherwise.} \end{cases} \quad (2)$$

Here, $f_\theta : X \times \mathbb{R} \to \mathbb{R}$ is the classifier predictor. The function $f_\theta(x, \rho)$ is dependent on tunable hyperparameters θ and an adjustable scalar ρ, which shifts the classification boundary, allowing for control over the classifier's performance, such as adjusting the false positive rate. Any classifier, $\hat{f}(x)$, can be made adjustable by adding ρ as an offset: $f_\theta(x, \rho) = \hat{f}_\theta(x) + \rho$. A Support Vector Machine (SVM) classifier can thus be adapted as $f_\theta(x, \rho) = w^T \varphi(x) - b + \rho$, where w is the vector of the learned weights, φ is a feature map and b is the offset.

For each point x, we define $\bar{\rho}(x)$ as the ρ value where x is on the decision boundary, i.e., $f_\theta(x, \bar{\rho}(x)) = 0$. This framework enables defining the ρ-safe set:

$$S(\rho) = \{x \in X : f_\theta(x, \rho) < 0\}, \quad (3)$$

which is the region classified as safe ($+1$). However, this set alone does not ensure a probabilistic guarantee, only that the classifier predicts $+1$ within this region. To obtain a probabilistic safety region S_ϵ that satisfies $P(y = -1|x \in S_\epsilon) \leq \epsilon$ with confidence $1 - \delta$, techniques from the field of order statistics can be used, such as probabilistic scaling and conformal prediction.

Probabilistic Scaling. Probabilistic scaling (SP) constructs safety regions based on the order statistics of the calibration dataset $Z_c = \{(x_i, y_i)\}_{i=1}^{n_c} \subset X \times Y$. We define the generalized maximum $\max_{(r)}(\Gamma)$ for a set $\Gamma = \{\gamma_i\}_{i=1}^n \in \mathbb{R}^n$ as the r-th largest value, ensuring no more than $r - 1$ elements of Γ exceed $\max_{(r)}(\Gamma)$. Assuming a continuous and monotonically increasing $f_\theta(x, \rho)$ on ρ, probabilistic scaling yields a ρ_ϵ such that:

$$S_\epsilon = S(\rho_\epsilon), \tag{4}$$

where ρ_ϵ is computed to satisfy $P(y = -1|x \in S_\epsilon) \leq \epsilon$ with probability $1 - \delta$. Details and assumptions for this method are provided in [5].

Conformal Prediction. Conformal prediction (CP), as developed in [38], provides a post-hoc assessment of classification conformity. Using a score function $s : X \times Y \to \mathbb{R}$, such as $s(x, \hat{y}) = -\hat{y}\bar{\rho}(x)$, that encodes the agreement between a sample x and a candidate label $\hat{y}$, CP defines a prediction region $C_\epsilon(x)$:

$$C_\epsilon(x) = \{\hat{y} \in \{-1, +1\} : s(x, \hat{y}) \leq s_\epsilon\}, \tag{5}$$

ensuring marginal coverage $P(\hat{y} \in C_\epsilon(x)) \geq 1 - \epsilon$. From this, the conformal safety region Σ_ϵ for input x with class $+1$ can be derived, i.e.:

$$\Sigma_\varepsilon = \{x \in X : s(x, +1) \leq s_\varepsilon,\ s(x, -1) > s_\varepsilon\}, \tag{6}$$

which is such that $S_\epsilon \subseteq \Sigma_\epsilon$. In [6] is shown that if $s_\epsilon \leq 0$ then $S_\epsilon = \Sigma_\epsilon$, achieving the desired confidence region. Details about conformal safety region (CSR) are provided in [6].

In the following, we will denote the safety region S_ε using the two methods as S_ε^{PS} for the probabilistic scaling method and S_ε^{CP} for the conformal prediction method.

3.3 Rule-Based Models Background

Rule-based classifiers are machine learning models that provide outputs as sets of decision rules (rulesets), offering interpretability [25,34]. Different techniques for rule-based classification are typically grouped by their scope, based on whether they aim at providing explanations globally valid on the whole dataset, or locally on specific instances [23].

Global Rule-Based Classifiers. In this kind of approach, the model learns a set of rules that represent the entire logic of the dataset, making it suitable for application to any data sample. The rules are "native" as they arise directly from the learning process without needing any intermediary steps.

Formally, a rule-based classifier trained on a dataset $T = \{(x_j, y_j)\}_{j=1}^{N} \in X \times Y$, where $x_j \in \mathbb{R}^d$ and $y_j \in \{-1, +1\}$, generates a ruleset $\mathcal{R} = \{r_k\}_{k=1}^{M}$. Each rule r_k has a premise, or antecedent, expressed as a conjunction of conditions:

$$\text{premise}(r_k) = \bigwedge_{i=1_k}^{N_k} c_{ik},$$

where each condition c_{ik} specifies an interval on the input features, either bounded, left-bounded, or right-bounded. The rule's consequence specifies the target class $\hat{y}_k \in \{-1, +1\}$ associated with the premise.

Local Rule Extraction via Anchors. Anchors is a model-agnostic local rule extraction technique that generates high-precision rules for explaining individual predictions of any black-box classifier. While locally faithful, these rules also hold in a neighborhood (or perturbation space) of the instance being explained. An anchor A for an instance x is a set of predicates that satisfies the precision threshold λ_{prec} with a confidence level $1 - \delta$:

$$\Pr\{\text{Prec}(A) \geq \lambda_{\text{prec}}\} \geq 1 - \delta,$$

where $\delta \in [0, 1]$ and $\lambda_{\text{prec}} \in [0, 1]$ sets the precision requirement for the anchor. Precision $\text{Prec}(A)$ is defined as:

$$\text{Prec}(A) = \mathbb{E}_{D_x(z|A)} \left[\mathbb{1}_{f(x) = f(z)} \right],$$

where f is the black-box model, and $D_x(z|A)$ is the distribution of perturbations z around x when the anchor applies. Optimal anchors are searched using reinforcement learning, and the process is formulated as a combinatorial optimization problem:

$$\max_{A} \quad C(A) \quad \text{s.t.} \quad \Pr\{\text{Prec}(A) \geq \lambda_{\text{prec}}\} \geq 1 - \delta,$$

where $C(A)$ represents the coverage for candidate anchor A.

Rule Evaluation. For rule-based classifiers, the performance of each rule r_k can be measured with two key metrics—coverage $C(r_k)$ and error $E(r_k)$—that allow us to evaluate the rule's ability to generalize to unseen data. Before defining the metrics, it is worth underlining that a 'positive' instance, in this context, refers to any instance that satisfies the considered rule, regardless of the output class. Similarly, the term 'negative' is used to denote the case when points do not satisfy the rule.

Coverage $C(r_k)$: this measures the proportion of correctly classified positive samples by rule r_k:

$$C(r_k) = \frac{\text{TP}(r_k)}{\text{TP}(r_k) + \text{FN}(r_k)},$$

where $\text{TP}(r_k)$ is the count of true positives and $\text{FN}(r_k)$ is the count of false negatives associated with the rule.

Error $E(r_k)$: it represents the proportion of false positives in the total predictions, helping to gauge rule precision:

$$E(r_k) = \frac{\text{FP}(r_k)}{\text{TN}(r_k) + \text{FP}(r_k)},$$

where $\text{FP}(r_k)$ and $\text{TN}(r_k)$ represent false positives and true negatives, respectively.

Combined, coverage and error contribute to the **relevance** $R(r_k)$ of each rule, which indicates its generalizability:

$$R(r_k) = C(r_k) \cdot (1 - E(r_k)).$$

3.4 Simulation of Social Robotics Navigation

Hinted by its name, Navground[2] is a playground to experiment with navigation algorithms. The Navground social navigation simulator allows for experimentation with various navigation algorithms. At its core, the simulator operates with multi-agent (robots) systems that carry out specific navigation tasks, ensuring they avoid collisions with both static obstacles and other robots, and deadlocks. Each robot is represented as a circular disc, with its state defined by a $2D$ pose (x and y), its orientation angle and its *twist*; the velocity of the robot in the x-axis direction, its velocity in the y-axis direction and its rotational speed, in radians per second, around its central axis, which represents how fast the robot turns. Robots navigate using one of several reactive navigation behaviors, which consider the current state of the environment to generate control commands that guide them toward their targets while avoiding collisions.

In this article, robots are modelled after the Thymio robot, a small robot with a size of 8 cm and two-wheel differential-drive kinematics, which is a very common kinematics[3] shared by many ground robots. Each simulated robot executes a specific behavior. In this article, robots will follow the *human-like* (HL) navigation [15], which is a bio-inspired, computationally light, local navigation algorithm for robotics, adapting a heuristic model for pedestrian motion. It addresses engineering aspects such as trajectory effectiveness and scalability, as well as societal aspects by producing human-friendly, predictable trajectories. In other words, this behavior is inspired by the way the pedestrian moves.

---

[2] https://github.com/idsia-robotics/navground.
[3] Kinematics is the study of the relationship between a robot's joint coordinates and its spatial layout, and is a fundamental and classical topic in robotics.

The HL navigation algorithm operates in regular time intervals by following three key steps: first, it selects the best direction toward the target while avoiding potential collisions by considering a safety margin around the robot and the velocity of nearby entities. Second, it determines an appropriate speed that allows the robot to stop within a safe distance if needed. Finally, the velocity is smoothly adjusted over time to ensure natural movement transitions. The safety of the resulting trajectories depends on various parameters (see Table 1 for the explanation of some HL parameters), such as the safety margin σ, which helps account for modeling and perception errors.

Table 1. Description of HL Parameters

Parameter	Description
v_{opt}	The desired optimal speed
τ_{rot}	The relaxation time to rotate towards a desired orientation
σ (safety margin)	The minimal safety margin (distance) to keep away from obstacles or other robots
η (eta)	The time that the behavior keeps away from collisions
τ (tau)	The relaxation time controlling the smoothness of the motion

Additionally, Navground provides different scenarios, where robots can navigate, in order to test and analyze their behavior. In this article, we will use the *crossings* scenario. In this scenario, we define the variable s as the length of each side of the square area containing the target waypoints and define the operational space for robots. The four target waypoints are located at the following coordinates: $(\frac{-s}{2}, 0)$, $(\frac{s}{2}, 0)$, $(0, \frac{-s}{2})$, and $(0, \frac{-s}{2})$. Half of the robots are tasked to pendle between the two vertically aligned waypoints, and half between the horizontally aligned waypoints (see Fig. 3). The scenario tests how robots cross in the middle, where the 4 opposing flows meet. In the case of the cross scenario, we must be clear that the positions of the robots go on the x-axis from $\frac{-s}{2}$ to the value set in $\frac{s}{2}$ of the scenario, and on the y-axis similarly.

In addition, in the context of social navigation between robots, deadlocks and collisions refer to two different types of issues that can arise during the interaction and navigation of multiple robots in a shared environment. A deadlock in robot navigation occurs when one or more robots become trapped in a situation where they cannot move due to the positions of other robots, waiting for the other to move in order to take up the movement again. A collision occurs when two or more robots collide or when a robot collides with static obstacles in the environment. This can result from uncoordinated movements or errors in navigation planning and control. We will also focus on these two negative events in experiments. Notice that a simulation can be considered safe if there is no collision between robots, efficient if no robot enters a deadlock state at any point during the simulation, and compliant if there are neither collisions nor deadlocks.

Fig. 3. In the *crossings* scenario, simulated robots navigate between predefined waypoints (colored cylinders) along the x-axis and y-axis, creating intersecting flows at the center. (Color figure online)

4 Topology-Driven Safety Methodology

Once all preliminary concepts have been defined, we can present the core contribution of this paper: a **topology-driven methodology** for defining safety regions in robot simulations. By combining topological tools with entropy-based analysis, we provide a systematic approach to avoid/prevent unsafe events such as robot collisions or deadlocks.

At a high level, our methodology consists of the following steps (see Fig. 4 for an example):

1. **Simulate:** Generate multiple navigation scenarios where a fleet of mobile robots moves between opposing targets, potentially leading to collisions or deadlocks.
2. **Build a dataset:** Extract topological features from each simulation and assign a binary safety label based on observed events (e.g., presence or absence of collisions). This process consists of the following steps:
    (a) **Extract point clouds:** From each simulation run performed by Navground, we extract the positions of all robots at each time step, resulting in n point clouds. Then, for each point cloud, we perform steps b–e.
    (b) **Compute persistent homology:** We compute the persistent homology of the point cloud, using the Vietoris-Rips complex. This yields a **persistence barcode**, focusing only on 0-dimensional features.
    (c) **Analyze birth-death intervals:** From the persistence barcode, we extract the lengths of the intervals that correspond to the 0-dimensional topological features.
    (d) **Normalize interval lengths:** We compute the sum of all interval lengths and normalize each length by this sum, obtaining a probability distribution of interval lengths of the topological features.

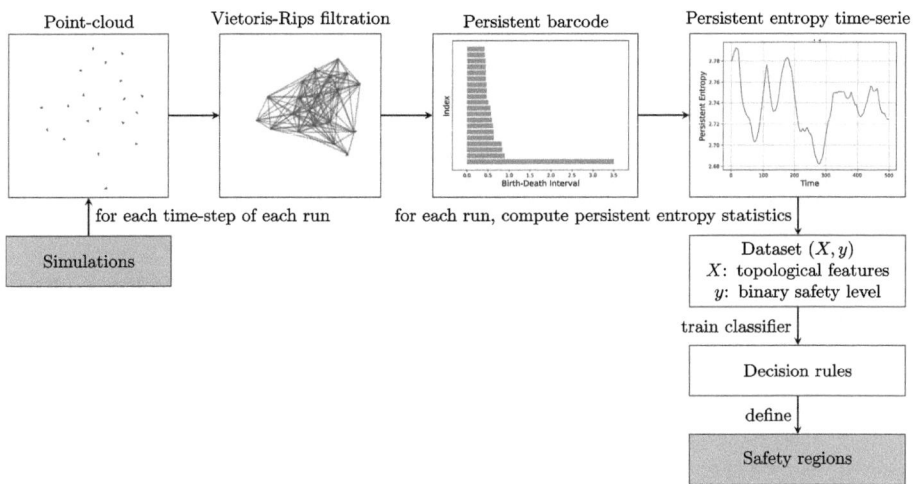

Fig. 4. Illustrative example of methodology pipeline.

(e) **Calculate persistent entropy:** We compute the entropy of the topological features probability distribution, using the Shannon entropy formula Eq. (1). See Fig. 5 for an example of a point cloud corresponding to the position of the robots in a specific time step, the corresponding persistence barcode of dimension 0, and the corresponding persistent entropy.

(f) **Generate persistent entropy time series and compute statistical parameters**. Once the above process is done for each time step of the simulation, we obtain a persistent entropy time series for the whole simulation. Finally, we compute four key statistical parameters for this time series: **mean, median, standard deviation and interquartile range (IQR)**. See Fig. 6 for an example of persistent entropy time series over a 500-step simulation.

Once the topological features are extracted, we construct a labeled dataset to train a classifier. The dataset is defined as:

- Input x: A feature vector extracted from the topological data of the simulation, defined as: $x = (meanEntropy, medianEntropy, stdEntropy, iqrEntropy)$. These features are derived from the 6-step methodology explained above.
- Output y: A binary label indicating whether the simulation is safe(+1) or unsafe(-1). The definition of "safe" depends on the context. Given a set of simulations, we assign each simulation a binary level indicating its safety level, depending on the avoidance event, for example, for safe analysis (collision or not collision):

$$y_i = \begin{cases} +1 & \text{if the number of collisions during the simulation } i \text{ equals 0,} \\ -1 & \text{if the number of collisions during the simulation } i \text{ is greater than 0.} \end{cases}$$

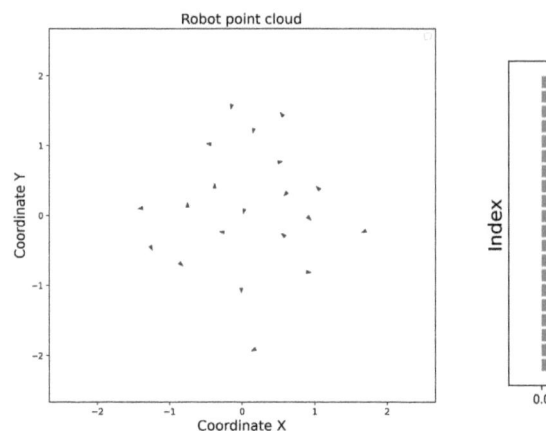
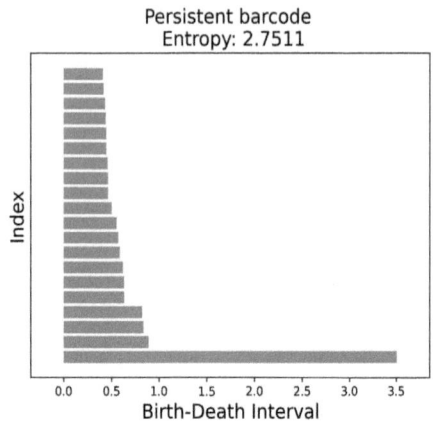

(a) Point cloud example of the robots in a specific time step.

(b) Persistence barcode of dimension 0 with corresponding persistent entropy of 2.7511.

Fig. 5. Illustrative example of computing the persistent entropy of a robot point cloud.

3. **Train a Classifier:** Using this dataset, we train a Support Vector Machine (SVM) classifier with adjustable margins to learn the decision function separating safe and unsafe simulations.
4. **Define Safety Regions:** Once the classifier is trained, we use it to construct probabilistic safety regions, which define zones in the topological feature space where simulations are likely to be safe. These regions are constructed using order statistics methods to the classifier, such as probabilistic scaling and conformal prediction. In addition, we extract local rules from these safety regions using Anchors.

Note that a specific time step in a simulation with a higher persistent entropy indicates a greater dispersion among the robots in relation how they are distributed around the space, without clusters of robots in certain areas and without empty areas or areas with few robots, being less likely to have empty areas and to form cluster of robots very grouped and another ones very far away, while a lower entropy indicates that less dispersion between the robots, being more likely to occupy specific regions of space and form clusters. See Fig. 7 for an illustrative example where we can compare the robot point cloud from two different time steps. The point cloud on the left has lower entropy than the one on the right (where the points are more dispersed).

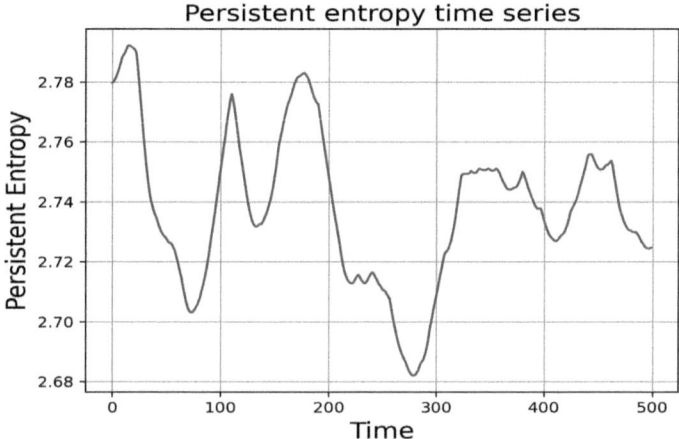

Fig. 6. Persistent entropy time series example of a simulation.

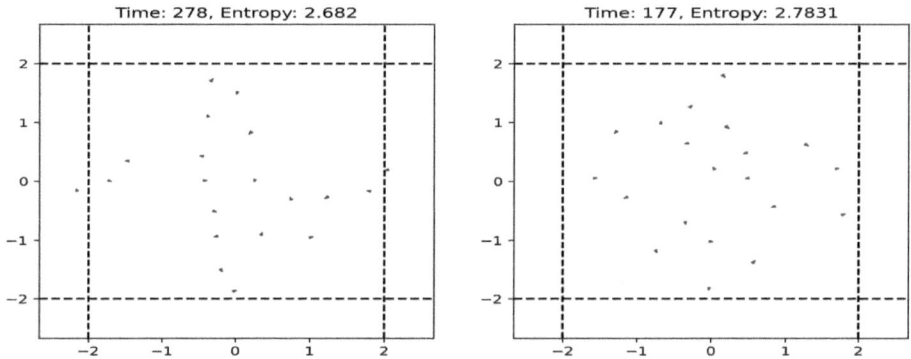

Fig. 7. Point clouds of two different time steps with the corresponding persistent entropy on top.

5 Experiments

In this section, we present the experiments and results we carried out by putting together the simulator, the safety regions and the illustrated topological techniques. After data collection through Navground simulator, we study the problem of collision avoidance, comparing our methodology with the one that uses behavior parameters (σ, η and τ, which are defined in Table 1 for the construction of safety regions [29] (instead of the topological features), then studying the problem of deadlock avoidance, and finally combining them for safe and efficient (free of collisions and deadlocks) navigations.

5.1 Data Collection

Using Navground, we generated a suitable dataset to study the safety of robots' movement while avoiding collisions, deadlocks, and both of them, via probabilistic scaling and conformal prediction methods, with interpretation via rule-based classifiers. We executed $N = 10000$ simulation runs, each with 2000 time steps, each one separated from the previous one in 0.1 s, with a group of 20 robots modelled after the Thymio robot. Each simulated robot executes the HL navigation with the following parameters (behavior parameters of the simulations):

- $v_{opt} = 0.12$ m/s
- $\tau_{rot} = 0.5$ s
- σ sampled uniformly from $[0.0$ m$, 0.1$ m$]$ for collision avoidance, and from $[0.0$ m$, 0.5$ m$]$ for deadlock avoidance and for safe and efficient simulations (since there are hardly any simulations with deadlocks if we limit this parameter to 0.1).
- τ and η sampled uniformly from $[0.0$ s$, 1.0$ s$]$

These HL parameters (σ, η and τ) have been sampled to generate simulations of all types, including safe, aggressive, cautious, or efficient simulations. Please, see Table 1 for an explanation of the HL parameters.

For each simulation run, we apply the methodology explained previously (Sect. 4), recording the following values:

$$\mathbf{x} = (meanEntropy, medianEntropy, stdEntropy, iqrEntropy).$$

According to the computational cost of calculating persistent entropy, for instance, the calculation time for persistent entropy for a point cloud at a given time i is less than 10 ms on a single core of a modern CPU (approximately 0.003 s), and the total time for computing the entire persistent entropy time series for a simulation with the mentioned characteristics is approximately 0.2 s. These times suggest that the method is efficient enough for real-time performance in practical applications.

Then, we assigned a binary label y to each simulation through the following criteria, depending on the avoidance event:

- Safe simulation (avoiding collision):

$$y = \begin{cases} +1 & \text{if number of collisions} = 0, \\ -1 & \text{if number of collisions} > 0 \end{cases}.$$

- Efficient simulation (avoiding deadlocks):

$$y = \begin{cases} +1 & \text{if number of deadlocks} = 0, \\ -1 & \text{if number of deadlocks} > 0 \end{cases}.$$

– Compliant simulation (avoiding both, collision and deadlocks):

$$y = \begin{cases} +1 & \text{if number of collisions/deadlocks} = 0, \\ -1 & \text{if number of collisions/deadlocks} > 0 \end{cases}.$$

Finally, we obtained the dataset $T_{\text{nav}} = \{(\mathbf{x}_j, y_j) \mid j = 1, \ldots, N\}$. In Sect. 5.3, we present and analyze the results obtained using reliable AI techniques for this dataset.

5.2 Data Exploration

Before entering in the results in terms of confidence regions and explainability, a first visual inspection of how classes are distributed in the dataset is useful to understand the non-trivial nature of the problem. In Figs. 8a, 8b and 8c, the relationships among the four persistent entropy-based metrics mean entropy, median entropy, standard deviation of entropy (stdEntropy), and interquartile range of entropy (iqrsEntropy) are visualized for three binary classifications: collision avoidance, deadlock avoidance, and compliant simulations (collision and deadlock avoidance). Each plot displays pairwise scatterplots, overlaid with KDE (Kernel Density Estimation) curves along the diagonals to depict distributions for each class.

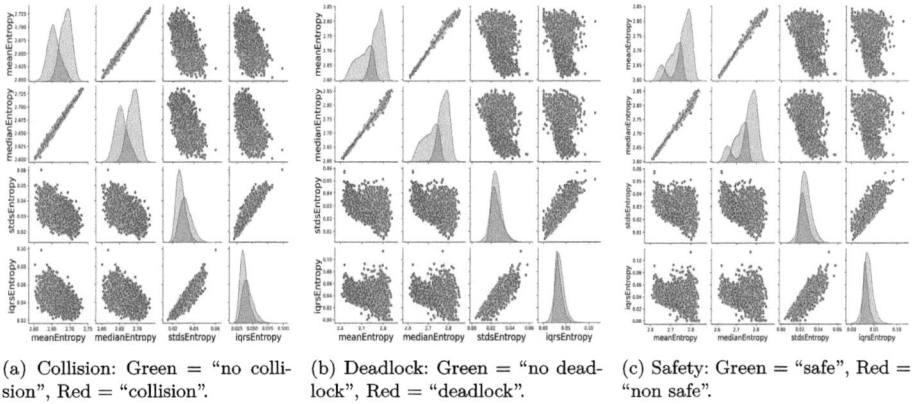

(a) Collision: Green = "no collision", Red = "collision".
(b) Deadlock: Green = "no deadlock", Red = "deadlock".
(c) Safety: Green = "safe", Red = "non safe".

Fig. 8. Pairwise class distributions of the features in T_{nav}.

Across all three classifications—collision avoidance, deadlock avoidance, and compliant simulations (collision and deadlock avoidance)—**mean entropy and median entropy** stand out as the most informative features for distinguishing between classes. While stdEntropy and iqrsEntropy provide less individual discriminatory power, they may still offer complementary information when used in combination with the other metrics. These insights highlight the potential of persistent entropy-based metrics for identifying critical system states and suggest a strong basis for further model development and optimization.

Lower values of mean entropy and median entropy are more closely associated with the "collision" class, indicating that decreased entropy in the system could signal potential collisions between robots. Higher values of mean entropy and median entropy are more closely associated with the "deadlock" class, indicating that increased entropy in the system could signal potential deadlock situations. In this way, we can observe how safe and efficient safe simulations, without collisions or deadlocks, have relatively stable values for mean entropy and median entropy, unless an extreme value occurs, either low or high.

The goal of this analysis is to characterize such a region in an interpretable way, via post-hoc rule extraction from confidence regions.

5.3 Results

First, we will compare training a rule-based model with the behavior parameters (as is done in [29]) against by training it with the topological features that have been extracted using the methodology proposed in this paper for the avoidance of collisions. For that, we will use Skope Rules. Skope Rules[4] is a rule-based ML algorithm, that learns interpretable and diversified rules for "scoping" a target class of interest, i.e. detecting samples from this class with high precision. In practical applications, skope-rules model has been applied to several safety-critical classification tasks, as well as anomaly detection problems or cluster description.

Table 2. Performance comparison between the adopted rule-based models. The first column reports the number of generated rules. The other columns refer to the following metrics (expressed in %): accuracy (ACC), F1-score (F1), true positive rate (TPR), false positive rate (FPR), false negative rate (FNR), true negative rate (TNR).

	# of rules	ACC	F1	TPR	FPR	FNR	TNR
SkopeRules-Behavior Parameters	9	78.6	75.1	70.8	15	29.2	85
SkopeRules-Topological Features	20	84.6	84.6	87.1	18.7	12.9	81.3

Table 2 highlights the superior performance of SkopeRules using topological features compared to behavior parameters. For a proper interpretation of the results, we remark that, based on the labeling criteria defined in Sect. 5.1, the positive class (i.e., $y = +1$) refers to our target situation (that is, either absence of collisions, deadlocks, or absence of both). As a result, true positives here denote their correct classification, with false positives reflecting how many hazardous cases (presence of collisions, deadlocks, or both, labeled as $y = -1$) are missed. In

---

[4] https://github.com/scikit-learn-contrib/skope-rules.

contrast, true negatives are associated to the dangerous situations being correctly classified, with false negatives representing false alarm cases.

The model using topological features as input features achieves higher accuracy (84.6% vs. 78.6%), F1-score (84.6% vs. 75.1%), and true positive rate (87.1% vs. 70.8%) while significantly reducing the false negative rate (12.9% vs. 29.2%). Although its true negative rate (81.3% vs. 85%) is slightly lower, and the false positive rate (18.7% vs. 15%) is higher, these trade-offs are outweighed by its improved balance across metrics. Remember that the positive class is the non-collision class (+1).

The use of 20 rules, compared to 9 for behavior parameters, suggests that the model that using topological features as input features, captures more complex relationships, enhancing its robustness. Models with fewer rules have the advantage of being more interpretable, but the richest ones may generate more fine-grained rules with better discriminative ability. Overall, topological features provide a more discriminative representation, making the model using them as input features preferable for scenarios where accuracy and minimising false positives are prioritised.

Also, we will compare the safety regions generated using these two types of input features. For that, the techniques detailed in Sect. 3.2 to derive the safety regions using Conformal Prediction and Probabilistic Scaling were applied by adopting an SVM as the classifier. Specifically, we considered a Gaussian kernel SVM, with a sigma set to 0.5, with regularization parameter set to 0.3, and a weighting of 0.5. These hyperparameters were selected manually to ensure a fair and controlled comparison across the different types of input features, rather than focusing on obtaining the best possible SVM performance. With this base model, prior to any error control, we achieve the following performance: 78.2% accuracy, 80.6% F1 Score, 82.8% TPR, 72.7% TNR, 27.3% FPR, 17.2% FNR using behavior parameters as input and 85% accuracy, 88.1% F1 Score, 91.6% TPR, 75% TNR, 25% FPR, 8.4% FNR using topological features as input.

Table 3. Performance comparison between the adopted techniques for finding safety regions at $\epsilon = 0.1$. The first column refers to the input features used for training the classification models, the second refers to the adopted techniques for finding safety regions, and the third one reports the optimal scaling parameter. The other columns refer to the following metrics (expressed in %): accuracy (ACC), F1-score (F1), true positive rate (TPR), false positive rate (FPR), false negative rate (FNR), true negative rate (TNR). Probabilistic Scaling denoted as PS, and Conformal Prediction denoted as CP.

	Method	ρ_ϵ	ACC	F1	TPR	FPR	FNR	TNR
Behavior parameters	PS	0.48	77.9	77	67.8	9.9	32.1	90.1
	CP	0.44	78.5	77.8	69	10.1	31	89.9
Topological Features	PS	0.42	79.8	81.6	74.3	11.9	25.7	88.1
	CP	0.21	83.7	86.2	84.1	16.9	15.9	83.1

Topological features consistently show better performance than behavior parameters across all metrics, both in baseline classification and in safety region generation. Among the methods for generating safety regions (see Table 3), Conformal Prediction demonstrates superior accuracy and F1 scores, particularly with topological features, making it the preferred approach for ensuring robust safety guarantees.

Now, we want to derive interpretable approximations for both regions in the form of decision rules. Local rule extraction via Anchors was performed on a set of instances labeled as $+1$ by the adjustable classifiers and sampled at a small distance $d \leq 0.05$ from their border.

Table 4. Performance comparison between the rules obtained using Anchors from the obtained adjustable classifiers (SVM). The first column refers to the input features used for training the adjustable classifiers, the second refers to the adopted techniques for finding safety regions, and the third column reports the number of generated rules (anchors). Covering and error percentages are reported for the logical union of the anchors being tested with respect to the labels assigned via PS (S_ε^{PS} output) and CP (S_ε^{CP} output) (Method labels column), and the real labels (Ground Truth column). Probabilistic Scaling is denoted as PS, and Conformal Prediction is denoted as CP.

	Method	# of anchors	Method labels		Ground Truth	
			Coverage	Error	Coverage	Error
Behavior Parameters	PS	5	86	36	73	29
	CP	5	85	35	73	29
Topological Features	PS	2	79	0	69	9
	CP	2	100	30	100	26

The results in Table 4 clearly demonstrate the advantages of using topological features over behavior parameters in the context of local rule extraction with Anchors. Notably, the number of generated rules (anchors) is significantly reduced when using topological features—only 2 rules ($meanEntropy > 2.68$ and $medianEntropy > 2.68$ for PS method, and $meanEntropy > 2.66$ and $medianEntropy > 2.65$ for CP method. Entropy above these values refers to simulations free of collision situations.) compared to 5 rules for behavior parameters (the same 5 rules for both methods: $\eta > 0.75, \tau \leq 0.5, \tau \leq 0.25, \tau \leq 0.76$ and $\sigma > 0.08$). This reduction highlights a key advantage: the rules obtained with topological features are simpler, more concise, and easier to interpret, which enhances their applicability in decision-making tasks.

In addition to reducing the complexity of the rules, the performance also improves. For topological features, the error rates are markedly lower. For instance, under Probabilistic Scaling (PS), the Coverage Error drops to 9%, compared to 29% with behavior parameters. Even with Conformal Prediction (CP), the Coverage Error decreases to 26% while achieving a perfect 100% coverage. Despite having fewer rules, topological features maintain competitive or superior coverage compared to behavior parameters.

These findings emphasize that topological features not only simplify the decision rules by reducing their number but also improve their accuracy and reliability, making them a more effective and interpretable choice for defining local decision regions.

Once we have verified that the proposed methodology achieves better results for differentiating between safe (without robots collisions) and non-safe simulations, we proceed to extend its use to the case of distinguishing between efficient (without deadlocks) and non-efficient simulations. We follow exactly the same steps, but this time we do not compare the results/performance with those obtained using behavior parameters (SafetyMargin, Eta and Tau).

Using the SkopeRules method and topological features to classify simulations with deadlock cases versus efficient simulations without them, we derive a total of 18 rules, achieving highly positive performance: 88.6% accuracy, 89% F1-score, 93% TPR, and 84% TNR. This demonstrates that these features achieve even better performance for deadlock avoidance than for collision avoidance when using SkopeRules.

Next, we generate the safety regions using these features in the same manner as before. We again considered a Gaussian kernel SVM, with a sigma set to 0.5, a regularization parameter set to 0.3, and a weighting of 0.5. With this base model, prior to any error control, we achieve the following performance: 86% accuracy, 82.3% F1 score, 74.7% TPR, 94.7% TNR. Using PS method we achieve the following performance: ρ_ϵ equal to -0.12, 87.2% accuracy, 84.6% F1 score, 80.1% TPR, 92.7% TNR; and using the CP method we achieve the following performance: ρ_ϵ equal to 0.17, 83.6% accuracy, 77.9% F1 score, 66% TPR, 97.3% TNR.

Again, local rule extraction via Anchors was performed on a set of instances labeled as +1 by the adjustable classifiers and sampled at a small distance $d \leq 0.05$ from their border. The number of generated rules (anchors) is 2 (same for both methods: $meanEntropy \leq 2.75$ and $medianEntropy \leq 2.75$. Entropy below these values refers to simulations free of deadlock situations.), so again, the rules obtained are very simpler and easier to interpret. We evaluate the logical union of the anchors being tested with respect to the labels assigned via the method used, and the real labels, obtaining the following results:

- 91% coverage and 21% error for ground truth labels, and 100% coverage and 22.5% for method labels for PS method.
- 91% coverage and 21% error for ground truth labels, and 100% coverage and 40% for method labels for CP method.

We can see how with the PS method we obtain a better performance in terms of error, although the rules are exactly the same, obviously obtaining the same performance for the real labels. Considering the non-trivial nature of the problem and of approximating a complex SVM shape via hyper-rectangular shapes (rules) while keeping the error bound as low as possible, we can consider our results as a promising compromise between safety and transparency.

Thus, if we focus on distinguishing between safe and efficient (compliant) simulations (free of collisions and deadlocks) and not compliant simulations, we obtain very simple rules for both methods:

- $2.68 \leq meanEntropy \leq 2.75$ and $2.68 \leq medianEntropy \leq 2.75$ for PS method.
- $2.66 \leq meanEntropy \leq 2.75$ and $2.65 \leq medianEntropy \leq 2.75$ for CP method.

In summary, our results highlight the advantages of using topological features in rule-based explanations and the generation of safety regions for classification. First, for differentiating between safe and non-safe simulations, we achieve better and more efficient results compared to not using these topological features. The results were even more favorable for distinguishing between efficient and non-efficient simulations, ultimately yielding a very simple rule for differentiating between compliant and non-compliant simulations. These findings confirm the suitability of topological features for enhancing transparency and reliability in classification and safety detection tasks.

6 Conclusions and Future Works

In this research, we presented an ML-based approach to compliant simulation, free of both collision and deadlock events, in mobile robot navigation. The proposed methodology contributes significantly to the field of eXplainable Artificial Intelligence (XAI) by integrating topological data analysis (TDA) and rule-based explanations to enhance interpretability in mobile robot navigation. The use of adjustable SVM classifiers and order statistics to define safety regions, followed by the extraction of Anchor rules, ensures that the decision-making process remains transparent and comprehensible. Overall, the proposed methodology achieves better and more efficient (simpler) results for collision avoidance compared to those obtained without using topological features as input in [29]. Furthermore, we extend this approach to deadlock avoidance and, ultimately, we combine the safety regions and rules for both events, obtaining the corresponding safety region and rules for safe and efficient (compliant) simulations, avoiding these two negative events (collisions and deadlocks), obtaining accurate and promising results for that. Beyond the immediate application in mobile robotics, the principles introduced in this work offer broader implications for xAI. The combination of topological insights with rule-based models presents a novel approach for generating explainable and robust decision boundaries in machine learning systems. In fields such as autonomous driving, industrial automation, and swarm robotics, where safety and efficacy are critical, the ability to construct interpretable safety regions could lead to more reliable and trustworthy AI-driven solutions.

While in this work the focus was to provide safety guarantees based on topological features, future research could explore more complex scenarios and behaviors, as well as incorporate additional topological parameters into the analysis.

This could further enhance the quality of the generated safety regions, improving the interpretability, and optimizing the overall performance.

Finally, since the rules are obtained a posteriori to the simulations —-meaning that we need to have the complete simulation and calculate the topological features to determine whether the simulation falls within the safety margins defined by the obtained rules—-we leave as future work the definition of the simulation parameters a prior so that the resulting simulations exhibit a safe entropy value, that is, within the range identified as safe by the rules.

Acknowledgements. This work was partially supported by REXASI-PRO H-EU project (HORIZON-CL4-2021-HUMAN-01-01, Grant Agreement ID: 101070028), the Departmental Research Budget of the Department of Applied Mathematics I of Universidad de Sevilla, and the Future Artificial Intelligence Research (FAIR) project under the Italian National Recovery and Resilience Plan (Piano Nazionale di Ripresa e Resilienza - PNRR), Spoke 3 - ResilientAI.

Code Availability. The code for the data and the experiments is available on a GitHub repository (https://github.com/Cimagroup/Topological-Features-and-Explainable-Safety-Regions.).

References

1. Anjomshoae, S., Najjar, A., Calvaresi, D., Främling, K.: Explainable agents and robots: results from a systematic literature review. In: 18th International Conference on Autonomous Agents and Multiagent Systems (AAMAS 2019), Montreal, Canada, May 13–17, 2019, pp. 1078–1088. International Foundation for Autonomous Agents and Multiagent Systems (2019)
2. Atakishiyev, S., Salameh, M., Yao, H., Goebel, R.: Explainable artificial intelligence for autonomous driving: a comprehensive overview and field guide for future research directions. IEEE Access (2024)
3. Atienza, N., Gonzalez-Diaz, R., Rucco, M.: Persistent entropy for separating topological features from noise in vietoris-rips complexes. J. Intell. Inf. Syst. **52**, 637–655 (2019)
4. Atienza, N., González-Diaz, R., Soriano-Trigueros, M.: On the stability of persistent entropy and new summary functions for topological data analysis. Pattern Recogn. **107**, 107509 (2020). https://doi.org/10.1016/j.patcog.2020.107509
5. Carlevaro, A., Alamo, T., Dabbene, F., Mongelli, M.: Probabilistic safety regions via finite families of scalable classifiers. arXiv preprint arXiv:2309.04627 (2023)
6. Carlevaro, A., Alamo, T., Dabbene, F., Mongelli, M.: Conformal predictions for probabilistically robust scalable machine learning classification. Mach. Learn. **113**(9), 6645–6661 (2024)
7. Carlsson, G.: Topological methods for data modelling. Nat. Rev. Phys. **2**(12), 697–708 (2020)
8. Chintakunta, H., Gentimis, T., Gonzalez-Diaz, R., Jimenez, M.J., Krim, H.: An entropy-based persistence barcode. Pattern Recogn. **48**(2), 391–401 (2015)
9. Cohen-Steiner, D., Edelsbrunner, H., Harer, J.: Stability of persistence diagrams. Discrete Comput. Geom. **37**(1), 103–120 (2006). https://doi.org/10.1007/s00454-006-1276-5

10. Dwivedi, R., et al.: Explainable ai (XAI): core ideas, techniques, and solutions. ACM Comput. Surv. **55**(9), 1–33 (2023)
11. Edelsbrunner, H., Harer, J.L.: Computational topology: an introduction. Am. Math. Soc. (2022)
12. Esteve, M., Falcó, A.: tramoTDA: a trajectory monitoring system using topological data analysis. SoftwareX **28**, 101953 (2024). https://doi.org/10.1016/j.softx.2024.101953
13. Garcia-Fidalgo, E., Ortiz, A.: Vision-based topological mapping and localization methods: a survey. Robot. Auton. Syst. **64**, 1–20 (2015)
14. Ghrist, R.: Barcodes: the persistent topology of data. Bull. Am. Math. Soc. **45**(1), 61–75 (2008). https://doi.org/10.1090/S0273-0979-07-01191-3
15. Guzzi, J., Giusti, A., Gambardella, L.M., Theraulaz, G., Di Caro, G.A.: Human-friendly robot navigation in dynamic environments. In: 2013 IEEE International Conference on Robotics and Automation, pp. 423–430 (2013). https://doi.org/10.1109/ICRA.2013.6630610
16. Hassija, V., et al.: Interpreting black-box models: a review on explainable artificial intelligence. Cogn. Comput. **16**(1), 45–74 (2024)
17. Hatcher, A.: Algebraic Topology. Cambridge University Press (2005)
18. Hossain, J., Faridee, A.Z.M., Roy, N., Freeman, J., Gregory, T., Trout, T.: TopoNav: topological navigation for efficient exploration in sparse reward environments. In: 2024 IEEE/RSJ International Conference on Intelligent Robots and Systems (IROS), Abu Dhabi, United Arab Emirates, pp. 693–700 (2024). https://doi.org/10.1109/IROS58592.2024.10802380
19. Islam, N., Haseeb, K., Almogren, A., Din, I.U., Guizani, M., Altameem, A.: A framework for topological based map building: a solution to autonomous robot navigation in smart cities. Futur. Gener. Comput. Syst. **111**, 644–653 (2020)
20. Jonsson, J.: Simplicial Complexes of Graphs, vol. 1928. Springer (2008)
21. Kaur, D., Uslu, S., Rittichier, K.J., Durresi, A.: Trustworthy artificial intelligence: a review. ACM Comput. Surv (CSUR) **55**(2), 1–38 (2022)
22. Koopman, P., Wagner, M.: Autonomous vehicle safety: an interdisciplinary challenge. IEEE Intell. Transp. Syst. Mag. **9**(1), 90–96 (2017)
23. Longo, L., et al.: Explainable artificial intelligence (XAI) 2.0: a manifesto of open challenges and interdisciplinary research directions. Inf. Fus. **106**, 102301 (2024). https://doi.org/10.1016/j.inffus.2024.102301
24. Lum, P.Y., et al.: Extracting insights from the shape of complex data using topology. Sci. Rep. **3**(1), 1236 (2013)
25. Molnar, C.: Interpretable Machine Learning, 2 edn. (2022). https://christophm.github.io/interpretable-ml-book
26. Mouha, R.: Deep learning for robotics. J. Data Anal. Inf. Process. **9**, 63–76 (2021). https://doi.org/10.4236/jdaip.2021.92005
27. Munkres, J.R.: Elements of Algebraic Topology. CRC Press (2018)
28. Murphy, R.R.: Introduction to AI Robotics. MIT Press (2019)
29. Narteni, S., Carlevaro, A., Guzzi, J., Mongelli, M.: Ensuring safe social navigation via explainable probabilistic and conformal safety regions. In: Longo, L., Lapuschkin, S., Seifert, C. (eds.) Explainable Artificial Intelligence, pp. 396–417. Springer Nature Switzerland, Cham (2024). https://doi.org/10.1007/978-3-031-63803-9_22
30. de la Paz López, F., álvarez Sánchez, J.R.: Topological maps for robot's navigation: a conceptual approach. In: Mira, J., Prieto, A. (eds.) Bio-Inspired Applications of Connectionism, pp. 459–467. Springer Berlin Heidelberg, Berlin, Heidelberg (2001)

31. Pierson, H.A., Gashler, M.S.: Deep learning in robotics: a review of recent research. Adv. Rob. **31**, 821 – 835 (2017). https://api.semanticscholar.org/CorpusID:25670768
32. Rao, V.S., Satish, M.A., Prasad, M.B.: Artificial intelligence: principles and applications. Leilani Katie Publication (2024)
33. Ribeiro, M.T., Singh, S., Guestrin, C.: Anchors: high-precision model-agnostic explanations. In: Proceedings of the AAAI Conference on Artificial Intelligence, vol. 32 (2018)
34. Rizzo, L., Verda, D., Berretta, S., Longo, L.: A novel integration of data-driven rule generation and computational argumentation for enhanced explainable AI. Mach. Learn. Knowl. Extr. **6**(3), 2049–2073 (2024). https://doi.org/10.3390/make6030101, https://www.mdpi.com/2504-4990/6/3/101
35. Rucco, M., Castiglione, F., Merelli, E., Pettini, M.: Characterisation of the idiotypic immune network through persistent entropy. In: Proceedings of ECCS 2014: European conference on complex systems, pp. 117–128. Springer (2016)
36. Rucco, M., et al.: A new topological entropy-based approach for measuring similarities among piecewise linear functions. Signal Process. **134**, 130–138 (2017)
37. Saeed, W., Omlin, C.: Explainable ai (XAI): a systematic meta-survey of current challenges and future opportunities. Knowl.-Based Syst. **263**, 110273 (2023)
38. Vovk, V.: Cross-conformal predictors. Ann. Math. Artif. Intell. **74**, 9–28 (2015)
39. Vrontis, D., Christofi, M., Pereira, V., Tarba, S., Makrides, A., Trichina, E.: Artificial intelligence, robotics, advanced technologies and human resource management: a systematic review. Artif. Intell. Int. HRM, 172–201 (2023)

Open Access This chapter is licensed under the terms of the Creative Commons Attribution 4.0 International License (http://creativecommons.org/licenses/by/4.0/), which permits use, sharing, adaptation, distribution and reproduction in any medium or format, as long as you give appropriate credit to the original author(s) and the source, provide a link to the Creative Commons license and indicate if changes were made.

The images or other third party material in this chapter are included in the chapter's Creative Commons license, unless indicated otherwise in a credit line to the material. If material is not included in the chapter's Creative Commons license and your intended use is not permitted by statutory regulation or exceeds the permitted use, you will need to obtain permission directly from the copyright holder.

A Biologically Inspired Filter Significance Assessment Method for Model Explanation

Emirhan Böge[1](✉)[iD], Yasemin Gunindi[2,3][iD], Murat Bilgehan Ertan[4][iD], Erchan Aptoula[3][iD], Nihan Alp[2][iD], and Huseyin Ozkan[3][iD]

[1] School of Informatics, University of Edinburgh, Edinburgh, UK
e.boge@sms.ed.ac.uk
[2] Faculty of Arts and Social Sciences, AlViNlab, Sabanci University, Istanbul, Turkey
{yasemingunindi,nihan.alp}@sabanciuniv.edu
[3] Faculty of Engineering and Natural Sciences, VPAlab, Sabanci University, Istanbul, Turkey
{erchan.aptoula,huseyin.ozkan}@sabanciuniv.edu
[4] Centrum Wiskunde & Informatica (CWI), Amsterdam, The Netherlands
bilgehan.ertan@cwi.nl

Abstract. The interpretability of deep learning models remains a significant challenge, particularly in convolutional neural networks (CNNs) where understanding the contributions of individual filters is crucial for explainability. In this work, we propose a biologically inspired filter significance assessment method based on Steady-State Visually Evoked Potentials (SSVEPs), a well-established neuroscience principle. Our approach leverages frequency tagging techniques to quantify the importance of convolutional filters by analyzing their frequency-locked responses to periodic contrast modulations in input images. By blending SSVEP-based filter selection into Class Activation Mapping (CAM) frameworks such as Grad-CAM, Grad-CAM++, EigenCAM, and LayerCAM, we enhance model interpretability while reducing attribution noise. Experimental evaluations on ImageNet using VGG-16, ResNet-50, and ResNeXt-50 demonstrate that SSVEP-enhanced CAM methods improve spatial focus in visual explanations, yielding higher energy concentration while maintaining competitive localization accuracy. These findings suggest that our biologically inspired approach offers a robust mechanism for identifying key filters in CNNs, paving the way for more interpretable and transparent deep learning models.

Keywords: Explainable AI · Interpretability · Neuroscience-inspired AI · SSVEP · Filter Importance · CAM

1 Introduction

Convolutional neural networks (CNNs) have demonstrated remarkable performance across various computer vision tasks, but understanding their decision-making processes remains a challenge. eXplainable Artificial Intelligence (XAI)

techniques aim to bridge this gap by offering insights into network activations [10]. One of the key challenges in XAI is assessing the importance of individual neurons and filters within deep learning models [20]. Identifying critical neurons aids in model pruning, robustness analysis, and fairness evaluation, while also contributing to a deeper understanding of network behavior [37].

In this work, we build upon the Steady-State Visually Evoked Potential (SSVEP)-based filter assessment framework [5], which draws inspiration from neuroscience [2,23,25]. SSVEPs describe neural responses to flickering visual stimuli at fixed frequencies, revealing frequency-specific tuning in biological neurons [25]. Previous research suggests that CNNs exhibit analogous responses, enabling a biologically inspired approach to filter selection [5]. This makes SSVEP-based filter analysis a promising direction for model interpretability. SSVEP analysis provides a stable measure of convolutional filter importance by leveraging frequency-domain representation of activations. This ability to capture fine-grained filter responses allows for precise identification of highly responsive filters [5]. Most importantly, by aligning with established neuroscience principles, this approach enhances the plausibility of AI explanations, offering a biologically grounded perspective on model behavior.

Our method incorporates SSVEP-based importance assessment with Class Activation Mapping (CAM) techniques, enhancing model interpretability by refining heatmap localization. Unlike traditional CAM methods [6,14,21,30], which consider all convolutional filters, our approach selectively focuses on the most responsive filters. This improves explanation quality by concentrating activation energy on the most relevant regions while reducing noise from less informative convolutional filters.

We evaluate our approach on VGG-16 [32], ResNet-50 [13], and ResNeXt-50 [35] using ImageNet [28]. The SSVEP-enhanced method is applied to Grad-CAM [30], GradCAM++ [6], EigenCAM [21], and LayerCAM [14], and its performance is compared against their respective baselines. Our findings demonstrate that SSVEP-enhanced CAM methods obtain more concentrated and focused explanations while maintaining competitive localization accuracy. *Source code is available at:* github.com/emirhanboge/SSVEP-CAM-Enhancement.

The remainder of this paper is structured as follows: Sect. 2 discusses related work and background, Sect. 3 details our proposed methodology, and Sect. 4 presents experimental findings along with an analysis of the results. Finally, Sect. 5 concludes with key insights and potential future directions.

2 Related Work

2.1 Explainable AI and Model Transparency

The rapid advancements in deep learning have led to significant breakthroughs in computer vision and decision-making systems. However, the black-box nature of these models presents a major challenge in critical applications, particularly in domains requiring fairness, accountability, and interpretability [1,7,11,12,15, 19,36]. Explainable AI (XAI) methods aim to provide insights into these models' predictions, making their reasoning more transparent. In vision-based applications, saliency methods and Class Activation Mapping (CAM) techniques are widely used to visualize model decisions.

2.2 Saliency-Based Methods and Attribution Techniques

Saliency-based methods highlight the most relevant regions of an input image that influence a model's decision. These approaches can be broadly classified into gradient-based, perturbation-based, and decomposition methods. Gradient-based approaches, such as Grad-CAM [30] and Integrated Gradients [34], compute the gradient of a model's output with respect to input features to determine their importance. Perturbation-based methods, such as LIME [26] and SHAP [18], approximate model behavior by altering input features and observing prediction changes. Decomposition techniques, such as Layer-wise Relevance Propagation (LRP) [3], redistribute the model output back to input features, ensuring the conservation of relevance.

2.3 Class Activation Mapping (CAM) Techniques

CAM-based techniques provide class-specific visualizations by aggregating feature importance scores across a model's activation maps. The original CAM approach [16,38] computes feature importance using global average pooling but requires architectural modifications. Grad-CAM [30] extends CAM by incorporating gradient information, making it applicable to a wider range of architectures. Further improvements were introduced with Grad-CAM++ [6], which refines pixel-wise gradient weighting to improve localization accuracy. Eigen-CAM [21] introduces principal component analysis (PCA) to derive discriminative feature representations without requiring gradients. LayerCAM [14] refines this approach by aggregating activations from multiple layers to improve localization precision. These techniques enable visualization of model focus areas, providing valuable insights into learned representations. While these CAM-based approaches enhance interpretability, the challenge remains in rigorously assessing the quality and faithfulness of the produced explanations. Samek et al. [29] emphasized that visualization methods should be evaluated not only on their perceptual appeal but also on their alignment with model decision-making processes. Their findings highlight the necessity of grounding interpretability techniques in well-defined validation frameworks that can systematically determine whether a heatmap truly reflects the model's reasoning or merely produces plausible-looking attributions.

3 Methodology

This section describes our approach to enhancing explainability in CNNs by utilizing SSVEP analysis for neuron/filter importance assessment. We propose

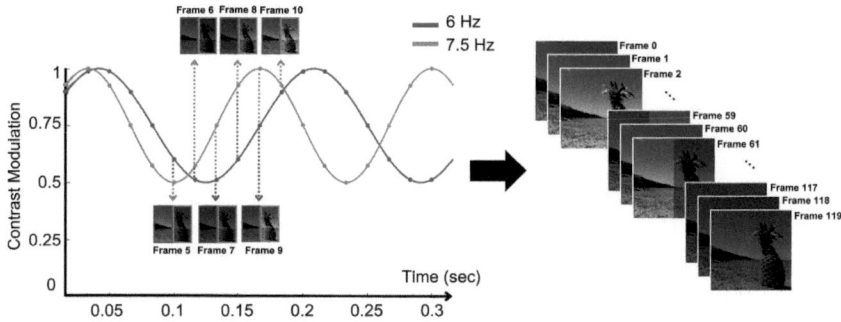

Fig. 1. Sinusoidal contrast modulation of an ImageNet image [28]. Left and right halves are modulated at 6 Hz and 7.5 Hz, respectively, generating 120 flickering frames.

a method that first identifies the most significant neuron filters using SSVEP-inspired frequency tagging and then applies CAM techniques using only the most critical filters.

3.1 Preliminaries: SSVEP-Based Filter Selection for Explainability

The work presented in this paper builds on the SSVEP-based neuron importance framework [5]. This method quantifies filter significance with a biologically inspired approach, and leverages frequency tagging to analyze filter activations under periodic contrast modulations. Analyzing this allows to identify the neurons that exhibit strong phase-locked responses to specific input stimuli.

We follow the SSVEP-based neuron importance setup introduced in [5], which builds upon frequency-tagging principles from neuroscience [2,4,23,25]. To analyze neural responses over time, we apply periodic contrast variations to a static input image using sinusoidal contrast modulation, as visualized in Fig. 1. This process generates a sequence of frames from the same image, where the contrast is dynamically modulated over time. The contrast of each frame i is adjusted on the basis of its temporal position within the sequence. Specifically, for each frame i, the modulation angle $\omega_i \in [0, 2\pi]$ is defined as:

$$\omega_i = 2\pi f \frac{i}{\text{FPS}} + \phi \qquad (1)$$

where $f \in \mathbb{R}^+$ is the modulation frequency, $\text{FPS} \in \mathbb{N}$ is the frame rate, $i \in \mathbb{N}$ is the sequential frame index, and $\phi \in \mathbb{R}$ is the phase shift, which is set to zero in our experiments. The method is generic and can be applied to various values of f and i. However, in our specific implementation, we use a sequence of 120 frames ($i \in [0, 119]$), with spatially distinct modulation frequencies. Specifically, following previous work [4], the left half of the image is modulated at $f_{\text{left}} = 6$ Hz and the right half at $f_{\text{right}} = 7.5$ Hz.

As shown in Fig. 1, the modulation is applied independently to each pixel, dynamically adjusting its intensity over time, thereby creating a periodic flickering effect. To modulate contrast at each pixel location, we scale the original intensity values I according to the sinusoidal function:

$$I' = \left(\frac{\sin(\omega_i) + 1}{2}(s_{\max} - s_{\min}) + s_{\min}\right) \cdot I \qquad (2)$$

where $I \in \mathbb{R}^{H \times W}$ represents the original image intensity values, with H and W denoting the image height and width, respectively. The parameters $s_{\max}, s_{\min} \in \mathbb{R}^+$ define the maximum and minimum modulation factors, set to $s_{\max} = 1.0$ and $s_{\min} = 0.5$ in our experiments. This periodic contrast modulation influences the frequency-specific activations in the network, and allows us to evaluate filter responses in the frequency domain, motivated by evidence that neural network exhibit frequency-tuning characteristics analogous to those of biological neurons [5]. As illustrated in Fig. 1, this process generates a sequence of 120 frames over a 2-second window at 60 FPS. Each frame is derived from the same static image, with pixel intensities oscillating according to their modulation frequency. No spatial transformations occur, which ensures that only the temporal flickering effect is introduced. This controlled contrast modulation is key to assessing how neurons respond to periodic visual changes. By analyzing how different convolutional filters in a pretrained network respond to these modulated inputs, we can quantify their frequency selectivity and importance.

These tagged images are forward-passed through a pretrained network, and the resulting activations of each filter are recorded over time. Later, the frequency response of each filter is analyzed using Fast Fourier Transform (FFT) to extract frequency components. To quantify the relevance of each filter, we compute Signal-to-Noise Ratio (SNR) in the frequency domain, using the FFT magnitudes of activations. The SNR at a given frequency f, denoted as $\text{SNR}(f) \in \mathbb{R}^+$, and is computed as follows [8,17]:

$$\text{SNR}(f) = \frac{F(f)}{\frac{1}{|\mathcal{N}(f)|} \sum_{k \in \mathcal{N}(f)} F(k)} \qquad (3)$$

where $F(f)$ denotes the Fourier magnitude at the discrete frequency bin f, representing the activation strength of a filter at that frequency. The set $\mathcal{N}(f) \subset \mathbb{R}^+$ consists of neighboring frequencies used to estimate the noise baseline, and $|\mathcal{N}(f)|$ is the total number of noise bins considered. To further improve numerical stability, we express SNR in decibels (dB), given by:

$$\text{SNR}_{\text{dB}}(f) = 10 \log_{10}(\text{SNR}(f)) \qquad (4)$$

A higher SNR value indicates that the filter exhibits a strong phase-locked response at the target frequency, which signifies its importance. Finally, as each convolutional filter produces SNR values across multiple discrete frequency bins, we summarize these values into a single scalar SNR score for each filter by computing the mean SNR across all frequencies. This metric is then used to rank all filters within the selected convolutional layers.

This ranking allows us to ensure that the explanation process is driven by filters with the strongest responses to specific stimuli. By selectively retraining only the top-K most responsive filters, we enforce a biologically inspired sparsity constraint on the explainability process.

3.2 Combining SSVEP-Based Filter Selection Into CAM

After identifying the most important neurons, we combine this information into the CAM generation process. Unlike traditional CAM methods, which compute class activation maps using a weighted sum of all convolutional feature maps based on either global average pooled classification weights [38] or gradient-based importance scores [30,31], our approach pre-selects only the most relevant filters based on their SSVEP responses. This ensures that only neurons with strong, frequency-locked activity contribute to the generated heatmaps, improving interpretability.

SSVEP-Guided CAM Generation: Traditional CAM techniques [30,31,38] compute interpretability maps by applying a weighted sum over all activation maps, where the weighting is determined either by classification-layer coefficients [38] or gradient-based saliency scores [30,31]. A broad formulation of CAM is given by:

$$M_{\text{CAM}}(x, y) = \sum_k w_k A_k(x, y), \quad (5)$$

where $A_k(x, y)$ represents the activation map for the k-th convolutional filter, and w_k denotes its corresponding importance weight [38].

However, this approach does not distinguish between relevant and irrelevant filters, potentially introducing noise and reducing interpretability and explainability. Many filters may activate in response to non-discriminative patterns, leading to scattered or misleading heatmaps [22,33]. To address this, we propose an SSVEP-guided filter selection strategy, which enhances interpretability and reduces noise by restricting heatmap computation to the top-K most relevant filters, ranked based on their SNR-derived importance from Eq. 3:

$$M_{\text{SSVEP-CAM}}(x, y) = \sum_{k \in \mathcal{K}} w_k A_k(x, y), \quad (6)$$

where $\mathcal{K}$ is the set containing the indices of the top-K filters identified through SSVEP analysis. By leveraging SSVEP-based filter selection, our approach ensures that heatmaps are more concentrated around salient regions, enhancing interpretability by improving localization and reducing irrelevant activations. Furthermore, by aligning with neuroscience-inspired principles, SSVEP-CAM provides a biologically plausible explainability method.

3.3 Evaluation and Metrics

To validate our method, we conducted various experiments. We compare traditional CAM methods that use all filters against our SSVEP-enhanced CAM approach. To assess the quality of the explanations, we use the following metrics.

Energy Concentration (EC): Quantifies how concentrated the CAM heatmap is in the most salient regions. Similar approaches have been explored in the evaluation of explainability methods, particularly in assessing the complexity and focus of neural network visualizations [29]. A higher EC score indicates that the explanation is more localized, avoiding unnecessary dispersion. It is defined as:

$$EC = \frac{\sum_{i \in S} H_i}{\sum_{j \in \Omega} H_j} \qquad (7)$$

where $H_i \in \mathbb{R}^+$ represents the heatmap intensity at pixel i, $S \subset \Omega$ denotes the subset of pixels corresponding to the top 20% highest heatmap intensities, and Ω is the set of all pixels in the heatmap. Specifically, this metric computes the proportion of the total heatmap energy that is concentrated within the most activated 20% of pixels. We expect this to be higher with CAM methods only using top-K filters, as they generate more concentrated attributions.

While we often observe that higher EC scores visually correlate with more spatially localized explanations, it is important to note that the EC metric itself is agnostic to spatial structure. It does not explicitly account for whether high-intensity pixels are spatially contiguous or scattered. Thus, while we observe that higher EC values tend to coincide with more spatially compact heatmaps in our qualitative results, this spatial localization is not guaranteed by the metric formulation alone. To assess spatial coherence more directly, qualitative visualizations are used in conjunction with EC in our evaluation.

Loc-1 and Loc-5 Localization Accuracy: We evaluate the localization accuracy of model explanations using the loc1 (Top-1) and loc5 (Top-5) metrics [6,30,38]. These metrics assess whether the most activated region correctly identifies the target class (loc1) or falls within the top five predicted bounding boxes (loc5).

Given a predicted bounding box $\hat{B}$ and a ground-truth bounding box B, localization accuracy is measured using the Intersection over Union (IoU), defined as [9]:

$$\text{IoU}(\hat{B}, B) = \frac{|B \cap \hat{B}|}{|B \cup \hat{B}|} \qquad (8)$$

where $\text{IoU} \in [0, 1]$, with higher values indicating greater spatial overlap. Localization is considered successful in loc1 if the highest-scoring predicted bounding box satisfies $\text{IoU} \geq \tau$, where τ is a predefined threshold (typically $\tau = 0.5$).

For loc5, at least one of the top five predicted bounding boxes must meet this criterion:

$$\max_{i=1,\ldots,5} \text{IoU}(\hat{B}_i, B) \geq \tau \tag{9}$$

Unlike conventional IoU-based evaluation, which measures spatial overlap between heatmaps and ground-truth annotations [9], loc1 and loc5 emphasize the interpretability of model explanations in classification tasks. These metrics ensure that the highlighted regions correspond to class-relevant areas rather than merely overlapping with object boundaries. For a detailed theoretical foundation of IoU, we refer to [9].

4 Experiments

This section presents a comprehensive evaluation of the SSVEP-enhanced CAM framework. The proposed methodology is compared against well-documented CAM techniques across three widely used architectures: VGG-16 [32], ResNet-50 [13], and ResNeXt-50 [35].

4.1 Experimental Setup

We identify the most relevant convolutional filters using the SSVEP-based frequency tagging method and select the top 100 filters for each model's explanation process. This selective approach ensures that only the most functionally significant filters contribute to the class activation maps. The final convolutional block before the fully connected layers is selected for all three models to generate the explanations as they capture high-level semantic features.

We conduct our experiments on the ImageNet (ILSVRC2012) validation dataset [28]. A subset of 5000 randomly sampled images is used to ensure diverse object classes while maintaining computational feasibility. All models used are pretrained on ImageNet, and are acquired using PyTorch's torchvision library [24]. The inputs are normalized using standard ImageNet mean and standard deviation values.

4.2 Experiment Results

Figure 2 presents visual comparisons between the methods. Across different methods, SSVEP-enhanced CAMs generate more spatially focused explanations by concentrating activation energy in regions most relevant to classification. Notably, EigenCAM shows significant improvements in spatial compactness, which reinforces our hypothesis that selecting functionally significant convolutional filters leads to more concentrated explanations.

Table 1 reports the Energy Concentration scores for each model and CAM method. This metric quantifies how concentrated the activation heatmap is in specific regions. Previous CAM methods assess their methods using conventional

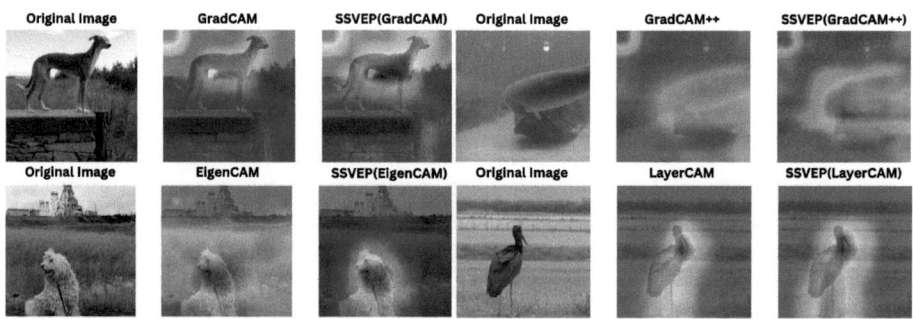

Fig. 2. Comparing baseline CAM methods and their SSVEP-enhanced counterparts.

Table 1. Energy Concentration (↑) (%) for Baseline and SSVEP CAM Methods, reported as **mean ± standard deviation** across 5000 validation samples.

Algorithm	VGG-16		ResNet-50		ResNeXt-50	
	Baseline	SSVEP	Baseline	SSVEP	Baseline	SSVEP
GradCAM	47.50 ± 8.26	**53.91 ± 11.05**	**45.24 ± 6.49**	44.31 ± 7.12	**42.02 ± 5.63**	39.39 ± 5.34
GradCAM++	39.18 ± 4.92	**44.89 ± 10.19**	39.31 ± 4.87	**42.68 ± 7.17**	**39.21 ± 4.06**	38.56 ± 5.04
EigenCAM	62.79 ± 17.33	**69.50 ± 13.52**	49.90 ± 11.48	**54.37 ± 11.68**	41.81 ± 7.28	**44.72 ± 7.60**
LayerCAM	46.63 ± 7.95	**47.09 ± 8.00**	45.66 ± 8.55	**46.48 ± 9.01**	44.27 ± 7.46	**44.75 ± 7.65**

metrics such as general alignment (e.g., IoU [9]) or impact on classification (e.g., ROAD [27]). Energy Concentration provides a direct measure of how focused an explanation is.

SSVEP-enhanced CAMs achieves higher Energy Concentration scores, which indicates that the activation energy is more focused. This confirms that selecting most responsive neurons enhances localization while reducing irrelevant activations. While localization accuracy measure overlap with ground-truth

Table 2. Localization Accuracy (↑) for Baseline and SSVEP CAM Methods.

Algorithm	Prediction Level	VGG-16		ResNet-50		ResNeXt-50	
		Baseline	SSVEP	Baseline	SSVEP	Baseline	SSVEP
GradCAM	loc1	**19.76%**	17.04%	18.52%	**18.92%**	**18.28%**	18.12%
	loc5	**24.50%**	21.16%	22.64%	**23.14%**	**22.18%**	21.86%
GradCAM++	loc1	**17.44%**	16.72%	18.72%	**19.90%**	18.12%	**18.52%**
	loc5	**21.54%**	20.66%	22.80%	**24.22%**	21.62%	**22.32%**
EigenCAM	loc1	**21.28%**	19.00%	25.06%	**26.12%**	21.72%	**22.78%**
	loc5	**25.78%**	22.78%	29.92%	**31.14%**	25.88%	**27.24%**
LayerCAM	loc1	21.84%	**22.00%**	**23.14%**	23.08%	**22.52%**	22.26%
	loc5	26.52%	**26.94%**	**28.16%**	28.06%	**27.04%**	26.82%

annotations, it does not account for the scattering of attributions. A heatmap may achieve a high IoU but it still can distribute energy across irrelevant areas. Therefore, it is important to find a balance between Energy Concentration and localization accuracy.

Table 2 presents localization accuracy results for each model and CAM method. Higher localization accuracy indicates a better match with human-annotated regions, and it does not necessarily reflect how precisely focused the explanation is. This distinction explains why SSVEP-enhanced CAMs do not always achieve higher localization accuracy in every case. However, they remain comparable to their baseline counterparts, and in some cases they even surpass the standard CAM methods despite utilizing only a subset of the all convolutional filters. This reinforces the idea that many activations may be redundant or even introduce noise for visual explanations.

4.3 Discussion

The results show that SSVEP-enhanced CAMs produce more focused and spatially compact explanations across multiple architectures. Higher Energy Concentration scores confirm that these methods reduce scattered attributions. This provides evidence that selecting only the most functionally significant filters improves interpretability by reducing noise from irrelevant activations.

Furthermore, localization accuracy results show that SSVEP-based filtering does not always achieve higher alignment with human-annotated ground truths. While some methods maintain or even improve loc1 and loc5 scores, others experience slight drops, particularly on VGG-16. Importantly, the most improvement in Energy Concentration score is seen on VGG-16 as well. This suggests that optimizing for focus and compactness sometimes comes at the cost of completeness in object localization. The trade-off between Energy Concentration and localization accuracy highlights the need for a balanced approach in evaluating explainability methods.

Variations in results across architectures indicate that model-specific characteristics can influence the impact of SSVEP filtering. For instance, ResNeXt-50 shows a more moderate gain in Energy Concentration compared to VGG-16 and ResNet-50, which suggests that the benefits of filter selection depend on how distributed a model's feature representation is.

Another limitation of our study is the scope of the evaluation dataset. All experiments were conducted on a subset of the ImageNet validation set consisting of 5000 randomly selected images. While this subset ensures class diversity, it does not capture the full variability of the dataset or test cross-dataset generalizability. A more comprehensive evaluation across multiple datasets is needed to robustly assess the general applicability of SSVEP-based filter selection.

It is also important to acknowledge that the three networks differ substantially in capacity: VGG-16 contains significantly more parameters than ResNet-50 and ResNeXt-50. Despite using the same number of top filters across models, this design choice may not normalize for architectural differences, potentially leading to performance disparities. A percentage-based selection strategy—e.g., retaining the top $K\%$ of filters per model could offer a fairer baseline across architectures. While this remains an open avenue for future work, we acknowledge that such a strategy may yield more consistent results and help disentangle architecture-specific effects.

These results underscore the importance of Energy Concentration as a complementary metric for evaluating explainability. While existing benchmarks primarily assess interpretability through localization accuracy or classification impact, our findings suggest that the spatial precision of attributions is equally critical. A more focused heatmap reduces ambiguity in model decision-making and offers better insights.

In summary, incorporating additional constraints to balance localization accuracy with Energy Concentration could further improve CAM-based explanations. Exploring different filter selection strategies across architectures may help optimize the trade-off between focus and completeness. These insights provide a strong foundation for improving model interpretability while maintaining practical usability across different architectures and datasets.

5 Conclusion

Our results demonstrate that SSVEP-based filter selection enhances the focus and interpretability of CAM-based explanations without significantly compromising localization accuracy. By concentrating activation energy in the most relevant regions, this method reduces noise and improves the clarity of attributions. While performance gains vary across architectures, the overall improvements in Energy Concentration suggest that selective filter activation is a promising direction for refining explainability methods. Future work could explore dynamic selection mechanisms that adapt to different network architectures and tasks, further optimizing the trade-off between focus and completeness in visual explanations.

References

1. Akhtar, N.: A survey of explainable AI in deep visual modeling: Methods and metrics. arXiv preprint arXiv:2301.13445 (2023)
2. Alp, N., Ozkan, H.: Neural correlates of integration processes during dynamic face perception. Sci. Rep. **12**(1), 118 (2022)
3. Bach, S., Binder, A., Montavon, G., Klauschen, F., Müller, K.R., Samek, W.: On pixel-wise explanations for non-linear classifier decisions by layer-wise relevance propagation. PLoS ONE **10**(7), e0130140 (2015)
4. Boremanse, A., Norcia, A.M., Rossion, B.: An objective signature for visual binding of face parts in the human brain. J. Vision **13**(11), 6–6 (09 2013). https://doi.org/10.1167/13.11.6, https://doi.org/10.1167/13.11.6
5. Böge, E., Gunindi, Y., Aptoula, E., Alp, N., Ozkan, H.: Adapting the biological ssvep response to artificial neural networks (2024). https://arxiv.org/abs/2411.10084

6. Chattopadhay, A., Sarkar, A., Howlader, P., Balasubramanian, V.N.: Gradcam++: Generalized gradient-based visual explanations for deep convolutional networks. In: 2018 IEEE Winter Conference on Applications of Computer Vision (WACV) (2018)
7. Doshi-Velez, F., Kim, B.: Towards a rigorous science of interpretable machine learning (2017). https://arxiv.org/abs/1702.08608
8. Dzhelyova, M., Rossion, B.: Supra-additive contribution of shape and surface information to individual face discrimination as revealed by fast periodic visual stimulation. J. Vision **14**(14), 15–15 (12 2014). https://doi.org/10.1167/14.14.15
9. Everingham, M., Van Gool, L., Williams, C.K., Winn, J., Zisserman, A.: The pascal visual object classes (voc) challenge. Int. J. Comput. Vision **88**, 303–338 (2010)
10. Ghorbani, A., Zou, J.Y.: Neuron shapley: Discovering the responsible neurons. In: Advances in Neural Information Processing Systems 33: Annual Conference on Neural Information Processing Systems 2020 (2020)
11. Gunning, D., Aha, D.: Darpa's explainable artificial intelligence (xai) program. AI Mag. **40**(2), 44–58 (2019)
12. Gunning, D., Stefik, M., Choi, J., Miller, T., Stumpf, S., Yang, G.Z.: Xai—explainable artificial intelligence. Sci. Robot. **4**(37), eaay7120 (2019)
13. He, K., Zhang, X., Ren, S., Sun, J.: Deep residual learning for image recognition. In: 2016 IEEE Conference on Computer Vision and Pattern Recognition, CVPR, pp. 770–778 (2016)
14. Jiang, P.T., Zhang, C.B., Hou, Q., Cheng, M.M., Wei, Y.: Layercam: exploring hierarchical class activation maps for localization. IEEE Trans. Image Process. **30**, 5875–5888 (2021)
15. Kazmierczak, R., Berthier, E., Frehse, G., Franchi, G.: Explainability for vision foundation models: A survey. arXiv preprint arXiv:2501.12203 (2025)
16. Li, K., Wu, Z., Peng, K.C., Ernst, J., Fu, Y.: Tell me where to look: Guided attention inference network (2018). https://arxiv.org/abs/1802.10171
17. Liu-Shuang, J., Norcia, A.M., Rossion, B.: An objective index of individual face discrimination in the right occipito-temporal cortex by means of fast periodic oddball stimulation. Neuropsychologia **52**, 57–72 (2014). https://doi.org/10.1016/j.neuropsychologia.2013.10.022
18. Lundberg, S., Lee, S.I.: A unified approach to interpreting model predictions (2017). https://arxiv.org/abs/1705.07874
19. Mersha, M., Lam, K., Wood, J., AlShami, A., Kalita, J.: Explainable artificial intelligence: a survey of needs, techniques, applications, and future direction. Neurocomputing p. 128111 (2024)
20. Molchanov, P., Mallya, A., Tyree, S., Frosio, I., Kautz, J.: Importance estimation for neural network pruning. In: IEEE Conference on Computer Vision and Pattern Recognition, CVPR, pp. 11264–11272 (2019)
21. Muhammad, M.B., Yeasin, M.: Eigen-cam: Class activation map using principal components. In: 2020 International Joint Conference on Neural Networks (IJCNN), pp. 1—-7 (Jul 2020)
22. Nielsen, I.E., Dera, D., Rasool, G., Ramachandran, R.P., Bouaynaya, N.C.: Robust explainability: a tutorial on gradient-based attribution methods for deep neural networks. IEEE Signal Process. Mag. **39**(4), 73–84 (2022)
23. Norcia, A.M., Appelbaum, L.G., Ales, J.M., Cottereau, B.R., Rossion, B.: The steady-state visual evoked potential in vision research: A review. J. Vision **15**(6) (2015)

24. Paszke, A., et al.: Pytorch: An imperative style, high-performance deep learning library. In: Advances in Neural Information Processing Systems 32: Annual Conference on Neural Information Processing Systems, pp. 8024–8035 (2019)
25. Regan, D.: An effect of stimulus colour on average steady-state potentials evoked in man. Nature **210**(5040), 1056–1057 (1966)
26. Ribeiro, M.T., Singh, S., Guestrin, C.: "why should i trust you?": Explaining the predictions of any classifier (2016). https://arxiv.org/abs/1602.04938
27. Rong, Y., Leemann, T., Borisov, V., Kasneci, G., Kasneci, E.: A consistent and efficient evaluation strategy for attribution methods (2022). https://arxiv.org/abs/2202.00449
28. Russakovsky, O., et al.: Imagenet large scale visual recognition challenge. Int. J. Comput. Vision **115**, 211–252 (2015)
29. Samek, W., Binder, A., Montavon, G., Lapuschkin, S., Müller, K.R.: Evaluating the visualization of what a deep neural network has learned. IEEE Trans. Neural Netw. Learn. Syst. **28**(11), 2660–2673 (2016)
30. Selvaraju, R.R., Cogswell, M., Das, A., Vedantam, R., Parikh, D., Batra, D.: Gradcam: visual explanations from deep networks via gradient-based localization. Int. J. Comput. Vision **128**(2), 336–359 (2019)
31. Selvaraju, R.R., Das, A., Vedantam, R., Cogswell, M., Parikh, D., Batra, D.: Gradcam: Why did you say that? (2017). https://arxiv.org/abs/1611.07450
32. Simonyan, K., Zisserman, A.: Very deep convolutional networks for large-scale image recognition. In: 3rd International Conference on Learning Representations, ICLR (2015)
33. Smilkov, D., Thorat, N., Kim, B., Viégas, F., Wattenberg, M.: Smoothgrad: removing noise by adding noise. arXiv preprint arXiv:1706.03825 (2017)
34. Sundararajan, M., Taly, A., Yan, Q.: Axiomatic attribution for deep networks (2017). https://arxiv.org/abs/1703.01365
35. Xie, S., Girshick, R., Dollár, P., Tu, Z., He, K.: Aggregated residual transformations for deep neural networks. In: Proceedings of the IEEE Conference on Computer Vision and Pattern Recognition, pp. 1492–1500 (2017)
36. Xu, F., Uszkoreit, H., Du, Y., Fan, W., Zhao, D., Zhu, J.: Explainable AI: a brief survey on history, research areas, approaches and challenges. In: Tang, J., Kan, M.-Y., Zhao, D., Li, S., Zan, H. (eds.) NLPCC 2019. LNCS (LNAI), vol. 11839, pp. 563–574. Springer, Cham (2019). https://doi.org/10.1007/978-3-030-32236-6_51
37. Yu, R., et al.: NISP: pruning networks using neuron importance score propagation. In: IEEE Conference on Computer Vision and Pattern Recognition, CVPR, pp. 9194–9203 (2018)
38. Zhou, B., Khosla, A., Lapedriza, A., Oliva, A., Torralba, A.: Learning deep features for discriminative localization. In: 2016 IEEE Conference on Computer Vision and Pattern Recognition (CVPR), pp. 2921–2929 (2016)

Open Access This chapter is licensed under the terms of the Creative Commons Attribution 4.0 International License (http://creativecommons.org/licenses/by/4.0/), which permits use, sharing, adaptation, distribution and reproduction in any medium or format, as long as you give appropriate credit to the original author(s) and the source, provide a link to the Creative Commons license and indicate if changes were made.

The images or other third party material in this chapter are included in the chapter's Creative Commons license, unless indicated otherwise in a credit line to the material. If material is not included in the chapter's Creative Commons license and your intended use is not permitted by statutory regulation or exceeds the permitted use, you will need to obtain permission directly from the copyright holder.

Author Index

A

Ademi, Luan 219
Alp, Nihan 422
Amling, Jonas 78
Aptoula, Erchan 422
Arrighi, Leonardo 271
Aru, Jaan 359

B

Barbiero, Pietro 319
Barbon Junior, Sylvio 271
Bartelt, Christian 28
Bauckhage, Christian 3
Böge, Emirhan 422
Bonabi Mobaraki, Ehsan 319
Bonchi, Filippo 294

C

Capaldo, Patrick 247
Carlevaro, Alberto 396
Cascione, Alessio 104
Ceschin, Matteo 271
Chakraborty, Tanmay 53
Colombini, Jacopo Joy 294

D

Dias, Braian Olmiro 359
Diligenti, Michelangelo 319
Domnich, Marharyta 359
Dormagen, Christian 78

E

Ertan, Murat Bilgehan 422

F

Frosini, Patrizio 294

G

Giannini, Francesco 294, 319
Giannotti, Fosca 294
Gonzalez-Diaz, Rocio 396
Gori, Marco 319
Guidotti, Riccardo 104
Gunindi, Yasemin 422
Guzzi, Jérôme 396

H

Hall, Mark 247
Horváth, Tamás 3
Hüllermeier, Eyke 131

J

Jullum, Martin 194

K

Ketheeswaran, Varniethan 247
Khajuria, Tarun 359
Klausen, René P. 383
Knab, Patrick 28
Kolpaczki, Patrick 131
Krasowski, Aleksander 383
Kretschmann, Marco 78

L

Landi, Cristiano 104
Lapuschkin, Sebastian 383
Liu, Weiru 169
Longo, Luca 271

M

Manerba, Marta Marchiori 104
Marton, Sascha 28
Mongelli, Maurizio 396
Müller, Sebastian 3

N
Nakanishi, Takafumi 332
Narteni, Sara 396
Naujoks, Jonas R. 383
Nielen, Tim 131
Noppel, Maximilian 219

O
Olsen, Lars Henry Berge 194
Ontiveros, Rodrigo Castellano 319
Ozkan, Huseyin 422

P
Pellungrini, Roberto 294
Pinto, Tiago 156

Q
Quintana-Amate, Santiago 247

S
Samek, Wojciech 383
Scheele, Stephan 78
Schlegel, Udo 28

S
Seifert, Christin 53
Sheldon, Dylan 247
Shi, Yiwei 169
Slany, Emanuel 78
Stevens, Delaney 247

T
Teixeira, Brígida 156
Toborek, Vanessa 3
Toscano-Duran, Victor 396

V
Vale, Zita 156

W
Weckbecker, Moritz 383
Wiegand, Thomas 383
Wirth, Christian 53
Wressnegger, Christian 219

Y
Yolcu, Galip Ümit 383

MIX
Papier aus verantwortungsvollen Quellen
Paper from responsible sources
FSC® C105338

If you have any concerns about our products,
you can contact us on
ProductSafety@springernature.com

In case Publisher is established outside the EU,
the EU authorized representative is:
Springer Nature Customer Service Center GmbH
Europaplatz 3, 69115 Heidelberg, Germany

Printed by Libri Plureos GmbH
in Hamburg, Germany